Ecosystems and Sustainable Development V

Ecological Sciences

Editorial Board

E. Tiezzi
University of Siena
Italy

J-L. Usó
Universitat Jaume I
Spain

W. Timmermans
Alterra Green World Research
The Netherlands

A. Viguri
Universitat Jaume I
Spain

R.E. Ulanowicz
UMCES
USA

Y. Villacampa
Universidad de Alicante
Spain

FIFTH INTERNATIONAL CONFERENCE ON ECOSYSTEMS AND SUSTAINABLE DEVELOPMENT

ECOSUD V

CONFERENCE CHAIRMEN

E. Tiezzi
University of Siena, Italy

C.A. Brebbia
Wessex Institute of Technology, UK

S.E. Jørgensen
University of Pharmaceutical Science, Denmark

D. Almorza Gomar
University of Cádiz, Spain

INTERNATIONAL SCIENTIFIC ADVISORY COMMITTEE

Organised by
Wessex Institute of Technology, UK,
University of Cádiz, Spain,
University of Siena, Italy,

In collaboration with:
International Journal of Ecodynamics

Ecosystems and Sustainable Development V

Editors:

E. Tiezzi
University of Siena, Italy

C.A. Brebbia
Wessex Institute of Technology, UK

S.E. Jørgensen
University of Pharmaceutical Science, Denmark

D. Almorza Gomar
University of Cádiz, Spain

WIT PRESS Southampton, Boston

E. Tiezzi
University of Siena, Italy

C.A. Brebbia
Wessex Institute of Technology, UK

S.E. Jørgensen
University of Pharmaceutical Science, Denmark

D. Almorza Gomar
University of Cádiz, Spain

Published by

WIT Press
Ashurst Lodge, Ashurst, Southampton, SO40 7AA, UK
Tel: 44 (0) 238 029 3223; Fax: 44 (0) 238 029 2853
E-Mail: witpress@witpress.com
http://www.witpress.com

For USA, Canada and Mexico

Computational Mechanics Inc
25 Bridge Street, Billerica, MA 01821, USA
Tel: 978 667 5841; Fax: 978 667 7582
E-Mail: infousa@witpress.com
http://www.witpress.com

British Library Cataloguing-in-Publication Data

A Catalogue record for this book is available
from the British Library

ISBN: 1-84564-013-6
ISSN: 1746-448X (print)
ISSN: 1743-3541 (on-line)

The texts of the papers in this volume were set individually by the authors or under their supervision. Only minor corrections to the text may have been carried out by the publisher.

Printed in Great Britain by Athenaeum Press Ltd, Gateshead.

Preface

Beyond the specific dimension of the individual, learning is a primary characteristic of life. Shifting our attention to local systems we can consider ecosystems and traditional communities as learning "minds", according with Bateson's thought. We call environmental wisdom the explicit knowledge that emerges from long periods of co-evolution of people and nature in local systems, cast in the same lot. Environmental wisdom rises both from trial-and-error and from more subtle kinds of knowledge, involving aesthetic and intuition. It sediments as tradition or religion and deeply contribute to landscapes creation, keeping ecosystems and humans alive together.

In line with this preliminary statement, ECOSUD is not only a forestage to present novel research related to ecological problems from all over the world; it also gives opportunities for new emergent ideas in science arising from the cross fertilization of different disciplines including mathematical models and eco-informatics, evolutionary thermodynamics and biodiversity, structures in ecosystems modelling and landscapes. ECOSUD is a challenge for the creation of a new science in line with Prigogine's statement that "at all levels we observe events associated with the emergence of novelties and narrative elements, which we may associate with the creative power of Nature".

It is our belief, that in order to survive, local communities should re-connect themselves with their biological basis. As a first option we need to pay new attention to our boundaries: not to avoid contacts, exchanges or cross-fertilization with other people and other lands, but to retain cultural biodiversity.

Only a network of self-centred communicating communities can provide a sufficient basis of diversity to achieve long-term sustainability. We believe we are living a moment of general crisis, a re-learning transition period that is inherently uncertain, and therefore we have to enlarge our cultural and technological basis, avoiding homogenization as the primary source of fragility.

The Editors
Cadiz, May 2005

Contents

Section 8: Economic issues

Section 9: Energy conservation and generation

Section 10: Environmental and ecological policies

Section 11: Environmental management

Section 12: Environmental risk

Section 13: Natural resources management

Section 14: Recovery of damaged areas

Section 15: Remote sensing

Section 1
Thermodynamics and ecology

Ecodynamics: the quest for evolutionary physics

E. Tiezzi
Department of Chemical and Biosystems Sciences, University of Siena, Italy

Abstract

The challenge for sustainable development needs a shift of paradigm towards an evolutionary point of view and also needs new modeling tools to investigate complex ecosystems and the related dynamics. This paper is an attempt to develop the new discipline of ecodynamics as a quest for evolutionary physics and ecoinformatics. Particular attention is devoted to goal functions, to the relation of conceptualizations surrounding matter, energy, space and time and to the interdisciplinary approach connecting thermodynamics and biology. The evolutionary dynamics of complex systems, ranging from open physical and chemical systems (strange attractors, oscillating reactions, dissipative structures) to ecosystems has to be investigated in terms of far from equilibrium thermodynamics (Prigogine). The theory of probability is discussed in light of new theoretical findings related to the role of events, also in terms of entropy and evolutionary thermodynamics.
Keywords: entropy, evolutionary thermodynamics, ecodynamics, probability.

1 Introduction

More than a hundred years ago, in 1886, Ludwig Boltzmann [1], one of the fathers of modern physical chemistry, was concerned with the relation between energy and matter in scientific terms. According to Boltzmann, the struggle for life is not a struggle for basic elements or energy but for the entropy (negative) available in the transfer from the hot sun to the cold Earth. Utilizing this transfer to a maximum, plants force solar energy to perform chemical reactions before it reaches the thermal level of the Earth's surface.

www.witpress.com, ISSN 1743-3541 (on-line)

To live and reproduce, plants and animals need a continuous flow of energy. The energy of the biosphere, which originates in the luminous energy of the sun, is captured by plants and passes from one living form to another along the food chain. The energy captured by chlorophyll is stored in carbohydrates (molecules rich in energy), and by means of photosynthesis, a term that means "to make things with light". This radiant pathway that provides us with great quantities of food, fibers, and energy—all of solar origin—has existed for about four billion years, a long time if we think that hominids appeared on the earth only three million years ago and that known history covers only two thousand years. Our ancestor, the blue alga, began to photosynthesize, thus assuming a fundamental role in biological evolution.

The organization of living beings in mature ecosystems slows the dispersal of energy fixed by plants to a minimum, enabling them to use it completely for their own complex mechanisms of regulation. This is made possible by large "reservoirs" of energy (biomasses) and by the diversification of living species. The stability of natural ecosystems, however, means that the final energy yield is zero, except for a relatively small quantity of biomass that is buried underground to form fossils for the future.

Photosynthesis counteracts entropic degradation insofar as it orders disordered matter: the plant takes up disordered material (low energy molecules of water and carbon dioxide in disorderly agitation) and orders it using solar energy. It organizes the material by building it into complex structures. Photosynthesis is therefore the process that, by capturing solar energy and decreasing the entropy of the planet, paved the way for evolution.

It is important to emphasize that biological activity is a planetary property, a continuous interaction of atmospheres, oceans, plants, animals, microorganisms, molecules, electrons, energies, and matter, all part of a global whole. The role of each of these components is essential for the maintenance of life.

The relations and activities of the global biogeochemical system are life. The aim of science is to maintain these relations and characteristics; to live in harmony with nature, not to conquer it. This type of science comprehends complexity and uncertainty, and moves away from a deterministic-mechanistic view of the world in favor of a holistic and evolutionary view. It refers to the "clinamen" of Lucretius and to the "disciples of Sais" of Novalis rather than to the clockwork world of Descartes and the reversible time of Newtonian mechanics. It considers the constraints not as halters or chains but as conditions that create diversity and mutations, all of which amounts to biological evolution: constraints as sources of creativity and presuppositions for evolution.

The basic laws of physics from Newton to the present day have been time reversible; on the contrary, reality is constituted by phenomenological aspects: macromolecular organization, cellular differentiation, life processes, characterized by irreversibility of time. The reason for this lies in dynamical interactions that take place in complex systems. The analysis of reality requires major modification of current physical chemistry equations and theories. What is now clear is that complex systems and their behaviour can only be analyzed by means of relations including time as directional factor.

On one hand, the use of time-reversible classical and quantum physical chemistry approaches for studying matter at the molecular level and the behaviour of simple molecular systems has greatly improved man's understanding. On the other hand, we need new approaches and new time-irreversible theories able to describe the behaviour of complex systems.

As Thomas Khun [2] remarks, the passing of time often brings anomalies which existing theories are no longer able to explain. The divergence between theory and reality may become enormous and consequently a source of serious problems. This is exactly what is happening today between current scientific theories and the natural situation of the planet. For this reason the sustainability theory needs this type of approach.

In Khun's terms this means a shift toward a new paradigm. As Palomar in Italo Calvino's novel observed: “if the model does not succeed in transforming reality, reality must succeed in transforming the model”.

Based on the assumption that the interaction between biophysical constraints and evolution is not satisfactorily described by current scientific theories, this paper is an attempt to present a new model to be used in ecological physical chemistry as concerns entropy, energy and time fluctuations in biological and ecological systems.

The epistemology of the model derives from interdisciplinary cross-fertilization between physical chemistry, mainly thermodynamics, and ecology, mainly systems ecology. The logical consequence is a complete change of point of view or a "gestalt" shift in modelling the relationship between biophysico-chemical parameters and the global environment.

Professor Ilya Prigogine, Nobel prize winner in chemistry, founded the basis of this new discipline. I do like to call this new discipline Ecodynamics or Evolutionary Physics.

2 Steps towards ecodynamics

In the framework of evolutionary physics we deal with goal functions instead of state functions, the ecodynamic models have to be based on relations evolving in time; “far from equilibrium thermodynamics” (Prigogine) assumes upon itself the role of foundation of a new description of nature.

In his autobiography, Nobel prize winner Ilya Prigogine recounts his first studies on far-from-equilibrium phenomena:
“It is difficult today to give an account of the hostility that such an approach was to meet. For example, I remember that towards the end of 1946, at the Brussels IUPAP meeting, after a presentation of the thermodynamics of irreversible processes, a specialist of great repute said to me, in substance: ‘I am surprised that you give more attention to irreversible phenomena, which are essentially transitory, than to the final result of their evolution, equilibrium’.”
He adds: “As we started from specific problems, such as the thermodynamic signification of non-equilibrium stationary states, or of transport phenomena in dense systems, we have been faced, almost against our will, with problems of great generality and complexity, which call for reconsideration of the relation of physico-chemical structures to biological ones, while they express the limits of

Hamiltonian description in physics. Indeed, all these problems have a common element: time."

Professor of physical chemistry at the University of Brussels, Ilya Prigogine was awarded the Nobel prize in chemistry in 1977. His studies opened a window on nature. For the first time in the history of physical chemistry, tools, methods, equations and models were developed to describe the essence of the evolutionary properties of nature. This was a true change of paradigm. This change in paradigm: a) implies that the intrinsic irreversibility of time has erupted in the basic equations of chemistry and physics; b) it sustains Pascal's view that the whole is greater than the sum of its parts and hence negates the statement of Descartes that the world should be divided into the smallest possible parts in order to understand it; c) it suggests that form and aesthetics (and hence quality as well as quantity) play a role in the evolution of nature. Nature is therefore conceived as φυσισ (*physis,* the word from which *physics* is derived) in the original Greek sense, a nature in which time, relations and aesthetics play a fundamental role.

In the foreword of "The Essence of Time" [3] Prigogine wrote:
"The first part of this book deals with the passage 'from a space to a time culture'. This is indeed an essential part of the scientific revolution we are witnessing at the end of the 20th century. Science is a dialogue with nature. In the past this dialogue has taken many forms. We feel that we are at the end of the period which started with Galileo, Copernicus and Newton and culminated with the discovery of quantum mechanics and relativity. This was a glorious period but in spite of all its marvelous achievements it led to an oversimplified picture of nature, a picture which neglected essential aspects. Classical science emphasized stability, order and equilibrium. Today we discover instabilities and fluctuations everywhere. Our view of nature is changing dramatically. At all levels we observe events associated with the creative power of nature. I like to say that *at equilibrium matter is blind, far from equilibrium it begins to 'see'*.

Although quantum mechanics and general relativity are revolutionary, as far as the concept of time is concerned, they are direct descendants of classical dynamics and carry a radical negation of the irreversibility of time.

Irreversibility is not related to Newtonian time or its Einsteinian generalization, but to an 'internal time' expressed in terms of the relations between the various units of which the system is composed, as are relations between particles."

This simply means that we no more deal with state functions, but rather with evolving ecodynamic functions.

Faced with the evolutionary character of nature and life, classical science (physics and chemistry) encounters three paradoxes:

- Prigogine's time paradox [3];
- the paradox of negentropy that cannot be calculated on the basis of conservative, deterministic and purely quantitative terms (energy and classical entropy) but which must consider information, forms and quality;
- the probability paradox (probability is an aseptic, atemporal mechanistic concept) which has to account for events, emerging phenomena, choices made

by plants, animals and ecosystems, random fluctuations of evolutionary biology and the phenomena of far-from-equilibrium systems.

3 The Belousov-Zhabotinsky reaction

Prigogine introduces the concept of the arrow of time to describe irreversible changes. The main issue derived from the theory of dissipative structures is that the evolution and maintenance of open systems far from equilibrium are possible only if irreversible thermodynamic processes occur. Such processes dissipate energy and matter, increasing Entropy in the environment.

The evolutionary process is such that systems become more and more complex and organized. Biological diversity is the product of long-term interactions at a genealogical and ecological level: the genealogical interactions regard the dissipation of Entropy by irreversible biological processes; the ecological interactions regard Entropy gradients in the environment.

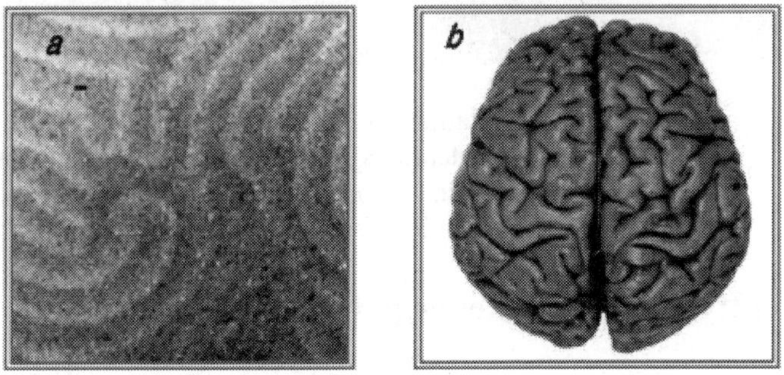

Figure 1: a) *Labyrinthine* chemical structure obtained with our reaction diffusion system (the Belousov-Zhabotinsky reaction) in lipid membrane b) Human brain.

There are also chemical systems that show phenomena of self-organization such as the formation of stationary spatial structures or periodic oscillatory states. Self-organizing chemical systems have been of relevant importance for the development of the theoretical biology, and nowadays they cover an important role in the evolution of systems biology. This science has been originated from the confluence between molecular biology, with its emphasis on individual macromolecules (DNA, proteins, enzymes…), and the molecular self-organization theories, in which thermodynamics plays the key role [4]. In his seminal work "*The Chemical Basis of Morphogenesis (1952)*" [5], Alan Turing theorized that tissues differentiation in the development of an organism starting from similar cells, could be due to a reaction-diffusion process in the cellar environment. This intuition remained only a theoretical speculation until 90s, when Dekepper's group in Paris found this kind of structure in an oscillating chemical system performed on a gel substrate [6]. Nowadays, the chemical pattern formation is deeply studied for its implications in biological systems, in particular a relatively simple chemical model can be used to explicate a lot of behaviors in cellar and tissue development. We performed a great number of experiments studying the Belousov-Zhabotinsky (BZ) oscillating reaction in membranes used as model for biological systems [7], and the figures 1 and 2 explain the similarities between the laboratory model and biological systems of several orders of complexity. The phenomenon is clearly related to the role of entropy in dissipative structures and to the input-output entropy flows.

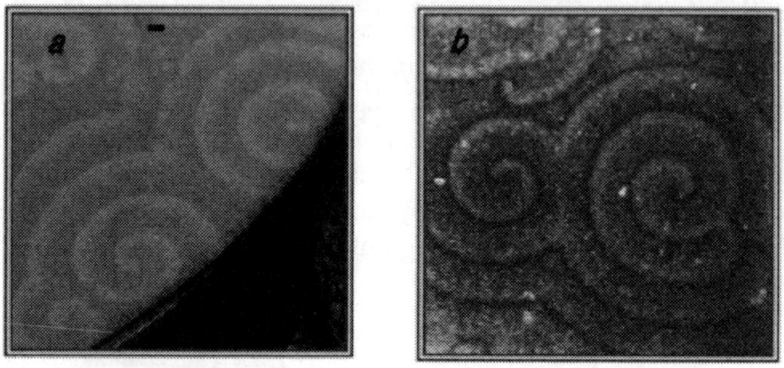

Figure 2: a) Spiral patterns obtained in our chemical systems; b) A colony of Dictyostelium Discoideum [8]. The spirals shown are caused by the movement of cells in response to cAMP waves periodically initiated by the aggregation center.

4 The entropy paradox: energy vs. entropy

In the far from equilibrium thermodynamics the role of entropy is fundamental. We may say that entropy exist *per se*, is a non-conservative function and is related to evolution. This conclusion is a big step because it overcomes the old dilemma of whether entropy was the shadow of energy or vice versa, and does not reduce the ingenious invention of entropy to a purely energy dogma. The First Principle formulates the concept of energy in a conservation framework; the Second formulates that of entropy in an evolutionary framework. This is where evolutionary biology and mechanics meet. Schrödinger's introduction of the concept of negentropy was an inspired one: a living system absorbs negentropy from the external environment, structuring itself and evolving on the basis of this interaction. In other words, energy and entropy can be related, as is done in classical thermodynamics and statistical thermodynamics, but from the point of view of time, the two concepts are irreducible and different. In an evolutionary Gestalt, entropy has an extra gear which is the key necessary for studying living systems and ecology. It is important to study flows of energy and matter, quantities which are intrinsically conserved; it is also important to study entropy flows, an intrinsically evolutionary and non conserved quantity. The appearance of a term of entropy production, or "source term" as Aoki [9] calls it, is the watershed dividing the evolutionary world from the special case of conserved energy and mass. *But if energy and mass are intrinsically conserved and entropy is intrinsically evolutionary, how can entropy be calculated on the basis of energy and mass quantities (entropy paradox)?* This question is still unanswered [10] and all we can do is to note that the ecodynamic viewpoint is different from that of classical physics and classical ecology.

Let us observe the different relations of energy and entropy vs. information. An energy flow can lead to destruction (increase in entropy, for example a cannon ball) or organization (decrease in entropy, for example photosynthesis). The same quantity of energy can destroy a wall or kill a man; obviously the loss of information and negentropy is much greater in the second case. Energy and information are never equivalent.

Entropy has the broken time symmetry of which Prigogine speaks. In other words, entropy has an energy term plus a time term that energy does not have. Entropy has an intrinsic temporal parameter. Energy obeys spatial and material constraints; entropy obeys spatial, material and temporal constraints.

If history and the succession of events are of scientific relevance, the concept of function of state should be revised at a higher level of complexity. The singularity of an event also becomes of particular importance: if a certain quantity of energy is spent to kill a caterpillar, we lose the information embodied in the caterpillar. But were this the last caterpillar, we should lose its unique genetic information forever. The last caterpillar is different from the nth caterpillar.

Stories take place in a setting, the details of which are not irrelevant to the story. What happens in the biosphere, the story of life, depends on the constraints of the biosphere itself. Hence it is important to have global models of the biosphere in terms of space, time, matter, energy, entropy, information, and their respective relations.

Table 1: The death of the deer.

Far from thermodynamic equilibrium	ENTROPIC WATERSHED	Towards thermodynamic equilibrium
m		m
E		E
S		$+\Delta S$
$-\Delta S$		$-\Delta S_{lost}$
information		Information lost

Finally if we consider the evolutionary transition from anaerobic to aerobic living systems, the ratio of energy to stored information is clearly different. The information that led to an evolution and organization of the two types of system is not proportional to the flow of energy.

Thus entropy breaks the symmetry of time and can change irrespective of changes of energy, being energy a conservative and reversible property, whereas entropy is evolutionary and irreversible *per se*. The flow of a non-conservative quantity, negentropy, makes life go and the occurrence of a negentropic production term is just the point that differs from analysis based on merely conservative terms (energy and matter).

The situation is explained in *table 1* "The death of the deer": mass and energy do not change, whereas entropy does. There is an entropic *watershed* between far from equilibrium (living) systems and classical systems (the dead deer or any inorganic-not living system).

We may conclude that in the far from thermodynamics equilibrium systems (biology and ecology) *entropy is not a state function, since has intrinsic evolutionary properties*, strikingly at variance with classical thermodynamics.

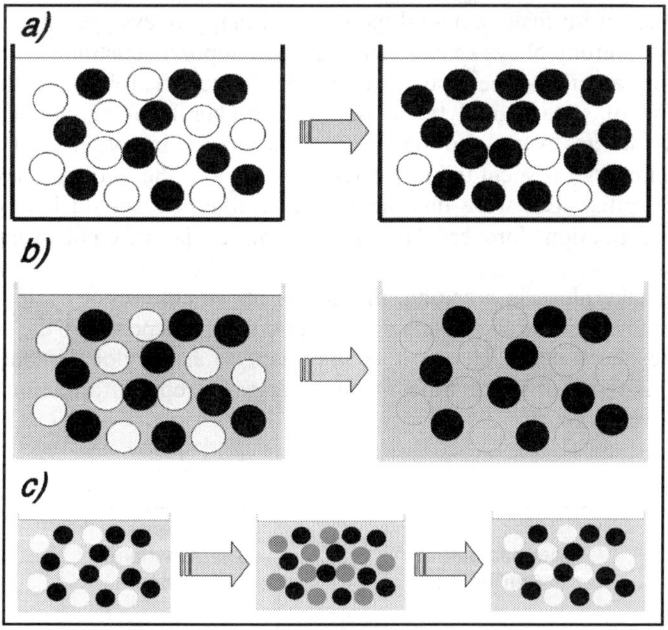

Figure 3: Unexpected events that may occur in living systems: a) oxidation; b) chameleon effect; c) oscillating reaction.

5 The probability paradox

An event occurs in a stochastic manner because it is preceded by others. There are genetic and environmental constraints. Evolutionary events proceed in a manner that depends on time: they show a direction of time; they are irreversible.

Past time has determined the constraints; the future is largely unpredictable, and always has a stochastic or probable element.

Previously unobserved events cannot be predictable; rare and extreme events may completely change the dynamics of complex systems.

Figure 3 shows the *emergence* of a probability paradox in the presence of events:

a) suppose that an oxidation (chemical event), unknown to the observer, arises in the classic "white and black spheres" game: the probability white/black is no more fifty-fifty (only if the oxidation is changing the white sphere to grey, I may know what happened),
b) suppose that an evolutionary event also occurs , related to the *"chameleon" effect* (sensible to the environment): again the probability is no more fifty-fifty; moreover the event's interval depends on the "chameleon";
c) suppose an oscillating event occurs, similar to the previously observed BZ reaction: the situation is more complex and depends on many parameters. Again the observer has no possibility to predict which sphere will be picked up from the container.

It is possible to conclude that in the far from equilibrium framework a classical probability approach does not apply and new models have probably to be developed for the Boltzmann's relation S = k lnW.

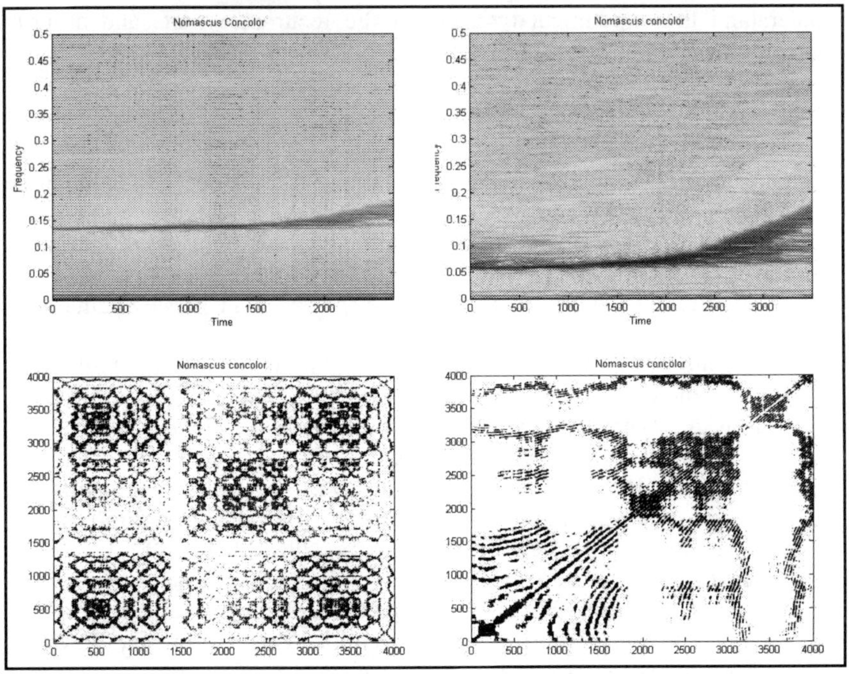

Figure 4: Recurrence Plot analysis of the calls of two different Nomascus Concolor gibbons. The spectrograms show two very similar signals, characterized by a light frequency modulation. On the contrary, the recurrence plots show completely different patterns.

6 Strange attractors

Because open ecosystems are self-organizing complex adaptive systems responding to current environmental conditions, we view the organizing principles as “orientors” or “attractors”

Again Prigogine underlines that the evolutionary dynamics of complex systems, (strange attractors, oscillating reactions, dissipative structures) has to be investigated in terms of far from equilibrium thermodynamics.

Figure 4 shows an experiment performed on gibbon vocalizations [11] . The comparison between the two lower figures (*recurrence plots of strange attractors*) is a clear *evidence of biodiversity* marked by *vocal fingerprint*. We have done similar experiments on Bat’s *vocal fingerprint* and on Sardinian deer [12]. Experiments on whales’ songs are in progress.

Again the role of Prigogine’s far from equilibrium thermodynamics is the theoretical basis of these calculations.

Biodiversity is strictly related to biological evolution and, also in this case, we have to refer to goal evolutionary functions: entropic change and flow is the key to understand the experimental results of the recurrence plots and a further incentive to develop new steps towards an evolutionary physics.

References

[1] Giacometti, G.: personal communication, from Hubel, R.; *Angewante Chemie*, (28), p.848, 1989.

[2] Khun, T.S., *The structure of scientific revolutions*, University of Chicago Press, Chicago, 1962.

[3] Prigogine, I., in Tiezzi, E. *The Essence of Time*, WIT press, Southampton, 2003.

[4] Westerhoff, H.V., Palsson, B.O.; “The evolution of molecular biology into systems biology”; *Nature Biotechnology*, 22 (10), pp. 1249-1252, 2004.

[5] Turing, A.; “The chemical basis of morphogenesis”; *Philos. Trans. R. Soc. London, Ser. B*, (327), pp. 37-52, 1952.

[6] Castets, V., Dulos, E., Boissonade, J., De Kepper, P.; “Experimental evidence of a sustained standing Turing-type nonequilibrium chemical pattern”; Physical Review Letters, (64), pp. 2953-2956, 1990.

[7] Magnani, A., Marchettini, N., Ristori, S., Rossi, C., Rossi, F., Rustici, M., Spalla, O. & Tiezzi, E.; “Chemical Waves and Pattern Formation in the 1, 2-Dipalmitoyl-sn-glycero-3-phosphocholine/Water lamellar system”; *Journal of the American Chemical Society*, 126 (37), pp. 11406-11407, 2004.

[8] Foerster, P., Müller, S. C., Hess B.; "Curvature and spiral geometry in aggregation patterns of Dictyostelium discoideum", *Development*, (109), pp. 11-16, 1990.

[9] Aoki, I., Entropy laws in ecological networks at steady state, *Ecological Modelling*, (42), pp.289-303,1988; Monthly variations of entropy production in lake Biwa. *Ecological Modelling*, (51), pp.227-232, 1990.

[10] See for example the interesting considerations of Coveney, P., Chaos, entropy and the arrow of time. *Chaos - a science for the real world,* ed. Hall, N., Italian translation Muzzio, F., Padua, pp. 203-212, 1992.

[11] Facchini, A., Kantz, H. & Tiezzi, E. "Recurrence plot analysis of nonstationary data: the understanding of curved patterns". Submitted to *Phys. Rev E*, 2004.

[12] Facchini, A., Bastianoni, S., Marchettini, N. & Rustici, M. "Characterization of chaotic dynamics in the vocalization of Cervus elaphus corsicanus". *J. Acoust. Soc. Am.* 114(6), pp. 3040-3043, 2003.

Replicator equations, response functions and entropy measures in science: mathematical background

Y. A. Pykh & I. G. Malkina-Pykh
Research Center for Interdisciplinary Environmental Cooperation (INENCO RAS), Russian Academy of Sciences

Abstract

Replicator dynamics is an evolutionary strategy well established in different disciplines of biological sciences. It describes the evolution of self-reproducing entities called replicators in various independent models of, e.g., genetics, ecology, prebiotic evolution, and sociobiology. Besides this, replicator selection has been applied to problem solving in combinatorial optimization and to learning in neural networks and also in fluid mechanics, game and laser theory. So, the replicator systems arise in an extraordinary variety of modeling situations. In this report we'll consider the new class of generalized replicator equations with nonlinear response functions and construct the Energy Lyapunov function and entropy measures for this system.
Keywords: replicator equations, Lyapunov functions, entropy, distance measure.

1 An overview and introduction

A *replicator* is a fundamental unit in evolutionary processes, representing a population *type*, and characterized by two attributes: $p_i(t)$, its proportion in the population at time t, and its non-negative fitness at time t. A replicator's fitness is a measure of its significance to the future evolution of the population. The proportions of replicators in a population change as a result of their mutual interactions, and their relative fitnesses.

The founding fathers of evolutionary genetics, Fisher, Haldane and Wright used mathematical models to generate a synthesis between Mendelian genetics and Darwinian evolution. Kimura's theory of neutral evolution, Hamilton's kin selection and Maynard Smith's evolutionary game theory are all based on mathematical descriptions of evolutionary dynamics. Concepts like fitness and natural selection are best defined in terms of mathematical equations.

The notion of a *replicator* – originally invented by Dawkins [6] – is now used in biology for "*an entity that passes on its structure largely intact in successive replications*" (Vrba [28]). The origin of life is characterized by the emergence of heritable information that, through the interplay of selection and variation, leads to Darwinian evolution.

Very recently the interest in evolutionary dynamical models has increased dramatically, mainly because in the game theoretic literature it is commonly thought that such models can provide a better understanding of the Nash equilibrium solution concept than traditional static game theory, as well as a description of the non-equilibrium behavior of the players. The replicator dynamics, introduced into the literature by Taylor and Jonker [27] for the special case of two player games in the late seventies of our century, is the classical example of such an evolutionary dynamical model.

Throughout last century the formal analogies between the mathematical models in population dynamics and certain models of different physical or chemical processes have been a source of inspiration both for biologists and physicists. As early as in 1911 Sharpe and Lotka [25] made an analogy between the stable age structure of human populations and an acoustical problem.

Autocatalytic reaction networks which in general involve two classes of catalytic processes – autocatalytic instruction for reproduction and additional material and process specific catalysis – were postulated as models for studies of prebiotic and early biological evolution scenarios Eigen, Schuster [7,8]. In the last decade it turned out that they serve also as models in very different fields like molecular biology, population genetics, theoretical ecology or dynamical game theory (Schuster and Sigmund [24]). A variety of self-replicating chemical systems have been constructed and investigated experimentally in the past 25 years since Spiegelman's [26].

Besides this fundamental importance in theoretical biology, replicator selection has been applied to problem solving in combinatorial optimization and to learning in neural networks (Bomze [3], Menon [11]). Recent results show that the same type of differential equations is also obtained by non-linear coordinate transformations from models in fluid mechanics and laser theory (Brenig and Goriely [4]). So, it is clear that replicator systems are a class of first order, nonlinear differential equations, arising in an extraordinary variety of modeling situations.

In this report we'll introduce the new class of generalized replicator equations with nonlinear response functions and construct Energy Lyapunov function and entropy measures for this systems.

2 Generalized replicator equations

First replicator-like equation was introduced by Fisher [9], who immediately recognized certain formal analogies between the mechanistic models introduced by Boltzmann [2] to analyze physical systems, and the selection models proposed by Darwin [5] to explain adaptation in biological systems. By considering the dynamical system which describes the changes in gene frequency of the population which occurs under natural selection, Fisher proved a directionality theorem, which he called the fundamental theorem of natural selection.

The absolute fitness of the zygote $\boldsymbol{A}_i\boldsymbol{A}_j$, denoted as w_{ij} is defined as the relative or fractional number of offspring per unit time that the genotype will produce that will grow to maturity and themselves reproduce.

The state of the genetical system at time t is simply the vector $p(t)=(p_1(t),\dots,p_n(t))$, which is clearly constrained to lie in the standard simplex σ in n-dimensional Euclidean space $\mathbb{R}^n$:

$$\sigma=\left\{p\in\mathbb{R}^n : p_i\geq 0,\quad i=1,\dots,n,\ \mathbf{e}^T p=1\right\}.$$

Here and in the sequel, the letter **e** is reserved for a vector of appropriate length, consisting of unit entries $\left(\text{hence } \mathbf{e}^T p=\sum_{i=1}^{n} p_i\right)$. The original Fisher's selection equation of haploid genotypes evolution is, then, written as:

$$\dot{p}_i=p_i\left(\sum_{j=1}^{n} w_{ij}p_j-\sum_k\sum_j w_{kj}p_k p_j\right)\quad i=1,\dots,n \tag{1}$$

where the dot is derivative w.r.t. time. The population state is then given as a point in simplex σ. Fisher took into account only zygote fitness. In this case $w_{ij}=w_{ji}$ i.e. matrix $W=(w_{ij})=W^T$. The difference between symmetric and nonsymmetrical matrices W is crucial. Indeed in the symmetric case the quadratic form $p(t)^T Wp(t)$ is increasing along trajectories of the selection dynamics (1) – this is the Fundamental Theorem of Natural Selection going back to R. A. Fisher.

Theorem 1. (Fisher [9]) *If $W=W^T$ then the function $p(t)^T Wp(t)$ is strictly increasing with increasing t along any non-stationary trajectory $p(t)$ under (1). Furthermore, any such trajectory converges to a stationary point.*□

Fisher claimed that the theorem was an analog of Boltzmann's [2] principle of entropy increase, and thus to be an analog of the Second Law. These claims have later been re-evaluated.

This theorem is tantamount to saying that mean fitness is an Energy Lyapunov function of the dynamical system (1). Let me recall that a single–valued function which is continuous and has continuous partial derivatives is called the Energy Lyapunov function (ELF) for dynamical system if it is monotonically increasing along the trajectories of this dynamical system (Meyer [12]). So, if we know ELF for dynamic system under consideration then we know practically everything about evolution of this system. It was shown by (Pykh [18]) what ELF may be also used as a measure of biodiversity.

In 1969 V.A. Ratner [23] showed that if we take into account also gamete selection when the fitness matrix $G = DW$, where $D = diag(d_i)$ is diagonal matrix with $d_i > 0$ and W is symmetrical matrix. In this case Fisher's theorem is a false. But, it was shown by Pykh [19, 22] that there exists an analog of Fisher's theorem. Let us denote by $\langle \cdot, \cdot \rangle$ the inner product of the two vectors.

Theorem 2. (Pykh [16,17]) *If matrix G has the next form: $G = D_1 B D_2$, where B is symmetrical, D_1 and D_2 are diagonal matrices and matrix $D = D_1^{-1} D_2 > 0$ then the function $E : \sigma \to \mathbb{R}^1$*

$$E(p) = \frac{p^T D_2 B D_2 p}{\langle d, p \rangle^2} \tag{2}$$

is ELF for system (6). □

3 Replicator equations with nonlinear response functions

In this report we'll restrict our consideration with generalized replicator equations Pykh [19] in the next form:

These equations are written as

$$\dot{p}_i = h(p) f_i(p_i) \left(\sum_{j=1}^{n} w_{ij} f_j(p_j) - \theta^{-1}(p) \sum_{j,k=1}^{n} w_{jk} f_j(p_j) f_k(p_k) \right) \quad i = 1, \ldots, n \tag{3}$$

Here, f_i are nonlinear response functions satisfying the conditions $f_i(0) = 0$, $\partial f_i / \partial p_i > 0 \;\; p_i > 0$, and $\partial f_i / \partial p_i \geqslant 0$ for $p_i = 0$; $W = (w_{ij})$ is the matrix of interactions; the function $h : \sigma \to (0, \infty]$ is determined by the particular problem under consideration; $\theta(p) = \langle \mathbf{e}, f(p) \rangle$; and $f(p) = (f_1(p_1), \ldots, f_n(p_n))$. Obviously, since $\langle \dot{p}(t), \mathbf{e} \rangle \equiv 0$ and $f_i(0) = 0$, the simplex σ and each of its faces are invariant sets of system (3). Examples of different response functions one can find in Pykh and Malkina-Pykh [22].

To state the main theorem, we need some preliminary results. First, it is convenient to pass to the matrix form of representation. In this form, system (3) becomes

$$\dot{p} = h(p) \mathcal{D}(f) \left(Wf - \mathbf{e} \theta^{-1}(p) \langle f, Wf \rangle \right) \tag{4}$$

where $\mathcal{D}(f) = diag(f_1, \ldots, f_n)$.

If the matrix W is nondegenerate, then system (4) has at most one isolated equilibrium point in $\mathrm{Int}\sigma$, which we call nontrivial.

Statement. (Pykh [16,19]). *System (3) has a unique nontrivial equilibrium point $\hat{p} \in \mathrm{Int}\sigma$ if and only if the vector $W^{-1}\mathbf{e}$ is either strictly positive or strictly negative.*□

The coordinates of this equilibrium point are determined from the system

$$\hat{f} / \langle \hat{f}, \mathbf{e} \rangle = W^{-1}\mathbf{e} / \langle \mathbf{e}, W^{-1}\mathbf{e} \rangle \quad (5)$$

where $\hat{f} = (f_1(\hat{p}_1), ..., f_n(\hat{p}_n))$. Let us introduce the notation $W^{-1}\mathbf{e} = b$; then, for $\hat{p}_i$, we obtain the following system of $(n+1)$ equations:

$$\hat{p}_i = f_i^{-1}(\lambda b_i) \qquad i = 1, ..., n, \qquad \sum_{i=1}^{n} \hat{f}_i^{-1}(\lambda b_i) = 1,$$

where λ - is an auxiliary variable similar to the Lagrange multiplier. Obviously, this system has a unique solution if all the b_i are of the same sign.

Theorem 3. (Pykh [19]). *If the matrix W is symmetric, then the function*

$$E(p) = \langle f(p), Wf(p) \rangle \theta^{-2}(p) \quad (4)$$

is a Lyapunov energy function for system (2). □

Corollary. (Pykh [14, 17]). If system (2) has a nontrivial equilibrium point $\hat{p} \in \text{Int}\sigma$, then it is totally stable in $\text{Int}\sigma$ if and only if the matrix W has $(n-1)$ negative characteristic numbers.□

Table 1: Different entropy measures.

Response function	Entropy	Name
Logariphmic $f_i(p_i) = (1 - \ln p_i)^{-1}$	$H_o(p) = \sum_{i=1}^{n} p_i \ln p_i$	Bolzmann entropy
Power-law $f_i(p_i) = p_i^{1-q};\ q \neq 1$	$H_o(p) = \frac{(\sum p_i^q - 1)}{1 - q}$	Tsallis entropy
Logistic $f_i(p_i) = \frac{1}{b + ce^{-\alpha p_i}}$ $b > 0,\ c > 0,\ \alpha > 0$	$H_o(p) = \sum_{i=1}^{n} \ln(1 - e^{-\alpha p_i})$	Logistic entropy

4 Entropy measures

Now, we can state the main result

Theorem 4. (Pykh [21]) *If system (4) has a nontrivial equilibrium point $\hat{p} \in Int\sigma$ and the matrix $(W^T + W)$ has $(n-1)$ negative characteristic value, then the function*

$$H_\varepsilon(p) = \sum_{i=1}^{n} \int_{\varepsilon_i}^{p_i} \frac{\hat{f}_i dx}{f_i(x)}$$

where $0 \leqslant \varepsilon_i \leqslant 1, i = 1,...n$ *are some constant is a Lyapunov energy function for system (4).* □

Based on this theorem we can receive a set of response function for existing entropy measures and construct new entropy and distance measures for any response functions. Short summary of this approach listed in tables 1 and 2.

Table 2: Different distance measure.

Response function	Interaction matrix	«Distance »	Name
Linear $f_i(p_i) = p_i$	Theorem 4	$H_{\hat{p}} = \sum \hat{p}_i \ln \frac{p_i}{\hat{p}_i}$	Relative entropy (Kullback [10])
Linear $f_i(p_i) = p_i$	$W = D_1 B D_2$	$H_{\hat{p}} = \sum_{i=1}^{n} d_i \hat{p}_i \ln \frac{p_i}{\hat{p}_i} - -\langle d, \hat{p} \rangle \ln \langle d, p \rangle$	Weighted relative entropy (Pykh [16,17])
logistic $f_i(p_i) = = \frac{1}{b + ce^{-\alpha p_i}}$ $b > 0, c > 0, \alpha > 0$	Theorem 4	$H_{\hat{p}} = \sum_{i=1}^{n} \hat{f}_i \ln \left(\frac{1 - e^{-\alpha p_i}}{1 - e^{-\alpha \hat{p}_i}} \right)$	Weighted logistic entropy (new)

5 Conclusion

It is seen from the examples given above that, if we consider entropy characteristics, then we should set $\varepsilon_i = 0$ in the expression for $H_\varepsilon(p)$, and if we are interested in "distances" between distributions, then we should take $\varepsilon_i = \hat{p}_i$. We also emphasize that there exists a relation between the derivative of the function $H_\varepsilon(p)$, which can be interpreted as a generalized entropy, and the function $E(p)$, which is often (in particular, in works on the theory of neural networks) considered as an analog of the energy. This relationship for entropy production was established by Pykh [20,21] and has the next form:

$$\dot{H}_\varepsilon = h(p)\theta\hat{\theta}\left(E(\hat{p}) - E(p)\right) \geqslant 0$$

In conclusion, we mention that all results stated above were obtained by formally analyzing systems of generalized replicator equations, which arise in very diverse fields of natural sciences and, therefore, can serve as a basis for finding analogies between these domains of natural sciences.

Also note that it was Ilya Prigogine who the first pointed out [13] the importance of the relationship between Lyapunov functions and entropy.

References

[1] Beck C. and Schlogl F., *Thermodynamics of Chaotic Systems*, Cambridge University Press, Cambridge, UK, 1995.

[2] Boltzmann L., *Vorlesungen űber Gas Theorie*, Leipzig, Germany: Barth, 1896.

[3] Bomze I.M., "Evolution towards the maximum clique", *Journal of Global Optimization*, no. 10, pp. 143 – 164, 1997.

[4] Brenig L. and Goriely A., "Universal canonical forms for time-continuous dynamical systems", *Phys. Rev. A*, no. 40, pp. 4119–4122, 1989.

[5] Darwin C., *On the Origin of Species*, London: Murray, 1859.

[6] Dawkins R., *The Selfish Gene*, Oxford University Press, Oxford, 1976.

[7] Eigen M., "Self-organization of matter and the evolution of biological macromolecules", *Natur-wissenschaften*, no. 58, pp. 465–526, 1971.

[8] Eigen M. and Schuster P., *The Hypercycle. A Principle of Natural Self-organization*, Springer-Verlag, Berlin, 1979.

[9] Fisher R.A., *The Genetical Theory of Natural Selection,* New York: Dover, 1930.

[10] Kullback S. and Leiber R. On information and sufficiency. *Ann. Math. Stat.,* Vol.22, N1, pp. 79-87, 1951.

[11] Menon A., *Replicators and Complementarity: Solving the Simplest Complex System without Simulation*, in: V.N. Alexandrov et.al., eds., ICCS 2001, LNCS 2074, pp. 922–931, 2001.

[12] Meyer K., "Energy functions for Morse-Smale systems", *Amer. J. Math.*, v. 90, no. 4, pp. 1031–1040, 1968.

[13] Prigogine I., Time, structure and fluctuations. Nobel lecture, 8 December, 1977

[14] Pykh Yu. A., *On the Global Stability of Some Ecological Models*, Mathematical Models of Cell Population, Inter-University Collection/Gorky State University, Gorky, pp. 70–74, 1981, (Russian).

[15] Pykh Yu. A., "On monostability of certain equations of population dynamics", *Biosphere Problems*, no. 2, pp. 71–80, USSR Academy of Sci., Moscow, 1981a (in Russian).

[16] Pykh Yu. A., *Steady-State and Stability in the Models of Population dynamics*, Nauka, Moscow, 1983 (Russian).

[17] Pykh Yu.A., "Lyapunov functions for Lotka-Volterra systems: an overview and problems", *Proceedings of 5th IFAC Symposium "Nonlinear Control Systems" 2001,* pp. 1655–1660. www.inenco.org/publications

[18] Pykh Yu.A., Liapunov function as a measure of biodiversity: theoretical background. *"Ecological indicators", 2 (2002) 123-133*

[19] Pykh Yu.A., Energy Lyapunov Function for Generalized Replicator Equations. *Proceedings of International Conference "Physics and Control",* 2003, pp.271-276 www.inenco.org/publications

[20] Pykh Yu.A., "Construction of entropy characteristics based on Lyapunov energy function". *Doclady Mathematics. V 69, N 3, 2004, pp.355-358* www.inenco.org/publications

[21] Pykh Yu.A., Construction of the entropy measures on the basis of replicator equation with nonsymmetrical interaction matrix. *Doclady Mathematics,* 2005, in press.

[22] Pykh Yu.A., Malkina-Pykh I.G. *The method of response function in ecology*. WIT Press, 2000, 275 p.

[23] Ratner V.A., *Mathematical Models in the Population genetics: Frequency-Dependent Deterministic Models,* in "Mathematical Models in Biology", VINITI, pp. 88–115, 1969 (Russian).

[24] Schuster P. and Sigmund K., "Replicator dynamics", J. Theor. Biol., no. 100, pp. 533–538, 1983.

[25] Sharpe F.R. and Lotka A.J., "A problem in age-distribution", *Philosophical Mag.*, no. 21, pp. 435–438, 1911.

[26] Spiegelman S., "An approach to the experimental analysis of precellular evolution", *Quarterly Review of Biophysics*, no. 4, pp. 213–251, 1971.

[27] Taylor P. G. and Jonker L., "Evolutionary stable strategies and game dynamics", *Math. Biosci.*, no. 40, pp. 145–156, 1978.

[28] Vrba E.S., *Levels of Selection and Sorting with Special Reference to the Species Level*, in Oxford Surveys in Evolutionary Biology, P.H. Harvey and L. Partridge, eds., Oxford University Press, no. 6, pp. 114–115, 1989.

Thermodynamic optimisation of the use of natural resources: an agroalimentary production in a Chianti farm (Italy)

S. Borsa[1,2], N. Marchettini[1,2], A. Pizzigallo[1] & F. M. Pulselli[1,2]
[1]*Dept. of Chemical and Biosystems Sciences, University of Siena, Italy*
[2]*A.R.C.A. Onlus, Siena, Italy*

Abstract

Agriculture is deeply based on the *in loco* availability of natural resources. They are mostly provided for free by the environment and often neglected by traditional accounting systems since it is difficult to measure their contribution or their physical weight with respect to the marketable input expressed in monetary units, more familiar to most people. The management of natural resources is a fundamental step toward the sustainability of a productive process. In this sense, it is necessary to answer some questions: how much does the local environment support the system? How high is the level of dependence of the system on other ecosystems? How much does the local environment contribute to make a given profit? This paper presents the environmental assessment of the use of resources for an agroalimentary production system located in the Chianti area (Province of Siena - Italy) by using Emergy evaluation, a thermodynamic based methodology introduced by Howard Odum during the '80s. The use of Emergy enables one to calculate some sustainability indicators (such as Environmental Loading Ratio, Emergy Yield Ratio, Emergy Density, Emergy Investment Ratio), able to give a systemic and holistic picture of the production process from an environmental point of view. Furthermore, this paper introduces the concept of "eMternality" to provide a monetary measure of the contribution of Natural Capital to the system. Starting from the economic result of the productive process, the method of "eMternalities" allows one to redistribute the income among all production factors, both marketable and environmental.
Keywords: agriculture, thermodynamic indicators, sustainable development, emergy evaluation, emternalities.

1 Introduction

How much does the environment support agroproductions? What is the real role of natural resources, that are not evaluated (but indirectly) by traditional economic instruments? How sustainable is a given agroproduction process with respect to other similar systems on the basis of the use of resources? Is it possible to measure the value of the environmental advantages of a biological production? Is it possible to estimate the economic value of the environmental contribution to the agricultural activity?

These are some of the questions that arise among policy makers, managers, environmentalists, scientists and farmers who are interested in agriculture.

Agriculture, as well as other human activity involving the environment, needs new tools to assess the level of sustainability and the capacity to survive indefinitely. Humans are threatening the basis of the life support system: loss of biodiversity, exhaustion of non renewable resources, depletion of natural capital, pollution and greenhouse effect are crucial elements never stressed by the traditional economic analyses. In the last decades, new methodologies has been developed, which are able to attribute an objective value to the environment on physical basis. They should be used together with economic parameters in order to better design the sustainable behaviour of human society.

2 Methods

All evaluations presented in this paper are based on eMergy methodology. Emergy was introduced by H.T. Odum during the '80s as a tool of environmental (but not only environmental) accounting [1-4]. On the basis of a thermodynamic hierarchy of energy, starting from solar energy, Odum's research has provided a measure of the environmental work necessary to generate an item or a flow.

Emergy is defined as the quantity of solar energy directly or indirectly necessary to support a given system and its level of organization. The emergy of all inputs to a system is calculated in terms of solar emjoules (sej) by means of suitable conversion factors called transformities (expressed in sej/J), or specific emergy (expressed in sej/g or other units). Emergy represents a measure able to evaluate the convergence of several inputs to a system on a common basis. This allows also to classify inputs in different categories (i.e. renewable, R, versus non renewable, N; local, L, versus purchased, F, etc.). On the basis of these classes, some indicators can be computed in order to assess the sustainability of the use of resources.

The *Environmental Loading Ratio* (ELR) is the ratio of purchased (F) and non-renewable local emergy (N) to renewable environmental emergy (R). A high value of the ELR indicates a lack of proportion between the use of non-renewable resources with respect to renewable ones, so that environmental cycles are overloaded. The *Emergy Yield Ratio* (EYR) is the ratio of total emergy (R+N+F) supporting the system to the emergy of the inputs from the economic sector (F) (i.e. not provided for free by the environment). It indicates whether a process can compete in supplying a primary energy source for an economy. The

Emergy Investment Ratio (EIR) is the emergy of purchased inputs (F) divided by local emergy both renewable and non-renewable (N+R). A high level of EIR represents a sort of fragility of the system because of its dependence on inputs from other economic systems. The *Emergy Flow Density* (ED) is given by the emergy flow (R+N+F) supporting a system divided by its area. If this ratio is high, a large quantity of emergy is used in a certain area: this can mean a high stress to the environment and points out the land surface as a limiting factor for future development.

Emternalities are defined as a measure of the environmental fraction that is embodied in economic products but which is not captured by commercial markets [5]. In the case of a production system, they could be defined as the environmental fraction which contributes to support the economic processes without leaving any footprint in the traditional economic accounting framework. In this paper the value of emternalities is calculated by using the ratio of money to emergy, that represents the value of one unit of emergy flowing through a given system, in monetary terms. This method enables to assign an economic value to those inputs without a market price, in order to redistribute the income on the basis of physical weights.

3 Results and discussion

The system under study is a farm, called Pacina, in the Chianti area (Province of Siena, central Italy). It is 63 hectares large and it is mainly devoted (10 ha) to a biological cultivation of Sangiovese vine, in order to produce a good Chianti wine. A wide portion of the area (30 ha) is devoted to satellite cultivations, such as olive production and fodder plants for zootechnic activity. The rest is covered by forests (23 ha). This enables to rotate crops and safeguard the territory in the long run. Biological production and rotation of crops represent a virtuous union towards sustainability, without neglecting the economic aspects of the activity.

The farm obtains 60 quintals (1 quintal = 220.46 lb.) of grapes per year. The market value of production is equal to 80 Euro per quintal, a low value with respect to the costs of production. For this reason, the subsequent phases of production (i.e. production of wine) are fundamental for the economic performance of the farm. In other words, grape production does not affect the earning capacity of the farm, probably because market prices do not remunerate the environmental production factors.

For emergy application to agricultural systems, see for example [6-10].

All the inputs to the system of grapes production and their emergy content are collected in Table 1. The analysis has been conducted for one hectare and one year (to avoid the seasonal oscillations of parameters). The total amount of emergy is equal to 7.84×10^{15} sej/ha/year and the main inputs, expressed in quantitative terms, are the environmental ones (in particular, rain and loss of topsoil). Other inputs are relevant, such as human labour and parasiticides. Biological production implies the absence of chemical items such as fertilizers. Machines (and related fuel consumption) are also used for other cultivations within the farm and their contribution to grapes production is very low.

Table 1: Emergy evaluation of grapes production in Pacina.

	Input	Unit	Unit/ha/yr	Emergy per unit (sej/unit)	Ref	Solar Emergy (sej/ha/yr)
	Local Renewable Resources					
1	Sunlight	J	4.59×10^{13}	1	[5]	4.59×10^{13}
2	Rain	g	8.50×10^{9}	1.45×10^{5}	[5]	1.23×10^{15}
3	Wind	J	2.12×10^{10}	2.47×10^{3}	[5]	5.24×10^{13}
4	Geothermal heat	J	3.15×10^{10}	1.20×10^{4}	[4]	3.78×10^{14}
	Local Non Renewable Resources					
5	Loss of topsoil	J	3.05×10^{10}	7.40×10^{4}	[4]	2.26×10^{15}
	Purchased Resources					
6	Nitrogen fertilizers	g	-	2.41×10^{10}	[5]	-
7	Phosphate fertilizers	g	-	2.02×10^{10}	[5]	-
8	Potash fertilizers	g	-	1.74×10^{9}	[5]	-
9	Human labour	J	1.50×10^{8}	1.24×10^{7}	[5]	1.86×10^{15}
10	Agr. machinery	g	6.02×10^{3}	1.13×10^{10}	[5]	6.80×10^{13}
11	Fuels	J	5.97×10^{7}	1.11×10^{5}	[11]	6.63×10^{12}
12	Wood	g	5.33×10^{4}	6.79×10^{8}	[5]	3.62×10^{13}
13	Iron ore	g	1.60×10^{4}	4.44×10^{9}	[5]	7.10×10^{13}
14	Organic manure	g	1.00×10^{6}	2.13×10^{8}	[5]	2.13×10^{14}
15	Parasiticide	g	6.90×10^{4}	2.49×10^{10}	[5]	1.72×10^{15}
	Total Emergy Flow		sej/ha/yr			7.84×10^{15}

A summary of emergy flows is shown in Table 2.

A relevant portion of emergy is directly dependent on local environment (R+N = 52.5%), without an economic counterpart (with the exception of 10% of human labour and 29% of organic manure). Soil erosion (non renewable) represents the 28.23% of total emergy.

Emergy of purchased inputs is less than 50% of total, putting on evidence a certain equilibrium between different categories of resources.

Emergy indices are able to corroborate these considerations and add information about the life of the system as a whole. They are useful to understand the direction of a system's development.

Table 2: Emergy flows and indices of the grape production in Pacina.

Summary of emergy flows and indices				
	expression	amount	unit	%
Local Renewable Resources	R[1]	1.86×10^{15}	sej/ha/yr	23.72
Local Non Renewable resources	N[2]	2.26×10^{15}	sej/ha/yr	28.83
Purchased Resources	F[3]	3.72×10^{15}	sej/ha/yr	47.45
Total Emergy Flow	Y[4]	7.84×10^{15}	sej/ha/yr	100

[1] **R** is given by the sum of items 1, 4, 10% of 9 and 29% of 14

[2] **N** is given by item 5

[3] **F** is given by the sum of items 6, 7, 8, 90% of 9, 10, 11, 12, 13, 71% of 14 and 15

[4] **Y** is given by the sum of (**R** + **N** + **F**)

ELR	**(N+F)/R**	3.21	
EYR	**Y/F**	2.11	
EIR	**F/(R+N)**	0.90	
ED	**Y/Area**	7.84×10^{11}	sej/m^2/yr

ELR is 3.21, meaning that the use of non-renewable inputs is three times larger than the use of renewable ones. EYR defines the importance of the environment in agroproductions. The farmer realizes value added thanks to natural resources, that contribute to the production together with the market goods and services. EIR is a measure of how much the system is dependent from the outside. The values of EYR and EIR are respectively 2.11 and 0.90, a good result as we will show afterwards. ED (7.84×10^{11} sej/m^2/yr) represents the convergence of inputs per unit of area, that is the measure of how intensive the agricultural activity is.

Table 3 presents the results of emergy evaluation for different grapes productions in Italy, two in Tuscany (Pacina and Montalcino) and two in Piedmont (Barbera of Montaldo Scarampi and Castelnuovo Boglione). All data are referred to the emergy flows per year for one hectare of cultivated land.

Pacina presents the highest environmental flows (both renewable – R – and non renewable – N), and the lowest level of purchased inputs due to the characteristics of biological production. Although the other farms produce more grapes per hectare, Pacina presents the best measure of efficiency because the specific emergy per unit is the lowest one.

ELR and ED values confirm how Pacina is following a sustainable trend in terms of environmental stress. At the same time, EYR and EIR represent the equilibrium in the use of resources: EYR emphasizes how the environment directly contribute to the production per unit of purchased input and EIR shows the low fragility of the system under study due to the low dependence of Pacina from other ecosystems or economic systems.

www.witpress.com, ISSN 1743-3541 (on-line)

Table 3: Comparing emergy flows and indices for different grapes productions.

Flows & Indices	Chianti Pacina	Brunello Montalcino	Barbera M.do Scarampi	Barbera C. Boglione
R [a]	1.86×10^{15}	1.47×10^{15}	1.63×10^{15}	1.73×10^{15}
N [a]	2.26×10^{15}	2.03×10^{15}	1.35×10^{15}	1.34×10^{15}
F [a]	3.72×10^{15}	8.98×10^{15}	1.26×10^{16}	1.64×10^{16}
Y [a]	7.84×10^{15}	1.25×10^{16}	1.56×10^{16}	1.95×10^{16}
Prod. (g/yr)	6.00×10^{6}	7.35×10^{6}	1.04×10^{7}	6.50×10^{6}
Emergy/unit [b]	1.31×10^{9}	1.70×10^{9}	1.50×10^{9}	3.00×10^{9}
ELR	3.21	7.48	8.56	10.25
EYR	2.11	1.39	1.24	1.19
EIR	0.90	2.56	4.23	5.34
ED [c]	7.84×10^{11}	1.25×10^{12}	1.56×10^{12}	1.95×10^{12}
Composite emt.	52.55%	28.04%	19.13%	15.77%
Renewable emt.	23.72%	11.78%	10.46%	8.89%

[a] **R**, **N**, **F** and **Y** are expressed in sej/ha/yr
[b] **Emergy/unit** values are expressed in sej/g
[c] **ED** values are expressed in sej/m^2/yr

Furthermore, the concept of emternalities can be introduced [5, 12, 13, 14]. Once we have environmentally dimensioned (in emergy) all the inputs to the system, it is possible to calculate the emternality ratios, i.e. the proportion (%) of the environmental fraction (R+N) in the entire set of inputs (Y). This index is called composite emternality ratio, while the ratio of R to Y is called Renewable emternality ratio. Table 3 show the importance of renewable resources in the production system of Pacina. The difference between the two ratios is defined as an indicator of unsustainability, but, in the case of Pacina, the flow of non-renewable resources (loss of topsoil) is overestimated, since the erosion rate is under control thanks to the rotation of crops.

The results of an emergy evaluation for a production system can be related to economic parameters, such as the value of production. In particular, the so-called "emergy/money ratio", attained by dividing the total annual emergy use (the sum of environmental resources used and imports) by the economic product, can indicate the amount of resources supporting the economic performance of a territorial system. The inverse of the Emergy/money ratio, vice versa, "may be calculated to put emergy wealth in economic terms familiar to most people" [2]. The last index, expressed in terms of Euro/sej, is useful in revealing assets not contemplated by economic accounting systems.

As we have seen, Pacina produces 60 quintals of grapes per hectare in the unit of time (one year). The economic value of production is equal to 80 Euro per quintal, so the total value of Pacina's production is 4,800 Euro/ha/yr. The production is supported by both economic and environmental inputs, hence the economic result should split up among all production factors.

The ratio of money to emergy is equal to 6.12×10^{-13} Euro/sej. On the basis of this conversion factor, the economic result is redistributed among all the inputs.

- Local environmental renewable resources (R) : 1,138 Euro/ha/yr
- Local environmental non renewable resources (N) : 1,381 Euro/ha/yr
- Purchased inputs (F) : 2,279 Euro/ha/yr

This could be a fairer redistribution of income among input: purchased inputs have a price (different from the above), but the amount of Euro calculated for R and N can be a useful environmental benchmark for resources management.

4 Conclusion

This paper has presented an environmental assessment of an agroproduction in Tuscany, called Pacina, by means of Odum's emergy evaluation. The analysis has been divided in three sections: 1) Assessment of the grapes production in Pacina by the collection of all the inputs supporting the system (in emergy terms) and the calculation of suitable indicators; 2) Comparison of four high quality different grapes production systems in Italy; 3) Evaluation of emternalities and the contribution of the environment to the production system. The results have put on evidence that the biological production is a crucial choice towards sustainability. It allows a better environmental performance of the system, without compromising its efficiency and the quality of the final product. Furthermore, the environmental inputs represent the fundamental elements which any agroproduction is based on. Integrating emergy and emternalities enables to evaluate this contribution in physical and economic terms respectively.

References

[1] Odum, H.T. Self organisation, transformity and information. *Science*, **242**, pp. 1132-1139, 1988.

[2] Odum, H.T. *Environmental Accounting. Emergy and Environmental Decision Making*. John Wiley and Sons. New York, 1996.

[3] Odum H.T., Brown M.T., Brandt-Williams S. Introduction and Global Budget, Folio #1. *Handbook of Emergy Evaluation.* Center for Environmental Policy, University of Florida, Gainesville, USA, 2000.

[4] Odum H.T. Emergy of Global Processes, Folio #2. *Handbook of Emergy Evaluation.* Center for Environmental Policy, University of Florida, Gainesville, USA, 2000.

[5] Pillet G. Emternalities as counterpart to economic externalities! *Ecological Modelling*, **178**, pp. 183-187, 2004.

[6] Brandt-Williams, S. Emergy of Florida Agriculture. Folio #4. *Handbook of Emergy Evaluation.* Center for Environmental Policy, University of Florida, Gainesville, USA, 2002.

[7] Bastianoni, S., Marchettini, N., Panzieri, M., Tiezzi, E. Sustainability assessment of a farm in the Chianti area (Italy). *Journal of Cleaner Production*, **9**, pp. 365-373, 2001.

[8] Principi I., Fugaro, L., Borsa, S. Assessing sustainability of the Chianti area: the role of agriculture. In *Ecosystems and Sustainable Development IV*, Vol. 1 (E. Tiezzi, C.A. Brebbia, J.L. Usò eds.), WIT Press, Southampton, pp. 723-729, 2003.

[9] Bastianoni, S., Marchettini. Ethanol production from biomass: analysis of process efficiency and sustainability. *Biomass and bioenergy*, **11**, pp. 411-418, 1996.

[10] Tiezzi E., Marchettini, N. *Che cos'è lo sviluppo sostenibile?* Donzelli, Roma, Italy, 1999.

[11] Susani L. Analisi termodinamica dei processi di produzione dell'energia termoelettrica mediante il calcolo di nuove transformity delle risorse petrolifere. Degree thesis in Chemistry, University of Siena, Italy, 2001.

[12] Pillet, G., Maradan, D., Zingg, N., Brandt-Williams, S. Emternalities - Theory and assessment. *Proc. of the 1st Biennial Emergy Conference.* Ed. by Brown M.T., University of Florida, Gainesville, USA, pp. 39-51, 2000.

[13] Brandt-Williams, S., Pillet, G. Fertilizer co-products as agricultural emternalities: quantifying environmental services used in production of food. *Proc. of the 2nd Biennial Emergy Conference*. Ed. by Brown M.T., Odum H.T., Tilley D., Ulgiati S., University of Florida, Gainsville, Florida, USA, pp. 327-338, 2003.

[14] Pulselli F.M., Pulselli R.M., Picchi M.P. Emergy evaluation of the "emternalities" in non-industrialized regions: the case of two mountain communities in Italy. *Proc. of the 2nd Biennial Emergy Conference*. Ed. by Brown M.T., Odum H.T., Tilley D., Ulgiati S., University of Florida, Gainsville, Florida, USA, pp. 397-407, 2003.

Section 2
Sustainability indicators

Quantifying possible pathways of sustainable development of a territorial system

S. Bastianoni[1,2], N. Marchettini[1,2] & R. Ridolfi[1,2]
[1]*Dept. of Chemical and Biosystems Sciences, University of Siena, Italy*
[2]*A.R.C.A. Onlus, Siena, Italy*

Abstract

The assessment of the environmental sustainability of a territorial system requires a holistic approach, based on thermodynamic functions and able to consider all the complex mechanisms that are involved in a system.

Many of the most used indicators focus their attention on single aspects, and they are not able to consider the system as a whole. Some authors have developed the use of different indicators such as emergy analysis and greenhouse gas inventory. The first methodologies point out their attention on the resource use. In particular, the Emergy Analysis measures the quantity and type of resources necessary to sustain the system. Greenhouse gas inventory is directly focused on the indirect impact of the system, i.e. the CO_2 equivalent emissions produced.

These methodologies have already been used in order to assess the sustainability of a territorial system while the suggested strategies and pathways for sustainability still need investigation. It is in fact very important to test if and how these methodologies are able to assess these possible paths of sustainability and to measure quantitatively the choices made.

The case study is the Province of Grosseto. The different indicators (emergy analysis and greenhouse inventory) define the Province of Grosseto as a system that makes a low impact on the territory. In this paper we formulate possible scenarios of sustainable development and we quantify how these developments affect indicators.

Keywords: sustainable pathways, emergy analysis, greenhouse gas inventory, territorial system, hydrogen production.

1 Introduction

A territorial system is a complex system in a steady state. Its structure is based on many levels of organizations; its openings to the outside, its irreversible dynamics are peculiar features of a complex system. This system requires resources and energy to enhance internal order and to self-organize, while increasing the entropy of the surroundings. The increase in entropy exceeds the internal entropy decrease of the system, so that the second principle of thermodynamics is observed. Hence a territory behaves like a dissipative structure [1]. When dealing with complex territorial systems, common indicators (i.e. analytical pollution measures) are not sufficient to address all the environmental aspects involved.

"Macro" indicators capable of evaluating the global environmental performance of a system are needed. A growing need has been felt to create instruments capable of monitoring more sensitive phenomena and elaborating more complex and meaningful information with greater portent than the usual stress, state and response data. In this paper, we present how it is possible to define sustainable pathways of development. The analysis is made on the province of Grosseto and uses two environmental approaches: emergy analysis and greenhouse gas inventory. The aim of this paper is to test if these environmental approaches are able to address quantitatively sustainability pathways and to describe which steps we have to use in order to analyse the sustainability options.

Our approach is focused either on the global scale, i.e. the system as whole in order to test the changes produced following different sustainable strategies or on the local scale in order to test the sustainability of the single option chosen.
The province of Grosseto is located in the southern part of Tuscany (Italy); its territory extends along the Tirrenic coast and it is delimited by the province of Livorno, Siena, Pisa and Viterbo. This territorial system produces a low impact on the environment [2]; its main activities are connected to agriculture and tourism. There is a production of electricity from geothermal heat that is very interesting from the point of view of sustainability. Another important characteristic of the system is, as we have said before, the presence of important agricultural activity, and then a great production of biomass residues.

The idea of using these environmental techniques to assess the sustainability pathways of a territorial system, comes form the fact that province of Grosseto has been characterized by a geothermal production and from the fact that there is a rising interest in hydrogen production for transport and energy production.

We test, with the two methodologies, the effect of considering electricity made by geothermal resources in spite of the Italian average resources used (mainly fossil fuel). Results from emergy analysis have tested using a graphical approach presented at 3rd Biennal Emergy Analysis Research Conference [3].

As our aim is to indicate sustainable pathways, in relation to the characteristics of the territory. We have checked the possibility of exploiting residues from agricultural activities in order to produce hydrogen. This study was a part of a national project entitled "Innovative Catalytic technologies for the

Production of Hydrogen and Syngas from Natural Gas, Biomass and CDR" a project financed by Italian Ministry of Instruction, University and Research (PRIN 2003).

As our aim is to construct a method able to identify sustainability pathways, we have performed the analysis of the territorial system considering two scenarios, one with electricity produced from average Italian fuel composition and another one considering the geothermal resources. Moreover we have tested, using emergy analysis, if it is sustainable the gasification of biomass for the production of hydrogen in comparison with fossil fuel. What we present is only the first part of an important project we are developing about technologies of hydrogen production.

2 Methodology

In this article we want to show how it is possible by the combination of different methodologies to follow the sustainable development of a system and therefore we do not spend much in the description of the methodologies but we indicate references for a better understanding.

Emergy analysis is an environmental methodology based on the laws of thermodynamics. Emergy is defined as the quantity of solar emergy necessary (directly or indirectly) to obtain a product in a given process. It can be used to assess complex relationships between the economy and its supporting environment since the work of both is expressed in equivalent terms. By calculating the emergy indicators we are able to understand how far from the sustainability the territorial system is [4,5]. Transformity is an intensive quantity measured in "solar emergy joules/Joules" (sej/J). It is an indicator of (in)efficiency since, for equivalent processes, giving the same product, the lower the transformity, the higher the efficiency of production.

In this paper we used one of the emergy indicators, i.e. the Environmental Loading Ratio (ELR) that is the ratio between non renewable and renewable resources used in a territory. The lower the indicator, the higher is the use of renewable resources with respect to non renewable ones.

The greenhouse gas inventory is realized according to the method proposed by IPCC [6]. We consider the emissions of the three greenhouse gases that give the largest contribution to global warming, i.e. CO_2, CH_4 and N_2O. The gas emissions were transformed into carbon dioxide equivalent using the Global Warming Potential (GWP). We calculated the emissions produced by the energetic sector, the livestock sector and the wastes. The quantity of CO_2 sequestered by the annual growth of forests was also considered in the greenhouse balance while forests cut and wood burnt were subtracted from the natural absorption. In this paper we use as indicator the total CO_2 eq emitted in the province of Grosseto.

3 Results and discussion

In the analysis of the Province of Grosseto, we have calculated emergy analysis and greenhouse gases inventory considering that electricity is produced from the

Italian average fuels (1st scenario) and from geothermal resources (2nd scenario). The results are showed in table 1.

Table 1: Results of the emergy and greenhouse gas inventory in the two scenarios.

Methodology	1st scenario	2nd scenario
ELR (Emergy analysis)	8.15	7.46
Total CO_2eq (Gg)	844.66	748.02

As we can see in the previous table, the two indicators present better value in the 2nd scenario when we use a renewable resource (geothermal) in spite of fossil fuel. To confirm this statement, as emergetic indicator (environmental loading ratio) express a relationship between two independent variables and the same indicator may be obtained using different values for the two variables in consideration (if the two parameters, renewable and non-renewable resources, are doubled or halved, the environmental loading ratio remains unchanged); we adopt an approach capable of simultaneously measuring both the value of the indicator and the variations brought about by the independent variables that give rise to it. We applied to the analysis of the Province of Grosseto the method proposed by Ridolfi et al. [3]. The graph is reported in figure 1.

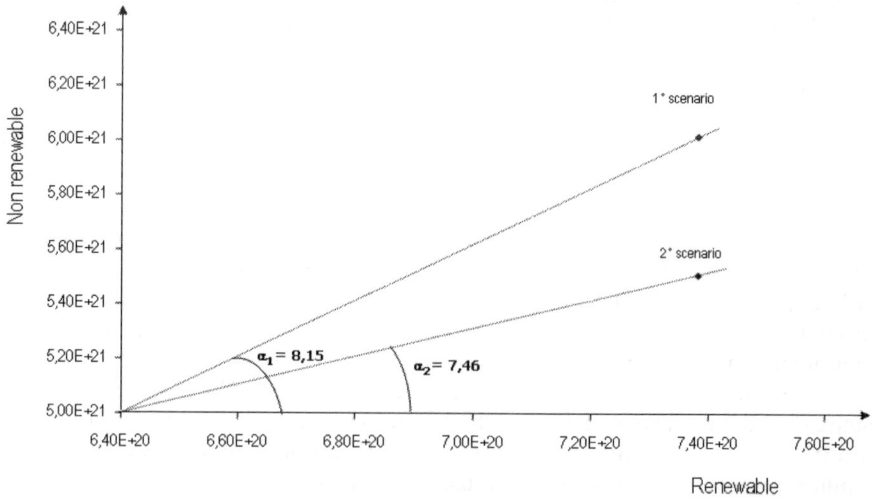

Figure 1: Graphic representation of ELR in the two scenarios.

As it can be seen in Figure 1, the decrease in the value of the angular coefficient shows an improvement in the sustainability of the system. This is due to the fact that, in the 2nd scenario, the system is using a renewable resource instead of a non renewable one. In the graph it is clear that the lower ELR of the system is not due to an increase in the use of renewable resources but to the decrease in the use of non renewable one. This diagram should be used to test the different pathways and to see what is really the best option chosen.

To develop sustainable strategies it is necessary to develop new productive activities in the territory, trying to choose the ones with the lowest impact. The option chosen should be adapted for the development of the system and in accordance with the characteristics of the territory. Then the alternatives should be tested with a methodological procedure in order to assess what is most advantageous from the point of view of sustainability.

We calculated the transformity of hydrogen from biomass: this indicator gives information about the emergy used to produce a J of product. Transformity is an indicator of inefficiency because for equivalent processes, giving the same product, the lower the transformity, the higher the efficiency of production. In the table 2 we present the emergy evaluation of hydrogen production from biomass; data are from Hamelinck et al. [7].

Table 2: Emergy analysis of hydrogen production from biomass.

	Item	**quantity**	**unit**	**transformity (sej/unit)**	**solar emergy (sej)**
1	Biomass	1.24E+16	J	4.40E+04	5.43E+20
2	Plant cost	2.37E+07	$	1.55E+12	3.67E+19
3	H_2	6.13E+15	J	**9.47E+04**	5.80E+20

The transformity of hydrogen from biomass gasification is compared to the one of fossil fuels used for transport. The latter one has a value of 1.11×10^5 sej/J. This means that hydrogen can be produced from biomass in a slightly more efficient way than fossil fuels from oil. Moreover ELR of fossil fuel production tends to infinite (the process is fed by non renewable resources), while for hydrogen from biomass we can imagine a finite (and quite low) number. What we still need to calculate to get ELR is the percentage of renewable to assign to biomass residues. The next step of this analysis is to study how this process can be integrated in the territory: we have to manage the size of a plant for hydrogen production, where it can be located, etc. The last step is then to estimate how the new production alters emergy analysis of the territory, and to imagine how the substitution of fossil fuel with hydrogen (considering all the necessary investments in terms of infrastructure) can change emergy indicators and in particularly environmental loading ratio. This change will be tested in the graphic method to understand if the pathway is going towards a more sustainable development.

4 Conclusions

The approach used is mainly based on two indicators: greenhouse gas inventory and emergy evaluation. The advantage of the latter methodology is that all flows of energy and matter sustaining the territorial system are accounted for and conducted to a single common denominator. In our approach we are able to assess the pathways of sustainability studying the system at the macro and micro scale. The latter scale permits us to test if the option chosen is a real alternative. The macro scale permits us to evaluate if the changes due to the introduction of a different way of production represents really a positive aspect to pursue sustainability. The use of a graphic method makes possible to take complete advantage of the information contained in the various components of the environmental loading ratio by making use of the information contained both in the emergy indicator itself as well as in their component variables.

In particular we have analyzed the territorial system in two different scenarios with a local geothermal production and without. The ELR and the CO_2eq decreases in the scenario with the geothermal production. For the ELR we have also used the graphic method, that is able to consider the index variation together with variables variation and so we can identify the reason of ELR decrease.

At the local level we have assessed hydrogen production from biomass in order to verify if it is an option to be followed for a sustainable development. This solution should be then investigated at the territorial level with all the necessary infrastructure to substitute fossil fuel with hydrogen and then it will be possible verify its sustainability with respect to the actual situation.

References

[1] Prigogine I. and Nicolis G., "Self Organization in Non-equilibrium Systems". John Wiley and Sons, New York, 1977.

[2] Ridolfi, et al., "A new environmental approach in the territory assessment", Brownfield Sites II Assessment, Rehabilitation and Development (C.A. Brebbia, A. Donati & C. Rossi eds.), WIT Press, Southampton, pp. 3-12, 2004.

[3] Ridolfi, et al., "The Use of Emergy Indices in the Environmental Certification of a Territory", 3rd Biennial Emergy Analysis Research Conference", Gainsville, Florida, USA, in press.

[4] Odum, H.T. 1996. Environmental Accounting: Emergy and Environmental Decision Making. John Wiley and Sons. New York.

[5] Odum, H.T., 1988. Self organisation, transformity and information. Science, 242: 1132-1139.

[6] IPCC, 1996. Greenhouse Gas Inventory. Reporting Instructions, 1996 (revised). IPCC, Intergovernmental Panel on Climate Change, 1,2,3.

[7] Carlo N. Hamelinck et al, "Future prospects for production of methanol and hydrogen production from biomass", Journal of Power Sources 111, 1-22 (2002).

How to measure the sustainability of an area: the SPIn-Eco project of the Province of Siena

S. Bastianoni[1,3], V. Niccolucci[1,3] & E. B. P. Tiezzi[2,3]
[1]*Dept. of Chemical and Biosystems Sciences, University of Siena, Italy*
[2]*Dept. of Mathematics and Informatics, University of Siena, Italy*
[3]*A.R.C.A. Onlus, Siena, Italy*

Abstract

The SPIn-Eco project has been proposed and funded with the aim of studying the Province of Siena (Italy) and the 36 municipalities into which it is divided from the viewpoint of sustainable development. Several sustainability indicators are used to point out the weak and the strong points for the territory with respect to sustainability. In this paper we have focused our attention on the following methodologies: emergy evaluation, ecological footprint, greenhouse gases balance.

The sustainability analysis made during the SPIn-Eco project has produced a data set that allows a practical comparison among these approaches by means of a correlation analysis. The correlations among several indicators based on the above data set are shown. The aim of this paper is to underline the similarities and differences among the three methodologies through correlation analysis.

Important correlations were found between ecological footprint and CO_2 emissions as well as with the non-renewable exogenous part of emergy flow. No correlation was found between total emergy flow and total ecological footprint.
Keywords: emergy evaluation, ecological footprint, greenhouse gases balance, correlation analysis, sustainability.

1 Introduction

Sustainability is a concept that requires a clear focus towards a scientific assessment and quantification. The SPIn-Eco project (Sustainability in Province

www.witpress.com, ISSN 1743-3541 (on-line)

of Siena through Ecodynamic Indicators) is a research program funded by the Siena Province administration and by the Monte dei Paschi Foundation with the purpose of assessing the environmental conditions and the relative level of sustainability of the Province of Siena (Tuscany, central Italy) and of the 36 municipalities within. It is a deep analysis of the state of the territorial system by a complete set of sustainability indicators.

The Province of Siena is generally recognized to be an area with a good harmony between human activities and environmental quality. Why study the level of sustainability of this zone? First of all because the results of an in depth analysis can give responses that are not in accordance with the general perception. This happens, for instance, when an area is characterized by low levels of pollution but also by an irrational use of the resources. Our goal has been to assess the resource use and to identify those aspects that could become limiting factors for the development of future generations.

The indicators used in this paper are linked to the following methodologies: Emergy evaluation; Ecological Footprint analysis; Greenhouse gases Inventory. During 2004, the SPIn-Eco project was completed at least for the part that concerns sustainability indicators of the Province of Siena and the 36 Communes that compose it. This project allowed the collection of a relevant data set of several indicators. In this paper, the correlations among several indicators based on the above methodologies are shown. Some kinds of correlations are expected between emergy and ecological footprint, since they both aim to measure the natural needs for sustaining a system on the basis of solar energy and area respectively. These correlations are obtained for very homogeneous systems and there is the possibility to find that there is a redundancy in the use of indicators, leading to a simplification of the procedure of assessment of the level of sustainability of a similar area.

2 The system

The Province of Siena is located in Tuscany, making it one of the largest provinces in Italy and the second largest province in the Tuscan region, with its 3821 km^2. Population is relatively low, around 250.000 people, making the density around 66 inhabitants per square kilometre. The Province's main commercial activities stem from the tourism, trade, banking and agricultural sectors; there is very little industrial activity. The province's principal commercial products are wine (Brunello di Montalcino, Chianti, Vino Nobile di Montepulciano and Vernaccia from San Gimignano), cheese and olive oil.

At an environmental level the Siena province is a quite peculiar system because, even though in a contest of an industrialized country, it has not many of the negative aspects generally related to this type of development. The low density of population and the careful attention to the natural and historical heritages make the Siena province an example of "different" development, as also stated in the OECD report, OECD [1]. In 1999, the GDP per capita was 17,822 euro.

3 Methods

3.1 Emergy analysis

Emergy accounting, Odum [2,3] uses the thermodynamic basis of all forms of energy, materials and human services, but converts them into equivalents of one form of energy. Emergy accounting is organized as a top down approach where first systems diagrams of processes are drawn to organize evaluations and account for all inputs and outflows from processes.

Emergy is the solar energy directly or indirectly necessary to obtain a product in a process; it is an extensive quantity and its unit is the solar emergy joule (sej). To convert energy inputs and other kinds of flows into the solar equivalent, it is necessary to know the *solar transformity*, which is the emergy necessary to obtain one unit energy of product. The transformity is an intensive quantity and usually measured in sej/J.

Total emergy necessary for the system is divided into local renewable (R), local non renewable (N) and imported from outside (F). Starting from this distinction it is possible to calculate a set of sustainability indicators that can be used to assess the relative sustainability of a system: in this contest we measure the effort that natural systems have to do in order to produce an item or to re-produce it after it has been consumed.

3.2 Greenhouse gas inventory

As a result of increasing warnings by members of the climatological and scientific community about the possible harmful effects of rising greenhouse gas concentrations, the IPCC [4] was established by the World Meteorological Organization and the United Nations Environment Programme in 1988 to assess the available scientific, technical, and socioeconomic information in the field of climate change.

The resulting Kyoto Protocol established binding emissions targets for developed nations, relative to their emissions levels in 1990, for an overall reduction of about 5 percent.

The greenhouse gases included in the targets of the Kyoto Protocol are carbon dioxide, methane, nitrous oxide, hydrofluorocarbons, perfluorocarbons, and sulphur-hexafluoride. The established targets must be achieved over the period 2008 to 2012, the first commitment period. Essentially, each country can average its emissions over that 5-year period to establish compliance, smoothing out short-term fluctuations that might result from economic cycles or extreme weather patterns.

Sources of emissions include fuel combustion, fugitive emissions from fuels, industrial processes, solvents, agriculture, and waste management and disposal.

3.3 Ecological footprint

The Ecological Footprint (EF), UNEP-WCMC e WWF [5], introduced by William Rees and Mathis Wackernagel, Wackernagel *et al* [6,7], Bagliani *et al*

[8] in the nineties as a measure of the consumption of renewable natural resources by a human population, be it that of a country, a region or the whole world. A population's EF is the total area of productive land or sea require to produce all the crops, meat, seafood, wood and fibers it consumes, to sustain its consumption and to give space for its infrastructure. It is interested, to compare the concept of ecological footprint with that, more used, of carrying capacity. This latter quantity is defined as the maximum weight, exercised from the population of a defined species, that a region can support without irreversibly compromising the productivity of the region itself. The ecological footprint represents the portion of carrying capacity used by the human population living in region. The ecological footprint analysis reverses the concept of carrying capacity evaluating the productive territory effectively used by a population, wherever this surface may be located (inside or outside the region under consideration), instead of the maximum human population that the area can support.

The EF classic formulation considers the average consumption of the population, based on the assumption that use of energy or matter derives, directly or indirectly, from a certain extension of land, hosting the ecosystems that support the resource drawing and/or guarantee the absorption of the emissions.

Available biological capacity is the total biological production capacity per year of a biologically productive space, expressed in global hectares. The ecological deficit is the difference between EF of a population and biological capacity of the space available to that population. This indicator measures the amount by which the area's footprint exceeds the ecological capacity of that system.

3.4 Correlation analysis

A correlation describes the strength of an association between variables. An association between variables means that the value of one variable can be predicted, to some extent, by the value of the other. A correlation is a special kind of association: there is a *linear* relation between the values of the variables. A non-linear relation can be transformed into a linear one before the correlation is calculated.

For a set of variable pairs, the correlation coefficient (R^2) gives the strength of the association. The square of the size of the correlation coefficient is the fraction of the variance of the one variable that can be explained from the variance of the other variable. The *relation* between the variables is called the *regression line.* The regression line is defined as the best fitting straight line through all value pairs, i.e., the one explaining the largest part of the variance.
In formulae:

$$y = \alpha + \beta x + \varepsilon \tag{1}$$

where x and y are the independent and dependent variable, respectively; α and β are the regression coefficients and ε is the error.

$$R^2 = \frac{Cov_{xy}^{\ 2}}{Var_x \times Var_y} \qquad (2)$$

4 Results

SPIn-Eco project created a data set of the mentioned indicators (and others) collected and calculated in the 36 municipalities that compose the Province of Siena. Correlation plots between indicators is shown. Limitations of these correlations are due to the fact that the differences within the Province are not so relevant and thus there is a high degree of homogeneity.

As it is clear from the definitions, there is a good level of similarity between Emergy evaluation and Ecological Footprint analysis. The poor correlation between Emergy flow per year and Total Ecological Footprint, that is the Ecological Footprint multiplied by the population of the area are shown in Figure 1.

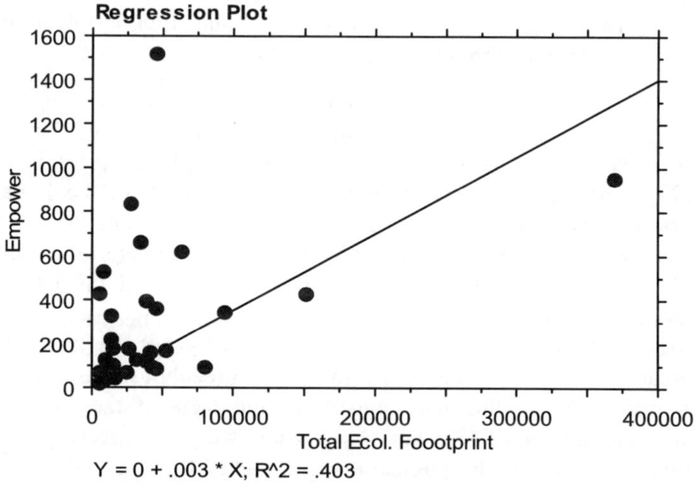

Figure 1: Correlation plot of Emergy flow (Empower measured in 10^{18} sej/year) to Total Ecological Footprint (in hectares), that shows a R^2=0.403.

How could this occur? A first reason can be the fact that in the Emergy analysis, all the inputs, both the natural (spontaneous) and the ones that are acquired for certain purposes are considered while the Ecological Footprint analysis considers only what is used for the population consumption. We have tested the hypothesis that just the F part of emergy can be correlated with the Total Ecological Footprint.

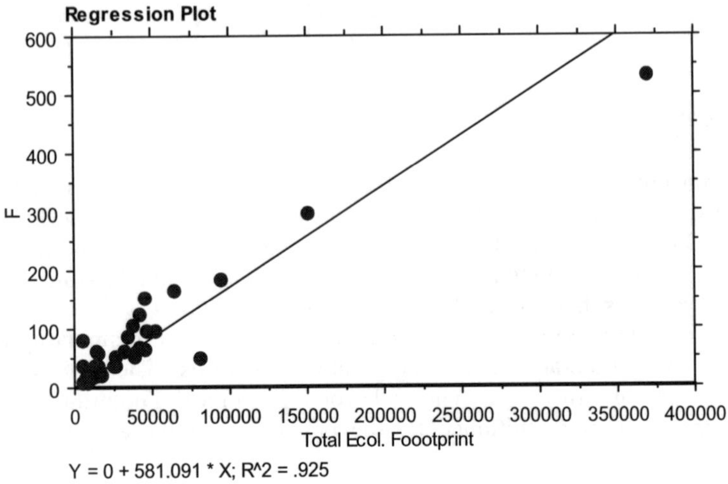

Figure 2: Correlation plot of F (non-renewable exogenous part of the Empower in 10^{18} sej/year) vs. Total Ecological Footprint (in hectares), with R^2=0.925.

Figure 2 shows an almost perfect correlation between these two indicators, confirming the validity of the hypothesis. On the contrary, the correlation between R+N (local emergy flows) and Ecological Footprint is negligible (R^2=0.179). The common aspects that are present both in the F part of the emergy flow) and in the Ecological Footprint are, for example the production of goods that are consumed and are included in both the numeraires, independently on the fact that the goods are not locally produced and the use of energy resources (both fuels and electricity).

Ecological Footprint considers (as a separate category) the "land for energy" that is what is required for the absorption of the greenhouse gases emissions. In the Province of Siena this part constitutes the 68% of the total Ecological Footprint, Bagliani *et al* [8]. For this reason we have investigated also the correlation between Total Ecological Footprint and CO_2 emissions.

The convergence of the two analyses is practically perfect (R^2=0.985), probably due to the fact that the 36 points of the plot are taken in an homogenous region, where the difference in the pattern of consumption within the population in the municipalities is very little. Therefore the relevance of the "land for energy" is reflected in the strong correlation with the CO_2 emissions.

We have decided to check also the plot of F versus CO_2 emissions. The good level of correlation was expectable: F includes fuels, and electricity from the national grid and other imported goods and services that should be considered non-renewable since the indirect use of fuels is anyway relevant on the total of the emergy required for their production.

Nevertheless it is relevant to show that there is a better correlation of the greenhouse gases emissions with Ecological Footprint than with non-renewable exogenous emergy flow F (R^2 is 0.938 in the latter case).

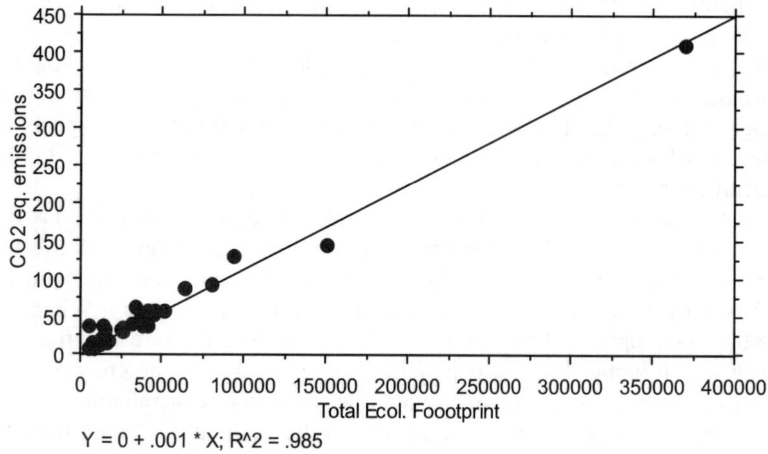

Figure 3: Correlation plot of CO2 emissions (in Gg) vs. Total Ecological Footprint (in hectares).

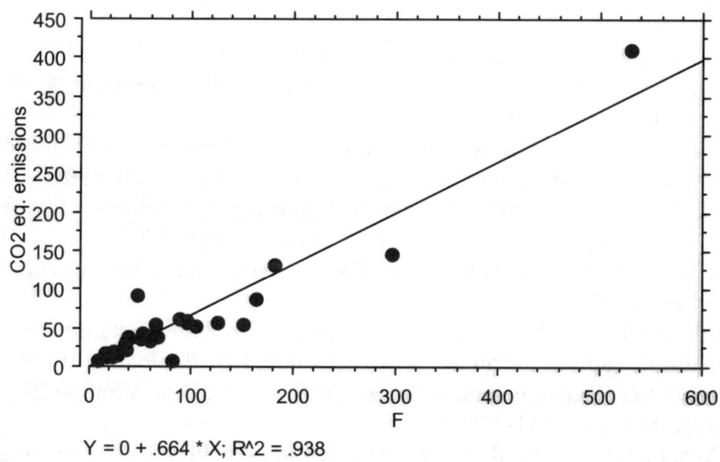

Figure 4: Correlation plot of CO2 emissions (in Gg) vs. F (in 10^{18} sej/year).

5 Conclusions

The sustainability analysis made during the SPIn_Eco project has produced a data set that allows a practical comparison among several approaches. We have started with the main three indicators, trying to understand what is the level of overlapping/complementarity of these approaches. A first negative result is the lack of accordance between Ecological Footprint and Emergy flow. Even though the general aim of the two methods is similar, these indicators seem to be complementary, at least in part. In fact the non renewable exogenous part of the emergy flow correlates quite well with the Ecological Footprint, showing that the R and the N part of the emergy flow have practically no relation with the Ecological Footprint. This means that Emergy evaluation shows aspects related to the use of local resources (materials storages for example) that Ecological Footprint does not.

It interesting to note that both F and Ecological Footprint have good accordance with the CO_2 emissions. This implies a good level of overlapping among the three indicators. For the calculation of Ecological Footprint a huge data base of personal consumption of the population is necessary. When it is not available, assumptions have to be made to reach a final result, that will be anyway less reliable. For the calculation of the F part of the emergy flow, the data set is very relevant and data are not always available or reliable.

We can therefore say that, in similar systems, as a first approximation, a greenhouse gases emissions assessment could substitute the Ecological Footprint evaluation or the calculation of the imported emergy flow. In fact the CO_2 emissions calculation is much easier and less time consuming that the other two.

References

[1] OECD, Territorial Reviews. Siena, Italy, 2002.

[2] Odum, H.T. Self organisation, transformity and information. *Science*, 242, pp. 1132-1139, 1988.

[3] Odum, H.T. Environmental Accounting: Emergy and Environmental Decision Making, John Wiley and Sons, Inc., pp. 1-370, 1996.

[4] IPCC. Greenhouse Gas Inventory. Reporting Instructions, 1996 (revised). IPCC, Intergovernmental Panel on Climate Change, 1,2,3.

[5] UNEP-WCMC e WWF, Living Planet Report, 2002, World wildlife found editor, 2002.

[6] Monfreda C., Wackernagel M. and D. Deumling Establishing national natural capital accounts based on detailed Ecological Footprint and biological capacity assessments. Land Use Policy, Volume 21, Issue 3, July 2004, pp. 231-246

[7] Wackernagel, M., Rees, W. The Ecological Footprint: reducing human impact on the Earth, New Society, Gabriola Island, BC, Canada, 1996.

[8] Bagliani, M., Contu, S., Coscia, I., Tiezzi, E. The evaluation of the Ecological Footprint of the Province of Siena (Italy). Ecosystems and Sustainable Development, Vol.1, pp. 387-396, 2003.

[9] Daly, H.E. Toward some operational principles of sustainable development. *Ecological Economics*, **2**, pp. 1-6, 1990.

[10] Daly, H.E.. Beyond growth: avoiding uneconomic growth, Isee Conference, Santiago, 1988.

Sustainable indicators in desertification phenomena: application to Calabria, Italy

G. Frega, P. Piro & R. Mangiardi
Dipartimento di Difesa del Suolo "V. Marone",
Università degli Studi della Calabria, Italy

Abstract

Italy is one of the Mediterranean countries that are menaced by desertification, particularly in the Southern regions: Sicily, Sardinia, Apulia, Basilicata and the Ionian areas of Calabria. In such a scenario it is evident that correct water resource planning is very important: reduced water resources, once considered meaningless, have now acquired notable importance. Environmentally Sensitive Areas (ESAs) [1] to desertification will be described in this paper, with particular reference to the Calabria region. Key indicators for the estimation of soil capacity to resist degradation processes will be found through the MEDALUS methodology (MEditerranean Desertification And Land USe: European Commission, 1999), which allows the assessment of desertification risks on a regional scale. Indicators will be grouped into four classes, on the basis of soil quality, climate quality, vegetation quality and management quality. Each index will be classified into three levels (high, moderate and low) according to the MEDALUS classification, and they will be entered into and employed by a Geographical Information System (GIS), which will define the different layers depending on the quality index considered. In this way, the contribution of each quality index will be defined and intervention and mitigation proposals will be developed through the description of the main sectors (soil protection, sustainable management of agricultural resources, decreased impact of production activities and territory re-equilibrium), allowing the definition of criteria used to limit the effects of the degradation and to allow correct land use.

1 Introduction

In Italy, desertification does not mean that landscape will turn into a desert one, but that it will be characterized by aridity, erosion, salinization, depletion of vegetable covering and organic substances, pollution and wrong soil use (effects of intensive agriculture on soil, effects of pasturing on vegetation, wood overexploitation in forest, irrigation mismanagement that have wasted land fertility). For this reason it is necessary to develop an efficient system for resources monitoring and models compatible with territory sustainable development. Being mainly a mountainous and hilly country, Italy is particularly vulnerable. Moreover, soil slope and its exposition are a further vulnerability factor in the climatic and geo-morphological context of the regions subjected to water stress conditions. In order to collect data concerning soil degradation and to describe its causes through measurements and observation, some indicators and indexes are employed. They are a whole of aggregated or weighed indicators or data, having great importance in the process that starts from the definition of the phenomenon and leads to decision making [2]. There is not a general consensus regarding the indicators to be used at a national scale. At the Mediterranean Basin scale, there exist many Community research projects. One of these projects, the MEDALUS, was designed to investigate climatic changes in the Mediterranean area, soil degradation in semi-arid areas, vegetation growth, socioeconomic changes and methods useful to integrate these factors through numerical models [3].

2 Project methodology

The methodology developed for the MEDALUS project, and illustrated in previous works [4] provided the definition for ESAs, through the evaluation of the so-called Environmentally Sensitive Areas index. This index is obtained by employing some key indicators grouped in four categories: Soil, Climate, Vegetation and Management. Through them, soil capacity to resist degradation processes or soil suitability to support and sustain specific uses can be evaluated. Each indicator has to belong to a class and each class is given a score varying from 1 ("lower weight") to 2 ("higher weight") depending on its influence on desertification process. The geometric mean of the groups of indicators belonging to each of the four categories, provides for four Quality Index (QI) [5]:

1) Vegetation Quality Index (VQI);
2) Soil Quality Index (SQI);
3) Climate Quality Index (CQI);
4) Management Quality Index and anthropic pressures (MQI).

The geometric mean of the four quality indexes gives the ESAs index which is used to classify the areas into four different sensibility categories (critical, fragile, potential, and unaffected by desertification) [6]:

$$ESAI = (VQI^{*}\ SQI^{*}CQI^{*}\ MQI)^{1/4}.$$

2.1 Vegetation Quality Index (VQI)

The biotic soil component able to contrast the desertification process is vegetable covering. Vegetation Quality can be obtained through indicators that "quantify" the capacity of each vegetable species (natural or agricultural) to resist to degradation. The key indicators developed for this purpose are:

1) Fire risk and recuperation capacity;
2) Soil protection from erosion;
3) Vegetation drought resistance;
4) Vegetable covering.

By combining these indicators [5] the Vegetation Quality Index (VQI) can be obtained. More specifically:

VQI = (Fire risk and recuperation capacity * Soil protection from erosion * Vegetation drought resistance * Vegetable covering)$^{1/4}$.

2.2 Soil Quality Index (SQI)

Soil, according to the definition of the Soil Conservation Society of America (1986), is a natural body composed of mineral and organic particles deriving from physical and chemophysical rock alterations and from the biological and biochemical transformation of organic residuals. Capable of supporting vegetation, it is characterized by inner atmosphere, flora and fauna determined by a particular water "economy". When soil lacks the characteristics necessary to support a vegetable covering (inadequate rooting depth and/or inadequate water capacity and/or lack of nutrients) a degradation process is triggered, leading in the end to land desertification. In this context, quality soil indicators can be related to soil water content and soil erosion through the evaluation of the proprieties or characteristics of the soil [5]. The procedure cannot be strictly applied to Calabria Region because the regional soil map is still missing. This map would have provided for a precise description of soil characteristics, thus giving the tools to estimate, in the totality of the area, the "value" of indicators such as soil depth, drainage, texture, and rock fragments [7]. At present, the indicators considered to represent soil quality are:

1) Parent rock;
2) Soil depth;
3) Slope.

Their combination gives a Soil Quality Index (SQI) equal to:

(SQI) = (Parent rock * soil depth * slope)$^{1/3}$.

2.3 Climate Quality Index (CQI)

The spatial distribution of the indicators in the territory is based on the values assumed in measurement stations. Rainfall observation period, for most stations, goes from 1921 to 2000, though in some cases the series are incomplete. Anyway, stations have always been run for more than 40 years, a period largely sufficient to give a very good estimation of the average value of annual total rainfall [8]. Calabria region is particularly rainy (average total annual rainfall is 1176 mm, higher than the Italian average value of 970 mm); the prevailing climate is humid (44%); hyperhumid climate characterizes Sila and Serre mountain chains, Aspromonte and Pollino massifs; in the areas of Catanzaro, Cosenza and Mileto climate is sub-humid; climate becomes arid in the most Southern areas and in the higher Ionian coastal areas (Villapiana). Irregular annual and pluriannual rainfall distribution, together with the occurrence of extreme events as well as rainfalls and vegetative periods out of season are the main climatic factors contributing to soil degradation in semi-arid and arid Mediterranean areas. According to recent studies [5], global climatic changes will affect the vulnerable Mediterranean areas: in the future, the hydrological deficit might leave the soil naked, thus favoring surface runoff and erosion, factors that may trigger the desertification process. Many proposals have been made regarding a rational classification of climate through the transformation of elementary data into synthetic climatic indexes, which should not consider pluviometry only, but also its relationship with the water need of soil and vegetation, that is real evapotranspiration meaning water quantity passing as vapor directly through soil evapotranspiration or indirectly through plant transpiration [9]. The indicators considered in this paper to represent climate quality are:

1) Climatic Thornthwaite index;
2) Average annual rainfall;
3) Slope aspect.

The combination of these indicators gives the Climate Quality Index (CQI). More specifically:

$$(CQI) = (\text{Clim. Thornthwaite ind.} * \text{Average annual rainfall} * \text{Slope aspect})^{1/3}.$$

2.4 Management Quality and anthropic pressures (MQI)

Paleoclimatic studies confirmed that the destabilization of natural ecosystems in general, and forest systems in particular, was a consequence of anthropic pressure on environment. In particular, the choice of some areas and not others was possibly a discriminating factor. Moreover, present changes in economic and social structures in some rural areas also have in many cases affected the hydrological cycle, exacerbating erosion phenomena and increasing surface runoff [3]. In the definition of desertification ESAs, the following key indicators regarding management quality and anthropic pressures should be considered:

1) Soil use intensity;
2) Land protection politics.

The highest score to soil use intensity has been given to sowable lands in irrigation areas and to urban areas because of soil subtraction associated with it. A low score for soil use intensity characterizes forested areas, the Tyrrhenian Coastal Chain, the Sila and Serre mountain chains, the Aspromonte massifs. The combination of these indicators gives the Management Quality Index and anthropic pressures (MQI). More specifically:

$$(MQI) = (\text{soil use intensity} * \text{management politics})^{1/2}.$$

3 Procedures and data

Among the most advanced instruments for the study of environmental variations in general, and desertification in particular, aerospace telemetering and Geographic Information Systems (GIS) are tools with powerful descriptive characteristics. Moreover, when data are introduced in a regional GIS, the immediate analysis and visualization of the phenomenon can be performed. Being relational databases, capable of implementing, manipulating and process any kind of georeferenced information, GIS is by its very nature suitable for the multifactorial analysis of ecological complex processes at a superregional scale. Moreover, ecological processes interact with economic and social factors difficult to quantify and analyze in the decision-making process for a sustainable land development. GIS allows a unitary representation of all these factors by attributing quantitative values to each of them depending on the "weight" that each has with respect to the others. This multidimensional matricial analysis method allows phenomenon interpretation and modeling of future events occurring in predetermined conditions. It can also optimize decision-making regarding environmental management on the basis of a maximum number of factors, thus minimizing the possibility of subjective evaluations [10]. In this paper, GIS ArcView 8.3 and the optional extensions ArcGIS Spatial Analyst were employed for data analysis. This software has many typical functions of the GIS environment, as map creation, data analysis and management. Map calculator function was employed to generate informative layers regarding quality indexes through the spatial distribution of point "values" assumed by the single indicators. The results are made available in a graphic environment, ready to be printed or to be employed for later processing, and in the alphanumerical format for their analysis, to be used in reports, and save the simulated scenario for later confrontation with other scenarios generated by parametric spatial analysis simulations. The following tools were employed in order to determine Desertification Sensible Areas:

1) Calabria Geological Map: scale 1:250.000 (Regional catchment Authority);
2) CORINE Land-Cover: scale 1:100.000 (Italian Geological service) - The surface area of the minimum mapped portion was 25 hectares, corresponding in the reference map (scale 1:100.000), to a square with a 5 mm side or a circle with a 2,8 mm radius;
3) DTM (Digital Terrain Model): square grid with a 250 m side (Italian Geological service).

4 Results and discussion

MEDALUS project methodology was applied to Calabria region. 41% of the area has elevations lower than 300 m.s.l.m. and in the remaining 59% elevations are higher. Mean regional altitude is 556 m.s.l.m. Plains are located near the coasts. Figure 1 shows the map of vegetation quality, which is the synthesis of the layers referring to fire risk, soil protection from erosion, drought resistance and vegetable covering [4]; Calabria territory resulted to be divided into areas with high (49,9%), moderate (18,4%) and low quality (31,7%). The best conditions characterize Reggio Calabria province; in this area, forested areas and perennial cultivations (olive groves) dominate, and they protect soil from degradation thanks to their resistance to drought, erosion protection and vegetable covering. The provinces of Catanzaro, Cosenza and Vibo Valentia include a higher percentage of areas with stronger tendency to degradation, though the values are less alarming than those reported for Crotone province.

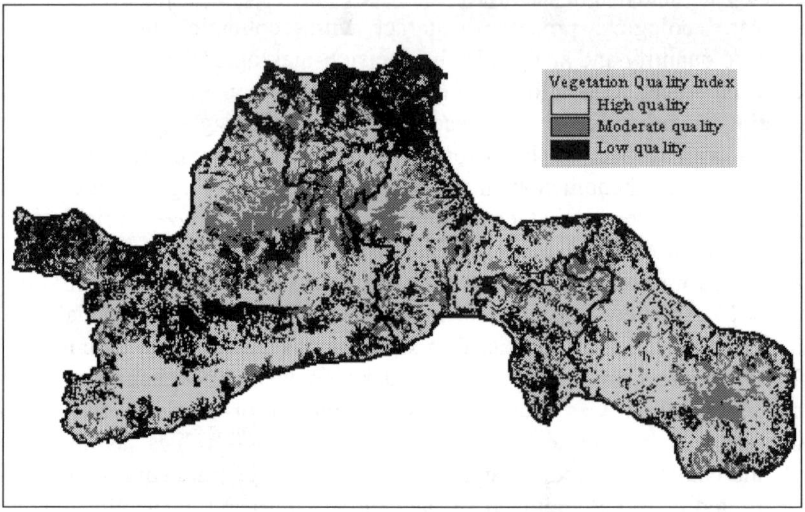

Figure 1: Vegetation quality map in Calabria region [4].

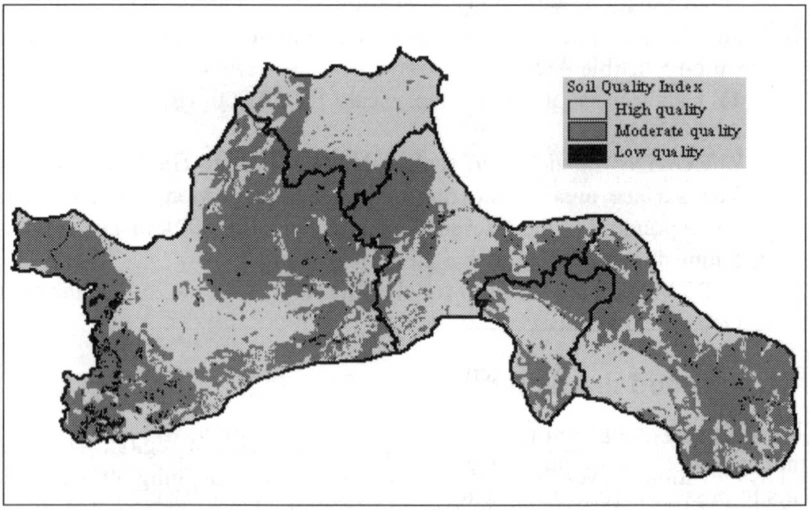

Figure 2: Soil quality map in Calabria region [7].

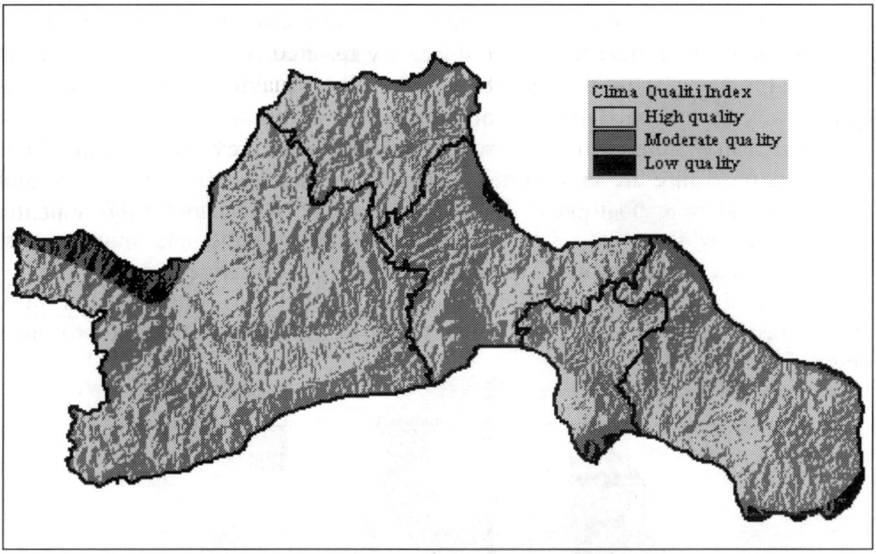

Figure 3: Climate quality map in Calabria region.

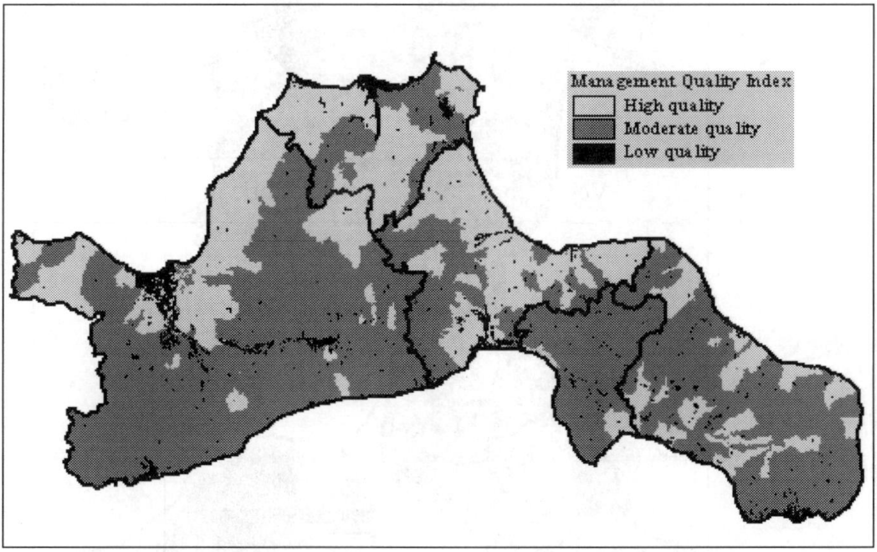

Figure 4: Management quality map in Calabria region.

Figure 2 shows the soil quality map of Calabria region, which is a synthesis of the layers relative to the indicators mother rock, soil depth and slope [7]. Soil results to possess different characteristics estimated on the basis of the indicators considered for the entire regional territory. Good quality soils, having a good water content and a good resistance to erosion, are located in coastal plains, in some portions of Crati valley where slopes are less than 6% and in most areas of Crotone province. Soils that do not resist well to desertification process (low quality) are located mainly in the Pollino massif.

Figure 3 shows climate quality map in Calabria region, which is a synthesis of the layers regarding the indicators Thornthwaite climatic index, average annual rainfall and slope exposition. A high climate quality characterizes 47 % of the regional area, while in 2% of the areas, located mainly in the most southern part of the region and in the higher Ionian area in Cosenza province, climate quality is low. In these areas, the occurrences of both scarce rainfalls and high evapotranspiration rates at the same time, significantly contribute to land desertification.

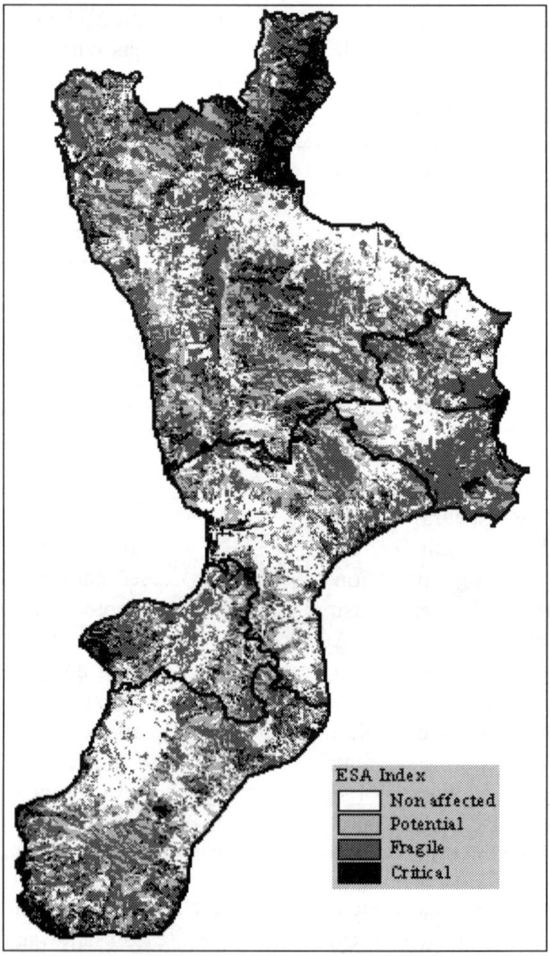

Figure 5: Map of sensible areas to desertification in Calabria region.

Figure 4 shows management quality map in Calabria region, which is a synthesis of the layers regarding the indicators soil use intensity, land politics and protection. In most regional areas, management quality is moderate. In particular, almost the entire territory of Vibo Valentia province has a moderate management quality, together with the territory of Reggio Calabria province. Areas with a low management quality are concentrated in a few zones. The theme final synthetic index (ESAI) is obtained by superimposing the theme of quality indexes previously considered. By grouping the results, the Desertification Sensible Areas map is obtained (Figure 5). The unaffected areas in Calabria region is about 26%; in Catanzaro province about 37%, in Vibo Valentia province about 24%, in Reggio Calabria province about 28%, in Cosenza province about 20% and in Crotone province about 26%. Most regional land, however, shows a “fragile” sensibility (41.5%). It should be considered that in “fragile” sensible areas the balance among natural factors and/or human activities is already particularly delicate. Finally, areas with “critical” sensibility are about 10%. These results reflect land geomorphologic characteristics, intensive and careless exploitation, and the presence of few forests, as well as the peculiar pluviometric regime, with rainfall below the seasonal average. For each area determined on the basis of the ESAs index, the quantitative contribution of each quality index can be obtained. For example, in Albidona municipality, there is an area classified as C3 (ESAs index of 1.57) whose contribution is given by a moderate SQI (1.34), a low CQI (1.93), a low VQI (1.68) and a moderate MQI (1.41). Thus, the most critical factors concern climatic conditions and vegetation typology. In this way, intervention politics aiming at solving specific problems peculiar to each area will be developed.

5 Conclusions

In Italy, Southern and insular regions, characterized by environmental stresses (seasonal aridity, several drought events, short and heavy rainfalls, soil erodibility, often unsustainable environmental pressures due to human activities) are menaced by desertification. Water shortage causes unbalances, and adaptation and mitigation measures should be adopted in order to prevent degradation and desertification. As for soil quality index, it is not very detailed because indicators concerning drainage and soil texture are not available due to the delayed publication of the Calabria soil map. Because soil use intensity is important, the indicators capable of representing management quality should be integrated. New thermopluviometric data will increase the network of measurement stations, they will support the analysis of temperature and rainfall trends to forecast possible future projections. By introducing a parameter that will consider fire probability, precious information concerning vegetation quality would be available. As for management quality, great importance should be given to environmental pressure and anthropic factors, fundamental elements in determining Environmentally Sensible Areas (ESAs) to desertification. The proposed methodology, based both on general and local knowledge of environmental processes, would thus be very useful in intervention planning, aiming at a rational management of the areas subjected to desertification and at the recovery of the menaced ones. After the definition of risk areas, the employment of Regional Indicators would undoubtedly allow planners to make informed decisions.

References

[1] Kosmas C., Kirkby M., Geeson N. Eds, *The MEDALUS project - Mediterranean Desertification And Land Use. Manual on key indicators of desertification and mapping Environmentally Sensitive Areas to desertification*, 1999.

[2] Agenzia Nazionale per la Protezione dell'Ambiente (ANPA) - Centro Tematico Nazionale Suolo e Siti Contaminati, *Sviluppo di indicatori per il Suolo e i Siti Contaminati*, Roma 2000.

[3] Ministero dell'Ambiente, *Comunicazione Nazionale per la Lotta alla Siccità e alla Desertificazione*, 1999.

[4] Frega G., Piro P., *Qualità della vegetazione e resistenza alla siccità: applicazione relativa alla regione Calabria*, Accademia Nazionale dei Lincei, Giornata Mondiale dell'Acqua "LA SICCITA' IN ITALIA", Roma Marzo 2003.

[5] Kosmas C., Ferrara A., Briassouli H., Imeson I., *Methodology for mapping ESAs to desertification*, In The MEDALUS project - Mediterranean Desertification And Land USe. Manual on key indicators of desertification and mapping Environmentally Sensitive Areas to desertification. Edited by: Kosmas C., Kirkby M., Geeson N.: EUR 18882, pp. 31-47, 1999.

[6] Frega G., Piro P., *Sulla procedura di identificazione delle Aree Sensibili alla Desertificazione (ESAs): il progetto MEDALUS (Mediterranean desertification and land use della UE (European Union)*, Memorie e Studi n° 353, Dipartimento di Difesa del Suolo, Università della Calabria, Dicembre 2000.

[7] Piro P., Frega F., Mangiardi R., *Identificazione delle Aree Sensibili alla Desertificazione e applicazione alla regione Calabria*, 24° corso di aggiornamento in Tecniche per la difesa dall'inquinamento, Guardia Piemontese Terme (CS) Giugno 2003.

[8] Moisello U., Idrologia tecnica, La Gogliardica Pavarese s.r.l, 1998.

[9] Thornthwaite C. W., *An approach toward a rational classification of climate*, Geograph. Rev., vol.38, 1948.

[10] Burrough P. A., *Principles of Geographical Information Systems for land resources assessment*, Clarendon Press, Oxford, 1986.

Section 3
Mathematical and system modelling

Wildfire hazard evaluation through a space-time point process conditional intensity model

J. Mateu, F. Saura, P. Gregori & P. Juan
Department of Mathematics, Campus Riu Sec, Universitat Jaume I, E-12071 Castellón, Spain

Abstract

Fire departments all over the world often use numerical indices to aid in wildfire management and hazard assessment. These indices are designed to summarize local meteorological and fuel information and provide an estimate of the current risk of fire.

In this paper we evaluate the effectiveness of the Burning Index (BI) (a collection of numerical indices designed to be used for fire planning and management) for predicting wildfire occurrences in the Valencian Community (Spain) using space-time point process models. The models are based on a particular decomposition of the conditional intensity, with separate terms to describe spatial and seasonal variability as well as contributions from the BI.
Keywords: burning index, conditional intensity function, spatio-temporal point processes, wildfires.

1 Introduction

A spatio-temporal point process is a random collection of points, where each point represents the time and location of an event. Examples of events include incidence of disease, sightings or births of a species, or the occurrences of fires, earthquakes, lightning strikes, tsunamis, or volcanic eruptions. Typically the spatial locations are recorded in three spatial coordinates, e.g. longitude, latitude, and height or depth, though sometimes only one or two spatial coordinates are available or of interest. Figure 1 displays some point process data consisting of microearthquake origin times and epicenters in Parkfield, CA, between 1988 and 1995, recorded by the US High-Resolution Seismographic Station Network (Nadeau *et al.* [12]). Figure 2 displays the centroids of wildfires occurring in 1994, 2000 and 2001 in Valencian Community, Spain (times of the events not shown).

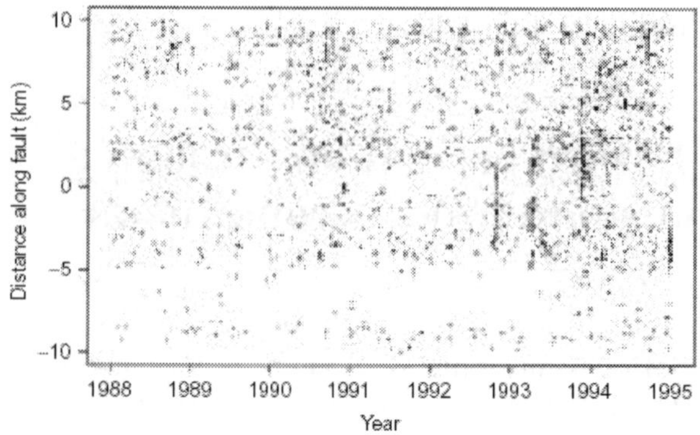

Figure 1: Microearthquake origin times and epicenters in Parkfield, CA, between 1988 and 1995.

Fire departments all over the world often use numerical indices to aid in wildfire management and hazard assessment. These indices are designed to summarize local meteorological and fuel information and provide an estimate of the current risk of fire. The Burning Index (BI) is part of the Spanish National Fire- Danger Rating System, a collection of numerical indices designed to be used for fire planning and management. While the usage of such indices is widespread, assessment of these indices in their respective regions of application is rare. In this paper we evaluate the effectiveness of the Burning Index (BI) for predicting wildfire occurrences in Valencian Community (Spain) using space-time point process models. The models are based on a particular decomposition of the conditional intensity, with separate terms to describe spatial and seasonal variability as well as contributions from the BI. The models are fit to wildfire and BI data from the years 2000-2001 using a combination of nonparametric kernel smoothing methods and parametric maximum likelihood. In addition to using AIC to compare competing models, new multi-dimensional residual methods based on approximate random thinning and rescaling are used to detect departures from the models and to ascertain the precise contribution of the BI to predicting wildfire occurrence. Residual analysis can identify specific areas where the performance is poor and suggest directions for improvement.

2 Characterizations

A spatio-temporal point process N is mathematically defined as a random measure on a region $S \subset \mathbb{R} \times \mathbb{R}^3$ of space-time, taking values in the non-negative integers

$\mathbb{Z}^+$ (or infinity). In this framework the measure $N(A)$ represents the number of points falling in the subset A of S. Attention is typically restricted to points in some time interval $[T_0, T_1]$, and to processes with only a finite number of points in any compact subset of S.

Traditionally the points of a point process are thought to be indistinguishable, other than by their times and locations. Often, however, there is other important information to be stored along with each point. For example, one may wish to analyze a list of points in time and space where a member of a certain species was observed, along with the size or age of the organism, or alternatively a catalog of arrival times and locations of hurricanes along with the amounts of damage attributed to each. Such processes may be viewed as marked spatio-temporal point processes, i.e. random collections of points where each point has associated with it a further random variable called a mark. Much of the theory of spatio-temporal point processes carries over from that of spatial point processes. However, the temporal aspect enables a natural ordering of the points that does not generally exist for spatial processes. Indeed, it may often be convenient to view a spatio-temporal point process as a purely temporal point process, with spatial marks associated with each point. Sometimes investigating the purely temporal (or purely spatial) behaviour of the resulting marginalized point process is of interest.

The spatial region of interest is often a rectangular portion of $\mathbb{R}^2$ or $\mathbb{R}^3$, but not always. Cases where the points are spatially distributed in a sphere or an ellipse are investigated by [1,2]. When the domain of possible spatial coordinates is discrete (e.g. a lattice) rather than continuous, it may be convenient to view the spatio-temporal point process as a sequence N_i of temporal point processes that may interact with one another. Any analytical spatio-temporal point process is characterized uniquely by its associated conditional rate process λ (Fishman and Snyder [5]). $\lambda(t, x, y, z)$ may be thought of as the frequency with which events are expected to occur around a particular location (t, x, y, z) in space-time, conditional on the prior history, H_t, of the point process up to time t. Note that in the statistical literature ([3,9]), is more commonly referred to as the conditional intensity rather than the conditional rate. However, the term intensity is also used in various environmental sciences, e.g. in describing the size or destructiveness of an earthquake, so to avoid confusion, the term rate may be preferred.

Formally, the conditional rate $\lambda(t, x, y, z)$ associated with a spatio-temporal point process N may be defined as a limiting conditional expectation, as follows. Fix any point $p = (t, x, y, z)$ in space-time. Let B_Δ denote the set $(t, t + \Delta t) \times (x, x + \Delta x) \times (y, y + \Delta y) \times (z, z + \Delta z)$ where Δ is the vector $(\Delta t, \Delta x, \Delta y, \Delta z)$. Then,

$$\lambda(p) = \lim_{\Delta \to 0} \frac{E[N(B_\Delta)|H_t]}{|\Delta|}$$

provided the limit exists. For orderly point processes (processes where $\lim_{|A| \downarrow \emptyset} Pr\{N(A) > 1\}/|A| = 0$ for interval A), the two definitions are equivalent. λ is a predictable process whose integral C (called the compensator) is such that $N - C$ is a martingale. There are different forms of conditioning corresponding to different types of martingales ([8], [10], [16]).

3 Models

The behaviour of a spatio-temporal point process N is typically modeled by specifying a functional form for $\lambda(t, x, y, z)$, which represents the infinitesimal expected rate of events at time t and location (x, y, z), given all the observations up to time t. Although λ may be estimated nonparametrically ([4, 6, 18]), it is more common to estimate it via a parametric model.

In general, $\lambda(t, x, y, z)$ depends not only on t, x, y and z but also on the times and locations of preceding events. When N is a Poisson process, however, λ is deterministic, i.e. depends only on t, x, y and z. The simplest model is the stationary Poisson, where the conditional rate is constant: $\lambda(t, x, y, z) = \mu$ for all t, x, y, z. In the case of modeling environmental disturbances, this model incorporates the idea that the risk of an event is the same at all times and locations, regardless of where and how frequently such disturbances have occurred previously. Processes that display substantial spatial heterogeneity, such as earthquake epicenters, are sometimes modeled as stationary in time but not space.

A commonly used form for self-exciting (clustered) point process models is a spatio-temporal generalization of the Hawkes model, where $\lambda(t, x, y, z)$ may be written as

$$\lambda(t, x, y, z) = \mu(t, x, y, z) + \sum_i \nu(t - t_i, x - x_i, y - y_i, z - z_i)$$

and the sum is over all points (t_i, x_i, y_i, z_i) with $t_i < t$. The functions μ and ν represent the deterministic background rate and clustering density, respectively. Often μ is modeled as merely a function of the spatial coordinates (x, y, z), and may be estimated nonparametrically as in Ogata [13]. When observed marks m associated with each point are posited to affect the rate at which future points accumulate, this information is typically incorporated into the function ν, i.e. the conditional rate λ is modeled as a background rate plus $\sum_i \nu(t - t_i, x - x_i, y - y_i, z - z_i, m - m_i)$. A variety of forms has been given for the clustering density ν. For instance, in modeling seismological data with two spatial parameters (x and y) and a mark (m) indicating magnitude, Musmeci and Vere-Jones [11] introduced explicit forms for ν, including the diffusion-type model where $\nu(t, x, y, m)$ is given by

$$\nu(t, x, y, m) = \frac{C}{2\pi\sigma_x\sigma_y t} \exp\left[\alpha m - \beta t - \frac{\left(\frac{x^2}{\sigma_x^2} + \frac{y^2}{\sigma_y^2}\right)}{2t}\right]$$

Ogata [13] investigated the case where

$$\nu(t, x, y, m) = \frac{K_0 \exp[\alpha(m - m_0)]}{(t + c)^p (x^2 + y^2 + d)^q}$$

as well as a variety of other models.

Several other forms for ν were suggested by Rathbun [14] and Kagan [7]. Sometimes λ is modeled as a product of marginal conditional intensities

$$\lambda(t,x,y,z) = \lambda_1(t)\lambda_2(x,y,z)$$

or even

$$\lambda(t,x,y,z) = \lambda_1(t)\lambda_2(x)\lambda_3(y)\lambda_4(z)$$

These forms embody the notion that the temporal behaviour of the process is independent of the spatial behaviour, and in the latter case that furthermore the behaviour along each of the spatial coordinates can be seen as independent. In such cases each of the functions λ_i may be estimated individually. Occasionally one subdivides the spatial region into a finite number of subregions and fits temporal point process models to the data within each subregion. In such a case the conditional intensity may be written

$$\lambda(t,x,y,z) = \sum_i \lambda_1(t)\mathbf{1}_i(x,y,z)$$

where the $\mathbf{1}_i$ are indicator functions denoting the relevant region.

3.1 Estimation and inference

All parameters for each of the possible models can be estimated by maximizing the log-likelihood function

$$\begin{aligned} L(\theta) = & \int_{T_0}^{T_1}\int_x\int_y\int_z \log[\lambda(t,x,y,z;\theta)]dN(t,x,y,z) \\ & - \int_{T_0}^{T_1}\int_x\int_y\int_z \lambda(t,x,y,z;\theta)dzdydxdt \end{aligned} \quad (1)$$

Asymptotic properties of the maximum likelihood estimator $\hat{\theta}$ have been derived under various conditions, along with formulas for standard errors; see Rathbun and Cressie [15]). Alternatively, simulations may be useful for obtaining approximate standard errors and for other types of inference. The estimated conditional rate $\lambda(t,x,y,z;\hat{\theta})$ can be used directly for prediction and risk assessment.

Spatiotemporal point processes may be evaluated via residual analysis, as described in Schoenberg [16]. One typically selects a spatial coordinate and rescales the point process in that direction. If the z coordinate is chosen, for example, then each point (t_i, x_i, y_i, z_i) of the observed point process is moved to a new point $(t_i, x_i, y_i, \int_{z_0}^{z_i} \lambda(t_i, x_i, y_i, z; \hat{\theta})dz)$, where z_0 is the lower boundary in the z direction of the spatial region being considered. The resulting rescaled process is stationary Poisson if and only if the model is correctly specified [17]. Hence a useful method for assessing the fit of a point process model is to examine whether the rescaled point process looks like a Poisson process with unit rate.

4 Wildfire modelling in the Valencian community

In this paper, in prescribing a model for λ, we use a spatial background component $m(x, y)$ which takes into account the spatial inhomogeneity of the wildfire occurrences. This component can be thought of as incorporating previous knowledge about where wildfires are more or less likely to occur. For example, it would be undesirable for the model to predict a wildfire occurrence inside a town. For this component a simple two-dimensional kernel smoother is used,

$$m(x, y) = \frac{1}{n_0} \sum_{j=1}^{n_0} \frac{1}{\phi_x \phi_y} K(\frac{x - x_{0j}}{\phi_x}) K(\frac{y - y_{0j}}{\phi_y}) \quad (2)$$

where K is a suitable kernel function. In estimating the spatial background $m(x, y)$, the smoother is not computed using the whole data set. Rather, the spatial locations of the wildfires occurring before the starting time of interest are smoothed, guaranteeing that the estimate of the conditional intensity at time t is based strictly on information from before time t. Here, n_0 is the number of wildfires in the full dataset occurring before the starting time of interest and (x_{0j}, y_{0j}) represents the spatial coordinates of the jth wildfire in that subset. Finally, ϕ_x, ϕ_y are positive parameters defining the degree of smoothness in function m.

A seasonal component $S(t)$ is used to describe the overall seasonal variation of the wildfire activity. Here, we smooth the times within each year of the past wildfires,

$$S(t) = \frac{1}{n_0} \sum_{j=1}^{n_0} \frac{1}{\phi_t} K(\frac{t^* - t^*_{0j}}{\phi_t}) \quad (3)$$

where t^* indicates the time since the beginning of the year and t^*_{0j} is the time since the beginning of the year for the jth wildfire occurrence before the starting date. Again, ϕ_t is a positive smoothing parameter.

Finally, a BI component $B(t, x, y)$ describes, for an arbitrary point (t, x, y), the contribution to the conditional intensity from the values of the BI at each station. Since the BI values are only observed at fixed locations, some form of interpolation is required to compute values at other locations. We consider a BI component of the form

$$BI(t, x, y) = \frac{1}{C} \sum_{s \in S_t} \left\{ \gamma_s K(\frac{x - x_s}{\beta_s}) K(\frac{y - y_s}{\beta_s}) BI(t, s) \right\} \quad (4)$$

where $BI(t, s)$ is the BI value recorded at time t from the sth station, (x_s, y_s) represents the location of the sth station, and S_t is the index set of stations in use at time t. The values γ_s are scaling coefficients for the BI values and are in units of events/(spatial unit$^2 \times$ day); the BI itself is dimensionless. The normalization constant C is simply the sum of the kernel weights. For each of the three components, the kernel function used is the standard normal density function.

One may consider as a basis of comparison simple baseline models such as a *homogeneous Poisson model* $\lambda^H(t, x, y) = \mu$, and the following *Spatial+Seasonal*

Figure 2: Wildfire locations in the Valencian Community during 1994 (left), 2000 (center) and 2001 (right).

model, $\lambda^0(t,x,y) = \nu m(x,y) + \alpha S(t)$, where ν and α are parameters to be estimated. The latter model does not include any information from the BI and serves as a model against which we can compare models incorporating BI information from each station. Thus, we take

$$\lambda(t,x,y) = \nu m(x,y) + \alpha S(t) + \beta I(t,x,y), \tag{5}$$

as our BI model and inspect the usefulness of the BI by comparing the performance of both λ and λ^0.

For our analysis, we focused on the wildfires recorded in the Valencian Community (Spain) during the years 2000-2001. Figure 4 shows the spatial coordinates of the wildfires recorded during the years 1994, 2000 and 2001.

We fitted several parametric families to the conditional intensity corresponding to: (a) A *purely spatial model* with $\lambda(t,x,y) = \nu m(x,y)$. Figure 4 shows an estimation of the $m()$ function and thus of the conditional intensity function; (b) A *purely temporal model* with $\lambda(t,x,y) = \alpha S(t)$. Figure 4 shows an estimation of the $S()$ function and thus of the conditional intensity function; (c) A *spatio-temporal model* with $\lambda(t,x,y) = \nu m(x,y) + \alpha S(t)$; (d) A *purely BI-based model* with $\lambda(t,x,y) = \beta I(t,x,y)$; (e) A *BI-based spatio-temporal model* with $\lambda(t,x,y) = \nu m(x,y) + \alpha S(t) + \beta I(t,x,y)$.

Two point process residual analysis techniques were employed to supplement a standard likelihood based model evaluation criterion (AIC). The random thinning method enabled us to check for residual space-time clustering on the same temporal and spatial scales as the data, while the rescaling method allowed for the closer inspection of temporal clustering in the residuals. Together, the methods

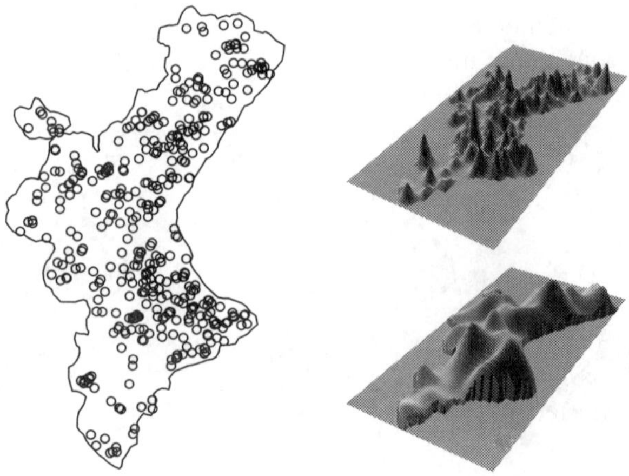

Figure 3: Accumulated wildfires locations for the period 2000-2001, and estimated $m()$ function for values of the smoothing parameters $\phi_x = 0.02$, $\phi_y = 0.02$ (top right) and $\phi_x = 0.05$, $\phi_y = 0.05$ (bottom right).

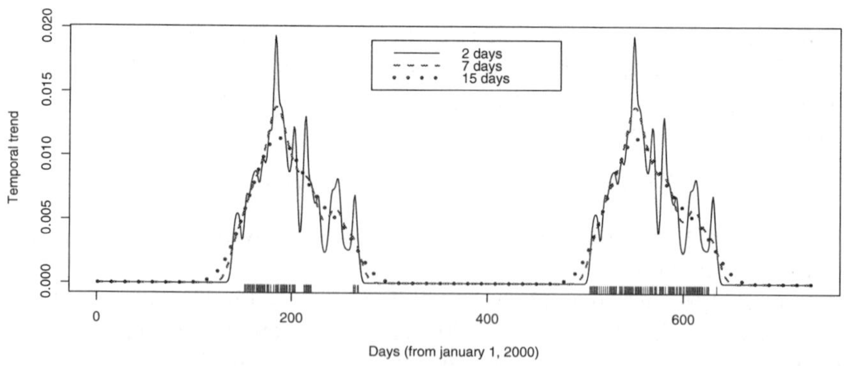

Figure 4: $S(t)$ function for the days in the period of 2000-2001. Over the horizontal axis, the days with wildfires have been marked.

provided greater insight into precisely where the BI model fit poorly and where it was making some (minimal) improvement.

5 Conclusions and discussion

We have developed an approach for evaluating a wildfire hazard index using space-time conditional intensity models. This approach has allowed for a detailed analysis of the performance of the Burning Index in predicting wildfire occurrence in Valencian Community, Spain. Our conclusions about the BI are based on an assessment of conditional intensity models which incorporate spatial, seasonal, and BI information. We found a model that outperformed a simple model which only takes into account natural spatial and seasonal variation.

References

[1] Brillinger, D.R., A particle migrating randomly on a sphere, *Journal of Theoretical Probability*, **10**, 429–443, 1997.

[2] Brillinger, D.R., Some examples of random process environmental data analysis, in *Handbook of Statistics*, Vol. **18**, C.R. Rao y P.K. Sen, eds, North-Holland, Amsterdam, pp. 33–56, 2000.

[3] Daley, D. & Vere-Jones, D., *An Introduction to the Theory of Point Processes*, Springer-Verlag, Berlin, 1988.

[4] Diggle, P., A kernel method for smoothing point process data, *Applied Statistics*, **34**, 138–147, 1985.

[5] Fishman, P.M. & Snyder, D.L., The statistical analysis of space–time point processes, *IEEE Transactions on Information Theory*, **22**, 257–274, 1976.

[6] Guttorp, P. & Thompson, M., Nonparametric estimation of intensities for sampled counting processes, *Journal of the Royal Statistical Society*, Series B **52**, 157–173, 1990.

[7] Kagan, Y.Y., Likelihood analysis of earthquake catalogs, *Journal of Geophysical Research*, **106**, 135–148, 1991.

[8] Kallenberg, O., *Random Measures*, 3rd Edition, Akademie-Verlag, Berlin, 1983.

[9] Karr, A., *Point Processes and Their Statistical Inference*, 2nd Edition, Marcel Dekker, New York, 1991.

[10] Merzbach, E. & Nualart, D., A characterization of the spatial Poisson process and changing time, *The Annals of Probability*, **14**, 1380–1390, 1986.

[11] Musmeci, F. & Vere-Jones, D., A space–time clustering model for historical earthquakes, *The Annals of the Institute of Statistical Mathematics*, **44**, 1–11, 1992.

[12] Nadeau, R., Antolik, M., Johnson, P.A., Foxall, W. & McEvilly, T.V., Seismological studies at Parkfield III: microearthquake clusters in the study of fault-zone dynamics, *Bulletin of the Seismic Society of America*, **84**, 247–263, 1994.

[13] Ogata, Y. Space–time point process models for earthquake occurrences, *The Annals of the Institute of Statistical Mathematics*, **50**, 379–402, 1998.

[14] Rathbun, S.L., Modeling marked spatio-temporal point patterns, *Bulletin of the International Statistical Institute*, **55**, 379–396, 1993.

[15] Rathbun, S. & Cressie, N., Asymptotic properties of estimators for the parameters of spatial inhomogeneous Poisson point processes, *Advances in Applied Probability*, **26**, 122–154, 1994.

[16] Schoenberg, F., Assessment of multi-dimensional point processes, Ph.D. Thesis, University of California, Berkeley, 1997.

WIT Transactions on Ecology and the Environment, Vol 81, © 2005 WIT Press
www.witpress.com, ISSN 1743-3541 (on-line)

[17] Schoenberg, F., Transforming spatial point processes into Poisson processes, *Stochastic Process Applications*, **81**, 155–164, 1999.
[18] Vere-Jones, D. Statistical methods for the description and display of earthquake catalogs, in Statistics in the Environmental and Earth Sciences, A. Walden & P. Guttorp, eds, Edward Arnold, London, pp. 220–246, 1992.

A cellular automata model for predicting fire spread

S. Hoya White[1], A. Martín del Rey[2] & G. Rodríguez Sánchez[2]
[1]*Iberdrola Generación, Salamanca, Spain*
[2]*Department of Applied Mathematics, University of Salamanca, Spain*

Abstract

A new model for predicting fire propagation in homogeneous environments, based on the transfer of a fractional burned area, is introduced in this paper. A particular type of discrete dynamical system, called a hexagonal bidimensional cellular automaton, is used in order to design the model. The simulations obtained are found to be in agreement with the experience of fire spreading in real forests.
Keywords: fire spreading, hexagonal cellular automata, mathematical modelling.

1 Introduction

As is well-known, forest fires is one of the major ecological agents in forest since they alter the structure and composition of forest and adversely affect human health and the supply of goods and services on which communities depend. Consequently, the study of forest fires have received increased public attention by the scientific community. Specifically, several mathematical models have been appeared in the literature in order to study the spreading of forest fire fronts. The efforts to model the growth of the fire front by means of mathematical models can be classified according to two approaches: vector models and cellular automata models. Vector models assume that the fire front spreads according to a well-defined growth law, and take a standard geometrical shape (see, for example, Vakalis *et al.* [6]). On the other hand, several types of cellular automata models for fire spreading have been introduced in the literature (see Karafyllidis [1, 2]).

The main goal of this work is to introduce a new discrete mathematical model for predicting the behaviour of the forest fire front based on a two-dimensional hexagonal cellular automata. Basically, it consists of a two-dimensional hexagonal array of a finite number of identical objects called cells, interacting locally with each other. Each cell can assume a state from a finite or infinite state set, which changes at every time step according to a fixed rule. The variables of such function are the states of some neighbour cells at the previous time step. The proposed model divides the forest into regular hexagonal areas, each one of them stands for a cell. The state of each cell is a real number from the interval [0,1]. If it is 0, then the cell is unburned, and if the state is 1, the cell is totally burned out. The evolution rule linearly depends on thirteen variables: the states of the twelve nearest cells to a given one and its own state. These variables are affected by some parameters which stand for wind speed and the topography.

The rest of the paper is organized as follows: In Section 2 a review of bidimensional cellular automata is given; the proposed model is introduced in Section 3; some graphical simulations are shown in Section 4; and, finally, the conclusions are presented in Section 5.

2 A review of cellular automata

In a precise way, a cellular automaton, CA for short, (see, for example, Sarkar [4], and Toffoli *et al.* [5]) can be defined as a 4-uplet $A=(C, S, V, f)$, where C is the cellular space formed by a bidimensional array of $r\times c$ cells, $\{(a,b), 1 \leq a \leq r, 1 \leq b \leq c\}$, such that each of which can assume a state. We can consider two types of cellular spaces: square cellular spaces, formed by a bidimensional array of identical square areas, each one of them stands for a cell, and hexagonal cellular spaces, where each cell stands for a regular hexagonal area. This work deals with this second type.

The state of each cell is an element of a state set, S. Furthermore, the state of a particular cell (a,b) at time t is denoted by $s_{ab}^{(t)}$.

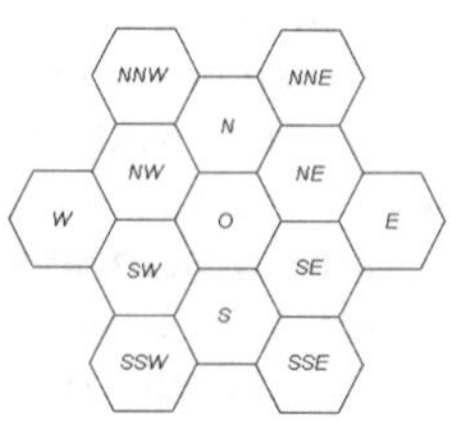

Figure 1: The neighborhood of the cell O.

The set of indices of the CA is the ordered finite subset $V \subset \mathbf{Z}\times\mathbf{Z}$, $|V| = m$, such that for every cell (a,b), its neighborhood $V_{(a,b)}$ is the ordered set of m cells given by $V_{(a,b)} = \{(a+\alpha_1, b+\beta_1), \ldots, (a+\alpha_m, b+\beta_m) : (\alpha_i, \beta_i) \in V\}$.

Depending on the process to be modelled, one can choose an appropriate neighbourhood. In this work, the neighbourhood of a particular cell $O = (a,b)$ is given by the set

$$V_O = \{O, N, NE, SE, S, SW, NW, NNE, E, SSE, SSW, W, NNW\}, \quad (1)$$

which is shown in Figure 1.

Due to the main features of the model for predicting fire spread proposed below, we must distinguish two types of neighbour cells of the cell O: near neighbour cells, $V^n = \{N, NE, SE, S, SW, NW\}$; and distant neighbour cells, $V^d = \{NNE, E, SSE, SSW, W, NNW\}$. Moreover, each distant neighbour cell, $(\alpha, \beta) \in V^d$, has two associated near neighbour cells: $(a+\alpha^+, b+\beta^+)$ and $(a+\alpha^-, b+\beta^-)$, that are given by those with common sides. For example, the associated near neighbor cells of NNE are N and NE, and so on. Furthermore, in this case the set defining the neighborhood, $V \subset \mathbf{Z}\times\mathbf{Z}$, depends on the cell $O = (a,b)$ to be considered. That is, if b is odd, then (see Figure 2), $V = \{(0,0), (-1,0), (0,1), (1,1), (1,0), (1,-1), (0,-1), (-1,1), (0,2), (2,1), (2,1),(0,-2), (-1,-1)\}$;

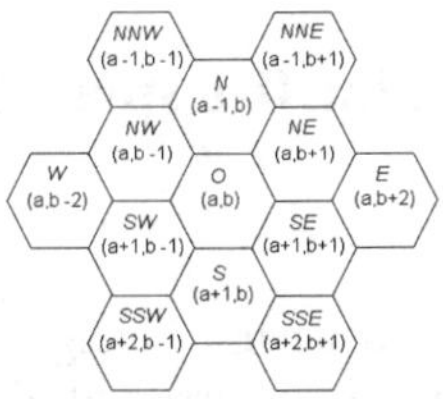

Figure 2: The labelled neighborhood when b is odd.

On the other hand, if b is even, then (see Figure 3), $V = \{(0,0), (-1,0), (-1,1), (0,1), (1,0), (0,-1), (-1,-1), (-2,1), (0,2), (1,1), (1,-1), (0,-2), (-2,-1)\}$.

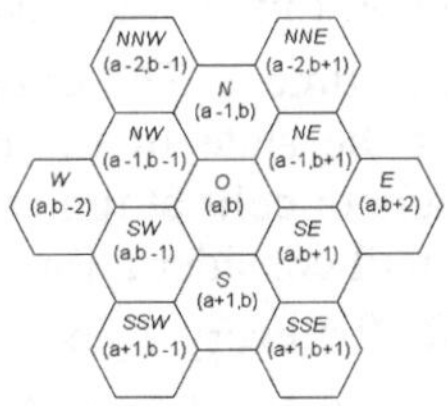

Figure 3: The labelled neighborhood when b is even.

For the sake of simplicity and, since it does not affect to the computations below, we will consider the generic neighborhood V_O given in eqn. (1).

The CA evolves deterministically in discrete time steps, changing the states of all cells according to a local transition function: $f: S^{13} \rightarrow S$. The updated state of the cell (a,b) depends on the thirteen variables of the local transition function, which are the previous states of the cells constituting its neighborhood, that is, $s_{ab}^{(t+1)} = f\left(s_{(a+\alpha_1,b+\beta_1)}^{(t)},\ldots,s_{(a+\alpha_{13},b+\beta_{13})}^{(t)}\right)$, with $(\alpha_i,\beta_i)\in V$, for every $1\leq i\leq 13$. Moreover, the matrix, $C^{(t)} = (s_{ij}^{(t)})$, is called the configuration at time t of the CA, with $C^{(0)}$ being the initial configuration. Since the number of cells of the CA is finite, boundary conditions must be considered in order to assure the well-defined dynamics of such CA. In this work null boundary conditions are considered: If $(a,b)\notin \{(u,v), 1\leq u\leq r, 1\leq v\leq c\}$, then $s_{ab}^{(t)} = 0$.

Linear CA are those whose local transition functions are linear with real coefficients. Note that, in this case, the state set is infinite: $S = \mathbf{R}$. Nevertheless, depending on the process to be modeled, the state set of the CA is usually finite and, consequently, a discretization function, $g:\mathbf{R}\rightarrow S$, must be considered. Thus, in this case, the local transition function is as follows:

$$s_{ab}^{(t+1)} = g\left(\sum_{(\alpha,\beta)\in V}\mu_{\alpha\beta}s_{a+\alpha,b+\beta}^{(t)}\right),\quad \mu_{\alpha\beta}\in\mathbf{R}.$$

3 The CA-based model for fire spreading

3.1 The state set

A forest area can be interpreted as the hexagonal cellular space of a CA by simply dividing it into a bidimensional array of identical regular hexagonal areas of side length L. Obviously, each one of this areas stands for a cell of the CA. The state of a cell (a,b) at a time t, is defined as follows:

$$s_{ab}^{(t)} = \frac{\text{burned out area of } (a,b) \text{ at } t}{\text{total area of } (a,b)} = \frac{\text{burned out area of } (a,b) \text{ at } t}{3\sqrt{3}L^2/2}.$$

If $s_{ab}^{(t)} = 0$, then the cell (a,b) is said to be unburned at time t; if $0 < s_{ab}^{(t)} < 1$, the cell (a,b) is partially burned out at time t, and finally, if $s_{ab}^{(t)} = 1$, the cell is said to be completely burned out at time t. The evolution of the CA used in the proposed model supposes that the state of the cell (a,b) at time t+1 linearly depends on the states of its neighbor cells at time t.

In the proposed model, we will consider a finite state set of order k, that is, $S = \{q_1,\ldots,q_k\}$, with $q_i\in\mathbf{R}$ for every i and $0\leq q_1\leq\ldots\leq q_k\leq 1$. Then, a suitable discretization function, $g:[0,1]\rightarrow S$, must be incorporated to the model as follows:

$$s_{ab}^{(t+1)} = g\left(s_{ab}^{(t)} + \sum_{(\alpha,\beta)\in V^n}\mu_{\alpha\beta}^{(a,b)}s_{a+\alpha,b+\beta}^{(t)} + \sum_{(\alpha,\beta)\in V^d}\mu_{\alpha\beta}^{(a,b)}s_{a+\alpha,b+\beta}^{(t)}\right), \tag{2}$$

where $\mu_{\alpha\beta}^{(a,b)}\in\mathbf{R}$ are parameters involving some physical magnitudes of the cells. Note that from eqn. (2), it is possible that the value $s_{ab}^{(t)}$ to be greater than 1. In this case, $s_{ab}^{(t)}$ is taken to be equal to 1.

3.2 Incorporating weather and topography conditions

Each cell O can be endowed with three parameters: The rate of fire spread, R, which is the same for all cells as the forest is homogeneous, the wind speed, W_O, and the height H_O. Specifically, the effect of the wind on the cell O is given by the set $W_O = \{\omega_{\alpha\beta}^{O}, (\alpha,\beta) \in V\}$, where $\omega_{\alpha\beta}^{O} > 0$, in such a way that if no wind is blowing on O, then $\omega_{\alpha\beta}^{O} = 1$ for every $(\alpha,\beta) \in V$; if the wind is blowing from North to South, then the coefficients ω_{NW}^{O}, ω_{NNW}^{O}, ω_{N}^{O}, ω_{NNE}^{O} and ω_{NE}^{O} must be larger than the rest of coefficients, and so on. The value of such coefficients stands for the magnitude of the wind. Furthermore, the height differences between various points in a forest also affect the fire spreading. As is well known, the fires show a higher rate of spread when they climb an upward slope, whereas fires show a smaller rate of spread when they descend a downward slope. The height influence of a near neighbor cell, $(a+\alpha, b+\beta)$, with $(\alpha,\beta) \in V$, on a cell $O =$ (a,b), is given by $h_{\alpha\beta}^{O} = \phi\left(H_{(a,b)} - H_{(a+\alpha,b+\beta)}\right)$. The function $y = \phi(x)$ must be determined according to the characteristic of the forest, and, also, it must satisfy the following conditions: If $x<0$, then $0< \phi(x)<1$; if $x = 0$, $\phi(x) = 1$, and, finally, if $x>0$, $\phi(x)>1$. Note that the first condition establishes that if $H_{(a,b)} > H_{(a+\alpha,b+\beta)}$, the fire increases its rate of spread; the second condition states that when $H_{(a,b)} = H_{(a+\alpha,b+\beta)}$, the topography does not affect the fire spread; and the third condition establishes that if $H_{(a,b)} < H_{(a+\alpha,b+\beta)}$, the fire restrains its spreading.

On the other hand, the height influence of a distant neighbor cell is affected by the influence of its associated near neighbor cells. For example, if the distant neighbor cell is NNE, then:

$$h_{NNE}^{O} = \frac{1}{4}\left(\phi\left(H_O - H_N\right) + \phi\left(H_N - H_{NNE}\right) + \phi\left(H_O - H_{NE}\right) - \phi\left(H_{NE} - H_{NNE}\right)\right).$$

Note that if the forest is flat (all cells have the same height), then $\phi(x) = 1$ and consequently $h_{\alpha\beta}^{(a,b)} = 1$ for every cell (a,b) and $(\alpha,\beta) \in V$. Consequently, $\mu_{\alpha\beta}^{(a,b)} = \omega_{\alpha\beta}^{(a,b)} \cdot h_{\alpha\beta}^{(a,b)}$, where $\omega_{\alpha\beta}^{(a,b)}$ and $h_{\alpha\beta}^{(a,b)}$ stand for the wind influence and the height influence respectively of the neighbor cell $(a+\alpha,b+\beta)$ on (a,b).

3.3 Determining the time step

In the proposed model, the size of the time step, $\tilde{t}$, is considered to be equal to the time needed for a one and only near neighbor cell to burn the main cell out. Consequently, the rate of fire spread of the cells, R, determines $\tilde{t}$, and it is assumed to be given by a different model (see, for example, [3]). As a consequence, it is easy to check that if all cells in the neighborhood of O are unburned at time t except for only one near neighbor cell, say for example N, then the time needed for O to be completely burned out is $\widetilde{t} = \sqrt{3}L/R$ (see Figure 4).

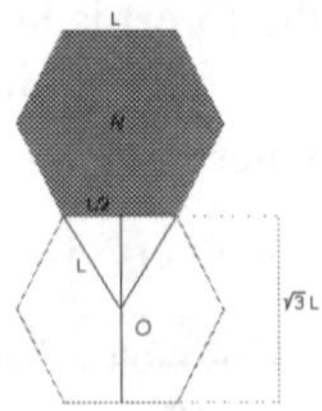

Figure 4: The size of the discrete step of time.

Thus, if all cells in the neighborhood of O are unburned at time t except only one adjacent cell, which is completely burned out, then at time t+1, the cell O is completely burned out: $s_O^{(t+1)} = 1$. Furthermore, if the only completely burned out neighbor cell at time t, is a distant neighbor cell of O, say NNE, then $s_O^{(t+1)} = \lambda < 1$. That value is calculated as follows. In a step time $\widetilde{t}$, the near neighbor cells, N and NE, and a little portion (a circular sector) of O will be burned out. Specifically, as the distance covered by the fire front in $\widetilde{t}$ with speed R is $\sqrt{3}L$, then the radius of the circular sector of O burned out is $\sqrt{3}L - L$ (see Figure 5).

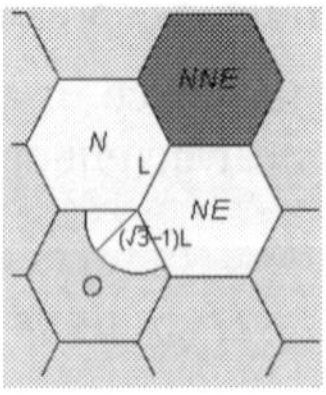

Figure 5: The calculus of λ.

As a consequence, the burned out area of the cell O is

$$\frac{\pi\left(\sqrt{3}-1\right)^2 L^2 \frac{\pi}{3}}{2\pi} = \frac{2-\sqrt{3}}{3}\pi L^2 .$$

So, if all neighbor cells of O are unburned at time t, except a distant neighbor cell which is fully burned out, then

$$s_O^{(t+1)} = \lambda = \frac{\frac{2-\sqrt{3}}{3}\pi L^2}{\frac{3\sqrt{3}}{2}L^2} = \frac{4\sqrt{3}-6}{27}\pi \approx 0.1080.$$

3.4 The local transition function

Taking into account the results from the previous sections, one can conclude that the local transition function of the hexagonal cellular automata for predicting forest fire spreading is as follows:

$$s_{ab}^{(t+1)} = g\left(s_{ab}^{(t)} + \sum_{(\alpha,\beta)\in V^n} \mu_{\alpha\beta}^{(a,b)} s_{a+\alpha,b+\beta}^{(t)} + \sum_{(\alpha,\beta)\in V^d} \mu_{\alpha\beta}^{(a,b)} s_{a+\alpha,b+\beta}^{(t)} \right),$$

with $\mu_{\alpha\beta}^{(a,b)} = \omega_{\alpha\beta}^{(a,b)} \cdot h_{\alpha\beta}^{(a,b)}$, where

$$h_{\alpha\beta}^{(a,b)} = \begin{cases} \phi\left(H_{(a,b)} - H_{(a+\alpha,b+\beta)}\right), \text{ if } (\alpha,\beta)\in V^n \\ \frac{1}{4}\Big[\phi\left(H_{(a,b)} - H_{(a+\alpha^+,b+\beta^+)}\right) + \phi\left(H_{(a+\alpha^+,b+\beta^+)} - H_{(a+\alpha,b+\beta)}\right) \\ \phi\left(H_{(a,b)} - H_{(a+\alpha^-,b+\beta^-)}\right) + \phi\left(H_{(a+\alpha^+,b+\beta^+)} - H_{(a+\alpha,b+\beta)}\right)\Big], \text{ if } (\alpha,\beta)\in V^d \end{cases}$$

and $g:[0,1]\to S$. Note that if there are no wind and topography conditions, the explicit expression of the transition function is as follows:

$$s_{ab}^{(t+1)} = g\left(s_{ab}^{(t)} + \sum_{(\alpha,\beta)\in V^n} s_{a+\alpha,b+\beta}^{(t)} + \lambda \sum_{(\alpha,\beta)\in V^d} s_{a+\alpha,b+\beta}^{(t)} \right).$$

4 Testing the proposed model

A good model for predicting forest fire spreading must pass some tests. In this work, we will consider four basic tests: (1) Modelization of a fire front spreading on a flat forest without wind conditions; (2) Modelization of a fire front spreading on a flat forest with wind conditions; (3) Modelization of a fire front spreading on a non-flat forest without wind conditions; and (4) Modelization of a fire front spreading on a non-flat forest with wind conditions. If an homogeneous flat forest without wind conditions is considered, the model must yield a circular fire front. If there are weather conditions, the wind speed and direction must affect the forest fire front. Furthermore, if the forest is non-flat, the topography conditions must be reflected in the dynamics of fire front since, as was mentioned above, fires show a higher rate of spread when they climb up an upward slope, whereas fires show a smaller rate of spread when they descend a downward slope.

An algorithm using the computer algebra system Mathematica has been implemented for the computational and graphical simulations of the fire fronts. The hypothetical forests used are modeled by means of a bidimensional array of 100×100 cells. In the initial configuration, there is only one cell (the central cell) burned out, whereas the rest of the cells are unburned, and 20 evolutions are calculated. In the figures below, only the configurations at times $t = 0, 5, 10, 15, 20$ are shown. Furthermore, in the simulations, the state set used is

$S = \{q_1 = 0, q_2 = 0.1, \ldots, q_{11} = 1\}$, and consequently, the discretization function, g:[0,1]→S, will be

$$g(t) = \begin{cases} 0, \text{if } t = 0 \\ q_i, \text{if } \frac{\text{i-1}}{10} \le t \le \frac{i}{10} \\ 1, \text{if } t = 1 \end{cases}$$

Moreover, the states of the cells are represented according to the following color code (see Figure 6).

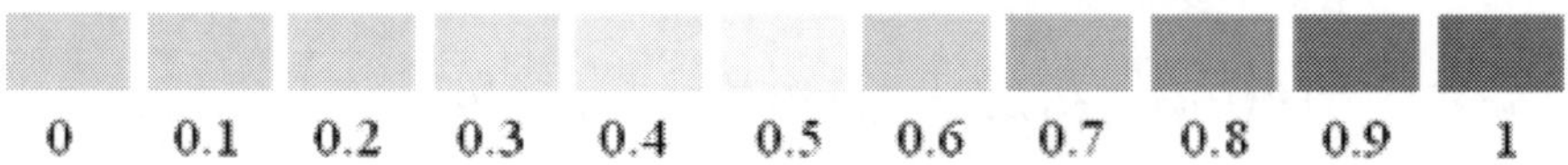

Figure 6: The color code.

Firstly, suppose that the forest is flat, and there are no wind conditions. Then, as is shown in Figure 7, the fire front is circular.

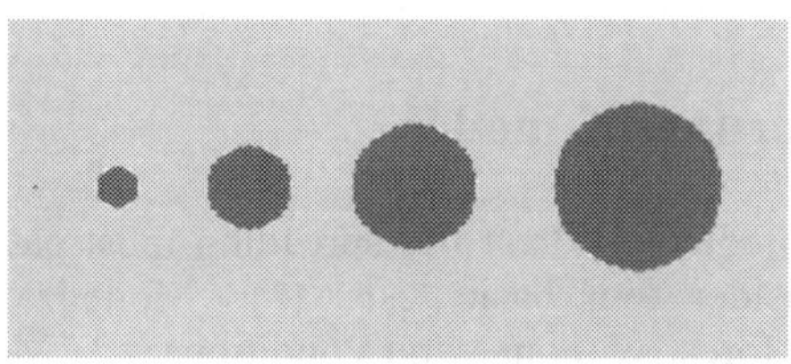

Figure 7: Simulation in a flat forest without wind conditions.

If the forest is flat and the wind is blowing from north to south according to the wind front given in Figure 8), then the simulation obtained is shown in Figure 9.

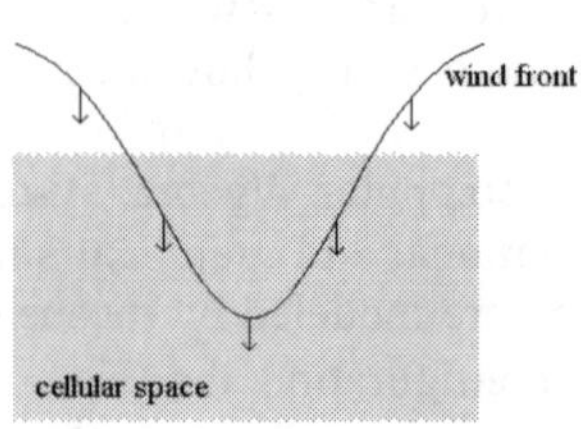

Figure 8: The wind front.

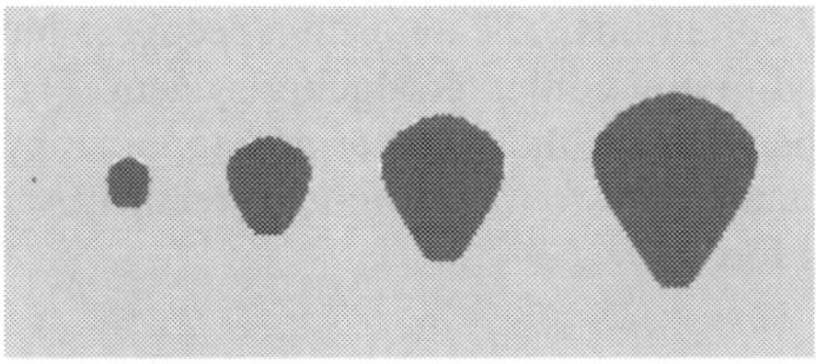

Figure 9: Simulation in a flat forest with wind conditions.

Now, suppose that the forest is non-flat, say for example, $H_{(a,b)} = b$ for each cell (a,b), and take, for example, the function

$$\phi(x) = \begin{cases} e^x, \text{if } x \leq 0 \\ 1 + \dfrac{\sqrt{x}}{10}, \text{if } x > 0 \end{cases}$$

If there are not wind conditions, the spreading of the fire forest is shown in Figure 10, and if the wind blows from north to south according to the above non-linear front, the fire forest evolves as is shown in Figure 11.

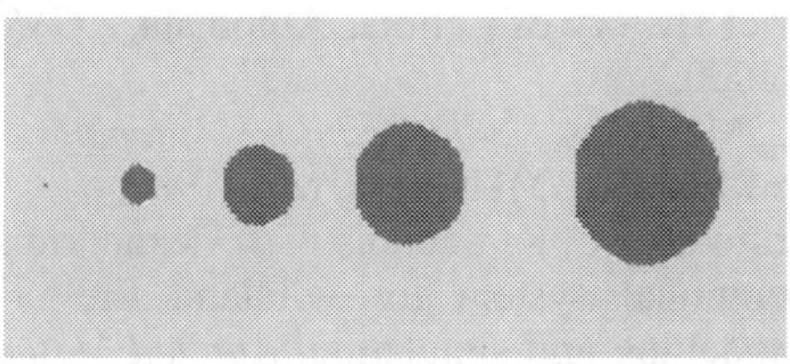

Figure 10: Simulation in a non-flat forest without wind conditions.

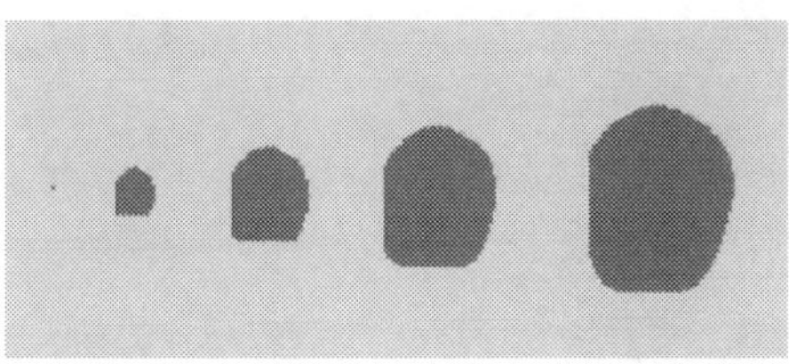

Figure 11: Simulation in a non-flat forest with wind conditions.

5 Conclusions

In this work, a new model for the prediction of forest fire spreading has been introduced. It is based on hexagonal cellular automata and incorporates weather and land topography conditions. The algorithm seems to be very efficient and it is easily implemented in any computer algebra system. The model is applied to four basic cases depending on the weather and topography conditions. All the graphical models obtained are found to be in agreement with the experience of fire spreading in real forests.

Acknowledgement

This work is supported by "Samuel Solórzano Barruso" Memorial Foundation of the University of Salamanca, Spain.

References

[1] Karafyllidis, I., Design of a dedicated parallel processor for the prediction of forest fire spreading using cellular automata and genetic algorithms. *Engineering Applications of Artificial Intelligence*, **17**, pp. 19-36, 2004.

[2] Karafyllidis, I. & Thanailakis, A., A model for predicting forest fire spreading using cellular automata. *Ecological Modelling*, **99**, pp. 87-97, 1997.

[3] McRae, R.H.D., Use of digital terrain data for calculating rates of fire spread with the PREPALN computer system. *Proc. of the 8th Conference and Bushfire Dynamics Workshop*. Canberra, pp. 579-585, 1989.

[4] Sarkar, P., A Brief History of Cellular Automata, *ACM Computing Surveys*, **32**, pp. 80-107, 2000.

[5] Toffoli, T. & Margolus, N., *Cellular Automata Machines. A New Environment for Modeling*, MIT Press, MA, 1987.

[6] Vakalis, D., Sarimveis, H., Kiranoudis, C., Alexandridis, A. & Bafas, G., A GIS based operational system for wildland fire crisis management I. Mathematical modelling and simulation. *Applied Mathematical Modellling*, **28**, pp. 389-410, 2004.

An evolutionary approach to simulate an industrial system

G. Confessore, G. Liotta & S. Rismondo
Istituto di Tecnologie Industriali e Automazione, Sezione di Roma, Consiglio Nazionale delle Ricerche, Area della Ricerca di Roma Tor Vergata, Via del Fosso del Cavaliere 100, 00133 Roma, Italy

Abstract

The Technology Transfer is successfully carried out by means of a strong partnership among industrial partners, banking systems, finance corporations, research institutes and public bodies. One of the main motivations for these partnerships is given by favourable boundary conditions such as local economic and legislative situations. On this point, Industrial Systems (ISs) represent at a world wide level an important example of Technology Transfer when they are defined in geographical areas (i.e., the Italian industrial districts). Therefore, an IS is characterized by strong interrelationships among partners. We focus on these interrelationships by taking into account a new scenario where, for instance, the research partners are geographically spread while the industrial partners are located in a specific area in which they could exploit the opportunities provided by local conditions.

We investigate these issues through the definition of a new model architecture able to represent and predict both the behaviour of the IS actors and the Technology Transfer effect. In particular, we introduce a Complex Adaptive System (CAS), that is, a flexible system: it reveals internal attributes able to exploit the diversity and to produce local innovations in response to environmental changes. In our CAS, we include some concepts of the evolution theory typical of the eco-system that well model the interrelationship we study.

1 Introduction

An Industrial System (IS) is composed of heterogeneous entities such companies, banking system, finance corporations, research institutes and public

WIT Transactions on Ecology and the Environment, Vol 81, © 2005 WIT Press
www.witpress.com, ISSN 1743-3541 (on-line)

body either working on a given geographical area and/or belonging to a common industrial sector. Nowadays, the actors of an IS have to be able to understand and control their way of work in order to exploit economic potential opportunities and to be competitive in the huge international. Therefore, the analysis, design and optimisation of ISs require methods, approaches, formalisms and tools to effective represent the main IS issues. Due to this fact, new needs arose for companies thus they would use adapted models considering physical and logical components of the company such as resources, products, information etc. Clearly, the goal of these models is to understand, engineer, evaluate, optimise and control the whole organisation of the company.

In the literature, many researchers propose new models for studying different IS issues and able to take into account various aspects. On the other hand, a critical point of classical models is their unsuitability to represent completely the IS due, for instance, to: the huge dimension of the network of firms; the hierarchical decisional level; the dynamic behaviour of the actors.

In this work we design a preliminary model architecture able to evolve getting the best IS configuration in response to the environment changes. In particular, we suppose the IS evolution mainly characterized by the self-organization and self-adapting properties. Classical optimization models are often monolithic and they do not allow to consider the IS dynamic behaviour. Moreover, the industrial actors could have different information, hard to manage with a (not always effective) centralized optimization model. On the other hand, we do not focus on classical system theory that better gets the IS dynamic.

In fact, to analyse the IS we provide a new model, called *SIM/OPT*, based on a discrete-event simulation general architecture where a combinatorial optimization and two decisional modules work. While simulation represents one of the main approaches of solving problems, the optimization module has to be usable in simulation module because ISs can not be studied easily with static classical modeling tools. We highlights that some of *SIM/OPT's* properties, such as self-organization, and self-adapting entities properties are not included in classical discrete-event simulation models. To introduce these properties and to study the growth and trend of the IS, we consider the complex adaptive system (CAS) simulation approach. In the literature, a CAS is a system that 'emerges over time into a coherent form, adapting and organizes itself without any singular entity controlling or managing it' (Holland [2]). In the latest years, CAS models have been applied in many research areas such as evolutionary biology, non-linear dynamical systems, and artificial intelligence due to their ability to represent complex system as is an IS (see for instance Maxfield and Lane [5]). In this preliminary work, the CAS approach is exploited to model an IS composed of manufacturers and suppliers (operating on a defined geographical region) that have to adapt themselves to the industrial environment. In particular, the main information guiding the evolution of the IS is the demand function.

A further goal of this paper, mainly related to the Technology Transfer issue, is to understand how the presence of research partners could produce IS changes.

The remainder of the paper is organized as follows. In Section 2, we formally define the CAS based simulation model. Sections 3 and 4 are devoted to the *SIM/OPT* modules description. Finally, Section 5 summarizes the results.

2 The CAS based system model

This paper investigates the design of the *SIM/OPT* model architecture, based on a discrete-event simulation general architecture where a combinatorial optimization and two decisional modules work. The *SIM/OPT* model architecture is able to represent the behaviour of the actors working in a complex Industrial System (IS). In particular, *SIM/OPT* is able to take into account the self-adapting, and the self-organization properties.

The next subsections describe the main topics of *SIM/OPT* and introduce the genetic algorithm schema as potential interpretation (and implementation) of the IS evolution in relation to the demand function.

2.1 The actors

In a CAS model, the actors refer to agents (or entities) acting in the complex system, where their behaviour gets spontaneous changes of the system.

We refer to an IS in which the manufacturers produce a single good, that is we consider each manufacturer belonging to the IS, having a specialized production process, able to produce a specific good. Let us suppose that the set of manufacturers constitutes an industrial cluster. In this setting, we consider the logistic model introduced by Gambarotto and Maggioni [1] and Maggioni [4]. The authors show how, by introducing specific preliminary hypothesis related to the industrial cluster properties, the trend of the total number of manufacturers belonging to the industrial cluster grow up following an *S*-curve. The *S*-curve represents a typical product life-cycle (that is flatter at the beginning and end, steeper in the middle), and can be stated as follows:

$$D(t) = \frac{c}{(1+be^{-at})},$$

where parameters a, b, c modify the slope of the curve, the function translation, and the maximum saturation value, respectively. We analyse a set of suppliers providing a single sub-item according to a demand function proportional to the number of manufacturers, that is we suppose for the suppliers a demand function given by an *S*-curve as well.

Therefore, starting by the logistic model, the main topic of this paper is the definition of a new IS model architecture representation based on CAS approach.

We introduce a set of actors S representing self-contained problem-solving entities. Each actor $j \in S$ operates collecting data from the environment, elaborating them, and applying strategies in order to achieve its goal. Moreover, each actor has incomplete information, there is not a centralized system control, the computations are asynchronous, and data are decentralized. The actors have logically and geographically spread information.

Given a time horizon of T periods, let S be the set of n_S^t suppliers at period $t=1, \ldots, T$ (i.e., $n_S^t = |S|$).

Let us assume the set of suppliers working on a specific regional area (where they exploit favourable boundary conditions such as local economic and legislative situation) and providing a single sub-item. In particular, we consider the set of suppliers S composed of three subsets, that is $S = S_1 \cup S_2 \cup S_3$. These subsets are related to a specific supplier property; in fact, we introduce parameter a_j for each $j \in S$, representing the supplier ability to modify its production process in order to best fit the demand function and then exploit this information as a business opportunity. Parameter a_j is set every time a new supplier is generated and it does not change during the IS simulation.

In the *SIM/OPT* model, we observe how the total number of suppliers n_S^t (i.e., $n_S^t = n_{S1}^t + n_{S2}^t + n_{S3}^t$) evolves during the simulation with respect to the demand variations.

Furthermore, we analyse how the innovation due to the Technology Transfer from research partners to the suppliers, produce IS changes. Due to this fact, we model the innovation given by the research partners as a function $I(t)$.

2.2 The *SIM/OPT* architecture description

Let us assume the demand function $D(t)$, and the innovation function $I(t)$ (for instance, given by the Research Institutes) being the input of *SIM/OPT* model. In particular, $D(t)$ acts directly on the optimization module (*OPT*), while $I(t)$ is the input for 'TT' module (where 'TT' is the acronym of Technology Transfer). This decisional module is able to code the information $I(t)$ in a simulation parameters changes, and then in a modified optimization scenario. The *SIM/OPT*'s output is the total number of suppliers n_S^t at period t (and n_{S1}^t, n_{S2}^t, n_{S3}^t). On the other hand, the number of suppliers n_S^t (and n_{S1}^t, n_{S2}^t, n_{S3}^t) for each $t = 1, \ldots, T$, represents the input of the 'E' module (Evaluator), that is able to modify the simulation parameters and then the optimization scenario.

Figure 1 depicts the *SIM/OPT* model general architecture.

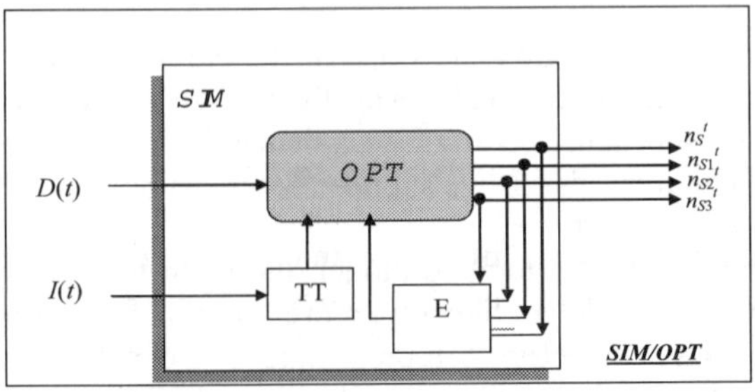

Figure 1: The SIM-OPT model architecture.

Next, we deeply explain how the *OPT* module works. We exploit the genetic algorithm basic idea in order to define an IS able to evolve with respect to the environment changes. For the biologists is consolidated the idea how the living adapt their environment in a short time (Kelley (1994)). In Computer Science this idea has been translated in what today we call genetic algorithm. This heuristic solution method adopts the concepts of natural selection, and natural genetics to find a near-optimal solution of a function. Therefore, we may assume that genetic algorithms approach the optimum of a given function in the same way nature selects the individual fittest to its environment.

In a genetic algorithm an individual (the chromosome) is represented as a string of bits, or genes (i.e., a string is a sequence of 1 and 0). This is not a restriction for the type of problem (for instance a route in a vehicle routing problem) since other data types can also be coded as bit strings. The chromosome, usually coded as a sequence of bits, represents a single solution for the analysed problem, and a given set of individuals constitutes a population.

The evolution of the population is guided by the genetic operators: *mutation*, and *crossover*. Mutation substitutes one or more genes of an individual randomly by a new value (e.g., the new value is selected at random in [0, 1]). Crossover exchanges parts, given by a single bit or a sub-string of bits, of one individual with the corresponding parts of another individual, both belonging to current population. Given a generation, the individuals are evaluated by the corresponding *fitness function* value. Let us suppose valid the *total generation replacement* representing the situation in which the whole offspring are selected while all parents are discarded. This is motivated by the biological model.

Next section aims at analysing the *SIM/OPT* model interpretation in terms of chromosome and the genetic operators definitions.

3 The *OPT* module functional schema

In this section, we explain how the *OPT* module follows the genetic algorithm schema. We define the chromosome composed of three genes, where each gene represents the total number of suppliers in a given subset (S_1, S_2, S_3). Therefore, recalling that n_{S1}^t, n_{S2}^t, n_{S3}^t are the number of suppliers in S_1, S_2 and S_3, respectively, a chromosome can be stated as follows:

n_{S1}^t	n_{S2}^t	n_{S3}^t

At simulation run t, a given chromosome represents an IS configuration of n_S^t suppliers. The fitness function (*ff*) value, that will be discussed in the experimental results, gives the difference among the individuals in a population. Figure 2 lists the main genetic algorithm steps with respect to the IS model. We introduce the population size n_z representing the number of individuals in a population, the demand value at period t, $D(t)$, the probability p^* guiding the genetic operators selection (crossover or mutation), and the number of IS observations T.

Concerning the genetic operators, the mutation selects an individual at random, and substitutes one gene randomly by a new value. The crossover selects two individuals and then exchange two genes of one individual with the corresponding of another individual. We implement a one-point crossover in which two individuals are aligned and one location on their chromosome is randomly chosen as the crossover site. The genes from the beginning of the individuals to the crossover site are exchanged between them. Between the resulting hybrid individuals is considered as the new offspring the one having the maximum fitness value.

```
▪ Set the population size (n_z)
▪ Set the initial Demand level (D(1)=D^0)
▪ Initialize the population with random chromosome according to D^0
▪ Evaluate all the chromosomes (compute the fitness function value)
▪ k = 1.
▪ Repeat{
      For i from 1 to n_z{
              Generate a probability value p at random
                      If (p > p*) Crossover
                      Else Mutation
              Evaluate the offspring in the next generation
      }
      Offspring replace parents
      k = k + 1
▪ }Until k < T
```

Figure 2: The *OPT* logical schema.

At each period t, we consider a fitness function that looks at encourage the chromosome that best fit the demand value $D(t)$. Therefore, all the IS configurations having a total number of suppliers $n_S^t >> D(t)$ ($n_S^t << D(t)$) are discouraged. Figure 3 depicts the trend of the *ff*. The maximum *ff* value is equal to 1 and corresponds to the chromosome that best fit the current demand level.

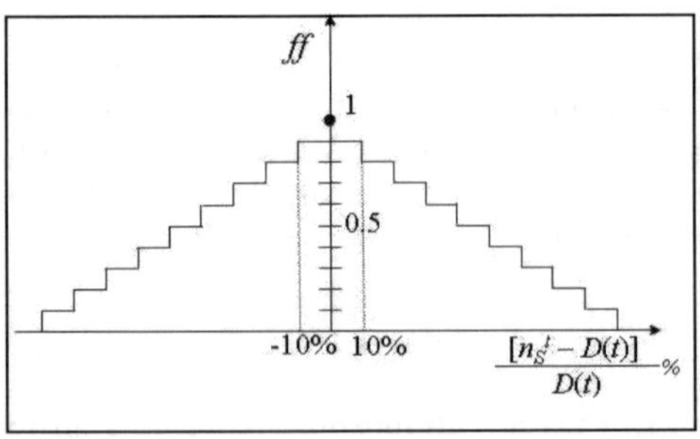

Figure 3: Fitness function trend.

4 EE and TT modules

The 'E' module acts on the *ff* value, then it modifies the optimization scenario. In particular, 'E' aims at modifying the *ff* value whenever the IS configuration (i.e. the chromosome) satisfy specific conditions. Due to this fact, at run t, the 'E' module penalises the *ff* value if the demand variation $\Delta D(t) = D(t) - D(t')$ computed in t and $t' = t - \Delta t$, respectively, is strongly meaningful, and $(n_{S1}^t + n_{S2}^t)$

$- n_{S3}^t > n^*$, where parameter n^* represents a threshold on the number of suppliers. In fact, we suppose the suppliers belonging to S_3 having more capability to survive in a strongly variable demand setting. Therefore, under these conditions, we must expect a low number of suppliers having low flexibility (n_{S1}^t) with respect to those one belonging to subsets S_2 and S_3, and in particular to suppliers belonging to S_3. In this way the IS configurations, namely the chromosomes, self-organize themselves in order to reach configurations which could assure a fast system stability in response to the demand level variation.

The 'TT' module modifies the optimization scenario whenever the innovation function $I(t)$ (i.e., the Technology Transfer result) value is not negligible. The effect of this function on the IS configuration is effective and appreciable if it represents a suppliers support towards an increasing degree of flexibility, that is an increasing capability to survive in strongly variable demand setting.

5 Conclusions and future works

This paper describe an innovative approach useful to model an IS. We then proposed the *SIM/OPT* model architecture based on the Complex Adaptive System (CAS) approach.

The model architecture aims at studying the trend of the total number of suppliers acting in a IS where a cluster of manufacturers produces a single good. We suppose to be valid the hypothesis given by the logistic model, and we observe the output of the *SIM/OPT* model, given by the trend of the total number of suppliers.

Future works and planned follow-up will be devoted to a detailed experimental analysis allowing the validation of the *SIM/OPT* model architecture, for instance either through the introduction of other typology of actors and the consideration of real data. In particular, future works aim at reproducing the opportunities given by the boundary conditions which often well reflect the competitive/collaborative environment within bounded geographical areas.

References

[1] Gambarotto, F. and Maggioni M.A., 1998. "Regional Development Strategies in Changing Environments: an Ecological Approach". *Regional Studies*, 32, 49-61.

[2] Holland, J.H., 1995. *Hidden Order*. Addison-Wesley, Reading, MA.

[3] Kelly, K., 1994. *Out of Control*. Addison-Wesley, Reading, MA.

[4] Maggioni M.A., 2001. *Clustering Dynamics and the Location of High-Tech Firms*. Heidelberg, Springer Verlag.

[5] Maxfield R. and Lane D.A., 1997. *Foresight, Complexity and Strategy*, in *Economy as a Complex, Evolving System II*, Arthur et al. (eds.), Addison-Wesley, Redwood City (CA).

Topological key players in communities: the network perspective

F. Jordán
Collegium Budapest, Institute for Advanced Study, Budapest, Hungary

Abstract

For both a general understanding of ecosystem functioning and the setting of conservation priorities is very important to have quantitative methods for quantifying the relative importance of species. We present an approach from the network perspective on ecology. Topological keystone species are those in critically important positions within the interaction network of an ecological community. Graph theory makes the quantification of the positional importance of nodes within networks possible. There are many ways to measure this and, in particular, we use some network indices recently introduced in social network analysis. These are suitable for the characterisation of both direct and indirect interactions. The key players of a hypothetical ecological community will be identified and the results of different methods will be compared. We emphasise that the need to find a quantitative, comparative approach to species importance is urgent and very important when outlining effective conservation efforts.
Keywords: keystone species, network perspective, graph theory, trophic field, indirect effects.

1 Introduction

The two main traditional strategies of conservation practice are to protect habitats and to save endangered species. Both have theoretical and practical difficulties and a possible third way could be to protect ecosystem functioning. This is easy to say but more abstract to imagine in everyday practice, or harder even to define. The recent claim for more objective and more quantitative studies in identifying keystone species [1] is a perspective offering a more functional approach to conservation biology. The characterisation and understanding of keystone, flagship, umbrella and other kinds of "important" species may be a bridge between habitat- and species-centric conservation plans [2].

However, the relative importance of species is not easy to define or quantify. Many ecologists intuitively agree that the importance of a species probably reflects the secondary effects of its local extinction (or removal). Through direct effects and indirect pathways of interspecific interactions, local extinctions can trigger secondary extinctions or, at least, may seriously influence other coexisting populations. If we accept the view that importance is a measure of triggering cascades through interspecific interactions, we might quantify important species by their "centrality" or positional importance within a community interaction network.

We present conceptual and methodological developments in outlining this quantitative view on species importance. Graph theory, as the basis of ecological network analysis helps in mapping the topology of a hypothetical interaction network. Species in critically important positions will be called *topological keystone species* [3] and their suitably defined topological interaction strength will be called their *trophic field* [4]. We suggest that developing the field theory of biology [5] could be useful in this area since understanding the relationship between species and ecosystems is a very topological problem, where the strength and the effective range [6] of spreading interactions is a cornerstone. We illustrate the application of some old and some new network indices in the quest for keystones in ecological networks.

2 Methods

2.1 The problem to be solved

We are interested in quantifying topological keystone species in the interaction network of a hypothetical community. The graph is shown in Figures 1 and 2. There are 34 "species" in this community and our concern is to rank them according to the relative importance of their network position. A couple of indices will be presented, the ranks for seven indices will be shown (see Table 1) and it will be shortly discussed under what circumstances they can be used suitably.

2.2 Degree (D) – the number of neighbours

The index that is most local but least informative about the topology of a network is the *degree* of a node (D). This is the number of other nodes connected directly to it. In a food web, the degree of a node i (D_i) is the sum of its prey (in-degree, $D_{in,i}$) and predators (out-degree, $D_{out,i}$):

$$D_i = D_{in,i} + D_{out,i}\,. \tag{1}$$

We note that the degree of a node is called its *degree centrality* in the sociological literature [7]. In ecology, several analyses on topological key species have been focusing on the number of neighbours in food webs, i.e. the degree of nodes in trophic networks [8, 9, 10, 11]. Since there are indirect effects spreading beyond the neighbours, degree gives only local information about a graph node. Social and ecological interaction networks are similar in many aspects and there are common technical roots partly presented in the followings.

2.3 Keystone index (*K*) – vertical interaction structure

Degree considers only the links directly connected to a node. We also consider network indices reflecting also short indirect effects, i.e. the neighbours of neighbours. We call these indices *mesoscale indices,* in contrast to the *local* nature of degree, and to the *global* nature of some indices to be presented later (defined on and characterising the whole network). The *keystone index* (*K*, see [3]) is derived predominantly from the application and modification of the "*net status*" index introduced in sociometry [12] but used also in ecology [13]. The keystone index of species *i* (K_i) is defined as:

$$K_i = K_{bu,i} + K_{td,i} = \sum_{c=1}^{n} \frac{1}{d_c}(1+K_{bc}) + \sum_{e=1}^{m} \frac{1}{f_e}(1+K_{te}), \tag{2}$$

where n is the number of predators eating species i, d_c is the number of prey of its cth predator and K_{bc} is the bottom-up keystone index of the cth predator. And symmetrically, m is the number of prey eaten by species i, f_e is the number of predators of its eth prey and K_{te} is the top-down keystone index of the eth prey. For node i, the first sum in the equation (*i.e.* $\sum 1/d_c(1+K_{bc})$) quantifies the bottom-up effect ($K_{bu,i}$) while the second sum (*i.e.* $\sum 1/f_e(1+K_{te})$) quantifies the top-down effect ($K_{td,i}$). After rearranging the equation, terms including K_{bc} and K_{te} (*i.e.* $\sum K_{bc}/d_c + \sum K_{te}/f_e$) refer to indirect effects for node i ($K_{indir,i}$), while terms not containing K_{bc} and K_{te} (*i.e.* $\sum 1/d_c + \sum 1/f_e$) refer to direct ones ($K_{dir,i}$). Both $K_{bu,i}$ + $K_{td,i}$ and $K_{indir,i}$ + $K_{dir,i}$ equals K_i. The keystone index emphasises vertical over horizontal interactions (*e.g.* trophic cascades as opposed to apparent competition). This index "measures" the trophic field of a species [4] in vertical direction and has been applied several times in network analysis [6]. Its important feature is the sensitivity to both distance and degree: it quantifies position at an intermediate scale rather than giving very local or very global information [14]. We calculated the keystone indices of trophic groups by the FLKS 1.1 programme (available on request).

2.4 Topological importance index (*TI*) – long, undirected effects

An index not biased for vertical interactions, i.e. taking into account also exploitative and apparent competition, is called *topological importance* index (*TI*). We use it for characterising long indirect effects [cf. 15] and the index itself is the extension of an earlier one proposed for the analysis of two-steps long, horizontal, apparent competition interactions in weighted host-parasitoid networks [16]. This index does not consider directed and signed interactions. Various indirect effects do spread in both bottom-up and top-down directions through trophic links and, as a result, horizontally, too. If non-trophic interactions are also considered, the network typically has direct horizontal links, too. In this case, trophically mediated indirect chain effects [17] as well as chemically and behaviourally mediated indirect effects are considered [18, 19]. In an unweighted network, we define $a_{n,ij}$ as the effect of j on i when i can be reached from j in n steps. The simplest mode of calculating $a_{n,ij}$ is when n=1 (*i.e.* the effect of j on i in 1 step): $a_{1,ij} = 1/D_i$, where D_i is the degree of node i (*i.e.* the number of its direct neighbours including both prey or predatory species). We assume that indirect chain effects are multiplicative and additive. For instance, we wish to determine the effect of j on i in 2 steps, and there are two such 2-step pathways from j to i: one is through k and the other is through h. The effects of j on i through k is defined as the product of two direct effects (*i.e.* $a_{1,kj} \times a_{1,ik}$), therefore the term multiplicative. Similarly, the effect of j on i through h equals to $a_{1,hj,1} \times a_{1,ih}$. To determine the 2-step effect of j on i ($a_{2,ij}$), we simply sum up those two individual 2-step effects (*i.e.* $a_{2,ij} = a_{1,kj} \times a_{1,ik} + a_{1,hj} \times a_{1,ih}$) and therefore the term additive. When the effect of step n is considered, we define the effect received by species i from all species in the same network as:

$$\psi_{n,i} = \sum_{j=1}^{N} a_{n,ij} \tag{3}$$

which is equal to 1 (*i.e.* each species is affected by the same unit effect). Furthermore, we define the n-step effect originated from a species i as:

$$\sigma_{n,i} = \sum_{j=1}^{N} a_{n,ji} \tag{4}$$

what may vary among different species (*i.e.* effects originated from different species may be different). Here, we define the topological importance of species i when effects "up to" n steps are considered as:

$$TI_i^n = \frac{\sum_{m=1}^{n} \sigma_{m,i}}{n} = \frac{\sum_{m=1}^{n}\sum_{j=1}^{N} a_{m,ji}}{n} \tag{5}$$

which is simply the sum of effects originated from species i up to n steps (one plus two plus three…up to n) averaged over by the maximum number of steps considered (*i.e.,* n).

2.5 KeyPlayer indices – position of groups of nodes

Recently, new network indices, search algorithms and a software (KeyPlayer 1.44) were developed for solving the "key player" problem [20]. This problem is composed of two related but distinct questions [21, 22]. The first, known as KPP-1, is: which k nodes have to be deleted in order to maximally disconnect the network, *i.e.* either increases the number of components or the average distance between remaining nodes. The second question, KPP-2, is: if we spread out an effect from *k* nodes, which *k* nodes have to be chosen in order to reach the others in the fastest way in the intact network. An optimal choice of *k* nodes is a *KP-set*.

The first index for the KPP-1 problem quantifies network fragmentation after node deletion:

$$F = 1 - \frac{\sum_i s_i(s_i - 1)}{N(N - 1)} \tag{6}$$

ranges from zero to 1 (for detailed explanation, see [20]). In eqn (6), s_i is the number of nodes in the ith component (*i.e.* disconnected subgraph). This index characterises network fragmentation or the reduction in "communication" between nodes, therefore large *F* values indicate more fragmented networks. If node deletion does not increase the number of components (leads to no fragmentation), it is still of interest how the average distance between nodes *i* and *j* changes. This is expressed as

$$F^D = 1 - \frac{2\sum_{i>j} \frac{1}{d_{ij}}}{N(N-1)}, \tag{7}$$

where d_{ij} is the distance between nodes *i* and *j*. The **R** reciprocal distance matrix is used in order to escape the problem of infinity appearing in the distance matrix **D** should disconnection yield isolated nodes [23, 24].

There are two possible approaches to the KPP-2 problem. One is simply the number of nodes (R_n) reachable within a given *n*-step distance from a given set of *M* nodes. The other is a distance-weighted reachability approach, R^D, considering differences between individual paths (not dichotomising them as equal or shorter than *n* or longer). This measure is:

$$R^D = \frac{\sum_j \frac{1}{d_{Mj}}}{N} \tag{8}$$

where d_{Mj} is the distance of any node *j* from a set of *M* nodes. When this measure reaches its largest value, our algorithm has found the optimal set of *M* nodes from which effects can most easily reach the remaining nodes. Here we only calculated F^D by using the optimisation algorithms of the KeyPlayer 1.44 software [20]. We looked for *KP-sets* of key-player nodes in order to examine the concept of "keystone species complexes" [25]. It is quite possible that the identification of single nodes as "keystones" might not tell the whole story on community organisation. It might even be misleading and difficult to interpret. These three indices are unique in the sense that the positional importance of *groups of nodes* can be quantified. Considering the claims for multispecies conservation biology, and the need for putting species into a multispecies context in order to understand their ecology, the future application of the *KP* indices in ecology seems to be probably fruitful.

Table 1: Positional importance ranks based on seven different network indices.

rank	D		K_{dir}		K_{indir}		K_{td}		K_{bu}		K		TI^{10}
2	10	**8**	4.92	**1**	26.83	**1**	31.17	**33**	7.44	**1**	31.50	**8**	2.41
8	10	**3**	4.78	**2**	14.82	**2**	18.49	**19**	4.37	**2**	18.34	**2**	2.18
1	9	**1**	4.33	**3**	5.34	**3**	10	**7**	3.35	**3**	9.95	**1**	2.01
22	9	**2**	3.78	**33**	4.94	**8**	6	**30**	3	**7**	7.46	**22**	2.01
7	8	**7**	2.89	**7**	4.51	**7**	4.01	**10**	2.59	**33**	7.44	**7**	1.82
3	7	**19**	2.78	**34**	2.68	**34**	3.68	**32**	2.26	**8**	7.27	**3**	1.64
15	7	**22**	2.78	**6**	2.46	**5**	2.68	**6**	2.11	**19**	4.62	**15**	1.54
19	7	**33**	2.5	**8**	2.18	**22**	2.41	**26**	1.72	**5**	3.81	**19**	1.53
14	6	**5**	2	**19**	1.83	**15**	1.79	**9**	1.29	**6**	3.81	**14**	1.33
18	6	**15**	1.83	**5**	1.79	**6**	1.68	**27**	1.28	**34**	3.81	**18**	1.33
23	6	**32**	1.7	**30**	1.55	**14**	1.59	**17**	1.19	**22**	3.46	**23**	1.32
12	5	**14**	1.67	**10**	1.45	**18**	1.38	**5**	1.11	**30**	3.11	**27**	1.1
27	5	**18**	1.5	**9**	0.83	**23**	0.83	**8**	1.1	**10**	2.59	**12**	1.06
9	4	**30**	1.5	**11**	0.72	**16**	0.54	**11**	1.1	**32**	2.20	**9**	0.91
11	4	**27**	1.37	**12**	0.72	**4**	0.5	**12**	1.1	**15**	2.15	**32**	0.89
26	4	**6**	1.33	**13**	0.68	**9**	0.5	**13**	1.1	**9**	1.79	**33**	0.89
32	4	**23**	1.19	**26**	0.66	**12**	0.46	**28**	0.69	**26**	1.78	**26**	0.86
33	4	**17**	1.16	**32**	0.56	**27**	0.33	**25**	0.67	**27**	1.67	**11**	0.84
13	3	**10**	1.14	**27**	0.25	**19**	0.25	**29**	0.67	**18**	1.57	**16**	0.65
16	3	**34**	1.11	**22**	0.17	**21**	0.25	**22**	0.54	**12**	1.56	**17**	0.65
25	3	**26**	1.07	**23**	0.17	**31**	0.25	**23**	0.54	**14**	1.44	**25**	0.65
28	3	**9**	0.95	**20**	0.16	**11**	0.21	**20**	0.3	**23**	1.37	**29**	0.65
29	3	**12**	0.84	**21**	0.16	**10**	0	**21**	0.3	**11**	1.31	**28**	0.64
30	3	**11**	0.59	**24**	0.16	**13**	0	**24**	0.3	**17**	1.19	**30**	0.64
5	2	**16**	0.58	**28**	0.16	**17**	0	**31**	0.26	**13**	1.10	**13**	0.63
6	2	**25**	0.57	**15**	0.15	**20**	0	**14**	0.19	**16**	0.73	**5**	0.59
10	2	**29**	0.57	**16**	0.15	**24**	0	**15**	0.19	**25**	0.73	**6**	0.54
17	2	**28**	0.53	**14**	0.1	**25**	0	**16**	0.19	**29**	0.73	**34**	0.53
21	2	**4**	0.5	**25**	0.1	**26**	0	**18**	0.19	**21**	0.55	**10**	0.46
31	2	**13**	0.42	**29**	0.1	**28**	0	**3**	0.12	**4**	0.50	**21**	0.45
34	2	**31**	0.42	**31**	0.09	**29**	0	**2**	0.11	**28**	0.45	**31**	0.44
4	1	**21**	0.39	**18**	0.06	**30**	0	**34**	0.11	**31**	0.44	**4**	0.35
20	1	**20**	0.14	**17**	0.02	**32**	0	**1**	0	**20**	0.30	**20**	0.23
24	1	**24**	0.14	**4**	0	**33**	0	**4**	0	**24**	0.30	**24**	0.23

3 Results and conclusions

Different indices give different importance ranks for the species of our hypothetical network. Table 1 shows the degree (D), keystone index (K and its direct, K_{dir}, indirect, K_{indir}, top-down, K_{td}, and bottom-up, K_{bu}, components) as well as the topological importance index for n=10 (TI^{10}); bold numbers correspond to species codes, while normal numbers are network index values.

The top row presents the actual index for ranking. Considering only the number of neighbours of the nodes (degree), species #2 and #8 are in the most critical positions but more developed indices reflecting also indirect effects (i.e. less local information) refine this view: species #8 has a weak indirect interaction structure (its K_{indir} rank is 8). The differences between the ranks of D and TI^{10} are caused by only the local versus global nature of information considered. But, since directed, K_{td} and K_{bu} are not expected to give similar results; these network indices reflect different aspects of network structure. For example, if a poison is being accumulated in a food web, K_{bu} can be the relevant characterisation of graph nodes. Thinking on long-term processes, we may more emphasise long indirect pathways being otherwise probably weak: in this case, TI^{10} is the adequate measure of positional importance. If, for any reason, trophic cascades are of primarily interest, K or its components are informative.

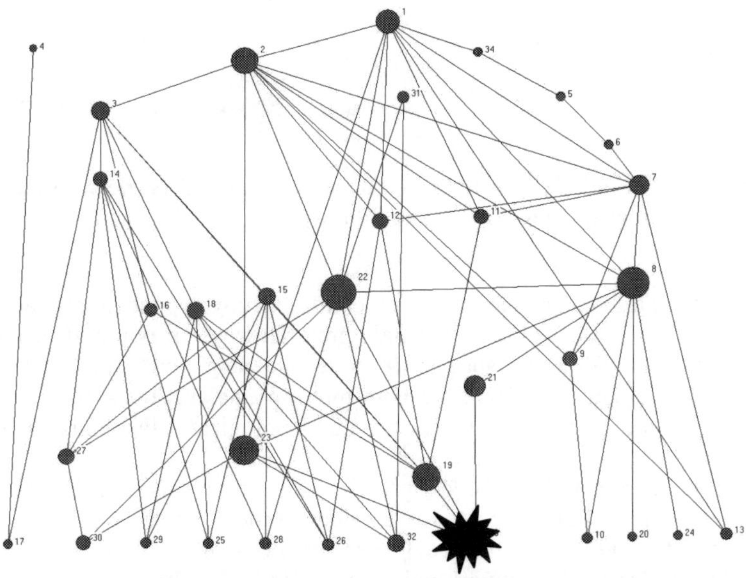

Figure 1: The relative strength of interactions different species have on species #33 marked by a dark star (drawn by the UCINET IV programme [26]). Radius of circles is proportional to topological interaction strength.

Apart of gaining importance ranks for species, it is also possible to map more deeply the interaction structure of the community. We present a more detailed study based on TI^{10} values. Figure 1 shows what is the relative strength of effects other species have on the arbitrarily chosen species #33 (a medium interactor based on its TI^{10} rank, Table 1). Figure 2 shows the relative strength of effects species #33 has on all other species.

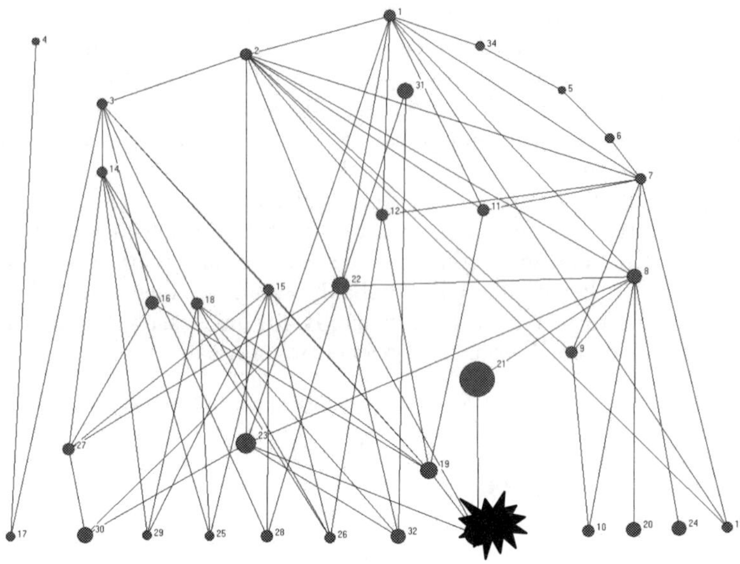

Figure 2: The relative strength of effects species #33 (dark star) has on all other species (drawn like Figure 1).

It can be noted that species #21 is evidently heavily dependent on our chosen species (Figure 2) since that is its single prey. However it is not affecting very strongly species #33, even species #8, a second neighbour can have a larger effect on #33 (Figure 1). Here we note that our analysis does not predict the dynamics of the system but calculates the topological constraints on system dynamics.

If our concern is to look for key groups of species, we use the KP indices not shown on Table 1. For example, if we calculate the F^D index for k=3, we have species #3, #8 and #33 in the KeyPlayer set. Looking at Table 1 we have to conclude that there is no network index suggesting a top three rank like this. We emphasise that thinking of group of species and developing techniques for quantifying and comparing their importance can be of high importance in future conservation biology, especially as the multispecies context is more an more actual and urgent to develop. The network perspective in ecology [27] and novel methodological developments [28, 29] are welcome, especially if bridging and cross-fertilising different scientific fields [3, 13, 30]. A lot of techniques developed in social network analysis seem to be useful and relevant in network ecology, and even some key questions are shared (e.g. how long indirect effects are still significant). The future task is to try to use these topological positional analyses in setting conservation priorities.

Acknowledgements

I thank S. Borgatti, W-C. Liu, I. Scheuring, A. J. Davis, T. Wyatt and V. Vasas for help and comments. K. Csankovszki and H. Erdős are kindly acknowledged for technical support. My research was funded by the Society in Science: The Branco Weiss Fellowship at ETH Zürich.

References

[1] Power, M.E., Tilman, D., Estes, J.A., Menge, B.A., Bond, W.J., Mills, L.S., Daily, G., Castilla, J.C., Lubchenco, J. & Paine, R.T., Challenges in the quest for keystones. *BioScience,* **46**, pp. 609-620, 1996.

[2] Simberloff, D., Flagships, umbrellas, and keystones: is single-species management passé in the landscape area? *Biological Conservation*, **83**, pp. 247-257, 1998.

[3] Jordán, F., Takács-Sánta, A. & Molnár, I., A reliability theoretical quest for keystones. *Oikos*, **86**, pp. 453-462, 1999.

[4] Jordán, F., Trophic fields. *Community Ecology*, **2**, pp. 181-185, 2001.

[5] Goodwin, B.C., A structuralist research programme in developmental biology. *Dynamic Structures in Biology*, ed. B.C. Goodwin, A. Sibatani & G. Webster, Edinburgh University Press, Edinburgh, pp. 49-61, 1989.

[6] Jordán, F., Liu, W.-C. & van Veen, F.J.F., Quantifying the importance of species and their interactions in a host-parasitoid community. *Community Ecology*, **4**, pp. 79-88, 2003.

[7] Wassermann, S. & Faust, K., *Social Network Analysis*, Cambridge University Press, Cambridge, 1994.

[8] Solé, R.V. & Montoya, J.M., Complexity and fragility in ecological networks. *Proceedings of the Royal Society of London, series B*, **268**, pp. 2039-2045, 2001.

[9] Dunne, J.A., Williams, R.J. & Martinez, N.D., Network structure and biodiversity loss in food webs: robustness increases with connectance. *Ecology Letters*, **5**, pp. 558-567, 2002.

[10] Montoya, J.M. & Solé, R.V., Small world patterns in food webs. *Journal of Theoretical Biology*, **214**, pp. 405-412, 2002.

[11] Williams, R.J., Berlow, E.L., Dunne, J.A., Barabási, A.-L. & Martinez, N.D., Two degrees of separation in complex food webs. *Proceedings of the National Academy of Sciences USA*, **99**, pp. 12913-12916, 2002.

[12] Harary, F., Status and contrastatus. *Sociometry*, **22**, pp. 23-43, 1959.

[13] Harary, F., Who eats whom? *General Systems*, **6**, pp. 41-44, 1961.

[14] Jordán, F. & Scheuring, I., Searching for keystones in ecological networks. *Oikos*, **99**, pp. 607-612, 2002.

[15] Yodzis, P., Must top predators be culled for the sake of fisheries? *Trends in Ecology and Evolution*, **16**, pp. 78-84, 2001.

[16] Müller, C.B., Adriaanse, I.C.T., Belshaw, R. & Godfray, H.C.J., The structure of an aphid-parasitoid community. *Journal of Animal Ecology*, **68**, pp. 346-370, 1999.

[17] Wootton, J.T., The nature and consequences of indirect effects in ecological communities. *Annual Reviews of Ecology and Systematics*, **25**, pp. 443-466, 1994.

[18] Menge, B.A., Indirect effects in marine rocky intertidal interaction webs: patterns and importance. *Ecological Monographs,* **65**, pp. 21-74, 1995.

[19] Abrams, P.A., Menge, B.A., Mittelbach, G.G., Spiller. D.A. & Yodzis, P., The role of indirect effects in food webs, *Food webs: integration of patterns and dynamics*, ed. G.A. Polis & K.O. Winemiller, Chapman and Hall, London, pp. 371-395, 1996.

[20] Borgatti, S.P., The Key Player Problem, *Dynamic Social Network Modeling and Analysis: Workshop Summary and Papers*, eds. R. Breiger, K. Carley & P. Pattison, Committee on Human Factors, National Research Council, pp. 241-252, 2003.

[21] Everett, M.G. & Borgatti, S.P., Analysing clique overlap. *Connections*, **21**, pp. 49-61, 1998.

[22] Everett, M.G. & Borgatti, S.P., The centrality of groups and classes. *Journal of Mathematical Sociology*, **23**, pp. 181-201, 1999.

[23] Ivanciuc, O., Balaban, T-S. & Balaban, A.T., Design of topological indices. Part 4. Reciprocal distance matrix, related local vertex invariants and topological indices. *Journal of Mathematical Chemistry*, **12**, pp. 309-318, 1993.

[24] Ricotta, C., Stanisci, A., Avena, G.C. & Blasi, C., Quantifying the network connectivity of landscape mosaics: a graph-theoretical approach. *Community Ecology*, **1**, pp. 89-94, 2000.

[25] Daily, G.C., Ehrlich, P.R. & Haddad, N.M., Double keystone bird in a keystone species complex. *Proceedings of the National Academy of Sciences USA*, **90**, pp. 592-594, 2003.

[26] Borgatti, S.P., Everett, M.G. & Freeman, L.C., UCINET IV Version 1.64. Natick, MA, Analytic Technologies, 1996.

[27] Margalef, R., Networks in ecology, *Theoretical Studies of Ecosystems - the Network Perspective*, eds. M. Higashi & T.P. Burns, Cambridge University Press, Cambridge, pp. 41-57, 1991.

[28] Jordán, F. & Scheuring, I., Network Ecology: topological constraints on ecosystems dynamics. *Physics of Life Reviews*, **1**, pp. 139-172, 2004.

[29] Allesina, S. & Bodini, A., Who dominates whom in the ecosystem? Energy flow bottlenecks and cascading extinctions. *Journal of Theoretical Biology* **230**, pp. 351-358, 2004.

[30] Luczkovich, J.J., Borgatti, S.P., Johnson, J.C. & Everett, M.G., Defining and measuring trophic role similarity in food webs using regular equivalence. *Journal of Theoretical Biology*, **220**, pp. 303-321, 2003.

An image of organization in a virtual environment

E. S. Tuzhikova
Department of Organizational Psychology, Herzen State Pedagogical University of Russia

Abstract

Scientific interest in various sorts of research opportunities using the Internet is very widespread and is an important and pressing question now as the concept of communication between Internet users receives wider investigation than everyday contact between people. The Internet creates a new space for information interchange and cooperation between all of its users. This space offers two basic features; firstly, the opportunity to find necessary information and the secondly, the opportunity to unite people in groups with shared interests. Likewise such features are available not only to each individual person, but also to whole companies that use the Internet in their daily operations.

Despite the small amount of scientific research about the Internet which has been carried out, attractive to psychological analysis is the connection between cyberspace problems and professional organizations and communities, representing themselves with the help of web-sites. One of the positive signs of the opportunity for social design in cyberspace is the active development of various network communities.

Any organization creates a corporate image and has a style that it purposefully forms and renders emotional - psychological influence, in both the external and the internal organizational environment. Web pages of the organizations contain not only reports of information about goods and services, where the basic purpose is advertising activity, but also create their own individual style in cyberspace. The above testifies to the necessity of psychological research into the image of organizations utilising cyberspace as a special form of corporate promotion, allowing them to attract a broader audience of consumers.

Keywords: web sites companies, image and style organizations in virtual environment.

1 Introduction

Scientific interest in various sorts of research opportunities using the Internet is very widespread and is an important and pressing question now as concepts of communication between Internet users receives wider investigation than everyday contact between people. The Internet creates a new space for information interchange and cooperation between people all over the users. This space offers two basic features; firstly, the opportunity to find necessary information and the secondly, the opportunity to unite people in groups with shared interests. Likewise such features are available not only to each individual person, but also to whole companies that use the Internet in their daily operations.

Despite the small amount of scientific research about the Internet which has been carried out, attractive to psychological analysis is the connection between cyberspace problems and professional organizations and communities, representing themselves with help of web-sites [8]. One of the positive sings of the opportunity for social design in cyberspace is the active development of various network communities.

It is necessary to mention that in psychology under the term "image" (from a Latin word "image" that meant figure, visual concept) one understands a purposefully formed fancied image, with which an image-bearer is endowed by means of associations, additional values that contributes to a more purposeful and emotional perception. Any company creates a corporate image of its own and has its own style that is being quite purposefully formed and has a certain emotionally psychological impact both on the outer and on the inner organization environment. Psychologists specializing on corporate studies underline that a favorable company image serves as an indicator of company's commercial success, stable financial position and active customer partners and community relations [4, 5].

Besides with the advent of the Internet a new kind of corporate image forming sprang up, it may be called a virtual image of the company that has its specific characteristics and offers new methods of company studies. Despite the fact that there are not many works devoted to the sphere of psychological corporate researches that can be found in the Internet these few works do not lose their topicality, they pose new problems that have to be investigated and given thought to [1, 6].

2 The main types of the virtual corporate sites

The existence of rather manifold sites that are presented in the Internet allows the singling out of the main types of the virtual corporate sites and giving them a certain description.

The most wildly applied type of corporate sites may be called "a company's visiting card". The basic aim of such sites is to promote the company's trademark on the Internet and image advertising. As a rule the most important information about the company is presented in such sites in quiet a laconic form.

"Visiting card" sites inform the potential clients and partners about the company's activity in the shortest terms.

The next site type may be called "electronic storefront". It is intended to promote the company's goods and services. The users are offered the chance of buying the goods or getting acquainted with the list of products that is presented in the form of a catalogue. Besides the site contains information about the company itself, about the products or services offered and provides possibilities of searching and sorting the information. The electronic catalogue may be provided with an order form that can be emailed to the manager. The peculiarity of this site lies in the necessity of keeping the information up to date and that means refreshing it regularly and on-the-fly.

Companies that specialize in selling their goods through the Internet offer the users the "electronic shop" type of site. The main function of such site type is, as you understand selling goods through the Internet. In this case the catalogue is more complicated, the navigation and ordering systems presuppose a further submission of the order form to the manager for the subsequent processing, after that the trading system is attached and a new trading cycle is carried out.

A number of corporate sites that may be called "promotion sites" are presented in virtual space. The function of such sites is advertising campaigns aimed at products, services or companies advancement and therefore the main task of any such promotion site is to activate a user to take the necessary decision while choosing a purchase or service. As a rule the contents, visualization, dynamics of the site are conditioned by the advertising campaign idea. Promotion site of the product advanced is oriented as a rule on ultimate consumers. The promotion sites are started simultaneously with the off-line advertising campaign, they are attached to it and are the source of advertising campaign information support. Advertisement in press, tele- and radio commercials awaken interest to the advertised good or service, "catch" the consumers' attention and the site offers a far more detailed information about the product/service.

There is another type of sites that is of interest. It offers the most detailed information concerning a certain topic and may be called "information site". In such sites some sort of topical information is presented in corpore in the form of numerous authors' articles, sometimes such sites offer a possibility to take part in a poll. The main task of information sites is to form the target audience of potential consumers. For this the users are offered the very information they need (news, newsreels, comparative analyses).

The next site type may be called "corporate site". The basic function of these sites is the automation of the company's activity in the Internet. They are characterized by a branchy structure, which is created in the aim of the image strengthening and company's multiple tasks realization. They embrace the company's subsidiaries in various cities and countries with developed dealer and partner networks. The sites of this type may besides the informative part include an electronic catalogue or shop.

It is necessary to mention the portal sites, which are created to provide the highest degree of company's information space attendance. The portal unites a great number of various Internet-resources in the company's information space, and interactive services as well.

Thus we may assume that virtual space combines various company site types that reflect the main targets and functions of the company. Besides, virtual companies' pages contain not only information about the offered goods and services thus serving as a means of carrying out the advertising campaign, but creates the individual style of the company in the virtual space. Each day the dynamics of the company's sites development keeps and broadens its image with the purpose of customer relations optimization, sale increase, the state of affairs improvement.

3 Psychological analyses of company's sites

In the virtual image of the company contents we may single out the two main component parts: the visual and the contansive sides of the site. To the visual side of the site image we may attribute the visual concept of the site created in the user's mind's eye after visiting the site. And to the contansive side we may refer the degree to which the site reflects the corporate style and image of the company by means of the information presented. We must nevertheless mention that this classification has rather a conventional character and the both parts are closely interrelated since the presented on the screen image of the company constitutes a single whole and appears to be a consequent stream of information to the user that programs and predetermines the figurative evaluative and emotional reaction. The estimation of the Internet site by the users is stimulated by information of various degree of intensity that bears a certain emotionally psychological reaction. The estimation is based on the previous experience, value orientations, generally accepted standards and principles. Thus the company image in the virtual space may by positive, negative or vague.

The main component part of the site's visual side is design. The new technologies of site creation give a possibility of using dynamic forms on Internet pages, creeping lines, applying multimedia for melodies or video tracks playing, which in its turn creates a positive image, while the congestion of the site with technical innovations may on the contrary lead to creating a negative impression. So organization psychologists state that certain functionality in the way of presenting the information and logical design connected with working out understandable for users models of information presenting turns out to be rather topical and important today [2, 7]. Besides we must pay attention to such psychological peculiarities of the users perception as the color spectrum of the site, the combination of the background color and the color of the print, the information presented, the comfort of the interface and the easiness of perception. For image creation and better memorization of facts in the stream of virtual pages the most successful for creating the positive corporate image seem to be the company's symbols and logotypes as well as easy to remember and print domain names and e-mail.

The contansive side of the site is analyzed through the information presented since in the virtual space the information is the main driving force. Therefore, presenting the information in time and in a comfortable and understandable form is the most important component of company's effectiveness and its successful development that in its turn creates a favorable impression. The stream of information presented in the company's sites as a rule depends on the politics, aims, and the current tasks of the company. These are mainly company's news, its products, services, and information about the stuff as well as various sorts of interrelations with the users that visit the site.

The interrelation of the company members with the clients may be defined as a separate component of the contansive side of the company site image that users pay attention to.

E-mail, forums, chats, and guest-books may be referred to the main types of interactive cooperation with the Internet users, besides we may specify another type of cooperation between company members - the Intranet. These types of communication have their peculiarities that are expressed in the mediated communication between people by means of written speech. It doesn't contain a number of non-verbal components that enrich the direct communication by means of gestures, mimicry, voice timbre and so on. It is necessary to mention that the interpersonal communication in the companies' sites has an official character. The inner network for communication between the company's employees reflex the corporate culture, psychological climate in the company, common aims, and socially psychological characteristics of interpersonal communications in the professional sphere. [3].

The most important component part of the contansive side of the company's site may be considered reliability and security. Companies that pay attention to them and foresee the possible variants of the hackers attacks try not to get into situations when image of the company may be injured, when the users can lose the information or money and also if there are difficulties with technical matters, that may hamper or simply stop the company's work.

Thus each side (visual and contansive) reflect the whole image of the company site presented in the Internet space and affect the effectiveness and success of the company's work in the today world. Any organization creates the corporate image of its own and has its own style, which is formed purposefully and renders emotionally psychological influence on the users. The theoretical analysis evidences the necessity of psychological studies of the companies' image presented in the virtual space as a special form of corporate image reflection that allows broadening the company's borders for a wider field of consumers.

References

[1] Bhatt G., Bringing virtual reality for commercial web sites. International Journal of Human – Computer Studies, 60 (2004), pp. 1-15.

[2] Chevalier A., Ivory M., Web sites designs: influences of designer's expertise and design constraints. International Journal of Human – Computer of Studies, 58(1), pp. 57-58.

[3] Igbaria M., Shayo C., Olfman L., Virtual Societies: their prospects and dilemmas (Chapter 10). Psychology and the Internet: intrapersonal, interpersonal, and transpersonal implications, ed. J. Gackenbach: Academic press: USA and UK, pp.239-247, 1998.
[4] Jewell L.N., Contemporary industrial/organizational psychology, Cole Publishing Company: USA, pp.145-168, 2000.
[5] Luthans F., Organizational behavior, McGraw-Hill: USA, pp. 185-196, 1998.
[6] Mahatanankoon P., Anandarajan M., Igbaria M., Development of a measure of personal web usage in the workplace, CyberPsychology&Behavior, 7(1), pp. 93-104, 2004.
[7] Palmer W., Griffith D., An emerging model of web site design for marketing, Communication of the ACM, 41(3), pp. 41-51, 1998.
[8] Rayport, J, Sviokla, J., Exploiting the virtual value chain, Harvard Business Review, 73 (6), pp. 75-85, 1995.

Section 4
Ecosystems modelling

Nonlinear time series analysis of ecological data collected in the Lagoon of Orbetello, Italy

A. Facchini[1], C. Mocenni[2], E. Tiezzi[1] & A. Vicino[2]
[1] *Department of Chemical and Biosystems Sciences, University of Siena, Italy*
[2] *Department Information Engineering, University of Siena, Italy*

Abstract

In this paper a nonlinear analysis of time series representing dissolved oxygen, temperature, pH and salinity data, collected in the Lagoon of Orbetello (Grosseto, Italy) is performed.

A first biological inspection of the data shows that the coastal area is highly eutrophic and subject to unexpected phenomena, like anoxic and distrofic crises. From a more theoretical point of view, the ecological complexity of this ecosystem suggests the need to consider nonlinear models for understanding the dynamics of the system.

The appearance of low dimensional deterministic chaos is demonstrated, using the nonlinear time series analysis approach by means of attractor reconstruction and the computation of the Maximum Lyapunov Exponent.

1 The Lagoon of Orbetello

The Orbetello lagoon is located in southern Tuscany, near Grosseto (Italian West Coast). This lagoon is an important ecosystem from environmental and economical point of view. In fact it is very rich in flora and fauna, as well as productive activities. The Orbetello lagoon is divided in two basins (Ponente and Levante) and covers a total area of about $27Km^2$. The meteorological and environmental situation is strongly influenced by the following data: the annual average temperature is $16°C$, the precipitation is scarce, the tides are limited ($10 \div 45\ cm$). Wind intensity is the unique important phenomenon that favors in summer the water movement. As a result of the above ecological status of the lagoon and the intensive agriculture, aquaculture and urban activities, a strong eutrophication affects

www.witpress.com, ISSN 1743-3541 (on-line)

the lagoon. The excessive concentration of nitrite, nitrate, ammonia, phosphorus and its compound produce an exaggerated growth of macroalgae and the decreasing of dissolved oxygen concentration in the water (about 7-8 ppm in average, 5-6 ppm in summer) [1]. In this situation a certain amount of hydrogen sulphide is produced by the anaerobic bacteria activity causing damage to the biological community, as for example the death of a lot of vegetables and animal organisms [2].

A continuous monitoring of oxygen, temperature, wind, nutrients and other indicators of the ecological status of the lagoon is fundamental for understanding and controlling these periodic phenomena [3].

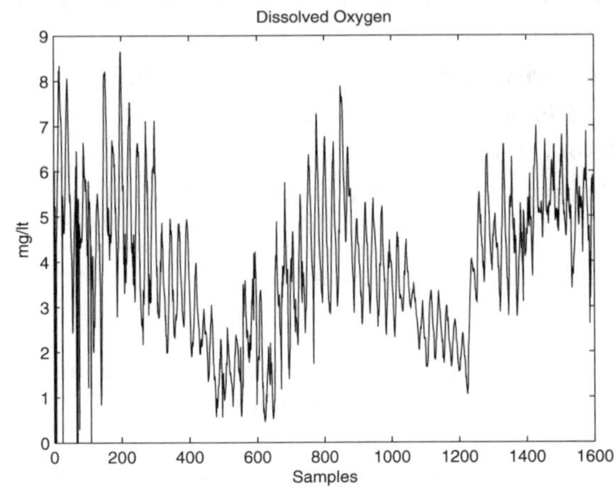

(a)

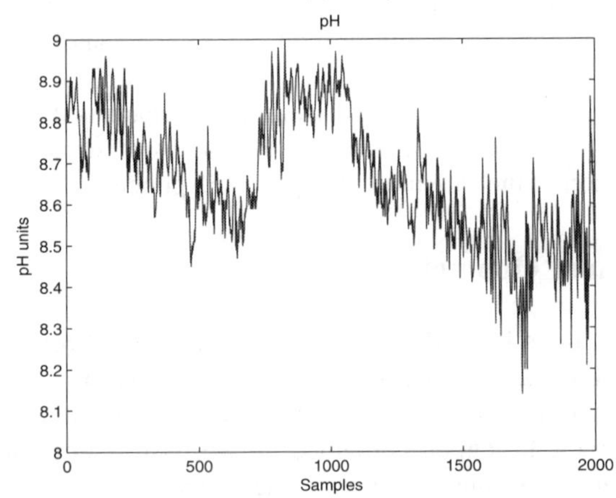

(b)

Figure 1: Time series analyzed: (a) Dissolved oxygen. (b) Water pH.

Table 1: Sensor characteristics of multiparametric devices.

Parameter	Interval of measurement	Sensitivity
Dissolved oxygen and saturation values	0-20 mg/lt.	0.2 mg/lt.
pH	0-14 pHU	0.2 pHU

2 Materials and methods

The time series were obtained with a network of 8 multiparametric devices located in 8 different survey stations. The following main parameters were measured:

- Dissolved oxygen.
- water pH.

Sensors were cleaned and calibrated 24 hours before the acquisition of the time series and, to avoid drift, just after acquisition. Several time series sampled at 60 seconds were collected and for the analysis we choose only the best avoiding noisy ones and those acquired in days with sensible weather variation.

3 Computational techniques

The analysis of the time series was performed using the software package TISEAN (TIme SEries ANalysis) [4], regarded as a robust algorithm set for nonlinear time series analysis. (The TISEAN software package is publicly available at http://www.mpipks-dresden.mpg.de/~tisean/TISEAN_2.1/index.html.) Typical steps are attractor reconstruction from time series and characterization of the chaotic dynamics by means of Lyapunov exponents and maximum Lyapunov exponent (MLE).

3.1 Attractor reconstruction

The attractor of the underlying dynamics was reconstructed in phase space by the time delay vector method [5, 6]. Starting from a time series $s(t) = [s_1, \ldots, s_N]$ the system dynamic can be reconstructed using the delay theorem of Takens and Mañe. The reconstructed trajectory $\mathbf{X}$ is expressed as a matrix in which each row is a phase space vector:

$$\mathbf{X} = [X_1, X_2, \ldots, X_M]^T \tag{1}$$

where $X_i = [s_i, s_{i+T}, \ldots, s_{i-(D_E-1)T}]$ and $M = N - (D_E - 1)T$. The matrix is characterized by two key parameters: the *Embedding Dimension* D_E and the *Delay Time* T. The embedding dimension is the minimum dimension at which the reconstructed attractor can be considered completely unfolded and there is no overlapping of the reconstructed trajectories. If the chosen dimension is lower than

www.witpress.com, ISSN 1743-3541 (on-line)

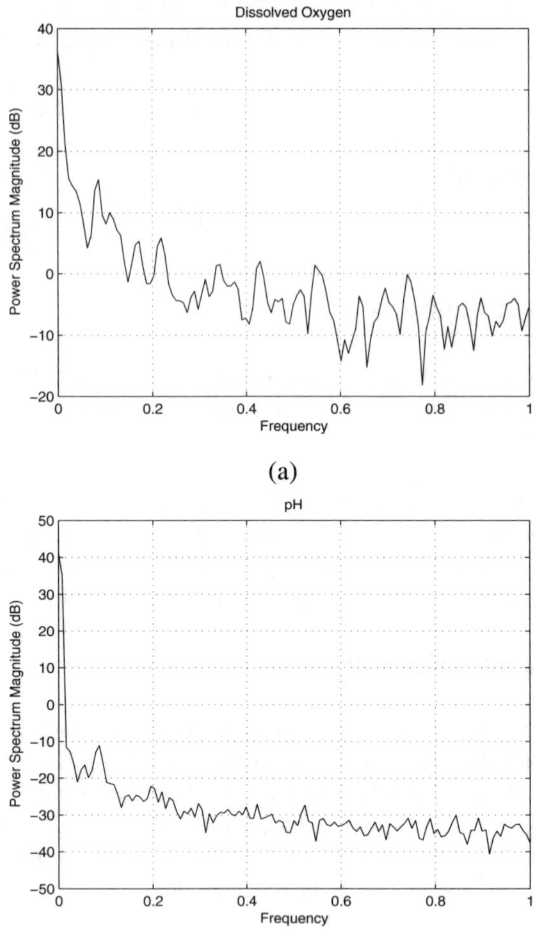

(a)

(b)

Figure 2: Power spectra of time series: (a) Dissolved oxygen. (b) Water pH. The broadband spectrum is a preliminary sign of nonlinear phenomena, but since these are natural phenomena, the contribution of noise must be taken in account.

D_E the attractor is not completely unfolded and the underlying dynamics cannot be investigated. Higher dimension was not used due to the increase in computational effort. D_E was computed by the method *False Nearest Neighbors* [6]. A false neighbor is a point of trajectory intersection in a poorly reconstructed attractor. As the dimension increases, the attractor unfolds with greater fidelity, and the number of false neighbors decreases to zero. The first dimension with no overlapping points is D_E. The delay time T represents a measure of correlation existing between two consecutive components of D_E-dimensional vectors used in the trajectory reconstruction. Following a commonly applied methodology, the time delay T is chosen in correspondence to the first minimum of the average mutual information function [7].

3.2 Lyapunov exponents

Chaotic systems display a sensitive dependence on initial conditions. Such a property deeply affects the time evolution of trajectories starting from infinitesimally close initial conditions, and Lyapunov exponents are a measure of this dependence. These characteristic exponents give a coordinate independent measure of the local stability properties of a trajectory. If the trajectory evolves in a N-dimensional state space there are N exponents arranged in decreasing order, referred to as the *Spectrum of Lyapunov Exponents (SLE)*:

$$\lambda_1 \geq \lambda_2 \geq \cdots \geq \lambda_n \tag{2}$$

Conceptually these exponents are a generalizations of eigenvalues used to characterize different types of equilibrium points.

A trajectory is chaotic if there is at least one positive exponent, the value of this exponent, known as *Maximum Lyapunov Exponent (MLE)* gives a measure of the divergence rate of infinitesimally close trajectories and of the unpredictability of the system and gives a good characterization of the underlying dynamics. Starting from the reconstructed attractor $\mathbf{X}$, it is possible to compute with the method of Sano and Sawada [8, 9] the SLE consisting of exactly $n = D_E$ exponents. This method is a qualitative one, and in presence of a positive exponents, λ_1, a more accurate method is necessary for the computation. The method of Rosenstein [10] is used to compute the MLE from the time series. This method measures in the reconstructed attractor the average divergence of two close trajectories in the time $d_j(i)$. The divergence can be expressed as:

$$d_j(i) = C_j e^{\lambda_1 (i\Delta t)} \tag{3}$$

where C_j is the initial separation. By taking the logarithm of both sides we obtain:

$$\ln d_j(i) = \ln C_j + \lambda_1 (i\Delta t) \tag{4}$$

This is a set of approximately parallel lines (for $j = 1, 2, \ldots, M$) each with a slope roughly proportional to λ_1. The MLE is easily calculated using a least-squares fit to the average line defined by

$$y(i) = \frac{1}{\Delta t} \langle \ln d_j(i) \rangle \tag{5}$$

where $\langle \cdot \rangle$ denotes the average over all values of j. Figure 4 shows some typical plot of $\langle \ln d_j(i) \rangle$: after a short transition there is a linear region that is used to extract MLE.

Table 2: Results.

	D_E	T_d	MLE
Dissolved oxygen	8	8	$\lambda_{DO} = 0.0892$
pH	8	6	$\lambda_{pH} = 0.0934$

4 Experimental results

The time series used in this analysis are shown in Figure 1, correlation was found between dissolved oxygen and pH. The spectra of these series are shown in Figure 2. The high density of the frequencies is a symptom of chaos, but is only a sufficient condition.

The parameters computed for attractor reconstruction are reported in Table 2. The reconstruction dimension D_E computed by the false nearest neighbors method was the same for each of the measured quantities, which is a sign of common underlying dynamic. This was confirmed by a visual inspection of the attractors showed in Figure 3. The shape of the two attractors was quite similar and was also similar to that reported in the book [6] (page 206) on the Great Salt Lake.

The structure of the attractor is a clear symptom of chaos, and the results of the computation of the Maximum Lyapunov Exponent are shown in Table 2. Since the exponents were positive we can say that chaotic dynamics exists and regulates the values of the major parameters. We must remark that the time series have a length of about 2000 samples and are characterized by a lightly colored noise. This aspect may influence the analysis, but from the point of view of qualitative results the method is not affected. More accurate analysis can be performed on longer time series, but due to the high non-stationary nature of the processes, the usual analysis techniques cannot be applied.

5 Conclusion

Natural systems are known to be self organized critical systems, and combine the equilibrium concept of criticality with non-equilibrium concept of self-organization, Kauffman would say at the *Edge of Chaos* [12]. With theoretical models, Jørgensen [13] shows that a lake ecosystem lays in this zone, and establishes a relationship between the level of information stored in the system and its evolution toward the edge of chaos.

Here we proposed a method based on nonlinear time series analysis to identify and describe evidence of chaotic dynamics regulating the ecological parameters of the Lagoon of Orbetello. Our analysis showed general chaotic dynamics clearly reflected by the parameters reported in Table 2. Since there is a direct link between the dynamics of an ecosystem and the quantity of information contained in it and since chaotic systems are known to produce information [14], we may think that

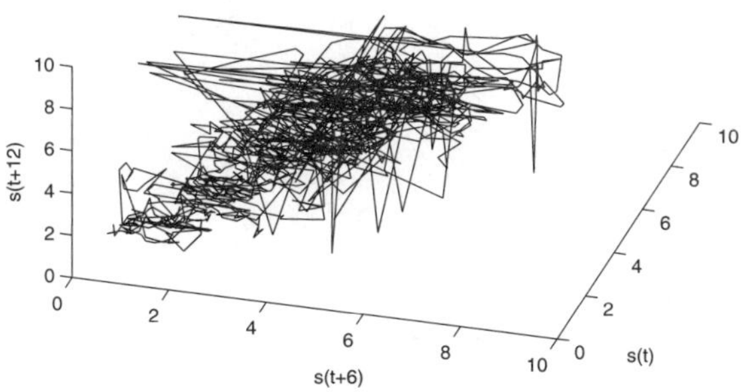

(a)

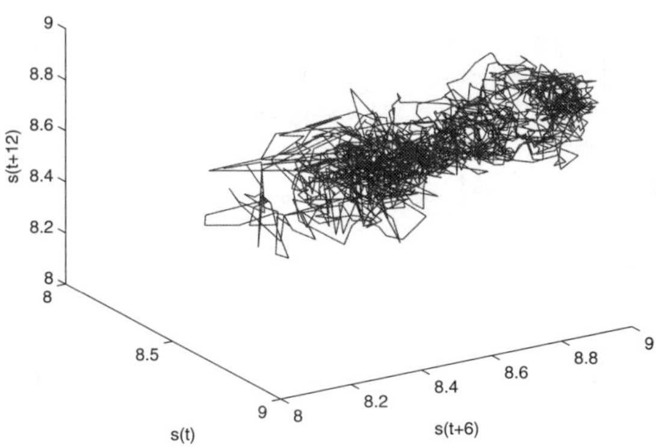

(b)

Figure 3: The reconstructed attractors of the four time series: (a) Dissolved oxygen. (b) Water pH. Visual inspection of the attractors we can show a common shape, very similar to that observed in [6].

the computed Lyapunov exponent represents a measure of the "chaoticity" of the lake, and in the meantime a measure of its quantity of information.

Future work will consist in the application of this investigation methodology to other different aquatic ecosystems, in order to establish a health scale based on the discussed indexes.

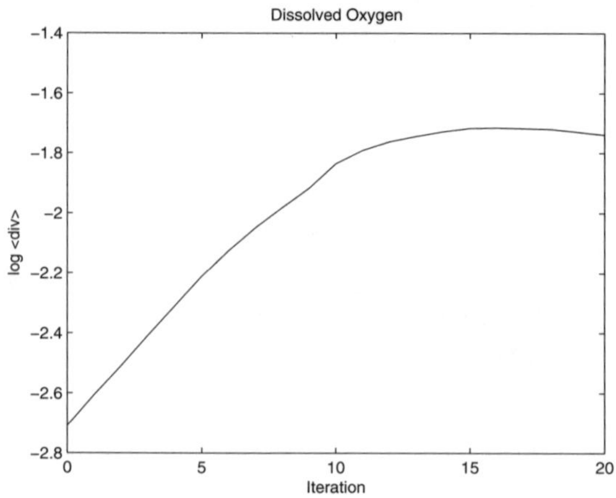

(a)

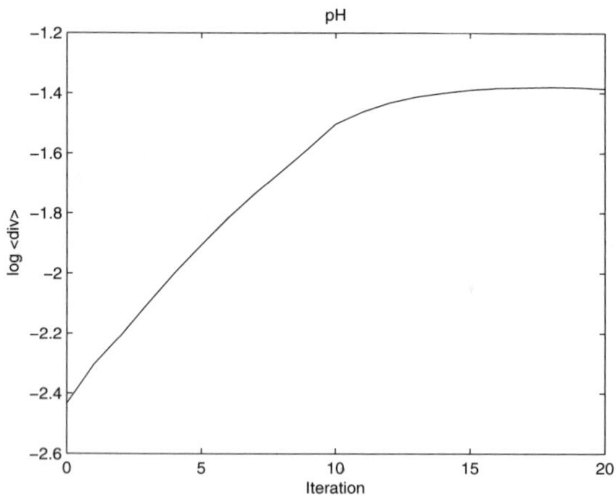

(b)

Figure 4: MLE calculated by Rosenstein algorithm: (a) Dissolved oxygen. (b) Water pH. The value of λ_1 for each exponent was obtained by linear regression of the curves in the area of the first 10 steps: $\lambda_{DO} = 0.0892$, $\lambda_{pH} = 0.0934$.

Acknowledgment

The data were provided by the Orbetello lagoon Authority. The data collection is performed in 2001-2003 for the lagoon Authority by ARPAT, (Regional Agency for the Environmental Protection of Tuscany).

References

[1] Lunardini, F. & DiCola, G., Oxygen dynamics in coastal and lagoon ecosystems. *Math and Computer Modelling*, **31**, pp. 135–141, 2000.

[2] Buffoni, G. & Cappelletti, A., Oxygen dynamics in a highly trophic aquatic environment. the case of orbetello coastal lagoon. *Estuarine, Coastal and Shelf Science*, **49**, pp. 763–774, 1999.

[3] Viaroli, P. & Christian, R., Description of trophic status, hyperautotrophy and distrophy of a coastal lagoon through a potential oxygen production and consumption index tosi: Trophic oxygen status index., 2004. Ecological Indicators, In press. Corrected proof available online.

[4] H.Kantz & T.Schreiber, *Nonlinear Time Series Analysis*. Cambridge University Press: UK, 1997.

[5] E.Ott, *Chaos in dynamical systems*. Cambridge University Press: UK, 1993.

[6] H.D.I.Abarbanel, *Analysis of observed chaotic data*. Springer-Verlag, 1996.

[7] A.M.Fraser & H.L.Swinney, Independent coordinates for strange attractors from mutual information. *Phys Rev A*, **33**, p. 1134, 1986.

[8] J.M.Greene & J.S.Kim, The calculation of lyapunov spectra. *Physica D*, **24**, pp. 213–225, 1987.

[9] M.Sano & Y.Sawada, Measurement of the lyapunov spectrum from a chaotic time series. *Phys Rev Lett*, **55**, p. 1082, 1985.

[10] M.T.Rosenstein, J.J.Collins & Luca, C., A practical method for calculating largest lyapunov exponent from small data set. *Physica D*, **65**, p. 117, 1993.

[11] Kantz, H., A robust method to estimate the maximal lyapunov exponent of a time series. *Phys Lett A*, **185**, p. 77, 1994.

[12] Kauffman, S., *The Origins of Order: Self-Organization and Selection in Evolution*. Oxford University Press, 1993.

[13] S.E., Jørgensen. *J theor Biol*, **175**, pp. 13–21, 1995.

[14] Sinai, Y., On the concept of entropy for dynamical systems. *Dokl Akad Nauk USSR*, **121**, pp. 768–, 1959. English Summary in Mathematical Reviews, Volume 21, p.286 (1960).

A model based estimation of the effect of population concentration in the urban areas in Eastern Asia in terms of nitrogen pollution

J. Shindo[1], K. Okamoto[1] & H. Kawashima[2]
[1]*National Institute for Agro-Environmental Sciences, Japan*
[2]*Graduate School of Agricultural and Life Sciences, University of Tokyo, Japan*

Abstract

We analyzed the current nitrogen cycle and compared it with previous data (from 1961 and 1980), in Eastern Asia including 10 countries in Southeast Asia, and three countries in East Asia, to clarify the environmental effect of the population concentration. Nitrogen loads from agricultural fields, livestock wastes, human wastes and NOx deposition of each country were estimated with a nitrogen cycle model based on the statistics on food production and consumption, NOx emission etc. They were assigned to 1km by 1km grid cells according to the landuse distribution and population distribution. Total nitrogen load was 56 x 10^6 t (3.8 t N/km^2) in 2000; 64% is from the agricultural sector including crop production, livestock waste and volatilized ammonium, and 13% is from human wastes. The extremely high nitrogen loads were localized to the restricted grid cells corresponding to large cities. We regarded the grid cells whose population was larger than 1000 as highly populated grids. We called them 'HPGs'. HPGs occupied only 1.31% of the whole study area, where 25% of people were living, and currently received 7.8% of the nitrogen loads (44% of which were from human wastes). The average nitrogen load in HPGs was 22 t N/km^2 and the maximum value was 230 t N/km^2. Compared with the results for 1961, total nitrogen load increased 3.8 times in the whole area and 6.2 times in HPGs. The highest nitrogen load and induced nitrogen pollution arose from urbanization. Further migration of people to urban areas is expected in Eastern Asia where 60% of people are still engaged in agriculture.
Keywords: nitrogen cycle, Eastern Asia, food production, population increase, urbanization.

1 Introduction

About two billion people, that are 30 % of the world population, are currently living in the Eastern Asia including 10 countries affiliated with Association of Southeast Asian Nations (ASEAN), China, Republic of Korea and Japan. Number of people in this area has been increasing rapidly during the latest several decades. In these countries, they are intensively growing rice that is a staple food for the people. As the land area and the farmland area are only 11 % and 17 % of the world, respectively (FAO [1]), much nitrogen fertilizer has to be used for producing sufficient food for the growing population in the relatively narrow farmland. Nitrogen fertilizer used in this area was 1.6 million t N in 1961 and it rapidly increased to 14.7 million t N in 1980 and 28.3 million t N in 2000. Amount of nitrogen fertilizer used in the area currently is about 37 % of the world consumption (FAO [1]).

Economic growth is also rapid in the Eastern Asia. The total GDP (at constant 1990 prices) has increased 3.5 times from 1.6 x 10^{12} US$ (1,275 $ per capita) in 1970 to 5.6 x 10^{12} US$ (2,869 $ per capita) in 2000 (Statistical Division, United Nation [2]) and energy consumption rate has accompanied with GDP growth (Energy Information Administration [3]). These rapid changes in artificial fertilizer use and in energy consumption affect the environment. Some researches have been conducted in respect with the effect of excess nitrogen on nitrogen riverine export and pollution in surface and ground water (Seitzinger and Kroeze [4], Van Drecht et al. [5]) in global scale. Shindo et al. [6, 7] evaluated the nitrogen load in Eastern Asian countries and showed that severe water pollution has possibly occurred in the upland areas with intensive agriculture in East China.

Economic growth generally brings about the population migration from agricultural sector to industrial sector, which promotes population concentration in urban areas. And it is disputed that rapid concentration of population into urban area without suitable construction of infrastructure (sanitary etc.) will cause severe environmental problems. Urban population has increased more rapidly than rural population also in our study area. In this study we evaluate nitrogen cycle from 1961 to 2000 and investigate the effect of population concentration by comparing the nitrogen load in urban areas with rural areas.

2 Method

The objective area of our study were the 13 countries mentioned in the previous section. For each country, we extract the "highly populated grid cells (HPGs)" that had population density larger than 1000 km^{-2} in 1995 according to the grid data of population at 1 km by 1 km scale derived from Deichmann [8] in order to evaluate the effect of population concentration in urban areas. Population at each HPG and at grid cell other than HPG in the arbitrary year was calculated by the following equations;

(For HPGs)

$$popG(y) = popG(1995) \times \frac{popU(y)}{popU(1995)}$$

(For other grid cells)

$$popG(y) = popG(1995) \times \frac{popT(y) - \sum_{HPGs} popG(y)}{popT(1995) - \sum_{HPGs} popG(1995)}$$

where *pop*G(*y*) indicates the population at a grid in the year *y*, and *pop*T(*y*) and *pop*U(*y*) are total and urban population , respectively, of each country in the year *y* derived from the FAO database (FAO [1]).

We evaluated the nitrogen load due to crop production (*NL*c), livestock waste (*NL*lv), human waste (*NL*w), energy production (*NL*e) and natural biological fixation (*NL*n) for each country based mainly on the "Food Balance Sheet" data (FAO [1]) according to the nitrogen cycle model shown in Figure 1. We also estimated spatial distributions of *NL*c, *NL*lv and *NL*n based on the landuse distribution and spatial distribution of *NL*w based on the population distributions. The concept of the model was similar with the model described in our previous papers (Shindo et al. [6, 7]) with the following revisions.

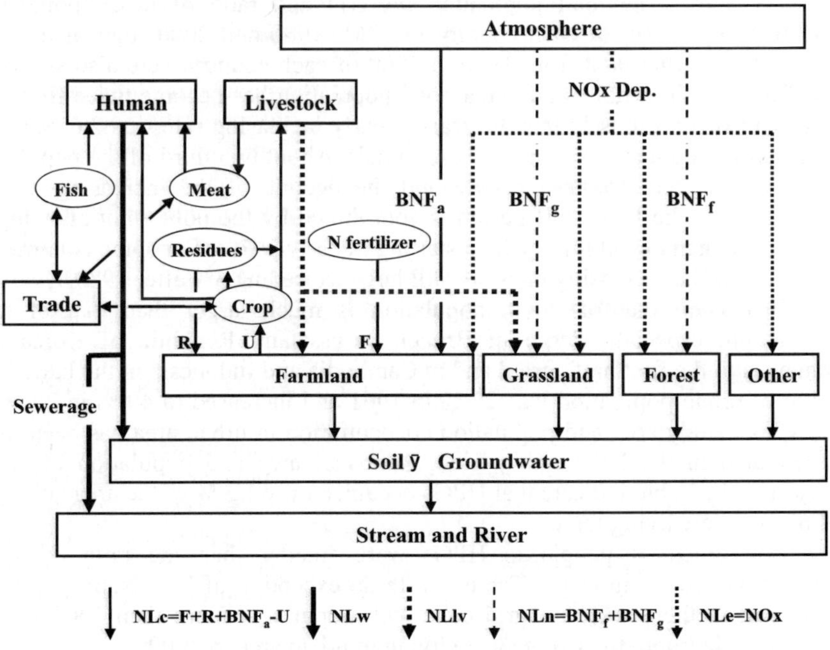

Figure 1: Nitrogen balance model to estimate environmental nitrogen model.

(1) Nitrogen from livestock wastes were evaluated separately based on the nitrogen balance between feed taken in by animals and meat (including eggs and milk) production.
(2) Province's data in China and Prefecture's data in Japan were used for nitrogen fertilizer consumption, rice and pulses production, heads of animals etc.
(3) Ammonium emissions from fertilizer and livestock waste were calculated assuming a constant emission rate for each type of fertilizer and animals proposed by Bounman et al. [9].
(4) Spatial resolution was changed from 0.5° by 0.5° to 1 km by 1 km grids in order to identify the urban area with dense population.
(5) Ammonium and nitrogen oxide emitted from grid cells were assumed to diffuse and deposit in a circle with 50 km diameter around the grid declining exponentially with distance.

Nitrogen loads in each HPG and also in regions made by HPGs adjoining each other that corresponded to the existing cities were compared with the other areas of the country.

3 Results and discussion

3.1 Population changes form 1961 to 2000

Table 1 shows the total population $pop\mathrm{T}(y)$ and ratio of urban population $pop\mathrm{U}(y)$ to $pop\mathrm{T}(y)$ of each country in 1961, 1980 and 2000. Increasing rates from 1961 to 1980 and from 1980 to 2000 of each country were also shown in the Table. In the whole study area, total population has become twice from one billion to two billions in this 40 years. Yearly increasing rate was 2.6 % in the first half period and 1.5 % in the second half. About two third of the population in this area were Chinese people and the decline of the increasing rate of population in the latter half period is contributed by the policy not allowing to have more than one child in China starting in early 1970s. For some countries in Southeast Asia, increasing rates are still large exceeding 3% after 1980.

Increasing rate of urban population is much larger than that of total population, especially large in Brunei Darussalam, Republic of Korea and Malaysia in the first half period and in Cambodia and Indonesia in the latter half. Ratio of urban population was 22 % in 1961 and increased to 40 % in 2000 for the whole study area and population concentration in urban area has been more accelerated in the latter half period. Ratios of area and population of HPGs shown in the Table indicate that HPGs occupied only 1.3 % of the area and 25 % of people were living there.

The ratios of people in HPGs were smaller than the ratio of urban population according to the Table 1 with an exception of Viet Nam. In Brunei Darussalam, there were no grid cells with population more than 1000 though many people (more than 70%) were living in urban area in 2000.

Table 1: Total and urban population, increasing rate, ratio of HPGS and per capital nitrogen load from human waste.

	Population (10^6) *pop* T(*y*)			Ratio of urban population (%)			Pop. increasing rate (%/y) Total		Urban		Ratio of HPGs (%)		NLw (kg/capita)		
Country/Year	1961	1980	2000	1961	1980	2000	1961-1980	1980-2000	1961-1980	1980-2000	area	pop. (2000)	1961	1980	2000
Brunei Darussalam	0.09	0.19	0.33	44.2	60.1	72.2	6.55	3.65	10.80	5.39	0.00	0.00	2.3	3.3	1.9
Cambodia	5.56	6.61	13.15	10.5	12.4	16.9	0.99	4.94	2.10	8.59	0.08	5.55	2.4	1.9	2.7
China	672.78	1004.17	1282.47	17.0	20.0	36.2	2.59	1.39	4.00	6.53	1.20	20.97	2.0	2.9	3.7
Indonesia	97.95	150.13	211.56	14.8	22.2	41.0	2.80	2.05	6.80	8.01	1.62	40.83	1.5	2.3	3.3
Japan	94.98	116.81	127.03	63.2	76.2	78.8	1.21	0.44	2.53	0.62	5.83	40.42	4.5	6.3	6.3
Republic of Korea	25.73	38.12	46.84	28.2	56.9	81.9	2.54	1.14	10.46	3.84	5.11	54.47	2.1	4.5	5.7
Laos	2.23	3.21	5.28	7.9	12.4	19.3	2.31	3.24	6.61	7.82	0.01	1.17	2.8	2.9	3.1
Malaysia	8.40	13.76	23.00	27.3	42.0	57.4	3.36	3.36	8.03	6.41	0.26	11.55	2.9	4.3	5.2
Myanmar	22.05	33.71	47.54	19.5	24.0	27.7	2.78	2.05	4.63	3.15	0.12	10.03	2.3	3.1	3.8
Philippines	27.91	48.09	75.71	30.4	37.5	58.6	3.81	2.87	5.90	7.30	1.17	20.77	2.2	2.7	3.2
Singapore	1.69	2.41	4.02	100.0	100.0	100.0	2.25	3.32	2.25	3.32	85.51	89.76	3.6	3.6	4.6
Thailand	27.47	46.34	60.93	12.7	17.0	19.8	3.62	1.57	6.69	2.65	0.48	13.70	2.3	3.0	4.0
Viet Nam	34.48	53.01	78.14	15.0	19.2	24.1	2.83	2.37	5.13	4.22	3.52	32.03	2.3	2.3	3.0
13 countries	1021.31	1516.56	1976.00	21.8	26.3	40.4	2.55	1.51	4.18	5.00	1.31	24.96	2.2	3.2	3.8

For other countries, HPGs contained 20% to 99% of urban population depending on countries, and therefore HPGs were considered to be the most populous urban area in each country. There were 381 regions made by adjoining HPGs in our study area and 61 regions among them had population exceeding one million. Many of these regions were identified as the existing large cities or a part of the city based on the location (longitude and latitude of the center of a region) and population in each region. As all the people in Singapore are citizens of Singapore city, we used the national data, not the data of HPGs, in evaluation of nitrogen load for cities in the following section.

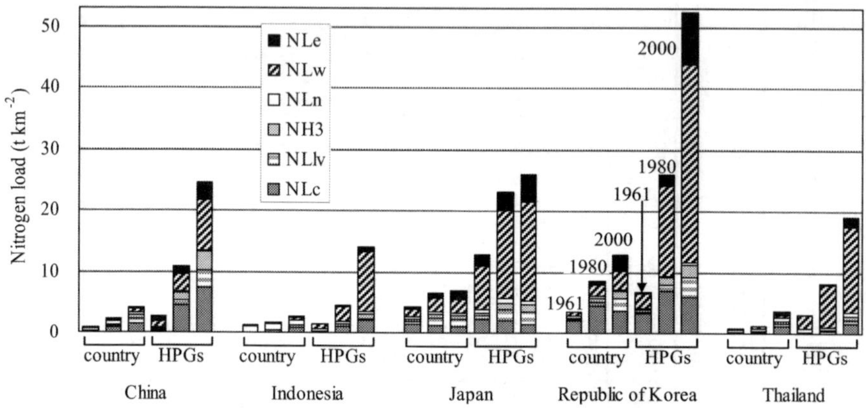

Figure 2: Yearly change of nitrogen load in several countries and in their HPGs in Eastern Asia.

3.2 Estimation of changes of nitrogen load

Figure 2 shows the Specific nitrogen load, which means nitrogen load per unit land area (t N km^{-2}), in 1961, 1980 and 2000 and contribution of each source for several countries estimated with the nitrogen balance model. Average nitrogen loads were calculated for whole country and for HPGs. Magnitude of nitrogen load and changing pattern in our whole study area was similar with those in China. Specific nitrogen load increased in every country in our study area from 1961 to 2000, though there is a large variation in nitrogen status from country to country (Shindo et al. [7]). In respect with the whole study area, specific nitrogen load increased 3.8 times from 1.0 t N km^{-2} in 1960 to 3.8 t N km^{-2} in 2000 and contributions of the various sources also changed. The contribution of natural fixation was maximum (56 %) and that of agricultural sector (*NL*c + *NL*lv + *NH3*) was only 20 % in 1961, while agricultural nitrogen load increased to 63 % in 2000. For HPGs, specific nitrogen loads and their increasing rates were much larger than the country averages as shown in Figure 2. Specific nitrogen load of the whole study area increased 6.2 times from 3.6 t N km^{-2} in 1960 to 22.6 t N km^{-2} in 2000. Nitrogen load due to human waste (*NL*w) were the maximum contributor in HPGs in many countries. The ratios of *NL*w in HPGs were 33 % and 39 % for China and for Viet Nam, respectively, while it ranged from 62 % to

www.witpress.com, ISSN 1743-3541 (on-line)

96 % in other countries. In case of Republic of Korea, for example, *NL*w in HPGs increased 13.6 times from 1960 to 2000 and it's share in total nitrogen load changed from 36 % to 62% during the same period. Increase of nitrogen load due to energy production was also marked in HPGs of Republic of Korea. In China and Viet Nam, agricultural contribution to the nitrogen load was large even in HPGs showing that agriculture was carried out still in the densely populated areas. It might be partly caused by the policy of Chinese government to control the migration of people to urban areas.

Figure 3 shows the specific nitrogen load in 1961, 1980 and 2000 of the 15 regions with HPGs corresponding to the existing cities, which had the largest specific nitrogen load among the identified regions in 2000. Cities with the largest specific nitrogen load were mainly detected in Indonesia, Singapore, Republic of Korea and China including Taiwan. In spite that country average of specific nitrogen load was very low in Indonesia (Figure 2), some cities like Medan, Makasar etc. had extremely high nitrogen load especially in 2000. These regions are particularly densely populated.

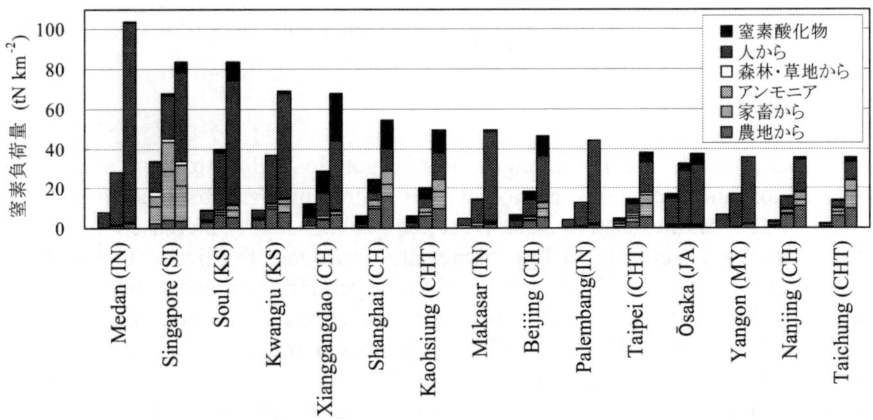

Figure 3: Yearly change of average nitrogen load in the region of HPGs corresponding to the large cities. SI: Singapore, IN: Indonesia, KS: Republic of Korea, CH: China, CHT: Taiwan China, JA: Japan, MY: Myanmar.

The estimation of increasing nitrogen load in HPGs and large cities might be still underestimates because of the following reasons. Although we assumed that *NL*w per capita was the same in urban and rural areas in the current estimation, urban people were considered to consume more food per capita than rural people. Table 2 shows the per capita consumption of major food in rural and urban households in China derived from Chinese statistics (National Bureau of Statistics [10]). According to this table, people in urban households are taking 1.5 – 2 times more animal proteins compared to the rural households in average. Total amount of meat consumption in Chinese households calculated from the values in Table 2 were 25 x 10^6 t, which was less than half of the country statistics of meat consumption appeared in FAO statistics and Chinese statistics.

Situations were same for the consumption of eggs and aquatic products. The balances between these amounts of consumption are considered to be used for food manufacturing and the food service industry etc. and are possibly consumed more in urban areas than in rural areas.

Table 2: Per capita consumption of major food in rural and urban Households in China in 1999 (kg $capita^{-1}$ y^{-1}) derived from [10].

Region	Grain	Vege-tables	Edible Oil	Pork, Beef and Mutton	Poultry	Eggs and Related Products	Aquatic Products
Rural	247.5	108.9	6.2	13.9	2.5	4.3	3.8
Urban*	—	114.9	8.2	20.0	4.9	10.9	5.5
Urban/ rural		1.06	1.34	1.44	1.98	2.55	1.43

* For the urban households, values are per capita purchases of major food.

4 Conclusion

We evaluated the yearly changes of nitrogen load due to food and energy production and their consumption with a simple nitrogen balance model from 1961 to 2000 in the Eastern Asia. Nitrogen load constantly increased mainly due to agricultural activities using increasing nitrogen fertilizer. There was a remarkable spatial variability in specific nitrogen load. By using the model of 1 km by 1 km grid scale and by extracting the HPGs as the populous grid cells (population density > 1000 km^{-2}), we estimated the environmental effect by urbanization in terms of nitrogen load. Increase of nitrogen load was more rapid in HPGs than in the other grid cells and HPGs are receiving much more nitrogen load. Singapore and some cities in Indonesia, Republic of Korea and China had the maximum nitrogen load exceeding 50 t N km^{-2}.

Agricultural population is still high (60 %) in the study area and growing number of people are expected to migrate from rural area to urban area along with the changes in industrial structure raised by the economic growth. High nitrogen load is and will be causing the serious effects on water environment such as nitrate pollution in groundwater, eutrophication in lakes and rivers, a red tide in coastal areas etc., unless suitable countermeasures such as sewage treatment are taken. Sanitation condition in the Eastern Asia is insufficient at present (WHO [11]) and the urbanizing areas with rapidly increasing population are considered to be the place that is facing the most serious environmental effect by nitrogen load.

Acknowledgments

This research was supported by the Global Environmental Research Fund of the Environment Agency of Japan for an "Assessment method for ecosystem acidification and eutrophication caused by acidic deposition on the basis of material cycles in catchments" and by the research fund from the Core Research for Evolution Science and Technology for "Modeling global hydrological cycles and world resources coupled with human activities". We thank Dr. S. Mishima who provided the Japanese statistical data on agriculture compiled for each city territory.

References

[1] FAO, Statistical Databases, http://apps.fao.org/page/collections, 2004.

[2] Statistical Division, United Nation, National Accounts Main Aggregates Database, http://unstats.un.org/unsd/snaama/Introduction.asp, 2004.

[3] Energy Information Administration, E.1c World Per Capita Total Primary Energy Consumption, 1980-2002, http://www.eia.doe.gov/pub/international/iealf/tablee1c.xls, 2004.

[4] Seitzinger, S.P. & Kroeze, C., Global distribution of nitrous oxide production and N inputs in freshwater and coastal marine ecosystems. Global Biogeochemical Cycles, 12, pp. 93–113, 1998.

[5] Van Drecht, G., Bouwman, A.F. Knoop, J.M., Meinardi, C. & Beusen, A., Global pollution of surface waters from point and nonpoint sources of nitrogen. The Scientific World, 1(S2): 632–641, 2001.

[6] Shindo, J., Okamoto, K., Toda, H. & Kawashima, H., Estimation of the environmental effects of excess nitrogen caused by intensive agriculture in East Asia based on global nitrogen balance. Ecosystems and Sustainable Development, Advances in Ecological Sciences 18, 49-58, 2003.

[7] Shindo, J., Okamoto, K. & Kawashima, H., A model based estimation of nitrogen flow in the food production–supply system and its environmental effects in East Asia. Ecological Modelling 169/1-2, 197-212, 2003.

[8] Deichmann, U., GNV197 - Human population and administrative boundaries databases for Asia. In http://www.grid.unep.ch/data/grid/gnv197.html, GRID-Geneva, United Nations Environmental Programme, Geneva, 1996.

[9] Bouwman, A.F., Lee, D.S., Asman, W.A.H, Dentener, F.J., Van der Hoek, K.W. & Olivier, G.J., A global high-resolution emission inventory for ammonia. Global Biogeochemical Cycles 11, 561-587, 1997.

[10] National Bureau of Statistics, China statistical Yearbook 2000, China Statistics Press, Beijing, 2000.

[11] WHO, Global Water Supply and Sanitation Assessment 2000 Report, World Health Organization, Geneva, http://www.who.int/docstore/water_sanitation_health/Globassessment/Global7-1.htm, 2005.

A simple empirical model of data fouling in marine fisheries

C. M. Wernerheim[1] & R. L. Haedrich[2]
[1]Department of Economics and Coasts Under Stress Project, Memorial University of Newfoundland, Canada
[2]Department of Biology and Coasts Under Stress Project, Memorial University of Newfoundland, Canada

Abstract

One of the most serious problems facing fisheries managers is how to improve estimates of the distortion ('fouling') of commercial landings data resulting from misreporting. Data fouling (legal or illegal) drives a wedge between what is caught and killed at sea, and what is landed and reported to the regulator. This can obscure the true state of the stock causing it to appear healthier than it is, resulting in quotas being set too high. We propose an analytical model of data fouling that can be used with empirical data to estimate what we call the data fouling factor. The model is solved analytically and numerically for the profit maximizing effort level and the associated number of high-grading operations. Some illustrative policy implications are derived.
Keywords: misreporting, high-grading, fisheries data, fisheries policy.

1 Introduction

The estimation of stock abundance and the determination of quotas alike depend in large measure on accurate and precise statistics on commercial landings. One of the most serious problems facing fisheries managers is how to improve estimates of the distortion resulting from misreporting. Failure to obtain an accurate account from harvesters about activities at sea undermines the reliability of catch data, which can in turn introduce an (avoidable) element of uncertainty into the outcomes of fisheries policy: the greater the inaccuracy in the data the wider the confidence intervals around the estimate of stock size. Our main contention is that unless official landings data are adjusted for the discrepancy between what is actually caught and killed at sea, and what is landed and reported to the regulator, quotas will be set too high. If the combined effect of data fouling in all its forms is sufficiently severe, resource decline may not be reversed.

The problems associated with data fouling have attracted increasing attention in the literature and popular media. From a science point of view, recent resource crises in Canada and elsewhere have raised questions about the reliability of scientific stock abundance estimates, recruitment, age class distributions, and other key population characteristics. There are also economic and purely environmental aspects to the wastage resulting from high-grading and dumping. From the standpoint of public policy, there is a growing recognition of the need for more effective management and enforcement given the unrelenting pressure on stocks from both domestic and foreign fleets. It is well known that activities that distort fisheries statistics occur in virtually all fisheries, and that they can cause entire fisheries to collapse (see e.g. Anon. [1]). But are some fisheries policy regimes 'better' than others in terms of the quality of the data made available for management? Our analysis suggests that the efficiency claims frequently made for IQs, and ITQs in particular, may be overstated. Some theoretical work exists in this area, but empirical work has been hampered by the lack of reliable data on activities at sea (legal or illegal) that are unobserved by the regulator. The empirical evidence is therefore scarce, and often indirect or anecdotal. This makes it very difficult to analyze the problem statistically.

Our purpose is to develop an analytical model of key elements that drive data fouling practices. The intent is to design a framework that can be used with empirical data to estimate what we call the data fouling factor. The analytical simplicity is attractive as it allows some key results with policy relevance to emerge, while keeping the assumptions transparent and the data requirement for implementation to a minimum. What makes this model potentially useful in the design of policy instruments focused on high-grading is that the data required are generally available. The model is solved analytically for the profit maximizing effort level and the associated optimal number of high-grading operations. Data on the biology, harvesting technology, prices and costs related to fishing, are then used to parameterize the model and solve it numerically. Sensitivity analysis can then be undertaken in order to inform policy.

A number of methods have been used to examine 'unreported fishing' for total catches (what happens at sea) versus landings (what is officially reported on land). (See Metuzals *et al.* [2] and the references cited therein.)

2 The model

Our previous survey research (Metuzals *et al.* [2]) confirms that it is appropriate to model these activities as the outcomes of individually rational action. Assume that each harvester has a property right to a portion of the catch in the form of a non-transferable individual quota (IQ) in a single-species fishery. The biomass comprises 'small' and 'large' fish, encountered with known probabilities. The IQs are reassigned arbitrarily on a seasonal basis, giving rise to myopic fishing behaviour and a desire to maximize the in-season value of the quota. The harvester maximizes profit by choosing (1) the fishing effort, and (2) the number of high-grading operations (n). The incentive to high-grade arises from a known market price premium charged on large fish.

Assume that identical vessels equipped with non-discriminatory gear are used by all harvesters so that the catch H per unit effort is constant across harvesters and proportional to the size of the stock in the standard fashion: $H/E=qX$, where E is nominal effort, q is the catchability coefficient, and X is the stock size. The regulator sets the aggregate quota Q for the current season on the on the basis of a biological growth function $F(x)$ of the Schaefer type, and the recorded catches in the previous season. Thus, $Q=H$ says that in aggregate the quota equals the sustainable equilibrium harvest. The quota share of each of the m fishers is then Q/m. But since catches in the previous season may have involved discarding and misreporting the current quota levels will, *ceteris paribus,* be set too high relative to the sustainable yield predicted from $F(x)$. The outcome is therefore not an equilibrium solution. This is the essential problem from the standpoint of the regulator: the biological equilibrium condition that growth or sustained yield equals the (aggregate) harvest is not satisfied (i.e. $F(x) \neq H$). It follows that this process is unsustainable and will lead to stock collapse if unchecked. The model is 'closed' in a heuristic manner by assuming that the regulator has information about the incentives at play, but not about the actual conduct at sea.

We define high-grading as the sorting and selective discarding of the portion of the catch comprising small fish for the purpose of replacing it with higher valued large fish. Assuming that each time a portion of the catch is replaced in this way the probability of catching large fish remains the same, the incentive to high-grade depends on the relative price of large fish, the cost of high-grading, and the cost of replacing the fish discarded by a new catch. Based on past experience fishers expect to catch large fish and small fish with probabilities π_L and $\pi_S = 1-\pi_L$ respectively. The harvest of large fish H_L and small fish H_S can then be written

$$H_i \equiv H \cdot \pi_i = q \cdot E \cdot x \cdot \pi_i, \quad i = L,\ S$$

The relationship between the corresponding market prices per unit weight is $p_L \equiv a \cdot p_S$, where $a \geq 1$ is the mark-up on large fish. Fishing revenue can thus be written: $p_L \cdot H_L + p_S \cdot H_S$. The opportunity cost of high-grading, $C_d(n)$, varies with the number of high-grading operations undertaken. It includes the costs of sorting, handling and storing large fish at sea. But it does not cover the cost of replacing discarded catch. Postulating that $C_d' > 0$ captures the practical aspect that high-grading gets increasingly more expensive due to on-deck congestion and time factors the more often the fish are discarded and replaced. The remaining portion of the opportunity cost of fishing $C(E,n;\phi)$ is attributable to fixed, vessel related costs, ϕ, such as insurance and licence or quota fees; the variable effort expended; and the number of high grading operations. This function is increasing in its arguments reflecting the increasing costs associated with longer time at sea. Specifically, $C_E'>0$ since the marginal cost increases with effort even if no high-grading occurs. Also, $C_n'>0$ since the marginal cost is increasing with the number of high-grading operations as this involves effort to replace discarded small fish with large fish. It stands to reason that if high-grading is profitable, the total effort expended in attempting to fill the quota can be considerably greater than otherwise. Hence, $Q=H\leq H_L+H_S$.

Each replacement catch adds additional weight of large fish H_L to the vessel hold. Suppose for illustrative purposes that $\pi_L=1/3$ and $\pi_S=2/3$. Successive replacements of the small catch with large fish will then increase revenue but at a decreasing rate since the size of the replacement catch declines continuously. This is because a portion of it (1/3) is retained with each high-grading whilst the rest is discarded. It follows that fishing revenue increases at a decreasing rate as the size (weight) of the catch continues to decline as the quota is gradually filled. For example, the weight of small fish discarded in the first high-grading operation is $H_S\pi_S$ whereas the value of the fish retained from the nth high-grading is $p_L H\pi_s^n\,\pi_L$ (Figure 1.)

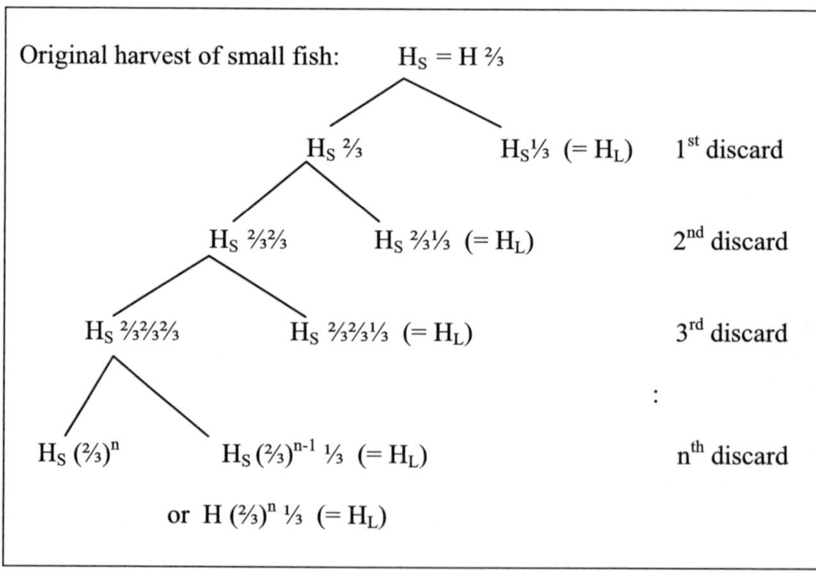

Figure 1: Determining the weight of large fish (H_L) retained from high-grading.

If costs were zero, fishing would continue until the entire hold (the full quota) consists of large fish. Since fishing and high-grading operations are both costly, a choice must be made simultaneously about the number of discarding operations, and the amount of effort expended in replacing the discards. When $n\geq 1$, profit becomes

$$\max_{E,n} \Pi = p_L \cdot H \cdot \pi_L + \sum_n a \cdot p_S \cdot H \cdot \pi_L \cdot \pi_S^n - c(E,n;\phi) - c_d(n)$$

$$= p_L H_L + p_L \cdot H_L \cdot \frac{\pi_s^n}{\pi_S - 1} - c(E,n;\phi) - c_d(n)$$

Using the definition of the harvest from above and dividing through by p_S, the first-order conditions can be expressed as

$$\frac{\partial \Pi}{\partial E} = \frac{p_L}{p_S} \cdot \pi_L \cdot q \cdot X \cdot \left(1 - \frac{\pi_S^n}{\pi_S - 1}\right) - \frac{c_E'(E,n;\phi)}{p_S} = 0 \tag{1}$$

and

$$\frac{\partial \Pi}{\partial n} = \frac{p_L}{p_S} \cdot \pi_L \cdot q \cdot X \cdot \left(-\frac{\ln \pi_S(\pi_S^n)}{\pi_S - 1}\right) - \frac{c_n'(E,n;\phi)}{p_S} - \frac{c_d'(n)}{p_S} = 0 \tag{2}$$

Note that the first term in the latter expression is positive for n ≥ 1since $\ln(\pi_S)\pi_S^n > 0$. Eqns. (1)-(2), satisfied for *E* and n** respectively, state a simple intuitive result. Use fishing effort to discard the catch of small fish and replace it with large fish until the marginal return (the incremental additions of large fish) equals the marginal cost (the incremental cost of another high-grading and catch replacement operation). It is easy to verify that the second-order conditions $\partial^2\Pi/\partial n^2<0$, and $\partial^2\Pi/\partial E^2<0$ hold.

2.1 Numerical solution: data and functional forms

The parameters estimated on empirical data come from a study of the Pacific Halibut fishery by Cook and Copes [3] and include the carrying capacity *K*, the catchability coefficient *q*, the intrinsic growth rate *r*, the aggregate effort expended by the fleet, the number of vessels, and actual catch rates. Cook & Copes estimate harvesting costs as a function of a standardized measure of nominal effort in this fishery (skate soaks), and provide a demand function for halibut. We use this demand function with the actual catch rates to determine on an *ad hoc* basis the relative price of 'large' and 'small' fish. We modify the cost function to account for high-grading, catch replacement, and the interactions between these elements and fishing effort. We posit a high-grading cost function that can be estimated empirically given more detailed data than we have available. The cost parameters relating to high-grading were thus constructed. The functional forms for the cost functions are:

$$C(E,n) = \beta_1 E + \beta_2 nE - \beta_3 E^2 \tag{3}$$

$$C_d(n) = \frac{n^{\delta_1+1}}{\delta_1 + 1}\delta_2 \tag{4}$$

www.witpress.com, ISSN 1743-3541 (on-line)

Eqn. (3) describes total harvesting costs (including the effort used for catch replacement following discarding). Eqn (4) captures total high-grading costs (the on-deck costs of sorting, handling, and storage using catch quality control). All parameter values are reported in Table 1.

2.2 Simulation results

Numerical solutions are obtained by solving the relevant first-order conditions. Calculating the elasticities of the dependent variables allows a quantitative assessment of the sensitivity of the optimal (solution) values to changes in the key parameters. This is useful for policy analysis since some of these parameters may be influenced directly or indirectly by policy means. In particular, what is the factor by which reported (observed) landings can be expected to differ from the unobserved actual kill at sea? Given the premium on 'large' fish, how many high-grading operations will maximize the profit on the quota in a given season? How sensitive is high-grading to the probability of finding large fish, to the price premium on large fish and fishing costs?

We report the elasticity coefficients η of effort and high-grading. A log-linear functional form is used for this purpose, except where changes in the independent variable are best thought of in incremental or unit terms, rather than in percentage terms. In such cases a semi-log functional form is derived by taking logs of the dependent variable. The interpretation of the elasticity coefficient is, of course, affected accordingly. The elasticity estimates show that the optimal effort level is much more sensitive to the relative price of fish than to the number of discards. This is consistent with the expected finding that optimal number of discards is also highly sensitive to the relative price of fish. The optimal effort level is 517,000 skate-soaks (with E measured in hundred thousand skate-soaks), and the optimal number of discards is five. The first four estimates (Table 2) refer to the sensitivity or responsiveness of E^* to each of four key parameters.

The remaining two results are measures of the responsiveness of n^* to two of the same parameters. We make the following observations: first, both E^* and n^* are remarkably sensitive to changes in the parameters in question. This is especially true of changes in the relative price of large fish, and interestingly, the opportunity cost of fishing. A one percent increase in the relative price elicits a very large positive response in effort. Similarly, a one percent increase in any fixed cost component, such as the quota fee, causes a disproportionate reduction in effort. Second, the probability of catching small fish increases as the optimal effort level falls continuously, while the optimal number of high-grading operations increases until most large fish are gone after which it also declines (Figure 2). The explanation is that at the margin, high-grading contributes more to profit than the required effort expended reduces it. High-grading thus continues, *ceteris paribus*, until the remaining large fish become too expensive to catch.

Table 1: Parameter values used to obtain a numerical solution.

Parameter	Value	Units	Parameter	Value	Units
α_1	10	-	p_S	2.5	\$
α_2	0.4	-	π_L	0.667	-
β_1	38.65	-	π_S	0.333	-
β_2	0.1	-	π_{dc}	0.5	-
β_3	0.45	-	K	$1098 \cdot 10^5$	tonnes
δ_1	1.1	-	q	$0.115 \cdot 10^{-5}$	-
δ_2	0.9	-	r	0.58	-
P	10	-	X	$3.66 \cdot 10^7$	tonnes
p_L	5	\$	a	2	-

Table 2: Optimal solution values and elasticity estimates.

	$E^* = 0.517$ $n^* = 5.139$ (≈ 5)	
From eqn.:	Elasticity of E^* with respect to the:	η
1	number of high-grading operations n	0.372[a]
1	probability of catching small fish π_S	-0.734[b]
1	relative price of fish p_L/p_S	3.278[b]
1	level of marginal cost β_1	-5.279[b]
	Elasticity of n^* with respect to:	
2	probability of catching small fish π_S	0.505[b]
2	the relative price of fish p_L/p_S	0.317[b]

Notes: a/ calculated from semi-log form
b/ calculated from log-linear form

This model also allows us to estimate the extent of error in the reported landings statistics as a result of high-grading. The 'data fouling factor', DFF, measures the discarded (unreported) catch as a proportion of the total fishing mortality. To see this, consider a quota set by the regulator (Table 3). Assuming that no high-grading occurs the quota is calculated as the equilibrium harvest using $Q=q \cdot X \cdot E$ and parameter estimates for the Schaefer model reported in

Table 1. The DFF can then be calculated as DFF = 1 – harvest reported / total fishing mortality. We calculate the DFF to be 56 percent. Interestingly, this is very close to a recent discard estimate by Canada's fisheries regulator, Department of Fisheries and Oceans, for the Newfoundland Region (Wellman [4]).

3 Conclusions and policy implications

From the evidence we have reviewed, the problem of data fouling is probably far greater than commonly believed. From a management perspective the problem is intractable in that data fouling encompasses a wide array of activities, many of which are not strictly illegal. Moreover, existing policy tools tend to be ill-designed for the purpose of curbing most data fouling behaviour. What data fouling practices have in common is the largely unsupervised environment in which they take place. This makes it exceedingly difficult to get reliable estimates on the extent to which such behaviours distort the statistics upon which sustainable fisheries management relies. Financially, it is difficult to argue for larger enforcement budgets, and greater expenditure on related education and moral suasion unless convincing statistical evidence support the putative benefits. Politically, decisive regulatory action is problematic because it pits the interest of the present generation against that of future generations. But if our moral obligation to future generations includes protection of ecosystems along with a capacity to generate economic well-being from the fishery, decision-makers need to face squarely any trade-offs between poverty-alleviation now and managing for a sustainable fishery.

Table 3: Data fouling results.

Harvest Measures	tonnes
Quota	475.24
Harvest reported (large fish)	433.39
Discards (small fish)	551.01
Total kill	984.49
Data fouling factor	0.56

This study lends further support to a conclusion drawn in several previous studies: that the role of education in changing long-established practices that undermine sustainability cannot be overemphasized. The implications for fisheries policy from the present research can be summarized as follows.

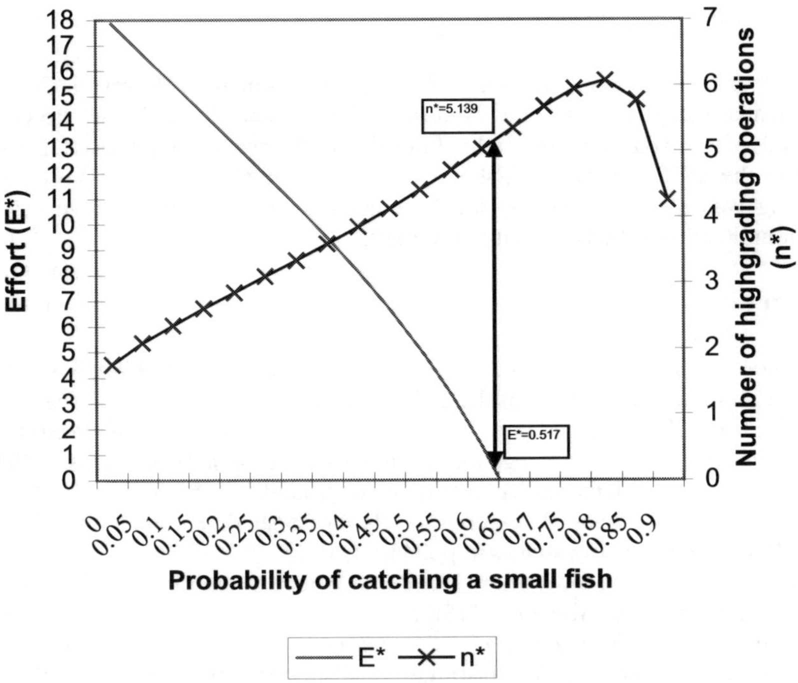

Figure 2: Optimal effort and discard rates.

Firstly, only in rare circumstances can IQs and ITQs be expected to substantially reduce the problem of data fouling. Since individual property rights under these regimes pertain to a portion of the harvest, and not to the productive asset itself (the stock), is seems clear that IQ and ITQ management can provide powerful incentives to high-grade and under-report catch (cf. Copes [5]).

Secondly, the Newfoundland groundfish community shows sustained shifts in overall size distribution and declines in average size of commercial species (see e.g. Haedrich and Barnes [6]). The present modelling indicates that while the economic incentive to high-grade is weakened as the probability of finding 'small' fish declines, it does not go to zero until 'large' fish are all but gone. This result is driven by the premium on large fish, relative to unit harvesting costs. The higher this ratio, all else being the same, the more high-grading there will be. This is worrisome in light of the fact that harvesting costs trend downward with technological change, while the price premium for large fish in the market can be expected to trend upward as the quality of the remaining resource is degraded. These factors thus combine to drive the price/cost ratio upward, which in turn fuels more high-grading. The damaging effects of this behaviour need to be given much more attention by policy makers. This suggests that the Norwegian approach (Gezelius [7]) of using a no-discard policy warrants closer examination.

Acknowledgments

The authors wish to thank the Social Sciences and Humanities Research Council of Canada (SSHRC), and the Natural Sciences and Engineering Research Council of Canada (NSERC) who funded the "Coasts Under Stress" Project through the SSHRC Major Collaborative Research Initiatives (MCRI) program. Funding was also provided by the host universities: Memorial University of Newfoundland and the University of Victoria.

References

[1] Anon., *Stopping Illegal, Unreported and Unregulated Fishing*, Food and Agriculture Organization of the UN: Rome, 2002.

[2] Metuzals, K.I., Wernerheim, C.M., Haedrich, R.L, Copes, P & Murrin, A. *When fish are foul: findings and a model for Newfoundland*, Coasts Under Stress Project, Memorial University of Newfoundland, St. John's, 2004.

[3] Cook, B.A. & Copes, P., Optimal levels for Canada's Pacific halibut Catch. *Marine Resource Economics* **4**, pp. 45-61, 1987.

[4] Wellman, J., Time for caution. The 2004 science of crab in Newfoundland and Labrador. *The Navigator* **7**(5), 2004.

[5] Copes, P., *Adverse impacts of individual quota systems on conservation and fish harvest productivity*, Institute of Fisheries Analysis, Simon Fraser University, Vancouver, June, Discussion Paper 00-2, 2000.

[6] Haedrich, R.L. & Barnes, S.M. Changes over time of the size structure in an exploited shelf fish community. *Fisheries Research* **31**, pp. 229-239-411, 1997.

[7] Gezelius, S. The morality of compliance in coastal fisheries. Cases from Norway and Newfoundland. *Proc. of the IASCP Northern Polar Regional Meeting*, Anchorage, Alaska. August 17-21, 2003.

Significance of carbonic anhydrase and its distribution in the Karst ecosystem

Y. Y. Wu[1], P. P. Li[1], B. L. Wang[2], C. Q Liu[2], X. T. Li[1] & X. Z. Zhao[1]
[1]*The Institute of the Agricultural Equipment Engineering, Jiangsu University, Zhenjiang, Jiangsu, 212013, People's Republic of China*
[2]*The State Key Laboratory of Environmental Geochemistry, Institute of Geochemistry, The Chinese Academy of Sciences, Guiyang 550002, People's Republic of China*

Abstract

Carbonic anhydrase (Carbonic anhydrase, CA; carbonate hydrolyase, EC 4.2.1.1) is a zinc-containing metalloenzyme that catalyzes the reversible conversion of CO_2 to bicarbonate. From the determination and analysis of CA in soil and water bodies in the karst ecosystem, such results may be obtained that show that the CA activities in soil are different among soil layers. In the upper layers of soil, the CA activities are greater than those below; the activities of CA in microalgae in different lakes are different. The determination and analysis of CA in plants in the Karst ecosystem show that CA activities vary from plant to plant. The order is as follows: *Parmrlia borreri* (4.71) < *Parmrlia caperata* (5.47) < *Pteridium aquilinum* (7.72) < *Tortula sinensis* (33.45) < *Barbula conslricla* (40.47) < *Euonymus sp.* (283.67) < *Toona sinensis* (976.47) < *Jasminum seguinii* (4895.76) (Unit: WAU/gFW). It can be seen from these results that the plant evolution coordinates with CA evolution, and CA may regulate the carbon cycle in the karst ecosystem. It is an important means for maintaining carbon balance to promote the plant succession of karst ecosystem and sustain the system.
Keywords: carbonic anhydrase, Karst, carbon cycle, carbonate rock, bicarbonate.

www.witpress.com, ISSN 1743-3541 (on-line)

1 Introduction

The biogeochemistry cycle, which regulates all biochemistry reaction, is the important "driving force" of the geo-environment. The carbon cycle is one of the most important element cycles. CO_2 is the important link and ligament of global carbon cycle [1].

Carbonic anhydrase (Carbonic anhydrase, CA; carbonate hydrolyase, EC 4.2.1.1), a zinc-containing metalloenzyme that catalyses the reversible conversion of CO_2 to bicarbonate, is widely distributed in animals, plants, archea and eubacteria, where it is involved in diverse physiological processes, such as ion exchange, acid-base balance, carboxylation/decarboxylation reactions and inorganic carbon diffusion between the cell and its environment as well as within the cell [2, 3]. Moreover, carbonic anhydrase may accelerate the dissolution and weathering of carbonate rock [4, 5] and large variations in CA activity among plants may result in a pervasive disequilibrium between leaf water and atmospheric CO_2 [6]. So, it is vital for the understanding of carbon cycle in karst areas to study the significance of carbonic anhydrase and its distribution in water, soil and plants in karst ecosystem.

2 Materials and methods

The research was performed in September 2003. The experimental sites were located in Guiyang city of Guizhou Province in the southwest of China. Soil samples from 0–5cm, 5-10cm, 10-15cm, 15-20cm and 20-25cm deep beneath the ground were obtained from one plot of cropland. Water samples were obtained from Hongfeng, Baihua and Aha Lakes. Plant samples were obtained from the hill of Lover Vale. The mother rock is limestone. The soil is calcareous. Lake water is CO_2 - HCO_3^- buffered. HCO_3^- is the main anion in those lakes.

Microalgae were collected from surface waters at Hongfeng, Baihua and Aha Lakes. 60L surface water from each lake was immediately filtered by 270 meshes fabric in order to remove impurities. Subsequent filtration with cellulose acetate membrane filters (1.2 μm pore size, Millipore) yielded the microalgae. Microalgae were scraped off the cellulose acetate membrane and diluted to 400mL by final filtrated surface water. This provided us with microalgae stock solution. These microalgae were immediately harvested by centrifugation at 1600g for 10min. CA activity was electrochemically determined by measuring the time required for the pH to drop from 8.2 to 7.2 in 15 ml of ice-cold barbital buffer (20 mM, pH 8.30) with these microalgae from different lakes and 10 ml of ice-cold CO_2-saturated distilled H_2O added into it. One unit [7] of activity was defined as: $WA=t_0/t-1$, where t_0 and t are the time taken respectively in the enzyme-free buffer (control) and the buffer containing enzyme sample.

10 g of fresh soils from different soil-layers were quickly frozen in liquid N_2, ground into powder with a mill, then homogenized with 30 ml of extracted buffer (20 mM veronal buffer with 50mM 2-mercaptoethanol, pH 8.2). The homogenate was centrifuged at 3200 g for 5 min. 15 ml of the ice-cold supernatants were added into 10 ml of ice-cold CO_2-saturated distilled H_2O to

measure the activity of CA. The measurement method of the activity of CA also conforms to Wilbur and Anderson's method [7].

The activities of CA of leaves of *Pteridium aquilinum*, *Euonymus sp.*, *Toona sinensis*, *Jasminum seguinii,* and plants of *Parmrlia borreri*, *Parmrlia caperata*, *Tortula sinensis*, *and Barbula conslricla* were measured. 0.5 g of leaves from *Pteridium aquilinum*, *Euonymus sp.*, *Toona sinensis* and *Jasminum seguinii* and 1 g of plants of *Parmrlia borreri*, *Parmrlia caperata*, *Tortula sinensis*, *Barbula conslricla* were quickly frozen in liquid N_2, ground into powder with a mill, then homogenized with 3 ml of extracted buffer (10 mM veronal buffer with 50 mM 2-mercaptoethanol, pH 8.2). The homogenate was centrifuged at 10000 g for 5 min. The supernatants were used to measure the activity of CA. The subsequent steps of determining CA activity were the same as those for soil CA activity.

3 Results

3.1 The activities of CA of microalgae in different lakes

Table 1 shows the diversity of the composition and CA activity of algae in different lakes. The total algae cell number in Lake Aha is the biggest while its CA activity is the lowest; and the total algae cell number in Lake Hongfeng is the smallest, but its CA activity is the strongest. It seems that CA activity is related not with total algae cell number but with that of *Cyanophyta*.

Table 1: The composition and CA activity of algae in different lakes (The CA activity values correspond to the mean±SD (n=3)).

Name of Lake	*Cyanophyta* cells • L^{-1}	*Chlorophyta* cells • L^{-1}	Total algae cells • L^{-1}	CA activity WAU • L^{-1}
Lake Aha	11.10×10^5	1.36×10^5	21.28×10^5	0.15 ± 0.03
Lake Hongfeng	12.17×10^5	1.75×10^5	16.15×10^5	0.24 ± 0.04
Lake Baihua	11.32×10^5	3.45×10^5	17.18×10^5	0.21 ± 0.05

3.2 The comparison of the activities of CA of soil from different depth

Table 2 shows the activity of CA in soil varies with depth. CA activity can be measured in the depths of 0-5cm and 5-10cm; the CA activity in 0-5cm-depth is the highest in all the soil layers. CA activity in the depths of 10-15cm, 15-20cm and 20-25cm cannot be measured.

3.3 The comparison of the activities of CA of plants

Table 3 shows the diversity of the CA activities in different plants. The activities of CA of lichens and *Pteridophyta* are very low, that of bryophyte relatively stronger, and angiosperm the highest. CA activities in angiosperm vary greatly. CA activity of *Jasminum seguinii* is about 170 times that of *Euonymus sp.*

Table 2: The CA activity of soil in different layers (The values correspond to the mean±SD (n=3)).

Depths	CA activity WAU • gFW^{-1}
0-5cm	2.22±0.18
5-10cm	1.86±0.24
10-15cm	NT
15-20cm	NT
20-25cm	NT

Table 3: The comparison of the activities of CA of plants (The values correspond to the mean±SD (n=3)).

Name of plants		CA activity WAU • gFW^{-1}
Lichens	*Parmrlia borreri*	4.71±0.61
	Parmrlia caperata	5.47±0.83
Pteridophyta	*Pteridium aquilinum*	7.72±1.06
Bryophyte	*Tortula sinensis*	33.45±3.14
	Barbula conslricla	40.47±3.69
Angiosperm	*Euonymus sp.*	283.67±20.93
	Toona sinensis	976.47±79.90
	Jasminum seguinii	4895.76±215.74

4 Discussion

Numerous carbonate rock outcropping and karstification are characteristic of karst landscape. Carbonate rocks consist mainly of $CaCO_3$ and $MgCa(CO_3)_2$. They are soluble and mobilizable by water under normal atmospheric temperature and pressure. Meanwhile, carbonate radical (CO_3^{2-}) acts in close coordination with atmospheric CO_2 in the process of solution. Chemical erosion of carbonate rock is a geochemical process between solid (carbonate minerals) and liquid (water) or/and gas phase (CO_2) in opening systems of gas-liquid exchange and solid-liquid solution in which water plays an important role as a solvent and a carrier. The processes involved in chemical erosion of carbonate minerals are presented as follows equation (1) and (2):

$$CaCO_3+CO_2+H_2O=2HCO_3^-+Ca^{2+} \quad (1)$$

$$MgCa(CO_3)_2+2CO_2+2H_2O=4HCO_3^-+Mg^{2+}+Ca^{2+} \quad (2)$$

It is indicated that the chemical composition of water in the karst region is dominated by HCO_3^-, Ca^{2+} and Mg^{2+}. It follows that the concentration of HCO_3^- in soil and water bodies of lake in karst area should increase gradually, but in the actual circumstance the concentration of HCO_3^- in karst hydro-environment remains relatively stable. On the one hand, it may have something to do with the velocity of the non-catalysed reversible reaction of $H^++HCO_3^- \leftrightarrows CO_2+H_2O$; on the other hand, it has something to do with the existence of CA in soil, water bodies and plants of karst ecosystem. The main role of CA is to catalyse the reversible conversion of bicarbonate to CO_2. The determined CA activity indicates the conversional ability of bicarbonate into CO_2. Therefore, the activities of CA of soil, water bodies and plants may express the ability to regulate carbon cycle in karst ecosystem.

The activities of CA of microalgae of water bodies of different lakes are different; the concentration of bicarbonate of water body is different, too. Because of the small capacity of the water body, the low activity of CA of microalgae in Lake Aha, which result in the higher concentration of bicarbonate in the water body (3.52 mM), water body's ability to regulate the reversible conversion of bicarbonate to CO_2 is weak. But the water bodies of Lakes Hongfeng and Baihua are large in capacity, the activities of CA of microalgae in the water bodies are high, and the concentrations of bicarbonate in the water bodies are low (1.29 and 0.89 mM, respectively), too [8].

The CA activity in the surface layer soil shows soil's ability to regulate the reversible conversion of bicarbonate to CO_2, too. The groundwater causes chemical erosion of carbonate minerals, which converts them into bicarbonate, and the bicarbonate of the soil solution moves towards the surface soil layer, where the reaction of the conversion of bicarbonate to CO_2 takes place. The concentration of bicarbonate in surface layer soil decreases, and the concentration of CO_2 increases to make up for the lost CO_2 participating in the chemical erosion of carbonate minerals.

The CA activities of plants are ordered from the lowest to the highest as the following. *Parmrlia borreri* (4.71) < *Parmrlia caperata* (5.47) < *Pteridium aquilinum* (7.72) < *Tortula sinensis* (33.45) < *Barbula conslricla* (40.47) < *Euonymus sp.* (283.67) < *Toona sinensis* (976.47) < *Jasminum seguinii* (4895.76). It is related to the plants' adaptation to the circumstance of water stress and the plants' ability to regulate the carbon balance. Except the soil's CA-catalyzed reversible conversion of bicarbonate to CO_2, with the action of CA in plants the bicarbonate of the soil solution that is absorbed by plants is converted into CO_2 and H_2O that are provided to plants for their photosynthesis. The angiosperm easily adapt themselves to the land environment, their CA activities strong. The activities of CA of lichens and *Pteridophyta* being very low, they adapt themselves to the land environment relatively weakly. *Tortula sinensis* and *Barbula conslricla* are the rock-grown bryophyte, have relatively higher adaptation to arid environment, and their CA activities are greater than that of

Pteridium aquilinums. To sum up, the activity of CA may be an important index of plant's adaptation to arid environment.

5 Conclusions

The quantity of carbon in the carbonate rock accounts for 99.55% of global total carbon. The reaction of chemical erosion of carbonate rock, the reversible conversion of bicarbonate to CO_2 and photosynthesis of plants are reactions key to carbon cycle. The carbon cycle of the karst area may be roughly illustrated with figure 1.

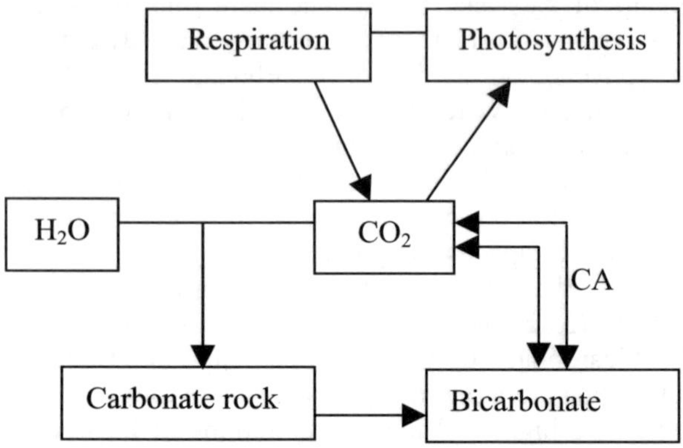

Figure 1: Carbon cycle sketch map in karst area.

CO_2 causes carbonate rock's dissolution into bicarbonate, which is converted into CO_2 either with CA catalysis or without catalysis. Soil-water-plant constitutes a continuous action system through CA. The activity of CA expresses the ability to regulate the carbon cycle in the ecosystem. Angiosperm in the karst ecosystem has an important part in regulating the carbon cycle. It is significant for sustaining of the ecological balance to protect the water and soil resources, and increase the vegetation coverage rate.

Acknowledgements

This work was supported by grant no. 40273038 of National Natural Science Foundation of China, no. KZCX3-SW-140 of the Knowledge-Innovation Program of Chinese Academy of Sciences, and no.2001-6-3 of Karst Dynamic Laboratory, Ministry of Land and Resources, P.R.C.

References

[1] Schindler, D.W., Carbon cycling: The mysterious missing sink. Nature, 398, pp. 105–107, 1999.

[2] Badger, M.R. & Price, G.D., The role of carbonic anhydrase in photosynthesis. Annual Review Plant Physiology, 45:pp.369-392, 1994.
[3] Sasaki, H., Hirose, T., Watanabe, Y. et al, Carbonic anhydrase activity and CO_2-transfer resistance in Zn-deficient rice leaves. Plant Physiol, 18: pp.929–934, 1998.
[4] Liu, Z.H., The role of carbonic anhydrase as an activator in carbonate rock dissolution and its significance in atmospheric CO_2 precipitation. Acta Geoscientia Sinica, 22(5), pp.470–480, 2000.
[5] Wu, Y.Y., Wang, B.L., Liu, C.Q., 2004, Chlamydomonas reinhardtii's influence on the corrosion of rocks. In: Martin-Duque, J.F., Brebbia, C.A., Godfrey, A.E. and Dian de Teran, J.R. eds. Geo-Environment 2004. WIT Press, Southampton, pp.145-150, 2004.
[6] Gillon, J. & Yaki, D., Influence of carbonic anhydrase activity in terrestrial vegetation on the ^{18}O content of atmospheric CO_2, Science, 291:pp.2584-2587, 2001.
[7] Wibur, K.M. & Anderson, N.G., Electrometric and colorimetric determination of carbonic anhydrase, Journal Biological Chemistry. 176,147-154, 1948.
[8] Wu, Y.Y., Li P.P., Liu, C.Q., et al, Influence of inorganic element and climate factor on growth of microalgae in karst lake, Journal of Nanjing Forestry University, 27(add):pp.67-70, 2003.

Section 5
Biodiversity

Several results of Simpson diversity indices and exploratory data analysis in the Pielou model

D. Almorza Gomar & M. H. García Nieto
Department of Statistics and O.R., Cádiz University, Spain

Abstract

The Pielou model is a model of the abundance of species in a habitat. In this paper, we apply Simpson diversity indices to the Pielou model and obtain a result that may be useful for testing the goodness of fit of the Pielou model. To obtain our results, we describe the broken stick model as a probability distribution and we present some results from exploratory data analysis of this model. The inequalities we present are useful in ecological studies that apply the Pielou model.
Keywords: Pielou model, probability distribution, diversity, Simpson index, exploratory data analysis.

1 Introduction

In the Pielou model the probability of finding an individual of the specie i in the habitat is $p_i = \frac{1}{S}\sum_{k=0}^{S-i}\frac{1}{S-k}$ where $0 \leq p_i \leq 1$, $\forall\, i = 1, 2,...., S$ and $\sum_{i=1}^{s} p_i = 1$, $p_i \geq p_j$, $\forall\ i \leq j$, with $i, j =1,\ldots, S$.

1.1 Pielou model as a probability distribution

The probability density function (pdf) given by $p_i = \frac{1}{S}\left[\frac{1}{S}+\frac{1}{S-1}+...+\frac{1}{i}\right]$ with $S>1$, provides a probability distribution that arises from the Pielou model.

Proof

The pdf is consistent with $0 \leq p_i \leq 1$, $\forall\, i = 1,2,...., S$ and $p_i \geq p_j$, $\forall\, i \leq j$, with $i, j =1, 2,\ldots, S$. Therefore, it is sufficient to prove that $\sum_{i=1}^{s} p_i = 1$.

$$\sum_{i=1}^{S} p_i = \frac{1}{S}\left[\frac{1}{S}+\frac{1}{S-1}+....+1\right]+\frac{1}{S}\left[\frac{1}{S}+\frac{1}{S-1}+....+\frac{1}{2}\right]+\frac{1}{S}\left[\frac{1}{S}+\frac{1}{S-1}+....+\frac{1}{3}\right]$$

$$+........+\frac{1}{S}\left[\frac{1}{S}+\frac{1}{S-1}\right]+\frac{1}{S}\left[\frac{1}{S}\right]=\frac{1}{S}\left[\frac{S}{S}+\frac{S-1}{S-1}+\frac{S-2}{S-2}+......+\frac{2}{2}+1\right]=\frac{1}{S}\cdot S=1$$

1.2 Cumulative distribution function

The cumulative distribution function is

$$F_S(i)=\begin{cases} 0 & i\le 1 \\ \frac{1}{S}\left[\frac{1}{S}+\frac{1}{S-1}+........+\frac{1}{2}+1\right] & 1\le i<2 \\ \frac{1}{S}\left[\frac{2}{S}+\frac{2}{S-1}+......+\frac{2}{3}+1+1\right] & 2\le i<3 \\ \frac{1}{S}\left[\frac{3}{S}+\frac{3}{S-1}+......+\frac{3}{4}+1+1+1\right] \quad \text{with} & 3\le i<4 \\ .... & .... \\ \frac{1}{S}\left[\frac{S-2}{S}+\frac{S-2}{S-1}+(S-2)\right] & S-2\le i<S-1 \\ \frac{1}{S}\left[\frac{S-1}{S}+(S-1)\right] & S-1\le i<S \\ \frac{1}{S}[S]=1 & S\le i \end{cases}$$

1.2.1 Result

Given two habitats with S_1 and S_2 species respectively, such as $S_1 > S_2$, in the case of the Pielou model, it is verified that: $F_{S_1}(i)<F_{S_2}(i) \quad \forall i$.

Proof

This result is going to be proved by induction.

If $i<1$ then $F_{S_1}(i)=F_{S_2}(i)$

If $1\le i<2 \Rightarrow F_{S_1}(i)<F_{S_2}(i)$ because:

$$F_{S_1}(i)=\frac{1}{S_1}\left[\frac{1}{S_1}+\frac{1}{S_1-1}+.....+\frac{1}{2}+1\right]<$$

$$\frac{1}{S_1-1}\left[\frac{1}{S_1-1}+\frac{1}{S_1-2}+.....+\frac{1}{2}+1\right]=F_{S_2}(i)$$

In general, if $j \le i < j+1$ then $F_{S_1}(i) < F_{S_2}(i)$ with $j = 1,2,....S_1 - 1$, because:

$$F_{S_1}(i) = \frac{1}{S_1}\left[\frac{j}{S_1} + \frac{j}{S_1 - 1} + ... + \frac{j}{j+1} + j\right]$$

$$F_{S_2}(i) = \frac{1}{S_1 - 1}\left[\frac{j}{S_1 - 1} + \frac{j}{S_1 - 2} + ... + \frac{j}{j+1} + j\right]$$

If $i \ge S_1 - 1$ then $F_{S_1}(i) < F_{S_2}(i)$ because:

$$F_{S_1}(i) = \frac{1}{S_1}\left[\frac{S_1 - 1}{S_1} + (S_1 - 1)\right] \text{ and } F_{S_2}(i) = 1$$

If $i \ge S_1$ then $F_{S_1}(i) = F_{S_2}(i)$

2 The Simpson reciprocal index and the Simpson direct index in the Pielou model

Simpson (1949) [8] defines the direct index, *D*, as the probability of interspecific encounter (PIE).

$$D = \sum_{i=1}^{S} p_i q_i = \sum_{i=1}^{S} p_i (1 - p_i) = \sum_{i=1}^{S} (p_i - p_i^2) = \sum_{i=1}^{S} p_i - \sum_{i=1}^{S} p_i^2 = 1 - \sum_{i=1}^{S} p_i^2$$

If the habitat is occupied by only one species, $S = 1$, then $D = 0$. The maximum value of Simpson's diversity index is $D = \dfrac{S-1}{S}$.

Another index of diversity that is known as Simpson reciprocal index is defined by:

$$D' = \frac{1}{\sum_{i=1}^{S} p_i^2}$$

If the habitat is occupied by only one species, $S = 1$, then $D' = 0$. The maximum value of Simpson's reciprocal index is $D' = S$.

2.1 Results on the Simpson's reciprocal index

2.1.1 Theorem

Given two habitats, with S_1 and S_2 species respectively, such that $S_1 > S_2$, for the Pielou model it is the case that $D'_1 > D'_2$.

www.witpress.com, ISSN 1743-3541 (on-line)

Proof

We are going first to prove that

$$D' = \frac{S^2}{2S-k}\ ,\ \text{with}\ k = \ln(S) + 0.577 + \frac{0.5}{S}.$$

Let call ξ to,

$$\xi = \sum_{i=1}^{S} p_i^2 = \frac{1}{S^2}\left[2S - \sum_{i=1}^{S}\frac{1}{i}\right] = \frac{1}{S^2}\left(\frac{1}{S}+\frac{1}{S-1}+.......+1\right)^2 +$$

$$+\frac{1}{S^2}\left(\frac{1}{S}+\frac{1}{S-1}+.......+\frac{1}{2}\right)^2 +.....+\frac{1}{S^2}\left(\frac{1}{S}+\frac{1}{S-1}\right)^2+\frac{1}{S^2}\left(\frac{1}{S}\right)^2$$

that can be also written as

$$=\frac{1}{S}+\frac{1}{S-1}+\frac{1}{S-2}+.....+\frac{1}{S-i+1}+....+\frac{1}{2}+1+$$
$$+\frac{2}{S}+$$
$$+\frac{2}{S}+\frac{2}{S-1}+$$
$$+\frac{2}{S}+\frac{2}{S-1}+\frac{2}{S-2}+$$
$$+..........+$$
$$+\frac{2}{S}+\frac{2}{S-1}+\frac{2}{S-2}+.....+\frac{2}{S-i-2}+$$
$$+..........+$$
$$+\frac{2}{S}+\frac{2}{S-1}+\frac{2}{S-2}+.....+\frac{2}{S-i-2}+......+\frac{2}{2}=$$
$$=\sum_{i=1}^{S}\frac{2(i-1)+1}{i}=\sum_{i=1}^{S}\frac{2i-1}{i}=2S-\sum_{i=1}^{S}\frac{1}{i}$$

and $\sum_{i=1}^{S}\frac{1}{i}$ is related to the constant $C = 0'577218$, obtained by Euler in 1734, in the following way:

$$\sum_{i=1}^{S}\frac{1}{i} = \ln S + C + o\left(\frac{1}{n}\right)$$

and verifies

$$\sum_{i=1}^{S}\frac{1}{i} \approx \ln S + C + \frac{0'5}{n}$$

Therefore

$$\xi = \frac{1}{S^2}\left[2S - \ln S - 0'577 - \frac{0'5}{n}\right]$$

Now we will consider $S_1 = S_2 - 1$ and S_2 and, so

$$D'_{S_1} = \frac{S_1^2}{2S_1 - k_1} = \frac{(S_2-1)^2}{2(S_2-1)-k_1} \quad ; \quad D'_{S_2} = \frac{S_2^2}{2S_2 - k_2}$$

being

$$k_1 = \ln S_1 + 0.577 + \frac{0.5}{S_1} = \ln(S_2 - 1) + 0.577 + \frac{0.5}{(S_2-1)}$$

$$k_2 = \ln S_2 + 0.577 + \frac{0.5}{S_2}$$

we obtain that $(S_2-1)^2 < S_2^2$ and we can consider $k_1 \cong k_2$, then

$$\frac{(S_2-1)^2}{2(S_2-1)} < \frac{S_2^2}{2S_2},$$

and therefore $\dfrac{(S_2-1)^2}{2(S_2-1)-k_1} < \dfrac{S_2^2}{2S_2-k_2}$. and also $D'_1 = D'_2$ when $S_1 = S_2$.

2.2 Results on the Simpson's direct index

2.2.1 Theorem

Given two habitats, with S_1 and S_2 species respectively, such that $S_1 > S_2$, for the Pielou model it is the case that $D_1 > D_2$.

Proof

For the demonstration we will consider the previous result (Almorza, Peinado, 2001) [2], where from they obtain

$$D = 1 - \sum_{i=1}^{S} p_i^2 = 1 - \frac{1}{D'} = \frac{D'-1}{D'} = \frac{\frac{S^2}{2S-k} - 1}{\frac{S^2}{2S-k}} = \frac{S^2 - 2S + k}{S^2}$$

and by considering the relation $D = 1 - \dfrac{1}{D'}$, the result is obtained.

3 Results of exploratory data analysis

3.1 Results on measures of position

3.1.1 Result

The median, for the Pielou model, is such that $M_d \geq \frac{(3+S)-\sqrt{S^2+4S+9}}{2}$

Proof

The median is a function of the number of species. It is clear that $1 \leq M_d \leq S$, and that

$$\frac{1}{S}\left[\frac{M_d}{S}+\frac{M_d}{S-1}+\frac{M_d}{S-2}+....+\frac{M_d}{S-M_d+1}+M_d\right] \geq 0.5$$

Hence

$$\frac{1}{S}\left[\frac{M_d}{S}+\frac{M_d}{S-1}+\frac{M_d}{S-2}+....+\frac{M_d}{S-M_d+1}+M_d\right] \leq \frac{M_d}{S}(S-M_d+3)$$

Therefore $\quad -M_d^2+(3+S)M_d-0.5S \geq 0$

Hence $\quad M_d \geq \frac{(3+S)-\sqrt{S^2+4S+9}}{2}$

3.1.2 Result

The third quartile (Q_3), for the Pielou model, is such that

$$Q_3 \geq \frac{(3+S)-\sqrt{S^2+3S+9}}{2}$$

Proof

The third quartile is a function of the number of species. In addition:

$$\frac{1}{S}\left[\frac{Q_3}{S}+\frac{Q_3}{S-1}+\frac{Q_3}{S-2}+....+\frac{Q_3}{S-Q_3+1}+Q_3\right] \geq 0.75$$

Hence $\quad \frac{1}{S}\left[\frac{Q_3}{S}+\frac{Q_3}{S-1}+\frac{Q_3}{S-2}+....+\frac{Q_3}{S-Q_3+1}+Q_3\right] \leq \frac{Q_3}{S}(S-Q_3+3)$

Therefore $\quad -Q_3^2+(3+S)Q_3-0.75S \geq 0$

Thus, $\quad Q_3 \geq \frac{(3+S)-\sqrt{S^2+3S+9}}{2}$

3.1.3 Result

The 90th percentile (C_{90}), for the Pielou model is such that

www.witpress.com, ISSN 1743-3541 (on-line)

$$C_{90} \geq \frac{(3+S)-\sqrt{S^2+2.4S+9}}{2}$$

Proof
The 90th percentile is a function of the number of species. In addition:

$$\frac{1}{S}\left[\frac{C_{90}}{S}+\frac{C_{90}}{S-1}+\frac{C_{90}}{S-2}+....+\frac{C_{90}}{S-C_{90}+1}+C_{90}\right] \geq 0.9$$

Hence $\frac{1}{S}\left[\frac{C_{90}}{S}+\frac{C_{90}}{S-1}+\frac{C_{90}}{S-2}+....+\frac{C_{90}}{S-C_{90}+1}+C_{90}\right] \leq \frac{C_{90}}{S}(S-C_{90}+3)$

Then $-C_{90}^2+(3+S)C_{90}-0.9S \geq 0$

Thus $C_{90} \geq \frac{(3+S)-\sqrt{S^2+2.4S+9}}{2}$

3.1.4 Result

The first quartil (Q_1), for the Pielou model, is such that

$$Q_1 \geq \frac{(3+S)-\sqrt{S^2+5S+9}}{2}$$

Proof
The first quartil is a function of the number of species. In addition:

$$\frac{1}{S}\left[\frac{Q_1}{S}+\frac{Q_1}{S-1}+\frac{Q_1}{S-2}+....+\frac{Q_1}{S-Q_1+1}+Q_1\right] \geq 0.25$$

Hence $\frac{1}{S}\left[\frac{Q_1}{S}+\frac{Q_1}{S-1}+\frac{Q_1}{S-2}+....+\frac{Q_1}{S-Q_1+1}+Q_1\right] \leq \frac{Q_1}{S}(S-Q_1+3)$

Then $-Q_1^2+(3+S)Q_1-0.25S \geq 0$

Thus $Q_1 \geq \frac{(3+S)-\sqrt{S^2+5S+9}}{2}$

3.1.5 Result

The 10th centile (C_{10}), for the Pielou model, is such that

$$C_{10} \geq \frac{(3+S)-\sqrt{S^2+5.6S+9}}{2}$$

Proof
The 10th centile is a function of the number of species. In addition:

$$\frac{1}{S}\left[\frac{C_{10}}{S}+\frac{C_{10}}{S-1}+\frac{C_{10}}{S-2}+....+\frac{C_{10}}{S-C_{10}+1}+C_{10}\right] \geq 0.1$$

Hence $\frac{1}{S}\left[\frac{C_{10}}{S}+\frac{C_{10}}{S-1}+\frac{C_{10}}{S-2}+....+\frac{C_{10}}{S-C_{10}+1}+C_{10}\right]\leq\frac{C_{10}}{S}(S-C_{10}+3)$

Then $-C_{10}^2+(3+S)C_{10}-0.1S\geq 0$

Thus $C_{10}\geq\frac{(3+S)-\sqrt{S^2+5.6S+9}}{2}$

3.1.6 Result

For the Pielou model, the interquartile range is such that

$$R_{IQ}\leq\frac{(S-3)+\sqrt{S^2+5S+9}}{2}$$

Proof

This follows trivially from

$$R_{IQ}\leq S-\frac{(3+S)-\sqrt{S^2+5S+9}}{2}=\frac{(S-3)+\sqrt{S^2+5S+9}}{2}$$

3.1.7 Result

For the Pielou model, the semi- interquartile range is such that

$$R_{SIQ}\leq\frac{(S-3)+\sqrt{S^2+5S+9}}{4}$$

Proof

As consequence of the previous result.

3.1.8 Result

For the Pielou model, the semi-interquartile range below the median is such that

$$R_{SIQ-M_d}\leq\frac{(S-3)+\sqrt{S^2+5S+9}}{(S+3)-\sqrt{S^2+4S+9}}$$

Proof

Results 3.1.1 and 3.1.6 imply that

$R_{IQ}\leq\frac{(S-3)+\sqrt{S^2+5S+9}}{2}$ and $M_d\geq\frac{(3+S)-\sqrt{S^2+4S+9}}{2}$, therefore:

$$R_{SIQ-M_d}=\frac{Q_3-Q_1}{M_d}\leq\frac{(S-3)+\sqrt{S^2+5S+9}}{(S+3)-\sqrt{S^2+4S+9}}$$

3.2 Results on other measures

3.2.1 Result

a) For the Pielou model, the interior frontiers are such that:

* Inferior interior frontier : $f_{INF} = Q_1 - 1.5R_{IQ} \geq -\frac{(S-15)+5\sqrt{S^2+5S+9}}{4}$

Proof $\quad Q_1 \geq \frac{(3+S)-\sqrt{S^2+5S+9}}{2}$ and $1.5R_{IQ} \leq \frac{3}{2}\cdot\frac{(S-3)+\sqrt{S^2+5S+9}}{2}$

Hence: $1.5R_{IQ} - Q_1 \leq \frac{(S-15)+5\sqrt{S^2+5S+9}}{4}$

* Superior interior frontier: $f_{SUP} = Q_3 + 1.5R_{IQ} \leq \frac{7S-9+3\sqrt{S^2+5S+9}}{4}$

Proof

We know that $1.5R_{IQ} \leq \frac{3}{2}\cdot\frac{(S-3)+\sqrt{S^2+5S+9}}{2}$

Then: $Q_3 + 1.5R_{IQ} \leq S + \frac{3}{2}\cdot\frac{(S-3)+\sqrt{S^2+5S+9}}{2}$

b) For the Pielou's model, the exterior frontiers verifies:

* Inferior exterior frontier: $F_{INF} = Q_1 - 3R_{IQ} \geq -\frac{2S-12+4\sqrt{S^2+5S+9}}{2}$

Proof $\quad Q_1 \geq \frac{(3+S)-\sqrt{S^2+5S+9}}{2}$ and $3R_{IQ} \leq \frac{3S-9+3\sqrt{S^2+5S+9}}{2}$

From 3.1.6 implies $3R_{IQ} - Q_1 \leq \frac{3S-9+3\sqrt{S^2+5S+9}}{2} - \frac{S+3-\sqrt{S^2+5S+9}}{2}$

* Superior exterior frontier: $F_{SUP} = Q_3 + 3R_{IQ} \leq \frac{5S-9+3\sqrt{S^2+5S+9}}{2}$

Proof

Results 3.1.6 implies $3R_{IQ} \leq \frac{3S-9+3\sqrt{S^2+5S+9}}{2}$

Therefore $F_{SUP} \leq \frac{5S-9+3\sqrt{S^2+5S+9}}{2}$

3.2.2 Result

For the Pielou model, the quartile average is such that:

$$\overline{Q} \geq \frac{2(S+3)-\sqrt{S^2+5S+9}-\sqrt{S^2+3S+9}}{4}$$

Proof

Given results 3.1.2 and 3.1.4, it follows that $Q_1 \geq \frac{(3+S)-\sqrt{S^2+5S+9}}{2}$ and $Q_3 \geq \frac{(3+S)-\sqrt{S^2+3S+9}}{2}$. Hence:

$$Q_1 + Q_3 \geq \frac{(S+3)-\sqrt{S^2+5S+9}}{2} + \frac{(S+3)-\sqrt{S^2+3S+9}}{2}$$

Therefore $\overline{Q} \geq \frac{2(S+3)-\sqrt{S^2+5S+9}-\sqrt{S^2+3S+9}}{4}$

3.2.3 Result

For the Pielou model, the trimean is such that:

$$TRIM \geq \frac{4(S+3)-\sqrt{S^2+5S+9}-\sqrt{S^2+3S+9}-2\sqrt{S^2+4S+9}}{8}$$

Proof

This follows trivially from results 3.1.1 , 3.1.2 and 3.1.4.

References

[1] Abad, M., Huete, M.D. and Vargas, M. (2001). *Estadística para las ciencias sociales y laborales*. Ed. José Carlos Urbano Delgado. Granada.

[2] Almorza, D. and Peinado, A. (2001). Análisis de diversidad a partir del modelo del bastón roto. *Información Tecnológica,* Vol.12 Número 5: 145-147.

[3] Baczkowski, A.J. (2000). The broken-stick model for species abundances: An initial investigation. Department of Statistics, University of Leeds. Internal Report STAT 00/10.

[4] Igelmo, A. (1998). *Análisis descriptivo de datos*. Universitat de les Illes Balears. Collecció Materials Didactics, 49. Palma.

[5] Pielou, E. C. (1969). *An Introduction to Mathematical Ecology*. Wiley, New York.

[6] Pielou , E. C. (1975). *Ecological Diversity*. Wiley, New York.

[7] Ruiz-Maya, L. and Martín, F.J. (1995). *Estadística II: Inferencia*. Editorial AC. Madrid.

[8] Simpson, E. H. (1949). Measurement of diversity, *Nature*: 163, 688.

Biodiversity conservation and rural sustainability: a case study of the Alexander Skutch Biological Corridor in Southern Costa Rica

H. E. Daugherty
Faculty of Environmental Studies, York University, Toronto, Canada

Abstract

The Alexander Skutch Biological Corridor links the Las Nubes Biological Reserve and Los Cusingos Neotropical Bird Sanctuary along the Río Peñas Blancas in southern Costa Rica and is part of the larger Mesoamerican Biological Corridor connecting Mexico and Panama. The Faculty of Environmental Studies of York University in Toronto and the Tropical Science Center in San José, Costa Rica, jointly manage the Las Nubes Center for Research and Conservation. The objective of the center is to restore and protect the biodiversity of the corridor through the promotion of sustainable agricultural practices on a regional landscape level. The focus is on the conversion of sun grown to shade grown organic coffee, stream bank enhancement and erosion control, reforestation of degraded areas, and the conversion of pasture land to more productive uses (e.g., reforestation for carbon sequestration). Local farmers are now producing a specialty coffee -- Las Nubes Sustainable Coffee -- that is marketed throughout Canada by Timothy's World Coffee—Canada's third largest specialty coffee retailer. The sale of this coffee contributes to rural sustainability of the region through a purchase price exceeding fair trade pricing, ecological production, and investment in social programs by the local farmers' cooperative. It is also an example of a partnership for sustainability between the private, public and civil society sectors.
Keywords: biodiversity, biological conservation, rural sustainability, sustainable development, biological corridor, sustainable coffee, Costa Rica.

1 Introduction

National parks and other protected areas alone are inadequate mechanisms to ensure the conservation of the world's biodiversity, particularly in tropical environments where most of the biological wealth of the planet is concentrated [1]. Similarly, sustainable community development in buffer zones around protected areas has proved to be elusive for rural dwellers adjacent to these areas. Deforestation has not only taken a heavy toll on tropical forests and their respective biotas, but forest fragmentation into terrestrial islands has also been a powerful force for the depletion of biological diversity. Creative alternatives are needed to ensure the long-term survival of biodiversity and to enhance the achievement of sustainable development at the local community level. Three such alternatives are the creation of biological corridors, "green consumerism" and financial support for environmental services.

The Los Cusingos—Las Nubes Biological Corridor in southern Costa Rica illustrates each of these three approaches to biodiversity protection and rural sustainability. This corridor is the focus of a joint research and development project of the Tropical Science Center (TSC) of Costa Rica and the Faculty of Environmental Studies (FES) of York University in Toronto. This partnership also involves the regional farmers' cooperative—COOPEAGRI, R.L.—of southern Costa Rica and Timothy's World Coffee, a specialty coffee corporation headquartered in Toronto.

2 Environmental description of the corridor region

Las Nubes, designated as a private biological reserve, is a montane rainforest at approximately 1200-1500 m on the Río Peñas Blancas on the Pacific slope of the Talamanca mountain range in southern Costa Rica. To the northeast is Chirripó National Park that continues into La Amistad, an international biosphere reserve which Costa Rica shares with Panama. Las Nubes thus forms part of one of the largest contiguous rainforest ecosystems in Central America.

The Río Peñas Blancas is the main river flowing through Las Nubes with its crystal-clear water cascading over rapids and waterfalls. Several deep gorges dissect Las Nubes, each presumably characterized by endemic species. Downstream is Los Cusingos, a lowland wet forest at approximately 700 m in the middle portion of the river basin. This is the former homestead of the world-renowned ornithologist Dr. Alexander Skutch. The Tropical Science Center now owns and protects Los Cusingos as a Neotropical bird sanctuary.

The Central American Commission on Environment and Development officially recognized this watershed as a portion of the Mesoamerican Biological Corridor that extends from Panama through Mexico. The Los Cusingos—Las Nubes Corridor is particularly significant in ecological terms because it connects forest fragments from the highest elevations to those nearer the Pacific coast, whereas most of the Mesoamerican Corridor connects fragments primarily at higher elevations. The significance of the highland—lowland connection is that the dryer lowlands forests are the most threatened ecosystems in Central America.

3 Development of the biological corridor

The corridor consists of forest patches of various sizes, ages and species composition; agricultural fields (primarily coffee and sugarcane); pastures; and degraded lands. There are several critical elements of the plan for the development of the corridor, the protection of its biological resources, and the sustainable development of its rural communities: (1) The transition from sun grown coffee to more ecologically sound production as a means toward stabilizing hydrological resources, enriching the soil, reducing soil erosion, and increasing biodiversity, particularly of resident tropical birds and Neotropical migrants and of the arthropod fauna essential for soil structure. The incentive for farmers to adopt a transition strategy is provided through a local cooperative of growers who sell certified sustainable coffee to Timothy's World Coffee, which is then marketed throughout Canada. (2) The creation of a model shade and organic coffee farm, "El Grano Tico," for demonstration of certifiably sustainable production practices. This is jointly financed by COOPEAGRI and the Fisher Fund for Neotropical Research and Conservation. Volunteer students from York University, working in collaboration with local coffee farmers, built the first nursery for trees identified as the most appropriate species for shade coffee, economic productivity and ecological sustainability. (3) The restoration of riverine forest to act as a hydrological corridor as well as a biological corridor. (4) The transition from degraded pasture lands to reforested land and agroforestry systems. The tree nurseries will ultimately provide the plants for reforestation of degraded pastures. However, considerable outreach and extension must be done to involve local cattle ranchers to participate in restoration efforts. (5) The transition to improved pastures, including the use of improved pasture grasses and partial tree cover. (6) Reforestation of degraded (non-pasture) lands, largely for regeneration of water resources and for erosion control. These lands consist of abandoned subsistence farms, sugar cane plantations, and coffee-eucalyptus plantations. (7) Future land acquisition through direct purchase of forest lands and other critical ecosystems within the Corridor. This is an attractive component of the strategic development plan jointly being implemented by TSC and FES. York University owns the Las Nubes Rainforest in the upper reaches of the watershed, Tropical Science Center owns the Los Cusingos Sanctuary in the lower portion. A program to purchase additional land would strengthen the long-range sustainability of the Biological Corridor by removing certain lands from potential threat. (8) Municipal provision of public lands to NGOs for forest protection and regeneration. One such example is the "Parque Natural" on the lower Río Peñas Blancas that is leased to TSC and managed by a local community group--COCOFORES--for restoration and environmental education activities. (9) Participation of local community groups in small business activities. A women's cooperative at Reserva San Luís in the Monteverde Biological Corridor, for example, is making bamboo furniture and paper products from bamboo wastes. A similar cooperative could be established in the Los Cusingos—Las Nubes Corridor for the manufacture of paper products from the wastes of coffee, banana, bamboo and sugar cane production. Organic fertilizers for coffee fields and home gardens could also be made from these waste products. There are numerous NWFPs that have potential market value. (10) The construction of a community environmental center (with library, laboratory and computer facilities) will serve as the focal point for joint research projects and for outreach and training activities.

4 Green consumerism

There have been numerous attempts to market ecologically certified products from the tropics, such as timber, coffee, cacao, tea and others [2]. The consensus, however, is that the pressures of commercial logging and deforestation for agriculture and pastures are of such a scale that the marketing of sustainable timber and agricultural products cannot prevent the loss of biodiversity on a large scale. Nevertheless, the opportunity remains to capitalize on green products to protect local and even regional biodiversity. In fact, regional landscape conservation—based on a mix of protected areas, buffer zones, sustainable forestry and agriculture, and international marketing—may offer the best hope for protection of biodiversity in some tropical areas, including southern Costa Rica. Furthermore the quality of the agroecological matrix in a tropical montane landscape is an important determinant of the maintenance of biodiversity—quite apart from the capacity of the landscape to produce certifiably "green" products.

Much of the coffee produced within the Los Cusingos—Las Nubes Corridor is "technified" sun-grown coffee that is produced with little to no shade cover, a high density of coffee plants, and significant inputs of agricultural chemicals (fertilizers, pesticides, herbicides and fungicides). Other coffee farms have varying amounts of shade cover provided by a small number of tree species, and a few follow traditional shade grown coffee production techniques.

A major objective of the research/development activities within the Los Cusingos—Las Nubes Corridor is to convert sun grown technified coffee to more traditional forms of shade grown organic production. The benefits from traditional production include erosion control, particularly on slope land susceptible to accelerated erosion; greater soil moisture retention; enriched soil fertility and improved soil structure through organic farming practices; and increased biodiversity, particularly of resident forest birds and Neotropical migrants [3]. An increase in the diversity and abundance of surface-dwelling beetles in more traditional forms of production has also been observed [4]. The species of ground-foraging ants was significantly higher in a landscape matrix of forest fragments and shade grown coffee than in one with forest fragments and technified coffee farms [5].

In spite of the natural values of shade grown, organic coffee, there has been a trend among many Latin American producers toward the technification of coffee production based on sun tolerant varieties, largely because of higher yields [6].

However, the world coffee market is saturated to the extent that many small producers are abandoning their coffee farms for other means of gaining a livelihood. Even larger producers are now leaving coffee unharvested because the cost of production and marketing exceeds the potential profit.

Small producers are better positioned to survive the currently saturated market by producing high quality shade grown organic coffee for the "boutique" or "specialty" coffee market in Europe and North America. The small farmers in the Corridor region of southern Costa Rica began to invest in the conservation practices associated with shade grown organic coffee, once guaranteed a fixed price for their product that will cover their investment and provide a wider profit margin.

The York University—Tropical Science Center project in the Corridor therefore has two thrusts: one is to aid the local farmer to convert to ecologically sound coffee production that can be certified as "sustainable," and the second is to secure a portion of the international market for the product.

A partnership between York University and Timothy's World Coffee provides the financial guarantee. The project supports the conversion from technified coffee to shade grown organic and farmers are guaranteed a price above current Fair Trade price for the sale of "Las Nubes Sustainable Coffee" throughout Canada. The remaining benefits are funneled into local community sustainability and to finance additional research and program activities.

Such a program is not likely to solve the problems of the loss of tropical biodiversity except at the local level. However, ecological production and green consumerism, together with other forms of alternative conservation practice and financing, will contribute toward saving tropical biota at the regional level. Furthermore, the successful marketing of green products yields other societal benefits such as forest protection, hydrological stabilization, and pollution reduction.

5 Financial incentives for conservation

Government payments to private landowners for the natural environmental services provided by forested ecosystems are a significant incentive for conservation. These services include carbon storage, erosion control, soil fertility, maintenance of water quality and quantity, and protection of biodiversity. Costa Rica has been a leader in developing such conservation grants. Administered by the environment ministry's National Fund for Forestry Financing (FONOFIFO), this is becoming an increasingly important mechanism for protecting forest land in Costa Rica. The Tropical Science Center, through its agreement to protect York University's Las Nubes Rainforest, receives an annual government payment from this program. Another objective of our project is to enlist a larger number of landowners within the corridor to participate. We anticipate considerable success from this effort since the maintenance of land under forest cover is now more profitable than conversion to coffee and other agricultural crops or pastures.

A "bold new approach" initiated by Conservation International, investment in "conservation concessions," is similar to the mechanism for the payment for environmental services. According to CI:

> conservation concessions provide a powerful way to expand the green market from its present dependence of products to the broader notion of green services—the opportunity to purchase biodiversity preservation directly [2].

Rather than leasing forested land in the tropics to logging and mining companies, governments and landowners lease land to conservationists at competitive prices. Contrary to popular opinion, conservation organizations can compete effectively with corporate users because of the relatively low costs. This system of conservation concessions contributes to biodiversity protection and sustainable development in several ways. As conceived by Hardner and Rice [2] the "New Green Market" has the following characteristics:

- It enables tropical countries to capitalize on their biological wealth and reduces their dependency on more volatile markets for timber and cash crops.
- It provides hard currency that pay government taxes and fees and that can be invested in part in local communities and social programs.
- It provides for the immediate protection of biodiversity of the leased forested land.
- It offers an investment opportunity for corporations wishing to promote a "greener" image.
- It is a potential conservation mechanism in areas where the establishment of national parks and other protected areas is problematical and/or more costly.
- It reduces risk by establishing ongoing economic incentives for continuing cooperation not susceptible to volatility and unpredictability.

6 The value of the biological corridor as a model

The Alexander Skutch Biological Corridor offers a possible model for the protection of tropical biodiversity within a framework of regional landscape conservation and rural sustainable development. It also represents a unique way to finance research and conservation efforts through land donation, private philanthropy, institutional collaboration, direct Costa Rican Government support through its payment for environmental services program, and indirect Canadian government support (in the form of research grants).

In summary, the objectives of this model are being achieved through:

- collaborative research and institutional capacity building
- private sector/university/cooperative partnership
- marketing of specialty "Las Nubes Sustainable Coffee" by a Canadian corporation

- reinvestment of profits from green products into research, improved farm efficiency, conservation practices, and in social services in local farm communities
- participation of local communities in landscape decision-making and small business
- promotion of a high quality agroecological matrix of mature forest fragments and productive sustainable farming systems which mimic natural systems.

The Faculty of Environmental Studies established The Fisher Fund for Neotropical Conservation to support joint research and conservation activities with the Tropical Science Center within the biological corridor encompassing the Las Nubes Biological Reserve and Los Cusingos Neotropical Bird Sanctuary. Both FES and TSC are committed to ecological protection and sustainable development through resource and information sharing, student and faculty research, and environmental education, local community involvement, and institutional capacity building. The success of the overall research and development program demonstrates the value of "partnership" in achieving conservation goals. It also illustrates a different approach to philanthropy and conservation in tropical environments that are so threatened by unwise economic development projects. It goes beyond the conventional way of thinking of conservation as "national parks" and "protected areas," explores new ways of problem-solving and international cooperation, encourages corporate social responsibility, and transforms traditional university thinking about social and environmental responsibilities.

References

[1] Bruner, A.G., Gullison, R.E. Rice, R.E., da Fonseca, G.A.B., Effectiveness of parks in protecting tropical biodiversity. *Science* **291**, pp. 125-128, 2001.

[2] Hardner, J. and Rice, .R., Rethinking green consumerism. *Scientific American* **286**, pp. 88-95, 2002.

[3] Znajda, S.K., Habitat conservation, avian diversity, and coffee agroecosystems in southern Costa Rica. MES Thesis, Faculty of Environmental Studies, York University, Toronto, 2000.

[4] Hall, S., Biodiversity Conservation in agroecosystems: a comparison of surface-dwelling beetle diversity in various shade coffee production systems in Costa Rica. MES Major Paper, Faculty of Environmental Studies, York University, Toronto, 2001.

[5] Perfecto, I. and Vandermeer, J., Quality of agroecological matrix in a tropical montane landscape: ants in coffee plantations in southern Mexico. *Conservation Biology* **16**, pp. 174-182, 2002.

[6] Moguel, P. and Toledo, V.M., 1999. Biodiversity conservation in traditional coffee systems of Mexico, *Conservation Biology* **13**, pp. 11-21.

Study of species changes under impact of the change in an ecological factor. Case study: the flood spreading project in Zanjan, Iran

F. B. Movahhed
Research Center of Agriculture and Natural Resources, Zanjan, Iran

Abstract

More than 90% of Iran is located in an arid and semi-arid area and water is one of the most important factors that can prevent sustainable development in all agricultural areas. Thus, water plays the important role in ecological condition changes, especially for plants. In this research, it was attempted to survey the water harvesting and its spreading impact on plant composition changes in a flood spreader. The study area is located in the part of the Zanjan plain, in the north-west of Zanjan city and between two rivers; Sorhain and Qarecharian, which includes rain fed and released lands that have been occupied by quaternary deposition. For this purpose, the amount of rainfall and diverted floodwater to the station was monitored and measured during the flooding period. In order to evaluate the plant composition changes in the three sites in spreading area and one in the control site, a total of 11 permanent transects (9 in spreading area and 2 as control) were stabilized using the Line Intercept Method, the canopy cover percentage of all species were noted and all species were distinguished. This study showed that some species under impact of floodwater spreading were omitted, some increased or decreased, and some new species were observed for the first time. The increase of vegetation cover and appearance of palatable plants in the last year showed that floodwater spreading can improve foliage production. Considering the life form of the observed species, although perennial forbs increased, floodwater spreading in the case of establishment of perennial grasses did not operate successfully. Therefore, the shortage of the studying period and changes in the amount of harvested floodwater make the correctness of these obtained results rather less valid.

Keywords: flood water spreading, life form, palatability, vegetation changes, Zanjan plain, Iran.

1 Introduction

Iran is a dry country and faces the problem of water shortages. The limited annual precipitation that falls during short and intense storms is mainly changed into floods. To overcome this problem, floodwater-spreading projects can be useful as one of the most suitable methods in most regions throughout the country. It was probably the first form of irrigation used by man. Its system consists of dams, dikes, ditches, or other means of diverting or collecting runoff from natural channels, and streams for spreading runoff from steep areas over adjacent flood plains (NRCS, 2002). This system allows infiltration of excess water with a minimum of control (Houston, [6]). The water that penetrates is then available for plant growth or deep percolation. The system has been applied effectively in some arid and semi-arid regions and used for improving forage quality and production on much of the dry and poor rangelands. Although range water spreaders are a well-known means of improving forage production, but compositional studies of changes that occur due to the practice are rare.

Kowsar (1987) has reported that barley yield was increased by 700 kg/ha under flood spreading system in Gharebayghan. Also the grazing capacity in this area has increased five times (Ebrahimi, [2]). There are a few reports on effect of flood spreading on plant composition. Perhaps the most detailed study of the effects of water spreading has been reported from Branson [1]. He indicated that herbage yield increased by an average of 160 percent. Total basal ground cover of vegetation increased in all parts of the system. The major compositional changes observed were a decrease in big sagebrush (*Artemisia tridentutu*) and plains prickly pear (*Opuntia pozyacantha*) and an increase in foxtail barley (*Hordeum jubatum*). In an intensive study of water spreading in New Mexico, Hubbell and Gardner [4] concluded that herbage yields were increased 4 to 9 times. The amount of increase was dependent on the duration of flooding. In studies conducted by Hubbard and Smoliak [5] increases in herbage production due to water spreading as high as 34 times were indicated.

This paper reports vegetation cover changes and composition on a water spreading system in a part of Zanjan plain in Iran from October 1998 to June 2003.

2 Materials and methods

The study area consists of a water spreader project within 250 ha with a diverted dam, a 2100 m transfer channel, a 2350 m transfer-spreading channel, and 15 spreading channels, located in north-west of Zanjan city, in the north-western part of Iran. This plain is located between two rivers of Sohrain and Gharecharian (Fig. 1). The most of the plain is under rain fed farming, fallow and abandoned lands. Dominant slope of plain varied between 2 and 5%. The plain has been occupied by quaternary deposition. The climate of the study area is Mediterranean, with hot summers and cold winters that are typical of the semi-arid area in Iran. Mean annual rainfall is about 297 mm and approximately 50 percent of the total precipitation falls during March to May with 15, 18.1 and

15.2% respectively. Mean annual temperature is 10.7°C with the mean maximum and minimum of 17.5 and 3.9°C respectively.

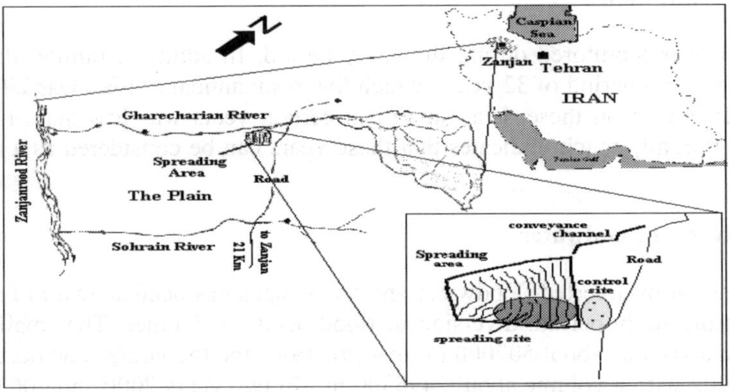

Figure 1: The location of study area.

The elevation of the study area is about 1800 m above sea level. The topsoil is loam with 10-20% gravel that changes with the depth to sandy loam with 40-50% gravel. The dominant species in this area are *Silen sp.*, *Ceratocarpus arenarius*, *Reseda lutea*, *Scariola orientalis*, *Carthamus lanatea*, and *Rosa persica* with some types of annual grasses.

The amount of diverted floodwater to the station was measured at all flooding times during five hydrological years from October 1998 to June 2003. Monitoring of vegetation changes was conducted in 11 transects (9 in spreading area and 2 in control area) by Line Intercept Method. The percentage of vegetation cover was measured and all of the species which intercepted the line, were identified and the percentage of canopy cover of each species were noted separately.

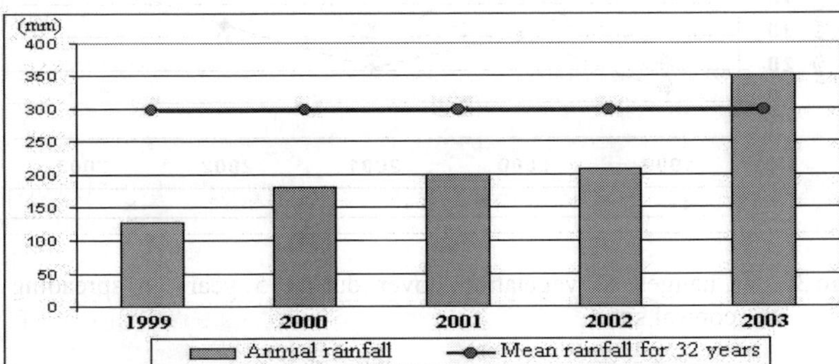

Figure 2: Annual rainfall during study period and mean rainfall of a period of 32 years.

3 Results

3.1 Precipitation

Rainfall was monitored during the study period. In addition, rainfall data was collected for a period of 32 years, which the mean annual rainfall was 297.1 mm (Fig. 2). Based on these data, rainfall in certain years was less than the mean annual rainfall, which, indicates that these years can be considered as a drought period.

3.2 Diverted floodwater

The amount of diverted floodwater and its changes has been shown in Figure 2. During the study period, diversion of flood occurred 5 times. The smallest one has had a volume about 507000 m^3 in April 1999 and the largest one occurred in May 2002 with a volume about 2496300 m^3. In two years 2000 and 2002, water diverting occurred along more than 30 days on April, so in these times the plants generally start to grow.

Table 1: Diverted floodwater data during study period.

Year	1999	2000	2001	2002	2003
Harvested water (1000m^3)	*507.6*	*2498*	*665*	*4500*	*7100*
Harvesting time (day)	*10*	*31*	*6*	*40*	*58*
Duration of Harvesting	*2-12 Apr.*	*25 Mar. – 24 Apr.*	*6-12 Apr.*	*2 Apr. – 12 May.*	*26 Mar. – 24 May*

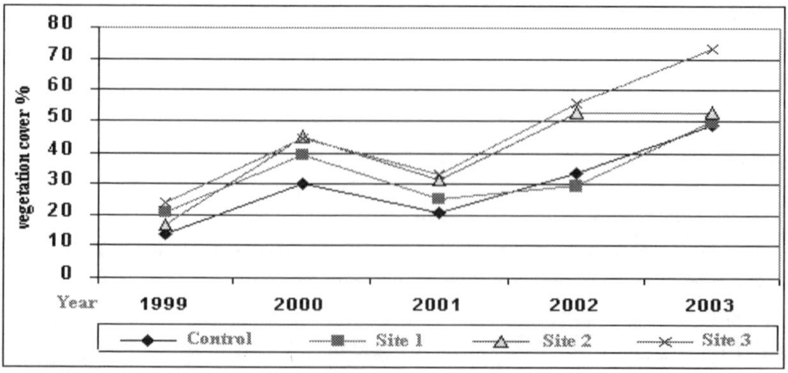

Figure 3: Changes of vegetation cover during 5 years in spreading and control sites.

3.3 Vegetation cover

The changes of vegetation cover during 5 years of study periods in three sites in spreading area and one site as control have been shown in Fig. 3. This figure shows that the vegetation cover changed with water spreading. On the other hand, more diverted floodwater causes more increase in vegetation cover. The mean vegetation cover in spreading area increased from 22 to 46% for 1999 and 2003, respectively.

3.4 Plant composition

3.4.1 Observed species changes

Total observed species in spreading area were 87 and plant diversity varied from 31 in 1999 to 65, 51, 59 and 60 for 2000 -2003 respectively. Whereas, in control area total observed species are 56 and have varied from 16 to 22, 29, 37 and 39 in these years (table 3). Some species observed only in 2000 and then omitted (e.g. *Poa bolbosa*), some of them gave positive response to water (e.g. *Carthamus lanatea, Henrardia persica,* and *Scariola orientalis*) and some of them gave negative response to water (e.g. *Silen sp., Nonea sp.,* and *Crambe orientalis*). Some species were increased from 1999 to 2003 (e.g. *Achillea sp., Centaurea virgata, and Eremopyrum bonaepartis*) and some of them decrease (e.g. *Reseda lutea, and Ceratocarpus arenarius*). The most striking vegetation changes on the spreader were a decrease in arial cover of *Silen sp.* and *Ceratocarpus arenarius* and an increase in *Eremopyrum bonaepartis.*

Table 2: Plant diversity, precipitation and harvested floodwater in spreading and control areas in 1999 – 2003.

	Location	*1999*	*2000*	*2001*	*2002*	*2003*
*No. of species**	Sprd[1]	31	65	51	59	60
	Cntl[2]	16	22	29	37	39
Precipitation (mm)		128.3	179.3	199.8	208	351
harvested floodwater (*1000 m^3)		507.6	2498	665	4500	7100

*1- spreading area, 2- control sites *: The number of observed species*

3.4.2 Species changes according to palatability

Due to plant palatability, there was not observed important change in site 1 for plant class 2 and only plant class 1 had a small increasing. This increasing was higher for site 2, specially in two last years and also, a small increasing on plant class 1 (Fig. 4). The observation of plants class 1 was the most important cases in site 3 and increasing of them in last year. In control site, the plants class 2 increased and nothing plant class 1 observed.

3.4.3 Species changes according to life form

According to life form of observed plants, only the one perennial shrub observed in spreading area and had small increasing from 0.46 to 1.09%. In the control site nothing of perennial shrub species was observed. Whereas in the spreading sites 35 perennial forbs species observed and total cover percentage of them changed from 5.9 to 22.6, in the control site observed perennial forbs were 26 and changed from 9.98 to 13.6%. Totally four perennial grasses were observed in the spreading sites and only 0.73 of cover in last year belong to them. But in the control site, this amount was 3.42% (Table 3).

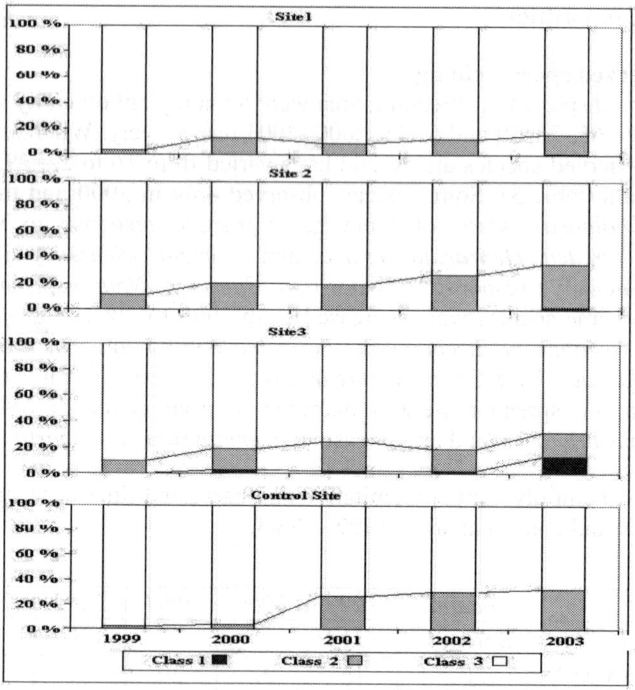

Figure 4: The cover percentage of observed species due to palatability.

4 Discussion

Based on the results obtained in this research, although the annual precipitation during 1999–2002 was about 30% less than the mean annual, but diverted floodwater and its spreading could prevent the effects of drought on vegetation.

This study also showed that floodwater harvesting caused to great changes in number of species and their cover in each year. Then, the species have shown different responses to presence of water as an environmental factor. In the other words, some of the plants response positively to increasing floodwater spreading and some of them showed negative reaction. This result, agrees with some part of Branson [1] finding that *Artemisia tridentata* and *Opuntia polyacantha* decreased and foxtail barley (*Hordeum jabatum*) increased in spreading area. The reason can be explained that remaining of water on the ground surface and saturation of soil and plant root zone for a long time can lead to welting, pale and falling of leaves and finally causes dying of sensitive plants (Kozlowski, 1974).

Table 3: Percentage of observed species cover due to life form.

Life form	**Species**	**Spreading**					**Control**				
		1999	***2000***	***2001***	***2002***	***2003***	***1999***	***2000***	***2001***	***2002***	***2003***
shrubs		0.47	0.86	1.16	1.53	1.10					
Total		**0.46**	**0.85**	**1.15**	**1.50**	**1.09**					
Perennial Forbs	*Achillea sp.*	0.08	0.48	1.04	1.87	1.69					0.2
	adonis			0.01	0.05					0.4	
	Anchusa sp.	0.01	0.10	0.05	0.01						
	Astragalus sp.		0.04	0.07	0.03	1.38				0.2	0.1
	Centaurea depressa	0.03	1.89	2.07	1.75	1.16		2.8	1.0	1.0	2.0
	Centaurea virgata	0.20	1.06	1.13	2.88	6.16	0.3	0.1	0.9	0.3	3.4
	Convolvulus arvensis	0.65	1.28	1.41	0.77	2.63	0.0	0.2	0.4	0.5	0.3
	Coronilla			0.01		1.83					
	Crambe orientalis	0.17	0.24	0.21	0.05	0.34	0.3		0.0	0.2	0.3
	Crepis sp.		0.07	0.00	0.24					0.1	
	Echinops sp.	0.24	0.01	0.63	0.16	2.04				0.0	0.2
	Euphorbia sp.	0.79	0.79	0.33	0.40	0.57	2.5	3.1	0.7	3.2	1.9
	Geranium		0.09	0.10				0.4			
	Gladiolus		0.18	0.22	0.18	0.09				0.1	0.2
	Haplophyllum	0.19	0.01			0.04	0.0	0.3			0.2
	Ixiolirion tataricum		0.01	0.09							
	lactuca					0.44					
	Linaria lineolata	0.05	0.04	0.03	0.03	0.08	0.4	0.3		0.5	1.0
	Linum	0.39	0.10	0.18	0.09	0.18			0.5	0.0	0.3
	Malabaila secacul		0.10	0.04	0.03	0.05					
	Medicago sativa	0.36	0.36		0.03	0.19				0.3	
	Noaea mucronata		0.06		0.02					0.2	
	Nonea sp.	0.28	0.03	0.09					0.2		0.4
	Onosma			0.08							
	Plantago lanceolata					0.06					
	Reseda lutea	1.75	1.20	0.51	0.52	0.27	6.1	4.2	0.5	0.9	1.4
	Sameraria sp.		0.11				0.1	2.4	0.1	0.3	
	Scorzonera sp.	0.10	0.22	0.25					0.1		
	Scrophularia ambros					1.64					
	Turgenia	0.20	4.74	2.53	2.07	1.01	0.3	1.7	0.4	0.1	0.9
	Allium		0.02	0.04	0.03				0.2		
	Hyoscyamus	0.02	0.01	0.10							
	Centaurea aucheri				0.51						0.5
	Cirsium sp.										0.5
	Onopordon sp.	0.38	0.08	0.37	0.06	0.25					
	Tragopogon sp.		0.21		0.30	0.49				0.2	
Total		**5.90**	**13.5**	**11.5**	**12.1**	**22.6**	**9.98**	**15.5**	**4.78**	**8.68**	**13.6**
Perennial Grass	Arrenetherum elatius					0.66					0.1
	Cynodon dactylon					0.04			1.7	3.2	3.3
	Poa bolbosa		0.02			0.03					
	Thevenotia persica		0.06	0.01							
Total			**0.08**	**0.01**		**0.73**			**1.68**	**3.19**	**3.42**
Annual Forb		**14.3**	**24.4**	**12.3**	**20.1**	**22.1**	**2.80**	**7.10**	**6.10**	**11.7**	**20.7**
Annual Grass		**0.21**	**3.79**	**4.06**	**12.2**	**10.2**	**1.16**	**7.60**	**8.74**	**9.82**	**14.2**

The increasing of the vegetation cover and appearance of palatable plants in last year showed that the floodwater spreading could improve the foliage production for livestock and their grazing capacity in such areas. This result, agrees with Hubbell and Gardner [4], Branson [1], Houston [6] findings and some reports from Iran (i.e. Ghaemi [3]; Shafie and Mollaee [11]). Considering to life form of observed species, although perennial forbs increased, but the floodwater spreading in the case of establishment of perennial grasses did not operate successfully.

As a result, it requested a long period for valid evaluating of the trend of vegetation changes under changes on this environmental factor toward improving of range vegetation via increasing of desirable plants (e.g. *Latyrus sp.*, *Vicia sp.* and *Astragalus sp.*) and reduction of the non desirable one. Therefore, shortage of studying period and changes on amount of harvested floodwater make correctitude of these obtained results rather less valid. Nevertheless, floodwater spreading has created a specific ecosystem that causes to improvement of environmental conditions in this region, so, it plays an important role for agricultural sustainable development and wild life.

References

[1] Branson, F. A., 1956, Range forage production changes on a water spreader in southeastern Montana, J. Range Manage., 9: 187-191.

[2] Ebrahimi, F. 1987, Work reporting, Natural Resources Fars Province.

[3] Ghaemi, M.T., 2003, the survey of aquifer management on trend and range vegetation changes in Poldasht, W. Azarbayjan, Iran, proceeding of third conference on aquifer management, Tehran, p. 181-191.

[4] Hubbell, D.S., and J.L. Gardner, 1944. Some edaphic and ecological effects of water spreading on range lands. Ecology, 25: 27-44.

[5] Hubbard, W.A. and S. Smoliak. 1953, Effect of Contour Dykes and Furrows on Short-Grass Prairie. Jour. Range Manag. 6: 55-62.

[6] Houston, W. R., 1960, Effect of water spreading on range vegetation on eastern Montana, Jour. Range Mange., 13: 289-293.

[7] Kowsar, S. A., 1995, An introduction to flood mitigation and optimization of floodwater utilization, Research Institute of Forests and Rangelands, No. 150, p. 522.

[8] Kozlowski, T.T. 1976, Water supply and leaf shedding. p. 191-231. In T.T. Kozlowski (ed.) Water deficits and plant growth, Vol. IV, Soil water measurement, plant responses, and breeding for drought resistance. Academic Press, New York.

[9] Natural Resources Conservation Service, 2002, Conservation Practice Standard for Water spreading, Washington D. C., P. 4.

[10] Pierson, R. K., 1955, Range Water Spreading as a Range Improvement Practice, Jour. Range Mangt, 8: 155-158.

[11] Shafiee, A. and A. Mollaee, 2003, Study of the impact of floodwater on vegetation in Ghachsaran, Iran, proceeding of 8th conference on irrigation and evaporating reduction, Kerman, p. 728-734.

Green roofs, storm water management, and biodiversity in Malmö, Sweden

A. Kruuse af Verchou
City of Malmö, Department of Public Works, Sweden

Abstract

The residential district Bo01 in Malmö, south Sweden, was built in the years 2000-2001 on former industrial land. Measures have been undertaken to counteract the negative impact of urban sprawl on the ecosystem. Houses are built close together to use the land efficiently. Still, it is a green district, thanks to two planning instruments, green space factor and green points, e.g. a majority of the buildings have green roofs. The greening of the area aims to present an attractive green surrounding for people, promote biodiversity, and minimise storm water run-off. Storm water is managed in an open system which includes ponds with native vegetation. The green space factor means that different types of surfaces are given different credits. Plant beds, climbing plants, green roofs, and ponds are given high credits. No credit is given to sealed surfaces. The green points include for example: a bird nesting box for each apartment, a courtyard containing at least 50 Swedish wild flower species, food for birds all year round in the yard. In the parks, semi-natural biotopes have been built comprising meadow, oak and beech woodland, and alder carr. The soil and the species composition of grasses, wild flowers, bushes and trees conform as far as possible with their natural counterparts. Before the area was developed, sea birds such as avocet and terns, nested on the old industrial sites. A compensation biotope for birds will be created in the northern harbour of Malmö. Studies show that the inhabitants are very satisfied with the quality of the parks and gardens. Biodiversity is lower than in a similar, but older residential district that has been used as a comparison. Biodiversity is expected to increase with time.
Keywords: urban, biodiversity, green roof, storm water management, biotope, habitat.

www.witpress.com, ISSN 1743-3541 (on-line)

1 Introduction

1.1 The residential district Bo01

The residential district Bo01 in Malmö, south Sweden, was built in the years 2000-2001 on former industrial land (fig. 1). The land is a landfill in the sea, Öresund (fig. 2).

The housing area has been built with focus on ecological sustainability, for example 100% locally renewable energy serves the area. Measures have been undertaken to counteract the negative impact of urban sprawl on the ecosystem. Houses are built close together to use the land efficiently (fig. 2). Still, it is a green district, thanks to two planning instruments, green space factor and green points, e.g. a majority of the buildings have green roofs. The greening of the area aims to present an attractive, green, healthy surrounding for people, promote biodiversity, and minimise storm water run-off. Storm water is managed in an open system which includes ponds with native vegetation.

1.2 Green environment is healthy environment

During the last decades research has shown that parks and nature can have an astonishing effect on people's health [1, 2]. The view through the hospital window effects the recovery after surgery: patients with a view over a park recovered significantly faster than patients with a view over a naked wall [1]. Stress recovery during exposure to natural environments, measured as i.e. blood pressure, happens within 4-6 minutes, while exposure to urban environments gives no recovery at all [2]. Children in day care centres with good admission to green areas are healthier, play better, and are more capable to concentrate than children with low admission to green areas [3]. Elderly people with a high demand of care are more active and less care demanding if they regularly visit parks than if they don't [4].

1.3 Green space factor

To achieve a certain amount of green space on the yards and to minimise the sealed areas, a green space factor is used. The green space factor means that different types of surfaces are given different credits. No credit is given to sealed surfaces. Low credits are given to unsealed but not green areas. Plant beds, climbing plants, green roofs, and ponds are given high credits. The use of green space factor has led to that almost all houses have at least one part with green roof. The green roofs are exclusively moss-sedum carpets, by far the most common type of green roof in Sweden. Most yards are very green, with trees, bushes and perennial herbs, and they all have a pond. In some of the yards there are biotopes with high qualities in terms of biodiversity, for example a sea shore meadow (fig. 3), and a pond (fig. 4). The green space factor is borrowed from Germany, where a similar system is used in Berlin and Hamburg.

Figure 1: Malmö is the third largest city in Sweden with 265,000 inhabitants.

Figure 2: An aerial picture of the housing district Bo01.

Figure 3: An artificial sea-shore meadow in one of the yards at Bo01.

1.4 Green points

On every yard the developer was to realise 10 out of 35 green points. The green points include for example:

- a bird nesting box for each apartment
- courtyard containing at least 50 Swedish wild flower species
- food for birds all year round on the yard
- bat boxes for each plot
- courtyard containing traditional cottage garden with various sections
- part of the courtyard left to grow by natural succession
- a habitat constructed for a specific insect group
- all unsealed areas in the courtyard has deep and good enough soil to allow vegetable cultivation
- courtyard consists of habitats that has regional nature as an example
- at least half the yard is covered by water
- all trees on the yard are fruit trees, and all bushes carry berries

1.5 Habitats in the parks

There are two parks in the area, Ankarparken and Daniaparken. In both of them, semi-natural biotopes have been built where the soil and the species composition of grasses, wild flowers, bushes and trees conform as far as possible with their natural counterparts. In Ankarparken, a beech woodland, an oak woodland and an alder carr are surrounded by maintained grass areas. The vegetation in these biotopes has been planted, not sown. A saltwater canal in which macro algae, fish and other creatures have been introduced, is also included in the park. Salt water is pumped into the canal from the sea, Öresund. In Daniaparken, a part of the grass area has been sown with typical Swedish meadow plants.

Figure 4: A pond with regional wetland vegetation in a yard at Bo01. In the background a green roof.

1.6 Replacement habitat for birds

Before this brown-field area was developed, sea birds such as avocet, little tern and common tern nested in the old industrial sites. Brown-fields of harbours, old industrial areas and marshalling yards often contain a species-rich fauna and flora. Work is under way in Malmö harbour on the creation of a replacement habitat similar to the one which disappeared.

1.7 Storm water management

Storm water in the Bo01 area is managed in an open system, with miniature canals and ponds in the courtyards, squares and streets. Most ponds have natural wetland vegetation, and increase the diversity of biotopes in the yards and in the streets. Green roofs and a high degree of green and unsealed areas aim to minimise the storm water run-off. Also the water quality should be improved by the high degree of infiltration, sedimentation and decomposition in the system.

Table 1: Number of breeding bird couples in Bo10 and Ön in the years 2002 and 2003.

	2002		2003	
Species	Bo01	Ön	Bo01	Ön
Larus canus	1	4-5	8-10	5-6
Passer domesticus	-	1-2	-	2-3
Anas platyrhynchos	0-3	-	1-3	1-3
Delichon urbica	-	12	-	13
Carduelis cannabina	-	1-3	-	3
Turdus merula	1	5-6	2-3	4-5
Hirundo rustica	-	-	-	2-3
Passer montanus	-	-	1	1
Columba palmumbus	1	4-5	1	1
Pica pica	1	1	1	1
Mergus serrator	0-1	-	-	1
Sturnus vulgaris	-	7-9	-	6-8
Oenanthe oenanthe	-	1	-	1
Haematopus ostralegus	-	-	1-2	1-2
Phoenicurus ochruros	-	4-5	-	3-4
Motacilla alba	2	1-2	3-4	4-5
Parus major	2	2	2-3	2-3
Apus apus	-	2	-	2-3
Sylvia communis	-	-	-	1
Sylvia curruca	-	-	-	1
Total number of breeding species	6-8	13-14	9	20
Total number of breeding couples	9-13	43-52	20-28	55-68

2 Evaluation

2.1 Biodiversity

Bird surveys quantify the diversity within this organism group, but abundance and breeding of birds may also be an indicator of biodiversity in a broader sense. A large abundance of birds indicates good food abundance – i.e. insects, other small animals, plant seeds and fruits. Good breeding by different bird species indicate a varied range of breeding places and/or habitats. Factors like the age of the area and human activities of course also effect the behaviour of the birds.

During 2002 and 2003 bird surveys have been performed in Bo01 and in another seaside residential area of approximately the same size in Malmö called Ön. The last construction work in Ön was completed five years earlier than in Bo01. Both years' species number and number of individuals are about twice as large in Ön as in Bo01 (table 1).

In Sweden there are 16 species of bats, of which at least eight have been found in Malmö. They eat flying insects, and prefer to hunt close to water where the abundance of food is high. Bats are good indicators of biodiversity of flying insects. Bo01 with all its ponds could be a good area for bats, especially behind the sheltering houses closest to the sea. Bat boxes have been placed in some of the yards. During the bat survey 2003, however, only one individual of the bat species *Pipistrellus pygmaeus* was found. In Ön, several hunting individuals of *Nyctalus noctula* were found, but were not regarded as nesting there.

In the park biotopes of Ankarparken, vegetation analyses have been performed once or twice a year during 2001 to 2003. The analyses show that the forest flora of the beech and oak woodlands has decreased in both species number and individuals. Simultaneously, a large number of weeds have colonised the biotopes. In the oak woodland a total of 152 species have been noted, of which only 22 were planted originally. In the alder carr, the more humid areas still hold much of its planted wetland flora, while the drier parts are colonised by weeds. In the meadow of Daniaparken, several of the meadow species that were sown in 2002 could not be found in 2003, and several could only be found in small amounts.

In the saltwater canal that goes alongside Ankarparken, algae, flowering plants and animals were introduced during 2001. In 2003 the flowering plants *Zostera marina*, *Ruppia cirrhosa*, *Potamogeton pectinatus* and *Zannichellia sp.*, had expanded in the sandy areas. The alga *Chorda filum* had disappeared, and the large plants of *Fucus vesiculosus* had died, but small individuals and spontaneously colonised individuals expand. Introduced creatures like e.g. *Gammarus sp.*, *Idothea sp.*, *Mytilus edulis*, *Theodoxus fluviatilis*, *Nereis diversicolor*, and *Gasterosteus aculeatus* have all increased in numbers. Filamentous algae of *Chlorophyta* and *Rhodophyta* have colonised spontaneously.

Vegetation analyses have been performed during 2001–2003 in five storm water ponds. The vegetation was introduced into them in the form of large, established plants wrapped up with their substrate in coconut fibre net. Throughout the investigation period, the vegetation has been rather constant, and is completely dominated by the planted species with a very small number of weeds.

2.2 Human values

In 2002 a questionnaire was sent to 210 inhabitants of Bo01, of which 142 answered. On the question if you did not agree at all (1) to if you agreed completely (5) with the statement that the own courtyard was attractive, the mean answer was 4,1. On the question if you were very unsatisfied (1) to very satisfied (5) with the quality and size of the parks and green areas, the mean answer was 4,4. A question if the open storm water system was good and safe was answered by the mean value 3,2.

A qualitative assessment of the courtyards showed that they are in many ways well designed. They were given high values for qualities like a well defined room, it is well managed and looks fresh, that it has development potentials and that there is shelter from the wind in the yard. Less high values were given for qualities like children can play in the yard, there is space for sitting down in the yard and it gives a green/lush impression. Low values are given for qualities like varied plant material, diversity of cultural plants, many insects in the yard, and the yard offers a lot of experiences.

In an interview, some of the Bo01 landscape architects expressed a certain dislike of the green space factor and the green points. But still they believed that their work with these planning instruments had given them an insight in the importance of the courtyard for sustainable development. They also thought they would bring this new insight into future projects.

3 Discussion

Number of bird and bat species was not as high as expected in Bo01, and in the case of the birds much lower than in the reference area. Two years is a very short time when dealing with biodiversity, and number of species in Bo01 is expected to increase in the future. The last buildings were completed several years earlier in the reference area as compared to Bo01, trees and bushes have grown larger and the vegetation has had time to establish, which can explain some of the difference. But even regarding these circumstances there are some problems in the green concept of Bo01. First, there are no areas left (except in the canal) for spontaneous plant colonisation. In the reference area, Ön, a non maintained grass area with high herbs and grasses and wild roses host several of the bird species that are not present at the Bo01 site. Second, the construction of biotopes that mimic nature is still a rather new topic in Sweden although there is some experience. More research and full-scale trials are needed to refine this art. Also the management of such biotopes needs more competence. Third, the ambition of the landscape architects of the yards and parks varied. Some had a large interest in biodiversity and therefore high ambitions, while others have given the green areas a conventional design.

Still, the focus on the outdoor environment in the planning stage has made Bo01 a green, lush area that is highly appreciated by its inhabitants. And, maybe most important, the green concept of Bo01 is a large and very important step towards seriously including biodiversity in city planning. The experience from Bo01 will be very important in the future, and will be carried by the people involved in the project as well as thousands of professional visitors from all over the world.

References

[1] Ulrich, R.S. View through a window may influence recovery from surgery. Science, Vol 224, pp 420-421, 1984.

[2] Ulrich, R.S., Simons, R.F., Losito, B.D., Fiorito, E., Miles, M.A. & Zelson, M. Stress recovery during exposure to natural and urban environments. Journal of environmental psychology, 11. 1991.
[3] Grahn, P., Mårtensson, F., Lindblad, B., Nilsson, P. & Ekman, A. Ute på dagis. Stad och Land 145, pp 1-101, 1997. (in Swedish)
[4] Ottosson, J. and Grahn, P. Utemiljöns betydelse för äldre med stort vårdbehov. Stad och Land 155, pp10-39. 1998. (in Swedish)

Section 6
Sustainability development studies

Collaboration for Local Agenda 21 implementation: a case-study of the Basque Country

I. Aguado[1], J. M. Barrutia[2] & C. Echebarria[1]
[1]*Department of Applied Economics V, University of the Basque Country, Spain*
[2]*Department of Financial Economics II, University of the Basque Country, Spain*

Abstract

A consensus exists regarding the idea that Local Agenda 21 (LA21) is a key tool for implementing a set of sustainability policies at a local level. Consequently, in the search of local sustainable development, networking and collaborative approaches to Local Agenda 21 can help local authorities not only to save resources but also to share knowledge and best practices. This is our principal hypothesis and we want to verify it in a real case study: the Basque Country experience. In this sense, the Basque Government has recently launched two innovative projects: Udaltalde (Groups of Municipalities) and Udalsarea (Network of Municipalities). Thanks to them, numerous municipalities have initiated their Local Agenda 21 and are developing, and even introducing their Local Agenda Action Plan. Additionally, we want to test if these two institutional instruments can serve for assessing the progress on Local Agenda 21 in the Basque Autonomous Region.
Keywords: local sustainable development, Local Agenda 21, environmental policy, local government, partnerships, Basque Country, Spain, international agreements, network of municipalities.

1 Introduction

Increasing environmental awareness coupled with the growing ecological consciousness of many politicians has led in the last decade to the emergence of concepts such as greening the economy, empowerment, intergenerational equity and interregional solidarity. Concern about the relevance of introducing sustainability issues in all policies is likewise increasing. The European Commission has prepared its Sustainable Development Strategies and encouraged national governments to develop their own. This encouragement prompted the Basque Government to prepare in 2002 a sustainability strategy entitled "Basque Environmental and Sustainable Development Strategy 2002-2020".

Within this general framework of sustainability policies, local authorities emerged as the most suitable level of government to set up actions, not only because of their closeness to people, but also because of the ability of local managers and politicians to adapt organisations to new managerial atmospheres and social demands. Since its approval ten years ago at the Rio Summit as a chapter of the Agenda 21 Program, Local Agenda 21 (hereafter, LA21) has revealed itself to be one of the most powerful instruments for environmental, social and economic management at local scale (Houghton, [10]). In this sense, local authorities, as the level of governance closest to the people, were identified as a key agent for visioning and implementing "sustainability" (Krueger and Agyeman, [14]). However, LA21 still encounters serious difficulties when attempting to introduce its principles into the citizenship arena and these are usually focused on public institution actions that do not produce the required changes in the behaviour of citizens, enterprises or in the institutions themselves. Starting with the establishment of the LA21 framework, this article then introduces the study area with a description of the Basque region, where the number of LA21 processes has grown spectacularly during the last three years. In the following sections, we put forward our hypothesis and in the fifth section reports on the state of play of LA21 in the Basque Country, highlighting the innovative experiences of Udaltalde (grouping municipalities together to prepare their LA21 Action Plans) and Udalsarea (a network of Basque municipalities that have finished their Action Plans). In the last section, we discuss the positive and less positive results, as well as potential assets for the future emerging from the introduction by LA21 processes of new schemes of governance in the municipal world.

2 Local Agenda 21: a framework

There is a growing, albeit reluctant, recognition of the links between global processes and local practices in the sustainability framework (Hewitt, [9]). In this sphere, Local Agenda 21 is part of the process of achieving Sustainable Development at local and regional levels, taking the general principles of Agenda 21 and translating them into specific plans and actions for specific communities (Twyman, [21]; Mehta, [16]). Besides demanding a proactive response from the local government sector, it also requires a serious and visible commitment by the local citizenship (Hutchinson and Frances, [11], Echebarria et al., [5]). In this sense, a consensus exists about the urgent need for 'bottom-up' strategies and citizen empowerment for improving local quality of life

(Scott, [17]; McMahon, [15]). Furthermore, as Gibbs [8] points out "sustainability can only be built around value and institutional shifts in society".

Local Agenda 21 places major emphasis on participatory structures and social learning processes (Kelly and Moles, [12]) and for this reason Local Authorities try to direct their efforts to the creation of forums and consultation processes. The community has to be accountable for long-term consequences and understand the need for radically altered perceptions of what contributes to quality of life (Hutchinson and Frances, [11]). But these processes usually become mere informative actions and do not highlight the importance of decision-making by the local community itself. In the end, the local community has to meet its own needs; it should therefore decide which initiatives to develop, with Local authorities taking the role of facilitator (Kitchen, Whitney and Littlewood, 1997).

There is apparently broad concern about LA21 processes being individual and about the lack of a "recipe book" of actions or a common methodology for implementing LA21 (Sharp, [19]). Key actors in each municipality need to search for innovative and local solutions to their own existing problems. However, numerous methodological guides have been prepared by governments and international organizations; the most commonly used is the one proposed by ICLEI (Hewit, [9]), which considers LA21 a process based on the agreement of a philosophy for the future of a city and culminating in the application of an Action Plan. It should previously have provided a framework for achieving consensus among stakeholders, while effective participatory structures need to be developed to ensure consensus on Sustainable Development strategies (Foh Lee, [6]; Freeman et al, [7]; Steinberg and Sara, [20]).

Although a system of sustainability indicators can be used to assess progress, it is important to connect this with a more detailed program that shows the specific subjects of each Local Agenda 21 (Valentin and Spangenberg, [22]). Indicators provide local authorities with a tool that supports the development of LA21 as it measures performance and progress in a way that is less bureaucratic and more meaningful to communities (McMahon, [15]). Most of the efforts made by local authorities to "internalise" the LA21 process are channelled through local government training. LA21 could also be effectively facilitated through regional networks of LA21 officers who, by sharing information, contribute to program diffusion and self-learning (Barrett and Usui, 2002). Last but by no means least, the participative structures created within the framework of LA21 play an important part in the development of LA21.

3 Study area

Located in the north of Spain, on the south-western border of France, the Basque Country (BAC) comprises the provinces of Álava, Guipúzcoa and Vizcaya. The three provincial capitals are Vitoria-Gasteiz, Donostia-San Sebastián and Bilbao respectively. Population density in the BAC is high, the region's industry is solid and its GDP higher than the Spanish one. It has an unusual culture and an ancient language about whose origins linguists still disagree. After the 1980 Statute of

Autonomy, BAC assumed a significant degree of self-government in different fields such as health, education, culture, public order, trade, etc.

One result of this decentralization process is a marked political hierarchy, in which the public bodies are divided into four categories: 1) the Spanish Government; 2) the Basque Parliament (Basque Government); 3) the Provincial Councils (provincial government) and 4) Town and Local Councils (municipal government). Within local government, we frequently find that Town Councils are grouped into *Mancomunidades* (*Cuadrillas* in the case of Álava), particularly where town councils govern small populations, in order to provide some public services, such as the water supply, waste management, environmental activities, etc. This local structure achieves a significant relevance when LA21 is adopted because in many cases the leadership in the implementation of these projects is assumed by the *Mancomunidad* or *Cuadrilla*.

4 Hypothesis

LA21 is understood as a process more than a product. Sharing experiences and information can help municipalities to improve their performance and to broaden the scope of shared know-how. Thus a first hypothesis is that working together, as is the case of Udaltalde, enhances the sharing of resources for LA21 implementation with the subsequent savings of financial and technical resources and the promotion of learning processes among the local authorities involved. Local authorities have overall responsibility for implementing their LA21 and a collaborative approach leads to improved information transfers (Mehta, [16]) and best practice analysis and other interesting experiences (Barrett and Usui, [1]; Selman, [18]). Networking also allows local authorities to acquire greater political weight, accessing other kinds of funds and higher representation at other government levels. Our second hypothesis is that networking municipalities, as in the case of *Udalsarea,* are a tool for self-assessment and for that reason networking reinforces the municipalities' commitment to LA21, and provides a way of taking part in other projects at EU, national or regional level. The importance of co-operation between municipalities emphasizes the challenge to local politicians and officials to open up to other international collaborative network.

For testing our hypothesis, we have reviewed policy documents, government reports, local diagnosis, local action plans and have realized diverse interviews to person involved (one technician from IHOBE, two technician from the Department of Land Planning and Environment of the Basque Government, three technician from the Delegation of Guipúzcoa, one political charge from the Delegation of Vizcaya, and six persons in charge of LA21 within the municipalities of Mungia, Errenteria, Alonsotegi, and Vitoria-Gasteiz). These interviews allow us knowing the personal opinion of persons that are working in the processes of implementation of LA21. They were asked about which are the performances developed in the Institution and which are the strengths and weak points of this performances. Also, in the years 2001-2002 we sent a survey to the 64 municipalities that had signed the Aalborg Charter or the Basque Government

Commitment of Sustainable Development. This preliminary survey helps us to notice that the municipalities of Basque Country were in initial phases of LA21 thanks to questions as if they have defined Sustainability Indicators or if they had realized the diagnosis or the Action Plan. In most cases, the answers were negatives. However, things today have changed a lot as it can be seen in the numerous policy documents developed by local authorities.

5 Local Agenda 21: the state of play in the Basque Country

General Law 3/1998 for the Protection of the Environment in the Basque Country establishes the need for an Environmental Frame Program for achieving Sustainable Development. The principal outcome deriving from this Law was the approval of the "Basque Environmental Strategy for Sustainable Development 2002-2020". Although not legally binding, this document includes more than 200 commitments and the high-priority objectives of Basque environmental policy. One of the targets set by the Basque Sustainable Development Strategy was for all municipalities with more than 5,000 inhabitants in the BAC to have completed LA21 design by 2006. In June 2003, 63% of these municipalities were in this phase or had finished their LA21 Action Plan.

The first steps in this direction given by the Basque Government Land Planning and Environment Department, in collaboration with the public environmental management company IHOBE, S.A. and the Basque Association of Municipalities, EUDEL was the coordination of the *"Program for the promotion of LA21 in Basque municipalities (2000-2003)"* (Basque Government, 2000). Generally, we can include Basque Government initiatives in one of four phases: Information, Training and Education, LA21 Design and LA21 Implementation. In the first phase, they use two tools: firstly, a web page (www.inguremena.net), which gathers information about the real situation in municipalities, Udaltalde- and Udalsarea-related performances and other issues of interest, such as financial funds, LA21 and Sustainable Development documentation. Basque government also launched an annual order concerning aid for the introduction of LA21 in city councils. Awards under this scheme are based on the following criteria: number of inhabitants, the town or city council's own economic contribution, its record of environmental action plan implementation and the quality of the proposal presented. To opt for these annual aids, town and city councils have to present an LA21 Project for 2, 3 or 4 years and prove that they will invest at least an amount equal to the aid they are applying for.

The other tool is a free information telephone number for Town Councils. The educational phase focuses on two features: methodological guides (covering best practices, indicators, LA21 methodology, key documents from international agreements, etc.) and training courses for town council personnel. The design phase included the launch of the Udaltalde program, involving city councils, generally grouped into *Mancomunidades* which work together on LA21 development. This phase also establishes a municipality promotion program offering councils the possibility of a web page and of participating in a local

Sustainable Development initiatives award. The implementation phase uses a network of sustainable municipalities, called Udalsarea, for municipalities that have made most progress on LA21.

6 The projects of Udaltalde and Udalsarea

Udaltalde 21 (translated as groups of municipalities) and Udalsarea 21 (translated as municipality network) projects are clearly the most innovative LA21-related performances undertaken by the Basque Government (in partnership with public environment management company IHOBE and Basque municipality association EUDEL). The project kicks off with group implementation of LA21, using a common methodology and regular meetings to ensure the continuous exchange of information between municipalities in the same work group. Each group is coordinated by a supra-municipal body, usually a *Mancomunidad* or a Development Agency, but generally employs external LA21 consultants.

Begun in 2000, the pilot project included the municipalities of Llodio and Amurrio in Álava, Santurce, Erandio and Basauri in Vizcaya and Zarauz, Legazpi and Azkoitia and Azpeitia in Guipúzcoa. (These two municipalities work together and share an LA21 technician.) Three firms of consultants, Minuartia, Sayma and Ingurune, formed a UTE (temporary business alliance). A Training Course was given at the beginning of the Project, and other specific advisory courses followed in each municipality. Regular meetings were hold throughout the process. A citizen participation forum and an internal committee were set up. An environmental diagnosis was produced for each municipality, with the outlines of the diagnosis providing the basis for a series of targets and objectives. Once these objectives had been classified by priority, a list of performances was compiled in the Action Plan document. To measure progress, twenty common indicators were proposed to facilitate comparisons between municipalities; each municipality then established between five to ten individual indicators. The original target of all these municipalities finishing LA21 implementation, including the take off of the Action Plan, by 2001 soon proved impossible, which is why most municipalities have joined the new Udaltaldes.

Later, in 2002, new commitments were signed with other groups of town councils, but here the groups of municipalities are arranged by communities, on the understanding that proximity helps create more benefits, because of the greater similarity between the municipalities involved. Each new Udaltalde has a coordinating body that is often the *Mancomunidad* itself or a development agency from the zone. Through its public company IHOBE, the Basque Government Land Planning and Environment Department and the County Council of Guipúzcoa provide technical assistance. Town councils are committed to acquiring their own policy commitment and appointing a process technician. The coordinating body must supervise financial funds and describe performances on a web page.

Udalsarea consists in the creation of a sustainable network of municipalities involving the town and city council that have made most progress on LA21. The regional government's most recent LA21-related performance is the Basque Network of Municipalities for Sustainability, officially presented on 20 December 2002. Beginning with 16 municipalities, the network has added 21 town councils since then. This activity was important because it makes municipalities fulfil several requirements before joining. Local authorities are required to draw up an Action Plan, including strategic lines of performances and specific programs. In this network, the Basque Government works with the municipalities that have made most progress towards LA21. The network now includes municipalities from the Udaltalde Pilot Project and others such as Donostia-San Sebastián and Vitoria-Gasteiz. Municipalities also have to produce a diagnosis and set up a participation forum. A technical secretary from IHOBE, in charge of administrative and coordinating tasks, helps these town councils. Two commissions were also created, one involving the mayors of the towns and the other technical staff from municipalities and other institutions, including the Guipúzcoa provincial council and EUDEL (Association of Basque Municipalities).

7 Discussions

Judging by the largely environmentally-oriented diagnoses and by LA21 action plan performances, LA21 processes are definitely affected by environmental imbalance, particularly as only environmental departments are usually empowered for LA21-related issues. In our view, the main cause of the imbalance between social and economic and environmental issues in local authority policy is the tendency to assign LA21 staff to environmental departments. To reduce the imbalance and ensure the success of such processes, all municipal action needs to be implicated in decision-making, with ongoing feedback and permanent evaluation. LA21 should act as an umbrella for all a municipality's local environment, social and economic improvement programs to avoid the duplication of activities and confusion, save public resources and achieve synergies. With this objective in view, networking and collaborative activities stand out as particularly useful instruments. Udaltalde and Udalsarea projects launched to date in the Basque Country have undoubtedly propped up the initiative of developing LA21 in local authorities in the Basque Country.

In the Udaltalde programs, guidance given by environmental consultants and the regional government's technical assistant is very valuable. However, despite the fact that each municipality has its own particular social, economic and environmental features, working with private consultants made it quite clear how remarkably similar most municipalities are. Consultants often produce exactly the same diagnosis, with at the most a very few changes, and the design of the action plans for all their municipalities is virtually identical. A very few consultants share LA21 for all municipalities. For the town councils involved in the Udaltalde Pilot Program, the consultants were Ingurumena, Minuartia and Sayma. New Udaltaldes can choose their consultants, but they usually work with a very limited number. Diagnosis and the definition of indicators must be addressed within the specific local context.

The methodology followed in the *Udaltaldes* is very similar to the one proposed by ICLEI (Hewitt, 1995) and the Basque Government (2000). One new departure is the promotion of meetings between participating town councils, which permit greater levels of cooperation and information exchange, as well as the joint production of various indicators. Agreeing to hold regular meetings helps to ensure a deeper commitment and that town councils promoting LA21 do not let their plans, usually prepared by overworked technical staff in the environmental department, degenerate into mere showcases. Having an LA21 technician ensures that someone is responsible for keeping the process moving, although it can also mean that local authorities do not get involved in the process or act as leading players.

The preparation in the pilot project of two types of indicators showed that common indicators enable municipalities to share a methodology for calculating them and allow comparisons of environmental situations and their future evolution. Specific indicators for each municipality can deal with the specific features of each municipality. The pilot project, which worked with independent town councils rather than with *Mancomunidades*, did not achieve synergies when implementing LA21, though it did help these town councils greatly in promoting LA21. With this initiative, they enjoyed the benefits of working together, reducing costs and sharing motivations and means. In defining tasks for the different organizations involved (municipalities, Basque government and consultants), greater control is exercised over target compliance. The initiative also promotes the exchange of experiences and more fluent access to Basque Government information. Moreover, they obtain financial support of 20% of the cost, thanks to collaboration between IHOBE and EUDEL.

Being a member of Udalsarea is a prestige move for town councils and a good number of them are encouraging LA21 processes to be able to join. To date, 37 municipalities belong to Udalsarea; all were required to have finished designing their LA21 Action before being admitted. Udalsarea 21 aims to support the transmission of information and promote more uniform criteria for the design of LA21 design, while facilitating the creation of citizen participation channels. The three Basque provincial councils have joined Udalsarea.

Nevertheless, it is still too early to say whether Udaltalde and Udalsarea projects will be a success in the Basque Country. Progress to date indicates that more municipalities have joined the Campaign for Sustainable Cities and Towns and have started on LA21 processes. Also, major commitments by the provincial councils and the Basque Government have been forthcoming. There is still no sustainable indicator measurement that would allow us to evaluate long-term progress on LA21 but the first steps have been taken by getting all public stakeholders in the BAC together on acquiring such objectives under the LA21 remit. Private agents and local communities now need to become involved and more participative structures developed. IHOBE's leadership with the Basque Government Department of the Environment, in providing strategic direction and, especially, producing of Sustainable Development and LA21 indicators is seen as a relevant instrument for the future evaluation of LA21 in the Basque Country. But LA21 implantation clearly requires greater coordination between

Basque administrative levels, since there are virtually no common inter-administrative programs and very few between different departments at the same administrative level. Besides, LA21 budgets from regional government, delegations and most of the municipalities are small. Furthermore, the economic resources allocated by municipalities are often totally conditional on the aid they themselves receive, which may in fact be the main constraint to the development of LA21 in the region.

Acknowledgements

Financial support from grants 9/UPV 00032.321-15908/2004 (University of the Basque Country) and UNESCO03/05 (Cathedra UNESCO) is gratefully acknowledged.

References

[1] Barrett, B. & Usui, M., Local Agenda 21 in Japan: transforming local environmental governance. *Local Environment,* **7(1),** pp. 49-67, 2001.

[2] Basque Government. *Guía práctica para la implantación y desarrollo de la Agenda 21 Local en los municipios de Euskadi.* Departamento de Ordenación del Territorio, Vivienda y Medio Ambiente: Vitoria-Gasteiz, 2000.

[3] Basque Government. *Programa de promoción de las Agendas 21 Locales en los municipios vascos 2000-2003.* Ihobe y Departamento de Ordenación del Territorio, Vivienda y Medio Ambiente: Vitoria-Gasteiz, 2000b.

[4] Basque Government. Estrategia Ambiental Vasca de desarrollo sostenible. Departamento de Ordenación del Territorio, Vivienda y Medio Ambiente: Vitoria-Gasteiz, 2002.

[5] Echebarria, C., Barrutia, J.M. & Aguado, I., Local Agenda 21: progress in Spain. *European Urban and Regional Studies*, **11(3),** pp. 273-281, 2004.

[6] Foh Lee, K., Sustainable tourism destinations: the importance of cleaner production. Journal of Cleaner Production, **9,** pp. 313–323,, 2001.

[7] Freeman, C., Littlewood, S. & Whitney, D., Local Government and Emerging Models of Participation in the Local Agenda 21 Process. *Journal of Environmental Planning and Management,* **39(1),** pp. 65-78, 1996.

[8] Gibbs, D., Ecological modernisation, regional economic development and regional development agencies. *Geoforum,* **31(1),** pp. 9-19, 2000.

[9] Hewitt, N., *European Local Agenda 21 Planning Guide. How to engage in long-term environmental action planning towards sustainability*, ICLEI: Friburg.

[10] Houghton, J., Place and the implications of 'the local' for sustainability: an investigation of the Ugu District Municipality in South Africa. *Geoforum* [In Press, Corrected Proof]

[11] Hutchinson, A. & Frances, G., Bioregionalism regeneration modelling: a holistic approach to health through environmental management. *Environmental Management and Health,* **7(3),** pp. 37–40, 1996.
[12] Kelly, R. & Moles, R., Towards sustainable development in the mid-west region of Ireland. *Environmental Management and Health,* **11(5),** pp. 422-432, 2000.
[13] Kitchen, T., Whitney, D. & Littlewood, S., Local Authority/Academic Collaboration and the Local Agenda 21 Policy Process. *Journal of Environmental Planning and Management,* **40(5),** pp. 645-659, 1997.
[14] Krueger, R. & Agyeman, J., Sustainability schizophrenia or actually existing sustainabilities? toward a broader understanding of the politics and promise of local sustainability in the US. *Geoforum* [In Press, Corrected Proof].
[15] McMahon, S.K., The development of quality of life indicators -a case study from the City of Bristol UK. *Ecological Indicators*, **2,** pp. 177-185, 2002.
[16] Mehta, P., Local Agenda 21: Practical Experiences and Emerging Issues from the South. *Environmental Impact Assessment Review,* **16(4),** pp. 309-320, 1996.
[17] Scott, A., Assessing Public Perception of Landscape: the LANDMAP experience. *Landscape Research,* **27(3),** pp. 271–295, 2002.
[18] Selman, P. (1998). Local Agenda 21: substance or spin? Journal of Environmental Planning and Management, 41(5), 533-54.
[19] Sharp, E., Local State of the Environment Reporting: lessons from Experience in Britain and Canada. *Planning Practice & Research,* **13(1),** pp. 81- 89, 1998.
[20] Steinberg, F. & Sara, L.M., The Peru Urban Management Education Programme (PEGUP) linking capacity building with local realities. *Habitat International*, **24**, pp. 417-431, 2000.
[21] Twyman, C., Rethinking community resource management: managing resources or managing people in western Botswana?. *Third World Quarterly*, **19(4)**, pp. 745- 770, 1998.
[22] Valentin, A.& Spangenberg, J.H., A guide to community sustainability indicators. *Environmental Impact Assessment Review*, **20**, pp. 381-392, 2000.

A conceptual approach to urban rejuvenation: a design intervention exercise in the historic silver triangle of Kuala Lumpur

S. S. Zubir & F. F. Silis
Faculty of Architecture, Planning & Surveying,
Universiti Teknologi MARA, Shah Alam, Malaysia

Abstract

The adaptive reuse of buildings and urban neighbourhoods are common in developed countries that have a long history of urbanization. This emerging trend of urban regeneration, which promotes tourism, is becoming an urgent agenda for many colonial cities in developing countries. The aim of this paper is to highlight an idea generated from our urban design studio that is based on the synoptic method so as rational strategies could be realized and transformed into design intervention. The crux of the design revolves around the idea of a return to historicism which could be summed up into the following 4 narratives of: - "redimere" vs. the voiceless genius loci; stabilitas loci vs. dynamics of change; reinterpretation of dialectics vs. IT as a faceless tool; and imago mundi vs. the language of money. The project aims at transforming the once active neighbourhood of Kuala Lumpur to become a vibrant mixed used colony of artisan, residential and other activities that are deemed appropriate for the vicinity. Primarily, the task is to project the area into a cultural enclave where unused shop houses, factories and warehouses are converted into galleries and lofts for artists and eventually establish the city as an art/cultural centre of the region.
Keywords: rejuvenation, morphology, metaphor, narrative, genius loci, intervention, historicism, development, heritage, built form.

1 Introduction

Urban rejuvenation is commonly an accepted norm in ensuring a sustainable future of historic cities in the developed countries particularly for its role in promoting urban tourism development (see Ashworth and Turnbidge [1], Prentice [2], Ashworth and Larkham [3], Morris [4], Herbert [5]). The case seems to be different in Malaysia where rapid urban developments have witnessed the decline in maintaining the overall quality of the built environment of the historic cities. Modern developments have transformed historic districts into fragmented building blocks that disregard the unique townscape of the historic centres. Sites of dilapidated buildings have been the target for new buildings and often are mediocre in design and failed to respond to the sense of place and the surrounding context. Only recently due to pressures from non-governmental agencies and society at large regarding the need to preserve the charm and character of historic districts have been an important agenda in new urban intervention projects. Nevertheless, due to the lack of legislative framework, new urban interventions are susceptible to further the degradation of the built form particularly buildings that are not protected by the Antiquities Act. Except for the new administrative capital city of Putrajaya, all other cities in Malaysia have no urban design guidance. The existing local plans for districts in the cities are inadequate to control new development or intervention in historic districts. The existing planning policies and development intensities that are based on plot-ratios are inadequate to controls development especially in maintaining the historic character of the place. Furthermore due to the repeal of the rent control act in many historical districts have exacerbated the situation due to the fact that the majority of the historical enclaves are strategically within the central business districts.

In order to protect our historic centres of becoming a complex switchboard of plug-in zones (Boyer [6]), the relevant government agencies must have a long term commitment and policies to preserving and maintaining the cities' cultural and historic identities, and at the same time able to accommodate the inevitable transition, growth and new uses. A comprehensive approach is urgently needed in handling new intervention projects in historic centres. As in the case of this paper, we believe that by adopting Rossi's idea that the "soul of the city" [7] resides in the history of the place and once the soul is given form, it becomes the sign of a place. As mentions by Durrell [8], "…you begin to realize that the important determinant of any culture is after all the spirit of place". Therefore, memory becomes the guide to the structure of the city and it is our task to critically reinterpret this sedimentary base of meaning where rejuvenation is the intervening tool for sustaining the history of the place.

In the broad field of historic preservation and adaptive reuse of buildings, there are many terms used interchangeably to describe urban rejuvenation. Nonetheless, the meaning is far more complicated than the synonyms used and lately, it has opened up for new avenues for urban interventions (Schittich [9]). Community participation is one of the important approaches to generate new/converted urban spaces and structures that satisfy the needs that benefits end users. Urban rejuvenation projects are not necessarily generated from the undeniable consideration to preserve historical continuity by establishing a balance symbiosis of the built heritage, culture, economy and technology. However, all of the commonly used "re" words – restore, rehabilitate recycle, remodel and so forth fall within the realm of the "change" category and some of the approaches have been reduced in meaning. Ashworth [10] introduces the terms "eradification" and "museumification" to denote the changes experienced in the European manipulation processes of built heritage.

The paper begins with an introduction to the project followed by a brief account of the study area highlighting key issues for urban intervention and elaborating the generated urban narratives. In any design problems, it is generally true that a number of alternative solutions appear possible, are not always explicit and sometimes no conclusion is entirely objective. It is not possible to delineate the contextual analysis in detail and it is hope that by a brief deliberation of design issues of the context would provide adequate information to support the narratives.

2 The project

The rejuvenation of one of the historic district in the city centre of Kuala Lumpur was an academic exercise to expose fifth year students of architecture at the Universiti Teknologi MARA with the appropriate techniques in solving urban design problems. The general idea of the project is that the interpretation of history cannot be discarded totally as it can generate innovative schemes that might be responsive to the context. By reviewing selected readings diachronically and synchronically, will enable students to enter into the dialogue as an auto critique of the city. These relationships start with the urban as the everyday and the lived, from which we must construct our utopias so as to clarify the possible/impossible, non fixed ideas and projects which are representational of the ever changing conjunctures and structures of the city. Understanding is not however closed or exhausted by analysis alone; there is always an opening for intuition.

Students are emphasized to conceptualize the city as a dynamic phenomenon, stressing dialectical movements, complexity, conflicts and contradictions. Concepts should be eminently applied openly and non-teleological dialectics should also be inherent in their thinking process for the fact that transformation and transposition thinking takes place in cities are evidently related with the wider context of the world.

From a number of schemes generated by students, the approach that emphasized a return to the *genius* of place seems to be the evocative solution for the urban context. In the urban design process, many alternative solutions have been realized. Based on Darwin's "survival of the fittest", many of the ideas were rejected leaving behind a collage of ideas as urban narratives to be translated into workable solutions in the design scheme.

2.1 Design process

The crux of this project was to expose students to the anatomy of judgment that was based on a synoptic method of urban/architectural analysis of criticism where operations, instruments and task play an integral part. In reviewing the students' works, the investigation of the three levels of evaluative criteria are taken into considerations i.e. the descriptive, the interpretative and the judging. In the process of evaluating the projects, questions such as how do we experience? How do we think? How do we respond? - will progressively evolved. In addition, communication analysis such as the study of ideologies, values, aesthetics, historical and contemporary expressive systems, ornament, form, reference, typological classifications are also considered. In a way, these criteria are reflected in the students' design process: to nurture and expand the creative mind required for judgment.

Although, we consider the use of urban morphology as the preferred method of analysis which investigates the dynamic of both the physical and spatial components of urban form, it requires further reinterpretation of the approach that includes modification and transformation of both the newly created as well as the context at where they are built. In the past, significant criticisms have been leveled against this study approach pointing out that it was of limited use as it only describes and explains historical phenomena but could not prescribe future design of the place. This might be true during its inception stage but in the last few decades or so, this approach has found a firm ground in urban design research and practice. (see Krier [11], Rossi [12], Vidler [13], Rowe and Koetter [14], Colquhoun [15]). The appropriate application from the study of urban morphology would be able to help in resolving contemporary urban design problems, especially in situations where there is a desire to rejuvenate a sense of place, both at the city and local urban scale. It is essential to note that the recognition of this approach does not provide an easy escape into historicism but will eventually provide architects and urban designers with a wider scope for operations in the creative reinterpretation and derivation of urban morphology.

2.2 Project objectives

Many have not realized that our lives are inundated with hierarchies of conceptual system, in terms of which we both think and act. These are fundamentally metaphorical in nature and when translated through our primary interpretive faculty, vision will generate representative drawings of the subject in mind. Therefore, these concepts that govern our thought and feeling are not just matters of the intellectual structure that we perceive, how we relate to people, and orientate ourselves in the environment. Our conceptual system thus plays an important role in defining everyday realities. If it is true to suggest that our conceptual system is largely metaphorical then the ways we think, experience and do things everyday are very much a matter of metaphor.

Metaphor is not just a matter of language or mere words (although it shares a common syntax with architecture) but in fact, the human conceptual system is metaphorically structured and defined. When metaphors are translated into architectural drawings then these become the conventional art of representing the ideas into workable solutions in terms of form, structure, space and so forth. We have been imbued with this mechanical operation of manual drawings for so long and that it is time to confront it. This practice from the conventional to the electronic media has taken place for quite sometime now and has become a prerequisite in the production of architectural drawings not only in architectural offices but also in schools of architecture.

Therefore, the ultimate aim of the project is for students to generate ways in which the existing built environment can be rejuvenated with their own innovative design. Since built heritage within the historic centre of the city tends to get weaker, it is the innovative design of the physical and spatial components that can enhance the brand identity of place by "(i) adding or creating distinct urban landscape, (ii) synchronizing spatially all the different social/cultural/economic groups; and (iii) generating new social solidarities among inhabitants related to their common and/or individual economic future" (Gospodini [16]). Students' projects have the choice to encapsulate these phenomena as the underlying basis for their design.

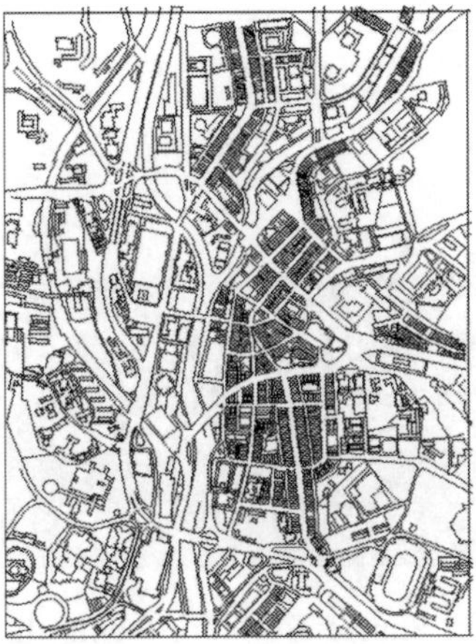

Figure 1: Site context.

3 Context

The proposed site of the project is located within the historic centre of Kuala Lumpur (Fig. 1). In the 1890's, multiracial communities settled within the vicinity of the area. Market Square (Fig. 2), east of the Klang River, became the commercial hub for the whole town. The Chinese communities settled around this Square and also towards the south into the present-day Chinatown. To the north, across Java Street (now Tun Perak Street), were the communities of the Malays. The Indian *Chettiars* and later the Indian Muslims traders set up businesses here. West of the river, the *Padang* (now Merdeka Square) was the focal point of the British administration (Fig.3). Kuala Lumpur continued to grow under the British until 1957. It gained the city status in 1972 and two years later became a Federal Territory.

Figure 2: Medan Pasar (Market Square) in 1920's (Source: National Archive Malaysia).

Figure 3: Sultan Abdul Samad Building facing the padang (parade ground). (Source: National Archive Malaysia).

Figure 4: Arial view of the site.

Even though many parts of the study area are filled with numerous office blocks, the typical shophouses still dominates the urban fabric. Over the years, it has played a central role in the life of the city in providing both workplace and home place and, in the present day, continues to house modern lives and work. Unfortunately, many of the buildings are in derelict conditions and tenantless. Due to the lack of design guidance and inadequate statutory backing for preservation have resulted in many of the historic buildings to be replaced by unsympathetic development. The existing urban fabric is a living testimony of the process in which urban development has encroached into the historic centre replacing not only the physical urban form but also the socio-cultural dimensions of the city (Fig. 4).

Figure 5: Concept plan.

4 Urban narratives

Perhaps, one approach to counter the prospect of our built environment becoming archaeological museums of so many dismembered architectural artifacts produced by the elementary, institutional and mechanistic typologies of the past, it is important to be constantly reminded of the full potential of understanding the history of the place. As Eric Owen Moss describes, "if one can understand the order of things past, then presumably one can account for the present, and predict the future" [17]. The following narratives were generated based on the above understanding to substantiate the urban rejuvenation proposals (Fig. 5).

4.1 Redimere vs. the voiceless genius loci

Jackson indicates that “localities have an attraction which gives us a certain indefinable sense of well-being and which we want to return to, time and again” [18]. To reinstate the loss sense of place, a reinterpretation of existing context into a concretize dimension is urgently needed and that tool used in the design was based on the phenomenological approach that clarifies itself as a method that urges a return to things. This concept underlies the proposed schemes of the urban intervention was also in spirit with L. Kahn’s statement that “the genius denotes what a thing is or what it wants to be” [19].

4.2 Stabilitas loci vs. dynamics of change

The character of a place is a function of time and it changes dynamically with it. The design task is to merge these two elements and hope this union will stimulate each other.

Stabilitas locus is the preeminent spirit or essence of a place that has transcendental qualities: immobile, substantially tangible, frozen in time, and also has the potentials in displaying immense historical significances of the built heritage of the urban context. By translating these elements in the design, the scheme usurped existing *genius locus* and to blend the concoction with the inevitable dynamic changes of the 21st Century, be it man-made innovations or the invisible qualities of information technology. These in turn creates the qualitative (foci) versus the quantitative (progress), or in other words, to bequeath the proposed site with the capacity of receiving different contents within certain limits. By doing so, it is hoped that the pace of urbanization is in tandem with the existing capacity and capability of the place.

As Kenneth Frampton idealizes *On Reading Heidegger*, “For where place is essentially qualitative and in and of itself concrete and static, production tends to stress quantity and to be in and of itself dynamic and abstract” [20].

4.3 Reinterpretation of dialectics vs. IT as a faceless tool

Having to reformulate the dialectical constituents of the place, there would be a possibility to misinterpret the context. However, the challenge does provide a few loopholes to be exploited.

Firstly, is how the integration of globalization into a historical context can paved the way for information technology to be a commanding tool in urban rejuvenation? This faceless tool reacts in tandem with the needs of the ‘timeless man’, of a globalized Malaysia, the collective ideal of the Modern World.

Secondly, we are able to predict future experiences derived from the existing fragmentary relationships between man and the environment, as such, man has identified built forms as a direct manifestation of existence. From this, it is imperative for us to offer the idea of renewal of art as a mean to rediscover Silver Triangle’s deepest essence, hence the manipulation of artistic concepts into event spaces that can be experienced by the masses: - psycho-physically and spiritually. This is not a new concept of which has been experienced from the transformation of SoHo and downtown New York into a hub of cultural activities that creates a sense of place identity. Since this idea works, and as abstract as a piece of art can be, it can also transcends human barriers and has the ability to conforms itself with the place of origin.

Mere objectification of art is however cautioned against the value it represents. Therefore, it is inherent for us to appraise the existing qualitative as opposed to the quantitative, in order to fabricate a vision of 'somewhere' which people can determined as their territorial space. To assimilate these existing qualitative, inside and outside, with the quantitative it represent, and by doing so, a reinterpretation of dialectics as a sustaining foci can have the capacity of morphing over time.

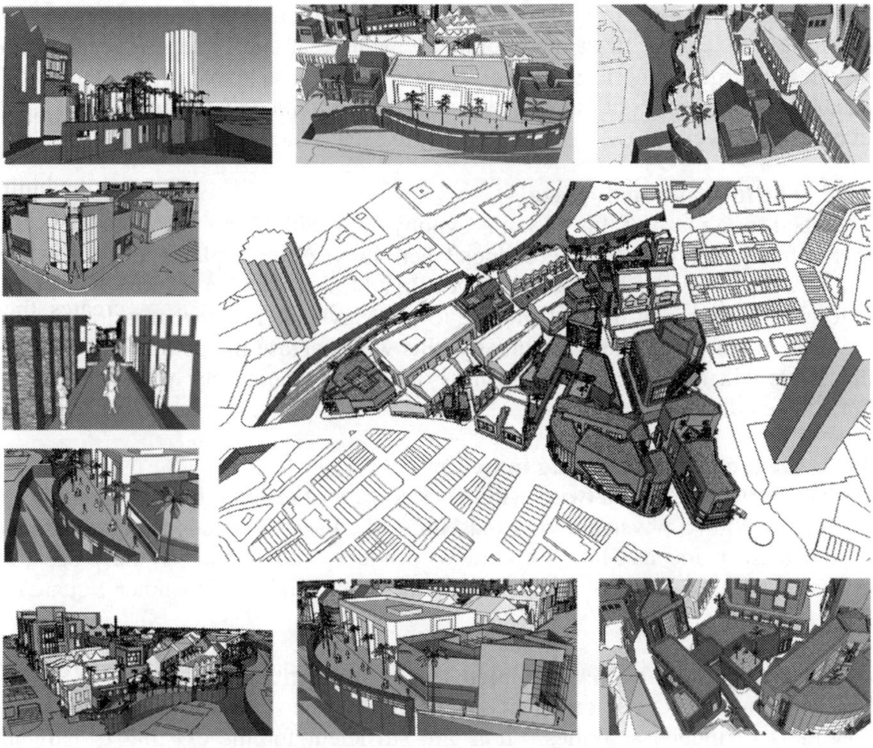

Figure 6: The proposed scheme.

4.4 Imago mundi vs. language of money

It is inevitable that money talks. The language of money possesses many status quo that can drive a traditionalist into embracing the capitalist realm. Hence, man total acceptances towards new and infused technological breakthroughs are indefinite. Our task is to coalesce the functional and visual quality of the place, which are inherent in 'imago-mundi' so as to display the power of art and money in an environment rich in built heritage.

The Central Market acts as one of the dominant foci and activity generator of the place. By transposing it into the overall development creates a new convivial focus that will expand the activities to a larger area and establish itself as the node within the historic neighbourhood. Within this environment, the introduction of commercialized programs and spaces are revealed into a larger context, from the internal spaces of the Central Market to the outside capitalist ambience of the city. The proposed scheme includes (Fig. 6):

4.4.1 The artists' capitalist neighbourhood

The sense of place with the projected architectural features of restored buildings can be a catalyst for artists to live, exhibit and promote their works. The setting of the artists' colony must incorporate elements that can generate creativity to produce 'memento-mori' works of distinctions. It also has the potential to become the hub for continuous artistic/cultural activities that promote local and international events.

4.4.2 The incorporated 'plaza'

The need for a plaza of this nature is synonymous with living in a city. The need to reinforce commercial and financial activities will complement and further enhance the business vitality of the place. In addition, the idea of creating a plaza is to establish a visual link of the site to the Maybank Tower that is located on the eastern part of the site. Eventually, this will increase the permeability of the place that will further enhance business opportunities not only in the study area but also to adjacent vicinities.

4.4.3 Medan Pasar-the living museum

A historical centre with a twist, with its collection of restored buildings clustered together to form a physical living museum. The Pasar Square will be a platform to showcase made in Malaysia cultural products and inevitably the place for artists' exhibitionist streak. It could culminate into a mini- Tiananmen Square of Kuala Lumpur.

4.4.4 Streets as a mishmash of open spaces and activities

Streets act as collective horizontal spaces that can be stretched to the maximum potentials to induce activities. It is not sufficient for the existing density to activate the place and the alternative mean is to create livable, rentable and functional outdoor spaces. Existing indoor activities can be extended outdoors within specific areas and hour. This proposal embraces and celebrates the streets by reinventing innovative events and space programs that are commercially viable within the context.

5 Conclusion

The proposals have generated metaphorical images about the architecture and the city with eminently conflicting dialectics: constraints and possibilities; meeting and solitude; gathering and separation; the trivial and surprisingly improvisation. The dialectics of architecture cannot be limited to a single school of thought but a spectrum of approaches that can enlightened the creative mind. Similarly, the city also cannot be limited to the opposition centre-periphery, although it implied and contained them. To look at the architecture and the city is to look at the world (thought as a relationship to the world), globality as totality, the universe, space-time, energies and information, but without valuing one rather another. The project considers the city as the model that has generated the urban derivatives. The definition of derivative is not any single item that is a by-product of the urban context, but rather components that one way or another has affected the generation of the built environment. One can hope that it will turn out well but the architecture and the city can become the centre of domination, dependence, exploitation, reformation and so forth.

By zeroing into the fragments as complete entities in themselves, students would be able to appreciate the hidden dimensions of the city and its artifacts. The study is not meant to expose students to abstract theories of architecture or the city but only to excite them in looking at things in a different way. The task is to look for functioning particularities rather than determining rules.

References

[1] Ashworth, G. J. & Turnbridge, J. E., The Tourist-historic City, Belhaven: London, 1990.

[2] Prentice, R., Tourism and Heritage Attractions, Routledge: London, 1993.

[3] Ashworth, G. J. & Larkham, P. J. (Eds) Building a New Heritage: Tourism, Culture and Identity in the New Europe, Routledge: London, 1994.

[4] Morris, E., Heritage and culture: a capita for the new Europe, in Ashworth, G. J. & Larkham, P. J. (Eds) Building a New Heritage: Tourism, Culture and Identity in the New Europe, Routledge: London, pp. 159-177, 1994.

[5] Herbert, D. T (Ed.) Heritage, Tourism and Society, Mansell: London, 1995.

[6] Boyer, M. C., Cyber Cities: Visual Perception in the Age of Electronic Communication, Princeton Architectural Press: New York, pp. 138-139, 1996.

[7] Rossi, A., The Architecture of the City, MIT Press: Cambridge, MA, p.7, 1982.

[8] Durrell, L., Spirit of Place, Pidgeon Audio Visual: London, p. 156, 1969.

[9] Schittich, C. (Ed.) Detail: Building in Existing Fabric- Refurbishment, Extensions, New Design, Birkhauser: Berlin, 2003.

[10] Ashworth, G. J., The conserved European city as a cultural symbol: the meaning of the text, in: B. Graham (Ed.) Modern Europe, Place, Culture, Identity, Arnold: London, pp. 261-286, 1998.

[11] Krier, R., Urban Space, Academy Editions: London, 1978.

[12] Rossi, A., The Architecture of the City, MIT Press: Cambridge, MA, 1982.
[13] Vidler, A., The Third Typology, in: A. Vidler (Ed.) Rational Architecture, Archives d'Architecture Moderne: Brussels, 1978.
[14] Rowe, C. & Koetter, F., Collage City, MIT Press: Cambridge, MA, 1978.
[15] Colquhoun, A., Modern architecture and historicity, in: A. Colquhoun (Ed.) Essays in Architectural Criticism, MIT Press: Cambridge, MA, pp 11-19, 1981.
[16] Gospodini, A., Built heritage and innovative design, Journal of Urban Design, 9 (2), pp. 242-243, 2004.
[17] Moss, E. O., Gnostic Architecture, Monacelli Press: NY, 1999
[18] Jackson, J. B., A Sense of Place, a Sense of Time, Yale University Press: New Haven, CT, pp.157-158, 1994.
[19] Lobell, J., Between Science and Light, Shambala: NY, 2000
[20] Frampton, K., On reading Heidegger, in: K. Nesbitt (Ed.) Theorizing a New Agenda for Architecture, Princeton Architectural Press: New York, pp. 440-446, 1996.

Linking equitable redevelopment to reduced damages from metropolitan sprawl

D. J. Hutch
University of Chicago,
U.S. Environmental Protection Agency

Abstract

New business, real estate and public investment dollars are skewed towards the predominantly white outlying suburbs, which fuels metropolitan sprawl, development of green spaces, and loss of farms. Many U.S. centre-cities are relegated to a preponderance of abandoned and potentially contaminated properties or brownfields. This unequal outward expansion is caused, in part, by unfair zoning and real estate practices that result in decreased development choices and increased social and economic inequality. Under-utilization of existing infrastructure potentially results in hundreds of billions of dollars in inefficiencies due to added costs and under-utilized capital. Exclusionary zoning, often based on minimum lot size requirements per household or exclusions of multifamily or accessory housing units, results in non-market limits to affordable housing. Unlike Europe's transit oriented developments, dispersed development in the U.S. increases automobile reliance and associated mobile source pollutants. Smart growth policies and brownfield redevelopment in the U.S. can help redress one-sided investment practices that have directed development and jobs away from older and poorer communities. However, market processes are distorted to under-price sprawling greenfield development, leading to sub-optimal land consumption and allocation of resources affecting the environment, community and regional economies, whilst exacerbating social-economic inequalities. More equitable urban redevelopment efforts can strengthen existing communities while promoting improved regional environmental performance along with fiscal and economic benefits.

Keywords: sustainable development, urban redevelopment, smart growth, brownfields, environmental justice, urban planning, growth management, fiscal impact, land use, equity.

1 Introduction

A perceived disconnect exists between U.S. smart growth policies to reign in urban sprawl, and the interests of disadvantaged communities. However, environmental protection and smart growth are related to the plight of older, and disadvantaged communities (Bullard et al [1]). The erosion of equality gains for African Americans since Brown v. Board of Education is associated with the emergence of sprawl development patterns aided by subsidized forms of business and residential development (Hutch [2]). The 2000 U.S. decennial census shows a strong and persistent national trend of whites and businesses leaving cities for environmentally destructive low density development, leaving less privileged groups to economically declining center-cities and inner-ring suburbs (Brookings [3]). Jobs have moved further from older communities while the tax base and even the social fabric of older communities have declined. This decline fuels crime, poor education, high unemployment and a continuing cycle of exodus to greener more sprawling areas along the metropolitan fringe. *The challenge for urban advocates is to rebalance growth to benefit older and poorer inner-rung communities while appealing to broader concerns including environmental, social, and fiscal concerns*. Providing alternative choices to existing low-density development in outlying or fringe areas would not only protect green space and our environmental quality, but also benefit entire metropolitan regions as well.

2 Existing development, water, and transportation investments

Planning commissions, economic development offices, transportation and environmental planning bodies exert significant influence on new developments. States and regions, influenced by federal programs, can determine whether existing communities or newer communities along the urban fringe will receive billions of dollars of capital investment, subsidies or water infrastructure or transportation improvements.

Many older cities are affected with a substantial $210 billion funding gap, projected over a twenty-year period, for sewer and water treatment improvements. However, the costs of constructing new sewer systems and waste water treatment systems for new suburban or outlying communities are higher" on a per capita basis than utilizing existing systems (McElfish et al [4]). In addition, state clean water revolving funds inefficiently favour construction of new sewer systems over upgrading and improving existing large scale urban sewer systems and combined sewer systems (McElfish et al [4]), which places poorer urban areas at a disadvantage. Although repair costs are considerable, the cost of not maintaining older infrastructure may be higher due to environmental risks and damages caused by poorly treated sewer overflows (Staff [5]). Watersheds often connect to one another so broader regional interests are at stake when an urban wastewater system fails (Orfield [6]). Also unchecked outward metropolitan development decreases the tax base and ability of poorer cities to maintain its infrastructure. Meanwhile building new systems in the suburbs could potentially double environmental burdens and costs in the future (Burchell and Shad [7]). This knowledge can help declining communities to more effectively participate in regional planning and investment decisions involving these funds (U.S. EPA [8]).

Inner cities have a huge role to play in reducing pressures from sprawl induced automobile dependency and the associated rise in air pollution levels. At stake are billions of dollars in transportation funding for many heavily polluted cities, whose future share of the $218 billion plus transportation pie is linked via the U.S. Clean Air Act to plans to improve air quality. Metropolitan Planning Organizations or MPO's are important to utilizing funding that can be applied to highways or transit (Rusk [9]). However, unlike Europe, transit in the U.S. receives far less funding priority while automobile or highways funding receives a much greater priority. Transit receives a lower proportion of the budget than roadway projects that can promote sprawl. Transit benefits are also inequitable. According to a report on transportation equity, the poorest fifth of urban residents in Southern California receive only 4% of transportation benefits (Dittmar and Chen [10]). Deficiencies for poorer communities exist in areas critical to development, including transportation enhancements, which allows for bicycling, pedestrian facilities, enhance the physical beauty of a corridor and possibly jumpstart revitalization efforts. Since U.S. MPO's must assure that all aspects of the population have been incorporated into the planning process (Rusk [9]), an opportunity exists for distressed communities to have influence in development decisions, including targeting existing communities with infill redevelopment – an important tenet of sustainable development and smart growth.

3 Smart growth can help declining communities

Instead of community specific effects, metropolitan wide or regional forces account for three quarters of the variance in poverty, which drives concentrated poverty outcomes for the region (Persky and Wievel [11]). A sustainable or "smart growth" land use strategy based upon compact or densely populated communities that channels new development towards existing communities, improves the jobs to housing balance by mixing commercial and residential development while decreasing auto-dependency is a potential remedy to growing regional inequities. More importantly, smart growth objectives mesh well with the benefits of strengthening and revitalizing older centre-cities and inner suburbs with large low income and minority populations. These communities are compact or more densely populated, unlike the dominant form of land consumptive forms of development. These poorer communities utilize existing public infrastructure and they offer architecturally distinct and historic sites to anchor new development upon.

4 The magnitude of the problem

Outward development of land is two and half times the rate of population growth (U.S. EPA, "Built…" [12]). A U.S. Federal Reserve Bank concludes that, "infrastructure investment that encourages decentralization may serve to undermine growth in productivity and social welfare" (Haughwout, [13]).

Metropolitan sprawl and the decline of center cities and older inner rung suburbs contribute towards negative economic and social welfare outcomes. In addition, social and economic segregation by race has dramatically increased. Four out of five poor whites and only one out of five poor blacks live in mixed income areas in cities (Chicago's [14]). Communities in outlying suburbs received larger levels of wealth building assistance related to infrastructure and housing relative to the center-city (Persky and Kurban [15]).

In a twenty-year span, $1 trillion was invested in a vast system of highways, and suburbs received a much greater share of highway funding than cities (Economist [16]). Transportation planning has influenced where and how hundreds of billions of dollars in U.S. federal transportation funds were over the last 6 year funding cycle. Yet the commuters who drive from their elite fringe communities to work pay only 25% of the true cost of their transport (Economist [16]).

Business and new residential development often follow government subsidies of sewers, parks, and schools. For example, U.S. federal investments in wastewater systems 1972-1990 totalled more than $60 billion (Singels [17]). Combined, state, federal and local contributions total $250 billion since 1970 (Staff U.S. House [5]). Unfortunately, these funds are not necessarily used for upgrading and repairing existing infrastructure at the core. Instead they are often directed towards the outer fringe areas of metropolitan areas that fuels a cycle of disinvestments and urban decline.

5 Appeals to more efficient growth

Inner city communities could assert that sprawl development is inefficient. Older denser and more compact communities, which typify disadvantaged communities, require less natural resources and generate less pollutants than more auto dependent and lower density sprawling communities (Bernstein [18]). Energy efficiencies obtained from district networks of heat, cooling and co-generation is better served by clustered or more densely populated urban developments (U.S. DOE [19]). In addition, sprawling development patterns require expensive investments in sewer, water and road extensions (Siegel [20]). The fiscal benefits of sustainable or smart growth planning initiative, including denser and more compact development, are substantial. Capital facility costs under current trends are 60% more expensive, school facilities are over 7% more costly and utilities are approximately 40% more costly than under a smart growth scenario (Burchell and Shad [21]).

Reducing travel times and improving the jobs to housing balance within communities is another benefit of the smart growth principle of strengthening existing communities. Chicago 's 2020 business confederation discovered efficiencies in decreased absenteeism and turnover rates if employees are not burdened by long commutes and reduced time for family life (IRP, Powell, [22]). This smart growth practice of tying jobs and housing to business development can improve the profits of businesses while increasing access to opportunities for the disadvantaged communities.

Divergence in from full cost pricing is another inefficient incentive for sprawl. Cross-subsidization or "average cost pricing in the provision of utility services has regressive impacts to older and poorer communities." Customers pay one uniform rate based on average costs despite location efficiencies associated with more centrally located or more compact developments, and despite the difficulties and higher costs of servicing sprawling communities. (Nelson [23]). As a result, residents of more urban, higher density areas subsidize new low-density developments in wealthier and more sprawling developments along the fringe. A recent Florida study of utility costs by development type found that it costs more than twice as much to service utilities in low-density developments than in more compact, higher density areas (Burchell [24]).

6 Environmental impacts related to inequitable development outcomes

Environmental damages result from sprawling development patterns. 12% to 55% of Water quality impairments can be explained by outward development influences (e.g., urban runoff) (U.S. EPA, "Our Built [12]). "Concentrating development in existing or more compact areas would produce 40% less water pollution than more dispersed development patterns" (U.S. EPA [12]). In fact, development pressures leading to polluted water runoff forced New York City's Catskill Delaware to consider spending \$4.57 billion on a new filtration system and increase drinking water bills by 45% unless plans to change future development patterns were considered (Clark and Stoner [25]).

Poorer air quality is linked to metropolitan sprawl via auto dependency. Metropolitan Sprawl has increased the number and length of trips, which increases automobile dependency, resulting in increased automobile emissions, including emissions of several harmful gases. Transportation sources (highway and off road sources) contribute up to half or 50% of the remaining overall pollution in the air, including 56% of NOx, 77 % of CO, 47 % of volatile organic compounds; and 25 % of particulate matter, (Brenner [26]). Also mobile sources represent the largest contributor to air toxics, which are associated with cancer or other serious health or environmental effects. The estimated annual costs of this motor-vehicle-based pollution are substantial, ranging from under \$30 billion to \$500 billion in increased health care costs, \$2.5 to \$4.6 billion in crop damage, \$6.0 to \$43.54 billion in damage due to reduced visibility (U.S. EPA, Our Built .. [12]). In the U.S., 159 million people live in metro regions that do not meet the safety standard for ozone.

Researchers have found that more compact smart growth development would reduce consumption of fragile lands by almost one-fifth (Burchell and Listofkin [27]). Ground level Ozone, exacerbated by traffic congestion, is responsible for 1 to 2 billion dollars in reduced crop production per year in the

U.S. (EPA Regional [28]). Concentrating development to central cities and older more dense communities can yield significant environmental benefits.

7 Critics of more sustainable or smart growth approaches

Critics fear that smart growth strategies such as growth management (or urban growth boundaries) will penalize the poor by increasing the price of land, restricting the supply of housing and increasing housing costs. However, "Local housing markets often adopt exclusionary large lot zoning, minimum house size requirements and bans on secondary units precisely to make their housing more expensive and thereby indirectly exclude lower income racial and ethnic minorities"(Nelson et al [29]). In fact, smart growth practices that discourage exclusionary or income based zoning in the outlying areas could benefit lower income and disadvantaged groups potentially more than the negative housing price effects observed by some studies. Also a $500 per month auto and transit savings from living in a more compact transit oriented community could be applied to mortgage payments and allow a family to qualify for a $50,000 more expensive mortgage (Holzclaw [30]).

8 Smart growth, economic efficiency and urban competitive advantage

Efficiency refers to the highest and best use of resources, however, externalities to market pricing for land markets, including subsidies and pollution, can lead to inefficient outcomes, including over provision of new sprawling residential developments (Hutch, "Market" [31]). More formally, it is the production of the best and optimal combination of outputs by means of the most efficient combination of input that produces output at the least cost (Pierce [32]). Centre cities or inner suburban or urban communities manifest sufficient densities and choices of input combinations to potentially meet the highest and best use criterion while sprawl influenced deconcentration diminishes social welfare (Haughwout [13]). Efforts to reconcentrate employment in the central city may increase the pie (or net fiscal benefits) by utilizing otherwise unemployed labour, land labour, buildings and infrastructure (Persky and Wievel [10]).

Revitalizing cities as opposed to sprawl can lead to efficiencies from shared inputs, scale efficiencies and synergistic business clusters (Haughwout [12]). In addition, marginal costs imposed by a new city household, especially with declining population, is less than the average costs of services while outer suburbs have trouble keeping marginal costs of new residents in line with the average costs for all residents (Persky and Wievel [10]). Even with high average expenditures, the marginal costs of the centre city are lower than that of suburbs in Chicago. For New York, marginal costs range from no costs for sewers, 25% for administration, 50% for fire police and sanitation and health and 75% of total average costs for education. Surprisingly, moves by new rich households to the centre city can create even higher fiscal surpluses; and poorer residential entrants can create even lower net costs due to abundant infrastructure and services in cities relative to fringe areas. (Persky and Wievel [10]). Therefore, policies that promote moves back to inner cities can tap into fiscal efficiencies despite higher average taxes and costs of service provision (for the poor). Unlike outer suburbs, cities do not have to expand fixed capital, or build new systems of provision (e.g., extend sewer lines, build schools) to accommodate new households. (Persky and Wievel [10]).

Over 20 year projected period, from 1990 to 2010, New Jersey could save $1.4 billion dollars from a smart growth or more compact form of planned development. And if these savings to schools, utilities, roads were extrapolated out to the nation, the annual savings would be $175 billion dollars for municipal governments and $500 billion per year for schools (Rami [33]). Utilizing existing infrastructure rather than developing greenfields can result in savings.

A Price Waterhouse study found that inner city communities have an unmet market potential of $85 billion dollars. (Boston [34]). In addition, assets such as a ready supply of untapped labour, strategic assess to key industries and markets and transportation make many inner cities potentially powerful places for businesses to expand. Meanwhile, development along the fringe, which threatens green space, endangers sensitive ecosystems and impairs water quality, is becoming less profitable. (Boston [33]).

9 Conclusion

Efforts to support more sustainable urban development have strong synergies with fiscal savings, environmental and economic benefits while providing alternatives to destructive greenfield developments in outlying areas. The U.S. could capture considerable benefits by providing for more development choices including compact developments and access to transit for people of varied incomes and backgrounds, while protecting greenspace and strengthening existing capital and infrastructure investments. By decreasing inequities in new capital investment that favor distant suburbs while upgrading and maintaining existing infrastructure in centre cities, the U.S. would help promote successful urban and brownfields redevelopment. Disadvantaged communities can certainly appeal to broader fiscal and environmental interests of the entire region and nation.

Acknowledgement

The views in this paper are solely those of the author, and do not represent the official policies or positions of the U.S. Environmental Protection Agency.

References

[1] Robert D. Bullard, Glenn S. Johnson PH.D. and Angel O. Torres, M.C. P., “Race, Equity and Smart Growth: Why People of Color Must Speak For Themselves”, A Discussion Paper, September, 2000, pp.2-3.

Environmental Justice Resource Center, Clark Atlanta University, available at: http://www.ejrc.cau.edu/raceequitysmartgrowth.htm

[2] Hutch, Daniel J., "The Rationale for Including Disadvantaged Communities in the Smart Growth Metropolitan Development Framework", Yale Law and Policy Review (Volume 20, Number 2, 2002, 2002), p.353.

[3] The Brookings Institution, Center on Urban and Metropolitan Policy, "Census 2000 Matters Racial Change in the Nation's Largest Cities: Evidence from the 2000 Census", April 2001, p. 1; website found at http://www.brookings.org/es/urban/census/citygrowth.htm.

[4] James McElfish Jr., Susan Casey Lefkowitz, Smart Growth and the Clean Water Act, (Washington: Northeast Midwest Institute, Smart Growth Network, 2001, Washington D.C. pp. 39-40. Web copy at: http://www.nemw.org/SGCleanWater.pdf.

[5] Staff of House Subcommittee on Water Resources and the Environment, 107th Congress, Water Infrastructure Needs (2001). Available at http://www.house.gov/transportation/water/03-28-01/03-28-01memo.html3#BACKGROUND (Last visited April 1, 2001).

[6] Orfield, Myron, Metropolitics, p. 10.

[7] Burchell, Robert W. and Shad, Naveed A.MCRP, "The National Perspective on Land Use Policy Alternatives and Consequences." National Public Policy Education Consequences, Prepared for the Farm Foundation, 1998. p. 9.

[8] U.S. EPA, CWSRF, "How the CWSRF Program Works" p.1, at http://www.epa.gov/owmitnet/cwfinance/cwsrf/basics.htm

[9] David Rusk, "Growth Management: The Core Regional Issue", in Bruce Katz ed. Reflections on Regionalism, (Washington: Brooking Institution Press, 2000) pp. 20, 100; available at: http://www.brookings.org /dybdocroot/es/urban/reflections/essay3.pdf. . pp. 20,100.

[10] Hank Dittmar and Don Chen, Surface Transportation Policy Project (STTP) "Equity in Transportation Investments", Background Paper, available at Http://www.fta.dot.gov/library/policy/envir-just/backcf.htm #equity p. 1-2

[11] Persky Joseph, and Wim Wievel, When Corporations Leave Town: The Costs and Benefits of Metropolitan Job Sprawl, (Detroit: Wayne State University Press, 2000) pp. 55-57, 126. Authors cite: Jargowsky, Paul, Poverty and Place: Ghettoes, Barriers and the American City. (New York Russell Sage Foundation, 1997) pp. 55-57,126-127.

[12] United States Environmental Protection Agency, EPA, Our Built and Natural Environments: A Technical Review of the interactions Between Land Use Transportation, and Environmental Quality, January 2001 (EPA 231-R-01-0020), pp. 5.11-15, 29, 42. Web copy at http://www.smartgrowth.org /pdf/built_environment/chapter2.pdf

[13] Haughwout, Andrew, Economist, "Infrastructure and Social Welfare in Metropolitan America", FRBNY Economic Policy Review, (Federal Reserve Bank of New York, December 2001, vol. 7, No. 3) pp. 1-2, 5-7.

[14] "Chicago's Regional Plan has a Message for Everyone", The Journal Sentinel (May 2, 1999), p.3. Web copy at http://www.jsonline.com /mews/editorials/may99/0502chicago.asp Reprinted from the Economist Newspaper Group.3.

[15] Joseph Persky, Hydar Kurban, "Do Federal Funds Better Support Cities or Suburbs", University of Illinois, Haydar Kurban, Department of Economics, Howard University, (A discussion Paper Prepared for the Brookings Institution, Center on Urban and Metropolitan Policy, November 2001), pp 7,.17. Available at: http://www.brookings.org /dybdocroot/es/urban/publications/persky.pdf : p.17:

[16] Economist Newspaper Ltd, "Urban Sprawl", August 21, 1999, U.S. Edition. pp. 1, 2.

[17] Singels, Nikos D. "Financing Priority Watershed Projects with the State Revolving Fund," Conference Proceedings, "Watershed 1996", 1996. p.1., available at http://www.epa.gov/OWOW/watershed/Proceed/singelis.html.

[18] Bernstein, Scott, The Center for Neighborhood Technologies, "Using The Hidden Assets of America's Communities and Regions to Ensure Sustainable Communities", Presented at the Symposium on the Future of Local Government in Michigan sponsored by the Municipal League Foundation",

[19] United States Department of Energy, Climate Change Technologies, "Combined Heat and Power", State and Local Climate Change Program, January 2000, p. 1. Available at: http://www.epa.gov/globalwarming /publications/outreach/technology/combinedheatandpower.pdf

[20] Siegle, Michael L, "The Effects of Land Use and Utility Service Costs, and Geographically Sensitive User Rates" 1998 Areas, Natural Resources Defence Council, pp. 16-18.

[21] Robert W. Burchell, Ph.D., Naveed A, Shad, MCRP, "_Costs of Sprawl Versus Compact Development", Emerging Trends Sensible Growth Seminar, Metropolitan Planning Council (Chicago Illinois, March 12, 1998), Table I, p.13.

[22] Institute on Race & Poverty (IRP) and John Powell, "Racism and Metropolitan Dynamics", Ford Foundation Briefing Paper August 2002 (Minneapolis: Ford Foundation and IRP) pp. 19, 21 available at: Instituteonraceandpoverty.org/fordinfo.html

[23] Nelson Arthur, James Duncan, Growth Management Principles and Practices, Chicago, IL., American Planning Association, 1995. p.113.

[24] Robert Burchell, PhD. Nancy Newman, PhD., Alex Zakrewsky, M.A./M.S., Stephanie E. Dipetrillo, M. Arch., M.C.R.P. Eastward Ho! Development Futures: Paths to Growth, Center for Urban Policy Research, Rutgers University, October 26, 1998, Prepared for the Florida Department of the Community Affairs and U.S. EPA, October 26, 1998. p. 30, 42.

[25] George Aponte Clark and Nancy Stoner, "Stormwater Strategies", Stormwater, January- February 2001, pg. 11. www.stormh2o.com; See also Henry L. Diamond and Patrick F. Noonan, Land Use In America:

Report of the Sustainable Use of Land Project, Lincoln Institute of Policy and Island Press 1996, Washington D.C., pg 78. "..leaking septic fields from proliferating vacation homes and non-point run-off from new suburban developments and agricultural lands threaten the purity of the water" (New York City's).

[26] Brenner, Robert, Acting Assistant Secretary Administrator, U.S. EPA, Testimony before the Committee on the Environment and Public Works, U.S. Senate, August 1, 2001. p. 1.

[27] Robert W. Burchell, PhD., David Listofkin, "Land, Infrastructure, Housing Costs And Fiscal Impacts Associated With Growth", Rutgers – The State University, New Brunswick, New Jersey, Prepared for "Rail-Volution 96": Building Successful Communities with Rail, September 8, 1996. p.9. See U.S. EPA, Our Built and Natural Environments, pp.11-13.

[28] "EPA Regional Approaches to Improving Air Quality, Office of Air Quality Planning and Standards", Research Triangle Park, NC 27711, (EPA/451-K-97-001) May 1997. (Pamphlet)

[29] Arthur C. Nelson, Rolf Pendall, Casey J. Dawkins, and Gerrit J. Knapp, "The Link between Growth Management and Housing Affordability: The Academic Evidence", The Center on Urban and Metropolitan Policy, Brookings, February 2002, available at: http://www.brookings.org /dybdocroot/urban/publications/growthmanagexsum.htm Also see: Note: #45.

[30] Holzclaw, John, "Using Residential Patterns and Transit to Decrease Automobile Auto Dependence and Costs", Natural Resources Defense Council, June , 1994, San Francisco, pp.6-7, web copy: http:/www.smartgrowth.org/library/articles.asp?art=190&res=800

[31] Hutch, Daniel, Brownfields, Market Efficiencies and Metropolitan Sprawl", Proceedings of the Brownfields 2001 Conference: Restoring the Environment, Revitalizing Communities, Chicago, p. 5-7. Available at: http://www.brownfields2002.org/proceedings2001/MOI-20-01.pdf

[32] Pierce, David W, "Allocative Efficiency", The MIT Dictionary of Modern Economics, 1986, pp.13-14.

[33] Rami, Matt, "Sprawl Subsidies and Smart Growth", Natural Resources Defence Council, p. 1. http://www.trasact.org/Reports/smartgrowth /fiscal.htm. Accessed 2/21/02.

[34] Boston Consulting Group, "The Business Case for Pursing Retail Opportunities for the Inner City", Institute for a Competitive Inner City, June 1998, p. 1. http://www.icic.org/research/pdf /pdf_2 _The_Business_Case.pdf

Sustainability planning: pushing against institutional barriers

D. Goudie
Centre for Tropical Urban and Regional Planning, James Cook University, Australia

Abstract

This paper describes a case study of an institution promoting sustainability goals but acting to restrict innovation and implementation of those same goals. The issue is important because institutions have cultures which may feel antipathy to a paradigm shift toward sustainability, whilst required to usher in sustainability. There are a multitude of conservative forces representing the Dominant Social Paradigm restricting innovation, despite sustainability policy. People engaging in sustainability implementation may come into conflict with institutional representatives of the old paradigm. Resistance to the New Environmental Paradigm may permeate our own organisations.

Trying to strike a balance between implementing ecologically sustainable development and respecting institutions' behaviour may require courage and perseverance. Institutions are often big, powerful, conservative and may tolerate bullying behaviour if threatened by innovation.

With most development takes place in urban settings, concepts of urban sustainability attempt to merge two very different fields of human endeavour - how we modify our landscape, our built environment, and how we behave in that environment.

Transport planning in Queensland, Australia displayed a tension between the infrastructure providers and the intending behaviour changers, so that project managers vested with encouraging travel behaviour change, badged as 'TravelSmart', appeared to fear innovation, fear action research which was, definitively, not under their full control. This paper explores this apparent 'internal dissonance' between the accepted need for, yet fear of change, via a case study attempting to introduce a pilot TravelSmart Destinations project to a provincial Queensland University, and the ways perseverance and maintaining focus on goals in both infrastructure and behaviour will make sustainability gains.

Keywords: sustainable, sustainability planning, institutional barriers, paradigm shift, implementation, impediments to change, ecologically sustainable development, urban travel change.

1 Introduction: plans and reality

A web search such as 'TravelSmart' shows much information and developed methods explaining ways to foster reduced solo urban car trips, as there is 'how-to' information about greenhouse gas abatement and energy conservation, health and environmental benefits of reducing car use.

This paper begins as a co-operative program between a TravelSmart coordinator at a University in North Queensland and the managing body of TravelSmart within the Queensland Department of Transport in Brisbane, the capital of Queensland, Australia, then provides a case study in the interplay of changing bureaucratic personnel and the way personalities can override stated goals.

Those most empowered to assist in implementing projects that require independence, initiative, local links and knowledge may be the ones who prove most obstructive to innovation Jarach [1], Phillips [2], ACF [3], Leibovitz [4].

The agreed aim of the pilot Destinations project for James Cook University in Townsville, North Queensland was to reduce solo car use by university students and staff, to develop and test innovative approaches and document the outcomes. Implementation was delayed from February to July 2004, the Unit manager claiming the contact was not legal, and refusing to make agreed payments so that innovation was stifled at the start of the academic year, and only allowed to properly commence toward the end of the academic year, when the university community is focused on assessment rather than travel modes and travel choices.

1.1 Background

In early 2003 the author, an adjunct Lecturer in sustainability planning at JCU, with a doctorate: *Toward sustainable urban travel* [5], was approached by a senior representative of SocialData, the key initiator of TravelSmart world wide, and a senior representative of the TravelSmart Unit, Queensland Department of Transport, Brisbane. I had wide experience in community engagement and an international paper on transport research methodology, [6]. It was agreed that I would implement both tried and innovative approaches to develop and test TravelSmart 'Destination' goals, using interactive 'social marketing' techniques at James Cook University. Details were formalised with the University and the Unit, a contract was refined and finalised in November 2003 and a project working group of experts and 'stakeholders' was formed in Townsville.
The agreed goals were:

1. "To research and develop a methodology for the planning, implementation and evaluation of TravelSmart Destinations Programs by
   - undertaking a literature review, web search and discussions with key agencies and Universities who have undertaken similar projects;
   - tailoring existing TravelSmart methodology to a 'Destinations' approach.
2. To concurrently implement and evaluate a pilot of the above TravelSmart Destinations methodology at James Cook University, Townsville..."

2 The problems begin

The TravelSmart Unit Manager only directly interacted with JCU personnel in early 2004. By then the senior project officer who had negotiated the contract left the Unit. Also, three project officers assigned to JCU left in quick succession over four months. They had all, in turn, left the Unit. By the forth link person in February 2004, I was alarmed to learn the latest project officer was ignoring the contract because she was unaware of it; nor would her office provide her with a copy. I sent a copy. There were problems from January onward.

2.1 Information and contracted funds withheld

For months the Unit, against their contractual undertaking, delayed sending results of the initial survey of 400 JCU commuters, including those nominating to help. Having been approved by Queensland Transport, the methodology was also detailed to and supported by senior university staff and the project working group. Until July 2004, the Unit withheld contracted funding both to support the project and to pay for contracted review material, effectively halting the project during the critical implementation months of the University's first semester. The Unit Manager declared the contract invalid, refusing to say how, or provide an alternative. Because contractural obligations were not being met by the Unit, others assisted in progressing the impass, arranging a meeting in July, when financial and procedural problems were satisfactorily resolved. The project was severely compromised by loss of confidence and a deeply uncertain future during semester one.

2.2 Time, trust and momentum lost

At the launch of TravelSmartJCU in Orientation week, February, 2004, we recorded details of 57 people who wanted to help. The future of the research project was very uncertain after withdrawal of Brisbane office support.

With firm support for the intended action research Cuthill [7] – research to develop and document socially and environmentally desired outcomes within sustainability principles – from the University, the Unit personnel involved in developing the contract and the overarching Project Working Group in the latter part of 2003, by February 2004, there was a profound shift from a shared, pilot methodological development of TravelSmart 'destination' approaches, to the Unit-imposed expectation that JCU would be subjected to a passive 'rollout' of Brisbane-adapted TravelSmart programs.

Withholding support had a clear impact on the development of participatory change, intended to flow from outcomes of a meeting held with 14 interested staff and students in March 2004. The drive of that meeting shrivelled over the months when Unit funds were withheld, under unsubstantiated claims that the contract was illegal. No alternative agreements were offered until late July, although repeatedly requested.

2.3 Institutional barriers to change – obstructions from within

Slowly pressure was brought to bear on the Unit manager from higher levels of his department, forcing a meeting mediated by a senior manager. Only then would the manager present his alternative proposal, remarkably similar to the original, except the new agreement insisted the University be a passive recipient of a methodology intended as pilot and developmental, to be reviewed as a passive, hand-off observational paper. That was submitted and available on the web through JCU's Centre for Tropical Urban and Regional Planning (http://www.tesag.jcu.edu.au/). Requests to have minutes taken were strongly rejected by the Unit manager.

3 The rocky road to some innovation

Despite these enervating and stressful obstructions, persistence produced an outcome on 11 November when the 'JCU Car less club' held its first meeting, preparatory to developing projects and events into 2005. Office bearers were elected, and five people offered to staff a stall in Orientation Week 2005, and ideas were flowing for greater impact of car less principles. Gaining support from the top is crucial to the success of any organisations' efforts at 'social marketing' [8]. I thank the Pro Vice Chancellor and his office for their unstinting support, sometimes in adversity. I also thank the numerous Heads of Schools and many others who expressed and gave support to the emergent car less project. Those who worked hard to set up the car less club deserve praise, along with supporters within Queensland Transport, and members of the Facilities management office.

3.1 Getting the infrastructure right

Townsville, North Queensland is largely a post 1950s growth city, with ample 'buildable' space. It has grown into a highly car dependent urban form. To turn a culture of car use around in a landscape designed for them will take time, but there are strong moves toward sustainability planing and behaviour change. Work has begun on the perceived main 'choke point' in the university path network, and the University is now highly responsive to concerns about provision of smooth, direct, safe, continuous and shaded paths. The thrust of this paper is that such endeavours are demanding enough with smooth, continuous projects. Having a project blocked for six months *by the support organisation* is a blatant example of institutional barriers to change.

3.2 The December 2004 report

Adapted extracts from the December 2004 report sent to the Unit follow. Some institutions will resist change. People and organisations who advocate change and attempt to play a contributory role may come up against subtle or bewildering resistance, perhaps from the most unexpected quarters. Persist.

3.2.1 Report executive summary

There are many ways to help people take more responsibility for their transport-related greenhouse gas emissions, and their health. Typing *TravelSmart* into a search engine will provide much well-presented detail: For destinations, engage staff and visitors, be patient with infrastructure providers as they begin to gear up for the time beyond car-dominated urban travel. This is central, along with copious, well targeted information, inducements both for change, and to support 'champion' volunteers.

Having 'focus' days for TravelSmart behaviour appears to have merit, as does nurturing local innovation to encourage more people to adopt TravelSmart behaviour. Survey and analysis by the Brisbane TravelSmart Unit indicated a drop in car use to JCU on Wednesdays, previously identified as the day with the highest car parking demand.

In areas where the urban form is low density and parking is relatively plentiful and cheap, an effective program needs to rely on promoting health aspects of reduced car use. Where there is a premium for parking and road space, helping people to learn how to use the public transport system or ride-share will also help reduce solo car use.

TravelSmart-type projects, whether badged as *Active Travel* or *Car less*, will greatly expand in coming years as the greenhouse gas crisis is properly appreciated. We will soon see depletion of cheap petrol, diesel and natural gas, with large price rises in transport fuels (websearch petroleum future).

A literature and web review showed that strong support from the parent body, access to TravelSmart information and incentives and room for local innovative response to specific local conditions is a winning combination. The example of 'Champions' whose input can be harnessed produces a rolling effect of travel behaviour change. Using easy-access data-based ride share programs has produced positive results, from ride to 'van' share.

In gauging the level of 'unmet demand' for travel alternatives, we need to carefully weigh the existing convenience of solo car travel and parking against the rewards and costs of alternatives.

3.2.2 Some review details

As with most destinations, schools or work places, JCU embraced and supported the TravelSmart approach because of concerns over parking availability, peak road congestion and the global aspects of vehicle emissions attached to travelling to and from the University. The TravelSmart project was also supported because it fulfilled some of the University's environmental policies of pursuing sustainability goals, including the health benefits of encouraging 'active' travel - walking and cycling. If the construction of extra parking areas could be postponed, there were clear and direct financial incentives as well. A student-based 'traffic count' survey [9] indicated some success of the JCU program.

3.2.3 TravelSmart meets a perceived need to reduce car use

Using 'champions' to lead and encourage by example is part of a broader process to get desired change. This is well understood in human geography's innovation theory: a simple way of conceptualising what all TravelSmart and like approaches attempt: a normative or innovation uptake model fig. 1 [10].

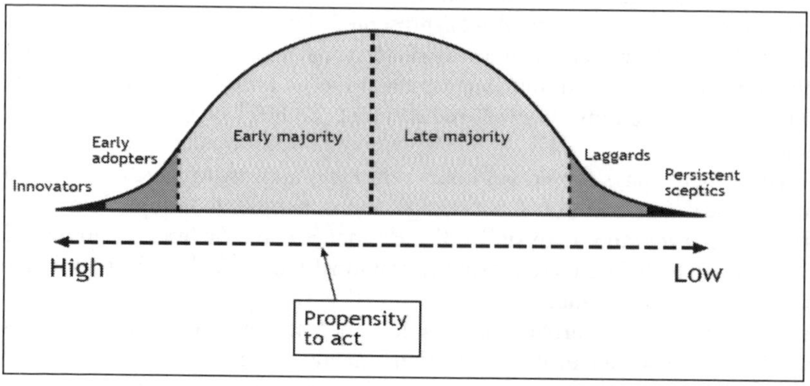

Figure 1: O'Neil's 2004 innovation uptake model.

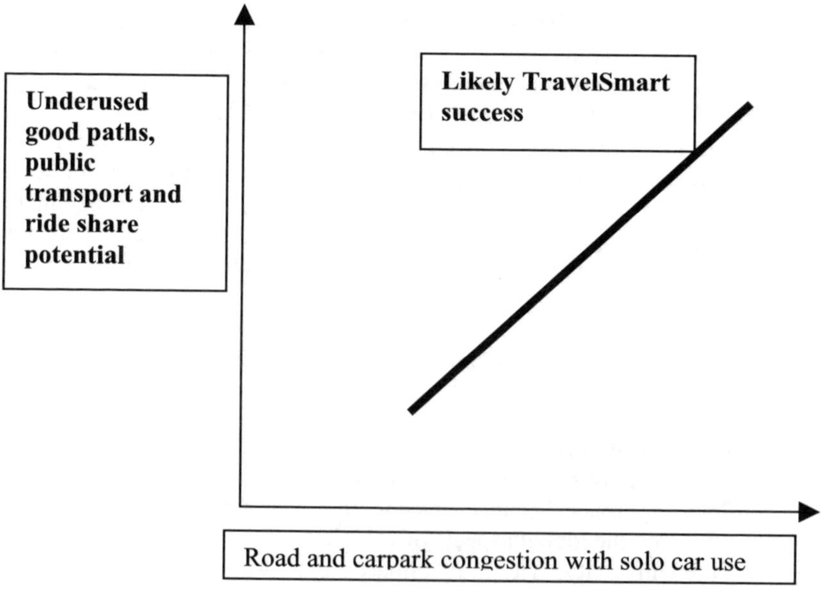

Figure 2: Relationship of likely TravelSmart success to existing access infrastructure and use.

With congested road and parking infrastructure dominated by solo car users and underused attractive alternatives, the TravelSmart process is easy, fig. 2.

The JCU 'before' Survey stimulated 20 pages of written comments from survey prompts, indicating strong interest in urban travel. The JCU coordinator fielded or generated a total of 867 emails in 2004. Bike use and walking were supported, with some concern about danger. There were concerns over price, frequency and reliability with bus use.

There was an expressed unmet demand for safe and attractive alternatives to solo car use. By October, T shirts were designed, printed and distributed, fig. 3, along with hundreds of 'car less' buttons. Central to the long term goals of establishing a self-sustaining reduction in car use, committed staff and students formed a JCU Car Less Club in November 2004, Fig. 3, and placed an article in the JCU student diary for 2005. Instant changes are unlikely, but a gradual, long term paradigm shift [11] is plausible. Infrastructure changes making walking and cycling safer, smoother, more direct and 'normal' is a process rather than a result.

Figure 3: The founding members of JCU car less club.

Figure 4: JCU upgrades identifies path chokepoints.

3.3 General lessons and recommendations (R).

R1. Develop trust and continuity with all stakeholders.

R2. Acknowledge the link of Destination, surroundings, and unmet demands for alternative transport, fig. 2.

R3. Allow that the host destination and surrounding councils will want to upgrade infrastructure (in all their sustainability policies). Allow that this will take time. In a spirit of cooperation, path continuity is now an open dialogue between the Facilities Management office and users. The University has proved willing to maximise path continuity and safety for users, fig 4. Figure 4 shows a destination of good will (indicated by embracing TravelSmart to begin with). Infrastructure upgrades are likely to follow the focus on TravelSmart behaviour and needs.

R4. Expand TravelSmart intervention programs to run for more than one calendar year. North Queenslanders have ‘Murri time’: some things can only mature at their own pace. Compacting a full start-to-finish project into one year does not allow much time for gestation or latent synergies to develop.

It is recommended that TravelSmart programs in future take a longer time frame than one year, that there is a ‘destination’ driven, rather than a ‘support provider’ time frame for implementation of the project. Safe paths and behaviour change may need time to self reinforce.

R5. Queensland Transport develop a free ride-share destination web based data base shell.

R6. Queensland Transport or other transport departments fund a public transport data base for all population centres in their jurisdiction. A web-accessible data base is already operating for SE Qld. Entered start and finish times and locations provide the user with details of how to best get from A to B.

R7. Allow the host Destination a reasonable degree of autonomy and encourage innovation. People; champions, who wish to promote alternatives to solo car use may come up with things like wearable buttons, fig. 5.

R8. Encourage identification of suitable once-per-week Focus Days, using e-distributed posters put up by supporters in each teaching and work area fig. 5.

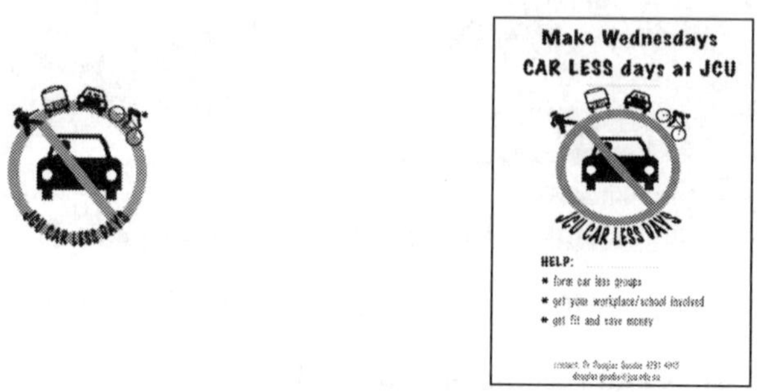

Figure 5: Distributed, locally designed button and e-poster to place in supporters’ work or study areas.

4 Conclusions

Service providers need to remain consistent in the undertakings of their work units, not allowing stress to override the agreed processes of projects. Consistency may be hard to achieve but bureaucratic processes need to support the stated goals of their own work units. Professional continuity is imperative for bureaucracies to support agreed projects. But for the strength and solidarity of people within JCU and Queensland Transport, the JCU project would have been destroyed. Any readers who have or may come up against seeming personality-based institutional barriers to sustainability change should persist, although there may be a personal cost. Despite the emergent resistance to this innovative pilot, there were successes, and useful lessons. Promoting Wednesdays as car less days achieved some success in travel behaviour change.

There are travel behaviour influences that are 'universal'. Convenience of car use is in tension with road congestion, parking ease, cost or stress and suitability of alternatives. When cars are easily and cheaply used and parked, with long distances from main residential areas, in an already car dependent, behaviour change without high petrol price increases may be small.

Each Destinations project must try to get as many supporters to the program as early in the process as possible, maintain professional continuity, and consider strategies that will maximise change within their unique situation. Long time frames and slowly updated path and end-of trip facilities are likely to flow from any well-managed TravelSmart process.

Developing and distributing free software for use by destinations to facilitate ride sharing was identified as highly desirable to further TravelSmart Destination goals.

Destinations can help badge themselves 'green' by embracing TravelSmart principles of reward, support and information on travel alternatives.

TravelSmart innovation and uptake will have an intrinsic pace for each destination. Flexible milestone dates, tailored to the rhythms of the host destination may help supporters feel ownership of the uptake process.

The methodology developed by TravelSmart Queensland and other TravelSmart proponents converge on engagement, commitment, support, information, inducements and rewards; relying on champions and volunteers to help in the normative shift to more sustainable urban travel. TravelSmart Queensland had a well developed draft Destinations program. With mutual respect in guiding and supporting host TravelSmart destinations, their methodology is sound, comprehensive, logical and likely to be as successful as the many other TravelSmart projects already working to reduce greenhouse gases and fossil fuel depletion, while promoting environmental and personal health. Under supportive leadership, TravelSmart Destinations, as refined by Queensland Transport, has a bright future.

References

[1] Jarach M. Overview of the literature on barriers to the diffusion of renewable energy sources in agriculture. Appl. En. 32:2 117- 131, 1989.

[2] Phillips R.. Long Range Planning. London. 27:4, 143-145, 1994.

[3] ACF Institutions for Sustainability. Australian Conservation Foundation ACF 1 -37. http://www.acfonline.org.au/docs/publications/tp007.pdf 2004

[4] Leibovitz J. 2003. Institutional barriers to associative city-region governance: the politics of institution-building and economic governance in 'Canada's Technology Triangle.' Urban Studies: 40:13, 2613-2642.

[5] Goudie D. Toward Sustainable Urban Travel. PhD thesis. James Cook University. 2001.

[6] Goudie D. Zonal method for urban travel surveys: sustainability and sample distance from the CBD. Journal of Transport Geography 10: 287 - 301. Elsevier, 2002.

[7] Cuthill M. Community well-being – the ultimate goal of democratic governance. Queensland Planner. 44:2. 8-11, 2004.

[8] O'Neill Y. Social marketing http://www.ses.nsw.gov.au/papers /young_oneill_1999.pdf

[9] Richardson AJ, Ampt ES and Meyburg AH. Survey methods for transport planning. Eucalyptus press. 459, 1995.

[10] O'Neill P. Why don't they listen – Developing a risk communication model to promote community safety behaviour. The International Emergency Management Society, 11th Annual Conference Proceedings, May 18-21, 2004, Melbourne, Victoria, Australia 160-169, 2004 .

[11] Fien J. Education for the environment- critical curriculum theorising and environmental education. Deakin University, Australia, 65, 1993.

After the revolution, sustainable development – Las Terrazas, Cuba

J. D. Davey
School of Architecture, Southern Illinois University, Carbondale, Illinois, U.S.A.

Abstract

West of Havana, in the heart of the Rosario Mountain Chain, this natural complex covers more than 5,000 hectares. Ecology-oriented, the Las Terrazas complex is associated with the Ecological Research Center for Sierra del Rosario Reserve, responsible for monitoring and studying the mountain chain's different ecosystems. The humid tropical climate results in the area's predominance of evergreen forests and abundant array of wildlife. Many beautiful bird species inhabit this area, including sparrows, nightingales and the Cuban trogon. Located in the heart of the Mountain range of the Rosary, declared by UNESCO a Reserve of the Biosphere, 50 km to the West of Havana, is the tourist complex "the Terraces". It is an experience of sustainable development, in a natural space of 5 000 hectares, with a laborious community of 1,000 inhabitants, where they harmonize natural and the moderate action of man, with an aesthetic sense, in a conservacionista scope with more than 30 years of experience. Las Terrazas sets an example of Cuba's concern with sustainability to include: (1) Raising the standard of living through satisfying in an integral manner the material and social needs of the population with emphasis on raising the educational and cultural level and including the environmental dimension in the economic and social development of the country, (2) Integration of economic, fiscal, commercial, energy, agriculture and industry policies to protect the environment and guarantee the sustainable use of natural resources in a framework of justice and equity, (3) Preserving for the next millennium the social achievements of the revolutionary process, (4) Defending collective access to the fundamental social services which are the guarantee of equity supporting sustainability, (5) Searching for greater efficiency in the productive processes, alternative sources of energy and sustainable agriculture practices, (6) Better education and dissemination processes aimed at increasing environmental awareness, and (7) Finding solutions to key environmental problems in the country such as land degradation, water contamination, sewage and environmental conditions in human settlements, deforestation, and loss of biological diversity.
Keywords: sustainable environments, conservation, environmental politics.

1 Introduction

According to the legend and lore of the revolution Che and his band of guerillas would retreat into the terrain and lush forests of Las Terrazas along the San Jaun River trail to regroup and rejuvenate before they continued their fight against the Batistia regime. Some also believe that these water have they same powers as does the In the early 1500's, Spanish conquistadors mounted expeditions to find the legendary spring whose magic waters could rejuvenate the elderly and heal the sick. In 1512, Ponce DeLeon failed in his attempt to reach the mysterious hidden valley containing a crystal fountain of healing water known as the "Fountain of Youth". Some forty-four years ago three Marxist Revolutionaries had big plans to change the structure of their country and thought education and land reform was one of the paths, after the machinegun.

Osmany Cienfugoes was the brother of Camille Cienfugoes one of the Marxist trinity together with Che Guevara and the bearded one (barbar). He was the party that led the land reform in 1968 that created *Las* Terrazas. Las Terrazas, a UNESCO world heritage site was an extensive reforestation project that turned what some call a desolate mountain into a beautiful Hawaii-like setting, with forests and a sustainable economy, which allows the residents to live a sustainable lifestyle in harmony with nature containing workshops with entrepreneurs, ecologists and residents who are creating a third way of sustainable development. Just 45 minutes west of Havana, in the heart of the *Rosario Mountain Chain*, you'll discover this natural complex that covers more than 5,000 hectares. A Experience of Sustainable Development, in a natural space of 5 000 hectares, with a laborious community of 1 000 inhabitants, where they harmonize natural and the moderate action of the man, with an aesthetic sense, in a conservacionista scope with more than 30 years of experience. Ecology-oriented, the *Las Terrazas* complex is associated with the *Ecological Research Center for Sierra del Rosario Reserve*, responsible for monitoring and studying the mountain chain different ecosystems. The humid tropical climate results in the area's predominance of evergreen forests and abundant array of wildlife. Many beautiful bird species inhabit this area, including sparrows, nightingales and the Cuban trogon.

2 A description of Las Terrazas

Its importance and interest is stressed by the fact that Las Terrazas is situated in the Sierra del Rosario, one of Cuba's natural strongholds, which was designated a Biosphere Reserve by the United Nations Educational, Scientific and Cultural Organization (UNESCO) in 1985. This experience was initially aimed at developing tourism in a beautiful mountainous area of high natural and historic values, as a major way to reanimate the zone's economy and improve the people's standard of living. Las Terrazas community was conceived as a miniature city, with basic facilities for its urban functioning and an architectural style whose key element is the harmonization of buildings with the landscape and the relief. The center of the leisure industry in that territory is at the Moka

Hotel, built in the San Juan Valley, at the foot of the Loma del Salón, or Salon Hill, with an architectural style that respects the local flora, which also contributes to embellishing that cozy establishment of 26 rooms (22 doubles, three triples and one suite). The complement to leisure lies in an infrastructure that aims to integrate tourism into the community, like in the case of the "Fonda de las Mercedes", conceived as an attraction that facilitates visitors' interaction with a local family and the rescue of Cuban culinary traditions. This rural community with a population of 850 was founded in 1971, as part of a global, cultural and natural preservation project that included a forest management approach involving terracing. Nestled in a small valley on the shores of San Juan Lake, the most striking aspect of this town is the very unusual and appealing architecture. Las Terrazas also serves as an artist commune with shops such as the craft boutique that uses recycled paper, wood and ceramic, a serigraphy store and a vegetable fiber weaving shop.

3 A socialist perspective on sustainable planning

Las Terrazas sets an example of Cuba's concern with sustainability to include: (1) Raising the standard of living through satisfying in an integral manner the material and social needs of the population with emphasis on raising the educational and cultural level and including the environmental dimension in the economic and social development of the country, (2) Integration of economic, fiscal, commercial, energy, agriculture and industry policies to protect the environment and guarantee the sustainable use of natural resources in a framework of justice and equity, (3) Preserve for the next millennium the social achievements of the revolutionary process, (4) Defend collective access to the fundamental social services which are the guarantee of equity supporting sustainability, (5) Search for greater efficiency in the productive processes, alternative sources of energy and sustainable agriculture practices, (6) Better education and dissemination processes aimed at increasing environmental awareness, and (7) Finding solutions to key environmental problems in the country such as land degradation, water contamination, sewage and environmental conditions in human settlements, deforestation, and loss of biological diversity.

4 A capitalist perspective of sustainable planning

What comprises sustainable planning and what does not is of course debatable to a point. Planning naturally is an activity, which incorporates business. The zoning of an area directs the types of development that can or can't happen. As discovered by Hawken and Lovins "the best solutions are based not on tradeoffs or "balance" between these objectives but on design integration achieving all of them together", (Natural Capitalism, p. xi). Sustainable Planning is ultimately about ensuring that development continues to occur in such a way that enables both society and nature to gain in the process. What this means at a practical level will be highly variable. In some cases this may involve the exclusion of areas from development altogether to ensure the conservation of biodiversity, which simply can't be replaced through re-vegetation programs. In other cases it will require development to observe strict 'sustainability' codes of conduct. Conditions may be placed on a development affecting the materials used, the orientation, the use of water, the sewage treatment, the building design and so on.

5 Green infrastructure: a framework for smart growth

"Green infrastructure" is the network of natural lands, open space, waterways, and smart growth design measures that form the framework for healthy and sustainable communities. With a green infrastructure in place, communities can protect native species and ecological processes, maintain clean air and water, reduce habitat fragmentation, pollution, and other threats to biodiversity, and improve the health and quality of life for people.

5.1 Natural

Natural areas are sites that are largely undisturbed by humans, with native vegetation areas distributed in naturally occurring patterns across the landscape. These patterns change over time under the influence of drought, flooding, fires, and the interactions between plants and wildlife. Among their benefits, natural areas:

- Provide a wide range of ecological services such as efficient nutrient cycling, soil enrichment and flood control.
- Provide valuable habitat for fish, wildlife and plants.
- Increase environmental flexibility in the face of natural disasters such as fire, drought and flooding.

5.2 Open

Open space is undeveloped sites that don't meet the criteria for natural areas because of human disturbance, but still provide habitat, scenery and other benefits. Open spaces can include areas such as farmland, recreational areas and utility corridors. Among its benefits, open space:

- Provide area for restoration to buffer natural areas.
- Provide recreational areas and visual relief in urban areas.
- Create a sense of community identity.

5.3 Greenways

Greenways are continuous or patchy areas of vegetation that provide corridors for the movement of humans and wildlife. They often follow natural waterways or land features, and may connect natural areas and open space. Highest quality greenways provide habitat and allow for the movement of wildlife, plants and water from one area to another. Greenways:

- Function as linkages and increase habitat connectivity and availability.
- Provide alternative transportation options (walking and cycling).
- Stimulate business development focused around recreation and tourism.

By prioritizing the protection of critical habitat and ecosystems, green infrastructure provides a link between the concentration of development in settled areas and the protection of rural and undeveloped areas, which are the two main elements of smart growth. When green infrastructure considerations are included in land use and transportation planning, biodiversity is protected, undeveloped areas are preserved, and corridors between natural areas are established, thus increasing the habitat value of protected areas in and around developed areas. Additionally, the increased natural vitality makes urban areas more attractive to residents, which is good for the economic health of communities.

6 Principles of green infrastructure

Green infrastructure adds a new set of tools and solutions to aid the fight against sprawl, including watershed management, the incorporation of biodiversity planning, and increasing public access to open spaces. There are several basic principles:

1. Protect, restore and maintain natural resources and ecosystem function, both in developed and undeveloped areas.
2. Use best available science to assess natural resources and determine areas of environmental vitality as the first step to land use planning.
3. Target for conservation areas of important ecological function, critical habitat, and corridors to connect such areas with already protected land.
4. Reduce the need for expensive storm-water management, flood control and restoration projects by protecting water resources, flood plains, wetlands and other buffers.
5. Limit the negative effects of development on habitat, air and water quality by ensuring decent vegetation cover and reducing paved surfaces.
6. Enhance stewardship of open space and natural areas by increasing environmental educational opportunities.
7. Engage citizens, organizations and agencies of the region to conserve biodiversity, and foster a sustainable relationship between society and nature in the region.
8. Enrich the quality of life for the region's citizenry, and support tourist and natural resource-based industries through increased access to open space.
9. Protect environmental quality by integrating green infrastructure with land use, transportation and water/sewer planning.

10. Create wildlife-friendly and environmentally sensitive regulations and incentive programs.

- awareness, training and education
- Local Government resourcing
- regional partnerships and planning
- legislative frameworks, and
- information and monitoring.

7 "Smart" development-guidelines and practices

Concentrate development in compact town centers. Town centers are developed at a higher density than surrounding land and defined by clear boundaries & identifiable hubs of activity.

- Site new development in or adjacent to existing settlements consistent with historic densities and patterns.
- Maximize average site density; minimize average lot area.
- Maximize floor area to site coverage ratio-build multi-story buildings.
- Site buildings close to street and close to each other-minimize setbacks and lot frontage.
- Minimize on-site parking-incorporate shared access, shared and on-street parking.
- Incorporate mixed uses into town centers to provide choices for all community members to meet their needs for housing, employment, goods, services, recreation, & social interaction.
- Promote projects that mix residential, commercial, and office uses.
- Site new housing within walking distance of commercial and employment centers.
- Provide a mix of housing types-single and multi-family, low and high income.

- Orient buildings to the street; break up the mass and facades of larger buildings.
- Screen and landscape parking areas; break-up large parking areas.
- Site parking under, to the rear, or to the side of buildings.
- Incorporate an internal network of paths, parks & commons for neighbourhood use.

- Organize streets in a coherent network-relate street design to the land use they serve.
- Maintain street connectivity (avoid dead ends) and integrate new roads within the existing street network-maintain variations on a traditional girded street pattern.

- Incorporate pedestrian circulation into street design-including sidewalks on at least one side of the street, well-defined pedestrian crossings.
- Provide internal network of pathways-incorporate off-street shortcuts for walkers and cyclists. Connect to regional path systems where possible.
- Design streets in central districts and neighbourhood for slow vehicle speeds.
- Maximize density and mix of development near transit and other transportation nodes.
- Maintain an overall low density by promoting projects that cluster small-lot developments and protect large tracts of continuous open land.
- Incorporate buffers between developed and resource land.

- Incorporate "green infrastructure" including natural features, drainage ways, floodplains and other functional open space.
- Define development and building envelopes to exclude environmentally sensitive areas.
- Minimize clearing & grading by using existing contours and vegetation in site design.
- Protect undisturbed vegetated stream buffers of sufficient width to protect water resources and wildlife habitat.
- Minimize fragmentation of wildlife habitats-core areas as well as connecting corridors.
- Incorporate non-structural and structural storm water treatment practices.

8 The Cuban position

Cuba has endured through the pre-Revolutionary stage, characterized by exploitation and depletion of the natural riches since the discovery (1492) up to the revolutionary triumph (1959), four centuries that include the neocolonial exploitation carried out by the United States of America. Among the aggressions carried out on the environment during the colonial as well as during the neocolonial stage stand out the depletion of large forest areas and the irrational use of land for agriculture and cattle, which resulted in degradation and erosion of soil, waters, relief and vegetation. To these can be added the deplorable conditions of health in the population due to the poor condition of services in this area and the serious social problems associated to extreme poverty, racial and sex discrimination, social inequality, illiteracy and exploitation in general. This panorama was inherited by the Revolution when it seized power in 1959, and because of its humanist character, it made its main principle the increase of the level and quality of life of its people in it's widest sense, principles upon which today the sustainability of development is argued. The most outstanding achievements during the first years of the creation of a new society are, in brief: Eradication of extreme poverty.

- Total transformation of the agricultural structure.
- Eradication of illiteracy, schooling of all the children and the creation of a significant autochthonous scientifical-technical capacity.
- Infant mortality rate was reduced from more than 60 to 9.4 per thousand and life expectancy rose from 61 to more than 75 years.
- Health programs against infectious diseases and health services were established, so today there is a doctor for every 203 persons.
- The population with access to piped water and sanitation facilities increased from 50% to 89.1% and 91.5% respectively.
- The population with electricity services increased from 56% to 94%
- Forest area in the country increased from 14% to 19.5%
- A process of territorial planning was developed, which allowed the introduction of an environmental element in most investment projects with a socioeconomic character.

Relevant moments of the Cuban environmental policy such as the creation of the National Commission for the Protection of the Environment and Conservation of Natural Resources, and in that same year, the inclusion in the Constitution of Article 27, which represented the reflection of the environmental protection in the Fundamental Law of the country, and how Law 33 of January 10 1981 -one of the pioneer laws in Latin America regarding the establishment a global protection of natural resources- established the basic tenets for conservation, protection and improvement and transformation of the environment and the rational use of natural resources, according to the integral policy for the development of Cuba. During the 1997 Rio Summit of Environment and Development Fidel Castro acknowledged the signing of the Convention on Biological Diversity and Framework Convention of the United Nations on Climate Change. It was a short time after the Summit Meeting, in Article 27 of the Constitution of the Cuban Republic; the concept of sustainable development was introduced. That same year, The Vienna Convention for the Protection of the Ozone Layer and the Montreal Protocol regarding substances that deplete the ozone layer were put into effect. In 1993 the National Program for Environment and Development was created and approved, which is the Cuban adaptation of Agenda 21 and includes additional topics in the interest of the developmental strategy of the country (Annex II). From this program spring the Territorial Program in order to adapt it to local demands and priorities. The paper remarks the creation in 1994 of the Ministry of Science, Technology and Environment as the ministry that will rule establishing the environmental policy of the country, with an adequate structure for carrying out this important task. Within the improvement of the legal framework, during 1995 and 1996 several legal bodies that reinforce environmental protection in different economical sectors were approved. It is worth mentioning those regarding Environmental Impact Assessment and Environmental State Inspection, Mine Law and the Tributary System. Likewise Cuban activity in the international environmental field is strengthened through concrete actions in several Conventions, which the country has signed. In 1995 activities dealing with environmental management were consolidated and strengthened in the country. With the IX Meeting of Latin American and Caribbean Ministers, with representatives from governments of 25 countries in the region and 26 international, regional and sub-regional organizations, NGOs and other sectors. As a colophon to the activities Cuba has carried out during these 5 years in the environmental sphere, there was the confection of the National Environmental Strategy and the Project for the Law for the Environment. That strategy offered a wide general conceptual frame for the National Program for Environment and Development, updating its scope and reach in according with the years that have passed since its creation in 1993. Project for the Law, took into consideration the economical, social and institutional changes that took place in the country, as well as the evolution of the international situation. It should be recognized that the difficult economic situation that has affected Cuba during the last years has affected the exploitation of the natural resources and has limited the actions for their conservation, but a search for a higher efficiency in production processes, the development of education and divulgence to achieve a higher environmental conscience, the search for alternative energy sources, the use of biological products in agriculture, will without doubt be essential actions for its recovery. Cuba with its entire struggle, to include the 1991 Russian collapse and the 40 plus years of embargo/blockade remains strong in their position on the environment.

9 Conclusion

J.R. McNeill (2000), in his work An Environmental History of the Twentieth-Century World, something new under the sun contents that "the Green Revolution was a child of the Cold War." This green revolution was a technical and managerial package exported from the First World to the Third beginning in the 1940s and making it greatest strides in the 1960s and 1970s. The new zeitgeist of sustainable/green-design and living that is heralded in today's agora is, as Solomon noted "nothing new under the sun". It is part and parcel a sleeping giant both in societies acts of omission and commission. To ignore the possible solutions of sustainable planning/development/living is due course for disaster, to embrace it as the "new solution" is to create a false representation one that does not acknowledge a rich past. A past and a present such as Las Terrazas.

References

[1] Carley, Rachel CUBA 400 Years of Architectural Heritage, (New York, 1997).

[2] Davidson Marshal B. in Joseph J. Thorndike, jr. ed., *Three Centuries of Notable American Architects*, (New York, 1981), 51-65.

[3] Davey Richard, *Cuba Past and Present*, (London, 1898), 31.

[4] Hawken, P, Lovins, A & Lovins, H *Natural Capitalism.* Bay Back Books (2000).

www.witpress.com, ISSN 1743-3541 (on-line)

[5] Locke, John. *Second Treatise of Government (1982)*. Harlan Davidson, Arlington Heights, Ill.
[6] Loomis John A., *Cuba's Forgotten Art Schools Revolution of Forms*, New York, 1999).
[7] McNeill J.R., in his work *An Environmental History of the Twentieth-Century World* (2000).

Regeneration and sustainable development in the transformation of Shanghai

Y. Chen
Department of Real estate and Housing, Faculty of Architecture, Delft University of Technology

Abstract

Globalisation has had an increasing impact on the transformation of Chinese cities ever since China adopted the open door policy in 1978. Many cities in China have been struggling with the challenges of urban regeneration created by the restructuring of the traditional economy and increasing competition between cities for resources, investment and business. The closure of docks, warehouses and industries, and the deteriorating position of traditional urban centres not only created problems but also created exceptional opportunities to reshape cities and create new functions. But this kind of process also generates a series of physical, economic and social consequences for cities to tackle. In many cases the problems exceed the capacity of the local community to adapt and respond. This paper examines a number of urban regeneration projects in Shanghai, in the hope of providing a better understanding of the process of urban regeneration in China and how best to ensure that such regeneration is sustainable. The paper reassesses the aims of regeneration, the mechanisms involved in the regeneration process and its physical, economic and social consequences, discusses how to achieve sustainable development in urban regeneration and makes recommendations for future action.

1 Introduction

Global market forces and increasing globalisation are clearly playing a role in the transformation of cities and towns. In most countries urban systems are experiencing dramatic changes brought about by economic restructuring, continuous mass migration and the arrival of immigrants. Over the last 20 years the same kind of urban transformation has been observed in almost all Chinese

WIT Transactions on Ecology and the Environment, Vol 81, © 2005 WIT Press
www.witpress.com, ISSN 1743-3541 (on-line)

towns and cities, many of which have experienced explosive economic growth, improvement of individuals' quality of life and rapid urbanisation. The opportunities for urban expansion and economic growth have left a legacy of physical, economic and social consequences. Old harbours and factories have been closed because of their failure to cope with technological change or the contraction in manufacturing, local shops and traditional business have been wiped out by severe competition from new types of retail outlet like supermarkets and shopping malls, old houses and run-down inner-city areas, long deprived of adequate maintenance, have been torn down to make room for new building, old communities have been relocated to the outskirts of the city and in most cases ripped apart. In many cases these types of problems have exceeded the capacity of the local community to adapt and respond.

Now that many parts of China are going through the same kind of transformation that is taking place in the cities of most developing countries, it is becoming important to bring together the lessons learned from experiences in areas that have already undergone the transformation process, as a way of achieving a better understanding of the process of regeneration and how best to promote it. A particular concern is how to ensure that the regeneration process is sustainable, not only to secure economic revitalisation and make the best use of existing resources but also to take account of the wider public interest.

The present paper examines the redevelopment of Lujiazui and Xintiandi, two urban regeneration projects carried out in Shanghai in the 1990s, to provide an understanding of the regeneration process in Shanghai and the general transformation in people's ideas about urban regeneration policy during the period, before going on to make suggestions about keys to success and lessons to be applied to further urban regeneration in Chinese cities.

2 Urban regeneration in Shanghai

'Urban regeneration' was seen as way of revitalising declining cities in North America and Western Europe, where urban dynamics were affected by economic restructuring, the decline of cities relying on traditional industries and increasing social isolation [1]. Schemes for urban reconstruction, revitalisation, renewal and redevelopment schemes drawn up between 1950 and 1990 [2] were followed in the 1990s by schemes for urban regeneration, designed to achieve 'the regrowth of economic activity where it has been lost; the restoration of social function where there has been dysfunction, or social inclusion where there has been exclusion; and the restoration of environmental quality or ecological balance where it has been lost' [3]. Unlike other such schemes, schemes for urban regeneration aim to achieve a mixture of economic, social and environmental targets, and are particularly concerned with the sustainability of the city's growth.

The development and growth of Chinese cities follow some of the patterns established in developed industrial countries, though everything is happening much faster and on a much shorter time-scale. The special thing about the growth of Chinese cities is that the reform and open policy implemented in 1978 freed the cities from years of imposed urban policies restricting their growth and forbidding population movement. Since then the new freedom has triggered explosive growth in towns and cities throughout the country. This growth and the resulting mass migration from rural to urban areas immediately encountered a huge shortage of public facilities, brought about by long-term neglect and lack of investment. Infrastructure, housing, offices, neglected neighbourhoods and the urban environment generally, all needed to catch up with an increasing demand fuelled by rapid economic growth.

Shanghai, an international metropolis in East Asia since the first half of the twentieth century, faced exactly this challenge, to upgrade its urban environment. Even though the local government cleared several slum areas in accordance with proposals made by the 1953 master plan, only a limited number of families benefited from the rehabilitation scheme. The lack of budget for infrastructure and housing led to deterioration in the physical environment of Shanghai, so that at the end of 1970s the city found itself overpopulated, underdeveloped and unattractive.

Many transformations in the post-reform era targeted run-down old inner city areas, areas of declining traditional industry and abandoned dockyards. Such changes can be seen in various places in the inner city and outskirts of Shanghai, where old houses have been torn down to make room for a more extensive road network, old neighbourhoods have given way to new shopping centres, traditional industries have moved out of the city centre to find more spacious accommodation, and docks were abandoned when new ports were established at locations nearer the sea. As many parts of Shanghai began to be transformed, local government was increasingly frustrated by the inadequate budget for infrastructure, housing construction and the renewal of inner-city areas, forcing practical consideration to be given to involving private finance and private developers in urban renewal programmes. In 1995 the SMG announced a series of policies to attract private finance to land development, the construction of infrastructure and, more particularly, urban renewal.

As the cost of leasehold land in city centres continued to increase, the cost of carrying out traditional rehabilitation projects in the city centre became impossibly high for both the public sector and the private developer. Many city dwellers were forced to move to new flats on the outskirts of the city. The pressure on developers forced many of them to tear down old buildings and replace them with high-rise buildings or high-density complexes in urban redevelopment projects. Efforts to preserve old buildings generally failed to compete with the compulsion to achieve the greatest possible commercial profit.

In the last few years, however, a change has begun to take place in people's way of thinking. People have become increasingly concerned about the lack of character displayed by new large-scale developments, not only in new satellite towns but also in Shanghai's historical centre. At the same time people started to become aware of a different approach, based on the 'adaptive reuse' of buildings and inspired by pioneering work in European and American cities. Originally such projects were limited to individual historical building with high preservation value. Old villas and apartments built in the early 1900s were converted into restaurants, teahouses or hotels. Later the experiment was extended to the larger-scale redevelopment of whole areas. The redevelopment of Xintiandi, as will be explained later in this paper, is a typical example. Not only has the adaptive reuse of buildings occupying an area of 30,000 m^2 preserved a historical physical continuum but, more significantly, finance for the project came from private sources rather than government subsidies, which meant that the project was deeply concerned with achieving economic sustainability.

Experience in Xintiandi has provided a fresh stimulus to local officials and private developers to look for alternative approaches to urban regeneration. In recent years the shift in thinking has reflected greater concern for the social consequences of these transformations to old neighbourhoods. Many critics of current urban regeneration programmes argue that historical continuity requires preservation of both the physical and the social environment if the pattern of historical and cultural development is not to be lost. Early projects totally ignored the issue of social justice: the end results only benefited a special group of upmarket consumers and certainly not the original communities. The new way of thinking has led to today's new style rehabilitation plan. In today's rehabilitation projects most of the original residents are relocated back to their old neighbourhood as soon the upgrading work is complete.

3 The challenge of sustainable development

While sustainable development aims to combine environmental sustainability, economic efficiency and attention to social needs [4], in practice it is easy to lose sight of the aim of urban regeneration and the factors that lead to success. Current experience with urban regeneration in Shanghai and other Chinese cities shows that the prevailing emphasis is still on economic growth, so that urban regeneration is often treated as property development and the success of the project is often mainly measured by the level of return on investment. These attempts take account of market forces and the interests of end users but fail to address the other two important aspects of urban development, social needs and environmental sustainability. In the process of urban regeneration in Shanghai, two issues have been ignored which need to be seriously addressed, social justice and the preservation of historical buildings.

Social justice means being concerned with the needs of the least well-off and ensuring that those needs are not ignored in the process of transformation. China has a series of policies at central and local level dealing with relocation and rehabilitation, most of which focus on economic compensation. This approach helps to reduce the economic loss suffered by displaced residents but takes little or no account of the existing historic and social fabric linking the local community with the place.

The idea of preserving old industrial buildings, folk housing and traditional city life, based on ecological considerations, is concerned with the minimisation of waste and the preservation of diversity. In Chinese cities old buildings are often seen as obstacles to new development but in fact they provide exceptional opportunities for the reuse of a historic legacy. Conservation can make possible the maintenance of the historic continuum of city life, something that is quite impossible if old buildings are replaced by new mass-produced high-rise. The lesson to be learnt from the failure of traditional conservation plans is that conservation needs to take into consideration the influence of market forces. The aim of conservation is not achieved when old buildings are left to rot inside a conservation area. Rather conservation needs to provide new functions and new driving forces for old buildings. A number of good examples of conservation can be found in America and Europe, for example the reuse of a Fiat factory in Italy as a shopping centre.

The key to improving the process is balanced incremental development, ensuring that the attraction of new functions takes place gradually and is recognised by the locals, rather than a sudden big bang approach, in which the traditional urban fabric is torn apart and a large amount of space and new faces with no interest in the local environment suddenly come on the market. Achieving this goal will require involvement by both the government and the private sector. Experience in Shanghai shows a continuing increase in private sector involvement in urban regeneration projects. Since the public sector lacks the experience, know-how and financial mechanisms required to put into practice all its plans for upgrading, it increasingly depends on private investment, as in the case of the redevelopment of Lujiazui, Shanghai's new central business district. The creation of public-private partnerships makes it necessary to define the way the two sectors are to share responsibility for ensuring the success and sustainability of the urban regeneration projects in which they are involved.

4 Lujiazui financial centre: Shanghai's new central business district

Lujiazui is a 1.7 km^2 area situated on the east bank of the Huangpu river in an area known as Pudong, which lies immediately opposite the Bund, Shanghai's historical centre and site of the former foreign settlement. Historically Lujiazui's development followed the growth of the port of Shanghai. But with no bridges or tunnels to link Pudong with downtown, the development of Lujiazui, as of other parts of Pudong, had lagged behind for years. In Mao's time, a number of heavy industries, with villages to house their workers, were established in the area adjoining the old harbour, ferries and warehouses. Over the years the quality of life in the Pudong area deteriorated steadily because of the lack of investment in public facilities and the lack of maintenance of the area's residential properties. Environmental pollution produced by the factories increased the problems of pollution faced by local communities.

The idea of redeveloping Lujiazui and its hinterland emerged at the end of the 1970s. In 1988, after years of research and feasibility studies by local planners, the city decided to reconstruct Lujiazui's 1.7 km^2 to create a central business district as the core of Pudong's 28 km^2 Lujiazui commercial and financial district. It is worth noting that this plan came about in part thanks to interaction with foreign expertise as provided for example by the Paris-based Institute d'Aménagement et d'Urbanisme de la Région Ile de France (IAURIF - Ile-de-

France Region Urban Planning Institute), which provides technical assistance to the Shanghai municipal government (SMG) on metropolitan planning issues [5]. Since the locals had little experience of developing central business districts on such a scale, in 1992 they called in architects of various nationalities, based in the UK, France, Japan and the US, to provide ideas and know-how for the project. The architects were invited to tender for the provision of consultancy services. A detailed plan for Lujiazui, based on the five plans, was finalised in the same year [6]. The plan focused on quality and sustainability, and took into account both economic sustainability and environmental quality.

The plan as finalised, like other plans prepared by the same architects, paid little attention to the existing situation on the site and the possibility of reusing old buildings, nor was proper consideration given to the social consequences of relocating the local community. This might be explained in part by the poor condition of the existing buildings. But the key factor was that the SMG wanted to create a memorable skyline for Shanghai's future central business district, and so wanted Lujiazui to be built as a futuristic 21st-century international financial centre, in sharp contrast to the 19th-century European-style Bund on the other side of the river.

Thanks to enormous publicity and a strong international profile, the redevelopment of Lujiazui attracted great interest not only from private developers in the region but also from foreign investors. To stimulate investment in Lujiazui, the public sector experimented with a series of public-public and public-private partnerships for projects in land development, infrastructure development and real estate development, involving not only different levels of government but also banks and private investors. Fortune World Company, a joint venture between a local public company and a Thai investor, is one successful example of public sector collaboration with the private sector. In this case funding was obtained through private financial channels to develop the 50 hectare site adjoining the Huangpu River in Lujiazui.

Massive investment has gradually managed to change the face of Lujiazui. In just ten years, with more and more banks, insurance companies and commercial businesses setting up branches in Lujiazui, old polluted factories have disappeared from the skyline of Lujiazui, to be replaced by offices, business centres, parks and large areas of green space. The new image of Lujiazui has attracted public attention and encouraged tourism. The resulting increased demand for entertainment, restaurants and shops led to l government to decide to add such functions to an area where originally only offices and hotels were permitted to be built. Substantial amounts of public money were invested in improving the quality of the urban environment. To increase accessibility the local government built roads, a metro, bridges and tunnels. It also cleaned up the once polluted river and replaced slum houses with green space.

The few traditional buildings which, thanks to the protection provided by the conservation plan, were left untouched by the redevelopment of Lujiazui, were converted into exhibition halls or museums. Most of the old industrial buildings, warehouses and homes were torn down to make way for new skyscrapers. This decision reflected the belief shared by many locals at the beginning of the 1990s:

the future of Shanghai was represented by economic growth and modern architecture designed by American and European architects; old buildings and neighbourhoods represented barriers to Shanghai achieving its ambitions for the future. Critics however argue that the lack of any historical memory in its internationalised architectural image has transformed Lujiazui into a western city and failed to provide the Shanghainese with a local identify. The debate continues, but there are no easy solutions. Some years later, the Xintiandi redevelopment project attracted much attention because of its alternative approach to urban redevelopment.

5 Xintiandi: where Shanghai's past meets its future

Xintiandi (Chinese for 'new heaven and earth') used to be a 30,000m^2 neighbourhood located near Huaihai Road, a well-known high-class shopping thoroughfare in the Luwuan district in central Shanghai. The houses in this neighbourhood were Shikumen lane houses, a typical local style of house combining traditional Chinese features with elements of European architecture, an architectural symbol of early 20th-century Shanghai. One of these old Shikumen houses, which later became a local museum, was the birthplace of the Chinese Communist Party. Over the years overcrowding and lack of maintenance had led to the neighbourhood becoming sadly dilapidated.

The idea of redeveloping Xintiandi emerged in 1997. The local district government wanted to redevelop the whole 52 hectare Taipingqiao area, of which Xintiandi formed part. It therefore asked Vincent Lo, director of Hong Kong's Shui On Group and a former business partner of the local officials, for advice. One stipulation was that the old party hall had to be preserved. Appreciating the prime position occupied by the Taipingqiao area, Lo decided to invite the famous US firm of Skidmore, Owings and Merril LLP (SOM) to prepare a plan. Accordingly, SOM devised a plan to redevelop, reuse and improve the functioning of and facilities provided by the inner city. The plan divided the area into four parts:

1. A historical area preserved as a business, restaurant, entertainment and tourism complex, with Xintiandi as its major part
2. The Corporate Avenue international business district
3. The Lakeville premier residential area
4. A shopping and entertainment centre and a 40,000 m^2 lake to form the centre of the area.

This plan was the first to introduce the idea of preserving the historic Shikumen houses. Vincent Lo invited the Boston architect Benjamin Wood and his firm Wood and Zapata, Inc. to take this bold idea further in his design. The original plan is said to have involved knocking down most of the Shikumen houses and replacing them by a new version of old Shanghai. Wood however wanted to take a different tack. Because the old Shikumen houses were cultural artefacts symbolising the meeting of East and West, he suggested that part of the historic fabric of Shanghai should be preserved and adapted for other purposes.

Singapore's Nikken Sekkei International Ltd assisted in the coordination of the construction work. Tongji University, a local university famous for the training it provides in architecture and urban planning, was invited to advise on the design and preservation of the Shikumen houses. The eventual design produced masterly interiors in beautifully renovated former houses, with stone gates in front, warm brick walls and terracotta roofs. It turned a dilapidated neighbourhood into a vibrant mixture of businesses thronged with shoppers, gourmands, filmgoers, coffee sippers, music mavens, and club hoppers.

Xintiandi was one of the earliest privately financed projects to preserve old buildings in a city, a task normally only undertaken by the public sector and publicly financed. The total amount invested in Xintiandi amounted to 1.3 billion Yuan (US$ 0.16 billion). The Shui On Group took a chance on the future of Xintiandi at its own risk. The idea for the project emerged at the beginning of the Asian economic crisis. The entire Asian real estate market slumped. The banks were doubtful about the economic return on the project, since the investment required to preserve an old building, 20,000 Yuan (US$2,415) per m^2, is several times higher than required for new building. In the end most of the investment in the project came from the company's own resources. The loan provided by the bank, US$45mn (30% of the total investment), only came through at the end of 1999, a year after the start of the project [7].

To the surprise of most investors, the Xintiandi project proved to be a hit, both critically and commercially. Xintiandi became a popular entertainment hub in a city centre imbued with Shanghai's historic and cultural legacy. Property values in the surrounding area have already risen - and continue to rise -more rapidly than in other parts of the city. The success of Xintiandi also received international attention. It was show-cased by Shanghai when the city hosted the APEC (Asian-Pacific Economic Cooperation) meeting in 2001. Xintiandi (the north block) has also won awards as winner of several competitions for excellence in redevelopment projects, including the 2003 Awards for Excellence competition held by the American Urban Land Institute, for the way it embraces the city's past and blends it with the commercial realities of modern urban living.

6 Conclusion

The Lujiazui redevelopment, the Xintiandi project and indeed many other ongoing urban projects in Shanghai, reflect an interesting transformation in the thinking about regeneration in the 1990s, a kind of paradigm shift. The first realisation was that there was no immediate conflict between economic return and the preservation of historic neighbourhoods. Alternative approaches to the reuse of old buildings could put new heart into a decayed area while still preserving its social atmosphere and traditional style of urban life. The approach selected depends on the aim of the project, the plan designated and the parties involved. A number of different approaches can often be used in combination to provide a more balanced development strategy.

Although each project has a unique development process, several things are required to ensure a successful result.

The first requirement is a clear vision that is not only responsive to market demand but also takes a long-term view of the future development of the area. The clarity of the goals set for the redevelopment of Lujiazui and Xintiandi set the direction for the area's future and attracted both potential investors and potential users. The same clarity of vision also plays a role in publicity and city marketing to enhance the projects' public reputation.

The second requirement is a strong commitment, a decisive element in the success of any project. Strong leadership, whether it comes from local government (as in the case of Lujiazui) or from the private sector (as in the case of Xintiandi) is essential to ensure that promises are kept and the line is held in the face of difficulties like the Asian economic crisis and the downturn in the local real estate market. This kind of commitment helps to strengthen the confidence of potential investors and buyers who are doubtful about a particular situation. It is also interesting to note that despite their strong commitment, the project leaders were not rigid about the strategies they put into practice. On the contrary, they became more flexible and adaptable in the way they dealt with changes in the market environment.

The third requirement is a proper attention to the balance between economic benefit and social and environmental goals. The clear proposals for Lujiazui and Xintiandi were not limited to property development but also took account of economic growth and social and environmental improvement, though to different extents. Both sets of proposals provided flexibility and sustainable development. Collaboration between government and the private sector provides a better chance of achieving a more balanced goal, which would be difficult for either side to achieve on its own.

As the regeneration process continues, increasing concern is being felt in Shanghai about the role of local communities and the effect the regeneration process has on them, a concern which was generally absent during the preparation of the two projects discussed above. The call for social justice and the preservation of historic buildings for alternative use has generated increasing interest among both academics and the public at large.

A number of later developments show signs of this new way of thinking. For example, a proposal to develop the waterfront of the Huangpu river, a major project involving the development of 73 km^2 of abandoned or under-utilised harbour, warehouse and industrial areas, has taken the continuity of the city's history into account by preserving old buildings in the area, and at the same time providing new uses and functions. Proposals have been tabled to reuse old industrial buildings by turning power stations and pumping stations into exhibition halls. A rehabilitation project in progress in the Jing'an District aims to improve the quality of life of the local residents. Although not all of those residents will be relocated back to their original homes (because the original density was unacceptably high), a good deal of effort will be put into ensuring that most of the original residents will be able to retain the local community's daily way of life.

Clearly there is still a long way to go before urban regeneration projects take a more integrated approach and become more responsive to social, economic and environmental issues, but the importance of sustainability is receiving more recognition than ever before in the daily practice of new urban regeneration schemes in Shanghai and other Chinese cities.

References

[1] Fraser, C (2003) Change in the European Industrial City, in Couch, C., Fraser, C. and Percy, S. (eds.)(2003), *Urban Regeneration in Europe*. Oxford: Blackwell. p. 20.

[2] Roberts, P. and Sykes, H. (2000) Urban Regeneration: a Handbook. Sage: London. p. 14.

[3] Couch, C. and Fraser, C. (2003) Introduction: the European Context and Theoretical Framework, in Couch, C., Fraser, C. and Percy, S. (eds.)(2003), *Urban Regeneration in Europe*. Oxford: Blackwell. p: 2.

[4] Percy, S (2003) New Agendas, in Couch, C., Fraser, C. and Percy, S. (eds.) (2003) *Urban regeneration in Europe* Oxford: Blackwell. pp. 200-209.

[5] Olds, K. (1997) Globalizing Shanghai: the 'global intelligence Corps' and the building of Pudong, in *Cities*, 14 (2), pp.109-123.

[6] Wang, A and Xia. L (2001): *Urban planning and Architecture of Shanghai Lujiazui Financial Central District: International consultation section*. Beijing: China Construction Industrial Publisher.2001: p. 130.

[7] Shanghai Xintiandi, http://www.xintiandi.com.

Section 7
Conservation and management of ecological areas

Alternative future growth scenarios for Utah's Wasatch Front: assessing the impacts of development on the loss of prime agricultural lands

G. Busch[1], R. J. Lilieholm[2], R. E. Toth[2] & T. C. Edwards, Jr.[3]
[1]*Bear River Association of Governments, USA*
[2]*Department of Environment and Society, College of Natural Resources, Utah State University, USA*
[3]*USGS Utah Cooperative Fish and Wildlife Research Unit, College of Natural Resources, Utah State University, USA*

Abstract

Utah's Wasatch Front spans a narrow corridor from Ogden and Salt Lake City south to Provo. Current forecasts predict that the region's population of 1.9 million will increase by 75% by 2030. This project developed a series of alternative future growth scenarios to predict the spread of future development within the 2.3 million ha study area. Satellite imagery from 1990 and 2000 was used to develop a logistic regression model to predict the probability of future development based on 30x30 m pixels. Independent variables included distance from roads and development, slope, location within city boundaries, and surrounding development density. Population forecasts were then allocated across the region at various assumed future settlement densities, and the resulting development footprint for the year 2030 was determined. We found that if future development increased from the current density of 15 people/ha to 25 people/ha, 36,900 fewer ha of open space would be lost to development. In addition, if future development occurs at the rate of 15 people/ha, the region will lose over 40,400 ha of prime agricultural lands over the next 30 years.
Keywords: demographics, economics, land use planning, logistic regression, sustainable development, urban growth models.

1 Introduction

The Wasatch Front is a rapidly urbanizing region of north-central Utah lying between the Wasatch Mountains to the east, and the Great Salt Lake to the west. The Greater Wasatch Area (GWA) closely follows the Interstate Highway 15 corridor from Provo north to Ogden. At roughly 2.3 million ha, the GWA encompasses all of the land area between the cities of Nephi in the south to Brigham City in the north, and from Tooele in the west to Kamas and Coalville in the east (Fig. 1).

The U.S. Census [1] found that the GWA was home to 1.9 million people in 2000. However, with an annual growth rate of 1.8%, the population is predicted to increase to 3.3 million by 2030, and as many as 5 million people could live in the region by 2050 (Envision Utah [2], GOPB [3], GOPB [5]). Due to this large population growth and an increasingly built-out land base, urban development is rapidly spreading to outlying cities and towns. If traditional sprawl-like development continues through 2050, the GWA will undergo substantial change. Indeed, while urban growth often provides opportunities for employment, income, entertainment, etc., it also typically results in increased air and water pollution, and the irreversible loss of wildlife habitat, open space, and agriculture lands.

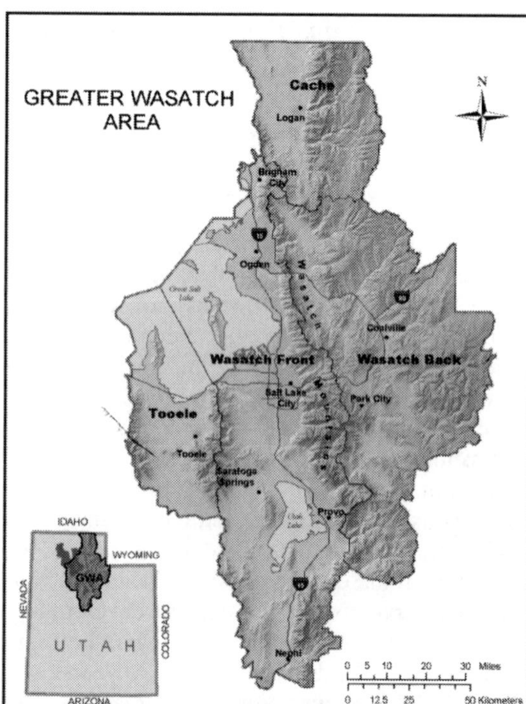

Figure 1: Utah's Greater Wasatch Area (GWA) is 2.3 million ha in size.

The goal of this research was to assess current development trends by examining how the GWA might develop over the next 30 years with the addition of 1.4 million new residents by creating hypothetical "alternative futures" (Toth [4]). We first assessed the location and scale of urbanization within the region from 1990 to 2000. Next, utilizing GIS and logistic regression, we developed a grid-based urban growth model to estimate the probability of future development for all undeveloped 30x30 m pixels in the study area. Finally, we calculated the potential loss of prime agricultural soils resulting from the conversion of open space to development under two estimates of future settlement density.

2 Methods

2.1 Modeling approach

Three main steps were followed to develop future growth scenarios for the GWA: (1) develop a logistic growth model for the region; (2) allocate future population growth across the study area; and (3) assess the impacts of future growth on environmental parameters – namely the loss of prime agricultural lands.

The first step was to develop a logistic regression growth model that predicted the probability of future development for undeveloped lands based on past growth patterns and each pixel's spatial characteristics. The result is a map showing the probability of any given location changing from undeveloped to developed status, based on the spatial attributes of that location. Logistic regression has been used to develop future growth scenarios for San Francisco (Landis [6]), the Mojave Desert (Hunter et al. [7]), and Camden County, New Jersey (Agung [8]).

The second step was population allocation. Allocation refers to placing a predicted future population across a landscape based on the most probable locations as determined by the logistic regression model. The result is a development "footprint" for the region at some point in the future.

The final step is an assessment of the effects that predicted future development will have on various parameters of concern. This is generally accomplished by overlaying the predicted development footprint onto a map of environmental factors to locate areas of overlap (Landis [6]). This process can be applied to any factor that has spatial overlap with the future development footprint. Here we calculated the expected loss of prime agricultural lands across the GWA.

The logistic growth model is a spatially oriented growth model. As such, the growth model's processes were, for the most part, modeled within a Geographic Information System (GIS), though some of the data were pre-processed using other software. Within the GIS, all spatial data were represented in a raster format using a 30x30 m pixel size.

2.2 Development of the logistic regression growth model

Logistic regression was used to calculate the probability of an undeveloped pixel becoming developed (the binary dependent variable) based on the pixel's location. The characteristics of each pixel (the independent variables) include site-specific and surrounding spatial factors that describe each pixel in context to neighboring pixels. Site-specific attributes include whether or not a pixel is developed, if the pixel is located within a municipal boundary, and the slope of the pixel. Spatial variables include the distance of a pixel to the nearest road, or the development density of surrounding pixels. Each variable has a different relationship with the dependent variable, but they typically follow a similar form:

Pr (development) = $f(-x_1 - x_2 - x_3 - x_4 + x_5 + x_6)$

where:

x_1 = distance from the nearest major road;
x_2 = distance from the nearest secondary road;
x_3 = slope;
x_4 = distance from existing development;
x_5 = location within a city boundary; and
x_6 = development density of surrounding cells within a 19x19 pixel window.

Logistic regression then determines the degree to which each variable contributes to the probability of a pixel being developed based on the relationship between these independent variables and development over some past time interval. When the logistic model is applied to each undeveloped pixel in the study area, it results in a future development probability gradient map.

2.2.1 Development, the dependent variable

Developed areas for both 1990 and 2000 were determined using remotely sensed data. Images from NASA's Landsat-5 platform were selected for its high temporal and spatial resolution. Full coverage of the GWA was acquired from two Landsat images, row38 path32 and row38 path31. Late season images were selected to highlight the variation between irrigated lands and drier natural landscapes within the GWA. Each image was corrected for sun angle, atmospheric attenuation, and instrument calibration as described in Chavez [9].

To assess the accuracy of the image classifications, the two 1990 images were joined into a complete development map for 1990. The two 2000 images were joined in a similar process. Accuracies of both development maps were assessed using 1996 aerial digital Ortho-photo quads (DOQ) (USGS [10]). An examination process was set up prior to the accuracy assessment. The overall classification accuracy of 94% and 95%, respectively, for the 1990 and 2000 images is quite good. The final step in processing the satellite imagery was to compare the 1990 development map to the 2000 development map to determine where new development had occurred during the 10-year interval. This new development dataset became the dependent variable used to calibrate the growth model.

2.2.2 The independent variables

2.2.2.1 Roads A 1986 dataset of roads was used for the 1990 time period due to a lack of temporal data. The 2000 road layer that came from TIGER was considered accurate for this analysis. Once editing was completed, the road layers were reclassified into two layers consisting of major and secondary roads.

The vector datasets were then rasterized to a 30-m pixel size. Finally, the Euclidian distance command was run in ARCINFO Grid to determine the distance from each pixel to the nearest road.

2.2.2.2 Slope Percent slope was derived from a Digital Elevation Model using the slope command in ARCINFO.

2.2.2.3 Development The origins of the 1990 and 2000 development datasets were explained above. These binary raster maps were processed further into two new data layers: development density and distance from development. Development density was calculated using a 19x19-pixel roving window, which calculated the percentage of developed pixels within the 361-pixel window. Development distance was calculated using the Euclidian distance command in ARCINFO Grid. Another development data set called the Water Related Land Use (WRLU) was obtained from the Utah Department of Water Resources. This vector-based data set delineates several land use categories using aerial photography from 1995 to 1997 (Utah Department of Natural Resources [11]). The WRLU was used to determine current population density, as well as areas to be excluded from new development (see "Exclusion Layer" below). These data also provided the 2000 development baseline from which future growth was allocated under the predictive scenarios.

2.2.2.4 City boundaries U.S. Census data provided both the 1990 and 2000 city boundary datasets. For this analysis, only incorporated cities were used, leaving out the Census Designated Places (U.S. Census Bureau [1]). Municipalities were then converted to a binary map such that pixels were either located within a city (1) or not (0).

2.2.2.5 Exclusion layer The exclusion layer is a combination of several datasets that represent areas unable to accommodate future development. Included are areas already developed, public lands, and water bodies, as well as local parks and designated open spaces.

2.2.3 Model calibration: establishing variable relationships

Logistic regression was used to calculate if and to what degree a statistical relationship exists between the dependent variable (areas developed between 1990 and 2000) and each of the six independent variables. The variables were run through the regression process in a stepwise, non-interacting manner. The result is a logistic regression growth model that, based on past growth patterns, calculates the probability of future development for each undeveloped pixel in the GWA that is available for development.

2.3 Population allocation

Population allocation is the process of populating the probability map with new residents in order to estimate the spatial extent of future development. This process includes three basic steps. First, future population within the region is estimated. Next, the average future settlement density for new residents is estimated to determine the amount of land that will likely be developed to accommodate these new residents. It should be noted that land is developed not just for residential homes, but also for streets, parks, commercial, and industrial uses, and can thus be thought of as a development footprint. Also note that the new development is allocated across currently undeveloped lands in the GWA based on the probability map derived above.

Population forecasts based on various economic indicators and the current demographic profile of the state project that the GWA's population will increase from 1.9 million in 2000 to 3.3 million by 2030 (Spendlove [12]). Next, an estimate of the density that future residents will settle across the landscape was needed. Two future settlement densities were modeled – the current density of 15 people/ha (6.8 people/ac), and a higher density of 25 people/ha (10 people/ac). Note that 25 people/ha is nearly the density of Los Angeles (Soule [13]) and would result in the conversion of far less land than the other alternative. While this density may be unrealistic to expect in more rural regions of the GWA, it is possible to consider for future development along the urbanized Wasatch Front, where the majority of Utah's population live. For comparison, U.S. metropolitan areas range from a high of 27.1 people/ha in Los Angeles, to a low of 6.9 people/ha in Atlanta (Soule [13]).

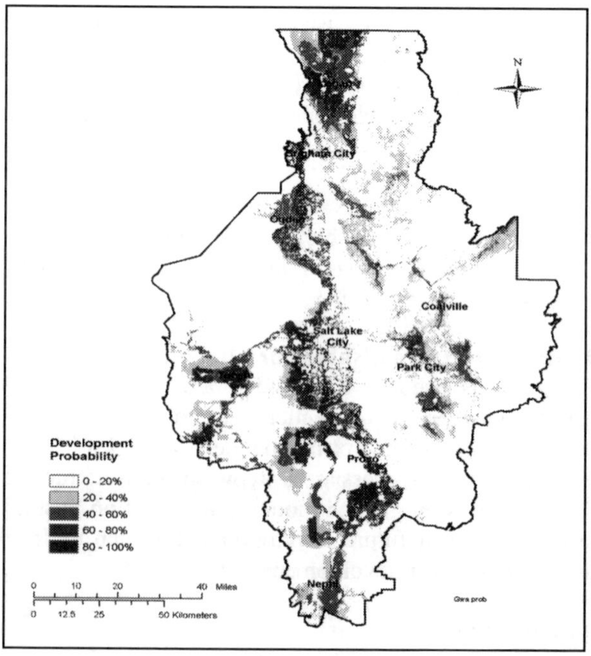

Figure 2: Probability of future development.

3 Results and discussion

3.1 Significant independent variables

Based on the logistic regression analysis, the final model fit the data well. The rescaled R^2 for the model was 0.6811, with the concordant pairs at 93%. Of the six independent variables considered, four stand out as important indicators of development between 1990 and 2000. These were percent slope, development density, the distance from existing development, and location within a city boundary. The slope coefficient was negative as expected, indicating that as slope increases, the probability of development decreases. Conceptually this makes sense since the majority of development in the GWA occurs on relatively flat farmlands formed on the bottom of ancient Lake Bonneville. In contrast, less development occurs on steep lands due to limited access and higher development costs. The coefficient for development density was positive, indicating that between 1990 and 2000, new development tended to cluster in locations of higher density development. The third variable, distance from existing development, had a negative coefficient, indicating that an increase in the distance from existing development brought a decrease in the likelihood of new development. The fourth variable, city boundaries, had a positive coefficient, indicating that locations within an incorporated area had a higher probability of new development. Figure 2 shows the probability gradient map for the GWA.

3.2 Future development in the GWA

Over the next 30 years, the population of the GWA is expected to increase from 1.9 million in 2000, to 3.3 million in 2030 -- an increase of 1.4 million people or 75%. The approximate footprint of urban development in 2000 was 115,807 hectares (447 mi^2). Depending on densities of future development, the new population could increase the developed area by as little as 48% (55,308 ha) at 25 people per ha, or as much as 80% (92,281 ha) at 15 people per hectare.

The allocation process used to create the development footprints is best understood through an example. Using the high density GWA scenario, in time period 2000 – 2010, 449,619 new residents are predicted to settle the area at a density of 25 people/ha, thus requiring 18,195 new hectares of development. Next the 18,195 ha is converted to 30 m pixels (11.111 pixels/ha), requiring 202,172 pixels to be converted. In other words, the 202,172 pixels with the highest probability for development are identified and designated for development for this time step. This process is continued for the next two time steps, resulting in the predicted development footprint for 2030 at 25 people/ha.

The spatial result of each of these density alternatives is then represented in map form showing the extent of the development footprint as it grows through time. The maps suggest that the GWA's new residents will be settling throughout the region. The model predicts significant new development along the I-15 corridor between Ogden and Brigham City, in the northern portion of Cache Valley, around Tooele, and west of Spanish Fork.

3.3 Development and the loss of prime agricultural lands

Throughout Utah, and especially within the GWA, urban and residential development is taking place on agriculturally productive lands. This trend is similar throughout the United States, where significant amounts of farmland are converted every year from the production of food to homes (Alterman [14]). In many respects, this conversion represents an irreversible process. Reporting potential trends of farmland loss is of political, social, and economic concern, and is one of many potential applications of this logistic growth model.

While the total area of farmland converted to development is of interest, the *quality* of the land is important as well. Indeed, not all soils are equal when it comes to producing crops. The Natural Resource Conservation Service (NRCS) describes soils according to several characteristics and ranks them into categories with prime soils being the most productive. For this analysis, prime soils were determined by the NRCS in the Soil Survey Geographic database (SSURGO) (Soil Survey Staff [15]).

Note that pre-settlement prime soils are those prime soils that existed before urban development removed them from agriculture. The amount of prime soils lost to development can be estimated by superimposing maps of development over the pre-settlement prime soils map. This analysis was done in two steps. First prime soils were compared to the existing urban footprint derived from the Water Relater Land Use to obtain an estimate of historic loss. This process establishes the baseline of prime soils which have already been lost to urban development since the arrival of settlers beginning around 1847. The second step is to compare the loss of remaining prime soils between 2000 and 2030 under the density scenarios. This analysis is expected to show that as density of urban development increases, the amount of prime soils lost to urban development will decrease.

Table 1: Actual and predicted prime soil loss from 2000 to 2030 for the GWA.

Total pre-settlement prime soils (hectares)	212,810			
Estimated prime soils loss using development footprint from WRLU (hectares)				
	Loss	% loss		
2000	49,486	23.25%		
Predicted prime soils loss using development density alternatives				
	25 people per hectare		**15 people per hectare**	
	Predicted loss	% loss	Predicted loss	% loss
2010	9,235	4.34%	14,992	7.04%
2020	8,986	4.22%	13,881	6.52%
2030	7,572	3.56%	11,511	5.41%
Predicted loss 2000 2030	25,794	12.12%	40,385	18.98%
Remaining prime soils	137,529	64.63%	122,938	57.77%

Of the 1,286,449 hectares of private lands within the GWA, 212,810 ha (16.5%) have the potential to be prime soil (Table 1). Of this potentially prime soil, 49,486 ha (23%) had been built upon by 2000. By 2030, 25,794 additional hectares of prime soil will be lost under the highest density alternative, and 40,385 hectares under the low-density alternative. Based on these scenarios, the GWA will retain as much as 63% or as little as 46% of its potentially prime soils by the year 2030.

Under these alternatives, the majority of prime soils remaining in 2030 are likely to be west and south of Utah Lake (See Fig. 1). This is an important result because it is doubtful that sufficient irrigation water would be available in those areas to provide for agricultural needs. Therefore, by 2030, it is likely that urbanization development will displace much of the GWA's economically viable farmland.

4 Conclusions

The population of Utah's GWA is expected to increase from 1.9 million to 3.3 million over the next 30 years. This growth will cause the built environment to increase and will lead to significant changes to the landscape of the GWA. While the scale of change will differ depending on the region, significant human-caused land use change will be a reality nonetheless.

The purpose of this research was threefold. First, it aimed to project present land use trends into the future to illustrate the likely outcomes of current land use decisions. Second, the research sought to explore the possible outcomes of alternative land use decisions in the form of higher development densities. Finally, the research applied the model results to look at potential loss of prime agricultural soils under the various density scenarios.

Based on the analysis presented here, if future populations continue to settle under the existing densities of 15 people/ha, new urban developments will likely cover an additional 92,281 ha (356 mi^2) by 2030. However, if settlement densities increased to 25 people/ha, the future developed area could be reduced to 55,368 ha (213 mi^2). Given these two scenarios, prime soils could be reduced by as much as 40,385 hectares at 15 people/ha, or as little as 25,794 hectares at 25 people/ha.

References

[1] U.S. Census Bureau, Appendix A, Census 2000 Geographic Terms and Concepts. www.census.gov/geo/www/tiger/glossary2.pdf.

[2] Envision Utah. Salt Lake City, UT, www.envisionutah.org.

[3] Governor's Office of Planning and Budget, Scenario Analysis, Review Draft. Salt Lake City, UT, 1999.

[4] Toth, R.E., Edwards, T.C. Jr., Lilieholm, R.J., Bell, D.L. & Buteau, E.R., Alternative futures for Utah's Wasatch Front: bioregional planning for the maintenance and conservation of open space. Final Project Report No.

2002-2, Utah Cooperative Fish and Wildlife Research Unit, Utah State University, Logan, UT 84322-5290 USA, 2002.

[5] Governor's Office of Planning and Budget, Quality growth and efficiency tools; Baseline 2003. Salt Lake City, UT, 2003.

[6] Landis, J., Imagining land use futures: applying the California urban futures model. *Journal of the American Planning Association,* **61(1)**, pp. 438-457, 1995.

[7] Hunter, L.M., Gonzales, M.J., Stevenson, M., Karish, K., Toth, R., Edwards, T.C. Jr., Lilieholm, R.J. & Cablk, M., Populations and land use change in the Mojave: natural habitat implications of alternative futures. *Population Research and Policy Review*, **22**, pp. 373 – 397, 2003.

[8] Agung, A.A.G., Grid-based urban growth model. Dissertation, New Brunswick Graduate School, Rutgers State University of New Jersey, 2000.

[9] Chavez, P.S. Jr., Image-based atmospheric corrections—revisited and revised. *Photogrammetric Engineering and Remote Sensing* **62(9)**, pp. 1025-1036, 1996.

[10] U.S. Geographical Society, Digital Orthophoto Quadrangles. geography.usgs.gov/digitalbackyard/doqbkyd.html.

[11] Utah Division of Natural Resources, A water-related land use summary of the State of Utah. Salt Lake City, Utah, 1999.

[12] Spendlove, R., Personal communication, 17 September 2004, Governor's Office of Planning and Budget, Salt Lake City, Utah.

[13] Soule, D., Confronting housing, transportation, and regional growth. *Land Lines*, Lincoln Institute of Land Policy, **16(2)**, pp. 12-14, 2004.

[14] Alterman, R., The challenge of farmland preservation: lessons from a six-nation comparison. *Journal of the American Planning Association,* **63(2)**, pp. 220-239, 1997.

[15] Soil Survey Staff, Natural Resources Conservation Service. *National Soil Survey Handbook*, Title 430-VI, Section 622.04, 2001.

Management of biodiversity in protected areas with sustainability control

K. Hellmann
*Centre for Sustainability Management (CSM),
University of Lueneburg, Germany*

Abstract

Protected areas are an important approach for safeguarding the world's biodiversity. The conservation of biodiversity needs to be planned, organized, put into practise and controlled, i.e. it needs to be managed. In order to serve this purpose, the kind of management of these protected areas (e.g. what kind of measures are taken, when they are to be applied) is of utmost importance. As stated by the Convention on Biological Diversity the notion of sustainable development is all-important within the scope of so called biodiversity management. This means the conservation of biodiversity needs to be managed not only according to ecological factors but also to social and economic aspects. There are, however, very few systematic management approaches for sustainable development of protected areas which ensure the realisation of the objectives of biodiversity conservation so far. Today biodiversity management mainly concentrates on ecological aspects while economic and social factors are considered only marginally. In various cases this results in economic problems to finance conservation strategies or in social problems with substantial economic and ecological side effects. In contrast hereto various tools to realise sustainable management in an efficient and effective way have been developed in the area of corporate sustainability management. The transfer of these management methods is reasonable: entrepreneurs as well as managers of protected areas need to realise specified objectives while resources are limited and stakeholder interests need to be taken into account. In the following the concept of sustainability control is analysed whether it is suitable to conserve biodiversity in protected areas in an efficient and effective way.
Keywords: management of protected areas, management of biodiversity, sustainabilitycontrol.

www.witpress.com, ISSN 1743-3541 (on-line)

1 Introduction

The notion of biodiversity has been widely known since 1992 when the United Nations Conference on Environment and Development took place in Rio de Janeiro. According to that biodiversity means "the variability among living organisms from all sources including, inter alia, terrestrial, marine and other aquatic ecosystems and the ecological complexes of which they are part; this includes diversity within species, between species and of ecosystems" [1, p.3]. Biodiversity is the basis for the life of human beings [1, 2]. By supporting functions of ecosystems fresh water is provided, grounds are protected, the regulation of climate is ensured, etc. Moreover, biodiversity provides food, medicine, raw material but also services like recreation, quality of life, etc. [3]. Biodiversity is the core for many cultural values [4]. However, the loss of biodiversity has rapidly accelerated during the last decades [5, 6]. This is mainly due to the impact of human beings on the environment, i.e. the manner how humans deal with goods of nature [5, 7]. According to the WBGU [8, p.61] the loss of biodiversity is one of the core problems of global change while other experts grade this as greatest international ecological danger [9, p.16].

At the conference in Rio de Janeiro in 1992 the Convention on Biological Diversity (CBD) was compiled as a frame concept for the protection of biodiversity [1]. According to article 8 of the CBD protected areas are an important instrument for the conservation of biodiversity. The conservation of biodiversity needs to be planned, organized, put into practise and be controlled, i.e. it needs to be managed. In order to serve this purpose, the kind of management of these protected areas (e.g. what kind of measures are taken, when are they applied) is of utmost importance.

2 Problems of the management of protected areas

There are several types of protected areas like national parks, nature parks or biosphere reserves which differ in their status of protection. Each country has its own criteria to specify the categories while the IUCN tries to enforce uniform categories on international level [10]. In Germany the categories are laid down by law (Bundesnaturschutzgesetz) [11]. Although the types of protected areas differ they all pursue the special target to protect and conserve biodiversity [10, p.7]. The problem hereby is that it remains unclear what exactly needs to be protected. Worldwide the dimension of the number of species is unknown and the description and mapping of species is a task hardly to cope with. The valuation of species is complicated as the ecological function and the potential benefit are hardly known [3, 12]. To cope with the lack of knowledge extensive research projects which take time and money need to be carried out. Due to the rapid loss of biodiversity there is no time to be lost and measures have to be taken immediately.

In addition to the challenge of conserving biodiversity the managers of protected areas are confronted with a lack of money. In Germany, for example, most of the protected areas are managed by the environmental authorities and get their budget from the state. Due to the financial shortness of the state the proceeds of the protected areas decrease. In order to deal with the problem more and more protected areas are managed by the private sector. Nevertheless, the managers of protected areas have to protect biodiversity effectively in spite of small funds [13, p.4ff.].

Moreover, the managers of protected areas have to consider the interests and demands of different groups. These groups of stakeholders are residents, farmers who have land within the protected area, tourists who want to visit the area, etc. They all have a certain stake in the protected area. If they do not accept the measures which have to be carried out to conserve biodiversity, the successful implementation is endangered [14].

As a result, the conservation of biodiversity needs to be managed not only according to ecological factors but also to social and economic aspects. There are, however, very few systematic management approaches for the sustainable development of protected areas which ensure the realisation of the objectives of biodiversity conservation so far. Today biodiversity management mainly concentrates on ecological aspects while economic and social factors are only marginally considered [15]. In Germany, for example, plans for maintenance and development are compiled for protected areas. They are the basis for comparison of the actual and the target state of the area [16]. However, financial aspects and the potential for social conflicts are disregarded. In various cases this results in economic problems to finance conservation strategies or in social problems with substantial economic and ecological side effects.

Consequently the question is, how the management of protected areas can be improved to ensure that protected areas are able to achieve their role to conserve biodiversity in the long run. In this context it seems to be reasonable to apply managerial concepts for the management of protected areas. On the one hand business concepts of information, evaluation and management allow more transparency. On the other hand the lack of money and the influence of stakeholders force the managers of protected areas to act more efficiently [17, p.249ff.]. The entrepreneurial way of thinking might contribute to find innovative solutions in order to procure resources and increase proceeds. The permanent search for improvement can increase the efficiency of measures.

Various tools to realise sustainability management in an efficient and effective way have been developed in the area of corporate sustainability management. One of these managerial concepts which is quite successful is *sustainabilitycontrol*. In the following it is discussed whether this concept is suitable to conserve biodiversity in protected areas in an efficient and effective way.

3 Sustainability-control for protected areas

The concept of control aims at creating a permanent, institutionalised, internal management process. The single procedures and management tools are coordinated in order to support the successful steering of procedures in a company [18, 19, 20]. Characteristics of the system are being targeted, being based on planning and control, being future-oriented, being adaptive and flexible. Not only

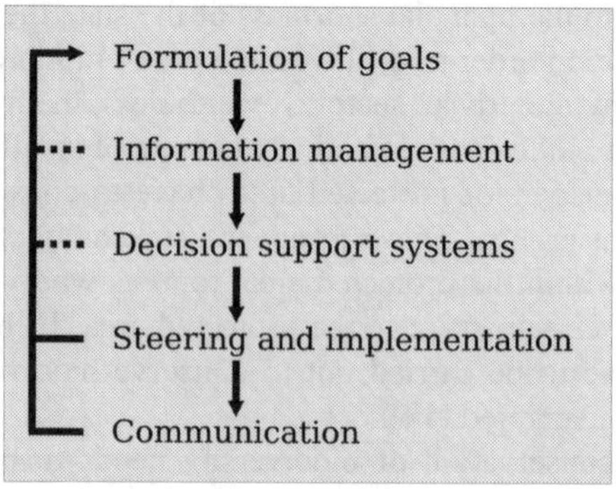

Figure 1: Process of sustainabilitycontrol. Source: based on Schaltegger and Sturm [24].

companies but also Non-Profit Organisations (NPO) and the public sector use the concept of control to support their management's decision-making [21, 22].

Within corporate environmental management the concept of eco-control has evolved as the decisive tool to support the sustainable development of a company in an efficient and effective way [23, 24]. Eco-control is concerned with the environmental and related financial impacts of a company. Based on data of material and energy flows eco-control is used for process control [25]. On the contrary controlling of the living world (flora, fauna and habitats) focuses on indicators which reflect criteria from the ecological perspective of sustainability [26].

The concept of sustainabilitycontrol goes one step beyond by integrating the social perspective in the process of control. For companies this is of particular importance as a careful and responsible dealing with social and ecological aspects is the precondition for economic success [27, 28]. The integrative approach makes conflicts transparent and makes it easier to deal with synergy effects and work simplification [29].

The concept of sustainabilitycontrol consists of several procedures: *formulation of goals, information management, decision support systems, steering and implementation and communication* [23, p.320ff.]. An overview of the process is shown in figure 1. Each procedure avails specific instruments of corporate environmental management. In the following the procedures are described with respect to the management of protected areas.

3.1 Formulation of goals

At the beginning of the controlling process the goals of the management of the protected area and its measures have to be formulated. This is a very important step for a successful controlling process. Usually the ecological goals for protected areas are itemised in a maintenance and development plan or a management plan [16, 30]. However, economic and social goals are usually not specified in the existing plans. But the management of social conflicts and financial problems is the prerequisite for the successful realisation of ecological goals. Therefore corresponding goals have to be formulated. In a first step they can be recorded in terms of a sustainability strategy for the protected area. In a second step they have to be specified on the operational level.

For an open landscape the goal might be to conserve its' characteristic flora and fauna and their habitats (e.g. heathland). In this example a traditional cultural landscape should be preserved on 75% of the area. On 25% of the area natural evolution should take place. To realise these goals different maintenance measures need to be implemented (e.g. cutting grass), fences have to be built to protect certain areas from the impact of human beings, etc. All these measures cost money so an economic goal might be to look for measures which show a large effect per spent Euro. Moreover, goals on the social level can be to integrate the critical stakeholders of the protected area in the planning process of measures to avoid conflicts.

3.2 Information management

In the next step information regarding the realisation of the ecological, economic and social goals needs to be collected. Data collection and information management is the most labour-intensive part of the process. In the first place species and ecosystems have to be mapped. The collection of data about species is a difficult task as species are not always easy to designate (e.g. lichens). In some areas like the tropical forests new species can be discovered every day so the number of species is unknown according to its dimension [31, 5]. However, the careful mapping of species and ecosystems for a protected area is an essential basis for the management of the protected area.

In addition, costs projections have to be made to allow the most efficient protection of biodiversity. These costs projections have to specify the investment (e.g. costs to build a stable for sheep) and regular payments (e.g. costs for regular maintenance measures, personnel costs) of the protected area. Besides, information has to be compiled about the needed funds for a certain period of time in the future.

Finally, data about stakeholders have to be collected. There are many different stakeholders in or near a protected area like tourists, residents, farmers, etc. with different interests. The managers of a protected area need to know which stakeholders are critical, i.e. which group has an influence on the successful realisation of measures. Thus, information about their interests and concerns is needed in order to be able to manage and avoid conflicts.

All the collected data should be summarised in a data base and be available at any time.

3.3 Decision support systems

To allow an efficient and effective controlling of the protected area the collected data has to be analysed carefully. Therefore a limited number of significant indicators has to be formulated. The indicators have to reflect the actual state of biodiversity within the protected area. Suitable indicators for ecological goals could be e.g. the number of individuals of an endangered plant within the protected area or the number of breeding birds within ten hectares. Moreover, indicators for the actual social and economic state have to be formulated as well (e.g. number of critical stakeholders, budget for certain measures).

Subsequently, target states have to be determined with respect to the indicators in order to allow a prioritisation for future measures of the protected area. From an ecological and economical point of view those measures have to be favoured which create the largest effect per invested Euro. In addition the social perspective has to be taken into account which favours those measures which are widely accepted by stakeholders. The frequency of critical media-reporting regarding the protected area or letters of complaint can be an indicator to assess the acceptance.

In the end a priority list should show the favoured measures and the optimal mix of measures by integrating the three perspectives of sustainability.

3.4 Steering and implementation

For the implementation and steering of the measures of the priority list responsibles have to be named for the implementation of single tasks. Normally the protected area's staff consists of very few persons, so it is particulary important to appoint the limited personnel well directed. For the success of the measures it is important that the participants have the necessary skills. Honorary assistants who often support the management of protected areas need to be considered according to their interests in order not to loose their assistance.

Target values per month and per year have to be determined for the named responsibles in order to allow periodical control. Such a target value can be the implementation of a certain maintenance measure (e.g. burning of heathland) within three months without worsening the acceptance of the stakeholders for this method and without exceeding a certain budget.

If the review of the realised measures shows any deviation from the target value, the manager of the protected area has to analyse the reason. As a result, goals and measures need to be reworked and adapted.

According to the organisational structure of the protected area (e.g. public or private management) it might make sense to create incentives for the realisation of certain measures. For example private owners often refuse the implementation of measures which restrict their land-use. In consequence the realisation of the goals to protect biodiversity is impaired. Financial, material, economic or social incentives might help to manage such conflicts.

3.5 Communication

It is also important to communicate the activities and plans of the management of the protected area. This can take place on an internal and external level. The external communication focusses on the improvement of the stakeholder's acceptance for certain measures and the protected area itself. On the one hand the distribution of know-how by media-reporting, information centres, guided tours, etc. plays an important role. On the other hand communication should also include stakeholder dialogues in order to foster the direct contact to stakeholders who are particulary affected by the management of the protected area. Moreover, communication is an important condition to receive sponsoring and funding.

On the internal level the integrated approach of management of the protected area can be communicated by advanced education, as this might be new to most of the employees in a protected area. Therefore, it is particulary important to build up an understanding by explaining the context.

Furthermore, internal communication is supposed to inspire the employees to find new solutions for more effective and efficient protection. For example the results of maintenance measures can be visualised with indices of eco-efficiency, e.g. the amount of money which was spent within a year to protect a certain number of one beetle species. If the amount of invested money is quite high and the number of conserved beetles is only low, the question arises whether the measure can be improved or substituted in order to achieve a better protection result. Like this the permanent search for improvement to increase the effect of measures to protect biodiversity is on its way.

4 Conclusion

The management of protected areas is confronted with various requirements to cope with. Not only the ecological goals need to be realised. At the same time the pressure to legitimise the protection goals and means increases, interests of different stakeholders have to be taken into account and the available financial resources from public funds decrease.

Improved management approaches are needed to allow an efficient and effective conservation of biodiversity in protected areas in the long run. Sustainabilitycontrol, a planning and guidance system, allows an integrated approach. The concept facilitates a systematic and strategic proceeding with a regular verification of goals and their realisation. This supports the permanent search for improvement. With the whole process ecological, economical and social aspects are taken into account. Thus the effect of measures to conserve biodiversity in an protected area can be assessed as a whole considering all perspectives of sustainability. Therefore, the process of sustainabilitycontrol induces more transparency, supports the decision-making of the manager of a protected area and facilitates the coordinating of different interests.

As a result sustainabilitycontrol seems to be a suitable approach to improve the management of biodiversity in protected areas. Further investigations have to analyse the managerial instruments within the different procedures of sustainabilitycontrol regarding their usefulness for the management of protected areas in practise.

References

[1] Secretariat of the Convention on Biological Diversity, Convention on biological diversity. 5 June 1992, 1992.

[2] Earthwatch Institute Europe, IUCN (The World Conservation Union) & WBCSD (World Business Council for Sustainable Development), *Business & Biodiversity. The Handbook for Corporate Action*. ATAR Roto Presse SA: Conches-Geneva, 2002.

[3] Gronemann, S. & Döring, R., Ökonomie der biodiversität. *Naturschutz in Entwicklungsländern. Neue Ansätze für den Erhalt der biologischen Vielfalt*, ed. GTZ & BfN, Kasparek: Heidelberg, pp. 129–134, 2000.

[4] Secretariat of the Convention on Biological Diversity, Convention on biological diversity. strategic plan, 2002.

[5] Brühl, T., *Bisherige Erfolge und Misserfolge der Biodiversitätskonvention. Gutachten im Auftrag der Enquete-Kommission "Globalisierung der Weltwirtschaft - Herausforderungen und Antworten"*. Johann Wolfgang Goethe - Universität Frankfurt am Main: Frankfurt am Main, 2002.

[6] Stone, D., Ringwood, K. & Vorhies, F., *Business & Biodiversity. A Guide for the Private Sector*. WBCSD (World Business Council for Sustainable Development) & IUCN (The World Conservation Union), 1997.

[7] Feit, U., Interdisziplinärer forschungsaustausch im rahmen des Übereinkommens über die biologische vielfalt. *Treffpunkt biologische Vielfalt. Interdisziplinärer Forschungsaustausch im Rahmen des Übereinkommens über die biologische Vielfalt*, eds. H. Korn & U. Feit, BfN (Bundesamt für Naturschutz): Bonn, Bad Godesberg, pp. 9–11, 2001.

[8] WBGU (Wissenschaftlicher Beirat der Bundesregierung Globale Umweltveränderungen), *Welt im Wandel: Herausforderung für die deutsche Wissenschaft. Jahresgutachten 1996*. Springer: Berlin, Heidelberg, 1996. Studie zu Defiziten des deutschen Beitrags zur Biodiversitätsforschung. als pdf gespeichert.

[9] Raustiala, K. & Victor, D.G., Biodiversity since rio: The future of the convention on biological diversity. *Environment*, **38(4)**, pp. 16–24, 1996.

[10] IUCN, *Richtlinien für Management-Kategorien von Schutzgebieten. Nationalparkkommission mit Unterstützung des WCMC, IUCN, Gland, Schweiz und Cambridge, Großbritannien, FÖNAD, Grafenau, Deutschland*. Morsak: Grafenau, 1994.

[11] Bundesministerium der Justiz & juris GmbH, Gesetz über naturschutz und landschaftspflege (bundesnaturschutzgesetz - bnatschg), 2002.

[12] Thuille, A., Forschungsstrategie für die biosphäre anforderungen und empfehlungen des wbgu-jahresgutachtens 1999. *Treffpunkt Biologische Vielfalt III*, ed. BfN (Bundesamt für Naturschutz), BfN: Bonn, Bad Godesberg, pp. 15–24, 2003.

[13] WCPA & IUCN, *Economic Values of Protected Areas. Guidelines for Protected Area Managers*. IUCN: Gland, Switzerland; Cambridge, UK, 1998. Total Economic Value (TEV), Kosten-Nutzen-Analyse, Potentieller

Nutzen für Schutzgebiete, Richtlinien für Schutzgebietsmanager (Zusammenarbeit mit Ökonomen), Definition Protected Areas (3), Bedeutung der CBD für Schutzgebiete (4f.), Client approach (Kundenbedürfnisse) (8f.), Ressourcenökonomik (23f.).

[14] Stoll, S., *Akzeptanzprobleme bei der Ausweisung von Großschutzgebieten*. Peter Lang: Frankfurt/Main, 1999.

[15] Gesellschaft für Ökologie (Hrsg.), Kappen, L. & Hörmann, G., *Ökosystemforschung und Ökosystem-Management. Kurzfassungen der Beiträge zur 30. Jahrestagung der Gesellschaft für Ökologie in Kiel vom 11. - 15.9.2000*. Parey: Berlin, 2000.

[16] Kaiser, T., Konzeptioneller aufbau eines pflege- und entwicklungsplanes dargestellt am beispiel des naturschutzgroßprojektes lüneburger heide. *Angewandte Landschaftsökologie 18*, ed. BfN (Bundesamt für Naturschutz), BfN: Bonn, Bad Godesberg, pp. 7–27, 1998.

[17] Schaltegger, S., Kubat, R., Hilber, C. & Vaterlaus, S., *Innovatives Management staatlicher Umweltpolitik. Das Konzept des New Public Environmental Management*. Birkhäuser: Basel, Boston, Berlin, 1996.

[18] Weber, J., *Einführung in das Controlling*. Schäffer-Poeschel: Stuttgart, 9th edition, 2002. Der Controlling Papst!, hier alle Konzepte übersichtlich zusammengefasst sowei sein eigenes dargestellt.

[19] Horváth, P., *Controlling*. Vahlen: München, 8th edition, 2002.

[20] Schwarz, R., *Controlling: Eine Einführung in Grundlagen, Komponenten und Methoden des Controlling*. Gabler: Wiesbaden, 2002.

[21] Eschenbach, R. & Horak, C., Rechnungswesen und controlling. *Handbuch der Nonprofit Organisation. Strukturen und Management*, ed. C. Badelt, Schäffer-Poeschel: Stuttgart, pp. 275–298, 1997. Controlling für NPOs, 285ff., Notwendigkeit, Ziele, Voraussetzungen.

[22] BMU (Bundesministerium für Umwelt, Naturschutz und Reaktorsicherheit) & UBA (Umweltbundesamt), *Handbuch Umweltcontrolling für die öffentliche Hand*. Vahlen: München, 2001.

[23] Schaltegger, S., Burritt, R. & Petersen, H., *An Introduction to Corporate Environmental Management. Striving for Sustainability*. Greenleaf: Sheffield, UK, 2003.

[24] Schaltegger, S. & Sturm, A., *Öko-Effizienz durch Öko-Controlling. Zur praktischen Umsetzung von EMAS und ISO 14001*. Schäffer Poeschel: Stuttgart, 1995.

[25] Schaltegger, S. & Kempke, S., Öko-controlling. Überblick über bisherige ansätze. *ZfB Zeitschrift für Betriebswirtschaft*, **2**, pp. 149–163, 1996.

[26] Buser, H. & Schaltegger, S., Öko-controlling für das firmenareal. *io Management Zeitschrift*, **64(5)**, pp. 77–82, 1995.

[27] Haasis, H.D., Unternehmensführung und nachhaltiges wirtschaften. *Unternehmensführung im Spannungsfeld zwischen Finanz- und Kulturtechnik: Handlungsspielräume und Gestaltungszwänge*, ed. H. Fischer, Kovac: Hamburg, 2001. Nachhaltigkeitscontrolling: 27ff.

[28] Weber, F.M. & Ammon, U., Nachhaltigkeits-controlling in mittelständischen unternehmen. *uwf UmweltWirtschaftsForum*, **12(2)**, pp. 49–53, 2004.
[29] Gehrlein, U., Von nachhaltigkeitsindikatoren zum kommunalen nachhaltigkeitscontrolling. grundzüge eines strategischen nachhaltigkeitscontrollings. *UVP-report*, **17(5)**, pp. 216–221, 2003.
[30] Bogner, D. & Golob, B., Die bedeutung betriebswirtschaftlicher aspekte in managementplänen am beispiel natura 2000. *Agrarökonomie zwischen Vision und Realität. Dokumentation der 10. ÖGA-Jahrestagung am 28./29. September 2000 in Wien*, ed. H.K. Wytrzens, pp. 262–267, 2002.
[31] Quintern, L., Integrative forschung zur erhaltung und nachhaltigen nutzung biologischer vielfalt. *Treffpunkt Biologische Vielfalt III*, ed. BfN (Bundesamt für Naturschutz), BfN: Bonn, Bad Godesberg, pp. 25–27, 2003. Gravierende Wissensdefizite.

The building's function in the containment and organization of activities in the Kiron system

E. C. Curiel-Carias
Facultad de Arquitectura y Urbanismo,
Universidad Central de Venezuela, Venezuela

Abstract

The dual purpose of meeting the great housing needs of inter-tropical zones, without further compromising the stability of their ecosystems, requires new concepts that help bridge the gap that exists between the organizational schemes of natural and artificial systems. Based on the wide scientific information available about living systems (LSs), this paper – through analogies and deductions – presents some of the attributes that must be included in the concept of containment and organization of buildings closely linked to LSs. To this end, the concept of the Kiron System (KS) is presented, which is a new level in the hierarchy of hybrid, semi-artificial nature, formed by three sub-systems: *ecosystem*, the human body as an organism or *biosystem*, and the building or *artificial system.* Its function is, precisely, to eliminate the dichotomy between the organizational logic of natural systems and artificial systems; an organization where these systems can link their matter, energy and information processes to form the functional components of KS. It is in the core of the KS where the concept of containment and organization of activities, traditionally assigned to buildings, is modified. The boundaries of the Kiron System become the new <container> in which the building or artificial system (AS) is transformed, simultaneously, into container and contained. In this scheme, the organizational role of AS is subordinated to the organizational characteristics of living systems in which it is nested, and its function is to organize, in a specific and gradual manner, the interactions between the natural elements present in each situation, to build the hybrid structural components in which the functional components of KS must be materialized.
Keywords: buildings, living systems, artificial systems, hybrid systems.

1 Introduction

The dual goal of meeting the increasing human needs in third world countries, without further compromising the stability of their natural systems, has proven difficult to reconcile. The difficulty lies, among other things, on the divorce that exists between the organizational schemes of natural systems, and the majority of artificial systems. In this paper, the discussion is limited to the issue of buildings as devices that contain and organize activities in the protected areas of the tropics, where construction restrictions make the problem more explicit. A possible explanation is that the traditional concept of these functions of buildings is insufficient given the growing demands imposed by the bio-requirements of their users, as well as the requirements of the natural systems where they are settled. This explanation is given in the context of other wider considerations discussed in a previous paper [1], which mentions our trend to deal more with imported images than with concepts, and to be more concerned about <*how*> things are built rather than <*what*> should be built [2]. Therefore, buildings become *artificial systems* generated by *conceptual systems* that are not linked and are even opposite to the demands of the *real system* in which they are inserted. This distortion is affected by the difficulty architects have to interpret – and apply- the knowledge that stems from the information contained in sciences that delve into many of the natural variables that affect, or should affect, the design of buildings.

Therefore the specific objective of this work is to develop the concept of buildings in relation to their function to contain and organize activities in regions with important and fragile ecosystems. That is, <what> a building located in the protected areas of those regions is or should be. This exercise is supported on the extensive information available in the natural sciences regarding living systems and, more specifically, a new concept derived from them (the Kiron concept) developed in a previous paper [3]. This study is justified by its possible application in similar areas that are not protected by special regulations, where housing demands (due to population growth and the fight against poverty) are rapidly devastating the inter-tropical biomas.

2 Method

Of the several functions of a building – environmental conditioning, symbolic, economic, and containment and organization of activities- this paper will focus on the latter, in light of the Kiron concept. Given the number and diversity of these functions, the Kiron function (which will be explained later on) was created based on the General Theory of Systems (GTS), which is sufficiently wide and flexible to facilitate the articulation of the several functions of the building. Given the importance of biophysical factors on this issue, the theories on living systems that are compatible with GTS will be stressed. By adopting elements of this theory as an initial proposal, it is possible to infer, through analogies and deductions, some of the attributes that must be included in the concept of buildings that are closely linked to said living systems. These analogies will not necessarily be used to establish a one to one correspondence between elements of living systems (LS) and those of the building or artificial system (AS), but between the system of relations that join the elements of each category of systems. Likewise, together with the isomorphisms we will look for the differences or *explanations* that define the conditions and specific aspects of each system. A rigorously logic deductive method will not be used (which provides conclusions given certain premises), but rather, heuristic inferences will be made, that is, to infer the possible consequences from the scientific knowledge available of living systems in the area of design; to work in the area where the concepts of science and design overlap, where *how* things are and *how they should be* are superimposed.

3 Fundamentals

The GTS studies general isomorphisms that are common to systems, and defines reality as *a hierarchy of organized wholes* [4]. From this universal group of systems, we are interested in the subgroup of systems that have a dynamic and complex nature, which tend to adopt certain particular states. These systems have been widely studied and described by authors like L. von Bertalanffy [4], W. R. Ashby [5], E. Laszlo [6], E. Goldsmith [7] and C. W. Churchman [8] among others, and based on their concepts and summarizing what was presented in previous studies [3, 9] – complex systems have been characterized by permanent *changes*, not at random but following a particular *order*. These *orderly changes* represent the tendency of systems to try to achieve certain specific states, that is, they are *goal-searchers* (not in the teleological sense). In these states free energy is minimized, and the system tends towards stability. This goal (a state of unstable balance or dynamic stability) is proportional to their level of organization.

3.1 Living Systems (LS)

Assuming that *Living Systems* (LSs) are a specific case of complex systems, and summarizing what authors like Járos [10], Miller [11], Mikulecky and Rosen [12], Odum [13], Maturana [14], Goldsmith [7], Acurero [15], Lovelock [16], Smith and Smith [17], Capra [18], Prigogine [19], Margulis [20], van Gigch [21], Langton [22] and Mosterin [23] have described and what was presented in [3] – we will try to characterize them systematically to infer some attributes of the artificial systems that are closely linked to them.

Ontology of LSs. Discussions to define LSs have led to two large tendencies: 1) One that states that is it not possible to clearly and satisfactorily answer the question *What is life*? since it is the result of a historic phenomenon, of a series of contingencies, and as such, "something that cannot be deduced from a general principle" [23]. 2) The other states that, in fact, an operational characterization of living systems is not possible from its common properties, but rather from its specific forms of organization, considered as the properties of <emerging> complexity [14]. By selecting the GTS as the foundation of this work, we are also selecting the second approach, since LSs are interpreted as emerging from complex systems. This perspective is consistent with the concept of reality presented by the GTS, that is, reality as a <hierarchy of organized wholes>. The idea of life herein assumed is one that understands it as the "continuous materialization of an autopoietic organizational pattern in a dissipative structure" [18]. *Objective of LSs.* Orderly changes in LSs are processes oriented towards achieving a goal or specific state, *homeostasis,* understood as the "... tendency of living systems to maintain the conditions of their inner environment constant", W. Cannon quoted in [24]. This is an important reference to evaluate the behavior of the system, and as indicated above, "is proportional to its level of organization" [7]. *Organization of LSs.* Opposite to the trend towards the disorganization implied in the second law of thermodynamics, a fundamental property of organisms is the ability to maintain their organization, so it could be considered that life is more a property of the organization of matter than a property of matter thus organized. [22]. In this way, there are constant <organization patterns> that are embodied (due to several processes) into dynamic physical structures [18]. *Processes of LSs.* Constitute the link between the pattern of organization and the structures in which it is constantly materialized [21]. Closely linked to these processes is the idea of the system's <functional components> (non material), which are totally dependent on the context and have no meaning without it. [12]. *Structural Coupling of LSs.* Living beings are structurally connected to their context through recurring interactions, "the organism itself becoming a representation of that interactions", K. Lorenz quoted in [15]. *Cognition of LSs.* For Evolutionary Epistemology, a structurally connected system is a system that learns through the coordination or mutual coupling of behaviors with other living beings. "Living beings gather more and more information about their environment through adaptation processes, and in this way represent the structure of the environment in which they live..." [15]. In this sense, knowledge is the proper reconstruction of its external structures within the system. Thus, the specific phenomenon that underlies the cognitive process is structural coupling [18]. *Symbiosis of LSs.* It is the above-mentioned close mutual adjustments, which explain the co-evolution of species. Lynn Margulis' theory of symbiogenesis compares the description of differences between species during evolution to another parallel process in which different organisms converge, thanks to symbiosis, to produce new hybrid entities [20] *Autopoiesis of LSs.* The mechanisms of symbiosis are implicit in the fundaments of the autopoietic school proposed by Maturana and Varela. *Autopoiesis* (that which generates itself) is a term used to describe the circular organizational pattern of LSs where the "function of each component is to participate in the production or transformation of other components" [18]. *Complexity of LSs.* The autopoiesis observed inside organisms is also observed in ecosystems and more clearly in the biosphere. So, one of the functions of all the components in a trophic chain in ecosystems is the transformation of other components in the same network. A consequence of this is the high degree of interdependence between the system's sub systems, between the systems, and between them and the supra system to which they belong. The variety of systems, subsystems, and components, as well as the number of relations between them constitute a fundamental trait of living beings, *complexity*. This is so because "complexity makes it more stable" [7]. *Hierarchy of levels of LSs.* Frequently, this complexity takes the form of a hierarchy [7], a multi-level structure of living systems that are nested within others. In the Theory of Living Systems, the hierarchy of levels consists of cells, organs, organisms, populations, organizations, communities, societies, and supranational systems [10]. However, natural systems coordinate their interfaces in the diverse hierarchies of nature [6]. Therefore, any system has a function to fulfill within a larger one of which it is a part [7], and the whole structure or organic function is "demonstrated" (justified?) directly not by its environment, but rather by the subsequent super-ordered system. [15]. *Limits, inlets, and outlets of LSs.* The systems of each hierarchical level have defined boundaries and decision-making entities, enabling them to exist (relatively) independent of each other [21]. On the other hand, links with other systems and/or levels are done in very specific points, like the *inlets and outlets* of matter, energy and information. These points are commonly associated to the concept of *transducers* or elements responsible to make the outlets of a system compatible with the inlets of another.

4 Discussion

4.1 An intermediate level, the Kiron System (KS)

As was said in [3], the innumerable consequences that the concepts previously depicted in the artificial systems design have, require some previous precisions. The entering into discussions about the rigorously transit through a deontic logic from LS ontology to a discussion on the axiology of those AS linked to them, surpasses the aims of the present work. This work simply limits, through a declarative or enunciatively logic, to walk from the product of the analytical reasoning that science offers, to others of heuristic feature that contribute to solve - in a more or less satisfactory way – the entropic dichotomy existent between the organized forms of LS and those of AS.

The various regions of the planet form a unique entity, the biosphere. This means that all its components are interdependent (natural as well as artificial), so they should be organized hierarchically to achieve an important common objective: the dynamic balance of the planet as a whole. This is inscribed in the context of wider discussions like the ones around the <GAIA hypothesis> [16], which debate whether the biosphere can be considered a living organism or not. In this sense, the thesis of autopoiesis is the support of works like the ones of D. Mikulecky, which establish that "the organisms stands apart from the machines by being closed to efficient cause" [12]. In other words, a machine needs a builder, since it cannot construct itself as living systems do. According to this idea, the biosphere is truly an organism [12]. The large flows of inert components of the biosphere (energy, water, air, chemicals) are so closely linked to living systems, that in fact constitute an intricate web, and thus it can be concluded that the biosphere is a single organism with a hybrid nature. This conclusion opens the possibility of considering anthropic production as one more process within this large hybrid organism.

The problem presented in the Introduction (how to reconcile housing and environmental demands) is thus located within the issue of this large complex, organized and hierarchical system, which we will call *global system* (GS). The four hierarchical levels mentioned in previous works [3] would initially be the *global system* (GS), the *ecosystem* (ES), the human body as an organism or *biosystem* (BS), and the building or *artificial system* (AS). Later on, certain modifications are introduced in this hierarchy, which will be explained.

Objectives and Limitations of the Kiron System (KS). In the described hierarchy, the sub-objective of the AS must be consistent with the ES and the BS, which in turn are subordinated and/or are compatible with the general objective of the GS. In the tree of hierarchies, and within the area of work selected (protected areas), the fundamental entity is the ecosystem, in which one of the <organisms> present (man) has specific functions to fulfill. To carry out these functions –and preserve his/her own homeostasis man requires certain <extensions> that enable him to do it, and are represented in this scheme by the AS. However, the dual purpose imposed on the AS to achieve the unstable balance between the ES and the BS simultaneously and by itself, is difficult to reconcile. A way to achieve this goal would be to involve the BS and the ES directly in the task of obtaining not only their own stability, but also that of a third system which, including the AS, constitutes a supra system that emerges in their confluence and whose function is to contribute to eliminate the dichotomy between the organizational logic of natural systems and of artificial systems. It is the emergence of a hybrid system, semi-artificial, integrated by the ES, BS, and AS subsystems, called the "*Kiron System*" (KS) for the purposes of this exercise [3]. This brings more resources (natural as well as artificial) and facilitates its organization since all the flows, cycles, and important activities of the problem are contained within the limits of the system under study. *Organization of the KS.* It is important to establish at least two differences between the organization of LSs and ASs: 1) LSs are systems with <organized complexity> whereas AS or "the non living have properties of organized simplicity or non-organized complexity" [21]. 2) There is a trend that establishes that "it is not possible to isolate the organization that defines living systems from their materiality, and therefore, it is not possible to make <organizational> representations based on the logic of life… living systems belong to a class of systems whose organization requires specific materialities..." [25]. In the semi artificial KS herein proposed, we don't try to rigorously reproduce an organization identical to living beings, but to join LSs and the AS in a third hybrid system (like in the biosphere) from which a specific organization must emerge to foster the symbiotic interaction between the ES and the BS. *Processes and Functional Components of the KS.* It is understood that the organization where LSs and the AS are joined would occur at the level of their matter, energy and information processes, or the functional subsystems identified by Miller [11]. The elements that form the organization of the KS would therefore be <functional components>. *Cognition of the KS.* The amount of entropy or uncertainty is the inverse of the amount of information available to reduce, and then select the different options. The explanation of the problem stated in the Introduction, corresponds to the difficulties to transfer the vast scientific information available on living systems, to the design of artificial systems directly related to them. As stated in a previous work [26], it can be said that the uncertainty (or entropy) contained in the chaotic diversity of possible building designs, is the result of the little information available regarding the peculiarities of the natural fabric in which they are inserted. Regarding this issue, the ample information available today about LSs provides the possibility of driving an intense process of self-organization (a basic principle of evolution) in the KS, through the learning generated in the process of structural coupling between the LSs involved. *Symbiosis in the KS.* The KS strives to achieve a deep knowledge of the ES and the BS to enable a mutually beneficial structural coupling. This would be one more process of the many studied by symbiogenesis, where different living systems converge to favor the emergence of new and beneficial hybrid entities. KS's *Autopoiesis.* The KS comes close to the autopoietic organizational form of living systems through the mutual benefit implied in symbiosis, where the product of said systems is the system itself (in this case the KS). In another scale, it would be a system that is isomorphic to the biosphere, that is, an organism formed by the mixing of living and non-living systems in the same network.

4.2 The function of containment and organization of the artificial system (AS) in the Kiron System

Implications of the KS in the functions of containment and organization of the AS:

Objective of the AS. The purpose containing and organizing activities, which is traditionally assigned to buildings, is to contribute to a more efficient, comfortable and safe behavior in the humans that carry out those activities within it. By introducing the Kiron system, this function is expanded because the objective of the AS is not only to contribute to the achievement of favorable conditions for the performance of the BS contained in it, but also to preserve and/or rehabilitate the ES that contains it.

The limits of the AS. The usual task of making an inventory of human activities within a building –and the later analysis of their relations- generally ends in their categorization according to their several functions. This allows the establishment of internal boundaries between the different <functional zones> of the building, and specifically, the boundary between the internal spaces and their environs. However, when the repertoire of <activities> of the natural environment must be inventoried, as well as its relations with itself, man and its artifacts, the usual physical boundaries between these zones, and between the container and its contents, disappear. The building now becomes precisely the container and contents. The components of the AS are no longer confined to the traditional boundaries, and are dispersed in the KS due to the better organizational possibilities that these new and close relations with the LS offer. In the Kiron system, it is necessary to redefine the internal boundaries around the new functional components that include activities of the ES, the BS and the AS; and the boundaries of the Kiron system become the new container. In it, the relations between its functional components would be similar to E. Tedeschi's description of the usual relations between the elements that constitute a building: "a set where the elements are added in a topological multi-level situation, not only by juxtaposition, but also by penetration, inclusion and articulation…" [27].

The AS in the functional components of the KS. The purpose of the basic activities or functions of the human body is to foster and preserve its wellbeing (associated to its *homeostasis*), which includes sleep, nourishment, the elimination of wastes, displacement, hygiene, communication, etc. In the case of a simple building like a house, the several functional zones (circulation areas, services, bathrooms, social areas, bedrooms, kitchen, etc.) are specialized in containing and ordering in a safe and efficient manner each of these categories of activities. These functional areas and their relations constitute the traditional *diagram of functions*- the foundation of the study of a building- which helps define its form and dimensions. By introducing the Kiron concept the diagram expands since it also has to unite the functional components of the BS and the AS, with the ES. This means assembling elements that belong to three different hierarchies, which share the fact of being integrated to the isomorphic processes that Miller identifies with 20 subsystems or functional components (neither material nor fragmentable).

The AS in the structural components of the KS. Once these functional components are identified, it is necessary to materialize them, by assembling simple and complex systems, living and inert, natural and artificial, into hybrid, semi-artificial structural components. Here the role of the AS as a <transducer> mentioned in [3] is essential. This approach allows, for example, a revalorization of the potential use of certain components and/or processes of the ES and the BS as substitutes of some of the traditional components of buildings, thus avoiding a redundancy of functions within the Kiron system and reducing the use of matter and energy. By delegating functions in the natural components and following its commonly reduced scales, it is also possible to reduce the dimensions of the AS, which favors even more its de-materialization and de-energization. It is an approach that also allows the use of several natural and artificial resources, like a pool of pieces and modules that can fulfill multiple functions in the structural components, in several situations depending on the form in which they alternate.

The organizational function of the AS. Given a set of limiting and determining factors, of activities and their corresponding affinities, the building designer focuses on the organization of all these factors. For E. Tedeschi "... coordination (organization) can be considered as a structure of interactions that tend to ensure a correct topological relationship between the elements that constitute a building, and a typology of coordination can also be established, analyzing the diverse possible associative forms of the elements and their different modes of interaction..." [27]. For Le Corbusier "… architecture is organization" [28]. The incidence of the Kiron concept in these ideas implies a review of the same processes that give rise to these organizations. The dissociation between the logic that rules the organization of natural and artificial systems, as already indicated, is one that can be charted saying that the former exhibit an autopoietic organization, and the product of such systems is the system itself. They do not respond to any explicit external instruction, bur rather, they gradually evolve towards an increasing diversity and complexity, starting from very simple interactions, producing a self-organized “bottom to top” solution as stated by R. Brooks [29]. Together, they are organizational forms that are also characterized by the endless recycling of the elements, interdependence, and the soft flow of matter and energy around the different biotic and abiotic components of the ecosystem. On the other hand, artificial systems (buildings, in our case) are not their own builders. They are the materialization of external instructions that specify globally, and for the future, the interactions of all its components. These are organizational forms imposed from “top to bottom” that contrary to the others, strive towards uniformity and simplicity to facilitate their execution and manipulation. The flow of matter and energy required for its construction, functioning and maintenance are unidirectional and unarticulated, which hinders the integration of its organization into its natural context. The core of the conflict is that both modalities of systems, forced to coexist in a single space, respond to totally opposite organizational schemes, which seriously compromises the viability of the global system in time.

What effect will the concept of the Kiron System have in the organizational function of the artificial modules of the structural components of the AS? Basically four: 1) The organization that the AS generates in the Kiron System must be partially modeled by the specific organizational characteristics of living systems (ES and BS) in which it is nested. 2) This means that the traditional organizational function of buildings is simultaneously restricted and expanded, since it not only organizes the activities contained within the building, but it must also contribute to preserve and/or rehabilitate the other natural organization that in turn contains it. 3) Also, this double function of the AS must be subordinated to the strategy of the Kiron system of dissolving the traditional separation between the organizational logic of the LS and the AS. 4) The organization favored by the AS must necessarily be the result of the specificities of each situation; an expression of the peculiarities that emerge in trying to gradually reach the organizational goal expected in a specific context. The AS will thus organize a set of simple and independent interactions between the available natural and artificial elements “bottom to top”. Here, the function of the AS is to enable the *emergence* of the self-organization of the KS.

Cognition of the AS. The resulting organization would be the product of the “influence of the whole over the parts” (the same way in which order is defined) enabled by the extensive information available on LS. This would reduce uncertainty (entropy) regarding the convenience or not, of the possible and several relations between the components. The hard task of detecting the infinite pertinent interactions between the elements present in each specific situation – until the best solutions are obtained (what evolution has done through mutations and selection) – could now be aided by today’s powerful search techniques, like the ones offered by genetic algorithms.

The AS in the ES and BS symbiosis. The AS is assumed as a simple implant or system that enables certain symbiotic relations between the LSs of the KS; it allows the BS and the ES to actively participate in the benefits of the other and of the KS as a whole.

The AS in the autopoiesis of KS. The AS would be a tool that allows the circular organization of the complex living systems that integrate it. That is, materialize a single organizational logic for all its components (partially separated in its base material due to the simple nature of artificial systems).

5 Conclusions

The fact that ASs and LSs belong to a single system, as well as the particular fact that there are situations where the former are nested in the latter – like the buildings located in protected ecosystems – must thwart in the AS the development of organizational forms besides those that are proper to the LSs. This leads, conceptually, to the need of a new intermediate and hybrid hierarchy (KS), formed by the ES, BS and AS subsystems, which could offer in said situations the required organizational unity to the LSs and the ASs. In the KS the traditional function of buildings of containing and organizing human activities would undergo significant changes. In this new concept, the building is not only the container but also the content; it organizes and is organized, and its function is to enable the coupling and active participation of the natural elements – present in each situation – in the construction of the hybrid structural components where the functional components of the KS will materialize.

References

[1] Curiel-Carias, E.C., Inconsequence of scientific knowledge in the field of design: Building in tropical coasts. Interciencias, 25 (7), pp. 346-350, 2000.

[2] Hillier, B., & Leaman, A., A new approach to architectural research. Ribaj, December, pp. 15-30, 1972.

[3] Curiel-Carias, E.C., The building concept in hybrid systems constitution (Kiron system). Building and Environment, (article in press), 2005.

[4] Bertalanffy, L., Teoría General de los Sistemas, Fondo de Cultura Económica: Madrid, 1981.

[5] Ashby, W. R., An Introduction to cybernetic, Wiley: New York, 1963.

[6] Laszlo, E., The systems view of the world, G. Braziller: New York, 1972.

[7] Goldsmith, E., Bringing the chaos in order. The Ecologist, September, pp. 11-18, 1972.

[8] Churchman, C.W., The Systems Approach, Delacorte: New York, 1968.

[9] Curiel-Carías, E.C., La tesis del tercer mundo en la comprensión de la teoría general de los sistemas. Tribuna del Investigador, 7 (1), pp. 60-76, 2000.

[10] Járos, G., Living Systems Theory of James Grier Miller and Teleonics. Systems Research and Behavioral Science, 17, pp. 289-300, 2000.

[11] Miller, J. G., Living Systems, McGraw-Hill: New York, 1978.

[12] Mikulecky, D. C., Robert Rosen: The Well-Posed Question and its Answer –Why Are Organisms Different from Machines? Systems Research and Behavioral Science, 17, pp. 419-432, 2000.

[13] Odum, H. T., Ecological and general systems: An introduction to systems ecology. University Press: Colorado, 1994.

[14] Maturana, H., Todo lo dice un observador. GAIA Implicaciones de la nueva biología, ed. W.I. Thompson, Kairós: Barcelona, pp. 63-79, 1995.

[15] Acurero, G., Filosofía de la biología, Fondo Editorial Acta Científica: Caracas, 1987.

[16] Lovelock, J., GAIA, Un modelo para la dinámica planetaria y celular. GAIA Implicaciones de la nueva biología, ed. W.I. Thompson, Kairós: Barcelona, pp. 80-94, 1995.

[17] Smith, R. L., & Smith, T. M., Elements of ecology, Benjamín/Cummings: California, 2002.

[18] Capra, F., La trama de la vida. Una nueva perspectiva de los sistemas vivos, Anagrama: Barcelona, 1998.

[19] Prigogine, I., El orden nació del caos. Los verdaderos pensadores de nuestro tiempo, ed. G. Sorman, Seix Barral: Barcelona, pp. 37-45, 1990.

[20] Margulis, L., Symbiotic planet: A new look at evolution. Basic Books: New York, 2000.

[21] van Gigch, J. P., Teoría General de Sistemas, Trillas: México, 1998.

[22] Langton, C.G., Preface. Proc. of the Artificial Life II. SFI Studies in the Sciences of Complexity, eds. C.G. Langton, C. Taylor, J. D. Farmer & S. Rasmussen, Addison-Wesley: Redwood City, Vol. X, pp. xiii-xviii, 1992.

[23] Mosterin, J. Apuntes del Seminario de Filosofía, 20 Octubre 2000, En búsqueda de una cosmovisión a la altura de nuestro tiempo, Universidad Central de Venezuela, Caracas, Venezuela.

[24] Villee, C. A., Biología, Ediciones McGraw-Hill: México, 1988.

[25] Ruiz-Mirazo, K., Moreno, A. Artificial life. An epistemologic study. Department of Logic and Philosophy of Science, Universidad del País Vasco, 2001. http://www.sc.ehu.es/sfwpbiog/KRuiz-Mirazo/Kepa.html.

[26] Curiel-Carias, E. C., Design in the integration of natural and artificial systems. Interciencia, 28 (8), pp. 482-486, 2003.

[27] Tedeschi, E., Teoría de la arquitectura, Ediciones Nueva Visión: Buenos Aires, 1972.

[28] Le Corbusier, Mensaje a los estudiantes de arquitectura, Ediciones Infinito: Buenos Aires, 1973.

[29] Brooks, R.A., How to build complete creatures rather than isolated cognitive simulators. Architectures for Intelligence, ed. K. van Lehn, Lawrence Erlbaum Associates: Hillsdale, pp. 225-239, 1991.

Section 8
Economic issues

Incorporating nature valuation in cost-benefit analysis

E. J. Bos[1] & J. M. Vleugel[2]
[1]*LEI B.V., The Netherlands*
[2]*OTB Research Institute, TU Delft, The Netherlands*

Abstract

In applications of cost-benefit analysis (CBA) the economic valuation of environmental impacts is perceived as being problematic. As a consequence, these impacts are usually not included in cost-benefit analysis. When part of the welfare effects of an investment scenario (project) is not included, CBA becomes incomplete, hence unreliable as a tool to support decision-making. It is not unlikely that if environmental concerns had been included in the CBA application, the outcome of the decision-making process would have been different. This article presents results from a Dutch case study in which a method to monetise part of these ecological costs and benefits was developed, while an application of the method shows how the balance of costs and benefit changes due to incorporation of the 'green' costs.
Keywords: nature valuation, social cost-benefit, rail, Dutch case study, policy.

1 Introduction

Cost-benefit Analysis (CBA) is recommended as most appropriate for supporting Dutch policy making on public investment projects [1]. However, the reliability of CBA largely depends on the appraisal of welfare-effects that are not normally expressed on a market, such as those associated with nature and the environment. It is the economic valuation of these welfare-effects that is perceived as being a major source of uncertainty. This especially holds for the adverse effects on nature, like the disturbance of ecosystems and the fragmentation of nature areas, as guidelines for the valuation of these ecological effects are currently not available. In reference to federal government plans to extend rail infrastructure in the Randstad area, the economic valuation of adverse ecological effects induced by infrastructure becomes particularly relevant. Therefore, in this paper guidelines were developed which contribute to the validity of economic assessment of these welfare-effects. When possible, use was made of existing guidelines, for instance U.S. guidelines on using non-market valuation methods. However, as guidelines for the economic valuation of ecological effects of infrastructure are a relatively underexploited subject in ecological economics, additional research was carried out.

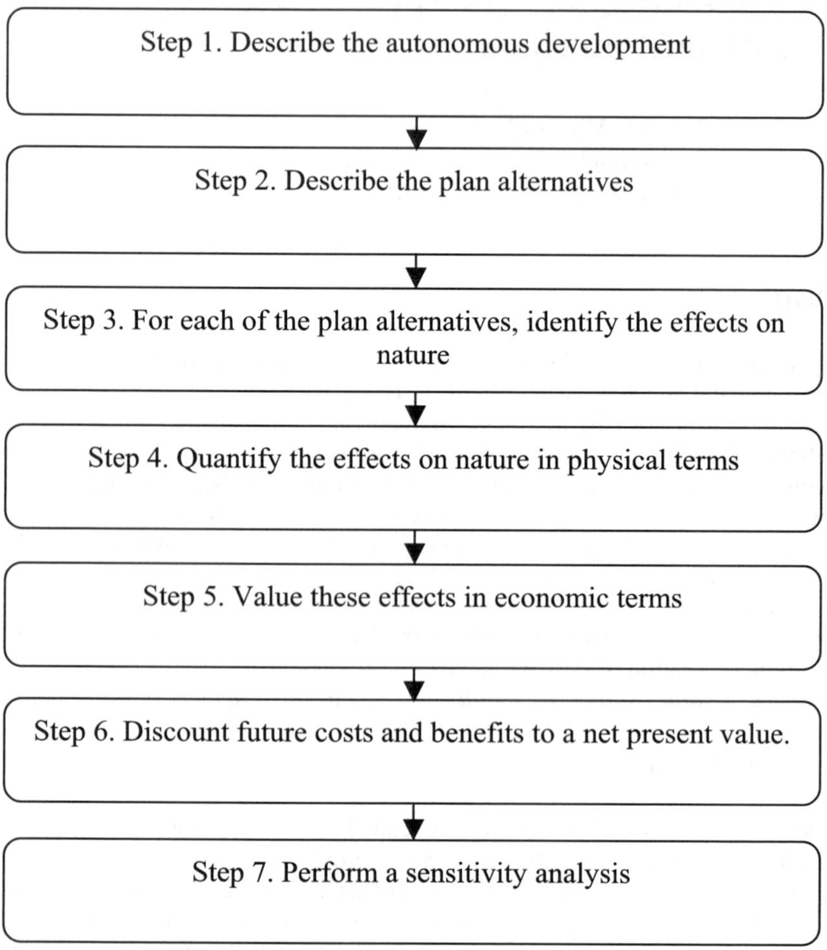

Figure 1: Step-by-step approach for CBA+.

2 Problem analysis

2.1 General framework for a nature inclusive CBA (CBA+)

After studying relevant existing environmental guidelines on how to carry out environmental appraisal studies, such as those by the U.S. Environmental Protection Agency (EPA), the National Oceanographic and Atmospheric Administration (NOAA) and OEEI [1], the decision was made to use the guidelines from EPA and OEEI as a basis for our own guidelines for the economic valuation of adverse ecological effects from infrastructure. This led to the step-by-step approach visualised in Figure 1.

For an extensive discussion of the approach, the reader is referred to [2]. In this paper the focus is on step 5, i.e. economic valuation of the adverse welfare effects from infrastructure, which are not revealed in market prices.

2.2 Relevant impacts

In this section the following welfare effects will be modelled:

- (i) disturbance of recreation;
- (ii) disturbance of ecosystems;
- (iii) fragmentation of ecosystems.

The reason that we focus on these welfare effects is that guidelines for the economic valuation of these effects are not available. Fragmentation and disturbance of nature areas a consequence of infrastructure is an underdeveloped area of research within CBA studies.

2.2.1 The disturbance of recreation

Disturbance reduces the utility (consumer surplus; see Appendix) consumers derive from recreation, as a result their willingness to pay for recreation is reduced.

The mathematical expression for the consumer surplus is as follows:

$$CS_{RN} = \frac{1}{2} \times \left\{ X_{RN} \times [P^{O}_{RN} - P^{MK}_{RN}] \right\} \tag{1}$$

It is assumed that recreational visitors do not have to pay an entrance fee. This implies that the only costs of visiting a nature area are the travel costs. If we assume that individuals make their trips always from the same location (usually their house), then individual travel costs are constant and the individual marginal cost curve is horizontal.

$$CS'_{RN} = \frac{1}{2} \times \left\{ \{ X_{RN} \times [P^{O}_{RN} - P^{MK}_{RN}] \} - \{ X'_{RN} \times [P'^{O}_{RN} - P^{MK}_{RN}] \} \right\} \tag{2}$$

When using this formula, collecting data for P'^{O}_{RN} is problematic in *ex ante* studies because the future shift of the demand curve is unknown. In order to solve this problem, the following alternative is used. The disturbance causes a reduction in the number of visits that equals (X_{RN} - X'_{RN}). The consumer surplus per visit before the shift of the demand curve was equal to: ½ × [P^{O}_{RN} - P^{MK}_{RN}].

Therefore, visiting the area X'_{RN} times per year instead of X_{RN} implies a total loss of individual surplus equal to CS'_{RN} = ½ × [P^{O}_{RN} - P^{MK}_{RN}] × [X_{RN} - X'_{RN}]. Then, the loss in consumer surplus for recreation is as follows:

$$CS'_{RN} = \tfrac{1}{2} \times [P^{O}_{RN} - P^{MK}_{RN}] \times [X_{RN} - X'_{RN}] \qquad (3)$$

The exclusion of variable 'P'^{O}_{RN}' simplifies collection of data significantly.

The US Environmental Protection Agency (EPA) recommends both the Travel Cost Method (TCM) and the Contingent Valuation Method (CVM) as methods to value recreation (i.e. P_{RN}) in economic terms. CVM implies that individuals are asked to reveal their willingness to pay for nature. TCM measures recreational benefits by means of the money and time people spend in travel to a site. OEEI considers the scientific basis and reliability of TCM as 'good', but the scientific basis of CVM is 'less good' and the reliability of CVM 'hard to verify and easily to manipulate'. Since OEEI [1] prefers TCM above CVM, we recommend CVM in cases where TCM and CVM are both applicable. Therefore, the preferred method to collect data for P_{RN} is TCM.

2.2.2 Disturbance of the ecosystem

This adverse welfare effect is related to the declining population of breeding birds in the area surrounding the railway. Empirical studies on the economic valuation of non-use values often express the underlying physical effect in terms of biodiversity [3, 4]. In such studies valuation based on surveying 'willingness to pay to conserve biodiversity' for a certain time period [3].

In case of non-use values, an individual does not have to make any costs to reap the benefits. So, in contrast to recreation, there is no marginal cost curve for non-use.

Based on the analysis presented in this paragraph the loss in consumer surplus from the disturbance of the ecosystem can be modelled as follows:

$$CS^{*}_{Biod} = \tfrac{1}{2} \times \left\{ [P^{*}_{Biod} - P_{Biod}] \times [X^{*}_{Biod} + X_{Biod}] \right\} \qquad (4)$$

US EPA recommends CVM as the method to value benefits of conserving biodiversity (i.e. P_{Biod} in our model) in economic terms. Note that TCM cannot be applied for assessing non-use values in economic terms, because this welfare effect is not revealed by changes in travelling behaviour.

2.2.3 Fragmentation of the ecosystem

Fragmentation reduces the number and variety of species. The modelling of this welfare effect, as well as the supply– and demand schedule and expression for consumer surplus, is analogous to the welfare effect 'disturbance of the ecosystem'.

3 Application

3.1 Introduction

The guidelines will be applied in a case study called 'Rondje Randstad' [5]. This ex ante valuation study is partially based on the findings of other, comparable cases. Therefore, the results of this case study are indicative. The case concerns plans to extend the rail infrastructure connecting the cities of Amsterdam, Utrecht, The Hague and Rotterdam.

These plans would imply adverse ecological effects, as the railway would intersect nature areas like the Green Heart area which is part of the so-called Ecological Main Structure of the Netherlands. CBA studies for Rondje Randstad have been performed according to the guidelines of OEEI [1] and thus do not include economised values for ecological effects that are not revealed on a market.

By applying the guidelines of section 2 these economised values can be added to available CBA studies for Rondje Randstad. In this way the impact of the economic valuation of ecological concerns on the outcome of CBA is shown.

3.2 Impacts

3.2.1 Disturbance of recreation

Variable 'P^{O}_{RN}' in formula (5) is the maximum amount that a visitor is willing to pay for a visit. If there is no entrance fee then only travel costs are concerned.

Willingness to pay values can be derived by using the nature valuation study of [6]. According to that study, visitors are willing to spend at most 46 minutes in travelling to a site. The formula for the Travel Cost Method is as follows:

$$P^{O}_{RN} = \gamma \text{ x } \{(AI / HW_{RN}) \text{ x } TT_{RN}\} + \{TC \text{ x } TD_{RN}\} \tag{5}$$

with

$\gamma = 0{,}4$ [source: OEEI [1]]

Average yearly income $AI = 26.000$ euro

Hours worked per year $HW_{RN} = 2.080$

Travel time $TT_{RN} = 1{,}5$ hours

Travel cost $TC = 0{,}036$ euro per kilometre per visitor (2,5 persons per car)

Travel distance $TD_{RN} = 100$ kilometre (deduced from travel time)

Therefore:

$$'P^{O}_{RN}' = 0{,}4 \times \{(26.000 / 2.080) \times 1{,}5\} + \{0{,}036 \times 100\} = 11{,}1 \text{ euro}$$

'$P^{MK}{}_{RN}$' concerns the actual travel cost of a visitor. We assume an average travel time of 30 minutes to the site relevant for our case. Again using the formula for the Travel Cost Method, the value for $P^{MK}{}_{RN}$ is:

$$\text{'}P^{MK}{}_{RN}\text{'} = 0{,}4 \times \{(26.000 / 2.080) \times 1{,}0\} + \{0{,}036 \times 100\} = 8{,}6 \text{ euro}$$

'X_{RN}' concerns average visiting frequency for the initial, undisturbed site. A study [1] about the 'Oostvaardersplassen' wetland, one of the largest green areas in the Netherlands, mentions an average visiting frequency of individuals living nearby the 'Oostvaardersplassen' of 4,22 visits per year. This value will be used as a proxy for the visiting frequency in the initially undisturbed planning region.

'X'_{RN}' concerns average visiting rate for the disturbed site. Estimations in [1] suggest that the visiting rate would decline more than 10% in case the 'IJzeren Rijn' railway line would be reactivated. This estimate will be used as an approximation for the decline of the visiting rate when Rondje Randstad would be implemented.

Now the loss in recreational consumer surplus due to the implementation of Rondje Randstad can be assessed as follows:

$$CS^{*}{}_{RN} = \left\{ \tfrac{1}{2} \times [11{,}1 - 8{,}6] \times [(4{,}22 - (0{,}90 \times 4{,}22)] \right\} = 0{,}53 \text{ euro}$$

per individual per year

3.2.2 Disturbance and fragmentation of the ecosystem

In order to collect CVM data for P_{biod} we use a CVM-study [4]. This study contains a mail survey sent to a random sample of 2.500 households in the province of South-Holland. The survey describes two project alternatives for the peat meadow area called the 'Alblasserwaard'. This is the largest of the four peat meadow areas in the Green Heart area.

The first project alternative concerns a further decline and eventual disappearance of rare meadow birds as well as a declining population of regular species. This concerns the expected autonomous development of the Alblasserwaard polder. The second project alternative concerns an improved situation for meadow birds and other species in the area. In this project alternative rare meadow birds will be protected and the population of regular species will grow. In the survey respondents where asked for their yearly willingness to pay for attaining the situation of the second project alternative. The survey included photo animations in order to visually illustrate the situation of the second project alternative.

CVM-study [4] satisfies NOAA guidelines in general terms. Accordingly, the project alternative is presented as a hypothetical situation. The fact that 'willingness to pay' is being surveyed instead of 'willingness to accept' also corresponds to the NOAA–guidelines. The same holds for the fact that photos are being used and that assessments are conservative. However, a mail survey instead of a personal interview does not correspond to the NOAA–guidelines.

The mean willingness to pay value (P_{biod}) of this study is 11 euro per individual per year.

3.3 Aggregation

3.3.1 Disturbance of recreation

The number of visitors of the Green Heart area is not available, but it can be derived as follows. According to [5] people living within a range of 1 kilometer from a railway line will have the burden of noise. Therefore, we assume that the parts of the nature area within a range of 1 kilometer from a railway line will be the relevant disturbed area for recreational visitors. As approximately 90 kilometer of the Rondje Randstad lines intersect peat meadow areas, the total area that would be disturbed equals 18.000 ha. Visiting rates (by bikers and hikers) for various types of nature are available [8]. For the type of nature in our case study region (i.e. open, accessible agricultural areas), [8] contains an average visiting rate of 1,2 to 2,4 persons per ha per day.

According to [2] a visiting rate in terms of persons per ha per day corresponds with 1,2 % of the total number of visitors per ha per year. From this it follows that a conservative estimate for the yearly number of visitors in the initially undisturbed area equals 1.8 mln. individuals.

3.3.2 Disturbance and fragmentation of the ecosystem

The number of visitors of the initially undisturbed area should be taken as an estimate for the population of these adverse welfare effects. Also in this case, the relevant population is 1.8 million people.

3.3.3 The total economic value of disturbance of recreation

Based on the preceding paragraphs, a conservative estimate for the total economic value of the adverse welfare effect 'disturbance of recreation' is as follows:

$$TEV_r = 0{,}53 \text{ euro} \times 1.8 \text{ mln. individuals} = 954.000 \text{ euro per year (a).}$$

3.3.4 The total economic value of disturbance and fragmentation

Based on the preceding paragraphs, a conservative estimate for the total economic value of the adverse welfare effects 'disturbance and fragmentation of ecosystems' is as follows:

$$TEV_{d+f} = 11 \text{ euro} \times 1.8 \text{ mln. individuals} = 19.8 \text{ mln. euro per year (b).}$$

In conclusion, a conservative estimate for the economised value of the total welfare loss that would occur as a consequence of adverse effects of Rondje Randstad on nature equals (a) + (b) or 20,75 mln. euro per year.

The estimates for the individual WTP are conservative. The real welfare loss will therefore be higher.

3.3.5 Summary of results

The impact of an investment project is felt during many decades. The social welfare loss should therefore be calculated for many years ahead. The standard approach is to use Net Present Values (NPV) for alternatives value of the time horizon and the discount rate.

It follows from Table 1 that the net present value of the negative impact of 'Rondje Randstad' on nature will vary between 111 and 341 million euro, thereby assuming that 'Rondje Randstad' will be implemented in 2010. This is a considerable amount compared to the net social costs found by [9]; a range of 0,59-5,5 bln. euro. This means that the adverse effects on nature can be up to 60 % of the total (debit) net present value. The case study illustrates that the impact of the economic valuation of ecological concerns on the outcome of CBA can be significant.

Table 1: Net Present Value (in mln. euros) for alternative time horizons and discount rates.

		Time horizon T (in years)		
		20	30	40
Discount rate r (%)	4	239,27	299,97	340,99
	10	111,42	122,13	126,25

4 Conclusions

This paper considered the deployment of guidelines for the economic valuation of ecological consequences of infrastructure projects. The case revealed that constructing new infrastructure, as well as extending existing infrastructure has adverse effects on nature. First there is the negative impact of railways and motorways on the recreational value of a nature area. Infrastructure use introduces noise in the area and reduces the scenic beauty of the landscape.

Second, infrastructure will have a negative impact on the ecosystem by intersecting nature areas and disturbing animal life. Railways and motorways become barriers to cross for various species. This will obstruct the interaction of species migrating between nature areas. Eventually, when this results in an isolation of nature areas, certain species might disappear when the areas become too small. Noise by infrastructure use reduces the number of species in the nature area. Negative impacts on ecosystems will (*ceteris paribus*) decrease welfare.

The result of our study is that guidelines for the economic valuation of the adverse effects of infrastructure on nature have become available. This contributes to the validity of economic assessment of the ecological effects from infrastructure projects. CBA+ therefore supports efficient decision-making about infrastructure investment projects.

Appendix: Loss in welfare (consumer surplus)

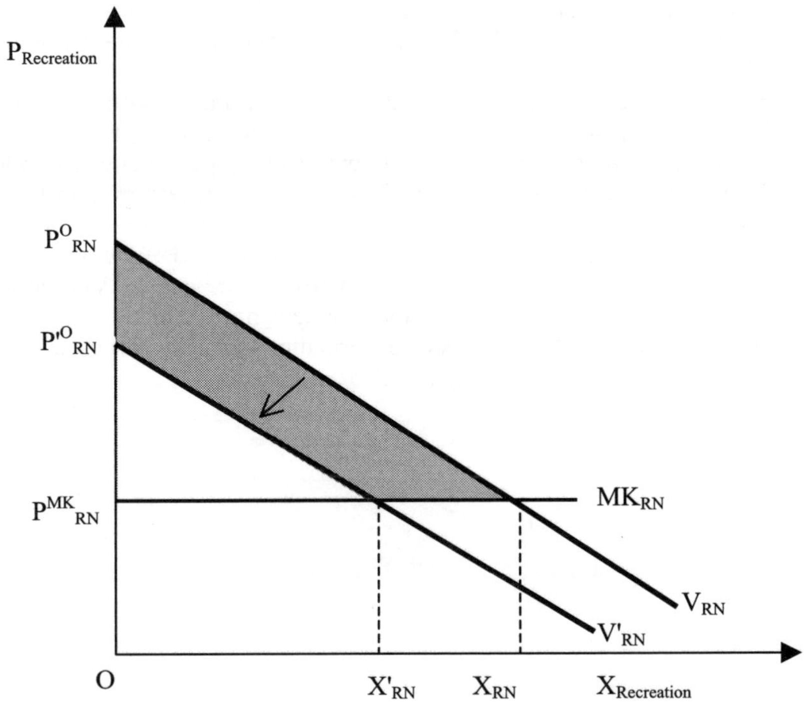

Figure A1: Loss of consumer surplus from disturbance of a nature area. The grey area corresponds with the loss in consumer surplus.

References

[1] OEEI, Onderzoeksprogramma Economische Effecten Infrastructuur, Welvaartsaspecten bij de evaluatie van infrastructuurprojecten, 2000.

[2] Goossen, C.M. and B. Ploeger, Selectie van Recreatievormen en Indicatoren voor het Beslissingsondersteunend Evaluatiesysteem voor de Landinrichting, SC-rapport 588, Wageningen, 1997.

[3] Ruijgrok, E.C.M., Valuation of Nature in Coastal Zones, Ph.D. Thesis, Free University, Amsterdam, 1997.

[4] Brouwer R. and F.A. Spaninks, The Validity of Environmental Benefit Transfer: further Empirical Testing, Environmental and Resource Economics, Vol. 14, 1999.

[5] Bos, E.J., De economische waardering van de effecten van infrastructuur op natuur: Case studie 'Rondje Randstad', rapport 4.04.02, LEI, Den Haag, 2003.

[6] Groot, A.W.M. de, K.H.S. van Buiren, I.W.D. Overtoom and M.Zijl, Natuurlijk Vermogen; een Emprirische Studie naar de Economische Waarderiing van Natuurgebieden in het Algemeen en de Oostvaardersplassen in het bijzonder, SEO, Universiteit van Amsterdam, 1998.

[7] Konijnenburg, P. van, J. Kortman, J. Jantzen and H. van der Woerd, Effecten van Reactivering van de IJzeren Rijn: Onderzoek naar de Effecten van Reactivering van de IJzeren Rijn op de Functies Recreëren, Wonen en Werken. IVAM en Universiteit van Amsterdam, Amsterdam, 2001.

[8] Vries, S. de, and C.M. Goossen, Recreatietekorten in de Provincie Noord-Holland: Een Globaal Zicht op de Effectiviteit van de Voorgestelde Plannen tot 2002, Alterra, rapport 488, Wageningen, 2002.

[9] NEI-Ecorys, KKBA van een snelle verbinding tussen de vier grote steden: Rondje Randstad, Rotterdam, 2001.

Financial efficiency versus social efficiency: a comparison using selected agrarian profiles in Andalusia

C. R. García
Department of Business Administration, ETEA, University of Córdoba, Spain

Abstract

In terms of sustainability, the agrarian policy of the European Union (CAP) is now facing a dilemma. In today's scenario of decreasing subsidies, some traditional agrarian enterprises may be not only financially inefficient but, even worse, totally unprofitable. These farms nowadays manage an employment level (family hand labour and external sources – immigration included) that helps to maintain people in the territory. The initial purpose of this paper is to classify selected agrarian profiles in a double entrance matrix by comparing the relative financial and employment efficiencies.

Using Data Envelopment Analysis (DEA), considering variable returns to scale input oriented BCC-DEA, all possible efficient frontiers are obtained. The methodology consists of removing sequentially the corresponding efficient agrarian profiles in the previous frontier, until there are not enough observations to perform the analysis. Both matrix axes represent these efficient frontiers – efficient sets of agrarian profiles – from the most efficient to the absolutely inefficient.

The position in the matrix of an agrarian profile defines the relationship between relative financial and employment efficiencies. Depending on its financial result (net margin) the analysed agrarian profile may or may not need subsidies to survive, that is maintaining its productive structure. In this situation, these aids may be conditioned both to financial and employment efficiencies in order to support good practices in terms of resource consumption and employment level. For example, a non profitable (with a negative or little net margin) but financially and socially (hand labour consumption) efficient agrarian profile may be subsidised to maintain a stable global environment. On the other hand, other situations should be restructured to improve their resource consumption (including hand labour) and/or their productive structure.

WIT Transactions on Ecology and the Environment, Vol 81, © 2005 WIT Press
www.witpress.com, ISSN 1743-3541 (on-line)

1 Introduction

Data Envelopment Analysis (DEA) is a well-known non-parametric method to evaluate the relative technical efficiency of several Decision Making Units (DMUs) described by many inputs and outputs (Charnes et al [1]). In an agrarian context, a DMU is an agrarian enterprise –known as a management unit, whose resource consumption represents the input structure and the production value of the farm is the output set -including subsidies, if necessary (García [2]).

Every farm has its own productive structure –resource consumption- due to a specific activity combination: crops and cattle. For both financial and efficiency analysis, it is very difficult to handle many individual agrarian enterprises because of statistical variability. The inner variability of the environment makes it difficult to achieve useful conclusions when individual observations –farms- are used. In order to make the sample more manageable, there are some methods to classify agrarian enterprises, for example: Technical and Economic Orientation (TEO, EU standard), Gross Value Added (GVA, standard method in input-output table development) and many more. Grouping farms in agrarian profiles have many advantages: for example, to obtain more global and useful information about a concrete agrarian type, to reduce the observation number, to make geographical studies –spatial analysis- easier, etc (García [2]). But, of course, this grouping process does not solve the variability problem although it is possible to use averages.

There are methods to manage such uncertain environments as above using, for example, Monte Carlo simulation (Seiford and Zhu [7], García [2]) but this paper only aims to design and check a classification method to compare financial and social efficiencies.

2 Materials and methods

Since 1991 three macro-surveys have been carried out in Andalusia funded by Consejería de Agricultura y Pesca (CAP) -1991, 1994 and 2000- and Instituto de Estadística de Andalucía (IEA) –2000, two organizations that belong to Junta de Andalucía, the regional government of Andalusia. Databases are the core of the AGROS information system that was designed as a decision support system in an agricultural policy context (García et al [5]). Real data are now available for classification, financial appraisal, simulation processes, and much more.

The statistical sample of surveyed farms was randomly designed to minimize the statistical error. It was based on three concepts: general structure of the farms (mainly, size –cultivated area and standard livestock units- and geographical location), their production structure (crops –both irrigated or not- and livestock combinations) and, finally, the value added of the different agrarian activities. This process was difficult because of the semi-unknown universe of farms in Andalusia since until 2002 we had no data from an updated agrarian census.

In order to classify the farm sample the GVA method was selected. Other methodologies like TEO are also considered standard, but it is proved that they have proved to show some, and very important, classification difficulties in dry farming environments with multiple agrarian activities in the same productive structure (García et al. [3, 4]). The GVA method is simple and robust and is also less sensitive to adverse weather conditions. This is why it is also chosen to design and develop input-output tables, a macroeconomic methodology. Using this method, an agrarian enterprise is classified by the activity –crop or cattle- with the greater individual GVA (García [2]).

Table 1: Agrarian profiles.

	Profiles	Abbreviation
1	Horticultural. Irrigated farming. Low costs and hand labour	HrA
2	Horticultural. Irrig. farming. Medium-low costs and h.labour	HrB
3	Industrial. Irrigated farming. Low costs and hand labour	IrA
4	Industrial. Irrig. farming. Medium-low costs and h.labour	IrB
5	Industrial. Irrig. farming. Medium-high costs and h.labour	IrC
6	Olive trees. Irrigated farming. Low costs and hand labour	OrA
7	Olive trees. Irrig. Farming. Medium-low costs and h.labour	OrB
8	Olive trees. Irrig. Farming. Medium-high costs and h.labour	OrC
9	Cereals. Irrigated farming. Low costs and hand labour	CrA
10	Cereals. Irrig. Farming. Medium-low costs and h.labour	CrB
11	Cereals. Irrig. Farming. Medium-high costs and h.labour	CrC
12	Cereals. Irrig. farming. High costs and hand labour	CrD
13	Citrus. Irrigated farming. Low costs and hand labour	CtrA
14	Fruit trees. Irrigated farming. Low costs and hand labour	FrA
15	Fruit trees. Irrig. farming. Medium-low costs and h.labour	FrB
16	Cereals. Dry farming. Low costs and hand labour	CsA
17	Cereals. Dry farming. Medium-low costs and h.labour	CsB
18	Cereals. Dry farming. Medium-high costs and h.labour	CsC
19	Cereals. Dry farming. High costs and hand labour	CsD
20	Fruit trees. Dry farming. Low costs and hand labour	FsA
21	Industrial. Dry farming. Low costs and hand labour	IsA
22	Industrial. Dry farming. Medium-low costs and h.labour	IsB
23	Olive trees. Dry farming. Low costs and hand labour	OsA
24	Olive trees. Dry farming. Medium-low costs and h.labour	OsB
25	Olive trees. Dry farming. Medium-high costs and h.labour	OsC
26	Olive trees. Dry farming. High costs and h.labour	OsD
27	Vineyards. Dry farming. Low costs and hand labour	VsA

After GVA classification was carried out, a frequency analysis was performed to determine statistical quartiles of both total crop costs and hand labour costs per hectare. Each GVA group was finally classified in agrarian profiles using the cross-quartile belonging of the observations, farms.

There are two main different methods to calculate the relative efficiency of the agrarian profiles: CCR-DEA (constant returns to scale) and BCC-DEA (variable returns-to-scale, Seiford [6]). Of course, there are also some extensions to the basic DEA methods: Imprecise DEA (IDEA), attractiveness analysis, Monte Carlo DEA, etc. There is no real evidence that in an agrarian context the constant returns-to-scale approach can be considered appropriate. Therefore, the BCC-DEA method (input oriented) was selected for relative efficiency appraisal using input and output averages.

In order to compare technical and social efficiencies, the employment level of each agrarian profile was considered first as input (it is a resource) and then as an output (it can be also considered as a social value). Only production-related parameters –financial- on average were initially selected for the BCC-DEA, Tables 2 and 3, removing financial, structural and non-agrarian ones. Parameter weights (minimum) were also controlled, Table 2, in the efficiency analysis to emphasize their participation in it. Considering the number of DMUs –27, the number of parameters was limited to seven-six inputs and one-two outputs to obtain an appropriate and discriminating enough classification.

The financial efficiency of each agrarian profile is determined using its Net Margin (NM) average –subsidies included. In order to obtain two financial-based groups within the 27 set of agrarian enterprises, a subjective 500 €/ha limit was fixed. Lower net margins per hectare mean a compromised financial situation.

Both the resource consumption and production values are measured in euros per hectare to eliminate farm size from the global analysis.

3 Results

Using the GVA method, 27 different agrarian profiles were detected from 2018 surveyed farms, Table 1. Each of them has more than 14 observations, therefore there is no problem about using basic statistics. Parameter averages are shown in Tables 3 and 4.

Applying the BCC-DEA method using averages, two different efficiency frontiers were determined, Table 4, both using hand labour costs per hectare as an input ([1] and [2]) and as output ([3] and [4]). In the first situation the relative efficiencies obtained are really "productive" ones. In the second, the obtained results can be related or associated to a "social" efficiency that considers to the agricultural enterprises to be employment sources.

From a technical point of view, the first efficiency frontier really (1st level) groups the efficient DMUs –efficiency equals one. Removing them from the sample, BCC-DEA immediately detects the second efficiency frontier (2nd level) and finally the inefficient DMUs, Table 4. Therefore, three different efficiency groups were determined.

There are efficient agrarian profiles (1st levels) both considering hand labour costs per hectare as an input and an output: HrB, OrA, CrA, FrA, FrB, FsA and IsA. The majority of them are in irrigated farming and absolutely all have low or medium-low total crop costs and hand labour costs per hectare. There are also totally inefficient agrarian profiles in irrigated farming like: IrC, OrB and CrD, in a very risky situation. The rest of the agrarian profiles have a mixed behaviour in terms of productive and social efficiencies. They can be efficient from a productive point of view and inefficient from a social point of view, or vice versa, Table 4.

Table 2: Production parameters.

Code	Parameter (€/ha)	Type of parameter	Min. weight (%)
1	Seed and plant costs	Input	0
2	Fertilizer costs	Input	10
3	Pesticides costs	Input	10
4	Machinery costs	Input	10
5	Hand labour costs	Input or Output	10
6	Electricity costs	Input	0
7	Fuel costs	Input	0
8	Total revenues without subsidies	Output	10

Table 3: Parameter averages.

	(1)	(2)	(3)	(4)	(5)	(6)	(7)	(8)
HrA	658.40	328.02	190.40	109.95	825.03	158.81	201.69	7264.87
HrB	1561.3	926.38	652.80	247.34	3823.5	650.44	549.79	27070.73
IrA	87.75	103.05	141.97	115.89	50.89	26.54	72.95	2342.44
IrB	131.07	178.19	209.39	245.60	146.64	78.69	68.40	2915.22
IrC	134.91	186.76	289.69	238.74	242.62	88.67	118.13	2598.98
OrA	4.65	76.82	32.04	5.18	285.48	21.83	68.75	2246.63
OrB	7.53	106.65	78.00	52.64	705.37	28.31	93.34	2186.25
OrC	3.15	198.62	74.66	48.27	1470.2	68.49	68.87	3000.35
CrA	35.37	42.96	8.54	28.25	18.84	10.57	23.90	494.78
CrB	45.21	50.67	16.73	44.75	54.69	37.65	29.58	617.88
CrC	105.80	87.95	49.94	92.68	135.56	34.23	74.70	1646.50
CrD	107.07	120.91	111.34	109.27	397.72	97.09	120.24	1635.88
CtrA	23.66	347.31	237.33	26.08	2643.1	113.53	141.93	5254.85
FrA	0.94	340.82	92.86	51.77	1591.0	174.39	96.18	5404.16
FrB	8.43	204.27	148.24	105.12	2930	150.64	306.57	10235.83
CsA	45.68	47.98	14.99	25.99	18.37	4.72	46.67	514.40
CsB	45.68	47.98	14.99	25.99	18.37	4.72	46.67	514.40
CsC	49.30	57.81	15.31	40.21	49.83	24.88	35.63	516.02
CsD	62.84	91.70	31.36	58.46	79.38	6.41	31.34	935.92
FsA	1.19	33.63	18.33	8.21	239.47	4.40	20.09	628.21
IsA	52.47	34.43	11.40	37.85	49.37	3.23	37.93	611.88
IsB	62.56	57.59	56.96	70.59	132.04	4.74	60.51	1064.11
OsA	18.29	81.81	28.42	20.92	195.66	13.67	56.88	1309.44
OsB	5.90	141.37	61.02	32.69	371.14	20.66	83.20	2391.81
OsC	2.20	106.65	52.39	96.42	589.86	16.84	72.28	2393.72
OsD	0.91	131.15	75.86	41.74	924.60	39.07	95.17	2955.27
VsA	3.70	67.48	56.34	17.84	808.92	59.63	94.33	1936.64

Table 4: Efficiency and financial results.

	Hand Labour costs as an input		Hand Labour costs as an output		Net Margin on average (€/ha)
	[1] 1st Eff. Frontier	[2] 2nd Eff. Frontier	[3] 1st Eff. frontier	[4] 2nd Eff. frontier	
HrA	1		0.7368	1	4,523.90
HrB	1		1		13,562.67
IrA	0.9549	1	0.3	0.601	1,425.86
IrB	0.6383	1	0.3828	0.6196	1,402.56
IrC	0.4592	0.6544	0.3325	0.4637	626.96
OrA	1		1		869.36
OrB	0.5859	0.9072	0.816	0.9946	-39.49
OrC	0.7456	1	1		-50.17
CrA	1		1		204.88
CrB	0.779	1	0.6924	1	87.55
CrC	0.7586	1	0.4586	0.7877	689.74
CrD	0.4069	0.6252	0.361	0.621	-202.28
CtrA	0.7089	1	1		542.46
FrA	1		1		1,499.96
FrB	1		1		5,992.05
CsA	1		0.8486	1	129.15
CsB	1		0.8986	1	279.33
CsC	0.6892	1	0.6821	1	88.96
CsD	0.8031	1	0.525	1	446.39
FsA	1		1		-141.01
IsA	1		1		346.05
IsB	0.6915	1	0.5798	0.9812	252.61
OsA	0.8436	1	0.7451	1	679.97
OsB	0.8168	1	0.3535	1	1,367.74
OsC	0.7348	1	0.9396	1	1,278.89
OsD	0.7526	1	0.9169	1	2,244.26
VsA	0.7269	1	1		400.95

CrA, FsA and IsA agrarian profiles are both productive and social efficient but their financial situation per hectare (agrarian year 2000) is not very appropriate (except in big cultivated areas), especially in FsA (negative net margin), Tables 4, 5 and 6. They will probably continue needing additional financial support to maintain their productive structures. On the other hand, CsA and CsB (high intensive production) are production efficient but they are located at a secondary level (high mechanised crops) from a social point of view. In this case, it is very difficult to improve their "social" contribution and they are also the unique productive alternatives in their geographical locations.

VsA and OrC are socially efficient but, in terms of production efficiency, both agrarian profiles are located at the second efficient frontier, Tables 5 and 6.

In the second case, the net margin per hectare on average is negative (Table 4) because it groups new olive tree plantations. Obviously, its revenues (without subsidies) were not enough to balance production and structural costs but its hand labour consumption is high enough to achieve social efficiency. Vineyards in dry farming, VsA, show a high employment level but their financial situation is risky. Therefore, subsidies can be socially justified to maintain their productive structure. Currently, the vineyard sector in Andalusia is being restructured removing plantations, using specific EU subsidies.

Table 5: Technical efficiency versus financial efficiency.

	Net Margin on average under than 500 €/ha	Net Margin on average over 500 €/ha
First level (Eff. Frontier)	CrA CsA, CsB FsA (-)* IsA	HrA, HrB OrA FrA, FrB
Second level (Eff. Frontier)	OrC (-) CrB CsC, CsD VsA IsB	IrA, IrB CrC CtrA OsA, OsB, OsC, OsD
Inefficient DMUs	OrB (-) CrD (-)	IrC

(*) Negative net margin on average.

Table 6: Social efficiency versus financial efficiency.

	Net Margin on average under than 500 €/ha	Net Margin on average over 500 €/ha
First level (Eff. Frontier)	OrC (-) CrA FsA (-) IsA VsA	HrB OrA CtrA FrA, FrB
Second level (Eff. Frontier)	CrB CsA, CsB, CsC (-), CsD	HrA OsA, OsB, OsC, OsD
Inefficient DMUs	OrB CrD (-) IsB	IrA, IrB, IrC CrC

CrB, CsC and CsD, cereal-based farms, are located in an intermediate position in both analysed efficiencies. Probably, they must improve their productive structures –resource consumption, including hand labour- to achieve a more appropriate level like CsA, CsB and CrA. Each of them have a compromised financial situation and subsidies can be also necessary like at present. Only the last profile can be easily restructured introducing new crops in irrigated farming.

IsB is not socially efficient and has an intermediate productive efficiency. This agrarian profile -financially compromised- is highly mechanised but its revenues, without subsidies, will not be able to maintain its productive structure. Only cereals, legumes and olive trees can substitute industrial crops in dry farming.

OrB and CrD are completely inefficient. In the first agrarian profile (new olive tree plantations that still have a low production), it is necessary to wait for a balanced production. The second has a very unstable productive structure that must be improved as soon as possible.

HrB, OrA, FrA and FrB have a very stable financial situation and all of them are productively and socially efficient. Only the second one has subsidies (production-based) nowadays but its net margin, including them, are enough to achieve a profitable level.

HrA and CtrA have an intermediate situation. Both without EU financial aids are profitable enough although certain improvements could be considered in the productive structure of CtrA and in the employment level in HrA.

Olive tree agrarian profiles in dry farming – OsA, OsB, OsC and OsD – are located in the second efficient level, both in productive and social cases. Their net margin per hectare shows a stable financial situation that can be improved in terms of resource consumption and employment level. Nowadays, their positive net margin is due to EU subsidies. These agrarian profiles are very difficult to restructure because of the lack of productive alternatives in dry farming.

Finally, industrial crop productive profiles – IrA, IrB and IrC – as well as CrC both in irrigated farming have a very risky situation considering productive and social efficiencies. In all of these structures EU subsidies are responsible for their positive and high net margins. In irrigated farming, could be relatively easy to restructure their productive structures.

4 Conclusions

BCC-DEA is a powerful methodology to classify agrarian profiles in terms of "productive" and "social" efficiencies. Adding their financial results (for example, net margin) and crossing the respective results, it is possible to classify complex farm types to obtain a global vision of the agrarian environment.

The lack of observations (agrarian profiles) is the most important difficulty in the classification process because of the limited number of financial parameters that can be chosen (conditioned by DEA). This problem can be solved grouping financial parameters. For example: productive, structural, hand labour, etc.

The inner variability of the sample is also a difficulty that has to be dealt with. Monte Carlo BCC-DEA methodology opens a new research subject to obtain new and more perfect agrarian profile classification. Monte Carlo financial appraisal can also be used to improve financial efficiency in terms of medium-term Net Present Value avoiding subjective limits.

Finally, the proposed methodology needs some historical data series or simulation processes to recommend productive, social or political improvements in the agrarian sector of Andalusia.

Acknowledgements

The survey processes were funded by CAP and IEA, both organizations of Junta de Andalusia. The author is especially grateful to Luis Rubio and his team in the Research and Studies Service of CAP and Marisa Asensio and her team in IEA.

References

[1] Charnes, A., Cooper, W.W. & Rhodes, E. Measuring the efficiency of decision making units. *European J. Oper. Res.* 2, pp.429-444, 1978.
[2] García, C.R. Efficiency of selected productive strategies with imprecise data. *Acta Horticulturae*, 659, pp.53-60, 2004.
[3] García, C.R., Martín, J.M. & Pérez, P.P. Socio-Economic Evolution of Horticultural Farms in Andalucía since 1991. *Acta Horticulturae*, 536, pp.207-214, 2000.
[4] García, C.R., Martín, J.M. & Pérez, P.P. Determinación y Análisis de Tipologías de Explotaciones Agrarias en un Espacio Rural Diversificado. *Empresa, Economía y* Sociedad, eds. A. Rodero & M.C. López, Publicaciones ETEA, pp.167-188, 2001.
[5] García, C.R., Martín, J.M. & Pérez, P.P. Estructura socioeconómica de las explotaciones agrarias de la Comunidad Autónoma de Andalucía. Final report of the project (non-published). Consejería de Agricultura y Pesca de la Comunidad Autónoma de Andalucía, 2003.
[6] Seiford, L.M. & Zhu, J. An investigation of returns to scale in data envelopment analysis. *Omega*, 27, pp.1-11, 1999.
[7] Seiford, L.M. & Zhu, J. Context-dependent data envelopment analysis – Measuring attractiveness and progress. *Omega*, 31, pp.397-408, 2003.

Establishing ecotourism in Mahabaleshwar and Panchgani, India

T. Woods
Institute of Development Studies, UK

Abstract

The hill stations of Mahabaleshwar and Panchgani in the Western Ghats, India, have been a popular location since British soldiers visited to escape the heat of the lowland plains. In recent years, the growth of India's consumer class, combined with increasing access to private and public transport, has led to damaging new tourist developments. Problems include the clearance of natural vegetation for hotels and facilities, the cutting of trees for fuel wood, increased pressure on water and electricity resources, pollution from vehicles, overcrowding and litter. These are serious concerns, due to the fragility and ecological importance of the forest and scrubland in the region. The character of Mahabaleshwar in particular has also changed, from a tranquil place for relaxing and appreciating nature to a busy commercialised resort.

Local authorities and environmental groups have made efforts to control these problems, but these have so far proved ineffective. Few people want to limit the growth of tourism in the region; most local residents, business owners and government planners favour the continued growth of mass tourism. This raises important questions about who should dictate the future pattern of tourism and whether environmental preservation is preferable to local economic growth, even when there are few alternative prospects.

This study examines why previous measures to make tourism more environmentally sustainable have been unsuccessful. A management plan is suggested which divides the region into zones of different tourism activity, with an emphasis on establishing ecotourism. This proposal is a new approach to solving the problems caused by tourism and, in theory, satisfies the conflicting aims of environmental preservation and economic development.

Keywords: carrying capacity, economic development, ecotourism, protected area management, zoning.

1 Introduction

The tourism industry has grown significantly in recent years. It is now one of the world's largest industries, contributing six percent of global Gross Domestic Product (PHDCCI [1]). This growth is set to continue, with global tourist numbers predicted to double between 1990 and 2010 to 1.018 million (Lindberg *et al* [2]). An important area of growth is ecotourism. There has been considerable debate regarding different forms of 'environmental tourism'. The terms and characteristics associated with these are widely discussed, for example by Mowforth and Munt [3]. One definition of ecotourism is 'responsible travel to natural areas that conserves the environment and improves the well-being of local people' (The International Ecotourism Society [4]). The World Tourism Organisation estimates that ecotourism is growing at an annual rate of five percent and almost every country now practices some form of ecotourism. India in particular has considerable potential for ecotourism, with 574 National Parks and wildlife sanctuaries, all open to the public. Competition between humans and the environment is also greater in India than any other region of Asia (Lew [5]).

The relationship between tourism and the environment is complex. Tourism has become a focus of criticism, because of its negative environmental impacts, and a focus of promotion, as a means of achieving sustainable development (Mowforth and Munt [6]). While it can be difficult to isolate tourism impacts from other forms of development, tourism does attract unfair criticism, as the impacts are more tangible than other forms of development (Buhalis and Flecher [7]). Previous research on ecotourism has often focused on the impacts and benefits of introducing tourism to previously undeveloped locations. However, to increase environmental protection further, ecotourism will need to be developed in areas where tourism already exists, rather than untouched 'wilderness' areas. This is the situation in Mahabaleshwar and Panchgani, where ecotourism is being considered as a mechanism for controlling the growth of tourism.

2 Study region

The Western Ghats mountain range is ecologically very important. Isolation from other rainforest areas in Asia means that many species in the Western Ghats are unique (Gadgil [8]). The diversity of plant and animal life has led to the Western Ghats, along with Sri Lanka, being declared one of 18 'biodiversity hotspots' in the world. The key criteria for these hotspots are the degree of endemism and the degree of threat. All hotspots have lost over 70 percent of their original vegetation cover. Identification of these hotspots enables prioritisation of conservation interests (Agrawal [9]). Mahabaleshwar and Panchgani are located within this region.

The variations in altitude, humidity and edaphic factors within the study region have produced a wide range of tropical, sub-tropical and temperate plant and animal species, many of which are endemic. Many plant species have adapted to withstand the strong winds and heavy rains of the monsoon and the near arid conditions of winter and mid-summer, making them unique sub-species. The region is also famous for several rare species of orchids. This vegetation is being cleared for agriculture and tourism purposes.

The loss of forest cover has affected the local fauna. Many animals once abundant in the region are now extinct and others are seriously endangered. The Malabar giant squirrel, the state animal of Maharashtra, is rarely seen. The last Black Panther sighted in Maharashtra was seen near Mahabaleshwar and the sloth bear has disappeared completely. These animals have declined due to habitat loss, a decline in prey for carnivores, disturbance to wildlife corridors in the region and the pollution of rivers and streams.

In recognition of the increasing pressures from tourism and agriculture, Mahabaleshwar, Panchgani and the surrounding forests were declared an Eco-Sensitive Zone (known as the MPEZ) under the Environment Protection Act in 2001 - the first area to be given this status in India.

3 Problems caused by tourism

Tourist numbers have risen steadily since the 1960s (Figure 1). This is partly due to increasing ownership of private vehicles, an increase in the number of private buses and improved road facilities (Dikshit [10]). This growth has had several impacts on the local environment.

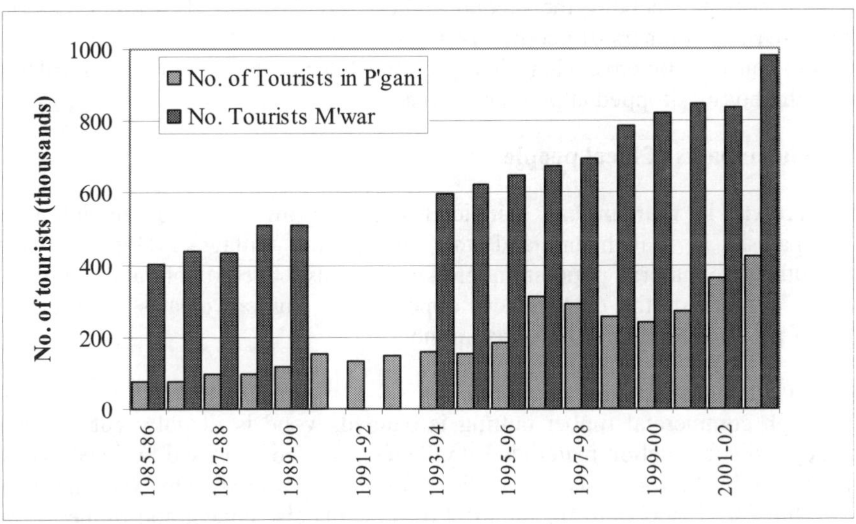

Figure 1: The growth of tourism in Mahabaleshwar and Panchgani. Source: Mahabaleshwar Tourist Office. (Data for Mahabaleshwar 1991-3 unavailable.)

3.1 New developments

The towns of Mahabaleshwar and Panchgani have both expanded to cater for tourism, encroaching into the natural vegetation. Large areas of forest have been cleared for new hotels and guesthouses. New buildings are now prohibited, but modifications and expansions still occur. It is difficult to enforce legal restrictions and corruption is widespread. Previous developments were not always designed in keeping with the character of the region. Many are several storeys high, emerging above the forest canopy. Others have used inappropriate materials. Once unsuitable buildings are established, it is difficult to change their appearance.

3.2 Litter and pollution

Traffic causes congestion, noise pollution and atmospheric pollution from exhaust fumes and the volume of traffic, both private and public, has increased steadily. In the early 1990s, this growth was estimated to be an annual increase of 15 to 20 percent each year; it is now even greater (Dikshit [11] Bharucha [12]). The villages around Mahabaleshwar have no solid or liquid waste management system, meaning sewage, litter and household waste pollute the forests and water bodies in the area (Paranjpye [13]).

Increasing tourist numbers exert considerable pressure on many resources and the local infrastructure. The increasing demand for electricity and fuel also causes problems, with power cuts common during the busy summer month. There are often water shortages during the summer months, despite Mahabaleshwar receiving the second highest level of rainfall in India. Besides the increasing numbers of people visiting the study area, the behaviour of many visitors causes problems. There is a growing litter problem, particularly plastic bags and bottles dropped at popular tourist spots.

3.3 The impacts of local people

The growth in tourism has coincided with a growth in the population of Mahabaleshwar, Panchgani and the surrounding villages. This is partly attributable to natural population growth, but also due to migration into the region because of the employment opportunities tourism creates. This causes further problem to the rise in tourist numbers.

3.3.1 Collection of forest products

Although commercial timber cutting is banned, wood is illegally cut for fuel, timber and construction materials by villagers. All the fuel used by local people is wood from the forest. There are fines for cutting wood (50 to 100 rupees per tree), but very few people are caught. Local people also collect non-timber forest products such as orchids, resins and oils for personal use and sale to tourists. Tourism has also caused an increase in poaching and smuggling of animal skins.

3.3.2 Agriculture

Rab cultivation is the traditional form of subsistence agriculture in the region. Local farmers burn tree branches and leaves to return nutrients to the soil. A new area is cleared when the land loses productivity. The area under cultivation continually shifts, until returning to the original plot. However, yields during the second cycle are invariably lower as the fertility of the soil has not had a chance to return to its original levels. Plots are discarded once they become infertile and the soil is easily eroded (Janah [14]). This unsustainable process means that forest regeneration is virtually impossible, either by natural processes or through plantation programmes. Land is also increasingly cleared for commercial agriculture to feed the growing number of tourists in the region.

Soil degradation has had further negative impacts in the region. During the monsoon, large quantities of topsoil from the slopes of the plateau are deposited in the nearby Koyna reservoir. The rate of siltation is estimated to be 9.63 hectare-metres per 100 km^2 each year. This could affect the economic life of the Koyna dam which supplies hydropower to Mumbai and other nearby towns and cities. It also reduces the storage capacity of the reservoir (Paranjpye [15]).

4 Discussion

The following discussion is based on data collected by the author through questionnaires, interviews and group discussions with the following groups: residents of Mahabaleshwar, Panchgani and surrounding villages; business owners in Mahabaleshwar and Panchgani; tourists visiting the region; members of local environmental groups; members of the Regional Land Use Committee, the Regional Environment Committee and the Regional Planning Board; officers at Mahabaleshwar municipal office and Panchgani municipal office.

4.1 Benefits of tourism

While causing several environmental problems, tourism brings many benefits to local people. This is a key element of ecotourism, according to several definitions. Employment in tourism is the major benefit for local people. Agriculture remains the most common form of employment but tourism provides a more reliable source of income and pays considerably higher wages. A shop or hotel worker can earn 1000 rupees a month, plus food; skilled labourers can earn up to 150 rupees per day. Wages for agricultural workers vary considerably, but are generally much lower than this. Tourism, in its current form, dominates the local economy and provides a good standard of living for many people in the region.

Local people identified improved road access and electricity and water supply systems as other benefits. New schools built in villages and secondary schools in Mahabaleshwar mean that local children can be educated to a higher level. The houses in villages have been improved with better building materials and the bank in Mahabaleshwar enables people to save money. Whilst these changes may have happened anyway, local people felt that tourism revenues helped to achieve them more quickly. Many people also identified interaction with tourists as a positive aspect of tourism.

4.2 Failure of previous ecotourism measures

Previous ecotourism activities have included putting up signs to prevent people from dropping litter and tree planting schemes to regenerate cleared forest areas.

However, these projects have all been unsuccessful. They have been small-scale and under promoted, with an emphasis on individual responsibility rather than collective regional schemes. Several environmental organisations have consequently demanded improved measures to reduce the impacts of tourism on the environment.

The introduction of a carrying capacity is one method for identifying a sustainable level of tourism. This has been suggested by some environmental groups with an interest in the area. Whilst several criteria exist for establishing carrying capacities, there are problems in achieving this. A carrying capacity for vehicles would require more detailed analysis than the total number, including factors such as type of vehicle, how polluting it is (such as exhaust fumes and oil leaks) and how much the vehicle is driven around the region. These impacts cannot always be easily identified or measured.

There is no universally accepted method for calculating carrying capacities for tourist numbers and there is often disagreement regarding which factors to consider and their relative importance. With disagreement over how a figure is determined, local people and businesses losing revenue from limited visitor numbers are likely to contest any legislation introduced. The issue of tourist numbers is also more complex than simply the total number of people entering the region. The areas where vehicles and tourists go within the region are important, as some areas are more ecologically sensitive than others. Visitor activities have become concentrated in a few popular tourist spots. High concentrations have a greater impact than if visitors were dispersed more evenly throughout the region. Furthermore, carrying capacities are not constant phenomena. During animal breeding seasons and periods of plant growth, the sustainable number of visitors is lower than at other times (Lindberg *et al* [16]).

4.3 Zoning plan

The problems identified suggest that restricting tourist numbers is not a realistic option. Any attempt to do so would meet with resistance from people dependent on tourism for their livelihoods, as well as from tourists. There is a strong possibility that a reduction in tourism revenue would force local people to seek alternative sources of income, such as the collection of fuel wood or subsistence farming, which are even more damaging to the environment. A restriction would be very difficult to enforce. Given that the impacts of tourism vary throughout the region, the most appropriate measures would be to:

- encourage greater spatial dispersal of tourists through the region, with restrictions on numbers in the most fragile areas
- encourage greater temporal dispersal of tourists through the year
- educate tourists, business owners and local people regarding the importance of the forests, to change behaviour patterns in all groups
- enforce measures regarding land use, buildings and resource consumption
- begin restoration work to alleviate the existing problems in the region.

The establishment of zoning systems is becoming a widespread management tool for many protected areas in India. Zoning is a compromise between the economic benefits of large-scale tourism and the need for effective environmental protection. I propose that the MPEZ is divided into four zones: ecotourism, nature tourism, commercial tourism and residential.

4.3.1 Ecotourism zone

The ecotourism zone would include the most ecologically valuable areas of forest around Mahabaleshwar and other important ecological sites. It should be closed to the general public and numbers limited to small groups, as happens in other protected areas in India. Visits will take the form of guided nature walks, with an emphasis on nature interpretation and identification. Eighty-one percent of tourists questioned said they would be interested in such activities. The impacts of visitors must be carefully monitored and group sizes adjusted accordingly. The roads in this zone would close to all traffic except for the major access roads to and from the towns.

4.3.2 Nature tourism zone

The nature tourism zone would include the major tourist attractions not covered by the ecotourism zone. These are in less fragile ecosystems and need fewer restrictions. A limited number of tickets would be made available for each point, to encourage a more even distribution of visitors. There would be a ban on private transport but an improved public transport system would be introduced: environmentally friendly buses can transport visitors around the major points in Mahabaleshwar. The hill station of Matheran provides an example of a tourist destination that successfully uses just public transport. There is a complete ban on motor vehicles and scooters and most visitors arrive by train. Alternative forms of transport, such as horses and hand-pulled rickshaws, are a major tourist attraction.

4.3.3 Commercial tourism zone

The commercial tourism zone would incorporate the town centres of Mahabaleshwar and Panchgani. These are currently very crowded and require reorganisation. The town centre of Mahabaleshwar will become a traffic free zone. It would be desirable to encourage more traditional crafts and products. Mahabaleshwar has a tradition of leather goods manufacturing, particularly shoes, and the making of wooden walking canes. These activities have almost vanished, overshadowed by mass tourism.

4.3.4 Residential zone

The residential zone would incorporate the residential areas in the two towns, hotels and guesthouses, as well as the villages between the two towns. Traffic should be permitted in this zone for access. Building restrictions need stricter enforcement to prevent the residential sector expanding further into the forests. It is also important to disperse where people can stay within the region to reduce congestion in the town centres. One method is introducing ‘home stays’ whereby tourists stay with local families. This would also provide another source of income, which will go directly for local people.

Establishing these zones within the MPEZ will require long-term planning and management. It is important that the changes occur as a gradual but definite process and that consultation with all stakeholders takes place before any changes are made. When considering the order in which to implement these changes, the initial emphasis must be on educating tourists and changing their behaviour patterns. Education for local people and business owners is important for obtaining support for these changes, but these groups are more likely to adapt if demands from tourists enforce this. If tourists express a desire for more environmentally friendly tourism, in terms of transport options, resource use, accommodation and location of activities, there will be more support for introducing these measures.

Only when ecotourism activities become widely available and well promoted will it be possible to ascertain how popular they are - this is a major problem in establishing ecotourism. Business owners, local people and the tourism planning authorities have all shown a strong preference for expanding current tourism activities, rather than introducing ecotourism. In interviews, these groups expressed a desire to increase tourist numbers and keep people in the town centres, where they will spend money in their businesses, rather than disperse them. It is these groups, particularly the planning authorities, who are largely responsible for the development of tourism. Tourists can only express a preference for environmental activities if these are available, but they are unlikely to be initiated by the stakeholders identified above. It is therefore vital that environmentalists begin to organise ecotourism activities independently, alongside educational activities about the benefits of ecotourism.

4.4 Temporal dispersal of tourists

Whilst dispersing tourists throughout the region will reduce congestion and overcrowding, reducing numbers at peak times, such as the summer months and weekends, is also desirable. This is when the negative impacts are most concentrated and there is most pressure on the resources in the area. This is a more difficult problem to resolve than spatial dispersal. People visit during these times as they are the holiday periods in India. Restricting people from visiting at these times will be difficult and unpopular. If tourists can be dispersed more evenly throughout the region and their behaviour patterns adapted to more sustainable activities, the concentration of tourists at peak times should become less of a problem.

5 Conclusions and policy implications

With a wealth of biodiversity, the Mahabaleshwar-Panchgani region has definite potential for ecotourism. However, previous developments mean that ecotourism cannot follow the pattern successful in other regions. Wilderness cannot be recreated and the established tourism infrastructure cannot simply be removed or ignored. Any ecotourism plan must seek to adapt the existing pattern of tourism, despite the difficulties in achieving this. Globally, ecotourism should focus more strongly on the problems in existing tourist destinations, such as Mahabaleshwar and Panchgani, rather than developing new destinations. There is an argument that mass tourism cannot be environmentally friendly or that ecotourism cannot be successful on a large scale (Fennell [17]; Barkin [18]). The presence of mass tourism in many destinations is unlikely to change, however, so the priority must be to adapt it to a more sustainable form of tourism, rather than focus on the preferences of the exclusive ecotourism sector.

The proposed zoning plan provides a new solution to the problems facing Mahabaleshwar and Panchgani. The implementation of this plan will require decisive action and legislation to ensure that the changes are enforced. This has not happened in the past because there is no desire for change amongst key stakeholders, notably business owners, planning committees and the local government. Education is important to changing attitudes and should remain an important component of any ecotourism proposal. However, in a region where tourism already exists, economic benefits will outweigh any amount of education. It is therefore imperative that ecotourism maintains the level of income generated by current tourism practices.

This study raises questions about the extent to which anyone has the right to modify the development path of a region. At present, most stakeholders are happy with the current pattern of tourism. It could be argued that agriculture causes more tangible damage in the region, without generating the same levels of employment or income, and that this should be the focus of restrictions and legislation, rather than tourism. Despite this criticism, however, the benefits of current tourism practices do not justify the extent of the damage caused. If more sustainable activities can maintain the level of income currently generated, then this must be the aim of all concerned. Further research is required to determine whether there is sufficient demand for environmental tourism to maintain current income levels. Whilst there is plenty of research regarding ecotourists from developed countries, there is very little research concerning tourists from developing nations and their perspectives on ecotourism. Van der Duim and Caalders [19] argue that a concern for nature is mainly a developed world interest. If ecotourism is to be successfully developed in the study region, it is important to determine the extent to which this is true.

A more sustainable, environmentally sound pattern of tourism in Mahabaleshwar and Panchgani will require a slow transition in behaviour and attitudes, instigated by environmentalists, supported by tourists and followed by local people and businesses, either through desire or necessity. If this can be achieved, then this region could provide a framework for promoting ecotourism in developed tourism destinations, both in India and throughout the world.

References

[1] PHD Chamber of Commerce and Industry (PHDCCI). *Eco-tourism and sustainable livelihoods*, Concept Paper, PHD House: New Delhi, 2003.

[2] Lindberg, K., Hawkins, D.E. & Western, D., *Ecotourism – a guide for planners and managers: volume 1*, Natraj Publishers: Dehra Dun, 1997.
[3] Mowforth, M. & Munt, I., *Tourism and sustainability – new tourism in the Third World*, Routledge: London, 1998.
[4] The International Ecotourism Society. *What is ecotourism?* Online www.ecotourism.org/index2.php?what-is-ecotourism.
[5] Lew, A.A., Asia. *The Encyclopaedia of ecotourism,* ed. D.B. Weaver, CABI: Wallingford, 2001.
[6] Mowforth, M. & Munt, I., *Tourism and sustainability – new tourism in the Third World*, Routledge: London, 1998.
[7] Buhalis, D. & Flecher, J., Environmental impacts on tourist destinations: an economic analysis. *Sustainable tourism development,* eds. H. Collossis & P. Nijkamp, Avebury: Aldershot, 1995.
[8] Gadgil, M., *Ecological journeys*, Permanent Black: New Delhi, 2001.
[9] Agrawal, K.C., *Global biodiversity: conservation, indigenous rights and biopiracy,* Nidhi Publishers: Bikaner, 2002.
[10] Dikshit, K.R., *Environment, forest ecology and man in the Western Ghats*, Rawat Publications: Jaipur, 1991.
[11] Dikshit, K.R., *Environment, forest ecology and man in the Western Ghats*, Rawat Publications: Jaipur, 1991.
[12] Bharucha, E.K. Personal communication, 26 July 2003, Director, Bharathi Vidyapeeth Institute of Environment Education and Research, Pune, India.
[13] Paranjpye, V., *Environmental status report of the Mahabaleshwar-Panchgani Eco-sensitive Zone*, Unpublished report, Pune, June 2000.
[14] Janah, S., *The tribals of India*, Oxford University Press: Oxford, 1993.
[15] Paranjpye, V., *Environmental status report of the Mahabaleshwar-Panchgani Eco-sensitive Zone*, Unpublished report, Pune, June 2000.
[16] Lindberg, K., Hawkins, D.E. & Western, D., *Ecotourism – a guide for planners and managers: volume 1*, Natraj Publishers: Dehra Dun, 1997.
[17] Fennell, D.A., *Ecotourism – an introduction*, Routledge: London, 1999.
[18] Barkin, D. The economic impacts of ecotourism: conflicts and solutions in Highland Mexico. *Tourism and development in mountain regions*, eds. P.M. Godde, M.F. Price & F.M. Zimmermann, CABI: Wallingford, 2000.
[19] Van der Duim, K. & Caalders, J., Biodiversity and tourism: impacts and interventions. *Annals of tourism research*, 29 **(3)**, pp. 743-761, 2002.

Financing the ecological city

R. R. White
Department of Geography, and Institute for Environmental Studies, University of Toronto, Canada

Abstract

A great deal of work has been accomplished on the physical aspects of the sustainable city, but relatively little has been done to explore the alternatives for financing sustainability in the urban context. This paper examines what has been accomplished already to encourage sustainability through the application of financial instruments such as traffic congestion charges, user fees for stormwater management, materials recycling, and similar initiatives.

Together these instruments may be seen as constituting the field of 'urban environmental finance' which may be defined as consisting of financial instruments which encourage a transition towards behaviour which supports the sustainability of urban systems. Whereas many examples exist of particular innovations in this area, no urban government appears to have approached the challenge in a comprehensive way using the framework of sustainable urban development. The reasons why this has not yet happened are not difficult to find. For example, politicians are usually reluctant to propose new charges even if they can promise that they will be revenue-neutral. Second, in many countries the urban level of government has very limited powers to impose such charges. Third, some schemes require significant costs for data collection and other implementation costs. Examples will be drawn from Canada, the United States, Europe and South-East Asia, with a focus on transportation, water and emissions to the air.
Keywords: urban finance, environmental finance, urban services, urban infrastructure, full cost pricing, urban metabolism, climate change and cities, ecological cities.

1 Introduction

A recent report of the U.S. National Research Council stated that: 'Over the next 30 years, most of the growth in the world's population is expected to occur in the cities and towns of poor countries. Cities are now the home to nearly half of the world's total population and over three-quarters of the population of high-income countries,' (National Research Council [1]). This development has many notable implications for urban living. First, as cities become the dominant settlement form and house more and more of the planet's population, it will become more difficult to export urban wastes – solid, liquid and gaseous – to non-urban areas. This is because there will be more of these wastes and rural dwellers will become more resistant to accepting them. Second, it is the poorest cities that are growing the fastest, and lack of financial resources makes it more difficult to design and maintain cities to provide the basic needs for their inhabitants.

For these and related reasons it is becoming increasingly important to re-think the way we build and inhabit cities. The present trajectory is unsustainable for numerous reasons – concerning health, economics, finance and social stability. We need to re-conceptualise urban life in terms of the Ecological City.

An Ecological City can be defined as 'a city that provides an acceptable standard of living for its human occupants without depleting the ecosystems and bio-geochemical cycles on which it depends' (White, 3 [2]). Ideally, this means that an Ecological City discharges *no* unwanted residuals to the components of the surrounding biosphere – atmospheric, terrestrial and hydrological. Specifically, this means that a city would emit *no* problematic gases, solids or liquids – no air pollution, no solid waste and no impure water. The only human habitats that have been designed to meet these exacting conditions are the 'biospheres' designed by the American and Soviet space programmes as prototypes for space ships capable of long distance journeys. The largest of these experimental habitats housed about a dozen people for several months. Clearly, the cities we live are a very long way from this kind of enforced equilibrium.

The notion of the Ecological City can be equated with the 'Sustainable City' with the physical parameters – required for sustainability – made more explicit. This paper goes beyond the physical parameters to examine some of the financial implications of sustainability. It does so by adapting the principles of the emerging field of environmental finance.

Modern cities are *not* 'ecological' in the sense defined above. Some are closer than others, but none are as close as we will need them to be if we are to develop a sustainable niche for humans on the planet. In fairness to urban planners and urban managers, cities were never designed for zero ecological impact. Cities were designed to provide shelter and services, and to manufacture goods. Some had loftier aesthetic and spiritual purposes, but most were based on short-term, least-cost reasoning.

This approach has produced cities that are extremely dysfunctional from an ecological standpoint. For example, traffic congestion is an almost universal feature of cities today. It is commonplace for 'travellers' to spend more of their journey time immobile than mobile. For example, even 15 years ago the engineers of the City of Toronto calculated that only 25% of the energy consumed by vehicles was used for motion – the rest is wasted (White [3]). The traffic situation in Toronto has greatly deteriorated since that time. For solid waste management the situation has declined even further. The City's waste used to be taken to a landfill just north of the city boundary. When that landfill was closed in 1998 the 'best solution' was identified as trucking the waste to a landfill in Michigan, some 450 km distant! Every day between 120 and 140 trucks make the round trip, each carrying approximately 30 tonnes of solid waste (Reguly [4]). For air pollution there have been some improvements for large particulates, carbon monoxide, lead and sulphates. However for hydrocarbons and carbon dioxide the situation has deteriorated further. Improvements in fuel and engine efficiency are far outweighed by increases in the number of vehicle-trips and the greater length of those trips. None of these trends is carrying us towards the goals of the Ecological City.

2 Water availability and climate change

Water quality is the single most important contributor to human health in both rural and urban areas. In urban areas the greater density of settlement increases the risk of the spread of contagious diseases associated with poor water quality, as has been witnessed on a regular basis, especially with typhoid, cholera and yellow fever. These diseases were largely checked in Western cities towards the close of the nineteenth century. They may still be a problem in poorer cities, along with other water-related diseases such as gastro-enteritis, hepatitis and malaria.

However, even in the richest cities we cannot afford to be complacent about water, either in quality or quantity. Cities like Los Angeles, located in a semi-arid region, are constantly looking for new sources of water. Even cities like Toronto and London face increasing costs for ensuring continuity of supply (City of Toronto [5]).

Climate change will introduce a host of new challenges, including many related directly to water supply. Although the global implications of climate change for average temperature are quite well understood and quite predictable under the 'business as usual' scenario, little else is predictable (IPCC [6]). Most fundamentally, business and government may not proceed 'as usual' but may become very proactive toward the reduction of greenhouse gas emissions. Under the 'business as usual' scenario, regional projections are subject to wide bands of uncertainty even for temperature, and more so for precipitation, wind and other atmospheric variables. What can be assumed is that the level of uncertainty for all these parameters will increase. It seems reasonable to further assume that, if we wish to maintain the same level of security under more uncertainty, then the costs of building and running urban infrastructure will increase.

The specific risks and uncertainties for the urban environment, under climate change, are:

- an increase in the probability of heavy precipitation events
- these storms may affect water quality, through increased overland flow and disease transmission, such as *Giardia, E. Coli and Cryptosporidium*
- these storms increase the probability of floods, including floods in urban areas

- an increase in the probability of droughts
- increased evapotranspiration, causing reservoir losses
- a shift in disease vectors, especially malaria
- more heat waves increase the probability of deaths from heat stress, especially when added to the temperature increase due to the urban heat island effect
- higher temperatures increase the risk of wildfires in wooded areas adjacent to urban areas, as we have seen recently in southern France, south-east Australia, California and British Columbia.

Thus climate change must be added to the main drivers that affect the future evolution of urban areas, along with population increase, an increasing percentage of the world's population living in urban areas, an increased level of material consumption and the disposal of residuals into the surrounding environment.

3 Urban environmental finance

Traditionally, urban services have been funded from revenue streams that might be completely unrelated to the use of the service or its impact on the environment. Specifically, many urban governments rely heavily on property taxes, residential and commercial. The tax is proportional to the value of the property and thus would be loosely correlated with the level of use of urban services. Transfers from senior levels of government are another important source of income. Urban governments also charge fees for a variety of services, such as parking fees and vending licences, as well as services such as the provision of water. Some urban governments have access to sales tax and some are able to tax company profits. None of these sources are linked closely enough to the environmental impacts of human behaviour to act in a way that might modify that behaviour.

Market-based instruments are now being designed and marketed to influence behaviour directly in several countries, and internationally through the Kyoto Protocol to the Framework Convention on Climate Change. The emerging field of environmental finance has been developed in order to address global environmental issues such as climate change and the extreme and unpredictable weather associated with it by using market-based instruments (Labatt and White [7]). Important products developed to date include trading credits for reducing emissions of pollutants (such as sulphur dioxide and carbon dioxide), weather derivatives (to hedge the risk of adverse weather), catastrophe bonds (to cover catastrophic risks such as hurricanes and earthquakes) and cost-cap-over-run insurance to cover unexpected costs for brownfield remediation. The field is expected to become an important force for improving environmental quality and reducing the financial impact of climate change. With reference to principles for the successful trading of credits for emission reductions, Richard Sandor observed: 'These core elements simultaneously assure environmental integrity, cost reduction, efficient trading and valid price discovery' (Sandor, 11 [8]).

In the urban context, local environmental issues are those associated with the basic elements of urban metabolism – inflows of water, energy and food, and outflows of solid waste, gaseous exhaust and wastewater (White, Chapter Three [3]). Can the market principles – identified by Sandor - be harnessed to provide more of what we need (goods and services) and less of what we do not need (wastes)?

The following sections provide a very brief survey of the main financial features of the use of water and energy and the generation of solid waste. Finance is the key, *both to raise revenue, and to change behaviour*. The reason we have so many avoidable problems in the urban environment is that we have sent the wrong price signals, and failed to internalise environmental externalities. The challenge is to understand the balance between these two facets – raising revenue and changing behaviour - because a radical change in behaviour may reduce the revenue stream, or fail to raise enough revenue to carry out the plan.

Another recurrent theme is the welfare implication of new charges. For example, if water is to be priced for full cost recovery, how can the necessary minimum use be assured for low-income people? Similar examples can be found for solid waste management, energy for heating and cooling homes, transportation for the disabled, and so on. In addition to the welfare implications there are direct health implications for all of these services, especially for water availability, air quality, climate change and waste management. All of these issues can be addressed on a case-by-case basis. A concern for the potential negative welfare implication of 'true pricing' should not be used as an excuse for delaying reform forever.

A further objection to privatising utilities and services is that the supposed competitive drive of the private sector does not come into play in these monopolistic situations. There is some validity to this observation because it is true that the visible competition that is present between shopkeepers, people selling homes, or other recognised commodities does not exist. However, there are *elements* of competition. In the case of the English water supply it is true that the consumers have only one supplier, but the economic regulator of the water industry – the Office of Water Services (OfWat) - has access to the pricing policies of ten companies operating in similar markets. Thus – in the sense that prices must be approved by OfWat – these companies are in competition with one another.

The other respect in which the competitive force can be brought into play is when the contract to design, build and operate a utility or service is put out to tender. Once awarded the contract should be regularly reviewed for performance. This requires the regulatory bodies to operate in an effective and transparent manner, which can not simply be assumed.

It is not easy to move from the traditional public sector supply system to one in which the private sector has an important role and in which prices are employed explicitly to move towards environmental targets, such as zero solid waste, zero harmful emissions to the air and 100% re-use of water. Pricing policy in a typical city today considers hardly any of these environmental quality issues, and none in a comprehensive manner. Many pricing structures actually encourage wasteful behaviour. The situation is generally better in Europe than in North America but nowhere does it approach the goal of the Ecological City.

3.1 Water

Water is not only the most critical resource but is also the one that is most seriously mismanaged. The biggest waste of water occurs outside the city on the irrigated farm and is therefore outside the scope of this paper. However, some cities, such as Beijing and Los Angeles are now in direct competition with their rural hinterlands for water. In the worst urban cases household water use is not even metered, but is simply made available in unlimited quantities for a fixed fee that is sometimes related to a property tax. This does nothing to encourage conservation. Indeed, it encourages a very inefficient peak use in the summer as residents who have gardens water them profligately.

The overall environmental objective should be to approach 100% re-use of the water supply, as in the 'biosphere' experiments. Technically there is no reason why this could not be done. It would be much more efficient that the current systems in which cities (until recently) assumed that they could operate as a 'free rider' on the natural hydrological cycle. As water becomes less freely available we need to move towards a system based on 100% metered use with ascending block prices to encourage conservation. The price charged to users should be sufficient to cover both capital and recurrent costs of water use and treatment. The welfare and public health issues can be dealt with by making the lowest price block affordable to low income people and sufficient to cover reasonable needs, such as 200 litres per person per day. Many cities are a very long way from this sort of target. In Toronto, even after recent price increases we still pay only CAD $ 1.22 per cubic metre for water, including sewage treatment. (This is the price for the first 80 cu.m in a four-month period. The next block is $1.26. As of December 30th 2003, the Canadian dollar was worth € 0.61.) Thus the daily charge for water use and treatment for a family of five people using 200 litres per person per day is less than the price of a single cup of coffee.

Stormwater management is also being brought into the fee-for-service realm with the introduction of stormwater user fees based on the quantity and quality of runoff. Although more than 400 such schemes are operating in the United States, only three are operating in Canada (Smeh [9]) These fees encourage the maintenance of porous surfaces and the control of contaminants discharged to the environment. Unfortunately they do not curb the significant deposition of contaminants from motor vehicle exhaust.

3.2 Energy

Like water pricing policy, energy pricing policy has evolved without any regard for environmental consequences. The general objective within the framework of the Ecological City is to provide energy for a variety of purposes (the provision of manufacturing, administration and services; mobility, lighting, space heating and cooling, cooking etc.) without damaging the environment or compromising human health. The transportation sector and its emissions to the air, which reduce air quality and change the climate, are major problems. Recently attention has focussed on the connection between the use of personal transportation and obesity. In North America, people in the suburbs, on average, weigh more than people living downtown who make more use of walking, cycling and public transport (Gilbert [10]). The final irony is that the automobile no longer delivers the service which people thought they had bought – an efficient means of personal mobility. As the suburbs sprawl and automobile use expands, more and more time on the road is spent in traffic jams.

There are various approaches to this conundrum. Many European cities have simply banned automobiles from the historic core, which was never designed for such traffic. Others have introduced congestion charges. The recent London example is not very sophisticated, being a set daily charge for entering the central part of the city. The price is fixed arbitrarily by the government. More ambitiously, Singapore has introduced a dynamic, market-based congestion charge that fluctuates with the degree of congestion. As congestion gets worse the fee (which is deducted from an account) increases. 'Electronic Road Pricing (ERP) … uses a dedicated short-range radio communication system to deduct ERP charges from 'smartcards' inserted in … vehicles each time they pass a pricing point when the system is in operation. The pay-when-you-use principle helps make motorists more aware of the true cost of driving' (Government of Singapore [11]).

Some cities have tolls on ring roads and cross-town expressways. Others charge nothing for road use other than the vehicle tax and fuel tax. To improve the situation we need to find financial instruments that will shift the transportation modal split from private automobiles to public transport, cycling and walking. This, in turn, will oblige energy-intensive travellers to pay for the environmental costs (as well as the congestion) which they generate.

3.3 Solid waste

As cities have become larger and more complex, their solid waste streams have become larger and more contaminated. In pre-industrial cities most of the waste stream was organic and could be left to decompose, *in situ*. Today the collection and disposal of solid waste – usually to a landfill outside the city – has become a significant municipal expenditure. Beyond the expense, a growing problem has evolved with resistance from local communities to accepting urban waste for various reasons, including odour, noise and dust, health fears, and impact on housing prices.

It is not unreasonable to expect a city to take care of its own solid waste, rather than exporting it to an unwilling host community. Several means have been attempted to move in this direction. Much of household solid waste can be recycled, keeping the organics for compost (if a garden is available) and having reusable material – such as paper, plastic, glass, and metals – collected by the municipality or a private body. In most cities where these options exist, compliance is voluntary. These measures alone can reduce solid waste going to landfill by 80% per participating household.

It is more effective to tackle the problem of solid waste generation at source by making the manufacturers and retailers accept 'producer responsibility'. This was introduced in the European Union in 1994 with the Directive on Packaging and Packaging Waste (McCallin [12]). Many municipalities have some form of take-back responsibility if only for certain types of bottle, such as those for beer and soft drinks.

A more price-oriented approach can developed in two ways – by paying the consumer for separating the recycled materials (as the in bottle-return programs), and by charging the consumer for any waste that has to go to landfill. There is some fear that the latter approach will encourage people to abandon their waste illegally but the evidence on this is inconclusive. Where consumers do have to pay per bag for waste removal there is more obvious political support for obliging the producers to reduce waste materials at source by providing appropriate packaging which can be returned, re-used or recycled.

4 The role of market forces and the role of privatisation

Without succumbing to a naïve belief that if 'we get the prices right' all our urban environmental problems will be solved, it should be evident that we can do much better than most cities currently do in attempting to get some of the prices moving in the right direction. It should be possible to agree that prices (or lack of them) should not encourage individuals to squander resources that are then paid for by the community at large. Whereas there is little support for insisting that everyone pay for the necessities of life there should be a great deal of support for the view that people should pay for the damage they choose to cause, the resources they choose to squander and the waste they choose to generate. Those choices could certainly be made subject to realistic (full cost recovery) charges.

The potential benefits from using prices to encourage more environmentally friendly behaviour are huge. For example, a city may not need a new sewage treatment plant if it can reduce both the contaminants entering the wastewater stream and the quantity of stormwater running into that stream.

The goal of using prices to encourage environmentally friendly behaviour is quite separate from the potential of privatisation for encouraging this change in behaviour to take place. After several years of recent experience the approach to this issue has become more pragmatic and less ideological. For those in favour of privatisation the advantages are that the private sector, driven by competition and the search for profits, is more efficient than the public sector. Prices may rise in the short term as investment deficiencies (in deferred maintenance and modernisation), are made good, but in the longer run prices would fall. For those opposed to privatisation the risks are seen as loss of employment as workforces are downsized and soaring prices as the consumers are sacrificed to the company's shareholders.

In practice, the quality of the outcome depends on the quality of the public regulation of private companies delivering services to the general public. In England, where the water supply and treatment sector was privatised in the early 1990s, there have been negative experiences such as lack of water supply and public health impacts, but also much has been learned (Bakker [13]). The process by which the system is monitored is much more transparent than it was when run by dozens of separate municipalities and public water boards.

5 Conclusion

There is little reason to fear that a coherent, environmentally oriented pricing policy for urban services will have negative welfare implications. On the contrary it is the lack of any coherent approach to pricing that is unjust. Why should the relatively poor pay for the relatively rich to water their lawns? Yet that is what happens if a water system is un-metered, or if there is a constant rate for water. Why should those who walk, cycle or take public transit absorb the environmental burden from automobiles? Why should the frugal pay for the disposal of the solid waste of the profligate?

Given that cities are very inefficient from a metabolic point of view and that many of their deficiencies are getting worse, why is more not being done? The will to change seems to be there as is evidenced by statements such as the Nagoya Declaration (1997) and the Charter of European Cities and Towns Towards Sustainability (the Aalborg Charter, 1994). The Council for Local Environmental Initiatives was established in 1990 and is associated with the International Union of Local Authorities (White Chapter 11, Appendices 1 and 2 [2]). From the Rio Earth Summit in 1992 a notable outcome was 'Local Agenda 21' which established environmental goals for local authorities throughout the world (Low et al. [14]).

Why - with all these activities and statements – is more not being done? It could even be argued that in most cities the situation is getting worse, despite some evidence of innovation. As poorer countries become richer most of them seem determined to follow the 'development path' of the richer countries despite the obvious dangers. (Daily we read of streets in China's big cities being closed to bicycles so that automobiles may have a freer passage.) The barriers to improvement are the usual barriers to innovation. Decision-makers and the public are preoccupied with seemingly more pressing matters. There is limited awareness of those cases where innovation has been successful. And, finally, the cost of implementation is often seen as a barrier.

Some lessons from the general field of environmental finance are encouraging. The first large-scale environmental market was established for credits for emission reductions for sulphur dioxide and nitrogen oxides in the north-eastern United States in 1995 through the Environmental Protection Agency (Sandor [8]). Despite widespread opposition on grounds of the expected cost of compliance, the credits traded at less than one quarter the price predicted by the opponents of the scheme, and the reduction targets were achieved ahead of schedule.

Similar savings should be possible within the urban context from using water more efficiently, reducing the amount of solid waste we produce, and shifting the transportation modal split to less destructive modes of travel. There is no technological obstacle to building an Ecological City. Perhaps there is no financial obstacle either.

References

[1] National Research Council, *Cities Transformed: Demographic Change and Its Implications in the Developing World*. Panel on Urban Population Dynamics, M. R. Montgomery, R. Stren, B. Cohen and H. E. Reed, eds., Committee on Population, Division of Behavioral and Social Sciences and Education. The National Academies Press, Washington, DC., 2003.

[2] White, R. R., *Building the Ecological City*. Woodhead Publishing in Environmental Management, Cambridge, 2002.

[3] White, R. R., *Urban Environmental Management – Environmental Change and Urban Design*. John Wiley & Sons, Chichester, 1994.

[4] Reguly, E., Toronto's landfill issue a big stinking mess. *Globe and Mail*, 9 September, p. B 2, 2003

[5] City of Toronto, *Water: Strategic Directions*. Toronto, Dept. of Works and Emergency Services, February 2000.

[6] IPCC, *Summary for Policymakers to Climate Change 2001: the Synthesis Report of the IPCC Third Assessment Report*. Available at http://www.ipcc.ch/, 2001.

[7] Labatt, S. and White R. R., *Environmental Finance: A Guide to Environmental Risk Assessment and Financial Products*. John Wiley & Sons, New York, 2002.

[8] Sandor, R., SO_2 market exceeds expectations. *Environmental Finance*, 1 (7), p. 11, 2000.

[9] Smeh, D. T., The Feasibility of User Pay Financing of Stormwater Management in Ottawa, Ontario. A Comparative Study with Regina, Saskatchewan. Unpublished document, Dept. of Geography, University of Toronto, 2003.

[10] Gilbert, R., personal communication, 2003

[11] Government of Singapore, 2004. Available at http://traffic.smart.1ta.gov.sg/erp/erp_main.jsp

[12] McCallin, J., Producer responsibility takes hold. *Environmental Finance*, 4 (9), p. 30, 2003.

[13] Bakker, K., Privatising water, producing scarcity: the Yorkshire drought of 1995. *Economic Geography*, 76,1, 4 – 27, 2000.

[14] Low, N., Gleeson, B., Elander, I. And Lidskog, R, *Consuming Cities: The Urban Environment in the Global Economy after the Rio Declaration*. Routledge, London and New York, 2000.

Section 9
Energy conservation and generation

Environmental impacts of commercial energy efficiency

K. Tiedemann
BC Hydro and Simon Fraser University, Canada

Abstract

The Government of Canada signed the Kyoto Protocol in December 1997 and committed itself to reducing greenhouse gas emissions by six percent below the levels in 1990 between 2008 and 2012. One of the Canadian initiatives to address global warming is the Dollars to Sense program. The Dollars to Sense program provides small and medium sized Canadian businesses with a set of three workshops that help participants find and implement energy cost savings measures and address global warming. The purpose of this paper is to report on discrete choice modeling and engineering analysis of commercial sector enterprises that were used to estimate the impact of the Dollars to Sense program on retrofit actions undertaken, energy savings, and reductions in carbon dioxide emissions.
Keywords: energy conservation, program evaluation, discrete choice models, greenhouse gas emissions.

1 Introduction

A key international program to address the problem of global warming is the Kyoto Protocol. The Government of Canada signed the Kyoto Protocol in December 1997 and committed itself to reducing greenhouse gas emissions by six percent below the levels in 1990 between 2008 and 2012. The Kyoto Protocol is the main response of the international community to strong and growing evidence that human economic activity is having quantifiable and potentially significant impacts on the earth's climate.

One of the Canadian initiatives to reduce greenhouse gas emissions is the Dollars to Sense program, which consists of three coordinated workshops for energy managers of business facilities sponsored by Natural Resources Canada

(NRCan). In the Energy Master Plan Workshop, participants learn to develop and implement a comprehensive energy management plan including assembling an appropriate team, using financing options and developing cost-effective energy solutions. In the Energy Monitoring and Tracking Workshop, participants learn to save money on energy costs by collecting data, developing an energy use baseline, analyzing energy use and establishing and implementing an improvement plan. In the Spot the Energy Savings Opportunities Workshop, participants learn to identify and capitalize on immediate savings opportunities including reviewing energy basics, identifying opportunities in electrical and thermal processes and assessing and quantifying benefits. From program launch in 1997 through 2003, about 3280 commercial sector representatives attended the Dollars to Sense workshops.

The rationale for the Dollars to Sense program is that providing business energy managers with detailed information on how to identify, analyze, implement and monitor energy savings opportunities will lead to reduced energy consumption and greenhouse gas emissions. The purpose of this paper is to report on discrete choice modeling and engineering analysis that was used to estimate the impact of the Dollars to Sense program on retrofit actions undertaken, energy savings, and reductions in carbon dioxide emissions in the Canadian commercial sector.

2 Background and previous research

Energy consumed in Canada by the commercial sector increased from 867.0 PJ in 1990 to 1130.1 PJ 2002. This represents an increase in commercial sector energy use of some 30.3 percent over twelve years and an annual growth rate of 2.2 percent. During the same period, overall energy consumption in Canada increased from 6,950.4 PJ in 2000 to 8,217.2 PJ in 2002. This in turn represents an increase in total energy use of 18.2 percent and an annual growth rate of 1.4 percent over twelve years. The Canadian commercial sector's share of energy use increased from about 12.5 percent in 2000 to some 13.8 percent in 2002. This pattern of increasing commercial sector energy use and rising commercial sector share is similar to that of other economically advanced OECD countries. Further information on trends in commercial sector energy use in Canada is included in Natural Resources Canada [1] and Statistics Canada [2].

A number of papers have examined energy use and the potential for energy savings in commercial buildings. These studies have found that the main uses of energy in commercial buildings include space heating, space cooling, ventilation, water heating, refrigeration, cooking, process equipment and lighting. Recent studies analyzing energy use in commercial buildings include BC Hydro [3], Davis and Swanson [4], Mortimer, Ashley, Elsayed, Kelly and Rix [5], Natural Resources Canada [6] and Schipper, Meyers and Ketoff [7]. A further group of studies have examined the impact of energy efficiency measures on energy use and greenhouse gas emissions in commercial buildings. These studies have found that there are a number of cost-effective technologies for reducing energy use and greenhouse gas emissions in the commercial sector. Recent studies examining energy savings and greenhouse gas reductions in commercial buildings include Southern California Edison and the California Measurement Advisory Council [8], Friedman [9], Krackler, Schipper, and Swegen, [10], Mortimer, Ashley, Moody, Rix, and Moss [11].

2.1 Data and approach

Based on a review of program documents and discussions with Natural Resources Canada, five key substantive issues were identified for study. These five issues can be summarized as follows: (1) estimate commercial sector energy consumption by end use; (2) develop gross measure savings rates; (3) estimate the attribution rate or share of the market impacts due to the program; (4) determine program impact on energy savings; and (5) determine program impact on carbon dioxide emissions. Table 1 summarizes the study issues, data sources and methodologies used for this study.

Table 1: Study issues, data sources and methodologies.

Study Issue	Data Sources	Methodologies
End use consumption	Customer survey NRCan data US DOE data	Engineering algorithms
Gross measure savings rate	File review Documents review	Engineering algorithms
Attribution rate	Customer survey NRCan data	Logit regressions
Energy savings	Customer survey NRCan data	Engineering algorithms
Emissions savings	Customer survey NRCan data	Engineering algorithms

3 Overview of commercial energy using technologies

This section summarizes key features of end use technologies employed in commercial buildings. There is no attempt to be comprehensive, rather the purpose is to provide the minimum amount of descriptive information needed to motivate the subsequent analysis.

Space Heating, Water Heating and Process Heating. Space heating, water heating and process heating requirements can be met through a variety of means such as steam boilers, water boilers, water heaters, heat pumps and electric resistance heat, but boilers dominate in the commercial market. In many commercial buildings, the boiler system is the single largest fuel user. Boiler efficiency varies depending on boiler design, age of the boiler, fuel used and ancillary equipment used for heat recovery. For modern boilers, thermal efficiencies can reach 85% or higher with additional efficiencies produced by non-condensing heat recovery systems, condensing heat recovery systems and regenerative burners that use computer systems to produce optimal mixes of fuel and air.

Space Cooling. Space cooling requirements can be met variously through room air conditioners, heat pumps or central air conditioning. Cooling requirements can be significant in some buildings, even in relatively mild climates, when the outdoor temperature is high compared to the indoor temperature, when there are significant solar gains or when there are major internal heat gains. High efficiency motors and pumps, airside economizers and ground-water economizers are means of reducing energy cooling needs.

Building Envelope. The building envelope is a major of heat loss (gain) with losses (gains) proportional to the conductivity of the envelope and to the difference between the indoor and outdoor temperatures. The thermal conductivity of a component of the building envelope is typically expressed in terms of watt loss per square meter per degree Celsius difference between indoor and outdoor temperatures. For the building shell, we assume that the roof is 20% of the shell area, the walls are 80% of the shell and that windows are 30% of the wall area. Ignoring the floor or foundation, this then gives shell area shares of 20% for the roof, 24% for windows and 56% for other wall components. We further assume that 20% of the heat loss is due to air exchange so that the heat loss (gain) through the envelope is the other 80%.

Cooking. Cooking loads are significant in restaurants, hotels, schools, hospitals and nursing homes. Most efficiency measures for cooking involve improved insulation, gaskets and controls. Microwave and flash ovens are major opportunities to reduce energy consumption, but are not suitable for all cooking applications.

Electro-chemical Processes. Electro-chemical processes are used in a wide variety of applications to produce metals through refining processes, form and fabricate a variety of manufactured products and deposit coatings on surfaces to protect against corrosion. These processes are relatively unimportant in the commercial sector and are not examined in this paper.

Refrigeration. Commercial facilities use refrigeration for processing and storage. Most efficiency measures for refrigeration systems are designed to increase the difference between the temperature at which condensation and evaporation occur, therby increasing the coefficient of performance. Other energy savings efforts aim to reduce the loss of cooled or chilled air.

Fans and Blowers. Fans and blowers provide the motive force to move air or another gas against the resistance of the air conveyance system. They typically include a motor, a fan or blower, a speed control device, a control vane or damper and a duct system. Up to one-half of the potential energy savings in a fan or blower system can be captured through appropriate sizing of the motor and its load, reducing unnecessary loads and minimizing motor idling.

Pumps. Pumps move liquids against the resistance of a piping system and uphill against gravity. Pumping systems typically include a motor, a pump or impeller, a speed control device, throttle or valve and piping. Again, up to one-half of the potential energy savings in a pumping system can be captured through appropriate sizing of the motor and its load, reducing unnecessary loads and minimizing motor idling.

Compression. Compressors increase the pressure of a gas to the point where it can do useful work, typically by increasing pressure from 15 psi (atmospheric pressure) to 100 psi. Compressed air systems typically include a motor, a speed control device, compressor, dryer/filter unit, throttle or vane or damper and a piping system. Key methods of saving energy include using as little compression as possible, minimizing air leaks and maintaining compressor efficiency.

Conveyance. A conveyance system is a vertical, horizontal or inclined device for moving people or bulk materials. It typically includes a motor, a speed control device and a belt, cable or pulley system. Since the conveyance systems themselves have high levels of efficiency, if properly maintained, main opportunities for energy efficiency involve high efficiency motors and adjustable speed drives.

Other Machine Drives. Other machine drives include hydraulic systems, cutting and milling equipment, and material shaping equipment. The main opportunities for energy efficiency involve maintenance, high efficiency motors and adjustable speed drives.

Lighting. Lighting technologies have improved substantially over the past decade, but many commercial establishments still use older, inefficient lighting technologies. The most obvious areas for improvement of lighting efficiency involve day-lighting, delamping and suitable scheduling and maintenance procedures, but there are also considerable opportunities to use light sources with high output levels. We assume that on average 10% of the connected load is for screw-type lamps, 80% for fluorescent tubes and 10% for large area lighting such as high bay and parking lighting. Cross effects of reduced lighting loads on space conditioning are ignored.

4 End use consumption

The first step was to estimate energy consumption by end use. The Office of Energy Efficiency [12] of Natural Resources Canada provided consumption shares by end use as well as estimated total energy consumption per square meter and some supplementary information. This information was made available for the following breakdown: space heating, space cooling, water heating, auxiliary motors, auxiliary equipment, and lighting. United States DOE [13] provided information on energy consumption shares for more detailed end uses, and this information was applied to the OEE data to estimate energy use shares for thirteen end uses. Annual consumption per end use per building was estimated using the following equation:

$$GJ_i = share_i * \text{consumption per square meter} * \text{average area}. \qquad (1)$$

Here, GJ_i is average consumption per building for end use i, $share_i$ is the share of end use i in total consumption, consumption per square meter is average consumption per square meter across all fuels and average area is 2207.9 square meters taken from the Office of Energy Efficiency [12]. Estimated energy consumption by end use for 2002 is shown in Table 2.

Table 2: Commercial energy consumption by end use in 2002.

End Use	Consumption (GJ/building)	Consumption (GJ/m^2)	Share
Water and process heat	366	0.166	0.092
Cooking	185	0.084	0.046
Process cooling/refrigeration	252	0.114	0.063
Pumps	40	0.018	0.010
Fans and blowers	230	0.104	0.057
Compressed air	26	0.012	0.007
Conveyance	40	0.018	0.010
Other machine drives	26	0.012	0.007
Electro-chemical processes	20	0.009	0.005
Space heating	1956	0.886	0.510
Space cooling	181	0.082	0.046
Facility lighting	581	0.263	0.145
Other uses	88	0.040	0.030
Total	3991	1.808	1.000

5 Gross measure savings ratios

The second step was to develop gross measure savings ratio estimates for 25 measures as shown in Table 3. We reviewed a wide variety of sources including Natural Resources Canada publications, technical reports on web sites, journal and conference literature and utility reports. The gross measure savings ratio was estimated for each measure using the following equation:

$$\text{Savings ratio}_i = (1 - \text{efficiency}_{st}/\text{efficiency}_{ef}). \qquad (2)$$

Here, the savings ratio is the ratio applied to the end use consumption for a given measure and efficiency_{st} and efficiency_{ef} are the percentage efficiency levels of the standard and the efficient technologies for each.

6 Market impacts

The third step was to estimate program impact using logit models as follows:

$$\text{Install}_i = F(\text{participant, industrial dummy, rate}). \qquad (3)$$

Here, install_i takes value 1 if measure i is installed/0 otherwise, participant takes value 1 for workshop participants/0 otherwise and rate is the average rate paid by commercial customers by service territory in dollars per MWh.

Table 3: Gross measure savings ratios.

Measure	End Use	Standard Efficiency Measure	Energy Efficient Measure	Savings Ratio
Drive/Controls	Fans/Blowers	Control vane 75%	ASD 95%	0.211
Fan Motor 1-5 HP	Fans/Blowers	Std efficiency 83.3%	Hi efficiency 87.5%	0.048
Drive/Controls	Pumps	Control valve 80%	ASD 95%	0.158
Pump Motor 6-25 HP	Pumps	Std efficiency 86.3%	Hi efficiency 90.1%	0.042
Drive/Controls	Compressed Air	Control throttle 83%	ASD 95%	0.126
Compressor Motor 1-5 HP	Compressed Air	Std efficiency 83.3%	Hi efficiency 87.5%	0.048
Reduce Air Leaks	Compressed Air	Average leaks 75%	Reduced leaks 85%	0.118
Coupling/ Drive	Conveyance	Worm gear/v belt/helical 85%	ASD 95%	0.105
Convey Motor 6-25 HP	Conveyance	Std. efficiency 86.3%	Hi efficiency 90.1%	0.042
Coupling/Drive	Other Process	Worm gear/v belt/helical 85%	ASD 95%	0.105
Process Motor 6-25 HP	Other Process	Std. efficiency 86.3%	Hi efficiency 90.1%	0.042
Ovens	Cooking	Standard	Microwave	0.100
Mid Efficiency Boiler	Space, Water, Process Heat	Std efficiency 75%	Mid efficiency 85%	0.118
Hi Efficiency boiler	Space, Water, Process Heat	Std efficiency 75%	Condensing 90%	0.167
Mid Efficiency furnace	Space Heating	Std efficiency 65%	Mid efficiency 78%	0.167
Hi Efficiency furnace	Space Heating	Std efficiency 65%	Condensing 90%	0.278
Economizer	Space Cooling	No economizer	Air side economizer	0.100
Drive/Controls	Refrigeration	Standard 85%	ASD 95%	0.105
CFL	Lighting	Type A 6%	CFL 24%	0.750*0.10 = 0.075
T8 Lamps	Lighting	T12 24%	T8 25.5%	0.059*0.80 = 0.047
HID Lamps	Lighting	Mercury vapor 15%	HID 30%	0.500*0.10 = 0.050
Window Shades	Space Cooling	No shades	Permanent shades	0.100
Roof Insulation	Space Heating	Standard 0.95W/m^2/C$^\circ$	Upgraded 0.48W/m^2/C$^\circ$	0.500*0.076 = 0.038
Wall Insulation	Space Heating	Standard 0.70W/m^2/C$^\circ$	Upgraded 0.35W/m^2/C$^\circ$	0.500*0.351 = 0.176
EE Windows	Space Heating	Single pane 5.70W/m^2/C$^\circ$	Double pane 2.85W/m^2/C$^\circ$	0.500*0.372 = 0.186

Table 4: Logit model results.

	Constant	Participant	Industrial	Rate	Chi^2
Fans	0.358 (0.873)	0.742 (0.268)	-1.155 (0.427)	-0.034 (0.014)	16.31 (0.001)
Pumps	-0.838 (0.706)	0.773 (0.257)	0.450 (0.388)	-0.015 (0.012)	10.91 (0.012)
Compressed Air	-2.383 (0.997)	1.053 (0.335)	0.364 (0.456)	-0.001 (0.015)	13.13 (0.004)
Conveyance	-4.719 (1.631)	1.105 (0.544)	1.912 (0.730)	0.003 (0.025)	19.24 (0.000)
Other Process	-2.335 (1.058)	0.789 (0.346)	0.393 (0.486)	-0.007 (0.106)	8.05 (0.045)
Oven	-3.467 (1.515)	0.012 (0.510)	-0.026 (0.782)	0.001 (0.022)	0.11 (0.991)
Mid Efficiency Boiler	-0.847 (0.880)	1.067 (0.294)	-1.949 (0.531)	-0.017 (0.014)	32.89 (0.000)
Hi Efficiency Boiler	0.215 (1.063)	0.542 (0.334)	-2.869 (0.816)	-0.030 (0.017)	23.79 (0.000)
Mid Efficiency Furnace	-0.544 (1.038)	0.956 (0.330)	-1.232 (0.519)	-0.030 (0.016)	15.08 (0.002)
Hi Efficiency Furnace	-0.400 (1.437)	0.822 (0.448)	1.265 (1.138)	-0.039 (0.023)	23.60 (0.000)
Economizer	-0.773 (0.851)	0.308 (0.272)	-0.634 (0.428)	-0.015 (0.013)	3.58 (0.311)
Refrigeration	-2.206 (0.892)	1.221 (0.312)	0.585 (0.428)	-0.002 (0.014)	19.66 (0.000)
CFL	-0.449 (0.659)	1.614 (0.221)	-0.925 (0.334)	-0.001 (0.010)	67.02 (0.000)
T8 Lamps	0.464 (0.681)	1.606 (0.228)	-1.643 (0.353)	-0.021 (0.011)	76.86 (0.000)
HID Lamps	-0.957 (0.692)	0.914 (0.226)	0.004 (0.336)	-0.001 (0.011)	17.69 (0.001)
Window Shades	0.812 (0.801)	0.451 (0.261)	-0.973 (0.424)	-0.012 (0.014)	9.21 (0.027)
Roof Insulation	-1.876 (0.860)	0.490 (0.285)	-0.290 (0.435)	-0.001 (0.013)	3.68 (0.298)
Wall Insulation	-2.765 (0.957)	0.759 (0.326)	-0.012 (0.473)	0.005 (0.014)	5.95 (0.114)
EE Windows	-1.586 (0.836)	0.947 (0.283)	-0.965 (0.445)	-0.005 (0.013)	18.41 (0.000)

7 Energy savings

The fourth step was to develop energy savings estimates by measure as shown in Table 5. Refer to previous tables for the full spelling of terms that are abbreviated in this table. Energy savings were estimated for each measure using the following:

$$\text{Energy savings}_i = \text{Use}_i\text{*saving rate}_i\text{*partial effect}_i\text{* part}_i. \qquad (4)$$

Here, energy savings for measure i is the product of the use rate, the savings rate, the partial effect as calculated from the logit model and the number of participants. Note that the partial effect or the estimated impact of program participation on the install decision is the partial derivative of the non-linear function F in equation (3). Because of the non-linearity of the function F, the partial effects cannot be read directly from the coefficients on the participation variable in Table 4.

Table 5: Energy savings.

Measure	End Use	Use per Build (GJ)	Saving Rate	Partial Effect	Particip (no.)	Energy Saving (TJ)
Drive/Controls	Fans/Blower	230	0.211	0.106	3283	16.9
Fan Motor	Fans/Blower	230	0.048	0.106	3283	3.8
Drive/Controls	Pumps	40	0.158	0.122	3283	2.5
Pump Motor	Pumps	40	0.042	0.122	3283	0.7
Drive/Controls	Comp Air	26	0.126	0.103	3283	1.1
Compress/Motor	Comp Air	26	0.048	0.103	3283	0.4
Reduce Air Leak	Comp Air	26	0.118	0.103	3283	1.0
Coupling/ Drive	Conveyance	40	0.105	0.032	3283	0.4
Convey/ Motor	Conveyance	40	0.042	0.032	3283	0.2
Coupling/Drive	Other Proc	26	0.105	0.069	3283	0.6
Process Motor	Other Proc	26	0.042	0.069	3283	0.2
Ovens	Cooking	185	0.100	0.004	3283	0.3
Mid Eff Boiler	All Heat	2323	0.118	0.125	3283	112.6
Hi Eff Boiler	All Heat	2323	0.167	0.040	3283	50.3
Mid Eff Furnace	Space Heat	1956	0.167	0.092	3283	98.3
Hi Eff Furnace	Space Heat	1956	0.278	0.003	3283	4.6
Economizer	Space Cool	181	0.100	0.042	3283	2.5
Drive/Controls	Refrigeration	252	0.105	0.142	3283	12.3
CFL	Lighting	581	0.075	0.398	3283	56.9
T8 Lamps	Lighting	581	0.047	0.386	3283	26.8
HID	Lighting	581	0.050	0.189	3283	16.9
Window Shades	Space Cool	181	0.100	0.066	3283	14.9
Roof Insulation	Space Heat	1956	0.038	0.061	3283	84.7
Wall Insulation	Space Heat	1956	0.176	0.075	3283	3.9
EE Windows	Space Heat	1956	0.186	0.125	3283	149.1
Total		3991				665.8

8 Emissions savings

The fifth step was to develop carbon dioxide savings estimates by measure as shown in Table 6. Estimated carbon dioxide savings are given by the following expression, disaggregated by fuel:

$$\text{Carbon dioxide savings}_i = \text{Energy savings}_i \text{*emission factor.} \qquad (5)$$

Here, carbon dioxide savings for the ith measure are the product of energy savings for the measure multiplied by the fuel specific emission factor. The emission factors, which were supplied by Natural Resources Canada, are: (1) electricity – 64.23 tonnes of CO_2E per TJ; (2) natural gas – 50.45 tonnes of CO_2E per TJ; (3) fuel oil – 75.43 tonnes of CO_2E per TJ; and (4) fossil fuels –

56.79 tonnes of CO_2E per TJ. The latter estimate is based on a fuel split of 74.6% natural gas and 25.4 % fuel oil.

Table 6: Emissions savings.

Measure	End Use	Energy Saving (TJ)	Main fuel	Emission Factor (tonnes CO_2 per TJ)	Emissions Saving (ktonne CO_2)
Drive/Controls	Fans/Blower	16.9	Electricity	64.23	1.09
Fan motor	Fans/Blower	3.8	Electricity	64.23	0.24
Drive/Controls	Pumps	2.5	Electricity	64.23	0.16
Pump Motor	Pumps	0.7	Electricity	64.23	0.04
Drive/Controls	Compressed Air	1.1	Electricity	64.23	0.07
Comp Motor	Compressed Air	0.4	Electricity	64.23	0.03
Reduce Leaks	Compressed Air	1.0	Electricity	64.23	0.06
Coup/Drive	Conveyance	0.4	Electricity	64.23	0.03
Convey Motor	Conveyance	0.2	Electricity	64.23	0.01
Coup/Drive	Other Process	0.6	Electricity	64.23	0.04
Process Motor	Other Process	0.2	Electricity	64.23	0.01
Ovens	Cooking	0.3	Gas/Oil	56.79	0.02
Mid Eff Boiler	Heating	112.6	Gas/Oil	56.79	6.39
Hi Eff Boiler	Heating	50.3	Gas/Oil	56.79	2.86
Mid Eff Furn	Space Heating	98.3	Gas/ Oil	56.79	5.58
Hi Eff Furn	Space Heating	4.6	Gas/ Oil	56.79	0.26
Economizer	Space Cooling	2.5	Gas/ Oil	56.79	0.14
Drive/Controls	Refrigeration	12.3	Electricity	64.23	0.79
CFL	Lighting	56.9	Electricity	64.23	3.65
T8 Lamps	Lighting	26.8	Electricity	64.23	1.72
HID Lamps	Lighting	16.9	Electricity	64.23	1.09
Win Shade	Space Cooling	14.9	Electricity	64.23	0.96
Roof Ins	Space Heating	84.7	Gas/ Oil	56.79	4.81
Wall Ins	Space Heating	3.9	Gas/Oil	56.79	0.22
EE Windows	Space Heating	149.1	Gas/Oil	56.79	8.47
Total		665.8			38.74

9 Conclusions

Canada signed the Kyoto Protocol in December 1997 and committed itself to reducing greenhouse gas emissions by six percent below the levels in 1990 between 2008 and 2012. As part of its Kyoto response, Natural Resources Canada launched the Dollars to Sense workshops in 1997. The Dollars to Sense program provides small and medium sized Canadian businesses with a set of three workshops that help participants find and implement cost effective energy savings measures and address global warming.

In this study we have analysed the impact of the Government of Canada's Dollars to Sense program using engineering algorithms and logit modeling. Five main issues are explored in this paper. First, estimate commercial sector energy consumption by end use. Second, develop estimates of gross measure savings rates. Third, estimate impact of program participation on the decision to install efficient measures. Fourth, determine program impact on energy savings. Fifth, determine program impact on carbon dioxide emissions. Key findings are as follows.

(1) Estimates of energy consumption for thirteen end uses were based on a customer survey combined with data from official sources. Average total energy consumption for commercial buildings is 1.8 GJ per square meter. The most important uses are space heating (0.89 GJ per square meter), lighting (0.26 GJ per square meter), water and process heat (0.17 GJ per square meter), process cooling and refrigeration (0.11 GJ per square meter) and fans and blowers (0.10 GJ per square meter).

(2) Estimates of gross measure savings rates for twenty-five technologies were based on energy use efficiency rates as obtained from a review of relevant literature and documents supplemented by interviews with experts. Estimates of the impact of individual measures were undertaken by comparing energy efficiency rates for standard and efficient measures. For lighting, the measure savings were normalized by the calculated share of lighting loads of 10% for screw-type fixtures, 80% for fluorescent tubes and 10% for large area lighting. For insulation, the measure savings were normalized by calculated share of losses of 7.6% for roof insulation, 35.1% for walls, 37.2% for windows and 20.0% for air leakage.

(3) Logit regressions were used to model the determinants of efficient measure installation and in particular the impact of program participation on efficient measure installation. The most important impacts of the program were on the installation of CFLs, T8 lamps, high intensity discharge lighting, efficient refrigeration, mid efficiency boilers, and efficient pumps, compressors, fans and blowers.

(4) Energy savings were estimated as the product of the use rate, the savings rate, partial effect on measure selection as calculated from the logit model and the number of participants. Total energy savings by commercial sector program participants totaled some 666 TJ per year.

(5) Carbon dioxide emission reductions were estimated as the product of energy savings by measure and a fuel specific emissions factor. Total emissions reductions were some 38.7 kilotonnes per year.

These results confirm that the program rationale is sound. Providing business energy managers with detailed information on how to identify, analyze, implement and monitor energy savings opportunities will lead to reduced energy consumption and greenhouse gas emissions.

References

[1] Natural Resources Canada, Energy Use Data Handbook: 1990 and 1996 to 2002, 2004.

[2] Statistics Canada, Report on Energy Supply-Demand in Canada: 1990-2002, 2003.

[3] BC Hydro, Electricity Conservation Potential Review, 1994.

[4] Davis, J. and Swanson, A. "Trends in Energy Use in Commercial Buildings – Sixteen Years of the EIA Commercial Buildings Energy

Conservation Survey," ACEEE Proceedings of the 1998 Summer Study on Energy Efficiency in Buildings, 1998.

[5] Mortimer, N., Ashley, A., Elsayed, M., Kelly, M., and Rix, J, "Developing a Database of Energy Use in the UK Non-domestic Building Stock," Energy Policy, Vol. 27, No. 8, 1999.

[6] Natural Resources Canada, CIPEC: Energy Efficiency Planning and Management Guide, 2002.

[7] Schipper, L., Meyers, S., and Ketoff, A., "Energy Use in the Service Sector: An International Perspective," Energy Policy, Vol. 14, No. 3, 1986.

[8] Southern California Edison and the California Measurement Advisory Council, California Summary Study of 2001 Energy Efficiency Programs, 2003.

[9] Friedman, R. "California Industry and Energy Efficiency," Proceedings of the 2001 Energy Program Evaluation Conference, 2001.

[10] Krackler, T., Schipper, L., and Swegen, O., "Carbon Dioxide in OECD Service Sectors: The Critical Role of Energy Use'" Energy Policy, Vol. 26, No. 15, 1998.

[11] Mortimer, N., Ashley, A., Moody, C., Rix, J., and Moss, S., "Carbon Dioxide Savings in the Commercial Sector: the Critical Role of Energy Use," Energy Policy, Vol. 26, No. 8, 1998.

[12] Office of Energy Efficiency. Improving Energy Efficiency in Canada: Report to Parliament under the Energy Efficiency Act 2002.

[13] United States Department of Energy. Commercial Consumption Tables. Table 2. Energy End-Use Intensities for Sum of Major Fuels, 1995.

[14] Office of Energy Efficiency. Commercial and Industrial Building Energy Use Survey, 2002.

[15] IPCC. Climate Change 2001: The Scientific Basis. Cambridge University Press, Cambridge, 2001.

Energy saving in building ventilation

A. D'Este, A. Gastaldello & L. Schibuola
Dipartimento di costruzione dell'Architettura,
Università IUAV di Venezia, Italy

Abstract

The actual trend of the new standards regarding indoor air quality is to increase the ventilation rates in order to improve the comfort and the healthy levels in buildings. As external air treatment cost in a HVAC system is a considerable quota of the global annual management charges, the possibility of reducing the energy consumption due to the ventilation is strongly suggested. A direct heat recovery from the exhaust air is the most used technique and a great variety of heat exchangers, with the ability to recover just the sensible heat or also the latent heat, are available. Another possibility is the use of the expulsion air as a cold source for a heat pump as its temperature level permits excellent *COP* (thermodynamic recovery). The heat pump can be installed alone or combined with the heat exchanger which should be installed before the heat pump evaporator to ensure the best performance. A comparison between these techniques has been carried out by simulating the performance of the different recovery system configurations in order to evaluate the energy and the economic saving. The results for different typical application cases, in terms of occupancy levels and ventilation rates, are presented here and discussed for various climatic conditions.
Keywords: indoor air quality, ventilation, heat recovery, heat pump, energy saving, economic saving.

1 Introduction

The new standards and the modern HVAC design tendency give increasingly importance to indoor air quality to achieve a full comfort in buildings. This involves to increase the ventilation rates in buildings such as schools, restaurants and offices and to impose the mechanical ventilation also where it was not usually compulsory in the past like for example in the smoking areas. In this way the external air treatment causes a considerable part of annual energy requirement of a building. This energy demand can be reduced by a heat recovery between inlet and outlet airflow rates. In this work some typical recovery strategies are analysed and compared.

2 The heat exchangers

Two kinds of heat exchangers have been considered: fixed plate and rotary wheels. Fixed plates are common air-to-air heat exchangers in which the airflow can't be in contact. In this case a spontaneous heat transmission due to the temperature gradient allows the recovering of the sensible heat. They are the most common kind of heat exchangers thanks to their simplicity, reliability and low cost. The modulation of the heat recovery is not very frequent. It can be done by using a by-pass duct to modulate or to exclude the external airflow through the heat exchanger when the thermal levels are not favourable. Different models for different airflows are available up to 180,000 m^3/h and efficiency between 50% and 70%; the pressure loss depends on airflow but it's usually between 180 and 250 Pa. The efficiency is defined in this way:

$$\eta_T = \frac{(t_{oae} - t_{iae}) \cdot \dot{m}_{ae}}{(t_{iar} - t_{iae}) \cdot \dot{m}_{ar}} \tag{1}$$

$\dot{m}_{ae}$ external airflow

$\dot{m}_{ar}$ return airflow

t_{iae} input external air flow temperature (= outside temperature)

t_{oae} output external airflow temperature

t_{iar} input return airflow temperature (= inside temperature)

input and output refers to the heat exchangers.

Rotary wheels are again air-to-air heat exchangers but they permit also a latent heat recovery thanks to the use of hygroscopic substances. For this reason the efficiency can achieve the 80% while the pressure loss depends on the features and it is usually between 80 and 250 Pa. The modulation is easy as it is possible to vary the rotary speed and so the heat recovery. Compare to fixed plate they are more expensive and less reliable, as they are not static.
The efficiency is defined in this way:

$$\eta_T = \frac{(h_{oae} - h_{iae}) \cdot \dot{m}_{ae}}{(h_{iar} - h_{iae}) \cdot \dot{m}_{ar}} \tag{2}$$

$\dot{m}_{ae}$ external airflow

$\dot{m}_{ar}$ return airflow

h_{iae} input external airflow enthalpy (= outside enthalpy)

h_{oae} *output external airflow enthalpy*
h_{iar} *input return airflow enthalpy (= inside enthalpy)*
input and output refers to the heat exchangers.

In the tests we have carried on the velocity of the rotary wheels is changed in order to have the inlet air humidity which ensures the comfort. This causes an efficiency penalization which makes these heat exchangers not suitable for each climatic condition.

3 The heat pump

Some HVAC designer and heat pump manufacturers suggest the heat pump use without heat exchangers in order to improve the *COP* and to have a simpler system. Their opinion is based on the fact that the heat exchanger pressure loss causes the presence of additional electric energy consumption. Furthermore as the heat pump performance is related to the cold source temperature, if the exhaust air is used to preheat the outdoor air by heat exchangers, there is a *COP* penalization. Usually outside air is used as cold source for heat pump and this causes problems as when there is the maximum heat needs the outside temperature is at lowest level and this means that the heat pump performance is at lowest level. If it's possible to use exhaust air as cold source the heat pump performance increase. On the other hand it is known and demonstrated [1] that if a heat pump is combined with a heat exchanger, the best performance for the whole system is obtained when the exhaust air is used to preheat the outdoor air and after as cold source for the heat pump even if this cause a *COP* penalization. Tests were carried on in order to realize which is the best configuration and so if it is not advantageous to avoid the installation of the heat exchangers.

4 Dynamic simulations

Simulations were carried on for four different Italian towns by knowing the UE Test Reference Year (TRY): Milan, Rome, Crotone and Trapani for the heating season. The analysis was about the energy cost due to the ventilation, so it refers only to primary air system. In each test there are three different occupancy level (1 person/13 m^2, 1 person/10 m^2, 1 person/7 m^2) and five ventilation rates (1.5, 2, 2.5, 3, 4 vol/h). The exhaust air rate is 0.5 vol/h less than the input air rate in order to have a positive air pressure to avoid uncontrolled infiltration. The three-storied building has 1000 m^2 floor area and 2.7 m high for each storey, total internal volume is 8100 m^3. Design internal conditions are 20°C and 50% relative humidity. The reference case for the comparison is without heat recovery and heat pump: the heating demand is supplied by a gas boiler, whose annual mean efficiency is 0.9, by a heat coil. See fig. 1 for detail of a typical primary air-handling unit. The first recovery system is shown in fig. 2 and it is characterized by a heat exchanger, fixed plate or rotary wheels, without heat pump. If the recovery heat is not enough the residual need is covered in the same way of the previous case. Plate heat exchanger efficiency is 0.5 and the pressure loss is 250 Pa while the rotary wheel efficiency is 0.6 and the pressure loss is 180 Pa. These values are meant to be a seasonal average, in fact during a long period several different working situations are possible and so the system doesn't work always in the nominal condition. On the other hand in this way we are quite sure not to overestimate the heat exchanger contribution. The pressure loss is covered by an additional fan and the related electric power can be easily evaluated by knowing the heat exchanger airflow and the fan efficiency which is fixed equal to 0.6.

$$P_{el} = \frac{\Delta p \cdot \dot{m}_a}{\eta_v} \tag{3}$$

P_{el}= *electric power due to the additional fan [W]*
$\dot{m}_a$ = *heat exchanger air flow [m³/s]*
η_v = *fan efficiency*

The second recovery system is shown in fig. 3 and it is characterized only by a heat pump; the cold source is the exhaust air from the inside where the temperature is 20 °C. The heat pump is sized by considering the extreme external condition; in fact, as it will be shown, the *COP* in this condition is always better than the value which ensures the economic benefit if compared with the traditional boiler. The performance of the heat pump is described by full load *COP* (nominal value equal to 3.92) at different thermal level and by a part load factor (*PLF*) which takes into account the penalization due to a part load functioning (UNI 10963). Two kinds of modulating control system have been considered: on-off and inverter. With the on-off modulating system there is always a penalization due to the part load functioning, while, with the inverter one, it is possible to obtain advantages by the part load functioning between the inverter functioning range [2, 3]. The previous heat coils are still present in order to cover the eventually exceeding heating needs.

In fig. 4 the last recovery system is shown. Now a heat exchanger, fixed plate or rotary wheels, and a heat pump are present. As already said the best performance is obtained when the exhaust air is used to heat the replacement air and then as cold source for the heat pump. Also in this case the auxiliary heat coils are present.

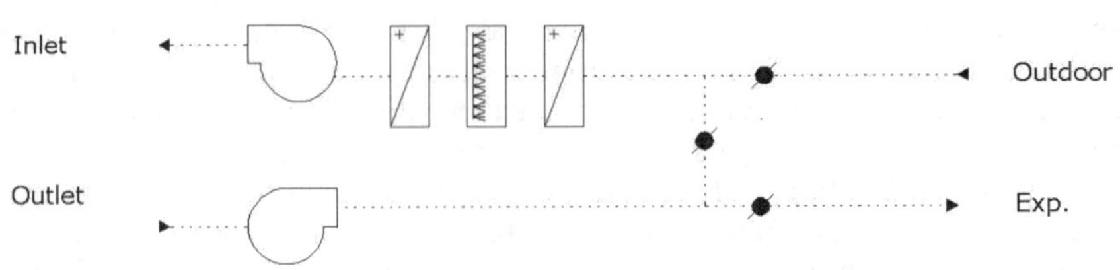

Figure 1: Traditional system for comparison.

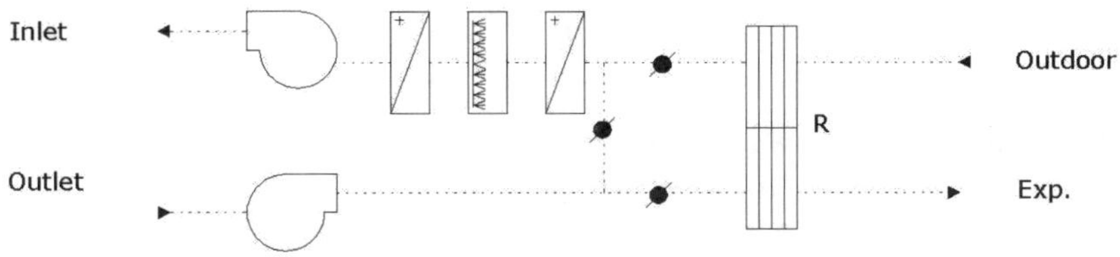

Figure 2: Heat exchanger system.

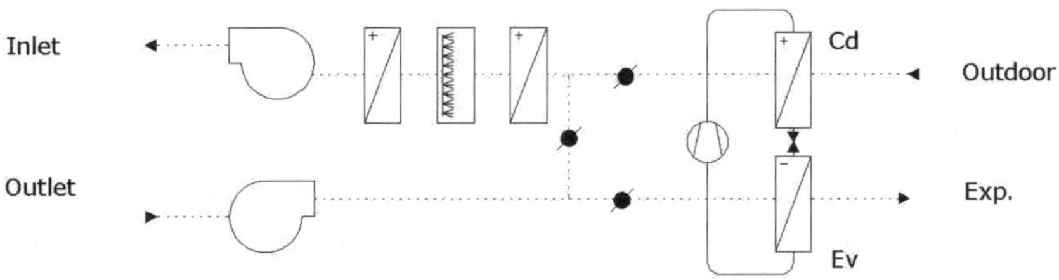

Figure 3: Heat pump system.

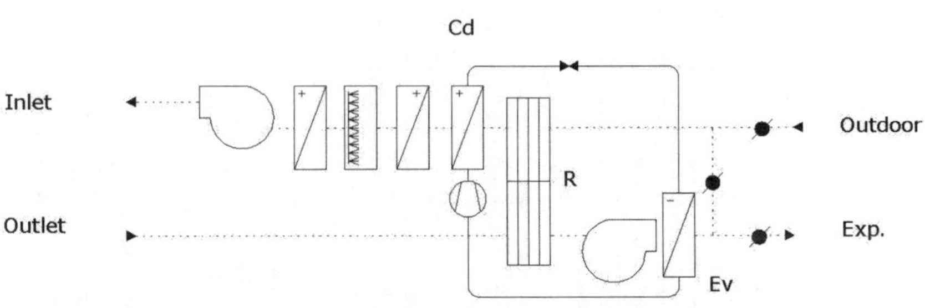

Figure 4: Heat pump and heat exchanger combined system.

In the end there are five different recovery systems: with plate heat exchanger (named "sensible"), with rotary wheel (named "total"), only with heat pump (named "HP1"), heat pump with plate heat exchanger (named "HP2") and heat pump with a rotary wheel ("HP3").

The comparison is done by considering the primary energy consumption and the economic saving. The electric energy is converted into primary energy consumption by dividing it for the Italian transformation ratio (0.36) from fuel energy to electric energy. The energy cost has been obtained by using the local charges which are different for the different towns.

Another important parameter for the comparison is the minimum value of the *COP* which ensures that the heat pump performances are better than the boiler ones (COP_l). The COP_l has been evaluated by the following ratio:

$$COP_l = \frac{CkW_e}{CkW_t} \quad (4)$$

CkW_e = *electric energy unit cost [€/kW*
CkW_t = *thermal energy unit cost[€/kWh]*

As the gas charge depends on the total consumption, for different occupancy and ventilation levels, the thermal unit cost is different and so also the COP_l is different.

5 Tests results

The heat exchanger effectivness is confirmed by the test results. Even though the heat pump without heat exchanger (HP1) is featured by the highest *COP*, this isn't enough to have the best global performance. Only for the Trapani clima, which is very warm, with an inverter heat pump, the HP1 performance are the best, but there the heat needs are not so significant. The extra electric cost due to the heat exchanger pressure loss is not so high to give up heat recovery.

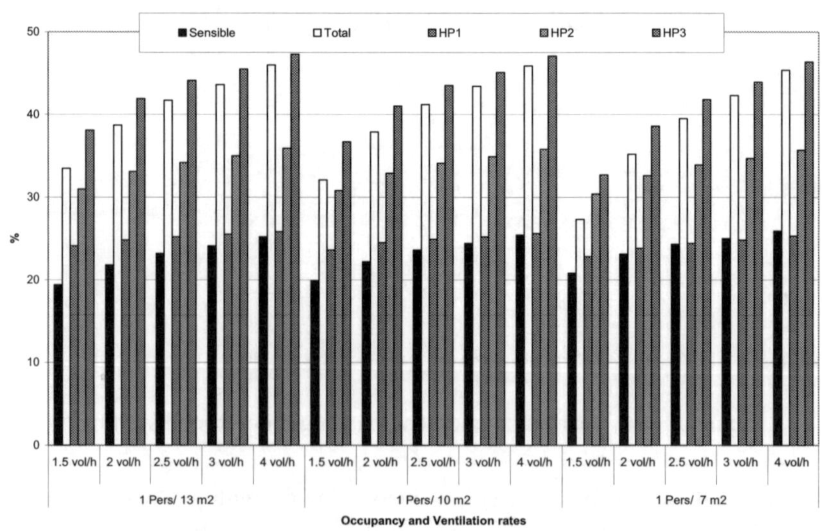

Figure 5: Energy saving for Milan.

The energetic analysis for Milan and Rome, fig. 5 and 6, show that the HP1 system performances are not less advantageous if compared to HP2 and HP3 system, but also if compared to total heat recovery. Only for Trapani the energetic analysis, fig. 7, shows that HP1 is comparable with HP2 and HP3. In these figures the heat pump results are referred to on-off control case.

The economic analysis, fig. 8-10, show that in general the use of the heat pump is convenient. This is clearly expressed, only for Milan, but the result is the same for the other towns, in fig. 11 where the *COP* for the different heat pump configuration is compared to the COP_l. In the same figure it is possible to note that actually the *COP* for the HP1 system are greater than HP2 and HP3 but, as already said, this doesn't mean that HP1 is the best solution.

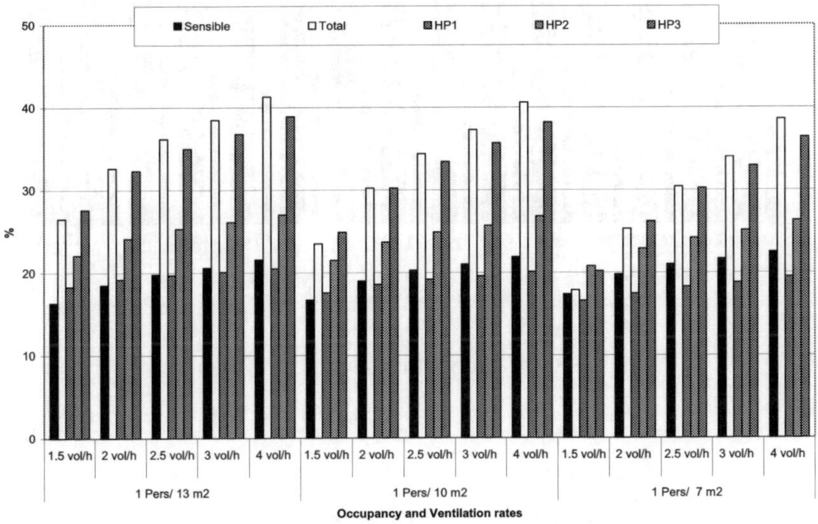

Figure 6: Energy saving for Rome.

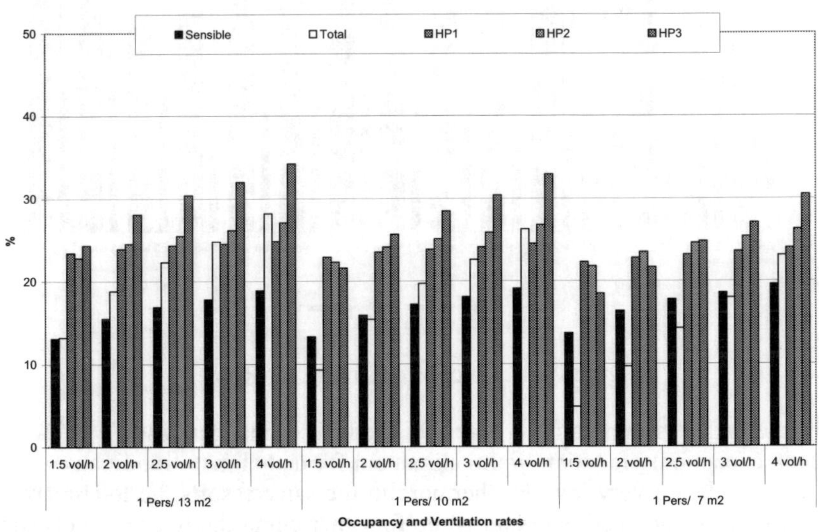

Figure 7: Energy saving for Trapani.

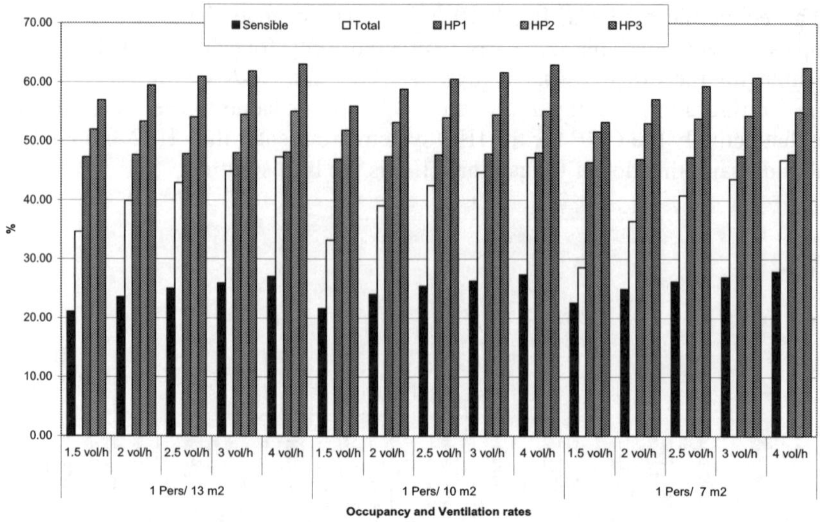

Figure 8: Economic saving for Milan.

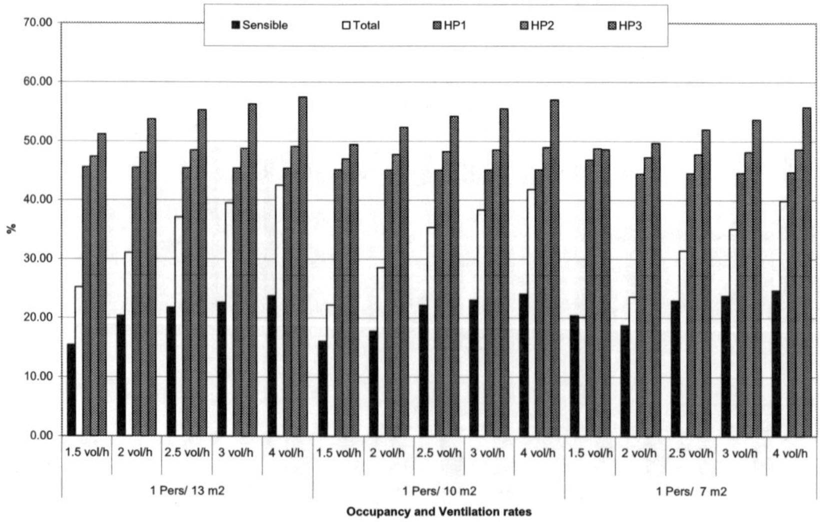

Figure 9: Economic saving for Rome.

In the end it is important to note that the heat exchangers should be always present, except only for some warm clima, but for that climate conditions usually the heat needs are very low. Furthermore in the same resorts the total recovery system performance isn't so good while for other clima the rotary wheels show great performance.

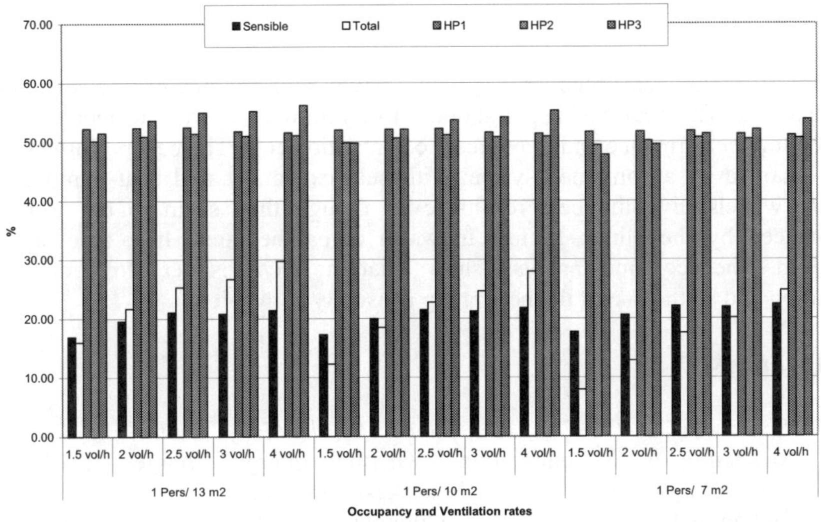

Figure 10: Economic saving for Trapani, on-off regulation.

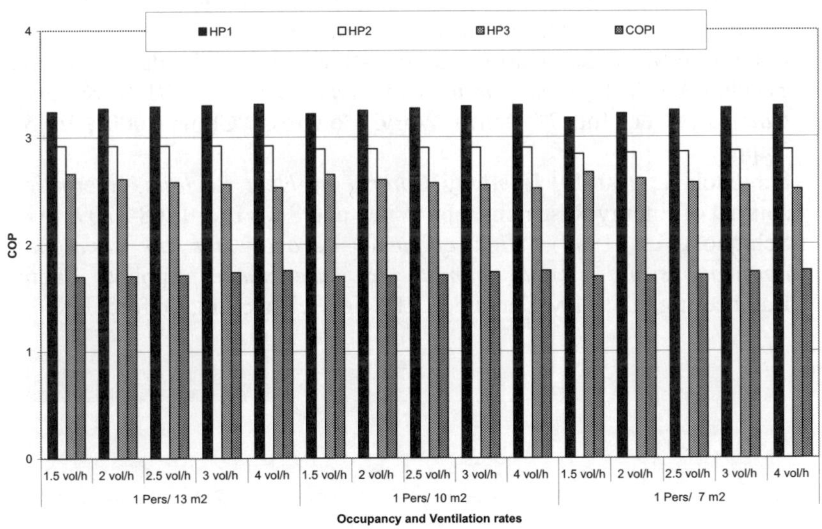

Figure 11: COP for Milan, on-off regulation.

All the tests show that for all systems featured with heat exchangers the energy and the economic saving increases with the ventilation rate and decreases with the occupancy rate, while the heat pump performance seems to be not influenced.

6 Conclusion

Some different heat recovery systems have been compared by dynamic simulations. The heat exchanger shouldn't be removed in order to increase the heat pump performance and to reduce the ventilation cost. The best performances are obtained by a combined system with heat exchanger and heat pump. The rotary wheels give the best results, even though they seem to be strongly influenced by the clima. In fact in warm clima the latent heat recovery is reduced. The economic analysis shows that the COP_l is very low for each situation and so the use of the heat pump is usually convenient.

References

[1] Schibuola L. (1993), *Heat pumps for humidity control in covered swimming pools*, International Thermal Energy Congress ITEC 93 Proceedings, vol. 2, 539-542, Marrakesh Morocco.

[2] Bettanini E., Gastaldello A., Schibuola L. (2003), *Simplified models to simulate part load performances of air conditioning equipments*, atti 8th International IBPSA Conference, Eindhoven.

[3] Schibuola L., Gastaldello A., Venco S. (2004), *Seasonal Performance Evaluation of Chillers characterized by new design solutions in air conditioning plants*, atti International Conference Climamed, Lisbona.

[4] Caberlotto M., Gastaldello A., Gerrard-Smith A., Schibuola L., Venco S., Zecchin R. (2001), *Tests Carried Out on a New Specific HVAC System for Cinemas,* Proc. Int. 7th Rehva World Congress "Clima 2000", ID 552, Napoli.

[5] Schibuola L. (2001), *Humidity Control by Heat Reclaim*, International Journal of Energy Research, John Wiley and Sons Ltd, 1208-1209.

[6] Schibuola L. (1997), *High efficiency recovery for air conditioning applications in a mild climate: a case study*, Applied Thermal Engineering, n.5, May, Pergamon Elsevier Science Ltd, Oxford, UK.

Viable and sustainable alternatives for post-consumed oil packages

L. H. S. M. Xavier[1], R. S. Cardoso[1], R. M. B. Matos[1], R. Valle[1] & P. L. González-Torre[2]
[1]*Universidade Federal do Rio de Janeiro – PEP/COPPE, Brazil*
[2]*Universidad de Oviedo – Gijón, Spain*

Abstract

In recent years, the increase in the number of vehicles has led to a major consumption of fuel and lubricants. Considerable amounts of lubricant oil and their packages are sent to waste deposits every year. On the other hand, the main oil industries in the world are looking at analyzing different alternatives to solve this kind of problem. Effective strategies for environmental management of residual oil waste and the lubricant oil packages are being studied in order to give the desired information to stakeholders all over the world. In Brazil, different states of the country bring possible solutions to this question through setting a solid waste management policy. Nevertheless, some specificities are not considered properly. This work brings an evaluation of possible perspectives for oil package disposal. In this paper, after a brief discussion about environment-related questions, 21 disposal alternatives for post-consumed lubricant oil packages were identified, 5 of which were considered viable. We concluded that economical, social and environmental aspects have great influence in the decision for each alternative considered in this work.
Keywords: environmental management, life cycle, reverse logistics.

1 Introduction

Manufacturing offers numerous products intended to meet human needs, but at the same time it generates many hazardous by-products.

Environmental policy is an interesting indicator of waste disposal problems [1], such as: emissions of substances and waste streams, dispersion in the atmosphere, changes in environmental quality and changes in the health of human, animals, plants and ecosystems.

In the modern world, the manufacturing of plastic resins is being considered prodigious due to its multiple purposes but, on the other hand, it is considered as a hazardous product by environmental specialists.

However, considering the production evolution, it is possible to recognize the ecological function of plastics resins that came to replace materials such as: skin, bones and other parts of animals and plants were used to produce different products for different purposes. Another consideration about plastics advantages is related with desirable conservation of products, mainly food and drugs because of plastics mechanical and chemical properties. Plastics have also other positive aspects as the low specific load (that reduces transport costs) or the low cost as raw material [2,3].

In the environmental point of view, plastics represent a small but significant element of waste management chain. There are many different kinds of plastics, with specific properties and purposes [4]. Nevertheless, the literature generally disregards these specificities and the different range of environmental impacts that plastic materials may cause.

The environmental impact is specially identified in one of the final phase of the plastic life cycle, the disposal one. The low capacity of degradation of plastic materials is responsible for the long period they remain and impact the environment.

The first question to make the decision about plastic waste disposal is to recognize correctly the type and the amount of waste plastic generated. After this, some possibilities can be studied in order to identify the more interesting one for each specific type of plastic.

Managers are increasingly encouraged to recognize their social responsibility regarding the future of the planet in their environmental decision-making process. Nevertheless, decisions must not be only based on manager's opinion. Instead of this, Sachs [5] emphasizes the importance of considering five sustainable development dimensions: economical, environmental, social, cultural and technical, considering different actors that could cooperate in order to add value to the decision-making process.

As stakeholders, those social actors are co-responsible for finding the most suitable alternative to environmental protection. Consequently, they face up to the usual difficulties of decision making: (first) correctly identifying feasible alternatives to solve the problem being studied and (second) prioritising them. Moreover, they recognize the need to include quantitative and qualitative aspects, which often conflicts with each other. In practice, each stakeholder tries to force its own values and criteria. It is easy to conclude that decision methods can be very useful to environmental decisions. In particular, reverse supply chains may become a primary subject for decision techniques.

Different methodologies were developed in order to answer the questions about waste management and reverse logistics. Many authors chose to run out solutions through Decision Support Systems (DSS) specially designed to environmental issues, named Environmental Decision Support Systems (EDSS).

Although, while some studies examine the opportunities of cost reductions and capacity improvement provided by supply chain management, reverse logistics seems to deserve more attention in the environmental decision-making process [6]. Important questions remain concerning subjects like location of facilities, management of different types of collection systems and transport problems.

This situation is changing fast; both the price of raw materials and disposal charges and the environmental consciousness are increased. Reverse supply chains can improve environmental practices (e.g., the reuse and recycling of waste) through the elaboration of a plan that includes the definition of [7]:

- the objectives of the reverse supply chains;
- the integration level and the type of the reverse supply chains;
- the characteristics of the waste materials and the definition of the target market for the recycled product;
- the location of the recycling facilities and others;
- the control and information systems for the reverse supply chain operations.

2 Plastic packages disposal

The main goal of this work is the analysis of different alternatives to post-consume plastic packages disposal according with its life cycle. Due to the unavailability of study all types of plastics, it was developed a case study about post-consume automotive lubricant plastic packages made in HDPE (high density polyethylene).

The recycling is currently used as a efficient alternative for post-consumed plastic packages. Nevertheless, packages with residual contents or produced with different mixed materials become a major problem to waste management decisions.

The lubricant oil packages are a specific case in which recycling types (mechanical, energetic or chemical recycling) must be carefully considered in order to process the correct disposal. The residual oil inside this post-consume package has chemical properties that turn the cleaning phase necessary even before the transportation and the recycling properly. Although a considerable amount of oil effluent is generated from the cleaning of these packages, what represents a considerable environmental problem to be solved.

Another relevant aspect of this previous evaluation is the interference of the residual oil inside these packages on the initial phases (extrusion and coloring) of mechanical recycling. Materials of worst quality may be produced due to the presence of the residual oil in the process.

According with this, we pretend analyse the possibilities to HDPE lubricant oil packages, considering the Industrial Ecology concept, which studies the relationship between industrial systems and environmental [8].

3 Supply chain modeling

As plastic and lubricant oil are products from petroleum, a simplified supply chain model can be designed according with Figure 1 [9]. This supply chain model describes the relation of suppliers and consumers in the production and consumption into lubricant oil chain.

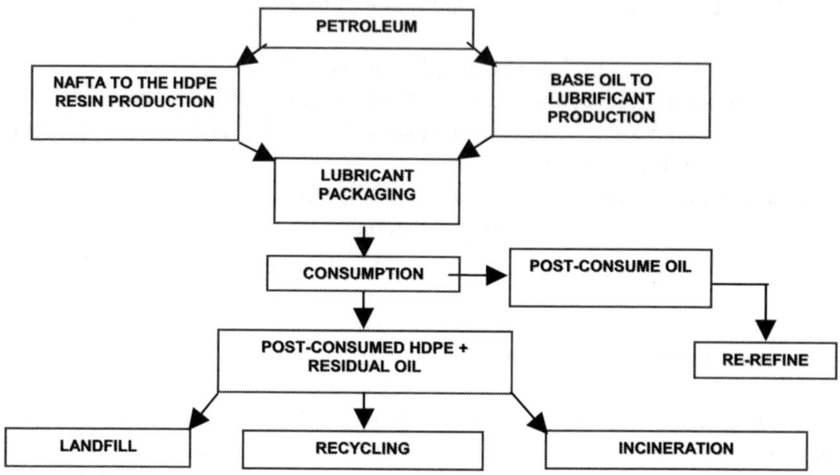

Figure 1: Lubricant oil package supply chain [9].

It is important to notice that in Figure 1 three possibilities to the packages disposal were considered but other possibilities should be considered to the waste reduction along the life cycle.

The HDPE packages are considered post-consumed in the final phase of the supply chain, but the residual oil, that remains inside the package, has not being consumed and, for this reason, it cannot be considered a post-consumed oil.

The residual oil has hazardous potential of soil and water contamination. If considerable percents of this residual oil could be recovered, it could represent important economical and environmental benefits in this supply chain.

In the last decade, in Brazil were produced about 880 thousand cubic meters per year of automotive lubricant oil production [10, 11].

Through the values observed in Table 1 it is possible to observe that, except for PETROBRAS, all the other organizations have a similar lubricant oil production. Thus, a consortium among these organizations could lead to the optimization of recovery of the lubricant oil packages.

Another important aspect showed by these figures is the representative potential of residual oil recovery from plastic packages. In one hand, the residual oil recover would provide social, economical and environmental benefits and, on the other hand, it could avoid potential environmental impact.

Table 1: Market-share of annual lubricant oil production in Brazil.

ORGANIZATION	MARKET-SHARE	ANNUAL VOLUME
PETROBRAS	23 %	202.4 thousands m^3
ESSO	10 %	88 thousands m^3
SHELL	15 %	132 thousands m^3
IPIRANGA	16 %	140 thousands m^3
TEXACO	20 %	176 thousands m^3
OTHERS	16 %	140 thousands m^3

4 Results

Despites the possibility of consortium of organizations to the lubricant oil packages recovery it was not carried on among Brazilian companies. Mainly legal and normative forces seemed to be an important aspect that contributes to the recovery optimization as can be observed with the Brazilian herbicides packages recovery.

Considering the supply chain model in Figure 1 and the need of reducing plastic wastes, there were defined four main groups to the definition of the possibilities to the packages disposal.

Environmental Decision Support Systems (EDSS) seemed to be an important tool in Environmental Management process during the last two decades. The unavailability of suitable data to produce relevant information remains as a critical point of this methodology. Nevertheless, important contributions on Decision Support Systems principles, applied to environmental problems, are still being developed. Gomes et al. [12] suggests the order of the main alternatives to plastic waste destination.

In Table 2 are presented the 21 possibilities and the respective group of classification.

For the Life Cycle Analysis group of criteria, were considered possibilities of new technologies developed. For example, the drainage apparatus for lubricant oil packages that are being currently used in Brazil. Nevertheless, its potentials could be improved if the time of lubricant oil package drainage was carefully observed [13].

Some characteristics may turn the alternative not viable, such as: the costs related with the package cutting/compacting alternative and the possibility of undesirable chemical and physical product changes brought through the gross sales consequences. An example of this is the 'stress-cracking' phenomenon that may compromises the quality of plastic packages during the time of usage.

The package reusing alternative can became interesting according with the lowest percentage of oil inside the package and the maintenance of chemical and physical properties of the package. The CO2 cleaning still represents a high investment cost possibility.

Table 2: Alternatives for post-consume oil lubricating package.

Life cycle analysis
Reduction
Environmental design
Alternative material analysis
Alternative technologies
Drainage apparatus/BOB (Bottom of the Bottle Oil Recovery System)
Package cutting/compacting processes
Gross sales
Package elimination
Landfill
Burning
Co-processing
Mechanical recycling
Chemical recycling
Thermal recycling
Incineration
Package reusing
CO_2 package cleaning
Reuse with lubricant oil
Triple washing
Reuse with another content
Legal aspects
Eco-taxes
Eco-labels
Deposit-refund program

Legal aspects are necessarily related with governmental decision-making areas. All of them take long periods of time to bring solutions to environmental problems.

Despite environmental impacts caused by the burning of plastic wastes (dioxins emissions, for example) the calorific value of plastic materials can provide considerable energetic recovery through the Thermal recycling alternative [1].

For each alternative, considering package elimination, a group of criteria was defined: (i) investments, (ii) operational costs, (iii) disposal/treatment costs, (iv) CO2 emissions, (v) corporate image and (vi) social/environmental benefits. Negative values for all criteria were settled, except for benefit and corporate image, in order to express their undesirable impact on the environmental performance. Appling the THOR Decision Support System [12], it was observed that five alternatives seemed to be more interesting than others. Landfill, Thermal recycling, Chemical recycling and Mechanical recycling were chosen as the best practices considering environmental, economic and social aspects of post-consume lubricant oil package disposal.

Then, as result of the viability analysis, it was observed that the alternative of drainage apparatus turns package cleaner and free of residual oil, improving the required quality to be accepted in other processes. According with THOR results, the alternatives of reuse and recycling (Mechanical, Chemical, Thermal) were considered the most interesting while Landfill was considered as easily implementation and able to bring environmental and social benefits through economic profits.

5 Conclusion

The environmental excellence concept is being settled in different management areas. Through this, is possible to carry on industrial development according to the economical, productive and environmental performance. This evolution leads some organizations to the environmental and managerial control integration in the most important spheres of decision. Responding to present questions and provide suitable answers do not seems to be enough.

Therefore, this work presents several proposals and much more questions to be solved in the plastic waste management. Nevertheless, some important possibilities were pointed out to be analysed and aggregated to petrochemical sector organizations, looking for social, economical and environmental viable solutions.

Acknowledgements

This research was funded by the Spanish Ministry of Science, contract number SEJ2004-07877-C02-01/ECON.

References

[1] Alter, H., The origins of Municipal Solid Waste. II Policy options for plastics waste management. *Waste Management & Research*, **11**, pp. 319-332, 1993.

[2] Cervera-Fantoni, A.L., *Envase y Embalaje,* Esic Editorial, Madrid, 1998.

[3] Diaz, A., Alvarez, M.J. & Gonzalez, P., *Logística Inversa y Medio Ambiente,* Mcgraw-Hill, Madrid, 2004.

[4] Tchobanoglous G., Theisen, H. & Vigil, S., *Integrated Solid Waste Management: Engineering Principle And Management Issues.* Mcgraw-Hill, New York, 1993.

[5] Sachs I., *Estratégias de transição para o século XXI. Desenvolvimento e Meio Ambiente.* São Paulo: Studio Noble, Brazil, 1993.

[6] González-Torre, P. L., Adenso-Díaz, B. & Artiba, H. Environmental and reverse logistics policies in european bottling and packaging firms. *International Journal of Production Economics*, **88(1)**, pp.95-104, 2004.

[7] Leite P.R., *Logística Reversa.* São Paulo: Prentice Hall, Brazil, 2003.

[8] Segger, T.P. & Theis, T.L., An Uniform and Quantitative Basis of Industrial Ecology, *Journal of Cleaner Production,* **10**, pp.225-235, 2002.

[9] Xavier, L.H.S.M. & Cardoso, R., 2002. Diagnóstico de alternativas para a destinação de embalagens plásticas em HDPE. PEP/UFRJ, 2002. Rio de Janeiro, Brazil.

[10] ANP, www.anp.gov.br

[11] SINDICOM, www.sindicom.com.br

[12] Gomes, C.F.S., Valle, R., Cardoso, R. & Xavier, L.H.S.M., Multiple Criteria Decision Making and Environmental Impact Assessment for Destination of Plastic Material Waste through THOR System. *XVII MCDM*, Canada, 2004. http://www.bus.sfu.ca/events/mcdm/ProgramF.pdf

[13] Valle, R., Xavier, L.H.S.M. & Cardoso, R., Aspectos legais da destinação de embalagens de óleo lubrificante. *Revista Meio Ambiente Industrial (RIMAI)*, 2005, *In Press.*

Section 10
Environmental and ecological policies

Adding coevolutionary principles to a holistic paradigm of sustainable development

M. B. Neace
Mercer University, U.S.A.

Abstract

In a previous paper (Neace 2003) I proposed an holistic model of sustainable development (SD) with science knowledge at its core. In this paper the models will be extended and deepened by incorporating several concepts from Norgaard's (1994) coevolutionary process. His basic thesis is that nature/environment and man, through knowledge, social structure/organization, values and technology co-evolve, not only within themselves but also with each other. My holistic thesis is all elements of nature, including man, are inseparably interconnected in an ongoing, dynamic, synergistic process. Merging the concepts results in a deeper, comprehensible appreciation of the many interconnections and complexities, including their fragilities, synergies and our own unknowing. I draw from his models, which overlap mine, and his six principles of coevolutionary cosmology. We agree, movement from anthropocentric processes and structures toward biocentrism requires a transition of values. Scientists, because of their unique professional status and ethos, are key catalysts in sustaining the unfolding process moving in the direction of coevolutionary harmony. Coming to grips with the man-biosphere process many truths are to be uncovered, including many stumbles along the way. Due to inherent uncertainty of the process the precautionary principle should serve as an operational underpinning. Movement toward SD is as much about future generations as it is the present generation.
Keywords: sustainable development, holistic, co-evolutionary cosmology.

1 Introduction

This is a work in progress. It has been and will continue to be a venture of discovery. The objective, beyond that of co-mingling two overlapping sustainability concepts, is to generate discussion, debate, and collaboration among scholars, professionals and policy makers. There are many models in both concepts. Two models from each concept are discussed in this paper.

Incorporating Norgaard's [3] coevolutionary concepts into my holistic model of sustainable development (SD) is the purpose of this paper. His basic thesis is nature/environment and man, through knowledge, social structure/organization, values/culture and technology co-evolve not only within themselves but also but also among each other. In my holistic models [1, 2] all elements of nature, especially *Homo sapiens*, are inseparably interconnected in a continuing unfolding process that is dynamic and synergistic. Merging the models leads to a deeper, more profound, and yes, more complex paradigm of SD. This conceptual paper is meant to generate discussion and stretch our individual constructs in a transdisciplinary fashion. It is not concerned with the difficult and often contentious issues of operationally defining, creating and implementing strategic designs – the work of SD. Let us begin by asking some hard questions regarding the process of sustainable development.

Norgaard [3, 4], as we all have, raises many very perturbing issues. Here are a few: (1) What should be sustained? (2) Who defines and determines the parameters of sustainability? (3) How to account for incongruities from the local level to the global? (4) Is sustainability feasible without factoring in poverty, justice, inequalities, cultural integrity and political sovereignty? (5) Is there sufficient trust, social capital and civil society - interconnectedness – among stakeholders to agree and carry forth SD programs? and (6) Can we expect movement toward SD unless our consciousness is holistic including a co-evolutionary mindset? There are many more. Both Norgaard [3] and I [2] emphasize the need for value transformation for SD processes to be viable.

2 Transformation of values necessary for holistic co-evolutionary paradigm

Not surprisingly, many in our established scientific community responded to these challenges, as have all established institutions throughout history when their intellectual underpinnings and power were challenged, with unequivocal denial [5]. Uncertainty wrought by these challenges spilled over to include philosophy, religion, social and political policy, and increasingly the physical interface between man and his natural environment. Research on this latter interface became irrefutable - there were mounting problems among man, his science, his economics and the natural environment. As environmental awareness swelled in the 1970s and 1980s so did the call for action from diverse stakeholder groups, resulting in a plethora of legislation throughout this period [6, 7, 8]. Beginning with denial of environmental problems in the late 60's, refuting the "questionable" scientific data, the science, technology, business/economic trilogy, began transforming their values from denial to reactive/anticipatory and, now, today, many are proactive/creative (Figure 1).

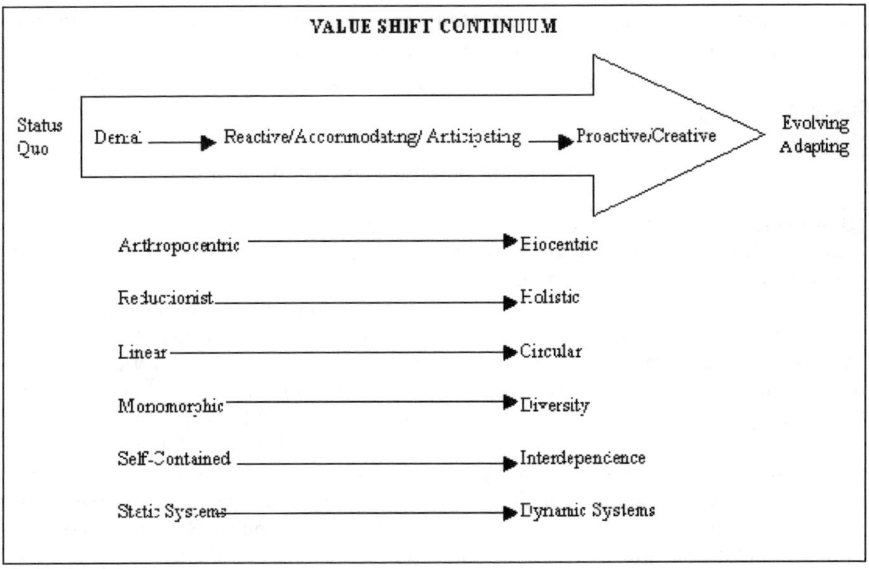

Figure 1: Transformation of values.

Science, under girded by the business/military coalition, was often viewed as the culprit for the manifold environmental problems: contamination of the Planet's soils, air, waters, loss of animal and plant life, disruption of ecosystems, and growing piles of toxic and solid wastes. Responses to environmental crises over the past five decades evolved through a process of value transformation as shown in Figure 1. Many of us refuted the "questionable" and growing science data base that clearly pointed to an interface between man and nature gone awry. Few took up the battle cry raised by Rachel Carson [9] when her information explicitly manifested the many industrial practices that were seriously damaging the delicate, complex, interactive relationship between man and the biosphere.

Denial is followed by a period of reactionary acquiescence, often resulting in rancorous disputations among stakeholders, even as research and observations pointed to an imbalance. Coevolutionary processes that underpin sustainable development were becoming tumultuous. Today, most stakeholders-not all-of all persuasions realize that continued utilization of the institutionalized Newtonian linear reductionist models at the pace of the past fifty years is unsustainable [10, 11, 7, 12, 13,14]. Capacity of the biosphere to withstand continual disruptions of its natural ecosystems, intrusions of wastes beyond Earth's absorption capabilities, increasing use of synthetic chemicals that are very difficult for Mother Nature to deconstruct, hinders her normal pattern of evolution. Harvesting of natural resources at rates faster than Mother Nature can replenish them is limited. The economic footprint of a few is overwhelming the biosphere at the expense of the many [10, 11, 12]. A basic principle of finance most of us attempt to abide by, sometimes not very successfully, is, use interest generated by investment capital and do not erode principle. Likewise, a basic principle of ecology and ecosystems is to maintain and refurbish the natural capital that underpins all life for long term survival of *Homo sapiens*, or for that matter, all living things. Do not erode natural capital at a rate that jeopardizes survival for this and future generations.

Table 1: Dominant and alternate premises (values).

Dominant Premises	**Alternate Premises**
Atomism: Systems consist of unchanging parts and are simply the sum of their parts.	*Holism*: Parts cannot be understood apart from their wholes and wholes are different from the sum of their parts.
Mechanism: Relationships between parts are fixed, systems move smoothly from one equilibrium to another, and changes are reversible.	Systems might be mechanical, but they might also be deterministic yet not predictable or smooth because they are chaotic or simply very discontinuous. Systems can also be evolutionary.
Universalism: Diverse, complex phenomena are the result of underlying universal principles which are few in number and unchanging over time and space.	*Contextualism*: Phenomena contingent upon a large number of factors particular to the time and place. Similar phenomena might well occur in different times and places due to widely different factors.
Objectivism: WE can stand apart from what we are trying to understand.	*Subjectivism*: Systems cannot be understood apart from us and our activities, our values, and how we have known and hence acted upon systems in the past.
Monism: Our separate individual ways of understanding complex systems are merging into a coherent whole.	*Pluralism*: Complex systems can only be known through alternate patterns of thinking which are necessarily simplifications of reality. Different patterns are inherently incongruent.

Source: Richard B. Norgaard, *Development Betrayed*, p. 62.

Conceptually, SD bridges the growing disharmony between ecology and economics. A broad range of disciplines, governments, NGOs, industries and professional groups have embraced SD, legitimized by the Brundtland report [15]. Although widely hailed conceptually, sustainable development is highly controversial regarding policies and practices bringing ecology and economy into harmony with each other. Conflicting values arise because of many different contextual interpretations these groups attach to the concept operationally. Williams and Millington [16] note that SD "…is a notoriously difficult, slippery and elusive concept to pin down." Their analysis of SD definitions led to a value continuum with "weak sustainability" at one end and "strong sustainability" at the other. The Brundtland Report definition rated weak on the value continuum as it has an anthropocentric view of development. Nature is viewed as a resource to be domineered and used. Deep ecologists [17] and eco-feminists [18, 19] are at the other end of the continuum, espousing value orientations supporting development that includes less consumption, equity, justice and the "rights" of Nature. Each end of the continuum, and those between, supports a different value position: human centered (anthropocentric) perspective to biocentrism, a non-human, biotic (humans included), inter-species perspective.

Norgaard [3, ch.6] posits that metaphysical and epistemological suppositions of atomism, mechanism, universalism objectivism (purisms) and monism dominated Western philosophy and science during the late nineteenth and twentieth centuries and formed the value basis of how society interacts with Mother Nature - modernism. Embeddedness of these value orientations, excluding alternate premises, is at the root of the debate, accounting for our many difficulties moving from "weak sustainability" toward a balanced perspective and acknowledgement of co-evolutionary principles that underpin man-biosphere relationships. There is considerable overlap of Figures 1 and 2. Norgaard views 'weak sustainability,' although anthropocentrically effective, as overly simplistic and not appropriate for understanding biospheric complexities: its pluralism, its interconnectedness, its great variety of inter-related, dynamic, cultures and ecosystems - a co-evolutionary cosmology. What is lacking is a paradigm, both theoretical and operational, that reunites man to 'his' biosphere [20]. Figure 2 and Norgaard's principles tackle this issue.

3 A holistic paradigm of sustainable development built on principles of co-evolutionary cosmology

Figure 2 postulates an integrated holistic paradigm for sustainable development. It is generic and applicable at any scale, from a cattle farmer in Brazil concerned with the vitality, quality and quantity of his forage, to regional and global issues such as river basins that overlap political boundaries, to concerns of disappearing snowcaps atop mountains worldwide. Figure 2 signals a shift in values: from simplistic, static systems to complex, evolving systems – pluralism. It also portends continuing research to understanding SD issues among the many branches of science - a transdisciplinary *modus operandi.* No one expects movement along the value continuum without some disputation. Disputation, questioning and healthy debate are necessary to reach higher levels of understanding, collaboration and respect for Planet Earth and its biosphere. For example, Caha [21] very realistically notes that in spite of many difficulties, Central and Eastern Europe are moving, albeit ratchetly, toward various forms of holistic alliances in which academic-science communities play major roles.

Movement along the value continuum from anthropocentric toward biocentric, including higher levels of assimilation, is necessary for various stakeholders to be willing to sit at a common table. As scale and number of players increase a major task is keeping an ever-diverse group of stakeholders, often of different cultures, some with competing agendas, at times contentious and mistrusting their counterparts, at the table, working collaboratively, if not always congenially, toward the common goal of SD. Today, the science community, academic and professional, plays a key role in making this happen. Through research, collaboration and knowledge dissemination they can create the social capital necessary for progress toward SD life styles. SD requires sustainable relationships among all elements of the holistic model. The science community providers of the core biospheric knowledge other stakeholders need for decision making. Biospheric knowledge is holistic, diverse and underpins life.

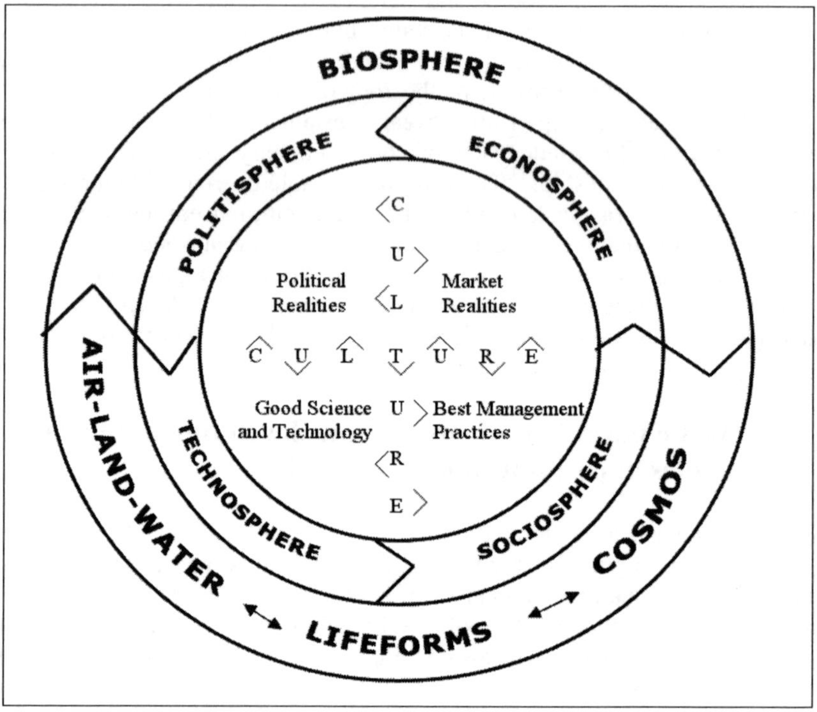

Figure 2: Integrated holistic paradigm.

Usefulness coevolutionary cosmologic holistic model requires frameworks that seek togetherness – a unification of elements, not in the concrete sense but in the vague sense that looks beyond dualism [22]. Norgaard [3, ch. 9] has constructed six principles – as a basis for understanding coevolutionary cosmology. They establish a framework for "working' the holistic model in Figure 2. Without this framework the model lacks the mortar to comprehend relationships, contexts, and its dynamic, integrated bricks of wholeness.

3.1 Principle 1

"First, people are within and effect both the state and the evolution of the cosmos we are trying to understand. The observer and the observed are interrelated." All behavior of all life, especially *Homo sapiens*, has some impact on the environment and other life, and in turn is affected by other life and the perceived environment. Co-interactions - exchanges - can be positive or negative, or both.

For example, anthropocentric relationships with their larger environments have had beneficial results based on simplistic, linear measures, such as GDP, and continue to do so even as their natural environments are being degraded at an unsustainable rate. Development experts from different cultures often have opposing views of common environmental issues, especially if they also come from different disciplines. For example, as has often happened, a development economist representing an undeveloped country views clearing forestland for agriculture differently than an environmental ecologist representing the UNDP. Cultures, perspectives and priorities all vary. Finding that common ground is not easy and the science community has a larger role to play than just providing facts. The holistic paradigm in Figure 2 regards relationships - social capital - as essential.

3.2 Principle 2

"Second, how we understand the cosmos determines how we affect the system, [and] how we know selects for properties of the evolving system we try to know." In Norgaard's second principle, causality is in the other direction, from the unit to the larger system in which it is embedded. How we reason and understand affects social and environmental systems and how they evolve. How we view and interpret environmental model paradigms, such as Figure 2, its scope, scale and context, determines our actions and the subsequent state of environments and their evolution.

3.3 Principle 3

"Third, the principle of conceptual pluralism. Different ways of knowing different aspects of the cosmos are really different and unlikely to merge into a [single] coherent understanding of the whole." Complex systems, such as Figure 2, do not lend themselves to simplistic, reductionist rationales. To do so lessens our chances of finding the truth and therefore reaching common ground where diversity is viewed as necessary and synergistic. Conceptual pluralism recognizes environmental diversity and the "...incommensurability of multiple models. Contentions and contradictions occur in environmental debates because our multiple models do not fit into a single coherent understanding." As Norgaard and other scholars of the complexity school argue, post-modern science (e.g., monism, positivism, etc.) will not provide realistic paradigms of holistic environments [3, ch. 6, 22, 23, 24]. Simplistic models are not wrong, they are insufficient when describing and determining policies regarding complex systems, such as the biosphere. It's the reality of multiple, simple, reductionist models that creates the necessity for complexity – the cultural and biotic pluralism implied in Figure 2.

3.4 Principle 4

"Fourth, people understand collectively; we are dependent on other people and how we are organized socially for much of what we know." We are also dependent on other people for our own development [25]. Scientists and other stakeholders increasingly rely on interdependency to understand complex systems. For example, browsing scientific journals one notes that single authorships are becoming less common. Many of these journals now lay claim to an interdisciplinary, multidisciplinary or multi-cultural means for disseminating information and knowledge. Much of their published works have multiple authors, often representing different disciplines, cultures and geographies.

Resolving environmental issues has become so important in terms of biospheric well being the larger society will not let any single constituency have sole responsibility for its caretaking and guidance [1, 2]. The sum of knowledge generated by multidisciplinary research is greater than the sum of its parts. Interdependency is not a panacea. Experiential intervention is often wrong. When risks are perceived as "high" the precautionary principal should hold sway [2]. Figure 2 was designed to take advantage of this interdependency of knowledge and its potential synergy – cultural pluralism in action.

3.5 Principles 5 and 6

"Fifth, parts and relations within systems are historically contingent." "And sixth, phenomena within systems of higher levels of complexity are contextual." These two principles are closely intertwined with respect to the contingent nature of historical events and the contextual character of parts within systems. As integral elements of schemas of understanding coevolutionary cosmologic processes they are interwoven and inseparable. Scientists using Figure 2 will have to develop relations with others of like minds to engage in transdisciplinary research: thinking out of the box collaboratively with colleagues from other disciplines. Holistic model building necessitates experientially putting parts together to see what works and what does not within specific contexts. Foucault [26] believes much of today's scientific rules of discourse are ungrounded in structure, lacking reality, being, more often than not, historically contingent and situationally reductionist, unable to loosen the bonds of their academic compartments apart from the whole. The episteme of co-evolutionary cosmology breaks down these barriers. This can occur exogenously or planned, as we are attempting to do with systems and processes that move toward SD. Figure 2 supports the creation of relationships within and between stakeholder groups at all levels and scopes, including the biotic world - social capital - to react to the contingent nature of exogenous events and the results of planned programs and processes. Each situation is unique and often dynamic. Behavior is contextualized.

For SD to be viable in terms of constructs/processes research, social organization, and strategically inclusive planning and polity, will require understanding that parts co-evolve holistically and can only be understood in context of whole systems in which they exist. Figure 2 is not unlike Lovelock's gaia hypothesis [27]: just as Earth is theorized as a living, evolving organism, searching for homeostasis, so are each of the parts when bundled together in various schemas to the benefits of those doing the "modeling," Whether bundling is a farmer tilling soil to grow crops, a housewife maintaining a clean household for her family, a professor of environmental economics developing a syllabus for her graduate students, or a manufacturer of cable wire considering the impact of new technology, all take account of available resources and outcomes of their decisions based on their social/physical environments and belief systems. All of these decisions will have some environmental impacts. They, and others in their system, will put various parts together within particular contexts. Although decision making may become habitual, over time the parts, the contexts and the social networks change, requiring reformulation, remodeling. The process, like nature, is always evolving. Of course, they are nature. Figure 2, is, in effect, a representation of a living organism. That living organism can be a single person or global corporation with activities in a hundred plus countries.

The holistic paradigm built on a co-evolutionary framework, recognizes cultural and scientific pluralism, reuniting man to the biosphere. We in the science community, because of our unique mission, biotic knowledge bearers, in our multistakeholder environments, have opportunities to make these models workable. We do this by fostering transdisciplinary programs in research, communications and polity, using the diversity we find all around us, in culture and biota, to create sustainable programs and structures that are in a continual state of evolving – of becoming. The models, as does the science of hermeneutics [3, p. 228], acknowledges pluralism in our sciences and in our cultures. Diversity provides opportunities for creative synergies to occur across disciplines and culture necessary for movement toward sustainable development.

References

[1] Neace, M.B., The catalytic role of the science community: making sustainability work. *Ecosystems and Sustainable Development*, vol. 1, eds. E. Tiezza, C. A. Brebbia & J.L. Usó; WITPress: Southampton, UK, pp. 603-611, 2003.

[2] Neace, M.B., Local culture: A key to the attainment of sustainable development. *Journal of American Culture*, **20(2)**, pp. 105-119, 1997.

[3] Norgaard, R.B., *Development Betrayed: The end of progress and a coevolutionary revisioning of the future*, Routledge: New York, 1994.

[4] Norgaard, R.B. Which we, whose wisdom, whither the mountain west? (Book Reviews). *Bioscience*, **53(3)**, pp. 278-281, 2003.

[5] Clark, M.E., *Ariadne's Thread*, St. Martin's Press: New York, 1989.

[6] Fischer, K. & Schot, J., (eds.). *Environmental Strategies for Industry*, Island Press: Washington, D.C., 1993.

[7] Hawken, P., *The Ecology of Commerce*, Harper Collins Publishers: New York, 1993.

[8] Schmidheiny, S., *Changing Course: A Global Business Perspective on Development and the Environment*, MIT Press: Cambridge, MA, 1992.

[9] Carson, R., *Silent Spring*, Houghton-Mifflin: Boston, 1962.

[10] Boulding, K.E., The economics of the coming spaceship earth. *Environmental Quality in a Growing Economy*, ed. H. Jarrett, Johns Hopkins Press: Baltimore, pp. 3-14, 1966.
[11] Daly, H.E., *Steady-State Economics*, 2nd ed., Island Press: Washington, D.C., 1991.
[12] Erhlich, P.H., *Human Nature: Genes, Cultures and Human Prospect*, Island Press: Washington, D.C., 2000.
[13] Rees, W.E., *Sustainable Development and the Biosphere*, ANIMA Books: Chambersburg, PA, 1990.
[14] Speth, J.G., Red Sky at Morning: America and the Crisis of the Global Environment, Yale University Press: New Haven, CT, 2004.
[15] World Commission on Environment and Development (WCED). *Our Common Future*, Oxford University Press: New York, 1987.
[16] Williams, C. & Millington, A., The diverse and contested meanings of sustainable development. *The Geographical Journal*, **170(2)**, pp. 99-104, 2004.
[17] Deval, B. & Sessions, G. *Deep Ecology: Living as if Natured Mattered*, Peregrine Smith Books: Salt Lake City.
[18] Karen, W. Feminism and ecology: Making connections, *Environmental Ethics*, **9(1)**, pp. 3-20, 1987.
[19] Buckingham, S. Ecofeminism in the twenty-first century. *The Geographic Journal*, **170(2)**, pp. 146-154, 2004.
[20] Teilhard, de Chardin, P., *The Phenomenon of Man*, Harper: New York, 1959.
[21] Caha, M. *Understanding Environmental Issues in Central and Eastern Europe: A Study Based on the Situation of the Czech Republic*, Regional Environmental Center for Central and Eastern Europe: Budapest, 1994.
[22] Grange, J., *Nature: An Environmental Cosmology*, State University of New York Press: Albany, NY, 1997.
[23] Byrne, D., *Complexity Theory and the Social Sciences*, Routledge: London, 1998.
[24] Eve, R., Horsfall, S., and Lee, M., (eds.) *Chaos, Complexity, and Sociology: Myths, Models and Theories*, Sage Publications: London, 1997.
[25] Durkheim, E., *The Division of Labor in Society*, Macmillan: New York, 1933.
[26] Foucault, M., *The Order of Things: An Archaeology of the Human Sciences*, Random House: New York, 1971.
[27] Lovelock, J., Gaia: A New Look at Life on Earth, Oxford University Press: Oxford, England, 1979.

Land use in the future – needs and limitations

R. Engström
Center for Environmental Strategies Research, fms, and Department of Industrial Ecology, Royal Institute of Technology (KTH), Sweden

Abstract

Suitable cropland is needed for production of food, forest products, bioenergy and other crops, and in all areas future projections have been made on the need for land. Projections of future contribution from biomass to the global energy system often take food production into consideration. But there is not only a conflict between different kinds of production: land has to be set aside also for protection of biological diversity. Saving species is important for reasons such as current and future commercial benefits, but also because of functional values of the ecosystems, to maintain productivity. In this study projections of future land use for different purposes are compared with total suitable land on a global scale. It discusses possibilities for realisation of the projections and potential strategies for making the fulfilment of the different needs compatible. Strategies for reducing land use are for example changed food consumption and energy saving measures. A main finding is that the available land can suffice for the needs according to the studied projections, but we might have to consider alterations for example in diet.

Keywords: land use, biodiversity, bioenergy, food security, agriculture, silviculture.

1 Introduction

The planet we live on has a limited land area, and there are many demands for this area. The land used for production purposes is primarily used for agriculture, but also silviculture is an important source of income for many countries. In the struggling for renewable energy sources bio fuels, both from agri- and silvicultural areas, are often proposed as an important contribution, in which case land will be used also for this purpose. In all of these areas: production of food, forest products and biomass for energy, projections are made on how much land will be used in the future to satisfy demands in each area. Projections of future production of bioenergy have often assessed also land use for food, and proposed use of excess land for bioenergy plantations (for example IIASA and WEC [1] and Rogner [2]). But the projections have seldom taken environmental issues and biodiversity conservation into consideration. After reviewing 17 studies of the contribution of biomass in the future global energy supply, Berndes et al [3], stated that 'the environmental consequences of a realization of the assessed bioenergy potentials are insufficiently analyzed. It is therefore unclear to what extent the assessed potentials harmonize with other environmental goals such as biodiversity and nature conservation' (p.19).

1.1 Aim and method

The purpose of this study is to compare projections of future land use for different purposes with total potential cropland, and to discuss priorities and options to reduce the land use, with a special focus on the importance of biodiversity. The study was made by means of literature studies. Databases were searched for projections of future land use for different purposes. Several projections could be found, and a few studies were chosen to represent each purpose. Thus, the study does not claim to show a complete overview of projections, but rather to give examples from the different areas of study.

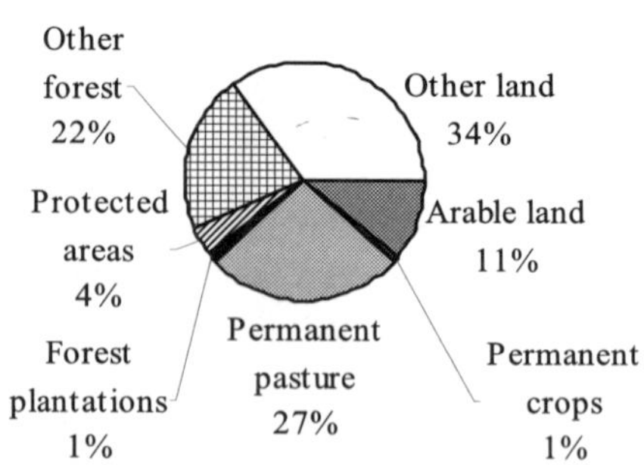

	Mha	Year
Total Land Area	13067	2002
Arable land	1404	2002
Permanent crops	130	2002
Permanent pasture	3485	2002
Forest plantations	187	2000
Protected areas	479	2000
Other forest	2819	2000
Other land	4562	2002

Figure 1: Current land use / land cover (FAO [4, 5]).

2 Review of projections for land use and production

2.1 Current land use

In 2002 approximately one third of the total land on a global scale was used for food production (arable land and permanent pasture), one third was forests (plantations and other forests together with protected areas, which, for a large part consist of forest land) and one-third other land (Figure 1). Figure 1 shows a mixture between land uses and types of land cover, which follows from the fact that not all of the land is actually used for production purposes.

2.2 Projections

Table 1 shows projections of future land use for different purposes. The projections are further discussed in the following sections.

Table 1: Projections of land use in 2050 for different purposes. See text for further explanations.

Land use type	Area 2050 (Mha)	Population (billion)	Diet	Yields (kg/ha)	Other assumptions	Reference
Agriculture						
Total arable land	1,690	10.1	Not specified	Not specified	High growth scenario	[1]
	2,033	8.296	Not specified	Not specified		[2]
Food	461	9.404	Vegetarian	10,000		[7]
	1,182	9.404	Vegetarian	3,900		[7]
	1,444	9.404	Affluent	10,000		[7]
	3,710	9.404	Affluent	3,900		[7]
Cereals only	725	9.104	(Moderate)	4,550		[8]
Biomaterials	101-276	Not specified	Not specified	Not specified		[6]
Forestry						
Plantations	103.3-234.2	Not specified				[9]
Total pulp and wood	402	Not specified				[6]
			Total primary energy use (EJ)	**Supply of bioenergy (EJ)**		
Bioenergy	390-610	10.1	1,047	Not specified	High growth scenario	[1]
	429	9.521	323	128.2	Renewables-intensive scenario	[10]
	1,280	8.296	Not specified	276	Max area for bioenergy	[2]
	6,592	(8.9)	1,780	1,780	Rich circumstances	[11]
	17,305	(8.9)	312	312	Poor circumstances	[11]
Species preservation	0.21-0.65	Not specified				[12]
Total min	1,253					
Total max	21,408					
Total potential cropland	4,144					[13]

2.2.1 Arable land

IIASA and WEC [1] and Rogner [2] calculated current and future land use for agriculture, to find out how much land could be used for bioenergy purposes. IIASA and WEC [1] estimated that in 2050 an additional 250 Mha, over the 1,440 Mha used for agriculture in 1995, will be used, while Rogner [2] arrived at an estimate around 2,000 Mha. Neither of the authors specify how the land is used: what areas are needed for different kinds of food, what kind of farming practices are used, how much of the land is for non-food crops, etc.

Hoogwijk et al [6] projected future land use for food, although no exact numbers were published. Their results showed however large difference depending on which diet (vegetarian, moderate or affluent) and kind of production system (high or low external input systems) was assumed. The same thing was shown by Penning de Vries et al [7]: based on numbers published in their paper it can be calculated that with a population size of 9.404 billion people land use for food can vary from 461 Mha (vegetarian diet and yield oriented production system) to 3,701 Mha (affluent diet and environmentally oriented production system).

Gilland [8] calculated the maximum attainable global cereal grain production in 2050 to 3,300 Mt on an area of 725 Mha. He assumed a world population of 9.104 billion in 2050, in which case a per capita consumption of on average 362 kg of grain could be allowed, or 600 kg in the more developed countries, 408 kg in China and 300 kg in the other less developed countries (about 20% over their current average level).

Hoogwijk et al [6] projected land use for biomaterials other than pulp and wood to 101-276 Mha. The biomaterials include for example cotton and rubber.

2.2.2 Forest products

FAO [9] projected future supply of resources from forest plantations, primarily round wood. They made three scenarios, of which they judged Scenario 2, with 160.2 Mha projected area of industrial forest plantations in 2050, as the most probable. Forest plantations are today only a small part, around 5 %, of the total forest area (see Figure 1). Also large parts of other forests are used for productive purposes: the major part of the northern boreal forests are not classified as plantations according to FAO's classification, but are used for large-scale production of pulp, paper and round wood. It has not been possible to find projections for future production from these areas, neither how much of them are situated at potential cropland and how much are on land with limited suitability for other kinds of land use. Hoogwijk et al [6] projected however total land use for pulp and wood to around 400 Mha.

2.2.3 Energy

An overview of projections of the contribution of biomass in the future global energy supply [3] showed that studies arrived at very different conclusions. The reason for this was uncertainties of future land availability and yield levels in energy crop production. IIASA and WEC [1] projected a need for 390-610 Mha of land for biomass cultivation in 2050 for their energy scenarios.

www.witpress.com, ISSN 1743-3541 (on-line)

Johansson et al [10] included 429 Mha of biomass cultivation, while Rogner [2] projected the maximum attainable area for biomass production to 1,280 Mha.

Nonhebel [11] projected future land use for food and renewable energy in the form of biomass plantations and photovoltaic (PV) systems, under two circumstances: rich (high yields of grain and bioenergy and high consumption of food and energy) and poor (low yields and low consumption). Land use for PV systems was much lower than for bioenergy plantations producing the same amount of energy. If using PV systems for the total energy use and assuming a population of 8.9 billion people (UN scenario [14]), the area needed on a global scale in rich circumstances was 230 Mha and in poor 41 Mha. This can be compared to 7,410 Mha for bioenergy-cultivation in rich circumstances and 17,305 Mha in poor circumstances based on Nonhebel's projections.

2.2.4 Biodiversity and species richness

Gowdy and McDaniel [15] forwarded the opinion that the 3,2% of the Earth's land area that is currently set aside (1989) is insufficient for the survival of biodiversity. Myers et al [12] on the other hand meant that if saving 25 hotspots with high numbers of endemic species, 44% of all (known) global plants and 35% of the vertebrates could be saved. The area of those hotspots were 0.21 Mha, or 1,4% of the total land surface on earth. In the Wildlands Project an ambitious conservation plan for North American biodiversity were drawn up [16]. According to that plan 23,4% of North America should be returned to wilderness, and another 26,2% severely restricted in terms of human use, to keep the natural ecological balance in nature.

There are evidently large differences between authors recommending how large areas that have to be set aside for species preservation. Swift et al [17] grouped the values of biodiversity in four types: intrinsic (the values biodiversity has on its own, such as cultural, social, aesthetic and ethical benefits), utilitarian (commercial benefits, for example as agricultural crops or for drugs), serependic (future but yet unknown values) and functional values (values beyond recognised direct utilitarian benefit, ecosystem services such as nutrient cycles, erosion control and water regulation). Saving species for their intrinsic, utilitarian or serependic values could be done in reserves, such as the plan proposed by Myers et al [12]. Functional values on the other hand are often part and prerequisite of the production systems. In the Convention of Biological Diversity [18] not only diversity between species is discussed, but also within species (genetic diversity) and between ecosystems. How large diversity is actually needed to maintain productivity is not known. It is commonly argued, however, that while only a few species are needed to sustain ecosystem services at a certain moment, a pool of species with slightly different niches and functions is needed in order to keep ecosystem functions at times of changes (e.g. Vandermeer et al [19]). The ability to absorb changes while maintaining function is often referred to as resilience. The concept of resilience is further set out in Folke et al [20], who also emphasises that 'by decreasing biodiversity and favouring monocultures, the capacity of ecosystems to sustain society with goods and services becomes more vulnerable to disturbances and environmental, social or political change' (p.27).

2.2.5 Total potential cropland

FAO [13] estimated total potential cropland on a global scale. Above the 1,463 Mha already (1994) cultivated, the authors found that another 2,386 Mha seemed to be available for further expansion. Protected areas on cultivable land and areas for settlements, which mainly were situated on arable land, were excluded in the assessment. Most of the potential additional cropland were found to be in Sub-Saharan Africa and in South and Central America [13].

Young [21] compared FAO's figures [13] with some other estimates (FAO [22, 23], Alexandratos [24], Fischer and Heilig [25] and Luyten [26]) of global total cultivable land, and found that they arrived at more or less the same area of available land. Young also questioned these figures: based on his own experience in selected countries and uncertainties in available data, he suggested that in reality only half or less of the estimated additional land (not under current cultivation) were available.

3 Discussion

3.1 Possibilities for reduced land use

Figure 2 shows the difference between the extremes in the reviewed land use projections, compared to the situation today and to total potential cropland. The figure focuses on the variation among the more central estimates and excludes the values from Nonhebel [11], that can be found in table 1. Differences in assumptions of food composition and production systems make huge differences in projected land use. Both extremes for food production came from Penning de Vries et al [7]: the minimal land use from a vegetarian diet and yield oriented agriculture, and the maximum from an affluent diet and environmentally oriented agriculture. With the maximum projection almost all available cropland (according to the FAO projections) is used for food production.

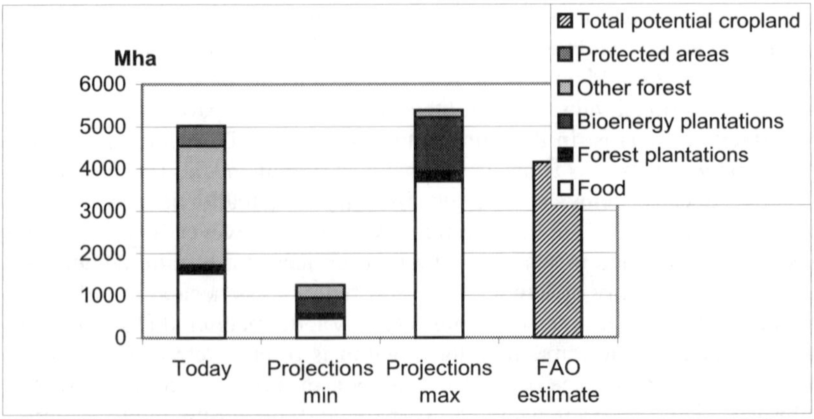

Figure 2: Extremes of projections in Table 1, compared to today's situation and to total potential cropland.

Changed diet has been suggested also by other authors as a mean to increase resource efficiency (Wirsenius [27]) and reduce emissions and energy use (Carlsson-Kanyama [28]) in food production. Decreased energy use in the food production can also contribute to reduced land use for bioenergy plantations.

Also assumptions regarding agricultural production systems are essential for calculated land use. If, again, using the assumptions by Penning de Vries et al [7] as example, yields in their environmentally oriented agriculture are less than half those of the yield oriented, which result in, for the affluent diet, a difference of more than 2,200 Mha between the production systems. The yield-oriented scenarios are dependent on high inputs of energy, fertilisers and pesticides. A review of 76 studies comparing the impact on biodiversity from organic and conventional farming practices showed that a wide range of taxa, from birds and mammals to micro organisms, have been found to benefit from organic practices (Hole et al [29]). It might be possible to keep a necessary biodiversity also with intensive farming practices, but as proposed by Swift et al [17] it might then be necessary to mix intensively farmed fields with areas with larger diversity on landscape level, that can provide new species in case of extinction of necessary species in the fields. In any case land is needed for maintaining biodiversity.

Future production systems will probably be affected in many ways by climate changes as a result of increased greenhouse effect. For example changes in temperature and precipitation will presumably lead to reduced yields in some areas and increased in others (Parry et al [30]). The overall result is not known, but preservation of biodiversity that increases the resilience in order to keep ecosystem functions despite changed environment appear even more important in the light of coming changes.

Gilland's projection [8] showed that the area demanded for cereal production was only about half compared to total crop production [1, 2]. If cultivation of crops such as tobacco, coffee and cotton could be substantially reduced, it seems as if much land could be saved. Non-food crops might however become more important: they serve increasingly to produce a wide range of biodegradable materials for example for packaging and other materials, but also pharmaceutical products (Penning de Vries et al [7]). With diminishing oil reserves such plantations are important replacements for many materials used today.

The contribution of biomass to the global energy use differs among different projections, but it often constitutes a significant part of the renewables, in some scenarios as much as half of total energy supply in 2050 (Berndes et al [3]). Scenarios assuming large share of bioenergy often include policies addressing climate change, although also scenarios not characterised as ecologically driven, for example IIASA and WEC's A2 and A3 scenarios [1], reach high levels of bioenergy. Bioenergy resources are often locally available; conversion into secondary energy carriers is feasible without high capital investments; it has positive effects on soil organic matters on degraded land; it can be used to reduce greenhouse gases from fossil fuels; and it may create new jobs in rural areas (Hoogwijk et al [6]). In contrast to many other renewables, such as PV systems, it is not intermittent, and functioning and affordable technique is available. It is therefore probable that the potential for biomass production for energy will be used in the future, if we keep goals of sustainability, and unless revolutionary developments on new energy sources or new techniques are made.

4 Conclusions and policy implications

Even if assuming that available calculations of total potential cropland is correct, it is clear from the projections reviewed in this paper that there is not enough suitable land to realise the highest projected levels of production of food, forest products and biomass for energy, if we care for biodiversity and future productivity. There are however options to reduce the land use, choices concerning diet, agricultural methods and composition and magnitude of future energy systems. It is evident that land is a limiting resource for the future, that has to be considered in policies for all activities using cultivable land. Studies arriving at the conclusion that there is spare land has to be taken with caution in light of the studies reviewed in this paper.

Countries with excess land, such as Sweden, should be aware of the lack of this resource on a global scale, and policies for e.g. bioenergy plantations should consider these limitations. According to the projections reviewed, assuming that there are large areas of spare land for bioenergy cultivation involve the assumption that not all people can have an affluent diet, based on an environmentally oriented agriculture. It is therefore important to find policies aiming at more sustainable consumption patterns, above all for food and energy.

Acknowledgements

Many thanks to Professor Dean Abrahamson for useful ideas and comments on an earlier manuscript. The work was carried out within a project funded by Formas.

References

[1] IIASA and WEC, *Global Energy Perspectives to 2050 and Beyond*, World Energy Council: London, 1995.

[2] Rogner, H.-H. Energy resources. *World energy assessment: energy and the challenge of sustainability*, ed. Goldemberg, J. United Nations Development Programme: New York, pp. 2000.

[3] Berndes, G., Hoogwijk, M. and van den Broek, R., The contribution of biomass in the future global energy supply: a review of 17 studies. *Biomass and Bioenergy*, **25** pp. 1-28, 2003.

[4] FAO, FAOSTAT Database, http://apps.fao.org.

[5] FAO *Global forest resources assessment 2000: main report*, FAO: Rome, 2001.

[6] Hoogwijk, M., Faaij, A., van den Broek, R., Berndes, G., Gielen, D. and Turkenburg, W., Exploration of the ranges of the global potential of biomass for energy. *Biomass and Bioenergy*, **25** pp. 119-133, 2003.

[7] Penning de Vries, F.W.T., Rabbinge, R. and Groot, J.J.R., Potential and attainable food production and food security in different regions. *Philosophical Transactions of the Royal Society in London*, **352** pp. 917-928, 1997.

[8] Gilland, B. World population and food supply Can food production keep pace with population growth in the next half-century? *Food Policy*, **27** pp. 47-63, 2002.

[9] FAO *The global outlook for future wood supply from forest plantations*, FAO Forestry Policy and Planning Division: Rome, 2000.

[10] Johansson, T.B., Kelly, H., Reddy, A.K.N. and Williams, R.H., A renewables-intensive global energy scenario. Appendix to Chapter 1. *Renewable Energy. Sources for Fuels and Electricity.*, ed. Johansson, T.B., Kelly, H., Reddy, A.K.N. and Williams, R.H., Earthscan Publications Ltd and Island Press: London and Washington D.C., pp. 1993.

[11] Nonhebel, S. Renewable energy and food supply: will there be enough land? *Renewable and Sustainable Energy Reviews*, **9 (2)**, pp. 191-201, 2005.

[12] Myers, N., Mittermeier, R.A., Mittermeier, C.G., da Fonseca, G.A.B. and Kent, J., Biodiversity hotspots for conservation priorities. *Nature*, **403** pp. 853-858, 2000.

[13] FAO *Land resource potential and constraints at regional and country levels*, FAO: Rome, 2000.

[14] United Nations Population Division *World Population Prospects. The 2002 Revision. Highlights*, UN: New York, 2003.

[15] Gowdy, J.M. and McDaniel, C.N., One world, one experiment: addressing the biodiversity - economics conflict. *Ecological Economics*, **15** pp. 181-192, 1995.

[16] Mann, C.C. and Plummer, M.L., The high cost of biodiversity. *Science*, **260** pp. 1868-1871, 1993.

[17] Swift, M.J., Izac, A.-M.N. and van Noordwijk, M., Biodiversity and ecosystem services in agricultural landscapes - are we asking the right questions? *Agriculture, Ecosystems and Environment*, **104** pp. 113-134, 2004.

[18] UNEP, http://www.biodiv.org/.

[19] Vandermeer, J., van Noordwijk, M., Anderson, J., Ong, C. and Perfecto, I., Global change and multi-species agroecosystems: Concepts and issues. *Agriculture, Ecosystems and Environment*, **67** pp. 1-22, 1998.

[20] Folke, C., Carpenter, S., Elmqvist, T., Gunderson, L., Holling, C., Walker, B., Bengtsson, J., Berkes, F., Colding, J., Danell, K., Falkenmark, M., Gordon, L., Kasperson, R., Kautsky, N., Kinzig, A., Levin, S., Mäler, K.-G., Moberg, F., Ohlsson, L., Olsson, P., Ostrom, E., Reid, W., Johan, R., Savenije, H. and Svedin, U., *Resilience and Sustainable Development: Building Adaptive Capacity in a world of Transformations*, Ministry of the Environment: Stockholm, 2002.

[21] Young, A. Is there really spare land? A critique of estimates of available cultivable land in developing countries. *Environment, Development and Sustainability*, **1** pp. 3-18, 1999.
[22] FAO *Agriculture: toward 2000*, FAO: Rome, 1981.
[23] FAO *Land, food and People*, FAO: Rome, 1984.
[24] Alexandratos, N. (ed). *World Agriculture: towards 2010. An FAO Study.*, FAO and John Wiley & Sons Ltd.: Chichester, 1995.
[25] Fischer, G. and Heilig, G.K., Population momentum and the demand on land and water resources. *Land Resources: on the edge of the Malthusian Precipice?*, ed. Greenland, D.J., Gregory, P.J. and Nye, P.H., CAB International: Wallingford, UK, pp. 9-29, 1998.
[26] Luyten, J.C. *Sustainable world food production and environment*, AB-DLO, Delft Hydraulics: Wageningen, 1995.
[27] Wirsenius, S. Efficiencies and biomass appropriation of food commodities on global and regional levels. *Agricultural Systems*, **77** pp. 219-255, 2003.
[28] Carlsson-Kanyama, A. Climate change and dietary choices: How can emissions of greenhouse gases from food consumption be reduced? *Food Policy*, **23 (3-4)**, pp. 277-293, 1998.
[29] Hole, D.G., Perkins, A.J., Wilson, J.D., Alexander, I.H., Grice, P.V. and Evans, A.D., Does organic farming benefit biodiversity? *Biological Conservation*, **122** pp. 113-130, 2005.
[30] Parry, M.L., Rosenzweig, C., Iglesias, A., Livermore, M. and Fischer, G., Effects of climate change on global food production under SRES emissions and socio-economic scenarios. *Global Environmental Change*, **14** pp. 53-67, 2004.

Incentive policy in the area of the housing market for the implementation of the Kyoto targets: the case of Austria

A. Hoeltl
Department of Economics and Management Science, Danube University Krems, Austria

Abstract

According to the Kyoto protocol and the EU burden sharing, Austria has to reduce its greenhouse gas emissions by 13 percent from the 1990 levels by 2008-2012. The subject of house heating has an enormous unused carbon dioxide emissions reduction potential, which indicates that existing institutional conditions do not induce the required energy saving investments.

The paper is aimed at developing an efficient incentive mechanism for implementing the Kyoto targets in the area of the residential housing stock. Current Austrian housing market regulations cause a cut-off of incentives for thermal-energetic renovation in the area of rental housing. Therefore the paper concentrates on developing an incentive scheme offering a solution for the investor/user problem on the strictly regulated rental housing market in Austria.
Keywords: Kyoto targets, housing market, emissions reduction, rent regulations, investor/user problem, thermal-energetic renovation, incentive mechanism, Nash solution.

1 Introduction

According to the EU burden sharing Austria has to reduce its greenhouse gas emissions by 13 percent. The Austrian climate strategy believes the largest reduction potential (28%) is found in the area of heating and other such private household utilities, due to the high consumption of energy in the housing sector and the mainly bad thermal repair of the housing stock.

From the economic point of view the greenhouse gas and carbon dioxide (CO_2) reduction is strongly correlated with the public good problem. This means that every household benefits from a CO_2 reduction and nobody can be excluded from the advantages. The existence of public goods leads to the classical situation of market failure. Individual rational behaviour causes socially unwelcome results. In view of the large unused reduction potential in the housing sector the existing institutional conditions do not induce the required energy and CO_2 saving investments. The paper is aimed at developing an efficient incentive mechanism for implementing the Kyoto targets in the area of the residential housing stock.

2 The housing sector in Austria

The amount of main residence flats in Austria in 2002 was 3,312.500 from which 39% (1,299.700) were rented. Most of these flats (76%) are situated in buildings which are in need of renovation. The CO_2 emissions, which have a lot to do with the burning of fossil fuels, are with a share of 80.5% the greatest problem of the greenhouse gas emissions. A quarter of the Austrian energy consumption is used in private households for general heating and heating of water, therefore they emit 18.5% of the Austrian CO_2 gases and/or 15% of the Austrian greenhouse gases. The economic reduction potential of energy in the area of housing is estimated at 25%. This means the total Austrian energy consumption could be reduced by 6.25% (on the basis of 1990) and one third of the Kyoto target for Austria could be fulfilled. About 80% of all new built and renovated flats are partly financed through public funding. The renovation of the housing stock receives 20% of these subsidies. The existing institutions in this area could be put to better use for the realisation of the enormous energy and CO_2 reduction potential in the housing sector.

3 General framework

3.1 3.1 Public good

Greenhouse gas emissions reduction is a global public good. A result of the economic theory of public goods is a lack of environmental measures in a system of voluntary contributions of the individuals. The inefficiency of such mechanisms increases with the number of beneficiaries of these measures. The higher the number of beneficiaries, the larger is the discrepancy between the efficient quantity of the public good and the actually available quantity.

The effects of the greenhouse gas emissions are still unclear und controversial, therefore it cannot be expected that the individuals know their marginal benefit from a reduction, even if they would be willing to reveal it truthfully. According to the economic theory individuals do not have preferences concerning the reduction of greenhouse effects.

Seeing as CO_2 reduction is fixed by the Kyoto protocol and the Austrian climate strategy, we do not have to find an efficient reduction scale in the area of housing. However, we do have to find the most cost effective way of reducing in order to reach our goals. An incentive mechanism for thermal-energetic housing renovation should encourage each individual to act according to the respective reduction costs.

3.2 Legal general framework

In Austria thermal-energetic renovation of flats which are subject to the price regulation has to be financed by a rent increase for a limited time. Such increases are approved by a specific court for a maximum of ten years and take effect six months after the lease has started. To be able to finance an energetic general renovation, a rent increase for ten years is necessary. Because of the legal general framework the approval of a rent increase is only realistic, if the duration of the lease is at least ten and a half years. According to the present method to ascertain the market value of real estate, thermal-energetic renovations do not cause an increase in value of the concerned buildings.

3.3 Partial analytical approach for the rental housing sector

Under certain conditions of information and assuming there is a competitive energy market and rational behaviour of the individuals, an energy tax is an efficient economic incentive instrument, one the one hand for thermal-energetic building renovation and on the other hand for appropriate behavior in energy use.

Due to the strict rental housing market regulations, an energy tax does not support the necessary building renovations, because the landlord in charge of the renovation is not affected by the level of the energy costs or does not profit from their reduction. A rational tenant will vary his or her energy consumption as much as possible depending on energy prices, but his or her possibilities of investments in energy saving renovations are restricted in a rented flat.

Due to the fact that 39% of all flats in Austria are rented and we are not confronted with competitive conditions on the housing market, this paper is aimed at developing an incentive system with a partial analytical approach particularly for the investor/user problem.

4 Thermal-energetic renovation at the status quo

The following analysis shows thermal-energetic renovation results for the rental housing market, that could be expected under the present legal situation in Austria. Only the thermal-energetic renovation sector has been examined, not the entire housing market. All other variables of the housing market have no influence on the model solution.

4.1 Assumptions

i. The examination concentrates on buildings with at least three rented flats under renting regulations.
ii. The amortization period for investments in thermal-energetic renovations (minus a possible public subsidy) is ten years, the technical life is twenty years. The investment costs comprise of only the costs which are directly

assigned to the thermal-energetic renovation, meaning only costs which directly induce energy reductions. The energy saving is 50% of the total energy costs, or 10% of the investment costs annually.

iii. A thermal-energetic renovation has to be financed by a rent increase for a limited time.

iv. A rent increase will not be approved by the court for more than ten years, at the earliest six months after the commencement of the lease, and at most on the level of the investment costs minus a public subsidy. The increase will be divided between the tenants according to the respective useable floor area of their flats in relation to the total useable floor area of the building. No rent increase will be approved, if the duration of the lease does not exceed four years and for flats of the category D (water and toilet on the corridor, rent > EUR 0,66/sm/month). Due to the fact that general thermal-energetic renovations need a rent increase for at least ten years and the duration of the lease must not end within this period, such increases for flats with time limited leases are feasible, if the duration of the lease exceeds ten and a half years.

v. The rent will fall back to the level before the renovation, after a period of not more than ten years, for which the court has approved the rent increase. However, the benefits of the energy costs reduction work still further ten years and after the amortization they go directly to the tenant because of the discontinuation of the rent increase (see figure 1).

vi. The advantage of the benefits for landlord and tenant is linear in money.

vii. The landlord does not know for certain if all flats in his or her building will be rented within the entire period of rent increase and by that the exact amount of the rent increase he or she can achieve.

viii. Due to the present method for determining the market value of real estate, thermal-energetic renovations do not imply an increase of the value of the concerned building.

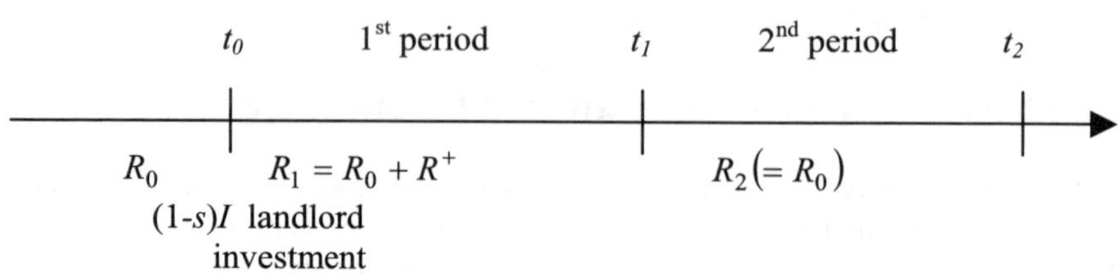

Figure 1: Changes in rent under thermal-energetic renovation R0...present rent, R1...level of rent in the period of rent increase, R+...rent increase, R2...level of rent after the period of rent increase.

4.2 The status quo model

The matrix of results in table 1 shows the benefits for the landlord in two different states of the environment. First under the conditions of a rent increase of zero (R^+=0) and second, if the court approves a rent increase at the highest possible level (R^+=(1-s)I). At best the landlord can achieve benefits of zero. The strategy „no renovation“ is the dominant one for the landlord, which means that he or she will always choose this strategy, because it is always better or at least has same result as the “renovation” strategy.

Table 1: Matrix of results for the landlord in the status quo model. I…investment in thermal-energetic renovation, s…share of subsidy from the investment costs, $0 \le s \le 1$.

		state of the environment	
		$R^+=0$	$R^+=(1-s)I$
strategy	*no renovation*	0	0
	renovation	$-(1-s)I$	0

A public subsidy for the thermal-energetic renovation is paid to the landlord as he or she is the owner and investor of the building which has to be renovated. However, this subsidy will be passed indirectly to the tenant due to the reduced rent increase by the amount of the subsidy. The present general framework does not support the political CO_2 reduction goals in the rental housing area.

5 Incentive model for the rental housing sector

The suggested model is based on the present institutional regulations, the assumptions from 4.1 are valid apart from iv. and v.

5.1 Incentive model

The most important factor of the suggested incentive system is the participation of the landlord with the benefits from the energy costs reduction. The benefits *B(I)* as a function of the investment correspond to the energy costs reduction minus the investment costs which the landlord has to pay:

$$B(I) = CR(I) - (1 - s)I \tag{1}$$

CR(I) describes the costs reduction for heating energy for the entire effected duration of the investment as a function of the investment. The costs reduction is influenced by the expected energy price. The aim of the landlord is the maximization of the benefits from the renovation investment. As soon as his or her share of the benefits exceeds zero, he or she maximizes this share, this is equal to the maximization of the total benefits from the renovation. For this the rent increase, considered over the entire effected duration of the investment, has to exceed the investment costs minus the subsidy ($R^+ > (1-s)I$) for guaranteeing a profit from the thermal-energetic renovation for the landlord. The matrix of results in table 2 shows the benefits for the landlord in two different states of the environment. First if the tenant gets a share of (1-a) of the benefits, with $0 < a < 1$, and second, the best case for the landlord, in which he or she gets the total benefits from the thermal-energetic renovation by means of the rent increase.

Table 2: Matrix of results for the landlord in the incentive model.

		state of the environment	
		R^+=CR-(1-a)B	R^+=CR
strategy	*no renovation*	0	0
	renovation	a(CR-(1-s)I)	CR-(1-s)I

In the first case the landlord can receive benefits from the thermal-energetic renovation as soon as a is positive. In the best case of the incentive system, he or she gets the total benefits as a difference between the energy costs reduction over the entire effected duration of the thermal-energetic measure, and the investment costs he or she has paid him- or herself. The tenant passes on the total energy costs reduction to the landlord via the rent increase, a is in this case 1. The condition for the feasibility of the renovation is that a as the landlord share at the benefits from the renovation is positive, which implies that $R^+ > (1\text{-}s)I$ must be valid.

5.2 Sharing out of the benefits

In the course of negotiations between the landlord and the tenant about the sharing out of the benefits in proportion a : (1-a), $0 \le a \le 1$, the result would be the Nash solution with $a = 0{,}5$, under the assumption of similar negotiations power of both parties. According to Nash´s idea (Nash [7]), the Nash solution is a fair negotiations solution which should be accepted by rational players. This solution is pareto optimal, meaning that no player can improve his or her position without worsening the position of the other player.

Assuming that the advantages from the benefits are linear in money for the landlord and the tenant, each point on the “benefits line” $B(I^*)$ in figure 3 shows a feasible sharing out of the benefits. In a two-person game the negotiation results for symmetrical games is on the 45° line. The point of intersection of the axis of symmetry with $B(I^*)$ is the Nash solution u^*. This point of intersection is unique, which means it only contains one element. Starting at the conflict point (0,0) (vector of paying out in the case of „no renovation“), the Nash solution means distributing the benefits in equal parts. Initially all the energy costs reduction $CR(I^*)$ goes to the tenant, due to his or her lower energy costs. Therefore, a correction of the sharing out from the point $CR(I^*)$ to the Nash solution at u' is required. This implies that the tenant passes on $\overline{CCR(I^*)}$ of the energy costs reduction to the landlord via the rent increase.

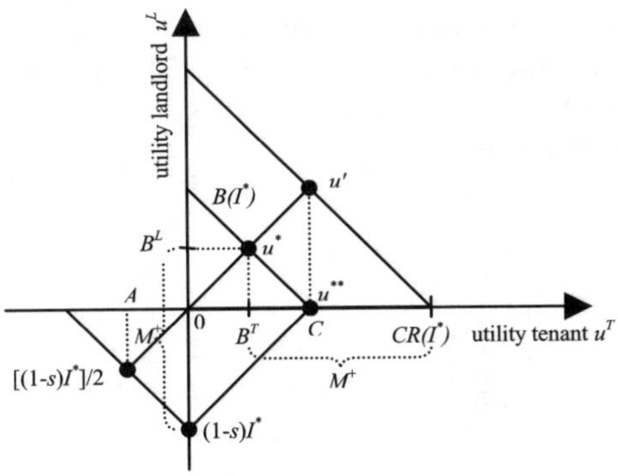

Figure 3: Nash solution for the sharing out of the benefits. According to Holler & Illing [3], B^T...benefits tenant, B^L...benefits landlord,

Because of the distribution of property, the landlord is in charge of the total investment costs. If we consider the resulting payments from that, at point $(1\text{-}s)I^*$ in figure 3, as the start of the rule about the distribution of the benefits, there would be a Nash solution u^{**}. This implies a lower share of the benefits as u^* for the landlord and a higher share for the tenant. The exact share of the benefits in this situation would be zero for the landlord, and the tenant would get the total benefits. The tenant would have to contribute half to the investment costs, with $[(1\text{-}s)I^*]/2$, to achieve u^* as the Nash solution from the negotiations. This is impossible due to the distribution of property. Therefore the tenant could not refund his or her investment costs share until he or she has received the benefits. This means that the resulting distribution of the benefits from the Nash solution u^{**} has to be corrected to the Nash solution u^*. Starting from the conflict point $(1\text{-}s)I^*$, not a plain, but a corrected Nash solution would be chosen. $\overline{B^T C}$ correspond to $\overline{A0}$, which means that the landlord would recoup the investment costs from the tenant. In total the landlord must have received an amount corresponding to $\overline{B^T CR(I^*)}$ via the rent increase, to realise the Nash solution in the negotiation game „thermal-energetic renovation".

5.3 The benefits of the tenant

Assuming that, in the status quo, a rational landlord will not enforce a thermal-energetic renovation, the suggested incentive system means a pareto improvement for the landlord as well as for the tenant. Before the thermal-energetic renovation the level of the rent is R, the energy costs are EC (see figure 4) and the tenant is willing to pay the amount LC for living costs (rent including overhands and energy costs). If a thermal-energetic renovation is carried out by the landlord, the tenant will have an energy costs reduction of *CR*. If the benefits are shared between the tenant and the landlord, the rent increase is R''^{+}, the present rent by that R'' (over the entire effected duration of the investment) and the living costs correspond to LC''. In the case of the thermal-energetic renovation and the above suggested sharing out of the benefits, the living costs for the tenant decreases. B^T in figure 4 shows the benefits for the tenant from the investment.

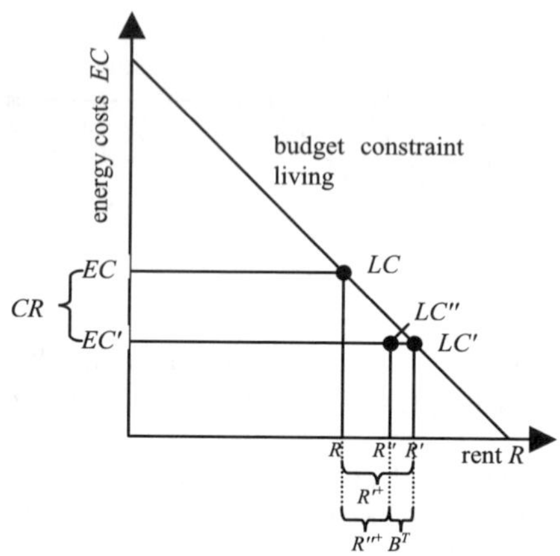

Figure 4: Budget contraint of the tenant for living.

In certain cases, if the court decides to give the entire benefits to the landlord, the rent increase for the tenant would be R'^{+} which corresponds to the entire energy costs reduction C*R*. The living costs LC′ would than still be on the budget constraint line of the tenant.

5.4 Incentive model on the aggregated level

The aggregated reduction function provides the government information about the optimum level of the thermal-energetic renovation in the regulated private rental housing area. It also provides information about possible CO_2 reduction and potential influence of subsidies. The optimum level of investment in thermal-energetic renovation on the aggregated level results from the maximization of the benefits:

$$\max_{I \geq 0} B(I) = CR(I) - (1-s)I \tag{2}$$

If I^* is the optimum level, the following first-order condition has to be fulfilled:

$$CR'(I^*) = (1-s) \quad for\ I^* > 0 \tag{3}$$

This means, that the level of investment is at its maximum at the point where the marginal heating costs reduction is equal to the marginal costs of a further unit of investment (minus the subsidy share).

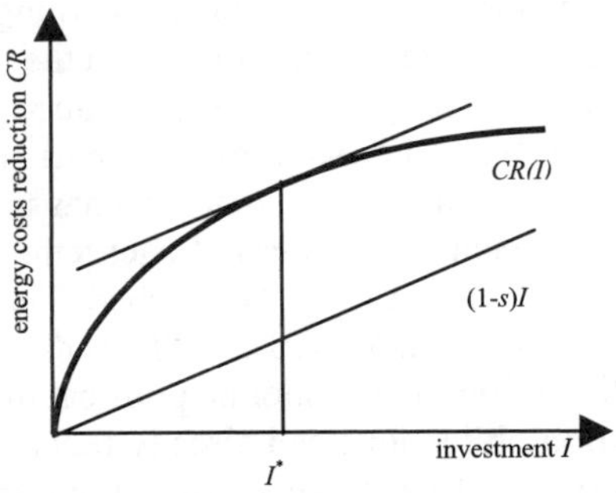

Figure 5: The optimum level of investment in thermal-energetic renovation on the aggregated level.

5.5 The Influence of the level of subsidies to I*

According to an increasing subsidy *s*, (1-*s*) decreases and by that the iso-profit line becomes flatter and the contact point between the iso-profit line and the reduction curve is situated more on the right side (under the assumption that the reduction function is concave). The level of the optimum investment increases with the level of the subsidy (see figure 6 with $s^A < s^B$).

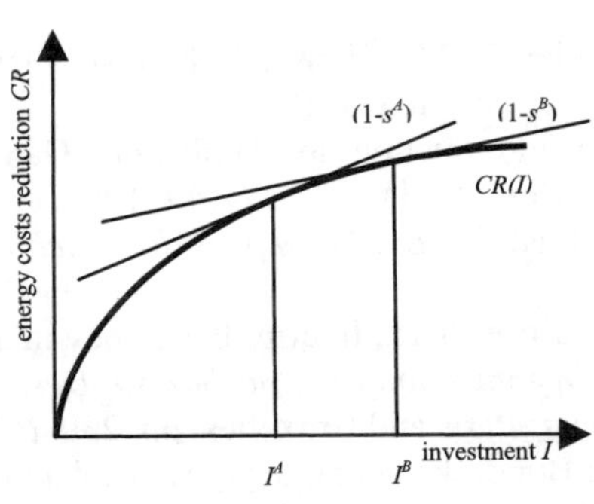

Figure 6: The influence of the level of subsidy to I^*.

The government is able to control the level of the thermal-energetic renovation, and by doing that, it also controls the level of the CO_2 reduction in the area of housing along the reduction goal, fixed in the climate strategy 2008/2012, by means of the fixing of the level of the subsidy in this area.

6 Conclusions

To reach the political target concerning the CO_2 reduction in the private rental housing sector, the landlord has to benefit from the thermal-energetic renovation. For this reason, the rent increase regulation concerning rental laws has to be changed. The level of the rent increase has to exceed the investment costs ($(1\text{-}s)I$) for which the landlord is in charge. The decision about the distribution of the benefits ($B(I)=CR(I)\text{-}(1\text{-}s)I$) can be made by the court which also approves the rent increase. The landlords benefit share a always has to exceed zero to give the rental housing sector an incentive for thermal-energetic renovation and then the climate political targets in this sector can be reached. The Nash solution with the landlords benefit share a=0,5 is suggested as a "fair" distribution.

Due to the realisation of pointed economic political measures, a quarter of the Austrian Kyoto reduction obligations can already be carried out. The suggested incentive system offers an efficient and easily implemented solution for the investor/user problem in the strictly regulated Austrian rental housing market. This is on the one hand a pareto improvement for the landlord as well as for the tenant, and on the other hand an important contribution in reaching the Austrian Kyoto targets without great charge to the public budget, if housing subsidies are used for renovating old buildings rather than building new ones.

Not only the international obligations in connection with the Kyoto protocol, but also the expected subsequent costs due to the climate change for Austria, necessitate a quick implementation of efficient solution concepts as the incentive scheme for thermal-energetic renovation in the rental housing sector suggests.

References

[1] Abele, H. & Winkler, G. M., Ökonomische Instrumente für den Post-Kyoto-Prozess. *Working paper*, Vienna, 1999.

[2] Gibbons, R., An Introduction to Applicable Game Theory. *Journal of Economic Perspectives,* **11(1)**, pp. 127-149, 1997.

[3] Holler, M.J. & Illing, G., *Einführung in die Spieltheorie*, Springer-Verlag: Berlin, 2003.

[4] Ledyard, J.O. & Palfrey, T.R., Interim Efficiency in a Public Good Problem. *Topics in Social Organization and Mechanism Design*, ed. C. d´Aspremont, De Broeck & Lacier: Paris and Bruxelles, pp. 239-261, 1999.

[5] Mietrechtsgesetz; Bundeskanzleramt. www.ris.bka.gv.at

[6] Myerson, R.B., Mechanism Design by an Informed Principal. *Econometrica,* **51(6)**, pp. 1767-1797, 1983.

[7] Nash, J.F., The Bargaining Problem. *Econometrica,* **18**, pp. 155-162, 1950.

[8] Stahl, K. (ed.). *Microeconomic Models of Housing Markets*, Springer-Verlag: Berlin and New York, 1985.

[9] Statistik Austria, *Wohnungen. Ergebnisse der Wohnungserhebung im Mikrozensus September 2002*, Vienna, 2003.

How nature and men could better interact: on ecosystem service evaluation and nutrient recycling in a principal-agent-framework

E. A. Nuppenau
Department of Agricultural Economics, University of Giessen, Germany

Abstract

This paper deals with the economic and ecological aspects of recycling organic matter to agriculture. It perceives nature as a service provider for such things as decomposing waste and enrichment of soil nutrients. As a novelty, nature's services are supported by human labour, external nutrient influx, and land assignment. Nature is perceived as seeking fitness and a quasi-objective function of nature is introduced, whereas humans are seeking services at minimal payments. 1. The paper starts with nature composed of an accumulating and a decomposing compartment. 2. Nature's fitness and human profits are simultaneously derived in a sequential process of optimal behaviour, i.e. we model the interaction by applying a principal agent framework whereas nature is an agent and humans are the principal. 3. As a result, an optimal exchange of services (recycling) and payments (labour) is endogenously determined. As a reference, we can consider alternative dumping costs of waste and have to refer to nutrient prices in agriculture. With respect to testing the economic viability of recycling, the competitiveness of organic matter recycling is assured against the dumping of waste. By this we receive the first suggestion of a frontier function that delineates fitness and welfare.
Keywords: recycling, evaluation of econ system services, principal-agent-model.

1 Introduction

Recycling organic matter, closing nutrient cycles, and improving energy efficiency is en vogue in agriculture. Generally speaking, to contemplate on ecological-economic efficiency of food and nutrient systems is popular [1]. In principle nature offers a double-dividend or cheap service to humans:

decomposing organic matter into nutrients (i.e. waste disposal) and providing soil nutrients for farming (i.e. organic fertilizer) [2]. However, the ecological economics of closing nutrient cycles appears not to be fully explored yet. In this paper, we will explore a new route using a principal-agent-framework [3]. This framework will help us to better understand nature's service provision in economic and ecological terms.

The new framework will enable us to draw better conclusions on the performance of system alternatives. We show how nature's services can be evaluated more correctly on basis of a joint concept of integrated evaluation. With respect to nutrient recycling we follow the tradition of Liebig, who suggested that urban waste should be recycled in rural areas, and that exergy-optimised systems are better than systems based on strong external energy inflows [4]. The paper is organised as follows: 1. We start with a conceptual outline. 2. An introduction to the formulation of objective functions will provide the groundwork for behavioural equations of nature and humans. 3. A quasi steady state outline will show how to evaluate the fitness of nature. 4. Humans as farmers and waste managers build their objectives and behaviour around nature. 5. The problem will be solved by the principal-agent principle of sequenced solutions and property rights are outlined.

2 Conceptual outline and basic framework

We start with Figure 1a which is a simplified description of a plant-nutrient-organic-matter cycle. Firstly, we have an accumulation unit of organic matter. This unit uses plant nutrients and sunlight to build up biomass based on species composition. With respect to explaining processes, which starts soon, we may take an economic-like approach of revealed preferences, now applied to nature. Organic matter production and species composition are specified simultaneously as given categories of a functional approach. The economic setting implies that a conceptual framework of fitness optimisation is given, which is a mixture of biomass and biodiversity [5], [6], and [7]. As a result we can explain observable specie combination. This allows us to derive parameters that depict the system. For it we, secondly, introduce a decomposing unit producing plant nutrients by recycling organics applying an approach of revealed goals and observable behaviour.

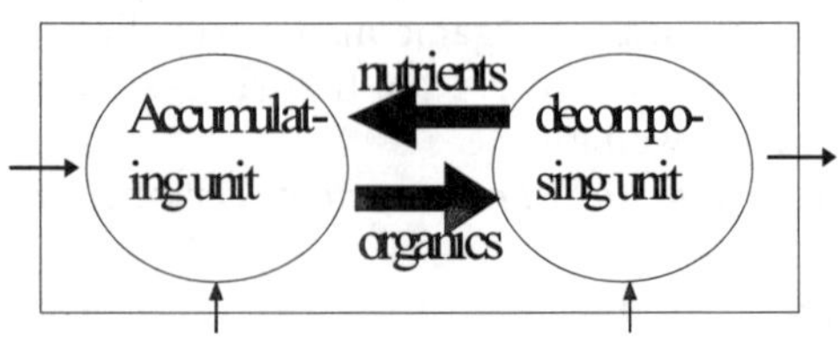

Figure 1a: Flows and recycling in nature.

As will be shown soon this conceptual outline of nature as an exchange system of plant nutrients and organic matter enables us to link functional aspects of nature's behaviour to human activities.

Note, no further structural insight is needed. Humans can work with revelation of "behaviour" of the accumulating and decomposing units. Next, in Figure 1b we add a decoupled farming and organic waste management system to make it clear. Humans use artificial fertiliser to produce food; food is consumed and remains are dumped outside the system including crop residues and human excrements. To describe the system as economically viable, farmers receive money and the system is viable as long as exogenous factors like income, labour, fertiliser, and energy are brought into it. Economic systems are described by financial flows and occupation. A human system may be so strong that the natural system diminishes and both are decoupled; in such cases humans are not recognizing ecological system services.

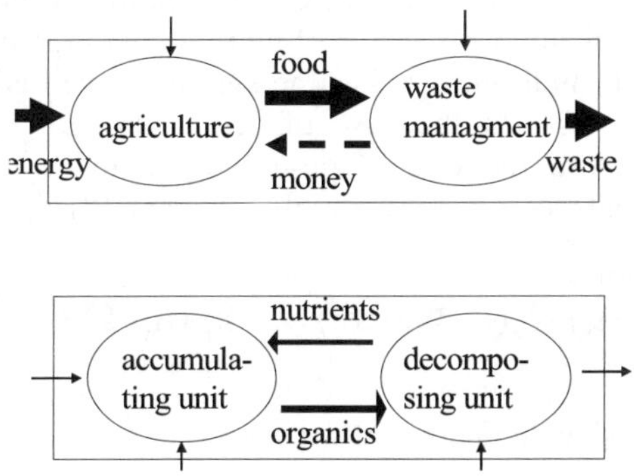

Figure 1b: Farming and waste management.

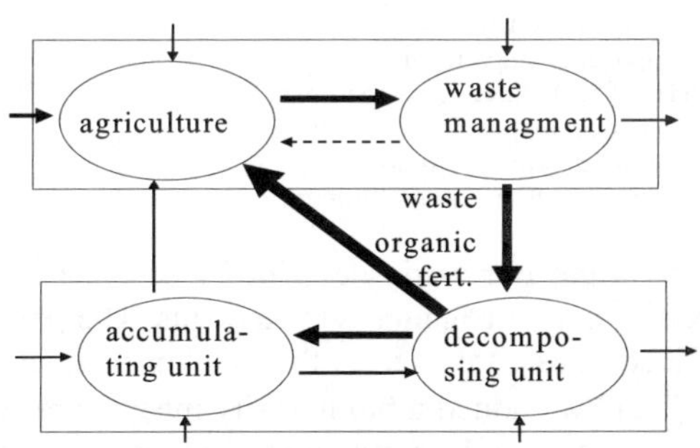

Figure 1c: Service flows.

In contrast in Figure 1c we see how the systems can be linked by physical exchange. Three types of physical service are explicitly modelled. 1. The decomposing unit takes over parts of the function of a human waste management unit by decomposing organic remains into plant nutrients. 2. Pant nutrients are supplied to agriculture as organic manure. 3. We further assume that a healthy nature supports agriculture as balance of prey and predatory. We need to comment on specific roles, functions, flows, and payments. With respect to the role of an accumulating unit, it has to be recognized that an equilibrium (steady state) has previously existed in a natural situation, characterising decomposing and accumulating units as open system. Hence, as a reference, we have to model how organic matter flows shift the healthiness and fitness of the eco-system, first.

3 Basic model outline and derivation of behavioural equations

3.1 Nature

A first step is to describe the eco-system under the criteria of an optimising system [5]. Hereby we can obtain a species composition [6] that is goal oriented, that describes physical flows by means of nutrient and organic matter exchange The idea is simply to indicate whether the system is well adapted to a certain environments or not [7]. In the case of plant nutrients and organic matter recycling, we are given the task of describing a flow-system that basically includes compartments being most simply. A goal [8] for the accumulation compartment is:

$$F_a = (1-\varpi)\tau_a s_a + \varpi s_a^{/}(1+s_a) - C_a(s_a - \Phi_{a1} n_d, n_x) + \lambda_{a,1}{}'(n_x + n_d - \Omega_{a2}(s_a + \dot{S}_a) + \lambda_{a,2}(1^{/}\Omega_{a3} s_a - a_0) \quad \text{(1a)}$$

and for the decomposing compartment we have:

$$F_d = (1-\varpi)\tau_d s_d + \varpi s_d^{/}(1+s_d) - C_d(\Omega_a s_d + \Phi_d n_d - s_a) + \lambda_d^1{}'(s_a - \Omega_{d,1} n_d - \Omega_{d,2} \dot{S}_d) \quad \text{(1b)}$$

where:

F_a	= fitness of accumulating compartment
F_d	= fitness of decomposing compartment
s_a	= vector of species of accumulating compartment
s_d	= vector of species of decomposing compartment
n_d	= vector of plant nutrients from decomposer
n_x	= vector of plant nutrients from external source

Equations (1) constitute our basic description of the eco-system as fitness optimising. Each goal function contains two elements. The positive component is organic matter production as contained in the number of species multiplied by a bodyweight "τ_a s_a ", and we added a biodiversity measurement $s_a^{/}(1+ s_a)$ ". The negative element or cost is a loss function. Losses are associated with the procurement of organic matter. We interpret costs as a loss of potential organic matter/energy acquisition. The difference to usual thinking is that conversion is incomplete: a loss s_l is an argument in a "cost function": $s_l = s_a - \Omega_{a,1} n_d$. An analogous argument applies to the decomposing compartment. Here, availability of organic matter from accumulation species and transformation in organic matter of decomposing species is a costly activity (energy consuming), i.e. organic net matter acquisition is the goal for species. Finally, we may think of inter-temporal storage of organic matter in compartments, i.e. growth. For further contemplation on the fruitfulness of the approach, please, do not consider the above presentation as absolutely "true"; rather it enables the construction of fitness. Admittedly, it is a hypothetical construct, but the fruitfulness can be demonstrated when we apply it in order to describe the interaction of the accumulating and decomposing unit.

Importantly, matter flows of the decomposer for nutrients are limited to the availability of organic matter from accumulators and vice versa. Then we have to specify cost functions as treatable mathematical formulations. We assume that cost components are quadratic, i.e. losses increase progressively, if species increase:

$$C_a(.) = \psi_a^{/} s_a - s_a^{/}[0.5\Psi_{a,1} s_a - \Phi_{a1} n_d] + s_a^{/}\Psi_{a,2} n_x + s_a^{/}\Psi_{a,3} l_a \tag{2a}$$

and

$$C_d(.) = \psi_d^{/} s_d + s_d^{/}[\Psi_{d,1} s_a - .5 \cdot \Omega_a s_d - \Phi_d n_d] \tag{2b}$$

Advantages can be seen soon, since quadratic goals provide linear behaviour.

3.2 Nature's behaviour and equilibrium

Note, behaviour in economics is defined as optimal behaviour (best fitted); behavioural equations are normally first order derivatives of goal functions. Then an optimisation of fitness provides a system of linear equations for accumulating:

$$\begin{aligned} &\varpi\tau_a + \varpi s_a - \psi_a - \Psi_{a,1}(s_a - \Phi_{a1} n_d) + \Psi_{a,2} n_x + \lambda_{a,1} + \Omega_{a3}\lambda_{a,2} = 0 \\ &n_x + n_d - \Omega_{a2}(s_a + \dot{S}_a) = 0 \\ &1^{/}\Omega_{a3} s_a - a_0 = 0 \end{aligned} \tag{3a}$$

and decomposing:

$$\begin{aligned} &\tau_d + \varpi s_d - \psi_d - \Psi_{d,1}(s_a - \Omega_a s_d - \Phi_d n_d) + \lambda_s = 0 \\ &s_d - \Omega_{d,1} n_d - \Omega_{d,2}\dot{S}_d = 0 \end{aligned} \tag{3b}$$

The systems (3a) and (3b) could also be stated ad-hoc. The advantage of deriving it from a goal function is the possibility to make inference from observation on "hidden" goals, i.e. in our case "fitness". A major problem is that the above system would initially contain three endogenous variables s_a, s_d, n_d. If no further restrictions are introduced, for instance on land use, the system is not scaled. For simplicity we may assume that a proportionality (3c) has been "designed" within "nature", and humans observe this proportionality as a revealed equilibrium:

$$s_d = \Omega_T s_a \tag{3c}$$

To clarify: we may help ourselves thinking that nature has arranged a proportional composition, made up of diversity, and we use "our" optimisation to describe "nature's technological plan", ex-post. When, we deduce the emergence of a composition of species as a black box and merely try to delineate nature's plan from observation. Equivalently, we may assume a limitation in area giving (3c').

$$a_0 = 1'a_d + 1'a_a = 1'\Omega_{T,d}s_d + 1'\Omega_{T,a}s_a \Leftrightarrow s_d = \Omega_{T,d}^{-1}[a_0 + \Omega_{T,a}s_a] \quad \text{(3c`)}$$

The idea for an equilibrium remains the same. Here decomposers need only minor areas of land, because they do not need sunlight; whence, they are omitted in a land use equation. Restrictions in land use are good when we later refer to farming, which normally needs a bulk of land; this is important for a joint welfare.

3.3 First introduction of humans as farmers and idea of linkage

Humans have two types of interest: to get plant nutrients for farming and to get rid of organic waste. Also we will later look at a situation where agriculture occupies land and farmland is associated with a reduction of area occupied by an accumulating nature. We commence with a description of agriculture in line with the above representation of our eco-system. As a simple representation we consider two elements for exchange: acquisition of plant nutrients by the farm and labour to improve ecosystems as payment. Furthermore land can be constrained

$$U_f = p_f s_f - p_m n_m - C_f(s_t, n_f + n_m, \mathrm{l_f}) + \mu \cdot [1 - I'[\mathrm{l_f} + l_\mathrm{a}] \cdot 1] - \rho' \mathrm{l_a'} \Phi\, \mathrm{l_a} \quad (4)$$

where additionally:

U_f = utility of farming measured as profit
s_f = vector of species raised in farming as sales
s_t = vector of species raised in farming as produce
n_m = nutrients purchased
n_f = nutrients from nature
l_f = labour in farming
l_a = labour to nature

This formulation is sufficient for the exchange in an "eco-economy" or "economy". However, some elements must be altered. In particular, the occupation of vast tracts of land means, that natural accumulation looses land, that decompositions becomes reliant on farm residues, and that farmers may pay special attention to providing residues for decomposition. This aspect will be discussed later. The situation for nature may improve since farmers have access to mineral fertilisers and an initial limited access to mineral nutrients is augmented. By equation

$$s_f = (I - \Omega_R)s_t \quad \textit{and} \quad s_{f,a} = \Omega_R s_t \Leftrightarrow s_f = (I - \Omega_R)\Omega_R^{-1} s_{f,a} \quad (5)$$

where additionally:

$s_{f,a}$ = vector of species raised in farming as sales,

a transformation, farmers provide organic matter. This introduction will help us to reformulate the interface of nature and humans whereas we see nature as agent.

4 Modification of objectives for fitting in principal-agent-nexus

4.1 Nature as agent

Seeing nature as agent we have to think about a type of payment for nature's service. Payments could be perceived as labour and land, both improving fitness of ecosystems. By such deliberations a new chart appears. Figure 2 shows links.

We have to qualify how farming has an impact on organic matter production in the ecosystem involving crops. We assume that there is a one-to-one substitution of organic crop residues for organic matter from natural plants. It is critical to think about this qualification, because we assumed in the initial outlet that there is a predetermined equilibrium between species in compartments of accumulation and decomposition. Organics used by humans appear in nature, for instance, as residues from grassland and grain fields. In the objective functions that were introduced (1), we now, in (1a'), see an externally fixed species set $s_{f,a}$, selected and decided by humans (farmers)!

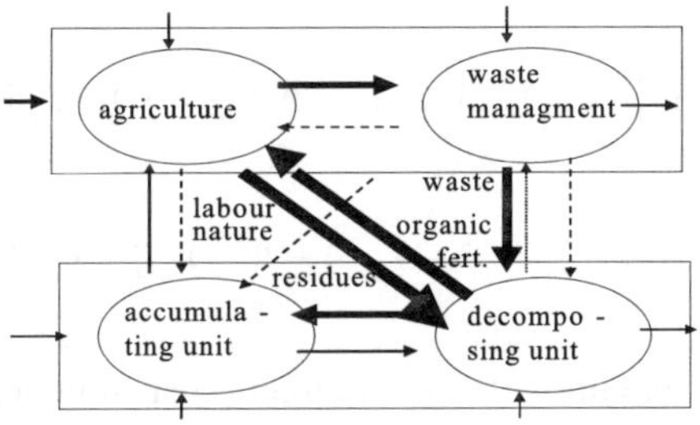

Figure 2: Integrated system.

$$F_a = (1-\varpi)\tau_a(s_a + s_{f,a}) + \varpi s_a'(1+s_a) - C_a(s_a + s_{f,a} - \Phi_{a1} n_d, n_x, l_a) + \lambda_a'(n_x + n_d + n_m - \Omega_{a2}(s_a + s_{f,a}) \qquad \text{(1a')}$$

As a further deviation in equation (1a') we find a contribution of human labour to nature's "cost" (reduction in costs) in acquiring nutrients. To perceive this, we foresee humans not only directly working for their immediate private products, but also allocating labour to nature that modifies the natural sphere by indirectly improving the functioning of ecosystems (for instance by building cultural landscapes, assuring better access to decomposed nutrients, etc.). This could mean any activity that is intended to improve the acquisition of needed nutrients (to seed, to plant, etc.). Finally, humans benefit indirectly from contributing labour. Next we have to specify where humans can use further labour with respect to supporting the decomposing compartment. We have to specify how they may interfere in decomposition and natural processing for the purpose of nutrient recycling as influenced by labour. For the decomposer we suggest equation (1b'):

$$F_d = (1-\varpi)\tau_d s_d + \varpi s_d^{/}(1+s_d) - C_d(\Omega_a s_d + \Phi_d n_d + \Phi_d n_f - s_a - s_{f,a}, s_{f,h}, l_d)$$
$$+\lambda_d^{/}(s_a + s_{f,a} + s_{f,h} - \Omega_{d,1} n_d - \Omega_{d,1} n_f - \Omega_{d,2}\dot{S}_a) \qquad) \tag{1b'}$$

where additionally:

$s_{f,h}$ = vector of waste to be recycled from households by the compartment

In (1b'), we again introduce human labour as a measure to reduce losses of organic matter (exergy). By introducing labour as a measure to put nature into a better position we think human activities improve the fitness of the whole system. Note, labour stands also for equipment produced by humans. But we have to specify costs. The approach is species oriented; so a labour vector can be designed to address species selectively and foster survival in competition for organic matter. Note not every species in the decomposition compartment will receive similar attention. For instance, humans may select certain bacteria and put efforts into the survival in order to maximise service received. Most simply we now assume that the initial cost component in the objective function alters in economic terms to

$$C_d(.) = \psi_d^{/} s_d + s_d^{/}[\Psi_{d,1}(s_a + s_{f,a}) - .5\cdot\Omega_a s_d - \Phi_d(n_d + n_f)] + s_d^{/}\Psi_{d,2} s_{f,h} + s_d^{/}\Psi_{d,3} l_d \tag{2a'}$$

and

$$C_a(.) = \psi_a^{/} s_a - s_a^{/}[0.5\Psi_{a,1}(s_a + s_{f,a}) - \Phi_{a1} n_d] + s_a^{/}\Psi_{a,2} n_x + s_a^{/}\Psi_{a,3} l_a \tag{2b'}$$

As a delineation of labour effects, indirect cost functions (2') depict the efficiency increase of compartments when using labour to reduce material losses.

4.2 Response function

With these amendments we get a new set of response functions (6) as compared to (3). To receive it, we arrived at new first-order-derivatives of goal functions.

$$\tau_d + \varpi s_d - \psi_d - \Psi_{d,1}(s_a + s_{f,a}) - \Psi_{d,2} s_{f,h} - \Omega_a s_d - \Phi_d n_d) + \Psi_{d,3} l_d + \lambda_s = 0$$
$$s_a - \Omega_{d,1} n_d - \Omega_{d,1} n_f - \Omega_{d,2}\dot{S}_a = 0 \tag{6a}$$

$$\varpi\tau_a + \varpi(s_a + s_r) - \psi_a - \Psi_{a,1}(s_a + s_r) - \Phi_{a1} n_d + \Psi_{a,2} n_x + \Psi_{a,3} l_a + \lambda_{a,1} + \lambda_{a,2} = 0$$
$$n_x + n_d + n_m - \Omega_{a2}(s_a + s_r) = 0 \tag{6b}$$
$$1^{/}\Omega_{a3} s_a - a_{0,a} = 0$$

Also the supposed composition criteria of decomposing and accumulating species

$$\mathrm{s_d} = \Omega_T \mathrm{s_a} \tag{6c}$$

is necessary. By (6) we receive a determination of an eco-system "behaviour" including an exchange system. The appendix gives a mathematical reformulation.

4.3 Second introduction of humans as principal

As already mentioned, humans primarily offer and decide on labour. We foresee a labour constraint and a special negative amenity of work for nature. Land is another issue. In the beginning we sketched an occupation by nature that did not recognise competition with agriculture. Now agriculture endogenously optimises land use. This requires an inclusion of specified and cleared land in (7a)

$$U_f = p_f s_f - p_m n_m - C_f(s_t, s_a, n_f + n_m, \mathrm{l_f}) + \mu_{f,1}[1 - I'[\mathrm{l_f} + \mathrm{l_a}]\cdot 1] - \rho' \mathrm{l}_a' \Phi_{\mathrm{f},1} \mathrm{l_a}$$
$$+ \mu_{f,2}[\mathrm{a}_0 \text{-} \mathrm{a}_{0,a} \text{-} 1' \Phi_{\mathrm{f},1} s_{f,a}] \tag{7a}$$

Equation (7a), as extension of (4), caters for labour and land for nature. For the interpretation of function (7a), as those of a principal, the interactions between species and agriculture (Appendix) can either be specified as a production approach, that foresees higher yields from maintained biodiversity and organic fertiliser, or expressed as a cost approach, that assumes an internal optimum for production. We take the cost approach and assume a net reduction of costs due to certain species. It means less net-labour is also a goal. For further contemplation, the waste management unit shall have the following objective function (7b):

$$U_w = \mu_w[1'(s_e + s_f - s_{f,h} - s_m)] - c_e \mathrm{l_e} + \mu_{w,1}[1 - I'[\mathrm{l_e} + \mathrm{l_d}]\cdot 1] - \rho' \mathrm{l}_d' \Phi_{\mathrm{f},1} \mathrm{l_d} + (C_o - C_w(l_e, s_{f,h})) - c_m s_m$$
$$: \tag{7b}$$

where additionally

U_w	= utility or cost of waste treatment measured as profit
$s_{e+}s_f$	= vector of waste to be recycled from organics and food from households (exogenous)
$s_{f,h}$	= vector of waste to be recycled in the natural decomposition system
s_m	= vector of waste exogenously recycled
C_o	= reference costs
l_d	= labour for waste compartment of nature
l_e	= labour for exogenous reycling

However, costs have to be minimised given the options for waste disposal available to humans. Note, with respect to ecological optimisation the system might react differently. An entropy increase is evident, but perhaps it can be minimised.

5 Solution to the interaction of humans and nature

To solve the problem we suggest humans are the principal and nature is the agent [3]. Nature is providing a contingent behaviour based on incentive [8]. We take the result from the Appendix on interaction (linear response), which is expressed as a residual form of behaviour, and substitute variables in the objective functions (7a and b). So finally we receive a new set of objective functions (8a and b):

$$U_f = p_f(I-\Omega_R)\Omega_R^{-1}s_{f,a} - p_m n_m - C_f(\Omega_R^{-1}s_{f,a}, s_a, \gamma_{41}l_a + \gamma_{42}l_d + \gamma_{43}s_{f,a} + \gamma_{44}a_{0,a}$$
$$+\gamma_{45}n_m, n_m, l_f) + \mu_{f,1}[1 - I'[l_f + l_a]\cdot 1] - \rho' l_a' \Phi_{f,1} l_a + \mu_{f,2}[a_0 - a_{0,a} - 1'\Phi_{f,1}s_{f,a}] \quad (8a)$$

Notably, expression (8a) reduces farm behaviour to decision-making on production ($s_{f,a}$: residues), labour (l_a: for nature), nutrient allocation (n_m: mineral fertiliser), and land ($a_{o,a}$: not farmed). But, also, we have to notice that farmers need information about labour l_d (devoted to nature by the recycling compartment for waste management). Simultaneous optimisation is necessary. In equation (8b) the objective function of the waste unit includes the eco-system reaction (Appendix.).

$$U_w = \mu_f[1'(s_e + (I-\Omega_R)\Omega_R^{-1}s_{f,a} - \gamma_{51}l_a - \gamma_{52}l_d - \gamma_{55}n_m + [I-\gamma_{54}]s_{f,a} + \gamma_{54}a_{0,a} - s_m)] - c_e l_e + \mu_{f,1}$$
$$[1 - I'[l_e + l_d]\cdot 1] - \rho' l_d' \Phi_{f,1} l_d + (C_o - C_w(l_e, \gamma_{51}l_a + \gamma_{52}l_d + \gamma_{55}n_m + \gamma_{54}s_{f,a} + \gamma_{53}a_{0,a})) - c_m s_m \quad (8b)$$

This formulation reveals a necessity to follow a joint optimisation of agriculture and waste management. For the moment we simply follow the strategy to sum up profits in the two sectors. Then we introduce the two quadratic cost functions:

$$C_f(.) = \psi_f' s_{f,a} - s_{f,a}'[0.5\Psi_{f,1}s_{f,a} + \Psi_{f,2}l_f + \Psi_{f,2}n_m + s_{f,a}'\Psi_{f,3}[\gamma_{41}l_a + \gamma_{42}l_d + \gamma_{45}n_m + \gamma_{44}s_{f,a} + \gamma_{44}a_{0a} + n_m] + \Psi_{f,1}n_m] \quad (9a)$$

$$C_w(.) = \psi_d' s - [\Psi_{w,2}l_e' + 0.5[\gamma_{51}l_a + \gamma_{52}l_d + \gamma_{53}n_m + \gamma_{54}s_{f,a} + \gamma_{5e}a_{0,a}]'\Psi_{w,1}][\gamma_{51}l_a + \gamma_{52}l_d + \gamma_{53}n_m + \gamma_{54}s_{f,a} + \gamma_{54}a_{0,a}] \quad (9b)$$

Inserting these functions (9) in (8) and optimising (8) we receive seven, interactive behavioural equations for the farm and waste sector (10a and b) which can be simultaneously solved for all endogenous variables. Seven variables concern the allocation of labour, food production, land, and mineral fertiliser. Hence, the compartments interact optimally. For the farm sector we find the derivatives:

$$p_f - \Phi_{f,1} 1\, \mu_{f,2}s_{f,a} + \psi_f' - \Psi_{f,1}s_{f,a} + \Psi_{f,2}l_f + \Psi_{f,2}n_m + \Psi_{f,3}[\gamma_{41}l_a + \gamma_{42}l_d + \gamma_{45}n_m + \gamma_{44}s_{f,a} + \gamma_{44}a_{0a} + n_m] + \Psi_{f,1}n_m = 0$$
$$p_m - \Psi_{f,2}s_{f,a} + \Psi_{f,3}(\gamma_{45}+1)s_{f,a}] + \Psi_{f,1}n_m = 0$$
$$1\mu_{f,1} + \Psi_{f,3}\gamma_{41}s_{f,a} + \Psi_{f,4}l_a + \Phi_{f,1}l_{a,1} = 0 \quad (10a)$$
$$1\mu_{f,1} + \Psi_{f,3}\gamma_{51}s_{f,a} + \Psi_{f,5}l_f = 0$$
$$\Psi_{f,3}\gamma_{44}s_{f,a} + \mu_{f,2} = 0$$

and for the waste recycling and management sector we have:

$$\gamma_{52}\mu_f + 1\mu_{f,1} + \rho\Phi_{f,1}l_d' - \Psi_{w,1}[\gamma_{51}l_a + \gamma_{52}l_d + \gamma_{54}n_m + \gamma_{54}s_{f,a} + \gamma_{54}a_{0,a}] = 0$$
$$c_e + 1\mu_{f,1} - \Psi_{w,2}[\gamma_{51}l_a + \gamma_{52}l_d + \gamma_{55}n_m + \gamma_{54}s_{f,a} + \gamma_{54}a_{0,a}] = 0 \quad (10b)$$

Additional three equations or constraints on labour and land (two for labour: farm and waste labour; and one for land) determine the system so that it becomes a linear system of 10 equations. This system is equivalent in numbers of equations and variables. Technically it is again a matter of matrix depiction. Preparing system (10) for the final determination of all endogenous variables, physical optimality results in a new exchange, qualified against dumping and fertiliser costs.

6 Summary

This paper provided an outline for a model of measuring the importance of nature services for humans. It pursued the idea of involving nature in organic waste recycling offering a double dividend. A double dividend means that we can get plant nutrients for agriculture cheaper from a decomposing nature than from a chemical industry; simultaneously nature offers organic waste recycling for citizens cheaper than dumping it outside the system. We introduced four actors: an accumulating nature, a decomposing nature, farmers and waste management. They interact and humans are principles and species in nature are agents. The model is solved sequentially and labour and nature service are exchanged. In doing so, nature is described by maximising fitness and humans maximize profits.

References

[1] Carlsson-Kanyama, A., Ekström, M., P., Shanahan, H., Food and life cycle energy inputs: consequences of diet and ways to increase efficiency. *Ecological Economics*, **44**, Issue: 2-3, March, pp. 293 – 307, 2003.

[2] Bouma, J., (Ed.) Eco-regional approaches for sustainable land use and food production. Dortrecht, 1995.

[3] Richter, G. Furubotn, E.G., Institutions and Economic Theory: An Introduction to and assessment of New Institutional Economics. Ann Arbor, 1997.

[4] Mayumi, K., The Originals of Ecological Economics. London,

[5] Herendeen, R. Do economics-like principles predict ecosystem behaviour under changing resource constraints?, pp. 261-287. In M. Higashi and T. Burns, (eds.), Theoretical Studies of Ecosystems: The Network Perspective. Cambridge, 1997.

[6] Joergensen, S.E., Development of models able to account for changes in species composition. Ecological Modelling, **62**, pp.165-208, 1992

[7] Ulanowicz, R.E., Ecology, the Ascendant Perspective. New York, 1997.

[8] Nuppenau, E.-A., Towards a genuine exchange value of nature: interactions between humans and nature in a principal-agent framework. *Ecological Economics*, **43**, pp.33-47

Appendix

The above system of the agent (nature) is constructed as a linear response system:

$$\begin{bmatrix} \Psi_{d,1}+\Omega_t(\varpi-\Omega_a) & 0 & \Phi_d & \Psi_{d,2} & 1 & 0 & 0 \\ 1 & 0 & \Omega_{d,1} & 0 & 0 & 0 & 0 \\ \varpi+\Psi_{a,1} & \varpi+\Psi_{a,1} & \Phi_{al} & \varpi & 0 & 1 & 1 \\ \Omega_{a2} & \Omega_{a2} & 1 & 0 & 0 & 0 & 0 \\ 1/\Omega_{a3} & 0 & 0 & 0 & 0 & 0 & 0 \\ 1 & 0 & \Omega_{d,1} & 1 & 0 & 0 & 0 \\ \Omega_{a2} & \Omega_{a2} & 1 & 0 & 0 & 0 & 1 \end{bmatrix} . \begin{bmatrix} [s_a] \\ [n_f] \\ [n_d] \\ [s_{f,h}] \\ \lambda_d \\ \lambda_{a,1} \\ \lambda_{a,2} \end{bmatrix} =$$

$$\begin{bmatrix} 0 & \Psi_{d,3} & 0 & 0 & 0 \\ 0 & 0 & \Omega_{d,1}0 & 0 & 0 \\ \Psi_{a,3} & 0 & 0 & 0 & 0 \\ 0 & 0 & 0 & 0 & 0 \\ 0 & 0 & 0 & 1 & 0 \\ 0 & 0 & -\Omega_{d,1} & 0 & 0 \\ 0 & 0 & 0 & 0 & 1 \end{bmatrix} \begin{bmatrix} [l_a] \\ [l_d] \\ [s_{f,a}] \\ a_{0,a} \\ [n_m] \end{bmatrix} + \begin{bmatrix} 1 & 0 & 1 & 0 \\ 0 & 1 & 0 & 0 \\ 1 & 0 & \Psi_{a,2} & 0 \\ 0 & 0 & 1 & 0 \\ 0 & 0 & 0 & 1 \\ 0 & 0 & 0 & 0 \\ 0 & 0 & 1 & 0 \end{bmatrix} \begin{bmatrix} \tau_d \\ \tau_a \\ n_x \\ a_0 \end{bmatrix} + \begin{bmatrix} 1 & 0 \\ \Omega_{d,2} & \dots \\ 1 & 0 \\ 0 & \Omega_{a,2}0 \\ 0 & 0 \\ \Omega_{d,2} & 0 \\ 0 & \Omega_{a,2} \end{bmatrix} \begin{bmatrix} \dot{S}_d \\ S_a \end{bmatrix}$$

Working with a steady state and not considering dynamics, residual behaviour is:

$$\begin{bmatrix} s_a \\ s_d \\ n_d \\ n_f \\ s_{f,h} \end{bmatrix} = \begin{bmatrix} \gamma_{30} \\ \gamma_{20} \\ \gamma_{20} \\ \gamma_{20} \\ \gamma_{20} \end{bmatrix} + \begin{bmatrix} \gamma_{11} & \gamma_{12} & \gamma_{13} & \gamma_{14} & \gamma_{15} \\ \gamma_{21} & \gamma_{22} & \gamma_{23} & \gamma_{24} & \gamma_{25} \\ \gamma_{31} & \gamma_{32} & \gamma_{33} & \gamma_{34} & \gamma_{35} \\ \gamma_{41} & \gamma_{42} & \gamma_{43} & \gamma_{44} & \gamma_{45} \\ \gamma_{51} & \gamma_{52} & \gamma_{53} & \gamma_{54} & \gamma_{55} \end{bmatrix} \begin{bmatrix} [l_a] \\ [l_d] \\ [s_{f,a}] \\ a_{0,a} \\ [n_m] \end{bmatrix} + [x]$$

A linear system prevails that contains information of a fitness-oriented system. which gives a new perspective for the objective function of the ecosystem.

Policy instruments for eliminating plastic bags from South Africa's environment

G. Nhamo
Environmental Education and Sustainability Unit,
Rhodes University, South Africa

Abstract

The South African Government, private sector and civic society signed, on 28 September 2001 the Polokwane Declaration stipulating that South Africa achieves zero waste status in all sectors by 2022. Prior to that, two key policy frameworks: the 1999 National Waste Management Strategy and the 2000 White Paper on Integrated Pollution and Waste Management had been put in place with legal mandates from the 1996 Constitution, National Environmental Management Act of 1998 and the National Environmental Management Policy of 1999. Given that single measure policy instruments such as self-regulation, command-and-control as well as market-based approaches fail to achieve set targets, this paper interrogates tensions, debates and responses around finding a proper mix of policy instruments to achieve zero plastic bags waste in the country. The main findings revealed that the government oriented command-and-control approach failed. This resulted in negotiations between industry, labour and government leading to the conclusion of the Plastic Bags Agreement in 2002, followed by the repulsion of the 2002 Plastic Bags Regulations in 2003 as well as the introduction of standards stipulating thickness of plastic bags and an estimated US half a cent (ZAR 3 cents) levy per bag. The impact has been an average drop of plastic bags demand by between 70-90%.

Keywords: waste, policy instruments, South Africa, Plastic Bag Regulations.

1 Introduction

The framework for South Africa's waste pollution and management is spelt out in the White Paper on Integrated Pollution and Waste Management of 2000 DEAT [1]. The White Paper is subsidiary to a number of other policies that include among them the Environmental Conservation Act of 1989, Constitution of 1996 and the National Environmental Management Act of 1998. The white Paper also incorporates the provisions of the National Waste Management Strategy and Action Plans of 1999 DEAT [1].

2 A paradigm shift in waste management

Of critical importance from the National Waste Management Strategy and Action Plans of 1999 was the introduction of a new thinking towards integrated pollution and waste management in South Africa. The document presents an internationally accepted waste management hierarchy that prioritises preventive as opposed to end-of-pipe measures to managing wastes. The full hierarchy promotes generating no waste, minimisation, re-use and recycling of waste products whenever possible, followed by approved treatment procedures before disposal on landfills as a last resort DEAT [1]. In 2001, the Government (represented by the Department of Environmental Affairs and Tourism – DEAT), private sector and the civil society ratified the Polokwane Declaration DEAT [2]. The Declaration stipulates that South Africa should achieve a zero waste status in all sectors by 2022.

3 Methodological framework

Latour [3] argues that the world is full of hybrid or quasi-object entities. They are hybrids because they are simultaneously real, discursive and socially constructed and actor/actant-network theory (AANT) was developed to analyse such hybrids. AANT denies that purely technical, scientific or social relations are possible as what may be viewed on the surface as social is partially technical or scientific and vice versa. AANT is constructed around a number of dimensions and processes including the actor (human), actant (non-human), actor/actant-networks. Analysis lenses in this framework are provided through the moments of translation (i.e., problematisation, interessement, enrolment and mobilisation) and these assist in tracing actors, actants and their networks so as to exam controversies and determine how they are resolved and/ or appear as black boxes Davies [4].

4 Presentation and discussion of findings

4.1 Command-and-control approach to regulation

In September 1999, the then Minister of Environmental Affairs and Tourism, Vali Moosa made a policy statement on his intention to ban thin film (14-17 microns) plastic shopping bags. Following his statement, the lead environment agency, DEAT promulgated and gazetted the draft Plastic Bag Regulations on 19 May 2000. An explanatory memorandum to the regulations indicated that the collection and disposal of plastic bags is a growing problem in South Africa as the use of plastic bags made of thin plastic film had increased significantly in recent years with large amounts of bags polluting and degrading the environment RSA [5].

The regulations were promulgated under the provisions of the Environment Conservation Act of 1989 and set the thickness of plastic shopping bags at 80 microns. A R100,000 fine (about US$ 17,000 as of January 2005) and 10 year jail term were also pronounced. The proposed regulations were not well received, especially by organised business, which pulled resources and started lobbying government to have the regulations reversed.

In its submission to the Parliamentary Portfolio Committee for Environmental Affairs and Tourism in October 2000 organised business indicated that public education and awareness raising were the most critical aspects in addressing environmental problems related to plastic shopping bags litter and waste in South Africa Botha [6]. Efforts that were being made by the plastics industry to address the problem associated with plastic shopping bags since the early 1980s were also highlighted. The Plastics Enviromark was indicated as one of the most successful initiatives. The Plastics Enviromark was started in January 1997 and incorporated the exclusive use of a logo by raw material suppliers and plastics converters who contract to support environmental education and awareness programmes PFSA [7]. The submission reported that as of October 2000, about 80% of the companies in the plastics packaging industry were contributing to the Plastics Enviromark initiative. Some of the awareness programmes covered by the Plastics Enviromark initiative PFSA *et al* [8] include: a series of publications aimed at schools and other environmental organisations for community and school use and the promotion of the Green Cage project that encourages recycling of plastic products through conveniently locating Green Cages around the country. At the time of submission, there were about 120 Green Cages throughout the country with more than 70 new job opportunities having been created.

Organised business claimed that plastics were vital packaging materials globally and assisted in promoting good environmental stewardship. In South Africa, plastic shopping bags were used in almost every retail outlet as carriers for the customer's purchases and were convenient and cost-effective PCSA [9] with an average of 8 billion circulated annually Nedlac [10]. In conclusion, the submission called for a holistic approach to the litter problem and warned that at least 3,800 jobs could be lost as most companies used modern equipment that could not 80 microns plastic bags. This is a position that was carried throughout the lobbying period by industry until 2002.

4.2 Regulations referred to Nedlac

After hearing the views from organised business and other submissions in October 2000, the Parliamentary Portfolio Committee declared a deadlock and referred the issue to Nedlac. Nedlac is South Africa’s national organisation that discusses and tries to reach consensus between government, organised labour, organised business and organised communities on issues affecting social and economic policy through social dialogue.

The draft regulations and the comments from the public were tabled by Nedlac for discussion on 23 November 2000 Nedlac [10] and affected parties, particularly Government agreed that a joint research project into the regulations be urgently undertaken. The scope was that this would assist parties to develop a shared understanding of the potential socio-economic impacts of the proposed regulations. The Nedlac report of 2001 revealed that the plastic shopping bag manufacturing industry consisted six large companies that shared between 70-75% of the local market, which entirely depended on plastic bag business. Nedlac recommended that it was not feasible to change existing equipment to manufacture firstly the required 30 microns plastic bag and later an 80 microns plastic bag and proposed regulations Nedlac [10].

4.3 Organised business and self-regulation

As negotiations were taking place, in March 20002, government finalised the Plastic Bag Regulations. Organised Business felt there were not significant changes compared to the original 2000 version of the regulations prompting it to come up with an alternative self-regulating plan. By that time organised business was, represented by the Plastic Federation of South Africa (as spokes organisation), the Plastic Recycling Employers Organisation and the Chemical and Allied Industries Association. The business plan was popularised as the e-Bag Initiative.

4.3.1 Concepts behind the e-Bag Initiative

The e-Bag Initiative aimed at reducing the number of plastic shopping bags that ended up in the waste stream. A levy was proposed at the point of sale of the plastic bag from the manufacturer to the retailer and the retailer in turn charging consumers for the bag at the point of sale. The retailer would also refund consumers for any bags that are returned to the point of sale. This arrangement was confirmed as having the impact to reduce the number of plastic shopping bags in circulation with the levy being used to stimulate the collection and recycling of plastic shopping bags. Industry would increase the thickness of plastic shopping bags to a minimum of 22 microns through regulation and further enhance the recycling content by developing a standard that would specify the characteristics of both shopping and refuse plastic bags.

Such a standard would include specifying a minimum thickness; ink to be used and its spread on the plastic shopping bag surface; the area of the bag that may be printed on and optimum size of bags. In respect of refuse bags, in addition to thickness the standard will specify a minimum recycled content. The e-Bag Initiative would be managed through a non-profit (Section 21 Company) to be named 'e-Bag South Africa'. The objectives of the Section 21 Company were outlined and these included among them the need to PFSA *et al* [8]:

a) promote efficiency in the use, re-use, collection, recycling and disposal of plastic shopping bags,
b) receive a levy from plastic shopping bag manufacturers and importers who were required to register with the South African Revenue Service,

c) follow appropriate international trends in the enhanced recycling of plastic shopping bags,
d) enter into partnerships with civil society organisations,
e) ensure that collection points are established within easy walking distance of all major settlements,
f) stimulate participation in education campaigns and recycling by small-scale and micro entrepreneurs and by organisations of civil society,
g) support government initiatives, and
h) investigate mechanisms to ensure participation in the company by all entities in the plastic shopping bag value chain.

4.3.2 Strategies for plastic bags collection

A Section 21 Company was supposed to have a managing director who would report to a Board, which in turn reported to the Minister of Environmental Affairs and Tourism. South Africa was to be divided into regional areas that employed Litter SWAT Teams to collect plastic shopping bags. Such Teams were to be formed either on an *ad hoc* basis when required or be integrated with existing community-based initiatives (figure 1). Regional Development Officers were proposed whose mandate was to manage Litter SWAT Teams and co-ordinate school and community activities. In this respect, about 36 fulltime posts were envisaged in addition to between 2,000 to 4,000 temporary jobs.

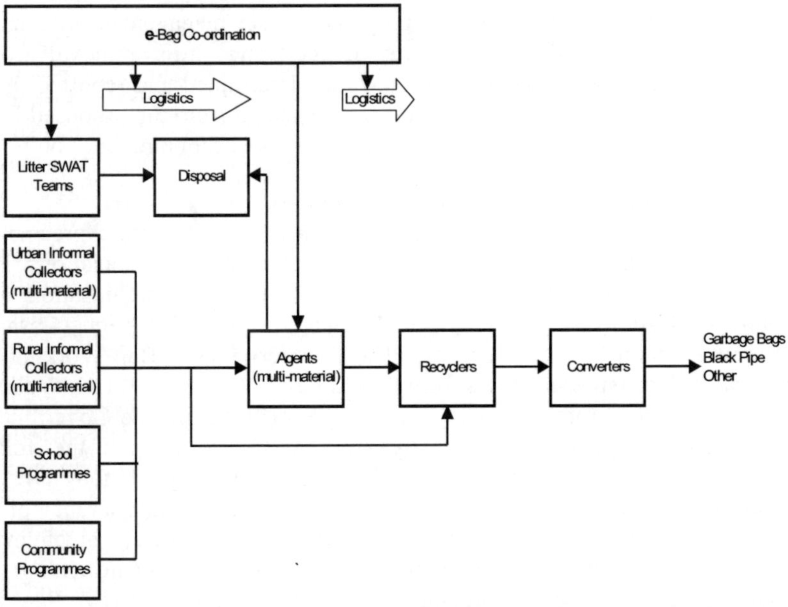

Figure 1: Plastic bags and other materials collection strategy (supplied by the PFSA, 2004).

The collectors would primarily collect plastic waste and sent it to collecting agents who would sell the collected plastic shopping bags to e-Bag Initiative or directly to recyclers who would in turn claim payment from the e-Bag Initiative (figure 1). In order to recover about 5% of the plastic shopping bags, the market price for recovered plastic shopping bag was set at R1,400 (about US$235 as of January 2005) per tonne.

4.3.3 Implementation

Polymer manufacturers and importers as well as plastic shopping bag manufacturers and importers, recyclers and retailers would register with e-Bag South Africa first PFSA *et al* [8]. Furthermore, these stakeholders were supposed to provide specific information to the e-Bag Initiative on a quarterly basis. This information included the total weight of polymer manufactured or imported and sold for plastic bag conversion as well as total weight of: plastic shopping bags manufactured or imported; those recovered through the litter collection strategy; those recovered through the refund system; those recovered from drop-off points; those provided to consumers; total weight of recyclate generated; recyclate to different end products; and material not suitable for recycling and disposed of to landfill.

At the other end, manufacturers were supposed to report on a monthly basis regarding the number of plastic shopping bags sold to retailers and the quantity of litter that is collected. This information would be collected at a local authority level and aggregated to a provincial and national level with DEAT providing information collected through the integrated waste management system. From the data generated, the annual rate of recycling, litter removal from the environment and waste reduction were to be determined and reported. In terms of finance, an estimated R84.5 million was expected from the proposed levy and this figure was based on locally manufactured plastic shopping bags only.

4.3.4 Plastic Bag Agreement and environmental law reforms

In September 2002 the Government entered into a Plastic Bag Agreement with organised business (Chemical and Allied Industries Association, Plastics Federation of South Africa, Plastic Recyclers Employers Organisation, and the Retailers Plastic Bag Working Group) and organised labour (Cosatu and National Council of Trade Unions). The Retailers Plastic Bag Working Group was made up of representatives from Pick'n Pay Retailers (Pty) Ltd, Woolworths (Pty) Ltd, Clicks Stores and Shoprite Checkers (Pty) Ltd. The Government and its partners adopted the e-Bag Initiative and agreed upon the following concerning the amendments to the 2002 Plastic Bag Regulations DEAT [5]: minimum thickness was set at 30 microns, disclosure and transparency of cost at checkout points, printing on plastic bags (to include a safety or environment related message, name of converter, e-mark, polymer identification grade, product purchase bar code and country of origin), creation of recycling market, creation of Buyisa-e-Bag South Africa and promotion of job creation, mandatory levy and prevention of illegal imports as well as the enforcement date that was set for 9 May 2003.

The Plastic Bag Agreement resulted in the repulsion of the May 2002 regulations that were replaced by the watered down May 2003 regulations. The Agreement also resulted in the June 2003 Compulsory Specifications for plastic shopping bags standards. Buyisa-e-Bag became operational in May 2004 with a government budget of R20 million allocated annually for the next three years. The reason why a budget line was established according to the Director of Waste Management in DEAT Moathse [12] was that the levy from the plastic shopping bags was not 'ring-fenced' and could not be collected specifically for activities related to dealing with plastic shopping bags.

To facilitate the collection of the levy, the Revenue Laws Amendment Act of 2002 was amended in 2003 to make provision for the imposition of environmental levies RSA [13]. Furthermore, in 2004 the Environmental Conservation Act of 1989 was amended to enable the Minister of Environmental Affairs and Tourism to make regulations regarding financial matters relating to specific waste types.

4.4 Results from implementation

4.4.1 Demand for plastic shopping bags and impacts on jobs

The following figures revealed the trend in demand for plastic shopping bags from the manufacturing plants. The figures and narratives were sourced from two manufacturing plants, one from Johannesburg and the other from Cape Town. Both plants belonged to the largest plastic shopping bag producer in South Africa. The first response indicated that the company had retrenched 150 (75%) of 200 employees Interview T11 [14]. The interview also revealed that the company used to produce 5 million bags per day and after the regulations, only 800,000 were being produced and as such operating a four-day shift from seven days previously. Another interview indicated that the plant was also operating on a five-day production week producing between 1.7 and 2 million bags per day. The total staff compliment was 225 compared to 166 that were left after retrenchments Email 13 [15].

Average figures from these two plants show that only 1,325 million plastic bags per day (about 311.4 million bags a year compared to 3.65 billion before the regulations) were being produced. This represents an estimated 92% cut in the actual number of plastic bags getting to the consumers. The 92% reduction in this company production figures also translate into a 42% slash of shopping plastic bags consumption and circulation at a national level just from a single producer if the base of 8 billion plastic shopping bags circulated annually previously in the county is used. On the jobs front, the figures represent about 49% of total (209 out of 425 employees).

The demand for plastic bags was also monitored for a complete year from two out of the three major groceries retail chains in Grahamstown between January 2003 and January 2004. The two retail chains are among the top three in the country. The period was selected to provide insights concerning demand before the regulations and demand after the regulations. Three distinctive phases emerged: one focusing on prior to the regulations (January to 8 May 2003), the other when the plastic bags were sold for between 26-46 cents (9 May to 11

August 2004) and when the plastic shopping bag 'war' erupted resulting in plastic bag prices being cut to between 10-17 cents (12 August and after). This is the price that plastic bags are being sold at to-date. Monitoring direct consumption was done in order to experience the real situation on the ground as events unfolded at the 'lowest' possible scale (local). The figures then presented a good case for comparison with sectoral and national patterns.

The demand situation from the observations is presented in graph 1. The figures presented in graph 1 show that demand trends at the local scale were similar to those experienced by the producers. The average monthly plastic shopping bag demand drastically fell by 98.8% (for Retailer A) and 99.1 (for Retailer B) during the first three months after the introduction of the Plastic Bags Regulation on 9 May 2003.

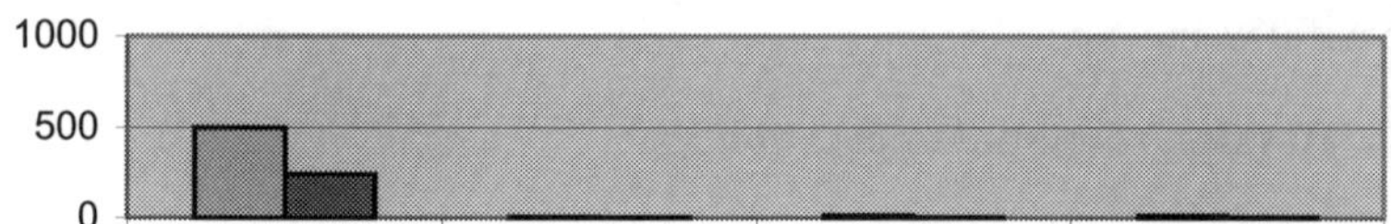

	Jan-April 2003	May-July 2003	August-Oct 2003	Nov 2003-Jan 2004
Retailer A	500	5.8	11.9	14
Retailer B	240	2.2	4.2	5.3

Monthly average (000s)

Graph 1: Retail plastic shopping bags monthly demand (000s).

However, the demand increased slightly after the reduction in plastic shopping bags prices on 12 August 2003 although overall, the demand remained subdued at 2.4% of the base average monthly consumption of 500,000 (for Retail A) and 1.8% (for Retail B) in the next three months between August to October. The trend improved slightly during the Christmas and New Year festive season. Average monthly demand rose slightly to 2.8% (from 2.4%) of average monthly base consumption of 500,000 (for Retail A) and 2.2% (from 1.8%) for Retail B. Overall, the monthly average demand for the two retail outlets fell by 98% from the period when the regulations were enforced to the end of the monitoring period in January 2004.

4.4.2 Environmental and social impacts

From a statement that appeared on the DEAT website on 16 July 2003 DEAT [16], the Wildlife and Environment Society of South Africa (WESSA) was one of the early beneficiaries of the introduction of the Plastic Bags Regulations. Its joint initiative with the Spar retail chain to introduce the Cloth Bags and EcoBag resulted in two sets of donations: a R16,000 donation for WESSA Border-Kei Region Office in October 2000 and another R50,000 on 18 July 2003 for the Head Office in Kwazulu-Natal. Follow-ups in separate interviews granted by Makana, Nelson Mandela Metro, City of Cape Town, Govarn Mbeki and Tswane local authorities also confirmed that the new law has led to a significant reduction in plastic shopping bags litter and pollution in the environment.

Another environmental benefit has already been discussed under the *Kids in Parks Programme*.

The Kids in Parks Programme DEAT [17] is an initiative aimed at transforming and developing the school curriculum. The programme was jointly launched by the Ministries of Education and Environmental Affairs and Tourism in partnership with Pick'n Pay and South African National Parks (SANParks) in October 2004. This environmental education programme aims to DEAT [17]: provide meaningful environmental education (within the framework of Outcomes-Based Education and Curriculum 2005) so as to equip future generations with the knowledge and skills needed to manage the environment, enhance cultural resource management and indigenous knowledge, strengthen community-parks relationships, and contribute to local economic development through subcontracting, community-driven enterprises, joint ventures, apprenticeships and employment. The programme received initiation funding of about R 9 million (about US$ 1.5 as of January 2005) from retail giant Pick'n Pay from its R1 donation per each Green Bag sold it pledged towards this environmental initiative Smith [18].

5 Conclusion

This paper presented two distinctive approaches to waste product regulation: government oriented command-and-control and organised business oriented self-regulation. The paper also discussed debates surrounding the initiatives and how the two approaches to regulation were married resulting in the repulsion of the May 2002 Plastic Bag Regulations through the Plastic Bag Agreement. The paper also revealed that the waste regulatory instruments managed to significantly benefit the environment with an estimated 83% (on average) of the plastic shopping bags having been removed from the environment a year later. A number of environmental programmes and organisations, among them, the Kids in Parks Programme and WESSA also benefited from the regulatory framework. The biggest challenge, however, is the sustainability of the initiative as well as the challenges the regulations presented to labour.

References

[1] DEAT, *White Paper on Integrated Pollution and Waste Management*, Government Printer: Pretoria, pp. 21-36, 2000.

[2] DEAT, *Polokwane Declaration*, Government Printer: Pretoria, pp. 1-6, 2001.

[3] Latour, B., On recalling ANT (Chapter 2). *Actor network theory and after*, ed. J.Law & J. Hassard, Blackwell Publishers: Oxford, pp. 15-25, 1999.

[4] Davies, A. R., Power, politics and networks: shaping partnerships for sustainable communities. *Area*, (34), pp. 190-203, 2002.

[5] RSA, *Proposed Regulations Under Section 24 of the Environmental Conservation Act, 1989 (Act N0. 73 of 1989)*. Government Printer: Pretoria, pp. 1-3, 2000.

[6] Botha, E., Industry wants more debate on plastic bag problem. *Daily Dispatch*, 14 September 2000.

[7] PFSA, *Plastics recycling: A survey of the South Africa recycling Industry 2000*. PFSA: Johannesburg, pp. 1-15, 2001.

[8] PFSA, PREO, & CAIA, *Towards eliminating plastic bags from the environment: A Plastics industry initiative*. PFSA, PREO & CAIA: Johannesburg, 5-15, 2002.

[9] PCSA, Dismay at revised regulations. *Packaging Review-May 2002*, (28), pp. 33, 2002.

[10] Nedlac, *Socio-economic impact of the proposed Plastic Bag Regulations*, Nedlac: Johannesburg, pp. 4-14, 2001.

[11] DEAT, *Plastic Bags Agreement*, Government Printer: Pretoria, pp. 3-10, 2002.

[12] Moathse, R. Personal communication, 8 September 2004, Director for Waste Management, DEAT, Pretoria, South Africa.

[13] RSA, *Revenue Laws Amendment Act (No. 45 of 2003)*. Government Printer: Pretoria, pp. 2-5, 2003.

[14] Interview T11, Impacts of plastic bags regulations implementation. 16 February 2004, Johannesburg, South Africa.

[15] Email 13, Request for information concerning shopping bag production. 16 February 2004, Cape Town, South Africa.

[16] DEAT, Moosa presents a R50,000 cheque to WESSA on behalf of Spar Supermarket. Department of Environmental Affairs and Tourism, http://www.environment.gov.za/, 2003.

[17] DEAT, Ministers van Schalkwyk and Pandor introduce the South African Kids to our national parks. Department of Environmental Affairs and Tourism. On-line http://www.environment.gov.za/, 2004

[18] Smith, N., Pick'n Pay to donate 20% of green bag price to environmental project. *Business Report*, 15 August, 2003.

Section 11
Environmental management

One-person households – a resource time bomb?

J. Williams
The Bartlett School of Planning, University College London, U.K.

Abstract

In the western world there is a trend towards the growth of small households, especially one-person households. In resource terms, one-person households are likely to consume more land, energy, goods and materials per person than those living in larger households where resources are shared amongst a greater number of people. Thus an increase in one-person households is likely to accelerate domestic consumption of resources over the next twenty years. This paper demonstrates the scale of the problem internationally and in the UK. It also investigates the UK Government's response and suggests ways in which it can be tackled in the future.
Keywords: resource consumption, one-person households, occupancy rates, household size, demographic change.

1 One-person household explosion and the potential consumption crisis

Household size has substantially reduced in Europe over the last 40 years. Average household size has decreased in the EU, while at the same time the absolute number of households has increased. More people are living in smaller households, while the proportion living in four or more person households is decreasing. The average household size in the EU in 1981/82 was 2.8 persons; in 2000/1 it was 2.5. However, there is variation throughout the EU. Spain, Portugal and Ireland have the largest households, while Sweden, Finland, Denmark and Germany, closely followed by the UK, have the smallest. The UNCHS-Habitat Indicators Programme, 1997 indicated an increase in Europe of one-person households from the 1960's onwards. It suggested that the number of one-person households was especially high in Northern and Western Europe, where the proportion of one-person households increased steadily between 1960-1988, although the size of the share varied from 8-20% in 1960 to 18-40% in the late eighties (10-20% growth). Greatest growth in one-person households during this period occurred in the Netherlands, Sweden and Switzerland, where the number of one-person households doubled (Van Diepen [1]). According to the Economic Commission for Europe by 2003 the smallest households were in Sweden (2.1 persons on average), followed by Denmark, Finland, Germany and Norway (2.2 persons on average). In Norway, more than 40 per cent were one-person households and in Sweden, Finland, Denmark and Germany this proportion was over 35 per cent (Economic Commission for Europe [2]). In the UK the number of one-person households has also grown significantly. Between 1971 and 1998 there was a 10% shift (18% of households in 1971 rising to 28% in 1998). Similar trends are already being experienced in the USA, Australia, New Zealand and Japan.

Evidence suggests that increase in one-person households is likely to have a detrimental environmental impact. The impact of changing demography on the environment has been widely studied (Lui et al [3]). More particularly the link between declining household size, diminishing biodiversity (Cincotta and Engelman [4]); increasing domestic energy consumption (INCPEN [5], Fawcett et al [6], Noorman and Uiterkamp [7], Roy and Caird [8]), increasing carbon dioxide emissions (Fawcett et al [6]) and household waste (INCPEN [5], Noorman and Uiterkamp [7]) has been researched. Lui et al [3] completed a global study to determine the impact of declining household size on biodiversity and natural resources. The study demonstrated that an increase in small households would lead to an increase in resource consumption and loss of biodiversity globally. More households would require more housing units (thus increasing land and materials needed for construction) and smaller households were less efficient in terms of resource use per capita than larger households. Increasing consumption of resources would also lead to a reduction in biodiversity through the loss of habitats and species.

Table 1: Effects of household size on the consumption of energy, materials and production of waste annually per capita (one-person household =100)

	1 person	2 person	4 person	Data Source
Products per capita	100	75	62.5	INCEPEN (UK data)
Packaging per capita	100	75	58	INCEPEN (UK data)
Indirect energy per capita	100	63	42	INCEPEN (UK data)
Electricity per capita	100	68.5	45	Noorman and Uiterkamp (Dutch data)
Gas per capita	100	64.5	39	Noorman and Uiterkamp (Dutch data)
Solid waste per capita	100	88.5	75.5	Noorman and Uiterkamp (Dutch data)

Source: Compiled using data from INCPEN [5], Noorman and Uiterkamp [7].

Further research supported the proposition that smaller households were less resource efficient than larger households. One study (INCPEN [5]) used UK data to determine how household size influenced consumption of goods, packaging and indirect energy. It demonstrated inverse relationships between the weight of goods, packaging and indirect energy consumed by a household and household size. Research also showed inverse relationships between direct energy consumption, carbon emissions, household waste and household size (Fawcett et al [6]; Noorman and Uiterkamp [7] and INCPEN [5]). Table 1 summarises the impact of household size on household resource consumption and waste production patterns.

Research by Roy and Caird [8] adopted a more holistic approach to determine the environmental impact of household size by deriving eco-footprints for a variety of households. The analysis studied 692 UK households. It showed that there was a decline in the size of the eco-footprint (per capita) as households got larger. It concluded that the shift to ever-smaller households would have a highly negative effect on the environment, especially in terms of energy consumption, personal transport and land for housing.

From the research it seems that an increase in one-person households could potentially have a significant impact on the environment in terms of resource consumption (materials and energy), waste production, carbon emissions and loss of biodiversity. The effects of these changes will be felt across the globe. The problems are also likely to escalate as other nations in the developed world experience similar demographic trends including USA, Australia, New Zealand, Japan and the rest of Europe.

2 The UK situation

Between 1996 and 2021 the number of households in England is projected to increase by about 3.8 million (19%) as a result of population change (46%); behavioural change (33%) and greater life expectancy (21%). In the UK by 2021 it is estimated that 8.5 million households will be one-person households (i.e. 35.5% of all households). Currently the majority of one-person households are aged over 65 and often widowed. However, the potential growth groups for the future appear to be single people of all ages and in particular single males aged 35-44. Historically, the group have tended to be less affluent, but as the characteristics of the group change in the future, so too may its level of affluence. However, according to the Office of National Statistics [9] the majority of one-person households still appear to be in the lowest income deciles, although this is largely because the majority are retired and receiving only a state pension. Retired one-person households with other forms of pension are more affluent than those on a state pension but still appear largely in the 2nd, 3rd and 4th deciles. Working one-person households are more economically diverse and are well represented in the 1st – 7th deciles. The upper deciles tend to be populated by employed, male, one-person households aged 35-54. Thus if this sector of the group expands in the future (as predicted) so too could average income amongst one-person households and as a result resource consumption.

Further research is needed to determine how changes in affluence amongst one-person households will affect consumption patterns in the future and the relative importance of one-person households in influencing consumption patterns when compared with larger households (especially two person households which are currently the most affluent).

A detailed statistical analysis of UK data (Williams [10]) was completed to determine in greater depth what the resource implications were of an increase in one-person households in the UK particularly amongst the growth groups (i.e. singles and single males aged 35-44) and the largest groups currently (i.e. those aged over 65 and widowed). The analysis showed that household size (when compared to other socio-economic and design variables) was a significant factor influencing resource consumption per capita. In terms of energy four key factors influenced consumption per capita: housing design, household income, age of occupants and household size. Design and affluence were found to be the key factors influencing energy consumption. Household size appeared to have the least influence of the 4 variables, but nevertheless the analysis suggested it was significant. Household size and income appeared to be the key determinants of the land consumption per capita. In this instance household size appeared to be a more significant factor influencing land consumption per capita than income. However, income was the key factor influencing expenditure on household goods per capita, but household size still appeared to have some limited effect. The analysis found that there was an inverse relationship between gas and electricity consumption per capita and household size. In fact one-person households consumed between 23 – 77% more electricity and 38 – 54% more gas than two or four person (all adult) households per capita respectively. There also appeared to be an inverse relationship between the quantity of space (land) consumed per capita and household size. The analysis showed that one-person households consumed between 45 – 65% more space than two or four person (all adult) households per capita respectively. The important finding from the research was not that one-person households consumed more than those living in larger households (per capita), but the scale of the difference. In terms of the current most predominant groups amongst one-person households and fastest growing groups, the analysis found that single males aged 35-44 are likely to have the largest ecological footprint (Table 2). Single males aged 35-44 also consume more energy, household goods and live in larger units than an average one-person household. Significantly this group is also the most affluent.

Table 2: Greatest consumers of resources amongst growth groups and largest groups of one-person households.

	average	male single 35-44	oph 65+	widowed	single never married
Annual energy consumption per capita (kwh)	14197	16073	14175	13380	7868
Floor space per capita (sqm)	67	72	68	62	28
Weekly expenditure on household goods per capita (£)	25	25	18	19	25

Source: Williams [10].

The analysis suggested a strong positive relationship between domestic resource consumption and income. Thus it seems that if affluence amongst one-person households increases in the future (as current trends suggest) so too could domestic resource consumption amongst the group. However, there are conflicting arguments relating to how consumption patterns alter with rising levels of affluence. For example Durning [11] argues that increasing affluence will result in "greener" consumption as households buy more environmentally-friendly products. Rothman [12] argues that there is no evidence to support this suggestion and that consumption will continue increase as affluence grows. Ropke [13] suggests that patterns of consumption will alter as affluence increases and that the share of spending will switch from food (in lower income groups) to housing and transport (in higher income groups). This was supported by the analysis conducted by Williams [10] which showed that singles (who tended to be less affluent than the other groups studied) tended to consume considerably less space and energy but spent more on household goods than the other more affluent groups (Table 2). The findings from the research conducted by Williams, Rothman and Ropke suggest that if affluence amongst one-person households increased the group's spending on resources (and more especially housing and energy) is also likely to increase. However more research is needed to determine the environmental outcome of increasing affluence amongst the group. Overall these findings suggest that the UK government needs to consider the environmental implications of growth in one-person households (particularly as affluence increases amongst the group) and introduce policies to manage the impact.

3 The Government response

The Government recognises the link between increase in one-person households and increase in domestic energy and land consumption, green house gas emissions and waste production. However, there are no policies that are specifically aimed at reducing consumption amongst smaller households or increasing household size (both of which are unlikely to be politically popular). General national targets have been set to reduce municipal waste going to land fill and greenhouse gas emissions from all sectors. The Government has also set national targets for the domestic sector, for reducing carbon consumption and increasing waste recycling. National targets have also been set for the development of new housing on existing brown field sites or recycling existing properties. Targets have also been set to increase residential densities (between 30 and 50 dwellings per hectare net). Overall Government policies and investment reflects a preference for recycling (e.g. waste and land), re-use (waste and land), recovery (energy) of resources or use of renewable resources (energy) rather than minimisation through the introduction of consumption controls (as it might slow economic growth and reduce international competitiveness).

Environmental targets create the stimulus for policy creation and release of funds needed to achieve the environmental goals set. The Government has introduced national targets for carbon savings and waste, but land supply targets do not exist. Land supply for housing is controlled to an extent through the planning system. Local planning authorities determine the location of new development, the scale and residential densities. Housing capacity studies completed by local planning authorities identify the sites available for redevelopment and should in theory control the land released for housing. However, in reality the market still largely dictates the quantity and type of accommodation built. Land supply is finite and particularly restricted in the UK. Thus it is very important that land supply targets are introduced to curb the market and protect the resource, especially with the growth in demand for housing that has been predicted. A national land use strategy is needed to identify and co-ordinate the environmental, economic and social goals for development and control the consumption of resources. This would provide the basis for national land targets for all forms of development including housing. In line with national land targets more stringent housing density targets should also be implemented that truly reflect the finite nature of the resource.

Finally, there are no policies or targets that specifically deal with the resource implications of a growth in one-person households generated by inefficiencies and increasing affluence. However, the economic cost of resources tends to restrict consumption amongst one-person households, which is particularly effective currently because of the economic characteristics of the group (i.e. generally low income). Working in opposition to these economic controls are subsidies for one-person households (e.g. reduction in council tax and fuel payments for older one-person households). Econometric predictions suggest that one-person households will become more affluent in the future which may lead to an increase in consumption. In order to ensure more efficient use of resources amongst the more affluent groups it is important that the environmental cost of living alone is truly reflected by the economic cost. Thus subsidies will need to be removed and the environmental costs of all resources will need to be more accurately reflected in the price. However, the economic diversity of the group means a variety of policies will be needed that encourage the affluent to be more resource efficient whilst ensuring low income households have reasonable living conditions.

4 A time for change

The resource inefficiencies arising from the growth in one-person households need to be addressed urgently at a policy level. Numerous policies will need to be evaluated in order to tackle the resource issue. Set out below are some possible policy solutions any of which would require considerable research prior to implementation if they were to be successful. Taxation can be used to internalise the environmental cost of living alone or of resource consumption and waste production. More direct fiscal mechanisms to deal with under occupancy and waste production are needed. Currently the cost of household waste collection is incorporated into the council tax and set at a fixed rate regardless of the quantity of waste collected. This system is far from transparent. Charges for refuse collection by volume would make the system more transparent and encourage waste minimisation and recycling. An occupancy tax could be charged to households living in under-occupied dwellings to encourage them to move to smaller properties. This would reduce the land, materials and energy inefficiencies generated by under-occupancy. A greater supply of smaller accommodation would be needed to enable the tax to be successful. The introduction of the tax could also encourage the formation of larger peer-shared households. New housing designs and forms of tenure will be needed to accommodate this trend. A relocation package is already in place to tackle under-occupancy in the social sector housing but not for private sector housing where the major problem exists. Similar relocation schemes funded by Government to encourage lower income households in the private sector to move into smaller properties could also be introduced. An alternative to introducing a separate occupancy tax would be to reform the way in which the council tax is assessed (i.e. based on property value only). The reformed tax would be calculated on the basis of household income, occupancy and property value which would better reflect the environmental impact of the household. It could also produce a more equitable charging system by taking into account households income and therefore ability to pay. These taxes could be introduced by local authorities using the information and infrastructure currently used for calculating and collecting income and council tax. Such taxes are likely to be particularly unpopular with more affluent smaller households. However, the proceeds could be recycled to fund the infrastructure and schemes needed (i.e. relocation packages, provision of waste recycling and recovery facilities) to support the behavioural changes needed to produce the desired outcome (i.e. less waste going to landfill and greater resource efficiency).

The need to conserve land has been largely overlooked by Government. The creation of a national land use strategy and the introduction of land targets could be used to restrict the consumption of this valuable resource. Housing allocations could be based both on brownfield and overall land targets. The targets could be monitored and enforced through the national land use database and planning system thus minimising costs of implementation and monitoring. Building regulations and subsidies could be used to encourage greater innovation in terms of environmental design. Higher land values may restrict growth in the construction industry itself and economic growth more generally. The number of units built does not necessarily diminish with the introduction of land targets, as densities could increase together with numbers of smaller units. Existing stock could also be recycled to provide alternative accommodation that better reflected the needs of smaller households. This could be further encouraged through the introduction of more stringent density targets for residential development. Appropriate density thresholds would need to be researched based on social and environmental criteria.

New and existing stock needs to be resource efficient and suitable for smaller households. Legislation and funding streams already support energy efficiency in new and existing stock. New techniques are being used to reduce the environmental impact of the construction and refurbishment processes. In both the private and social sectors new housing is also becoming more space efficient.

But there is still a lack of one-bedroom stock available in the private sector. However, there appears to be an over supply of one-bedroom units in the social sector with insufficient numbers to fill the units (OPDM [14]). The higher density requirements and alternative lifestyles now emerging mean that there will be a need for more innovative design in existing and new housing stock in the future to address current resource inefficiencies. For peer-shared households the recent introduction of common-hold as a legitimate form of tenure in the UK may increase the ease of buying and selling property that is owned by a group of unrelated individuals, which could increase the potential for ownership and investment in this form of accommodation. Demonstration projects and funds for research and development could be provided by Government to encourage the development of the new design solutions and research potential markets. This would provide house-builders with the opportunity to innovate and help to generate markets for new housing forms. It would also enable house builders to develop expertise and experience that may help increase their competitiveness outside the UK.

In the short-term fiscal policy, design solutions, legislation and targets are likely to be the most successful instruments for change. However, longer-term there will need to be a profound cultural shift towards greener consumption patterns (i.e. a reduction in consumption and consumption of more environmentally friendly products). Education provides an instrument, through which these long-term changes might be achieved, by providing people with the information that enables them to understand why change is needed and how it can be best achieved. A programme to raise awareness of the environmental impacts of under-occupancy and benefits of greener household consumption is needed for all households. It would be useful to direct a specific campaign at one-person households to make them aware of their particular impact and provide them with greener lifestyle options that particularly reflect their needs and preferences.

5 Conclusions

In conclusion, the growth in one-person households is potentially a resource time bomb. The rapid growth in household numbers, resource inefficiencies and increasing affluence amongst one-person households make the group potentially a major resource consumer and waste producer. More research is needed to determine the future levels of affluence and consumption patterns amongst the group in order to estimate its impact more accurately as these estimates are extrapolated from current trends. The Government has recognised the potential environmental implications of the growth in one-person households but is yet to introduce any specific policies to tackle the problem. This paper presents some possible instruments for reducing the environmental impact of the domestic sector. All of these would require considerable research prior to their adoption as would any similar policies aimed at defusing the resource time-bomb identified in this paper.

References

[1] Van Diepen, A., Developments In Household Composition In Europe. In (Ed.) Noorman, K and Uiterkamp, T *Green Households: Domestic Consumers, Environment And Sustainability.* London: Earthscan Publications, pp 82-101, 1998

[2] Economic Commission for Europe, *Trends In Europe And North America: The Statistical Yearbook,* 2003.

[3] Liu, Daily, Ehrich and Luck, Effects of Household Dynamics on Resource Consumption and Biodiversity. *Nature*, 421, pp530 – 533, 2003

[4] Cincotta, R. P. & Engelman, R. Nature's Place: Human Population and the Future of Biological Diversity, *Population Action International*, Washington DC, 2000.

[5] International Consumer Protection and Enforcement Network, *Towards Greener Households – Producers, Packaging and Energy.* London: INCPEN, 2001..

[6] Fawcett, T, Hurst, A, and Boardman, B, *Carbon in the UK Economy.* Oxford: Oxford University Press, 2002.

[7] Noorman, K and Uiterkamp, T, *Green Households: Domestic Consumers, Environment And Sustainability.* London: Earthscan Publications, 1998

[8] Roy, R and Caird, S, Footprints on the Carpet. *Town and Country Planning,* 70 (10) pp277-279, 2001.

[9] Office of National Statistics, *Family spending 2001-02*, London: HMSO, 2003.

[10] Williams, J, *Homes for the Future – A Means for Managing the Singletons Consumption Crisis*, unpublished PhD Thesis, Department of Planning. London, University College London, 2003.

[11] Durning, A, *How much is enough? The consumer society and the future of the earth*, Earthscan Publications, London, 1992.

[12] Rothman, D, *Environmental kuznets curves – real progress or passing the buck?* 1998.

[13] Ropke, I, The environmental impact of changing consumption patterns: a survey. *International Journal of Environment and Pollution*, 15 (2) pp127-145, 2001.

[14] Office of Deputy Prime Minister, *Under-occupation in social housing.* London: OPDM, 2000.

www.witpress.com, ISSN 1743-3541 (on-line)

Environmental impacts of the regulation of the Shinano River, Niigata prefecture, Japan

M. Sane[1], H. Yamagishi[2], M. Tateishi[2] & T. Izumia[3]
[1]Graduate School of Science and Technology, Department of Environmental Sciences, Niigata University Japan
[2]Faculty of Sciences, Niigata University, Japan
[3]Faculty of Engineering, Niigata University, Japan

Abstract

The coastal zone of Niigata Prefecture is severely affected by erosion. This study was developed to investigate the relationships between river regulation and changes to the coastal zone. Regulation of the Shinano River began during the Meiji Period with the construction of a long jetty. The jetty was built to avoid the silting of the river mouth, and allow the significant maritime trade to continue with inland transport via the Shinano River. Additional regulation involved the dredging of two channels southward from the mouth of the Shinano River, the Sekiya and the Ohkozu, for the purpose of flood mitigation in the Niigata Plain. To evaluate changes to the coastline, several approaches were used. Firstly, six sets of aerial photographs were examined. Then, the sediments grain-size parameters and mineral variation were analyzed to find the correspondence with shoreline changes. As a third approach, field surveys were conducted and historical data on the coastal process was assessed. The coast in the vicinity of the artificial channels accreted and there was erosion on the down-drift side of the river mouth.
Keywords: Shinano River, jetty-Ohkozu channel, Sekiya channel, erosion.

1 Introduction

In Japan, coastal erosion affects most of the shoreline along the Sea of Japan, though seldom along the Pacific coast. The most significant changes are observed along the coast of Niigata Prefecture especially from the mouth of the Shinano River to the district of Joetsu. Erosion is due to several factors, mainly the reduction in river sediment supply to the coast caused by the construction of diversion channels such as the Ohkozu and Sekiya channels. Changes to the shoreline have also occurred from the interference of coastal protective structures with the natural longshore transport, causing a sand deficit on their down-drift side. Indeed, Niigata is the biggest port along the Sea of Japan and it prospered in the feudal age by transporting rice from the Echigo Plain. The city was also an important place for maritime trade and inland transport via the Shinano River. In those days, the mouth of the Shinano River was so frequently filled with sediment carried by the river that the port's business was often hampered. Following the river reform on the Niigata Plain in the latter part of the nineteenth century, a jetty was constructed on the west side of the river mouth in 1906 to move the sandbar further seaward to maintain a deeper channel for navigation. This resulted in a larger volume of sand being retained that is more difficult for sediments to move down the shoreline. This inhibition of sand movement continued further along the coast. The beaches between the welding of the bar and the river entrance suffer great erosion. With respect to Ohkozu and Sekiya channels, their main purpose was to mitigate the flooding that affected the low lands in Niigata Prefecture.

This was widely discussed by Isobe [5], Tanaka [14], Takeyama [13], Tsuchiya et al. [9] and Yoshikawa et al. [15]. Several investigators also believe that a series of tectonic disturbances in the geological past, together with the natural geomorphology of the coastal zone, led to the coastline being vulnerable to hazards. This is based on indications of a high subsidence rate Nakano and Takehisa [7], the low topography, the geomorphologic units consisting of mainly low resistant materials such as natural levees, sand dunes and swamps Urban Kubota [1], and exceptional winter tidal waves. However, there has been little investigation on the effect of river regulation on changes to the coastal environment, especially the drop in river sediment supplied to the coast, as shown by the sorting pattern of heavy minerals and textures of beaches sand.

2 The study area

The study area (Figure 1) is located in a very sensitive coastline stretching between the mouth of the Shinano River and the Ohkozu channel, Niigata Prefecture, Japan. It has a well- developed social and economic infrastructure. The coastal plain in the region has large-scale irrigation schemes where crops such as rice and vegetables are grown. The study area was formed by both fluvial and marine deposits in the Quaternary age. It has been affected by worldwide sea- level changes as well as local tectonic movements. It consists mostly of alluvial lowland, less than 5 m high, with a few, very scattered remnants of terraces Yoshikawa et al. [15]. Geomorphologic units consist mainly of Late Quaternary units such as coastal sand dunes (III- II 600- 500 years BP) Urban Kubota [1]. These units are backed by alluvial depression of the Niigata Plain and natural levees. Beach types found along the Japanese coast show the occurrence of multi- bar beaches which also occur along the study area Mogi [6].

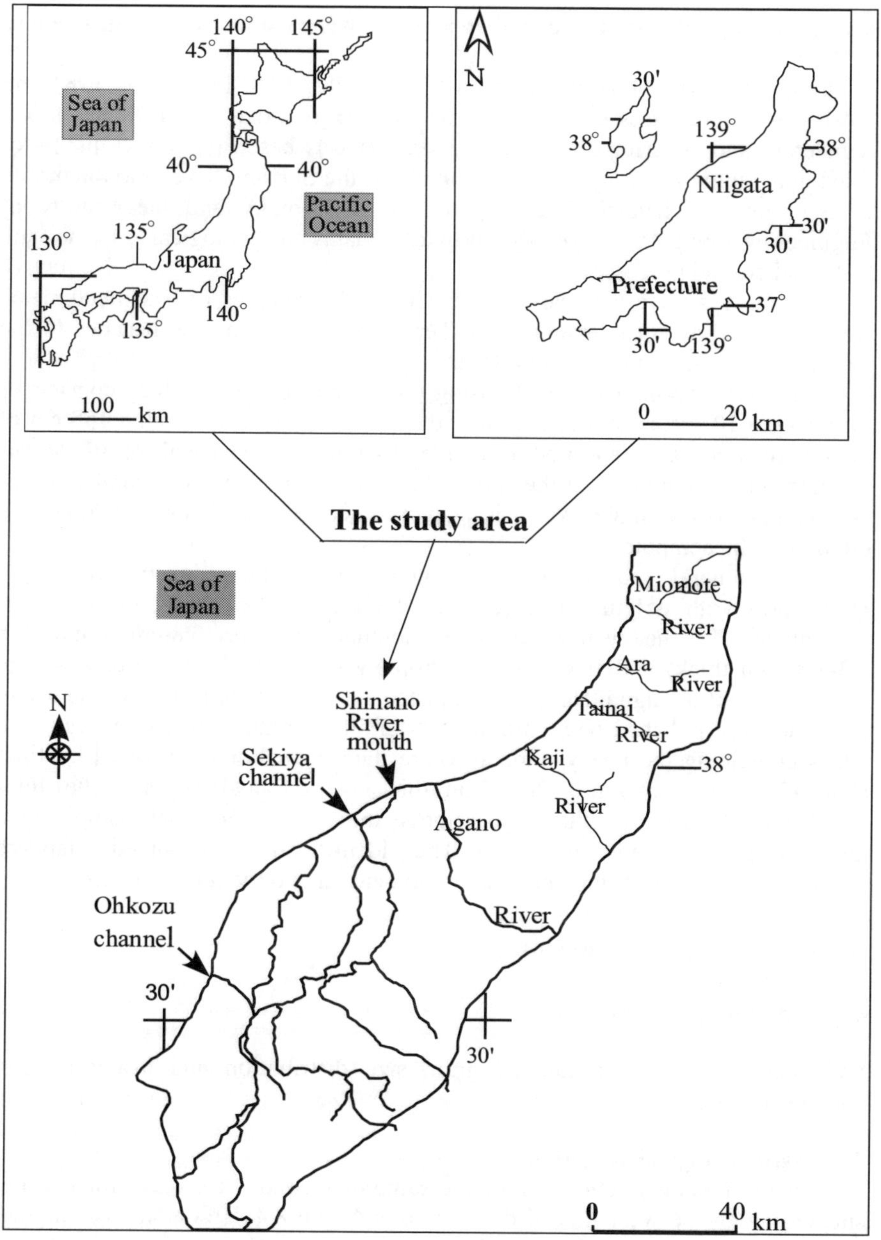

Figure 1: Location map of the study area.

3 Data collection

In this study, a survey was carried out to examine the impacts of river regulation on a portion of the Niigata shoreline from the mouth of the Shinano River to the beaches along Teradomari. Several approaches were use to evaluate the changes to the shoreline.

Firstly, six aerial photographs from 1914, 1928, 1958, 1972-1974, 1981 and 1991-1995 were assessed. These images were rectified to the same scale, registered, and superimposed. The registration was based on control points of fixed geographic features such as the mouth of the Shinano River and the mouth of the Ohkozu channel. The Department of Geology and the Faculty of Engineering, Niigata University, provided data on geological aspects and historical coastal processes.

Field surveys were also carried out. Up to 100 samples of beach sediments were collected at 5m intervals along Teradomari coast and the beaches to the west of the mouth of the Shinano River.

Grain size analyses were made using the method of Drop, which consists of introducing 10 grams of sediment into the analyzer bottle containing 155 cm of volume of water, and deposited on a slide of Aluminum. The analyzer bottle was connected to a computer. At the end of the timing (10 to tens of seconds), grain-size parameters (grain-size, kurtosis, skewness, standard deviation) are translated directly to the computer.

Heavy mineral grains were separated from light sediments by using bromoform with polytungstate (density 2.82g), weighed and converted into percentages. The heavy minerals were mounted on slides (28mm×48mm and 1.3-1.4 mm thick) and fixed using Petropoxy (10 parts Resin hardener). The slides were put on digital Hot Plates adjusted at 75°to let the resin set. The heavy minerals were polished with carbon 1500 grains to reduce their thickness. The slides containing the heavy minerals were then heated and recovered by finer slides (24mm×32mm and 0.12-0.17mm thick) using Canada Balsam. The slides have been cleaned by Ethanol to remove the carbon. For each sample, two hundred grains were analyzed. The identification accounted standard petrographic criteria (color, specific gravity, etc.) and optic microscope.

4 Results and discussion

4.1 Sediment patterns

Sediments parameters accounted grain size distribution and heavy mineral contents (figure 2).

4.1.1 Mineralogical variations

The heavy mineral fractions in all the samples ranged 0.1%-0.2% for beaches situated along the west side of the river mouth and 8%-10% along Teradomari beaches. Several mineral species have been identified and classified into minerals of high specific gravity and minerals of low specific gravity. The mineral procession is dominated by three of the most stable heavy minerals such as apatite, rutile and tourmaline. The grouping of the heavy minerals in minerals of low specific gravity and minerals of high specific gravity made it possible to identify the portions of strong agitation and low agitation.

The high percentage of minerals with high specific gravity (83%) such as rutile and tourmaline along the beaches to the west of the river mouth suggests a portion with strong agitation, which is not favorable for the accumulation of sands. Heavy minerals of lower densities are selectively entrained and transported offshore by the swash of waves on the beach face, tending to leave as a lag the minerals that have higher densities Li and Komar [4]. Similar results were obtained by Frihy and Lofty [2] and Idrissi et al [3] in their analyses along the northern Sinai coast of Egypt and on the coastal zone of Casablanca, Morocco.

Conversely, beaches along Teradomari coast tend to have heavy minerals with lower specific gravity dominated by opaques (magnetites and ilmenites), which constitute 88% with smaller concentrations of apatite and tourmaline. The increase in the proportion of minerals with lower specific gravity suggests a portion of shoreline with weak agitation that is favorable for the accretion of sediments.

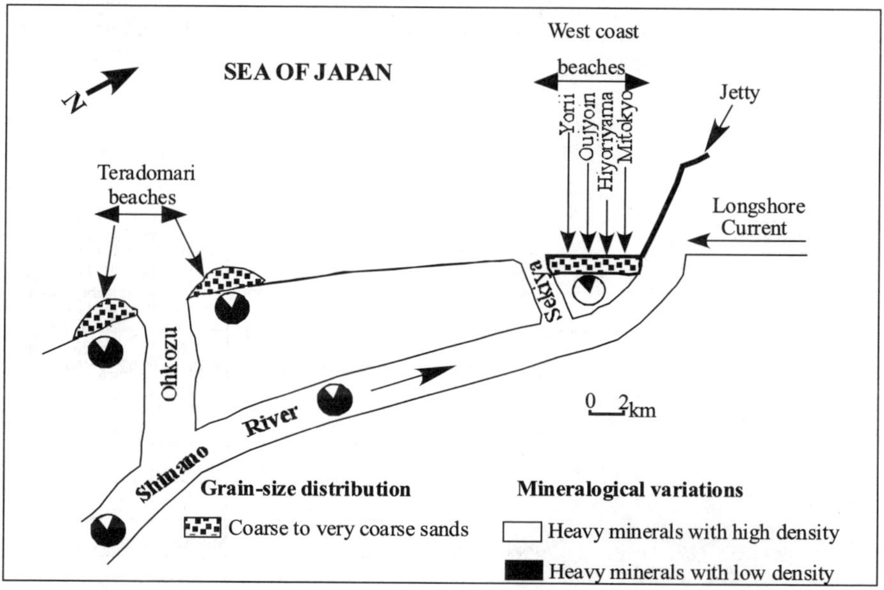

Figure 2: Grain-size and mineralogic distribution of sediments.

4.1.2 Grain-size distribution

The granulometric analysis of the sands taken along the beaches of Teradomari shows a generally coarse fraction dominated by sediments ranging 0.5mm-1mm (94.415% of the samples), classified as very well sorted (So=0.21) and strongly coarse-skewed (Sk= -1.50 in average). The granulometric analysis of the sands taken in the Ohkozu channel and further upstream of the Shinano River shows the same pattern since 93.476% of sediments range 0.5mm-0.25mm, very well sorted (So=0.22) and strongly coarse-skewed with terms for skewness averaging -1.5. The resemblance between the granulometric characteristics of sediments of the beaches along Teradomari coast and those of the main channel of the Shinano River indicates significant river sediment supply to the beaches along Teradomari coast.

In the other hand, grain-size distribution along the coast to the west of the mouth of the Shinano River shows a slight distinctive pattern with a more important fraction of coarser grains since 74.532% of the sediments range 1mm-1.25mm. The beaches of his section are separated from the river mouth by the protruding jetty, which prevents sediment supply to this section and indicates that river sediment supply to the coast has become inexistent or negligible. This is confirmed by the difference between the granulometric characteristics of the channel sediments and beaches of this section. The lack of river sediment supply and the absence of longshore sediment transport have amplified the erosive trend observed along this portion by reducing the sedimentary input necessary for the balance of the beaches.

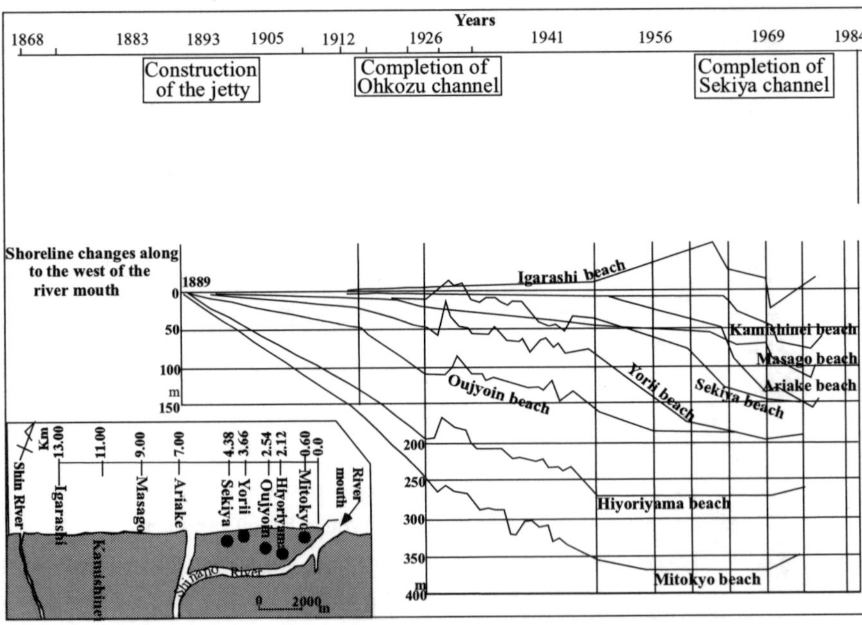

Figure 3: Changes to the shoreline along the west side of the river mouth following the regulation of the Shinano River, Urban Kubota (1). The bold circles indicate the sampling sites along this portion.

4.2 Eroded beaches

Beaches along the west side of the river mouth have undergone a significant and almost continuous retreat since the construction of the long jetty on the river mouth in 1906. The construction of the jetty disturbed the North-South oriented littoral sediment transport, causing erosion of the beaches to the west of the river mouth, located downdrift. The completion of the Ohkozu and Sekiya channels then aggravated the sedimentation imbalance and accelerated the regressive evolution of the beaches along this portion. The lack of longshore and river sediment supply led this portion being exposed to the erosive action of the swell that is particularly strong during winter. The retreat of the shoreline to the west of the river mouth is estimated at 400m during the eighty years considered for this study, that is to say a rate of erosion of 5m/year. Except for the Igarashi beach, which shows localized sediment deposition, the beaches of this portion (Mitokyo, Hyoriyama, Oujyoin and Yori) underwent significant erosion (Figure 3). This led the decision maker to undertake a vast program to mitigate the erosion by a large scale of coastal hardening involving engineering structures such as detached breakwaters and artificial reefs.

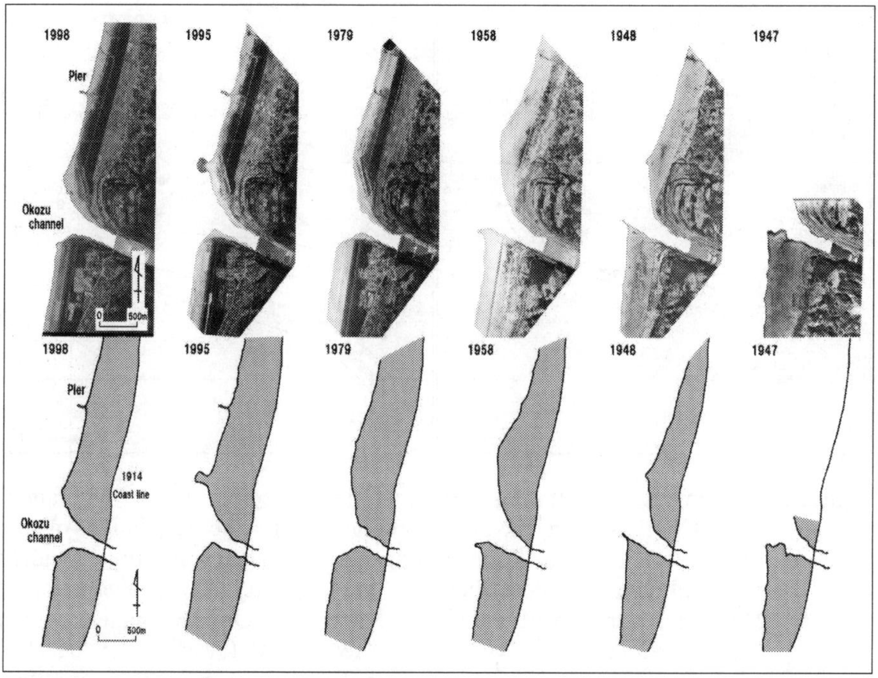

Figure 4: Changes to the shoreline along Teradomari following the completion of the Ohkozu channel, Yamagishi et al [11].

4.3 Prograding beaches

The beaches of Teradomari prograded substantially following the completion of the Ohkozu channel. The sedimentary contributions accumulated along this portion come essentially from the Shinano River by way of the excavated channel. The coast to the west of the river mouth was deprived of almost 90% of volumes of sediment that are diverted towards the beaches of Teradomari. Indeed, prior to its regulation, the Shinano River discharged to the coast a total volume of sediments estimated at 1,000,000 m^3/y. After the completion of the Ohkozu channel in 1932 and the Sekiya channel in 1972, up to 900,000m^3/y of volume of sediments was diverted mainly towards the Ohkozu channel (oral communication, 2004). As a result, the coastal zone surrounding the Ohkozu channel shows sedimentary progradation of more than 700 meters as shown in figure 4.

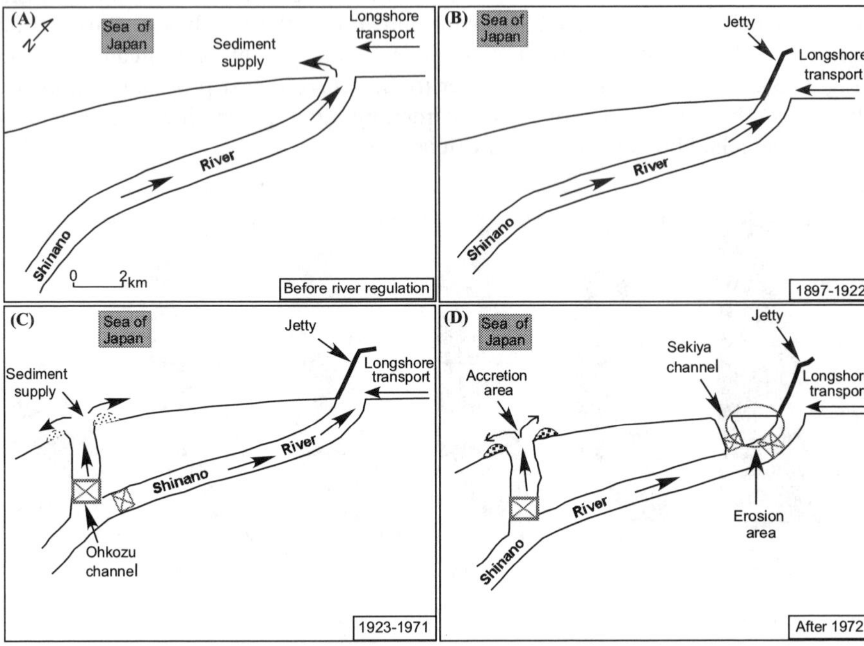

Figure 5: Schematic illustration of the impacts of river regulation. (A): Configuration of the shoreline before the regulation of the Shinano River. (B): Drop in longshore sediment transport downdrift side following the construction of the long jetty. (C): Exacerbation of the erosive trend with the construction of the Ohkozu channel, which discharges 90% in volume of sediments towards the beaches Teradomari. (D): The beaches of Teradomari accreted more than 700m of sediments to the detriment of those to the west of the river mouth, which undergone significant erosion averaging 400m.

5 Conclusion

We attempted to understand the relationship between river regulation and changes in the coastal area along a portion of the Niigata Prefecture shoreline over an eighty-year period. The geomorphology showed a predominance of low topography and low resistant units, with significant ground subsidence and influence from strong tidal waves in winter. Before river regulation, fluctuations in the shoreline were due to typical seasonal changes such as the retreat of the beaches due to the increase of the swell energy in winter with rough-seas and accretion again when the seas were calm. Seasonal surveying made it possible to determine the variations of height on the beaches along the study area. This natural erosion and accretion process had been altered by engineering works. With construction of a long jetty on the western side of the mouth of the Shinano River, there was a significant reduction in sediment delivery by the longshore current and a drop in sediment supply to the coast leading to impoverishment of the majority of the beaches to the west of the river mouth and resulting in rapid erosion.

Construction of the Ohkozu and Sekiya channels further reduced the sediment discharge to the coast by more than 90% (Yamagishi [16]). The coast to the vicinity of the mouth of the Ohkozu channel accreted more than 700 meters of sediment since 1912, and the coast to the west of the mouth of the Shinano River eroded significantly, averaging 400 m. A schematic illustration depicting the regulation of the Shinano River and induced impacts is given below (figure 5).

Considering river regulation has affected the coastal landscape, we encourage efficient mitigation of coastal degradation by both engineering methods and with integrated management. For successful and sustainable management actions in the coastal zones, the management action must be technologically feasible, economically viable, socially desirable, legislatively permissible administratively achievable, also environmentally sustainable Elliot and de Jonge [12]. Environmentally sustainable management action is highly welcomed for the coastal zone of Niigata Prefecture in particular since it has suffered so far major damages and has been threatened by several hazards such as flooding and high waves, while at the same time coastal erosion has worsened.

References

[1] Urban, K., *Geomorphology of Niigata Prefecture*. Niigata University, Graduate School of Science and Technology, Faculty of Sciences, pp 10-47, 1979.

[2] Frihy, O.E. & Lofty, M.F., *Shoreline changes and beach-sand sorting along the northern Sinai coast of Egypt.* Springer-Verlaag:Geo-Marine Letters (17), pp 140-146, 1997.

[3] Idrissi, M., Ait Laamel, M., Hourimeche, M., Chadgali, M., *Impacts of the swell on the current morphological and sedimentary evolution of the coastal zone of Casablanca-Mohammedia (Morocco).* Elsevier: Journal of African Earth Sciences (39), pp 541-548, 2004.

[4] Li, Z. & Komar, P.D, *Longshore grain sorting and beach placer formation adjacent to the Colombia River*. Journal of Sedimentary Petrology (62), pp 429-441, 1992.

[5] Isobe, M., *A theory of integrated coastal zone management in Japan.* Department of Civil Engineering, University of Tokyo, p 18, 2001.

[6] Mogi, A., *On the shore types of the coasts of Japanese Islands*. Geogr. Rev. Japan, 36, 245-266 (J+E), 1963.

[7] Nakano, T., and Takehisa, Y., *Ground subsidence in the Niigata Plain*. Geogr. Rev. Japan, 33, 1-9. (J+E), 1960.

[8] Sakaguchi, Y., *Notes on the problems of the paleogeography of the Echigo Plain, Niigata Prefecture*. Quat. Res (Japan), 3, 284-289. (J), 1964a.

[9] Tsuchiya, Y., Shibano, T., and Nakanishi, T., *Long- term shoreline change of the Naoetsu harbor*. Coastal Eng. In Japan 19: 109-20, 1976.

[10] Uda, T. Shoichi, K., and Torao, T., *Beach changes caused by the construction of coastal structure on the Ichibouri Coast in Niigata Prefecture*. J Japanese Geomorphological Union, Vol 9, No 1, Jan 1988.

[11] Yamagishi H., Takashi, I., Ayalew, L.& Ota, Y., *Environmental geology of the Kakuda-Yahiko Range- geomorphic sequence and landslide susceptibility*- Department of Environmental Science, Faculty of Science, Niigata University, Japan, pp. 57-59, 2003

[12] Elliot, M., and de Jonge, V.N., *Responses of estuaries to natural and anthropogenic changes: perspectives and a global view*. ECSA 37 ERF 2004 conference Ballina (Australia) June 20-24, Proceedings. P: 21, 2004.

[13] Takeyama, S., *Changes of river bed in the middle reaches of "Tones" River*. Geogr. Rev. Japan, 31, 486-495. (J+E), 1958.

[14] Tanaka, M., *Rate of erosion in the Tanzawa Mountains, central Japan*. Geogr. Ann., 3, Ser. A, 155-163, 1976.

[15] Yoshikawa, T. Kaizuka, S. & Ota, Y., *The landform of Japan*. University of Tokyo Press, 222 p, 1981.

[16] Yamagishi, T. *Personal communication*, 15th July 2004, Consultant, Kitac. Co. Ltd, Niigata city, Japan.

Groundwater flow and flushing of animal burrows in tropical mangrove swamps

A. Susilo
Department of Physics, Geophysics Laboratory, Brawijaya University, Indonesia

Abstract

Tidal groundwater in a mangrove swamp can return to the mangrove creek by one of two mechanisms: (a) flowing through the swamp soil due to water table difference between the creek and the groundwater in the swamp; or (b) flowing via tidal flushing of animal burrows. This paper compares the magnitude of these two mechanisms for different regions of a mangrove swamp. Direct groundwater flow rates resulted from water stored in the sediment as a consequence of infiltration, especially during and after tidal inundation, were calculated for every square meter in the surface of a mangrove forest from piezometer data. Flow rates of water due to burrow flushing were determined based on published surveys, by estimating the burrow volume and the percentage of the burrow water that was flushed at each tidal inundation. Although direct groundwater flux was found to decrease further away from the creek compared to that close to the creek, it has similar range to burrow flushing flow. The direct groundwater flow ranged from 0.004 to 0.04 $m^3/m^2/day$, whilst burrow flushing flux ranged from 0.01 to 0.04 $m^3/m^2/day$. Considering the errors involved in the experiments and calculations, these ranges can be considered as being the same and neither of the two processes can be considered as superior to the other. As a consequence, surveys of groundwater processes in mangrove areas, and more generally in swamp and tidal areas where animal burrows are present, will need to consider both mechanisms. Investigations of the influence over flushing mechanisms of different residence times of the water in burrows and in the sediment body would also be recommended in order to establish salt and nutrient budget in mangrove swamps.
Keywords: burrow flushing, groundwater flow, mangrove swamp, piezometer.

1 Introduction

Groundwater flow in mangrove creeks has attracted a number of scientific researches in recent years [1-7] because it might have a significant influence on the salt balance and other processes such as nutrient cycling. Groundwater flow is a main pathway for the transport of terrestrial nutrient from the land to the creek along with surface flow from rain runoff or tidal inundation [4]. Mazda *et al.* [8] and Wolanski [9] predicted that groundwater flow through mangrove swamps is an important factor in determining the nutrient budget and water properties of the receiving mangrove creek.

Burrow flushing during inundation may be an important factor in exchanging solutes (oxygen, nutrients, toxins and salts) between surface and burrow water [1]. Recent researches have investigated the mechanism driving this process [10] and attempted to quantify it [11]. Flushing of burrow water occurs during tidal inundation and is caused by a pressure difference across the numerous openings of the burrow due to the surface water slope [10]. It was estimated that about 30% of burrow water was flushed per tide during that process [11], entraining salts and other materials out of the burrows and into the creek.

As outlined above, tidal water in a mangrove swamp can flow to the creek by two mechanisms, which are;

(a) Groundwater that flows through the sediment as interstitial pore-water from the swamp to the creek. This flow is a consequence of water infiltration, especially during and after tidal inundation, and is due to the hydraulic gradient between the swamp and the creek. In this paper it will be called "direct groundwater flow".

(b) Flushing of free water through animal burrows during tidal inundation. This will be called "burrow flushing flow".

In this work, I compared the importance of water flow rates due to direct groundwater flow and burrow flushing in mangrove swamps, assuming that both mechanisms occur.

2 Study sites

The three study sites were located in the upper reaches of the Cocoa Creek (approximately 55 km east of Townsville (19°15'S; 146°50'E), North Queensland), the Gordon Creek (approximately 5 km southeast of Townsville), and Situbondo, East Java, Indonesia. These sites were selected because they contained extensive mangrove communities and well developed creek network. Besides, experiments on the hydraulic conductivity of mangrove sediment had been carried out previously in the first two areas [12]. Finally, investigations on the morphology of burrows (using resin casts [13] and on the proportion of burrow water flushed during each inundation [11] had also been conducted in the *Rhizophora stylosa* mangrove forest at Gordon Creek.

The Cocoa Creek (Figure 1b) is an undisturbed area within the Cape Bowling Green National Park. Its length is about 7 km and its width ranges from approximately 50 m at the mouth to less than 10 m at the head. The width of the mangrove fringe that grows along the creek varies along its length from a few meters to 50 m. The Cocoa Creek is ebb-tide dominated [14].

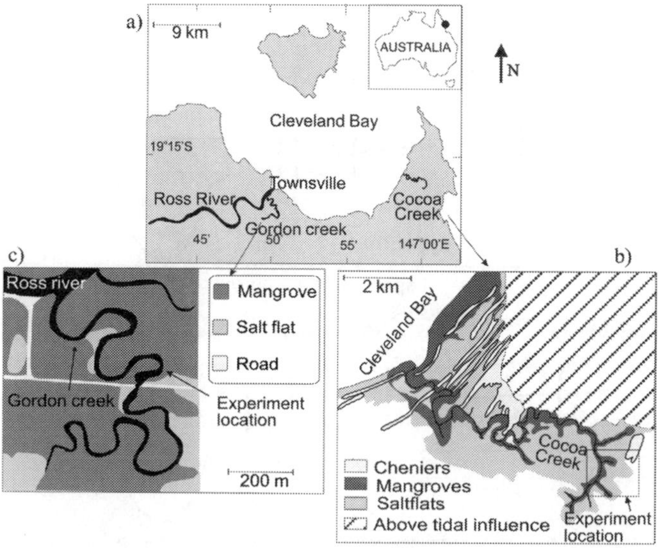

Figure 1: Study sites in the mangrove forests near Townsville (a), in the upper reaches of Cocoa Creek (b) and in the middle section of Gordon Creek.

The second study site, the Gordon Creek, is a small creek that drains into a much larger Ross River. It is *ca.* 5 km long, 16 m wide at the mouth and 4 m wide at the head. The mangrove forest growing along the Gordon Creek is mainly composed of *Rhizophora stylosa* and *Ceriops spp.*at the edge of the creek.

The third study site was only to measure the hydraulic conductivity of the mangrove sediment. The detail of this area is not explained here.

3 Methods

3.1 Piezometer arrays

Four piezometers were installed at the Cocoa Creek amongst the living and dead mangrove trees at irregular intervals, at 2 and/or 4 m depth depending on the site, and water level was logged continuously from 14 June through 27 September 2001 (Figure 2a). A fifth piezometer was deployed in the middle of the creek for 2 weeks to compare tidal variations on site with tidal predictions at Townsville. Dataflow Systems Pty. Ltd. (Australia) pressure sensors were then mounted inside PVC tubes and the data logger was attached on top of a stand.

At the Gordon Creek, 5 piezometers were installed from October 2001 to April 2002, at approximately 1 m depth mostly in the *Rhizophora stylosa* area, except for one piezometer that was installed at the border between *Rhizophora stylosa* (O5) and *Ceriops spp* (Figure 2b). The depth of 1 m was chosen to position the bottom of each piezometer in a burrow and to record water level inside the burrows.

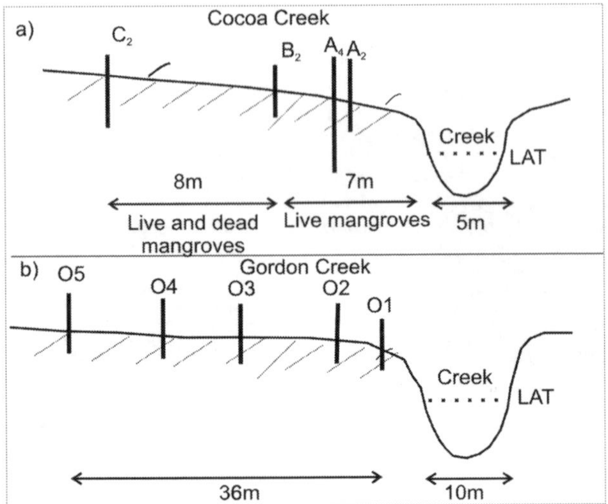

Figure 2: Piezometers transects as installed (a) in the upper reaches of the Cocoa Creek, with three instruments amongst the live mangrove area and one in the mixed zone with dead and live trees, and (b) at the Gordon Creek.

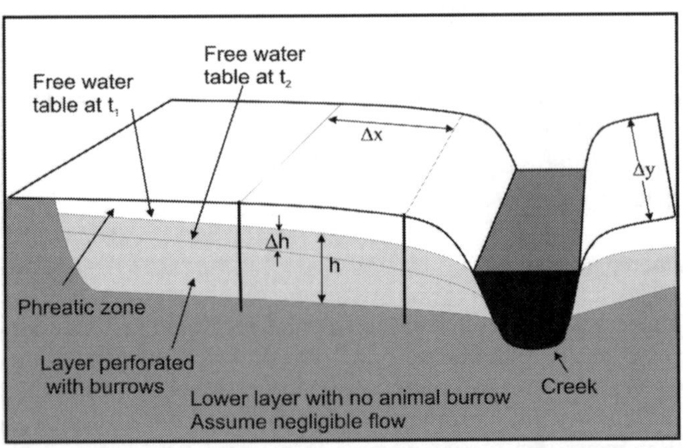

Figure 3: Position of the underground water table during ebb tide. During a few hours (days), when ebb or small high tides occur, the water table in the sediment will drop in relation to the porosity of the sediment.

3.2 Model description

When tidal height is lower than the swamp sediment surface and there is no tidal inundation, the water table level in the mangrove forest is located below the swamp sediment surface and infiltration will not occur. However, the tidal influence is still present in the sediment body, as the water level in the sediment will follow the tidal signature, up to a certain distance from the creek. Further away from the creek, groundwater level in the sediment will slowly fall because it will be out of range of the horizontal pressure caused by tidal fluctuations.

Regardless of the tide height, level with respect to the swamp sediment surface, the water table level will gradually fall during ebbing periods until the next flooding tide. Moreover, in both cases where the water level is lower than the sediment surface (i.e. at ebbing tide of high tides, and during flooding and ebbing of small high tides), the rate of groundwater loss from the mangrove sediment pores to the creek over a period Δt can be calculated from the piezometer water level (see Equation (1) referring to Figure 3).

Based on Figure 3, the equation for direct groundwater flow can be defined as:

$$\Delta V/\Delta t = \left(\Delta h/\Delta t - E\right)\Delta x\,\Delta y\left(1 - F_S(t)\right)p\left(1 - F_b\right) + \left(\Delta h/\Delta t - E\right)\Delta x \Delta y F_b \quad (1)$$

where $\Delta V/\Delta t$ = volume change rate of water stored in the sediment; $\Delta h/\Delta t$ = change rate of the water table level (measured with the piezometers);

E = evapotranspiration rate;
Δx and Δy are defined in Figure 3;
$F_s(t)$ = degree of saturation of the sediment;
p = porosity of the sediment;
F_b= fraction of sediment layer that is occupied by animal burrows.

The first term on the right hand side of Equation 1 is the rate of change of water volume stored in the sediment pores, and the second term is the volume of free water that is stored in the burrows. Both terms refer to a period Δt. Hence Equation 1 expresses the total amount of tidal water that is stored in a slab of sediment of surface area $\Delta x\Delta y$ over a period Δt.

The groundwater fluctuations recorded by the piezometers were used to determine the value of $\Delta V/\Delta t$ in Equation 1 and to calculate the rate of change of water volume stored in the sediment. The water level was calculated and averaged for each piezometer over periods of hours or days, depending on the available data.

Tidal flushing of the burrow was also modeled for the same slab of surface area $\Delta x\Delta y$, over a period of time Δt. The average volume of water that was removed from the burrows over approximately a lunar cycle period (Δt = 1 month) was calculated. Since water was removed from the burrows at each swamp inundation, the number of inundations per month (N) was first determined. Different mangrove swamps will undergo different numbers of inundations over a lunar cycle, depending on the level of the swamp sediment surface and characteristics of the tide. From the physical characteristics of the mangrove swamp, the flow rate of the water flushed from a burrow, Q_{wf}, can be described as follows:

$$Q_{wf} = \Delta x \, \Delta y \, D_b \, F_b \, F_{wf} \, N / \Delta t \tag{2}$$

where: D_b = depth of the burrow;
F_b = fraction of burrow volume compared to sediment volume;
F_{wf} = fraction of burrow water flushed per inundation;

This flow rate is expressed in m^3/day, but it can be reduced to a rate in metre of depth/day or in metre of depth /s within an area of 1 m^2 of sediment surface.

4 Results and discussions

4.1 Fluctuations of groundwater levels at Cocoa Creek

Figure 4 shows the results of groundwater fluctuations recorded at the Cocoa Creek over approximately 2 weeks (14 - 28 June 2001) during dry season (no rainfall occurred during that period). Although measurements were recorded over 3.5 months in total, only a 2-week sample covering a spring-neap cycle is presented here for clarity. Other spring-neap cycles not presented in the figure displayed a similar pattern. Because the swamp sediment surface of the mangrove forest at the Cocoa Creek was relatively high (3.2 m above LAT), the sites were rarely inundated with only 9 inundations occurring per month on a yearly average, with the maximum number of inundations in March (15), and the minimum number in June (5), including the period shown on Figure 4.

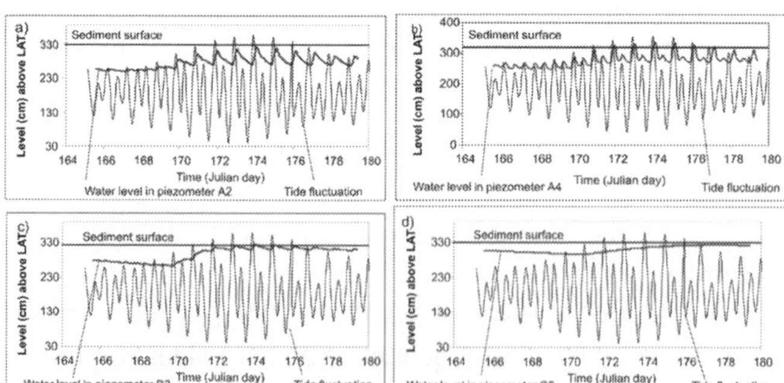

Figure 1: Fluctuations of groundwater level and tides at Cocoa Creek sites with respect to the sediment surface level.

The delay of water level fluctuations in the piezometers over the tidal cycles was 3 to 5 hours, depending on the distance of the piezometer from the creek and on the depth of the piezometer. The greater the distance from the creek, the longer the time lag between tide height and groundwater response. In addition, at sites A4 and A2 which were close to each other but at different depths, the time lag was similar for both piezometers, but the deepest piezometer (A4) followed the tidal signature more closely in term of amplitude of response.

4.2 Fluctuations of groundwater levels at Gordon Creek

There was no period over which reliable data was recorded simultaneously at all sites at Gordon Creek due to battery failure, faulty pressure sensors, and PVC screens not touching the burrows. Therefore, the data presented in Figure 5 cover different periods for different sites, but there was no rain throughout the duration of the study and thus conditions were consistent. All sites were inundated by the tides 19 times per month on average, which was therefore also the frequency at which the crab burrows were flushed.

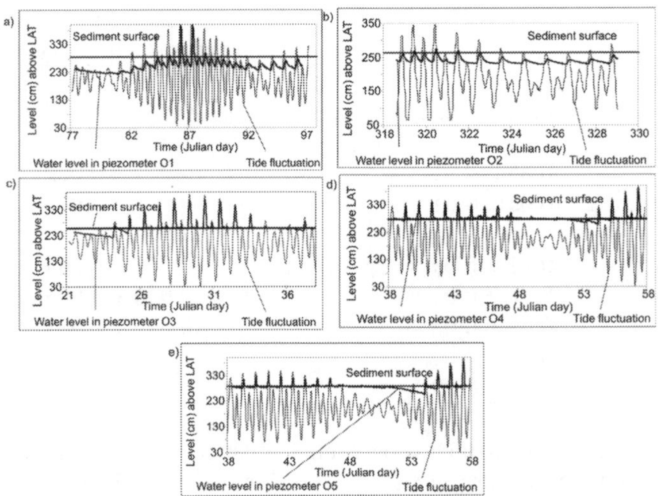

Figure 4: Fluctuations of groundwater level (from piezometer records) and tides (from tide table) at Gordon Creek sites.

Water level fluctuations at Gordon Creek show a similar pattern at sites O3, O4 and O5 (Figures 5c, d and e). These patterns show that the water level fluctuations followed the tidal signature when the tide was higher than the swamp sediment surface. In contrast, fluctuations disappeared when the tide did not reach the swamp sediment surface. There was no delay between tidal height and groundwater level peaks, which indicates that the piezometers were well connected to the burrows.

At site O1, groundwater fluctuations followed tidal variations only for the highest tides, and without a time lag. A lag occurred only when the tide was below the swamp sediment surface, with a *ca.* 1 hour lag. During the rest of the study period, water height fluctuations displayed only one oscillation per day with a sharp rise and a slow fall, which were least pronounced at the end of the neap period. Site O2 showed only one oscillation per day, which also tended to disappear at the end of the neap period. The time lag in groundwater level for this site was *ca.* 1 hour, similar to site O1. This lag suggests that sites O1 and O2 were not connected to a burrow.

4.3 Direct groundwater flow

Calculation results for direct groundwater flow and for rate of change of water volume stored in the sediment are shown in Table 1.

Table 1: Piezometers name, average and standard deviation of speed of infiltration obtained from each piezometer in both field areas (Cocoa and Gordon Creeks), and volume of infiltrated water at each site.

Site name	Rate of change of the water table level $\Delta h/\Delta t$ in (m/day)	Rate of change of water volume stored in the sediment $\Delta V/\Delta t$ per unit of sediment surface area (m^3/m^2day)
Cocoa		
A2	0.13 ± 0.03	0.020 ± 0.004
A4		
B2	0.05 ± 0.01	0.007 ± 0.002
C2	0.03 ± 0.01	0.005 ± 0.001
Gordon		
O1	0.12 ± 0.09	0.020 ± 0.004
O2	0.18 ± 0.02	0.030 ± 0.005
O3	0.09 ± 0.02	0.015 ± 0.003
O4	0.11 ± 0.02	0.017 ± 0.003
O5	0.10 ± 0.02	0.016 ± 0.003

From the above results, the average rate of change of water volume stored in a slab of sediment per unit area is 0.016 ± 0.003 m^3/m^2/day. The maximum rates of groundwater stored in the sediment body per unit area were 0.020 ± 0.004 m^3/m^2/day and 0.030 ± 0.005 m^3/m^2/day for Cocoa and Gordon Creek areas respectively, both occurred at *ca.* 5 m from the creek. Further away from the creek, the rate was about half of these values and seemed to stabilise past the maximum point.

4.4 Calculation of burrow flushing during tidal inundation

The burrow flushing flow was calculated based on Equation 2 with the following parameters: the average monthly numbers of tides that inundated the sediment surface in our field experiment at Cocoa and Gordon Creeks were 9 and 19 respectively, D_b = 0.9 -1.3 m and F_b = 0.05 - 0.15 [3], and F_{wf} = 0.25 - 0.35 [11]. Hence, the average amount of water flushed per day through the burrows was 0.01 – 0.04 m^3/m^2/day. In this calculation I assumed that the parameters were constant for the entire swamp areas.

5 Conclusions

Using the data from previous experiments in the same field areas [3, 11, 12], direct groundwater flow to the creek and burrow flushing flow mechanisms were compared. More specifically, the amount of groundwater returning to the creek appeared to decrease by half at a distance of *ca.* 5 to 10 m from the creek compared to the section within the first 5 m from the creek. This decrease in flux with distance from the creek is expected as this is the region where the water table slopes are the highest. In comparison to the groundwater flux range (0.005 - 0.03 m^3/m^2day), the burrow flushing flux was found to have a similar flux range (0.01 - 0.04 m^3/m^2day). Considering the errors involved in the experiments and calculations in an order of 50-100%, these ranges can be considered as being similar, and neither processes can be considered dominant. Instead, both seem to be significant in term of flow, and as a consequence in term of their potential contribution to the flushing of salts and nutrients from the swamp sediment to the creek.

This result suggests that a new approach to studies of groundwater processes in mangrove swamps is required. In the past, direct groundwater flow has been considered as the most important factor in transporting nutrients and flushing salts in mangrove environments [15, 5-6]. However, most researchers [4, 8-9] have drawn this conclusion qualitatively rather than quantitatively. One exception is a study by Hughes *et al* [7] that provides calculation from piezometer measurements of groundwater flux caused by tidal water. This earlier study shows that the groundwater flux was dependent on the rainfall and, therefore, season with a variation by a factor of three between dry and wet seasons (from 0.22 m^3/day to 0.61 m^3/day per meter width of the creek respectively).

In this paper, I quantify both mechanisms (groundwater flow and burrow flushing) in two areas, and compare their relative importance for the first time. It appears that both have the same order of magnitude, with burrow flushing showing a slightly wider range than groundwater flow. As a consequence, surveys of groundwater processes in mangrove areas, and more generally in swamp and tidal areas where animal burrows are present, will need to consider both mechanisms.

Acknowledgements

I would like to thank Paul Givney for his help in drilling and installing the piezometers, Fikriyati H. Suwardani for helping to download the data of groundwater fluctuation and Drs. P. V. Ridd and. Johan Noor for checking the manuscript.

References

[1] Heron, S. F., Tidal Flushing of animal burrows in Mangrove Swamps, PhD dissertation, James Cook University, School of Mathematical and Physical Sciences, Townsville, Australia, 2001.

[2] Hollins, S. E., Ridd, P. V. and Read, W. W., Measurement of the diffusion coefficient for salt in salt flat and mangrove soils. *Wetland Ecology and Management* 8, 257-262, 2000.

[3] Stieglitz, T., Ridd, P. V. and Muller, P., Passive irrigation and functional morphology of crustacean burrows in a tropical mangrove swamp. *Hydrobiologia* 421: 69-76, 2000.

[4] Lara, R. J. and Dittmar T., Nutrient dynamics in a mangrove Creek (North Brazil) during the dry season. *Mangroves and salt Marshes* 3: 185-195, 1999.

[5] Cohen, M. C. L., Lara, R. J., Ramos, J. F. and Dittmar, T., Factors influencing the variability of Mg, Ca and K in water in a mangrove Creek in Braganca, North Bazil. *Mangrove and Salt Marshes* 3: 9-15, 1999.

[6] Kitheka, J. U., Mwashote, B. M., Ohowa, B. O. and Kamu, J., Water circulation, groundwater outflow and nutrient dynamics in Mida Creek, Kenya. *Mangrove and salt marshes* 3:135-146, 1999.

[7] Hughes, C. E., Binning, P. and Willgoose, G. R., Characterisation of the hydrology of an estuarine wetland. *Journal of Hydrology* 211, 34-49, 1998.

[8] Mazda, Y, Yokochi H. and Sato, Y., Groundwater flow in the Bashita-Minato Mangrove Area, and its Influence on Water and Bottom Mud Properties, *Estuarine, Coastal and Shelf Science* 31:621-638, 1990.

[9] Wolanski, E., Hydrodynamics of mangrove swamps and their coastal waters, *Hydrobiologia* 247: 141-161, 1992.

[10] Aucan, J. and Ridd, P. V., Tidal asymmetry in Creek surrounded by saltflats and mangroves with small swamp slopes. *Wetlands Ecology and Management* 8: 223-231, 2000

[11] Hollins and Ridd, (accepted). The concentration and consumption of oxygen in large animal burrows in tropical mangrove swamp. *Estuarine, Coastal and Shelf Science*

[12] Susilo, A. & Ridd, P. V., (*in press*). A method for measuring bulk hydraulic conductivity in mangrove swamps. *Wetland Ecology and Management.*

[13] Stieglitz, T., Ridd, P. V. and Hollins, S. E., A small sensor for detecting animal burrows and monitoring burrow water conductivity. *Wetland Ecology and Management* 8: 1-7, 2000.

[14] Bryce, S. M., Controlling factors on sediment transport in mangrove Creek systems of North-East Queensland, PhD dissertation, James Cook University, School of Earth Sciences, Townsville, Australia, 2001.

[15] Wolanski, E and Gardiner R., Flushing salt from Mangrove Swamps. *Australian Journal of Marine and Freshwater Research* 32: 681-683, 1981.

Carbon dioxide long-term emissions and its storage options in the Baltic Region

I. Kavaliauskaite[1], M. Uibu[2], S. Teir[3], R. Kuusik[2], R. Zevenhoven[3] & G. Denafas[1]
[1]*Kaunas University of Technology, Lithuania*
[2]*Tallinn University of Technology, Estonia*
[3]*Helsinki University of Technology, Finland*

Abstract

Among other greenhouse gases mainly carbon dioxide (CO_2) is responsible for the so-called enhanced greenhouse effect that causes global warming. The majority of carbon dioxide emissions are from combustion of fossil fuels and from industrial processes. Carbon dioxide emissions from fossil fuel combustion could be reduced by capture and storage. One potential storage option is mineral carbonation. Magnesium and calcium oxide-based minerals as well as waste materials may be used for long-term storage of CO_2 in the form of environmentally stable carbonates. Helsinki University of Technology has investigated the options for storing CO_2 in the form of thermodynamically stable and environmentally inert magnesium carbonate by utilizing mineral carbonation. Large resources of minerals suitable for mineral carbonation appear to exist in Finland and at many other locations worldwide. A combination of thermodynamic and experimental investigations have been carried out at Tallinn University of Technology proving the concept of abatement of CO_2 emissions in Estonia's oil shale-based heat and power generation by wet carbonization of alkaline waste ashes. CO_2 emissions from the Baltic power sector utilizing local fossil fuels are high. Although at present the Baltic States fulfil Kyoto protocol requirements, their carbon dioxide emissions are expected to grow in the near future. Upcoming markets for emission trading makes the research on storage options valuable as well. This encourages evaluation of the main CO_2 emissions sources in the Baltic region. Also different storage options of CO_2 in these countries are discussed.
Keywords: carbon dioxide, mineral carbonation, storage, Baltic.

1 Introduction

Carbon dioxide (CO_2), which is the most dominant greenhouse gas (GHG), is responsible for global warming and leads to the enhancement of the natural greenhouse effect. Today the concentration of CO_2 in the atmosphere is about 370 ppm, which is 30 % higher than the pre-industrial level of 280 ppm Newall *et al.* [1]. It has been estimated that to stabilise the atmospheric concentration of CO_2 at a level not more than 50 % above its current level, emissions would need to be reduced by more than 60 % during the first decades of this century. Achieving such large reductions will require development of new and improved technologies Koljonen *et al.* [2]. CO_2 emissions are primarily caused by using fossil fuel in the energy sector. To stop using fossil fuel makes little sense while fossil energy resources are huge Lackner *et al.* [3]. Thus, fossil fuel may continue to be used if carbon dioxide emitted was captured and put into long-term storage Koljonen *et al.* [2].

2 CO_2 emissions in Baltic Sea area – situation and dynamics

The Baltic States became EU members on the 1st of May 2004 and these countries currently fulfil Kyoto protocol requirements for carbon dioxide emissions. But their CO_2 emissions are expected to grow in the near future followed by the reorganization of Baltic power sector. Estonian and Latvian power sectors will be reconstructed but however the biggest consequences will be brought by the closure of the Ignalina Nuclear Power Plant (Lithuania) Denafas *et al.* [4].

Finland, as EU member, according to the Kyoto protocol has to reduce its greenhouse emissions to the level of 1990. At the moment it seems that the only known alternative for Finland is mineral carbonation, as Finland has widespread deposits of the minerals needed Koljonen *et al.* [2].

2.1 CO_2 emissions in Lithuania

Lithuania has ratified the United Nations Framework Convention on Climate Change in 1995 and signed the Kyoto Protocol in 1998. By signing the Kyoto protocol, Lithuania has been obligated to reduce GHG emissions by 8 % below the 1990 level during 2008-2012 [5].

The largest source of carbon dioxide emissions in Lithuania is the energy sector together with transportation. Lithuania currently fulfils Kyoto protocol requirements under CO_2 emissions: in 1990, the emissions of carbon dioxide in Lithuania were the largest and amounted to 42 Mt while in 2000 this number was only 16.1 Mt Denafas *et al.* [4]. This decrease was an outcome of a decline in industry. The CO_2 emission data for various sectors in Lithuania are shown in Table 1.

The main reason why Lithuania meets this international agreement is the Ignalina Nuclear Power Plant (INPP), the primary electricity producer for Lithuania. Over the last 5 years, it generated 80-85 % of the total electricity in

Lithuania Denafas *et al.* [4]. But this will change in the near future: it is already known that the first block of INPP will be closed on the 31st of December 2004; the second block has to be closed at the end of 2009. After the full closure of INPP the fulfilment of Kyoto Protocol might be complicated. Other Lithuanian power plants, mainly condensing power plants and combined heat-power (CHP) plants, will have to replace the INPP power output. According to the National Energy Strategy, once the INPP shuts down the Lithuanian Power Plant (LPP) will be the country's primary source of power [7]. The LPP, which can run on both oil and gas, was built between 1962 and 1972 and operated at full capacity until 1992. Although the LPP has used over 80 % of its technical lifetime, a Lithuanian government study has shown that it is cheaper to modernise the plant than to build a modern plant of similar size [8].

Table 1: Sources of CO2 emissions in Lithuania [6].

Sources	CO_2 emissions, Mt		
	1990	1999	2000
Energy sector	17.4	5.4	4.0
Non-industrial combustion facilities	9.0	3.6	3.5
Manufacturing	3.6	2.0	2.2
Production sector	2.2	0.5	0.4
Transport	3.1	3.3	2.9
Other mobile sources	3.5	0.3	0.3
Land use change and forestry	2.8	2.8	2.8

The development of renewable energy sources is not a priority in Lithuania; increased demand will be covered by a number of inefficient oil and gas based power plants. For future compliance with Kyoto protocol, proper ways have to be found for emitted carbon dioxide capture and long-term storage.

2.2 CO_2 emissions in Estonia

In 1990-1993 during the shift in Estonia's economy from planned to market the GDP dropped sharply followed by a decrease in energy demand and production. At the same time energy related activities are the most significant contributors to GHG emissions in Estonia. A total of 17.2 Mt of CO_2 from fossil fuel combustion was emitted in 2002. Most of Estonia's energy demand is satisfied by oil shale and approximately 67 % of the CO_2 emissions come from its combustion. During the combustion of pulverised oil shale CO_2 is not formed as a burning product of organic carbon, but also as a decomposition product of the mineral fuel part (*i.e.* carbonates), which makes its carbon emission factor relatively high, being 29.1 tC/TJ. The transport sector is also an important source of carbon dioxide and in 1999, CO_2 emission from transport was 1.203 Mt, accounting for about 7 % of Estonia's total CO_2 emissions [9] – see Table 2.

Mainly due to the reduction of industrial production and re-structuring, Estonia has reduced its GHG emissions for 2002 by 56 % compared to 1990. At the same time Estonia is among the ten largest emitters of CO_2 per capita in the world (12.2 tons of CO_2 per capita) [10].

Table 2: Sources of CO_2 emissions/removals in Estonia [9].

Sources/Sinks	Sources of CO_2 emissions, Mt		
	1990	1999	2002
Total fossil fuel consumption	37.493	16.424	16.971
Energy industries	29.753	13.478	13.911
Manufacturing	2.655	0.660	0.421
Transport	2.693	1.203	2.174
Residential	1.556	1.036	0.135
Agriculture	0.386	0.013	0
Commercial	0.45	0.034	0.087
Industrial processes	0.614	0.347	0.319
Cement production	0.468	0.321	0.232
Lime production	0.146	0.026	0.087
Land use change and forestry	-6.320	-8.107	-8.563
Total net emissions	31.787	8.664	8.726

Several mitigation strategies, projections, legal acts and programmes (Estonian National Environmental Strategy, GHG Emission Reduction Programme for 2003 – 2012) have been elaborated and enforced in Estonia. The main goal is to improve energy efficiency in both the energy sector and industry, but also for demand side developments. A significant effect on the reduction of CO_2 emission in Estonia is expected from the introduction of an up-to-date combustion technology – the fluidised bed combustion of oil shale – in the Narva Power Plants. Increasing the share of natural gas in primary energy consumption will also be an important factor affecting CO_2 emissions, due to the fact that natural gas is the least carbon-intensive fossil fuel. An important option for reducing CO_2 emissions is a wider use of renewable energy sources. In Estonia biomass is the most important renewable option, while wind energy has smaller and small-scale hydropower minor importance [9].

2.3 CO_2 emissions in Finland

According to the United Nations Framework Convention on Climate Change (UNFCCC) and the Kyoto Protocol, Finland is committed to reduce its GHG emissions during 2008–2012 to the level of 1990, and must report annually its inventory of anthropogenic greenhouse gas emissions. The Finnish national climate strategy promotes renewable energy, energy taxation and the energy conservation as main measures for reducing GHG emissions [11]. Currently, the most significant mitigation measure taken to reduce greenhouse gas emissions has been the commissioning of the construction of a fifth nuclear reactor. However, the fifth nuclear reactor will not directly replace any active fossil fuel-based power station; it will only satisfy the current national demand for electric power. Additional GHG emission abatement measures are needed.

In 2002, Finland's carbon dioxide emissions were 69 Mt (11 % above 1990 baseline level), and its share was as high as 85 % of Finland's total GHG emissions. The largest source of CO_2 in Finland is fuel combustion in the energy sector – see Table 3. Other sources of CO_2 are manufacturing industries, transport, and small-scale industrial processes and agriculture [12]. During 2003, the CO_2 emissions from the energy sector alone rose by 13 % up to 70 Mt [13].

Although Finland's current national strategies do not include the use of CO_2 capture and storage as a GHG emission abatement option, the development of these technologies and the need for more effective reduction measures will probably make them attractive in the near future. According to Koljonen *et al.* [2], the lack of CO_2 storage sites and long transmission distances to the closest storage sites abroad are the greatest barriers to overcome, if CO_2 capture and storage would be implemented in Finland. They recognised mineral carbonation as the only known option for storing CO_2 in Finland.

Table 3: Sources of CO_2 emissions/removals in Finland [12].

Sources/Sinks	Sources of CO_2 emissions, Mt		
	1990	1999	2002
Fuel combustion	53.9	56.8	62.2
Fugitive emissions from fuels (peat, oil and natural gas)	3.5	3.5	3.5
Industrial processes	1.2	1.0	1.0
Agricultural soils	3.2	2.0	2.1
Others	0.6	0.8	0.7
Land use change and forestry	-23.8	-10.8	-18.0

3 Mineral carbonation

When certain natural minerals and industrial wastes react with carbon dioxide, various carbonates are formed, eqn (1). This process is called mineral carbonation or mineralization. Carbonation of mineral silicates occurs spontaneously in nature as the natural weathering of rocks, but this process takes a million years to complete. The overall reaction is exothermic and for a metallic cation Min (typically Mg or Ca):

$$(MinO)_x \cdot (SiO_2)_y \cdot (H_2O)_z(s) + xCO_2 \leftrightarrow xMinCO_3(s) + ySiO_2(s) + zH_2O \qquad (1)$$

Mineral carbonation could provide a means to safe disposal and storage of CO_2 Lackner [14]. The main motivation for developing an industrial process for carbonating minerals is the superior storage potential and storage time of mineral carbonates in comparison with other CO_2 storage options. In fact, the global mineral reserves (mainly calcium and magnesium silicates) are larger than the fossil fuel reserves. Several mineral carbonation processes for storing CO_2 have been developed during the last ten years, but most of them suffer from being too expensive due to a high energy demand.

Another application of mineral carbonation is to carbonate industrial wastes followed by separation of individual carbonates. For instance calcium carbonate is widely used, *e.g.* as a paper filler and construction material, and could therefore be a valuable product. Magnesium carbonate has fewer industrial applications than calcium carbonate.

3.1 CO_2 mineralization using natural silicates

Finland has access to vast amounts of natural magnesium silicates (serpentine and serpentinite), often found as tailings from mineral or metal processing industries Zevenhoven and Teir [15]. Natural calcium silicate resources (mainly wollastonite) are too few and too expensive for being a feasible CO_2 storage alternative Teir *et al.* [16]. During the last five years, gas-solid carbonation of minerals has been studied at the Helsinki University of Technology (HUT). The objective of the work has been to develop a magnesium oxide-based mineral carbonation process for long-term storage of CO_2. The main focus has been upon improving the kinetics and energy efficiency of large-scale mineral carbonation. Tests have been made with magnesium hydroxide ($Mg(OH)_2$) in a pressurized thermogravimetric analyser (PTGA), using a humid CO_2 atmosphere at pressures ranging from 1 to 35 bar. Recent results show that elevated pressure levels significantly increase the carbonation rate, but the reaction rate (2 % conversion of 75-125 μm particles in 2 hours) is still far too slow to be applied in an industrial process. The experiments show also clearly that the dehydroxylation of $Mg(OH)_2$, eqn (2), should be avoided, since dehydroxylated $Mg(OH)_2$, *i.e.* magnesium oxide (MgO), appears to carbonate much slower than $Mg(OH)_2$.

$$Mg(OH)_2 \longrightarrow MgO + H_2O(g) \tag{2}$$

In addition to TGA experiments, tests with $Mg(OH)_2$ in an atmospheric bubbling fluidized bed batch reactor were conducted. One interesting result was that attrition, abrasion *etc.* continuously remove small amounts of material from the particles' surface. These fine particles, which are entrained from the reactor, show higher levels of carbonation than (larger) particles sampled from the bed. The highest achieved carbonation of these fines was 8 %. In the same facility, experiments were made with Lithuanian mineral glauconite as well, assuming that the oxides of Mg, Ca, Na and K could be carbonated Teir *et al.* [17].

3.2 CO_2 mineralization using wastes from iron and steel production

Recently, HUT has started investigating the possibility to carbonate slag from iron and steel works by extracting calcium and magnesium ions with acetic acid. The calcium oxide-content of iron and steel slag is actually higher than that of natural calcium silicates found in Finland (wollastonite). If impurities can be removed in the carbonation process, the product could be sold as precipitated calcium carbonate (PCC), which has a market price of about ten times higher than that of iron and steel slag. Therefore, carbonation of slag could provide a way to reduce CO_2 emissions from iron and steel works, utilizing the waste slag and producing a commercial product.

3.3 CO_2 mineralization by alkali of oil shale ash

Besides being the largest CO_2 emitter in Estonia, the energy sector also produces huge amounts of alkaline waste ashes. About 5 milj. tons of oil shale ash is transported to the ash fields every year. Oil shale ash contains up to 30 % of free Ca and Mg oxides, which can be binders of acidic gases like SO_2 and CO_2 Kaljuvee and Kuusik [18], Kuusik *et al.* [19]. Free CaO and MgO containing ash causes formation of strongly alkaline ash transportation water (pH 13) and is considered to be hazardous waste. Carbonation of these free oxides would have dual environmental benefits: decreasing CO_2 emissions and neutralization of alkaline ashes.

Thermodynamic analysis of CO_2 binding reactions in the system ash-water-flue gas indicated that if the equilibrium is reached, the CO_2-binding capacity of oil shale ash pulp is fully utilized. The binding capacity of 1 ton of oil shale ash on the base of free CaO and MgO would be about 200 kg CO_2 Kuusik *et al.* [20]. Laboratory experiments were carried out to investigate the carbonation of aqueous suspensions of ash (Table 4) Kuusik *et al.* [21]. Distilled water and transport water that has a high content of salts and where Ca^{2+} ions were beforehand precipitated were used for preparing aqueous ash suspensions.

Table 4: Main characteristics of oil shale ashes.

Ash	Content, %		SSA, m^2/g	Screenings, mm						
	CaO_f	CO_2		+0.63	+0.40	+0.16	+0.1	+0.071	+0.045	-0.045
Mix98	20.12	2.25	1.49	0.61	1.21	5.45	9.7	7.07	15.76	60.2
Mix03	18.1	1.04	0.383	1.0	1.8	13.8	21.4	21.4	17.6	33.2

The extent of carbonation was described by index N, which indicates how many times the amount of CO_2 entrained into suspensions exceeds the stoichiometric ratio calculated according to eqn (3):

$$CaO + CO_2 \leftrightarrow CaCO_3 \tag{3}$$

The effectiveness of carbonation process was described by the CO_2-binding degree (BD_{CO2}) expressing which part of the theoretical binding capacity of the ash is utilized. (Figure 1).

The carbonation kinetics of ash depends on its several parameters including size of particles, porosity, specific surface area (SSA), the presence and amount of glassy phase etc. CO_2-binding degree over 100 % can be explained by the carbonation of MgO and $CaSiO_3$ that were not taken into account. If total utilization of free CaO (CaO_f) is accomplished, 1 ton of ash can bind 140 – 196 kg CO_2. This would allow 712 – 996 thousands of tons of CO_2 to be bound on the production level of SC Narva Power Plants in year 2002 making up 7-9.9 % of total CO_2 emissions.

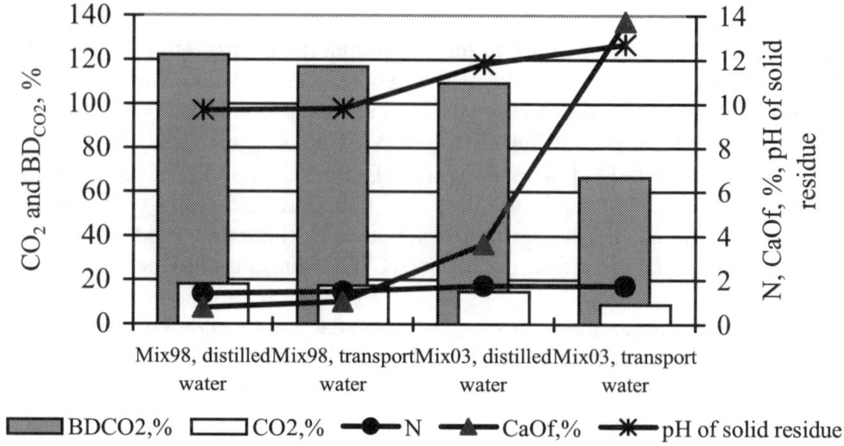

Figure 1: Main characteristics of carbonation process and carbonated ashes.

Figure 2: SEM pictures of fluidized bed combustion ash (left) and pulverized firing ash (right).

Until now, electricity production in Estonia was based on pulverized firing of oil shale, however as of year 2004 combustion in circulating fluidized beds was introduced. Fluidized bed combustion occurs at much lower temperature (about 750 – 800 °C) than pulverized firing (1300 – 1400 °C). Therefore the residue ash contains less glassy phases, has higher SSA (up to 10 times compared to pulverized firing ashes) and is expected to have higher reactivity towards CO_2. SEM pictures show the different surface properties of these ashes- see Figure 2.

4 Conclusions

Carbon dioxide emissions from the power sector in the Baltic Region are high. Although at the moment Baltic States satisfy Kyoto protocol requirements, their growing emissions and the upcoming market of emission trading force these three countries (Estonia, Latvia, Lithuania) to take special actions for CO_2 emission reduction.

The biggest consequences for Lithuanian CO_2 emissions will be brought by the closure of INPP. After that, other Lithuanian power plants will have to replace INPP power output. Carbon dioxide emissions will grow and proper ways for CO_2 storage have to be found.

Estonia is among the ten largest emitters of CO_2 per capita in the world and most of Estonia's energy demand is satisfied by oil shale. Oil shale ashes, which are formed in huge amounts in the energy sector, contain up to 30 % of free Ca and Mg oxides. Laboratory experiments and calculations show that up to 7–10% of the CO_2 emitted could be mineralized by these ashes.

It seems that for Finland the mineral carbonation is the only possibility for storing carbon dioxide inside country's borders. However, currently achievable carbonation rates make it not yet possible to apply this on a large scale. One of the promising technologies to reduce carbon dioxide emissions from iron and steel works seems to be CO_2 mineralization by waste slag from that sector.

Acknowledgments

The work was partially funded by the Nordic Energy Research Programme project "Nordic CO_2 sequestration" (2003-2006).

References

[1] Newall, P., Clarke, S., Haywood, H., Scholes, H., Clarke, N., King, P., Barley, R., "CO_2 storage as carbonate minerals", IEA Greenhouse gas R&D programme, Report Number PH3/17, 1999.

[2] Koljonen, T., Siikavirta, H., Zevenhoven, R., "CO_2 capture, storage and utilisation in Finland". Project report PRO4/T7504/02, VTT Processes, Espoo, Finland 2002. www.eny.hut.fi/research/combustion_waste/publications/other/co2capt.pdf

[3] Lackner, K. & Ziock, H., From low to no emissions. *Modern Power Systems*, **20(3)**, pp.31-32, 2000.

[4] Denafas, G., Sitnikovas, D., Galinis, A., Kudrenickis, I., Klavs, G., Kuusik, R., Predicting CO_2 and SO_2 emissions in the Baltic States through reorganization of energy infrastructure. *Environment International*, **30(3)**, pp. 1046-1053, 2004.

[5] EnergyStart.lt. Energy and atmospheric pollution, www.energystart.lt/en/content.php?id=112&sid=67 .

[6] Atmosferos skyriaus duomenys (2000). Aplinkos ministerija.

[7] National energy strategy 2002, www.rst.lt /Print/teisaktai_nacenergstrategija.htm
[8] Country profile - Lithuania. Review of Status of Emissions Trading Activities in CG11 Countries. http://r0.unctad.org/ghg /sitecurrent/projects/cg11/country_p/Lithuania_Country_Profile.doc.
[9] Estonia's Third National Communication under the UN Framework Convention on Climate Change, Estonia, November 2001.
[10] Estonian Energy 2002, www.mkm.ee/failid /Estonian%20Energy%202002%20ENG.doc
[11] Ministry of Trade and Industry, Implementation including emissions trading, Web page, http://www.ktm.fi, updated 22.6.2004.
[12] Finnish Ministry of the Environment, Greenhouse Gas Emissions in Finland 1990-2002, National Inventory Report to the UNFCCC Secretariat, 2004.
[13] Statistics Finland, Preliminary Energy Statistics 2003, 2004.
[14] Lackner, K.S., A Guide to CO_2 Sequestration, *Science*, **300**, pp. 1677-1678, 2003.
[15] Zevenhoven R., Teir S., Long-Term Storage of CO_2 as Magnesium Carbonate in Finland, *Proc of the 3rd Annual Conference on Carbon Capture and Sequestration*, Alexandria (VI), USA, 2004. paper 217
[16] Teir S., Eloneva S., Zevenhoven R., Production of precipitated calcium carbonate from calcium silicates and carbon dioxide, article submitted to *Energy Conversion and Management*, August 2004.
[17] Teir, S., Raiski, T., Kavaliauskaite, I., Denafas, G., Zevenhoven, R. Mineral carbonation and the Finnish pulp and paper industry. *Proc. of the 29th Int. Conf. on Coal Utilization and Fuel Systems*, Clearwater (FL), April, 2004. paper 11, pp. 127-138
[18] Kaljuvee, T. & Kuusik, R., Desulfurization of flue gases by oil shale ash. *Oil shale*. **10(1)**, pp. 33-43, 1993.
[19] Kuusik, R., Kaljuvee, T., Trikkel, A., Maarend, J., Roundyguine, J., Dry desulphurization of flue gases by Estonian lime containing materials. *Proc. 10th World Clean Air Congr.*, Finland, Espoo, pp. 037-040, 1995.
[20] Kuusik, R., Türn, L., Trikkel, A., Uibu, M., Carbon Dioxide Binding in the Heterogeneous Systems Formed by Combustion of Oil Shale. Integrations of system components – thermodynamic analysis. *Oil Shale*, **19(2)**, pp. 143-160, 2002.
[21] Kuusik, R., Veskimäe, H., Uibu, M. Carbon Dioxide Binding in the Heterogeneous Systems Formed by Combustion of Oil Shale. Transformations in the system suspension of ash – flue gases. *Oil Shale*. **19(3)**, pp. 277-288, 2002.

Section 12
Environmental risk

Effect of wrack accumulation on salt marsh vegetation, Jamaica Bay Wildlife Refuge, New York City, New York

R. Stalter[1], A. Jung[1] & M. D. Byer[2]
[1]Department of Biological Sciences, St. John's University, Jamaica, New York, U.S.A.
[2]Division of Natural Resources, Gateway National Recreation Area, National Park Service, New York, U.S.A.

Abstract

In April 2004, five arrays in different types of salt marsh vegetation were covered with 15-20cm of wrack secured in place, in an attempt to duplicate the natural deposition of wrack on the marsh by tides and storms, and to quantify and extend anecdotal observations and the results of previous studies. A control plot in each array was left uncovered; another plot was covered with only 2-3cm. The wrack was removed from one plot in each array at one, two, four, and six month intervals. Up to two months of wrack coverage appeared to have little effect on either density or standing crop (recorded six months after initial coverage) of the principal marsh species, *Spartina alterniflora, S. patens, Distichlis spicata, Juncus gerardii,* and marsh margin *Phragmites australis.* Except for *Phragmites,* however, these species appeared to be strongly inhibited after four months of continual coverage, and killed or extremely inhibited after six months. Wrack 2-3cm thick (never removed) appeared to inhibit the aforementioned species after six months, but not as much as the 15-20cm wrack mat. These results are fairly consistent with those of an earlier study that focused on *Spartina alterniflora* only, except that two months' coverage seemed sufficient to kill back most of the *S. alterniflora* in that study. *Phragmites'* apparent resistance to wrack cover can be explained by the considerable energy reserves of its large rhizomes and the ability of its awl-like shoots to penetrate a thick wrack mat. Future studies should focus on recovery of the vegetation once the wrack has been removed, and on chemical changes in the soil caused by the decaying wrack, which may in turn affect the future course of vegetation development.
Keywords: salt marsh, wrack, Jamaica Bay, wildlife refuge, New York.

1 Introduction

Wrack, composed mostly of dead marsh plant stems and leaves, primarily *Spartina alterniflora* (salt marsh cordgrass) with lesser amounts of *Phragmites australis* (tall reed), is naturally deposited upon salt marsh vegetation by tidal action. If wrack is thick enough and covers the marsh grasses and forbs for a sufficient period of time, it will smother and kill the salt marsh plants, with the exception of the woodier, more robust *Iva frutescens* ssp. *oraria* (high tide bush). In an earlier study [3], *Spartina alterniflora,* at least its above-ground parts, at Jamaica Bay Wildlife Refuge was killed in plots covered with wrack for 60 consecutive days or longer.

Spartina alterniflora is the dominant plant over approximately 70 percent of the total area of salt marsh at Jamaica Bay Wildlife Refuge [1, 3]. Monocultures of this coarse rhizomatous perennial grass occupy two of the arbitrarily determined vegetation zones within the salt marsh described by Stalter and Lamont [6], the high low marsh and low low marsh or creek bank marsh. Other important salt marsh species are *Spartina patens* (salt meadow grass), *Distichlis spicata* (spike grass), and *Salicornia spp.* (salt wort/glass wort). *S. alterniflora* occasionally may be found in a third sub community, the lower upper marsh, dominated by *Distichlis spicata* and *Spartina patens*. A fourth community, the high upper marsh, is dominated by *Iva frutescens* ssp. *oraria*. A fifth sub community, dominated by *Juncus gerardii* (black rush) occupies a small portion of the Jamaica Bay salt marsh.

1.1 The problem

In the aforementioned study, Byer et al. [3] examined the effect of the accumulation of wrack only in plots where *Spartina alterniflora* was dominant. The objective of this present study was to investigate the effect of extended wrack coverage in five vegetation zones including the *Spartina alterniflora* monoculture. Monitoring of the experimental manipulation of wrack mats may provide quantitative information useful in interpreting the following: (1) the time needed to smother and kill major salt marsh species within several undisturbed salt marsh vegetation types, (2) successional relationships as various salt marsh species invade plots uncovered following extended wrack coverage, (3) the time needed for each of the original species in each sub community to reach parity with that species' importance before the artificial disturbance, (4) how long it takes wrack mats to decompose on site in each vegetation type.

1.2 Site description

The following vegetation types can be identified in Jamaica Bay salt marshes:

1) The *Phragmites australis* community that colonizes fresh to brackish marshes, a near-monoculture of the named species. This is not a salt marsh community, but is included in this study because it often borders salt marshes at Jamaica Bay.

2) The *Spartina patens/Distichlis spicata* community occupies higher elevations within the marsh. This community may be dominated by either species, and may also contain *Limonium carolinianum* (sea lavender) and *Salicornia europaea* (glass wort).
3) The *Juncus gerardii* (black rush) community, essentially a monoculture, generally occupies ground over an abandoned road bed at Jamaica Bay Wildlife Refuge.
4) The *Spartina alterniflora* community, also a near monoculture, is found at relatively low elevations. A tall form up to 2m occupies creek banks while a shorter form, generally less than 1m, occupies "higher" ground. Environmental factors may be responsible for the different growth forms [3]. Our study site was confined to the zone occupied by the tall form.

2 Methods

Five arrays of permanent experimental plots were established in the above communities, with two arrays in the *Spartina patens/Distichlis* community. The dominant taxa in these arrays were the most abundant salt marsh species at Jamaica Bay Wildlife Refuge (Table 1). Vegetation in each of the above consisted of nearly pure stands of each species with the exception of the *S. patens/Distichlis* community. Within the latter, one array was placed at a site where *S. patens* was dominant and *Distichlis* a less abundant associate; the second, where *Distichlis* was dominant and *S. patens* an unimportant associate. Each array was 1.5m wide and consisted of eight 1m x 1.5m plots in a row roughly parallel to the water's edge. In each of these plots, a central 0.5m x 1m sample plot was marked off, surrounded by a 0.25m wide buffer zone (0.5m between adjacent sample plots). Each array was GPS-located and permanently marked at the corners, as were the 1m x 1.5m and the 0.5m x 1m plots.

Table 1: Relative abundance of salt marsh species, Jamaica Bay, New York. Abundance data from Stalter and Lamont [6]. Vascular plant species classified according to Gleason and Cronquist [4].

Species	Abundance
Aster tenuifolius	infrequent
Atriplex hastate	infrequent
Distichlis spicata	frequent
Iva frutescens ssp. *oraria*	infrequent
Juncus gerardii	frequent
Limonium carolinianum	infrequent
Salicornia europaea	frequent
Spartina alterniflora	frequent
Spartina patens	frequent
Suaeda calceoliformis	infrequent
Suaeda maritima	infrequent

At the start of the experiment, October 2003, all plots were sampled to provide baseline data. The parameters sampled, in the initial and all subsequent observations, were: number of shoots by species, plant height as a mean of three measurements taken in each of four quarters of the sample plot and in the center, and visual cover estimates.

In early April 2004, wrack was collected and placed upon each array, except for one control plot and one plot designated to duplicate the conditions used by Bertness and Ellison [2] in their experiments, at a thickness of 15-20cm. The latter plot, hereinafter called the "Bertness Plot", was covered with only 2-3cm of wrack. Wrack was oriented parallel to the long axis of the arrays insofar as possible. To secure the wrack for the duration of the study, fish netting with 6.5cm mesh was laid over the wrack-covered arrays and held in place with a peripheral rope tied to stakes at the corners of the array and attached to the netting with special snap clips purchased from Forestry Suppliers of Jackson MS. Fifteen cm wire staples were used to fasten the rope to the ground. An additional rope was attached at each end of the array at the center and stretched taut down the length of the array.

Table 2: Denisty (stems/m^2) of salt marsh species in five sub communities at a Jamaica Bay salt marsh. The plant communities (arrays) are (1) *Spartina alterniflora* community, (2) *Spartina patens/Distichlis spicata* community dominated by *S. patens*, (3) *Spartina patens/Distichlis spicata* community dominated by *Distichlis*, (4) *Juncus gerardii* community, (5) *Phragmites australis* salt marsh border community. All plots were sampled between 1 and 15 October, 2004 in plots covered with wrack in early April 2004, wrack removed after the number of months indicated.

Array	Species	Control	1 month	2 months	4 months	6 months	Bertness
1	*Spartina alterniflora*	1,400	1,600	1,400	100	-	100
2	*Spartina patens*	5,735	4,276	2,500	700	-	100
	Distichlis spicata	-	-	900	2,300	500	100
	Phragmites australis	100	-	-	-	-	-
3	*Distichlis spicata*	3,958	2,700	1,900	1,100	-	1,100
	Spartina patens	1,200	-	-	-	-	-
	Phragmites australis	-	100	100	-	-	-
4	*Juncus gerardii*	4,433	1,556	2,179	2,288	400*	200*
5	*Phragmites australis*	64	144	64	32	32	32

In May 2004, one plot in each array was uncovered and sampled. Subsequently, one plot in each array was uncovered and sampled in June, August and October 2004. During all marking, manipulation, and sampling of the arrays and plots, attention was given to minimize trampling and disturbance of the study plots.

During 1-15 October 2004, vegetation within each experimental plot and the control were sampled with three randomly located 10x10cm quadrats. Stems were first counted, by species. Then, the vegetation was cut at ground level. Standing crop (gms. of vegetation/m^2) was determined. Data is presented in Tables 2 and 3.

Table 3: Standing crop (gms/m^2) of salt marsh species in five sub communities at a Jamaica Bay salt marsh. Plant communities (arrays) and wrack covering and removal schedule as in Table 2. Sampling was done between 1 and 15 October 2004.

Array	Species	Control	1 month	2 months	4 months	6 months	Bertness
1	*Spartina alterniflora*	579.8	886.5	813.4	122.7	-	3.5
2	*Spartina patens*	546.1	641.5	346.2	26.7	-	171.4
	Distichlis spicata	-	-	163.7	0155.7	182.9	31.6
	Phragmites australis	173.9	-	-	-	-	-
3	*Distichlis spicata*	476.6	290.4	267.1	61.6	-	252.3
	Spartina patens	98.2	-	-	-	-	-
	Phragmites australis	-	44.8	117.1	-	-	-
4	*Juncus gerardii*	240.1	152.4	229.7	296.8	26.1	104.3
5	*Phragmites australis*	1,591.0	703.0	93.9	353.0	786.0	678.0

3 Results and discussion

Taking into account the small sample size, most of the species, in most of the arrays, show no tendency to decline in either density or standing crop after one or two months of wrack coverage. After four months of coverage, some species, e.g. *S. alterniflora* in Array 1, *S. patens* in Array 2 and *Distichlis* in Array 3, appear to show a marked tendency to decline in both density and standing crop. After six months of coverage, most of the species in most arrays have been completely killed back, or at least drastically reduced in both numbers and standing crop.

Compared to results from an earlier study [3], in which two months of wrack coverage was found to kill most of the above-ground parts of *S. alterniflora,* here a notable reduction was not evident, including in the latter species, until wrack had remained on the plots for four months. At this time we can suggest no reason for this difference.

Distichlis was present in the two, four and six month plots in Array 2. It appeared to tolerate wrack cover at this site better than the dominant *S. patens. Distichlis* produces thicker culms than those of *S. patens,* which may have enabled spike grass to penetrate wrack cover. Also, most *Distichlis* biomass was rhizomes, which, unlike photosynthetic tissue, may be little impacted by exclusion of light so long as their energy reserves are not exhausted. Why, then. *Distichlis* in Array 3, where it is the dominant species, appears to be more vulnerable is hard to explain. Perhaps differences in one or more environmental factors between the two arrays are responsible.

Phragmites is the lone species that showed no declining trend with long-term wrack coverage. The large size of this grass, the large energy reserves of its rhizomes, and an ability of its awl-like shoots to penetrate 15-20cm of wrack may provide it relative immunity to wrack impact.

In the Bertness plots, from which wrack was not removed before observations were made in October 2004, both density and standing crop of all species were somewhat to considerably less than in the controls of the same arrays. It thus appears that even the relatively thin wrack layer placed on these plots was somewhat effective in killing the plants underneath and/or in suppressing their growth, although not as effective after six months as the thicker, 15-20cm layer that had been placed on the other experimental plots.

In general, the results of this experiment are consistent with those of the earlier study cited [3] involving *Spartina alterniflora* alone, and with the anecdotal observations of many ecologists [2, 5]. Long-term residence of wrack on salt marsh vegetation tends to kill it back, as one would expect of any substance or object that excludes sunlight from the vegetation. After the wrack is removed, either by human hands or by natural forces such as tides and storms, a bare patch may be exposed. This, however, does not appear to lead to permanent change in the marsh vegetation. The patch is soon recolonized. If the wrack has not remained on the area long enough to kill the rhizomes beneath it, these may produce new shoots of the same species that were killed back, or rhizomes may grow into the area from the un-impacted surrounding vegetation. Sometimes the bare patch is invaded by the annual *Salicornia europaea*; numerous dense patches of this species can be seen within the marsh. Although further studies will be necessary to clarify the role of *Salicornia* in salt marsh dynamics, it seems probable that it is a stage in a micro-succession, and that these patches will soon be re-invaded by the original dominant species.

Another question deserving of further study is how the presence of wrack on an area may change the soil chemistry, and how this may affect the subsequent dynamics of the vegetation.

A comparison of Bertness and Ellison's [2] results with our own shows that, when continuously covered with only 2-3cm of wrack in a Rhode Island salt marsh, the same species involved in our study were completely killed much more quickly (within 35 to 70 days depending upon the species) than when covered with 15-20cm in our own plots (4 to 6 months, or ~120-180 days). An examination of the methods used by these authors may provide the key to these differences. They uncovered their plots briefly each week for monitoring purposes, then replaced the wrack and netting. This regimen likely resulted in much disturbance and mechanical damage to the plants as wrack and netting were repeatedly removed and replaced. This could have been a major factor in the relatively rapid demise of Bertness and Ellison's plants. We think that our protocol of using plots covered for differing periods of time, covering and uncovering each plot only once, caused less disturbance and gave a truer indication of the impact of the wrack itself on the plants.

Acknowledgements

We are most grateful to Shadrack Ngene, whose enthusiastic efforts in lifting and hauling wrack and doing associated tasks saved our time and our backs. We thank Superintendent Billy Garrett and Division of Natural Resources Chief Doug Adamo of Gateway National Recreation Area, U. S. National Park Service, for their support and cooperation. The staff of the Jamaica Bay Wildlife Refuge was also helpful and supportive, as was the Aquatic Research and Environmental Assessment Center (AREAC) and its head, Dr. Martin P. Schreibman, of Brooklyn College, partners with the National Park Service in ongoing research projects at Jamaica Bay. Gratitude is due the Maintenance Division of St. John's University, who prepared the stakes used in our wrack hold-down system.

References

[1] Alderson, C. and G.W. Frame 1999. Monitoring the salt marsh at Schmitt's Marina in Big Egg Marsh, Jamaica Bay, New York, using permanent plots. New York City Department of Parks and Recreation and Division Natural Resources, Gateway National Recreation Area. Draft manuscript with maps and photographs, October 1999.

[2] Bertness, M., and A.M. Ellison, 1987. Determinants of pattern in a New England salt marsh plant community. Ecological Monographs 57: 129-147.

[3] Byer, M. D., G. W. Frame, W. Panagakos, M. Waaijer, Z. Aranbayev, Y. Michaels, R. Stalter & M. P. Schreibman. 2004. Effects of wrack accumulation on Spartina alterniflora, Jamaica Bay Wildlife Refuge, New York City. In: C. A. Brebbia, J. M. Saval Perez & L. Garcia Andion (eds.), Coastal Environment V, Incorporating Oil Spill Studies. Pp. 183-190.

[4] Gleason, A.A., and A. Cronquist, 1991. Manual of vascular plants of northeastern United States and adjacent Canada, New York Botanical Garden, Bronx, New York 910pp.

[5] Reidenbaugh, T.G. and W.C. Banta 1980. Origins and effects of Spartina wrack in a Virginia salt marsh. Gulf Research Reports 6 (4): 393-401

[6] Stalter, R. and E.E. Lamont. 2002. Vascular flora of Jamaica Bay Wildlife Refuge, Long Island, New York. Journal of the Torrey Botanical Club 129 (4):346-358.

Geochemical and geophysical characterisation of a municipal solid waste landfill

G. Siracusa[1], A. D. La Rosa[1], G. Giuffrida[2] & A. Leotta[2]
[1]*Department of Physical and Chemical Methodologies for Engineering (DMFCI), Faculty of Engineering, Catania, Italy*
[2]*Geovertical s.r.l, Catania, Italy*

Abstract

An application of an integrated approach including geochemical analyses and geophysical investigations, aimed at the detection of possible leaks originating from an urban solid landfill, is proposed. The objective of the subsurface geophysical investigation was to use non invasive methods to delineate buried waste zones. The information collected in this investigation may be useful to locate possible leachate pockets and to optimize subsequent sampling and remediation.

Methods used at the site focused on the electrical insulating properties of the nonmetallic (glass, plastic) containers and the electrical conducting properties of possible leaking fluids and clay soil.

As a case study the example of a municipal solid waste landfill, located in SE Sicily, is presented.

Keywords: geophysics, resistivity, tomography, landfill, liquid percolation, leachate.

1 Introduction

Leachate plumes originating from municipal solid waste (MSW) landfills are potential sources of contamination for water resources, including ground and surface water and littoral environments, where the naturalistic equilibrium may be severely influenced if exposed to pollution [1,2]. The related consequences for the mentioned ecosystems are difficult to be evaluated and sometimes cannot be predicted. For these reasons and in order to prevent leakage from MSW landfills, a preliminary detailed geological investigation is usually done to choose the most proper landfill site. Additionally, particular attention is devoted during the various construction phases that are generally regulated by national and local authorities. Even in this case, post-closure monitoring of possible leachate dispersion into the surrounding environment must be continuously checked through the establishment of a comprehensive water quality monitoring and control program. Monitoring programs are usually based upon the chemical analysis of major, minor and trace elements of a number of leachate and water samples collected inside and in the immediate vicinity of the landfill itself and for long periods of time.

Furthermore, development of completed landfill sites, which has become highly desirable particularly in land-limited locations, is invariably hindered by its settlement. Estimating long term landfill settlements becomes an integral part of the plans for the final closure of a site and its ultimate reuse. The rate and magnitude of landfill settlement depend primarily on refuse composition and the presence of leachate pockets in the burial zones.

Taking into account these considerations, a cost-effective approach to the problem should be based upon the measurement of those physical properties which are mostly influenced by the presence of leachate in the subsurface, i.e. electrical resistivity.

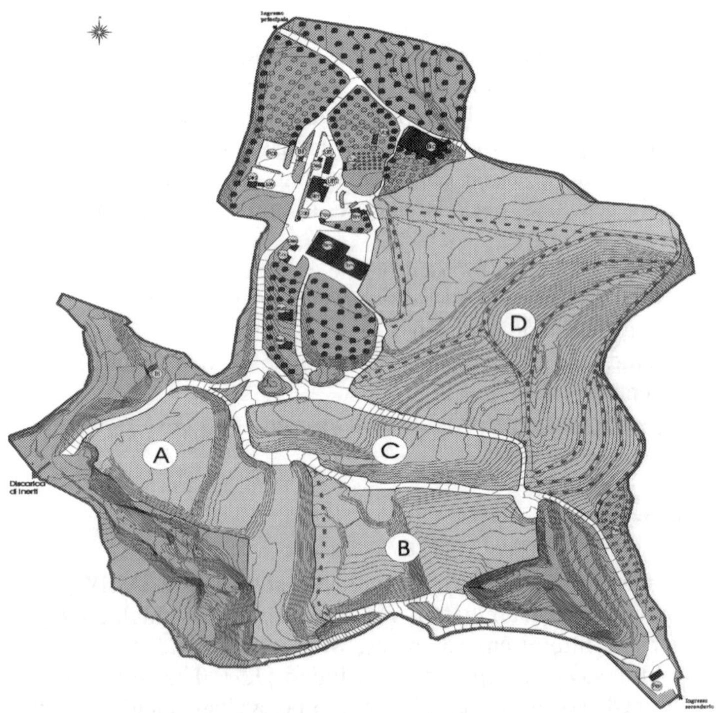

Figure 1: Landfill surface.

2 Site description

The municipal solid waste landfill is located between two urban Sicilian centres: Misterbianco and Motta S. Anastasia, and occupies a surface area of 34.7 ha which is divided into four main sectors (A,B,C and D) as shown in figure 1. The landfill has been activated in 1986 but an appropriate management has been applied only since 1999 due to the Council Directive 99/31/EC of 26 April 1999 on the landfill of waste entered into force on 16.07.1999 and implemented in the Member States within 16.07.2001.

According to the legislation, a landfill must be situated and designed so as to meet the necessary conditions for preventing pollution of the soil, groundwater or surface water and ensuring efficient collection of leachate as and when required. Protection of soil, groundwater and surface water is to be achieved by the combination of a geological barrier and a bottom liner during the operational/active phase and by the combination of a geological barrier and a top liner during the passive phase/post closure. The landfill under our study responds to all the law requests as both base and sides consist of a mineral layer (clay) which satisfies permeability and thickness requirements. Furthermore, the underground mapping reveals the absence of ground water underneath the waste disposal area.

3 Geo-chemical characterization

3.1 Geological description

The amount of garbage gathered in the landfill is 400-450 tons per day (e.g.: the total amount collected in 2004 was 135000 tons). The volume capacity of the landfill is 3155648 m^3 which correspond to a weight capacity of (3155648 m^3 * 0.9 t/ m^3) = 2840083.2 t (if we consider that the compaction degree is 0.9 t/ m^3). The weight of disposed waste up to May 2004 is 822831.38 t; the landfill further capacity is (2840083.20 t – 822831.38 t) = 2017251.82 t. The provision is that the landfill will be closed in 2019 and afterwards a post closure rehabilitation plan will be carried out.

The landfill soil is mainly marly clay with fine granulometry, water permeability values between 3.5 to 10-8 cm/sec, hydraulic conductivity of K ≈ 10-8 cm/sec and thickness of s = ~ 100 m.

The geological and hydrogeological conditions below and in the vicinity of the landfill site generate a geological barrierwhich provides sufficient attenuation capacity to prevent a potential risk to soil and groundwater.

3.2 Leachate management

Thanks to the natural waterproofing property of clay it was not necessary to install an artificial waterproofing system.

Every day the disposed wastes are covered with a 20 cm thick layer of soil in order to improve the leachate drainage. Furthermore, appropriate measures have been taken, with respect to the characteristics of the landfill and the meteorological conditions, in order to:

- control water from precipitations entering into the landfill body,
- prevent surface water and/or groundwater from entering into the landfilled waste,
- collect contaminated water and leachate.
- treat contaminated water and leachate collected from the landfill to the appropriate standard required for their discharge.

Table 1: Chemical analysis of the leachate.

PARAMETER	UNIT	LANDFILL	BIOGAS PIPE
pH		11	11
Conductivity at 25°C	mS/cm	39900	38064
COD	mg/l	4276	2213
BOD_5	mg/l	2118	1433
Chloride	mg/l	5864	4560
Ammonia (NH4+)	mg/l	2382	2443
Sulphate	mg/l	238	250
Arsenic, Barium, Cadmium, Cobalt, Chromium, Mercury, Nickel, Lead, Copper, Aluminium	mg/l	<1	<1
Iron	mg/l	3.85	3.78

3.3 Landfill settlement and refuse composition

The biodegradation of organic matter in municipal solid waste (MSW) landfills increases the void ratio and weakens the structural strength of the refuse within a landfill leading to a substantial loss of volume and settlement [3]. Development of completed landfill sites, which has become highly desirable particularly in land limited locations, is invariably hindered by this settlement. Estimating longterm landfill settlements becomes an integral part of the plans for the final closure of a site and its ultimate reuse. The rate and magnitude of landfill settlement depend primarily on refuse composition (table 2) and operational management practices which affect biodegradation and stabilization processes within the landfill.

Table 2: Chemical analysis of the municipal wastes.

Number of samples	137
chemical-physical composition	
Water (%)	49.1
Burning materials (%)	29.2
non burning materials (%)	21.7
heating capacity (kcal/kg)	1036
marketable composition	
wood matter (%)	18.7
plastics (%)	6.8
metals (%)	2.4
inerts (%)	5.4
organic matter (%)	46.5
fine materials (%)	20.2

3.4 Biogas collection and electricity production

The landfill provides an innovative and highly effective system of biogas collection and electricity production. The power plant has a capacity of 2.3 MWe while the current electricity production is 1.3 MWe.

In order to describe the working principle of the technology, municipal solid waste contains significant portions of organic materials that produce a variety of gaseous products when dumped, compacted, and covered in landfills. Anaerobic bacteria thrive in the oxygen-free environment, resulting in the decomposition of the organic materials and the production of primarily carbon dioxide and methane. Carbon dioxide is likely to leach out of the landfill because it is soluble in water. Methane, on the other hand, which is less soluble in water and lighter than air, is likely to migrate out of the landfill. Landfill gas energy facilities capture the methane (the principal component of natural gas) and combust it for energy.

4 Geophysical characterization: resistivity method

Electrical resistivity surveys are commonly used for hydrogeological, mining, geo-technical investigations, and environmental surveys [4]. Subsurface electrical resistivity is related to buried materials and various geological and hydrogeological parameters such as the mineral and fluid content, porosity and water saturation.

A 2D-DC (two-dimensional, direct-current) electrical survey was performed at the municipal solid waste landfill to determine the subsurface resistivity distribution by making measurements on the ground surface. The resistivity directly measured in the field survey is not the true resistivity of the subsurface but an "apparent" resistivity value. The apparent resistivity value equals that of the resistivity of a homogeneous ground measured from the same electrode arrangement. To determine the true subsurface resistivity, an inversion of the measured apparent resistivity values must be performed [4]. The 2D-DC resistivity system used at the waste landfill was the Sting/Swift resistivity system by Advanced Geosciences, Inc.(AGI). Of the three different arrays (Wenner, Schlumberger, and dipole-dipole) that were used initially, the dipole-dipole was the most successful because of its detailed resolution near the land surface. Three dipole-dipole profiles, which were collected at 2 metres electrode spacing, were further evaluated. From these measurements, the true resistivity of the subsurface could be estimated. There are several steps involved in producing a cross-sectional profile of "true" resistivity of the subsurface. The field measurements are spatially related to positions in the cross section and recorded by a data logger (figure 1). The field data are subsequently downloaded to a computer and input into an inversion model RES2INV [5] which inverts the data and creates a contoured profile of field apparent resistivity.

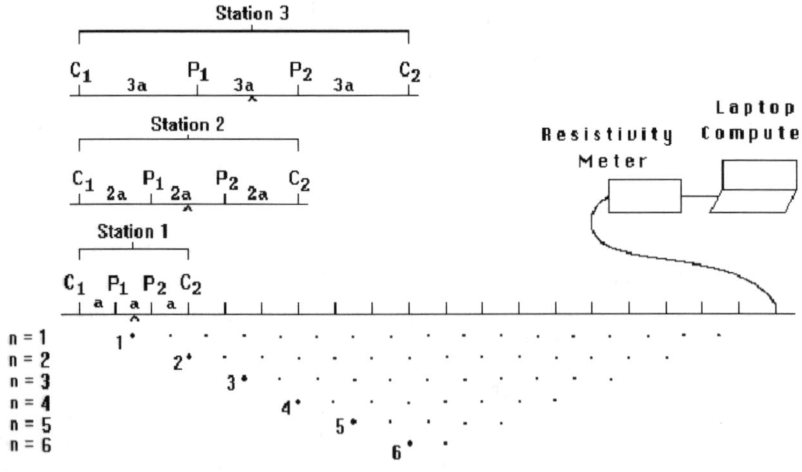

Figure 2: Sequence of measurements to build up a pseudosection using a computer controlled multi-electrode survey setup.

Two-dimensional (2D) electrical imaging surveys are now widely used to map areas of moderately complex geology where conventional 1D resistivity sounding and profiling techniques are inadequate. The results from such surveys are usually plotted in the form of a pseudosection (Figure 2) which gives an approximate picture of the subsurface geology. The RES2INV program uses the smoothness-constrained least-squares method inversion technique to produce a 2D model of the subsurface from the apparent resistivity data alone.

Through a trial-and-error process, the interpreted model is improved to create a modeled resistivity profile that closely resembles the field apparent resistivity profile. The interpreted model is then considered to have produced a representation of "true" resistivity of the subsurface when a close match is made between the modeled resistivity profile and the apparent resistivity inversion profile.

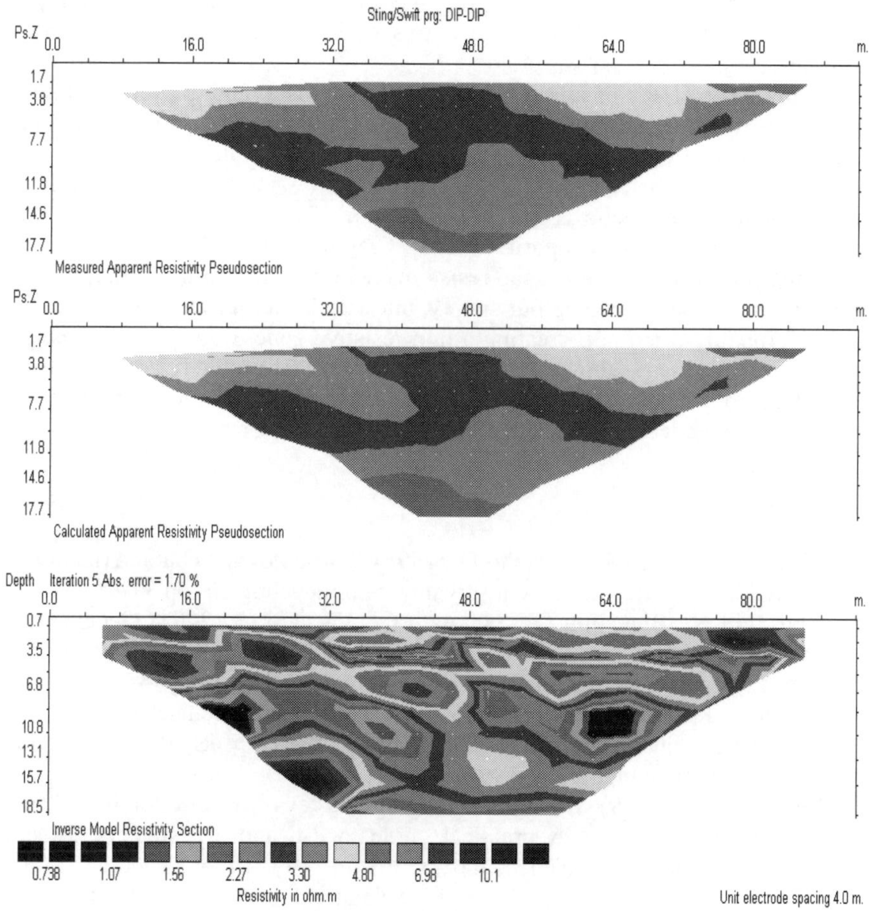

Figure 3: Electrical tomography.

5 Results and discussion

The Sting/Swift application carried out in the municipal landfill aims at the moisture detection in a post-closure burial zone which has already been stabilized. Moisture content is considered the most important parameter in refuse decomposition and gas production. It provides the aqueous environment necessary for anaerobic digestion and also serves as medium for transporting nutrients and bacteria throughout the landfill. Moisture movement in addition to moisture content has been demonstrated as a significant variable affecting methane gas production [6,7].

The result of our investigation is a contoured representation of the apparent and inverse modelled "true" resistivity in a cross-sectional format as shown in figure 2c.

The obtained tomography depends on the refuse composition: less conductive zones (shown in red or in brown) may correspond to plastics and/or to other inert materials.

In this format, the insulating quality of the glass and plastic containers thought to be present at the site are expected to appear as higher resistivity values among the lower resistivity values due to soil and water.

We notice first that the entire section has very low resistivity values (all less than 15 ohm-m). We believe that this is because of the high clay content of the soil, and the presence of evaporites (salts). Clay has a low electrical resistivity, and if the pore water is saline, the resistivity will be lower still. Furthermore, it rained in the weeks preceding our survey, but was dry during our fieldwork. The surface probably dried out, creating a thin resistive zone. Beneath this there are very conductive areas (shown in blue, <2 ohm-m) that probably corresponds to water leaching. The same conductive areas are shown at the bottom of the landfill where the leachate is generally collected.

References

[1] Chiampo F., Conti R., Cometto D. (1996) Morphological characterization of MSW landfills. Resources, conservation and recycling 17, pp 37-45.

[2] Abu-Zeid N., Bianchini G., Santarato G., Vaccaro C. (2004) Geochemical characterisation and geophysical mapping of Landfill leachates: the Marozzo canal case study (NE Italy) Environmental Geology, 45:439–447.

[3] Kylefors K., Lagerkvist A. (1997) Changes of leachate quality with degradation phase and time. Proceedings Sardinia, Sixth international landfill symposium, pp 133-149

[4] Loke, M.H. (1999) Electrical imaging surveys for environmental and engineering studies -- A practical guide to 2-d and 3-d surveys: Austin, Texas, Advanced Geosciences Inc., 57 p.

[5] Loke, M.H. (2001) Tutorial 2D and 3D electrical imaging surveys, Geotomo Software, Malaysia.

[6] Farquahar G., Rovers F.A. (1973) Gas production during Refuse decomposition. Water Air and Soil Pollution 2, p. 484-499.

[7] Zelunder A.J. et. al. (1982). Microbiology of Methane Bacteria in Anaerobic Digestion. Elsevier Biomedical Press. London UK.

Learning from Jonglei – enough compromises on our ecosystems!

A. Mustafa Ahmad
College of Architecture and Art, University of Petra, Jordan

Abstract

The Jonglei Canal Project in southern Sudan was planned to by-pass and thus drain part of the wetlands of the Bahr al-Jabal and Bahr az-Zaraf Rivers into the White Nile. While this will increase the Nile waters flowing northwards it will most probably have negative side effects on the local, and maybe the regional, environment, the benefits shared between Egypt and the Sudan and the probable damage falling on the already crippled southern Sudan. Harmful effects of government projects are rarely granted full, objective presentation in the Arab world and this is doubly harmful in countries like the Sudan where they escalate into other related evils, in this case warming and desert creep. The canal project, launched in 1978 and brought to a halt through armed force by rebels in 1984, has played a prominent role in the Sudanese political events of the past two decades which have at long last given way to the peace agreements of January 2005. This paper tries to outline the nature of the project, the peculiar Sudanese-Egyptian disputes in action, the advantages and possible hazards of the project and recommends that the region be developed in a manner that regards the wetlands as a valuable resource and protects the ecosystem from threats of destabilisation.
Keywords: conservation and management of ecological areas, environmental risk, natural resources management, water disputes.

1 Introduction

The title of this conference 'Ecosystems and Sustainable Development' brings to mind three retarded regions in the Sudan that demand urgent attention and action. The first is the Jonglei wetlands in the south; the second is the advancing desert belt now embracing the national capital, Khartoum; the third is Lake Nubia on the northern border created by the erection of the High Dam in

Egypt with its wealth of water, silt, fish, location as a port, archaeological sites and dramatic scenery all totally neglected for over forty years.

This paper focuses on the first region and attempts to analyze the Jonglei Canal Project since, unlike with the other two, interfering with the wetlands ecosystem is an action that can trigger abrupt and far reaching ecological changes and one that has fairly influential foreign parties pressing for action for their own guaranteed benefits regardless of local side effects.

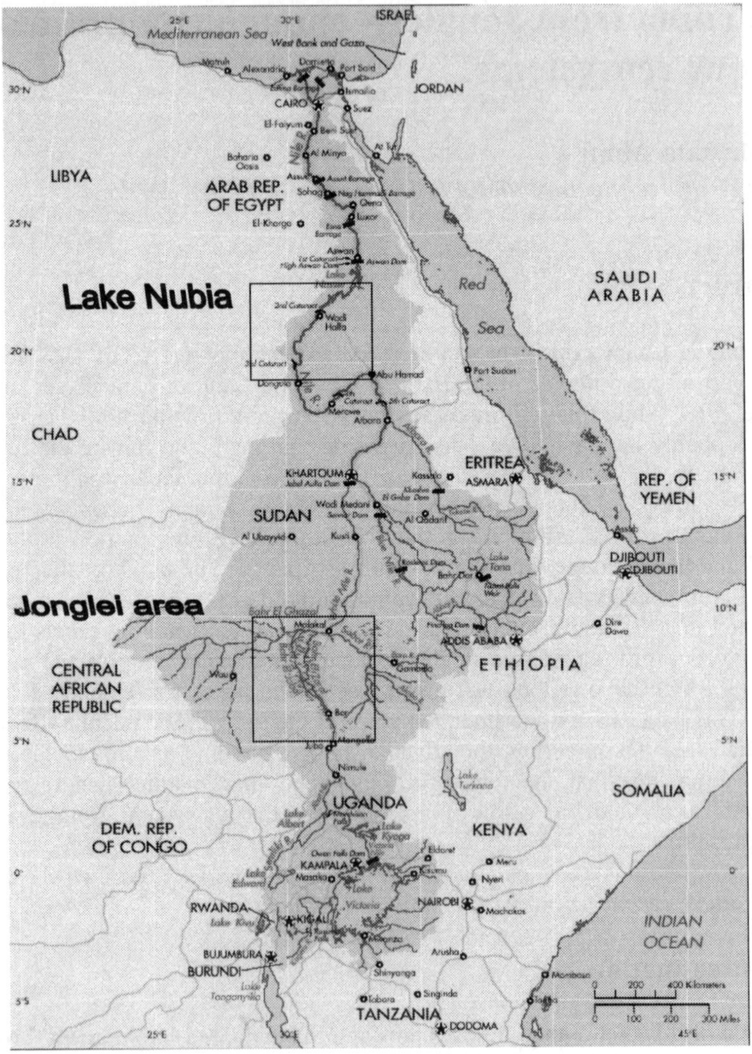

Figure 1: The Nile Basin with the Jonglei wetlands and Lake Nubia marked. (source: http://www.nilebasin.org/nilemap.htm)

2 The region

The Jonglei wetlands lie between latitudes 6 30 and 9 30 North and longitudes 30 10 and 31 45 East. As the waters flowing northwards from the Equatorial Lakes reach a point in the Jonglei area their course branches into two rivers: Bahr al-Jabal and Bahr az-Zaraf; they then overflow their banks and flood the adjacent low, almost flat plains (sloping at about 10 cm/km) thus creating the marshland. This is augmented by annual rainfall of 600-700 mm at the northern parts of the marshland and 800-1000 mm at its southern ones. The inundated area covers over 8000 sq. km and often extends to several times that much following the river discharge's seasonal and annual variation and the intensity of the rainfall, fig 2 [1].

The rainfall, the evaporation from the extensive water surface and the transpiration from the thick layer of floating vegetation all join to create the unique ecology of the region. Since the19th century, writings have reported on the rich biodiversity of the place. Various mammals, reptiles, fish and birds are reported. Moghraby (1985) reports that 'it probably harbours the largest population of crocodiles in the world' [2]. The flora include papyrus, reeds, acacia and water hyacinths. The Jonglei marshland is one of three in southern Sudan, the other two being the Mashar and the Bahr al-Ghazal ones.

In this region, isolated, inaccessible and plagued by wars around it, some 500,000 to 800,000 souls were estimated to live in the 1980s. They are cattle herders partly settled in villages on the higher land and partly following a semi-nomadic pattern over land and marshes. The harsh lives and vulnerable livelihoods characterising their existence apply, to a greater or lesser extent, to the rest of the south.

3 The project

A canal cut between Jonglei and the mouth of Sobat River would bypass, and thus ultimately reduce, the marshlands and channel part of the excess water directly to the White Nile thereby increasing its discharge. The proposal, first submitted in 1938, was subsequently modified more than once. In the final version the canal was 280 km long, 4 m deep, 52 m wide, sloping at 7-9 cm/km and calculated to deliver an average of 20 million cubic metres of water per day [3]. That has been estimated to shrink the permanent marshes by 34 to 43% [4]. In the second phase of the project the discharge of the canal will be raised to 43 million cubic metres per day by either increasing its cross section or digging a new one; this will dry up the marshes entirely. An irrigation canal of 5 million cubic metres capacity will run along the canal's west side [5].

In 1975 the Ministry of Irrigation and Hydro-electric Power issued a 70-page report dealing in considerable detail with the hydrological aspects of the project and touching on historical and socioeconomic ones. The central objective was to increase the Nile revenue by 4.7 billion cubic metres annually measured at Malakal equivalent to 3.8 measured at Aswan to be shared equally by the two countries. This will be raised to 7 billion if Phase II of the project is completed.

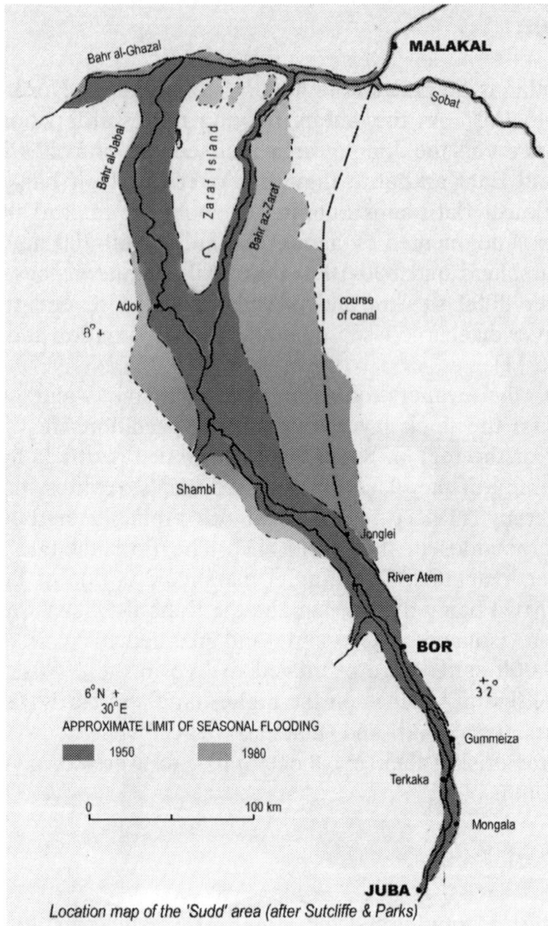

Figure 2: Location of the wetlands and course of the canal (adapted from Sutcliffe and Parks as cited in Moghraby and Sammani, [3]).

The report then mentions other benefits: providing a water source for livestock and wildlife; providing a road along one bank of the canal that can be used most of the year; reducing the flooded area by 10-20% during the flood season; shortening the river route Juba-Malakal (the two provincial capitals) by about 300 km (this figure seems exaggerated when checked against the map); reducing disease vectors and supporting the comprehensive national development plans. The report makes no mention of side effects. Admittedly, the biodiversity issue was not as articulated three decades ago as it is now. But the impact of the project on the climate specially the rainfall, the depletion of the flora and fauna, the aid to desert creep, etc. were needed to complete the picture. The vigilant southerners had additional worries: that tribes would be pushed closer together and conflicts over pasture would increase, that the canal would cut across the routes of their livestock and game and that drying out the wetlands would facilitate the movement of the government's troops.

The controversy is compounded by Egypt's subtle but persistent pressure for the implementation of the project; she welcomes the extra share of water and is prepared to meet half the project's expenses for it.

With such a variety of issues at play the Jonglei project was bound to spark as much controversy as the approval it gained. Excavation started in 1978 by the French *Compagnie de Construction International* and was forced to a halt by southern rebels in 1984 after most of the work had been completed.

Figure 3: Satellite map of northern Egypt showing the narrow habitable strip crossing the desert. (source: SPOT Images).

4 Egypt's role

Egypt's problems are considerable by Arab standards. Those that concern our present debate can be summed up in a few points. The country has a population of 68.6 million (2004 estimate, 2004 CIA Factbook) which, coupled with an annual growth rate of 1.96% (due principally to the arrival of a new-born every 23.6 seconds), is estimated to surpass the 100 million mark by 2025. Geography has squeezed this population into a small liveable strip along the Nile since only 4% of the land is arable; and although the government has succeeded in regularly increasing the cultivable area, this area *per capita* has continued to shrink. As such the country is stressfully overpopulated. Only a small proportion of the water needs is provided by rains and a slightly higher one by underground sources. Reliance on the Nile for fresh water is therefore high.

Egypt's helplessness in confronting her population explosion is matched only by her helplessness in confronting growing *nouveau riche* and *bourgeois* classes created in the 1970s characterised by an insatiable appetite for a wasteful, consumerist life style. It is matched also by her inefficiency in managing her water supply (of which more later).

It is obvious, due to other similar dictates of geography, that it is not in the interest of Egypt to have intensive irrigation, agriculture, industry or large cities flourishing in the Sudan or Ethiopia if this flourish relies on the Nile. Nor is it in her interest to have in these two states strong patriotic governments all too ready to lock horns with foreign interests when they conflict with national ones. The prospect of the separation of southern Sudan hence the creation of a new state in the Nile Basin has recently become another nightmare to Egypt similar to that of constructing dams in Ethiopia which will reduce the storage capacity of the High Dam and gradually shatter its functional (and symbolic) role.

In 1929 when all the region was under foreign domination the *Nile Waters Agreement* was ratified distributing the Nile waters between the Sudan and Egypt in the ratio 1:12 *i.e.* giving 4 billion cubic metres annually to the Sudan and 48 to Egypt. The agreement was revised in 1959 and the shares were raised to 18.5 billion cubic metres to the Sudan and 55.5 to Egypt. The other countries, where the river tributaries originate or through which it flows, were conveniently overlooked. Later, having let herself fall under the impression that the terms of this agreement are inviolable to the end of time, Egypt has been quick to threaten with a resort to arms if her share of the water was touched irrespective of what changes might have hit the region in three quarters of a century. An odd debate goes on as to whether it is geography or history that should predominate in settling the water shares *i.e.* whether it is the party that possesses the source of the stream or that which has for a longer period utilised its water.

This paradoxical mix of apprehension and *hauteur* on Egypt's side has increasingly coloured her relations with other Nile Basin countries and infused them with much tension and distrust. The Sudanese find no mention of the possible damage to their ecosystems in the work of Egyptian scientists when they discuss drying out the 'swamps' to increase the Nile discharge and no reference to the fact that this increase comes in large part from the heavy rainfall which is not part of any agreement on Nile waters and which will be a threatened element if the drying out actually happens. They are amazed when, for example, they come across an alarm raised by an Egyptian researcher warning of the loss of biodiversity in the small lakes of *Manzala* and *Mariout* in northern Egypt [6]; they are incredulous when the head of the Cairo sector in the Ministry of the Environment warns that Cairo Province loses annually one and a half billion cubic metres of *drinking* water 'through leaking water networks and the Egyptian citizen's lack of environmental awareness relating to the use of water' [7]; they are enraged when news transpires about an Egyptian-Israeli agreement to pipe Nile waters to the Negev Desert through the *Peace Canal*.

5 Winds of change

Only recently has promise of reform to the lopsided situation appeared. The Nile flows today through ten independent countries home to over 300 million souls and all their governments, except of course Egypt's, are intent on working out more reasonable agreements. First among these is Ethiopia (source of the Blue Nile which offers Egypt 84% of her fresh water) burdened by its 67 million citizens and hefty share of poverty, droughts, famines and wars. Agreements concluded during colonial times should not automatically continue to be binding, these countries rightly argue, and by the same common sense we must add those concluded by dictatorial regimes after Independence when they go glaringly against national interests. They have to be regularly re-examined *vis-à-vis* new developments. It is unfortunate that the world's longest stream is the one that carries by far the least amount of water in comparison to other great rivers.

The required reform involves two new considerations: that none of the Nile Basin countries is excluded from the agreements on the Nile issues and that it is not only the sharing of the waters which is at issue but the development and utilisation of the entire resources of the river in a comprehensive way to the benefit of all parties. On the first count we can mention the creation of the Nile Basin Council of Ministers and the December 2004 meetings of the Equatorial countries to discuss matters of mutual interest and resolve conflicts. On the second, the most prominent step is the World Bank's *Nile Basin Initiative* of 2001 [8]. This looks more comprehensively at the problem and proposes seven projects: Nile Transboundary Environmental Action, Nile Basin Regional Power Trade, Efficient Water Use for Agricultural Production, Water Resources Planning and Management, Confidence Building and Stakeholder Involvement, Applied Training and, finally, Socio-economic Development and Benefit Sharing. Egyptian reactions to the new situation have, on the whole, been distinctly negative [9].

As for the Sudan, the country suddenly found itself one of the major foci of world attention. This is due to the natural resources which have finally become a tangible reality and the ongoing resources wars, to borrow Suleiman's term [10] – oil, water, gold, uranium, livestock to mention a few. Under various pretexts industrial countries keep rushing to establish an early foothold in the promising coming state. Moreover, Federalism, officially adopted in 1971, imposes further conditions on the development scene; environmental issues, the development and management of animal and water resources, road networks within the province are now handled mainly at the level of the provinces not that of the central government. And although the main distinction in the federal state is that between the central government and the provincial governments, the Sudan has its peculiarities: the provinces have never carried equal weight. The distinction between north and south is predominant. The injustice inflicted on the south and the neglect it suffered for half a century is a nagging consideration. This introduces new obligations and particular emphasis must be laid, when planning the utilisation of resources, on placing the interest of the southern Sudanese before all others. It is further emphasized by the fact that one of the vital national resources, oil, is now being pumped out specifically from that region.

6 The suggested way forward

The Jonglei Canal Project is at present too riven with complexity and controversy to deserve a clear green light. Particularly in view of the approaching Nubian Desert front, drying up the wetlands partially or totally is almost certain to bring undesirable long-term environmental changes.

The issue is by no means a local one. The world has finally come to recognise the threats posed by global warming and desertification and feel the colossal efforts required to combat and overcome them. Awarding the Nobel Peace Prize to Kenyan environmental activist Wangari Maathai in 2004 has underlined this awareness and proven the link between peace and the environment or, to put it more directly, between environmental degradation and the rise of conflicts.

Unlike the hydrologist or the hydrobiologist whose materials gain extra richness by the region's remoteness and difficulty of access, the physical planner has little in his hand to aid his work. No population census has ever been conducted in southern Sudan and the civil war and resultant population displacements have undermined the reliability of old estimates. The patterns and conditions of settlements, except for the larger towns, must have changed considerably. Room for reform is huge. But even disregarding for a while the above side effects the notion of developing the region uncompromisingly as a wetland holds a thrilling attraction to the planner and under the present new conditions is not unrealistic.

Wetlands should be regarded as valuable assets and preserved and developed as such. Their potential as social, economic, environmental, scientific and entertainment resources needs careful assessment. Shrinking the permanent flooded area by up to a maximum of 43% as the Sutcliffe-Parks study predicts is certainly too high to permit the desired results.

In light of the entry of the country into an oil era and the termination of the civil war in the south upgrading the entire wetland to a healthy, productive state no longer seems as daunting a proposal as it once did, provided the political will is there to help the south catch up. It will involve activities like selective clearing of floating vegetation to facilitate navigation and increase the flow of water and its oxygen content, building dikes, roads and bridges, creating natural reserves, rehabilitating and reorganising settlements in a hierarchy over the whole region, revising land uses, revitalising human activities, fighting water-borne and water-related diseases and so on.

Due to the continual clashes in the region no convincing Environmental Impact Assessment (EIA) has been produced and the projects seem to have been viewed in isolation while what was needed was to see it in the context of a comprehensive regional development plan covering the southern region then the rest of the country. This should be illuminated also by studies of similar experiences, for example drying up the *Ahwar* marshes of southern Iraq.

Increasing the Nile waters is at present a lower priority than developing the marshland and can, in any case, be resorted to any time in future. And attempting to draw national environmental policies under pressure from a foreign party, in this case Egypt, must be ruled out. It is high time for Egypt to start demonstrating to others what positive, effective steps to take in numerous fields: the elimination of waste in water use, recycling of used water, modernisation of irrigation systems, utilisation of sea water, desalination, economic co-operation and complementation of other Nile Basin countries' activities and resources for shared benefits, stopping the pollution of her own waters but, above all, handling her population time bomb. Egypt has to start listening to critics like Saeed, the respected self-exiled Egyptian geologist, who kept arguing for decades that the whole idea of 'greening the desert', and in particular the *Toshki Project*, is basically wrong-headed and must give way to realistic alternatives [11].

The upgrading of human settlements in the region starting with the Upper Nile provincial capital, Malakal, is vital to all sustainable progress in the south and will be set on a firm track by the establishment of a specialised institution for development and wetland studies in Malakal to serve at different levels, from the local to the African Equatorial regional.

The Sudanese seem at present in a position to pose as demonstrators of how to respect the environment and live in harmony with it since little of the age's evils: consumerism, extravagance, exploitation, has yet been part of their way of life.

References

[1] Republic of the Sudan. Ministry of Irrigation & Hydro-electric Power. The Jonglei Canal project (Phase I).(Arabic). Khartoum, January 1975.

[2] Moghraby, Asim, The Jonglei Canal – needed development or potential ecodisaster? Environmental Conservation, 9(2), pp. 141-148, summer 1982.

[3] Moghraby, A. & Sammani, M.O., On the environmental and socioeconomic impact of the Jonglei canal, Environmental Conservation, 12(1), pp. 41-48, spring 1985.

[4] Sutcliffe, J. V. & Parks Y.P. A hydrological estimate of the effect of the Jonglei canal on areas of flooding, Institute of Hydrology, Wallingford, UK, 1982. (cited by Moghraby & Sammani, 1985).

[5] El Zein, Soghayroon, Jonglei Canal. Proceedings of the Fifth Erkowit Conference, Juba, n.d.

[6] Hinnawi, I., The future of the Egyptian environment in five scenarios, (Arabic), Al-Bee'a wat-Tanmiya (Environment & Development), 6(44), pp. 18-23, Beirut, November 2001.

[7] Anon. Egypt: waste of 1.5 billion cubic metres of water annually, Bada-il (Arabic edition of The Ecologist), 1(2), p. 10, Autumn 2004.

[8] World Bank & Nile Basin Initiative Secretariat, Nile Basin Initiative strategic action program: an overview, May 2001.
[9] for a typical Egyptian reaction see: Saeed, Rushdi, The world Bank prescription for the development of the Nile Basin (Arabic), Wijhat Nathar, issue no 32, The Egyptian Company for Arabic & International Publishing, Cairo, September 2001.
[10] Suleiman, M., The Sudan: resources and identity wars, (Arabic), Cambridge Academic Press, UK, 2000.
[11] Saeed, R. Egypt of the Future. (Arabic), Kitab al-Hilal, Cairo, 2004.

The methods of forecasting of SO_2 and suspended dust concentrations for warning purposes in the example of selected polluted regions in Poland

D. Foszcz, T. Niedoba & J. Siewior
[1]*Department of Mining and Geoengineering, University of Science and Technology in Krakow, Poland*
[2]*Provincial Inspectorate of Environment Protection, Katowice, Poland*

Abstract

The problems of air pollution monitoring is presented in this paper because of its harmful influence on the natural environment and the health conditions of people. In the example of the city of Krakow and cities of the Upper Silesia Industrial Area, the state of air pollution by suspended dust and SO_2 were characterised. Statistical analysis of the data from automatic monitoring stations from the region mentioned above was performed and analysis of dependencies between the state of air pollution and meteorological data was carried out. The methodology of pollution modelling for the warning purposes was discussed.

In this paper, on the basis of the measurement data from automatic monitoring stations, the forecast models of SO_2 concentration and suspended dust were determined (ARX models and models obtained from adaptive modelling), which can be generally used for the purposes mentioned above.
Keywords: air pollution monitoring, statistical methods, sulphur dioxide, suspended dust, ARX models, adaptive models.

1 Introduction

Sulphur dioxide (SO_2) is a colourless, reactive gas that is odourless at low concentrations but has a pungent smell at very high concentrations. Sulphur dioxide is highly soluble in water, resulting in the formation of sulphurous acid (VI). This can be done by homogenous oxidation and reactions in solution, with or without catalytic factor. It reacts on the surface of a variety of airborne solid particles and can be oxidised within airborne water droplets.

Sulphur dioxide, SO_2, enters the atmosphere as a result of both natural phenomena and anthropogenic activities e.g.: combustion of fossil fuels; oxidation of organic material in soils; volcanic eruptions; biomass burning.

Effects of volcanic eruptions may have an impact on air traffic, as such eruptions are important sources of ash (aerosols) and sulphur dioxide in the atmosphere. However, emissions are sporadic, intermittent and often occur in uninhabited regions.

Mainly power stations, combustion of fuel and vehicles are the anthropogenic sources of SO_2 pollution. Coal burning is the single largest man-made source of sulphur dioxide, accounting for about 50% of annual global emissions (e.g. from 1 tone of hard/brown carbon of 3% of sulphur 60 kg of SO_2 is leaking), with oil burning accounting for a further 25 to 30%.

Changes in the abundance of sulphur dioxide have an impact on atmospheric chemistry and on the radiation field, and hence on the climate. Consequently, global observations of sulphur dioxide are important for atmospheric and climate research.

The major health concerns associated with exposure to high concentrations of sulphur dioxide include effects on breathing, respiratory illness, alterations in pulmonary defenses, and aggravation of existing cardiovascular disease. In the atmosphere, sulphur dioxide mixes with water vapour producing sulphuric acid. This acidic pollution can be transported by wind over many hundreds of miles, and deposited as acid rain (www.temis.nl, [1], Szczepaniec-Cieciak and Koscielniak [2]).

According to the paper (Rutowski et al, [3]) it is proved that exposure of human beings to SO_2 results in increasing of total number of lymphocytes (the tests were carried on by using Amaya-Sugiura passive sampling and ion spectrophotometry)

The harmful influence of SO_2 depends on both of concentration and time of exposure, what is presented on fig. 1.

It occurs that even a small concentration of SO_2 in situation of longer exposure to people causes disadvantegous effect on health, mainly connected with respiratory and blood systems (Rutowski et al, [3]).

Aerosols are tiny particles suspended in the air. Some occur naturally, originating from volcanoes, dust stroms, forest and grassland fires, living vegetation, and sea spray. Human activities, such as the burning of fossil fuels, prescribed fires, and the alteration of natural surface cover, also generate aerosols. Many human-produced aerosols are small enough to be inhaled, so they present a serious health hazard around industrial centers or even hundreds of miles downwind. Another unfortunate aspect of the small sizes of respirable dusts is that they have a very low settling velocity and can remain suspended in air indefinitely.Additionally, thick dust or smoke plumes severely limit visibility and can make it hazardous to travel by air or road. New research shows that aerosol pollution can modify cloud properties to reduce or prevent precipitation in the polluted region. Aerosol containing black carbon can impact climate and possibly reduce formation of clouds (Carver, [4]).

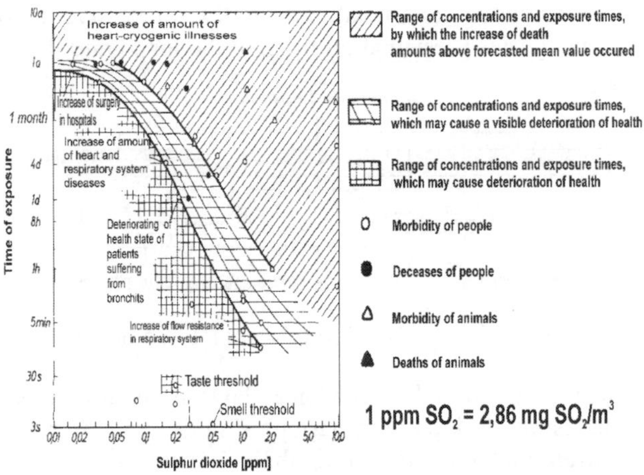

Figure 1: The dependence of health state of people and animals on SO_2 concentration and time of exposure.

Sources of atmospheric dust are winds blowing over dry earth (plowed fields, deserts, and roads), the various products of combustion, volcanic eruptions, salt spray from the oceans, pollen and other material from plants, and meteoric particles. The detonation of nuclear devices in the atmosphere creates radioactive dust

Dust sometimes settles quickly on surfaces, but vast quantities are carried to the upper layers of the air and suspended there for long periods of time.

Classification of dusts may be divided into five categories:

- Toxic dusts – these can cause chemical reactions within the respiratory system or allow toxic compounds to be absorbed into the bloodstream through the alveolar walls. They are poisonous to body tissue or to specific organs (Walli, [5]).
- Carcinogenic (cancer causing) dusts;
- Fibrogenic dusts;
- Explosive dusts;
- Nuisance dusts.

The Silesian province, as well the region of Krakow are ones of the most polluted regions in Poland. So, the forecasting and researches over SO_2 and dusts concentrations in this area are crucial and very important.

2 Methodology of pollution spreading modelling

Modelling of air pollution spreading bases on a reciprocal connection between the features conditioning dispersion of pollution. Among these features, influencing on expansion of pollutants, as: meteorological conditions, source and emission characteristics, reciprocal affection between pollution and ground surface, the most important are meteorological conditions. So, the modelling of atmospheric phenomenons is crucial. Generally, dispersive models may be divided into the categories presented on fig. 2. (Chodorski and Pietrzyk, [6]).

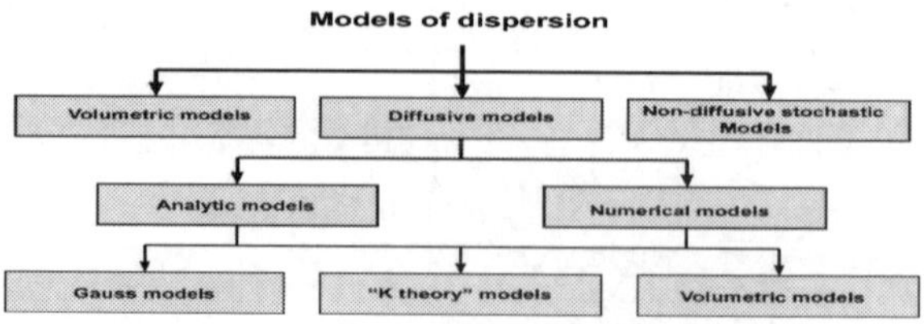

Figure 2: Division of dispersion models.

Diffusive models are based on physical laws of pollution propagation by hovering and diffusion, derived with various simplifying assumptions, In these models both differential equations and their coefficients of certain physical interpretation were applied [Chodorski and Pietrzyk, [6]; Borysiewicz and Stankiewicz, [7]; Juda and Chrosciel, [8]).

Gauss models are based on the assumption that the concentrations distribution function is a normal distribution with variances depended on distance from a source and atmosphere stratification. The models of "k theory" assume that the turbulent concentrations flow is proportional to mean concentration. This assumption is called the closing of first extent.

The point of start to the theroretical researches of pollution spreading in atmosphere are differential equations of diffusion in moving centre. The solution of these equations allow to determine the pollution concentration in any distance from a source and (for the point of pollution emission – a chimney) its height assuring optimal spreading of emitted pollution. The basic assumption in these equations is that the spreading is symmetrical round the „z" axis.

The general form of equation of turbulent diffusion in moving centre, being applied in further considerations, in rectangular co-ordinate system is presented by the following equation:

$$\frac{\mathrm{d}S}{\mathrm{d}\tau} = \mathrm{div}(KVS) - S\mathrm{div}\vec{c} + f \tag{1}$$

where: S – gas or dust pollution concentration, K – coefficient of atmospheric diffusion, $\vec{c}$ – vector of air movement velocity, f – a function expressing the action of volumetric emission source of pollution (decrease or increase of pollution).

Depending on the assumptions and simplifications we obtain various forms of solution of diffusion equation. As the most known and rated to the basic ones the solutions given by Sutton, Pasquille, Bosanquet, Pearson and Calder are considered, which differ among themselves by assumed vertical and horizontal diffusion coefficients. In the equations mentioned above the independence of atmosphere turbulence coefficients on co-ordinates x, y, z is assumed. The given solutions of diffusion equation are the base for the analytic solutions (Juda and Chrosciel, [8]).

The starting point to solving the diffusion equation in moving centre by Pasquille was the introduction of atmospheric diffusion coefficients, given by equations:

$$\sigma_x = \sqrt{\overline{u}^2}\,\frac{x}{\overline{u}} = T_x x,\ \sigma_y = \sqrt{\overline{\upsilon}^2}\,\frac{x}{\overline{u}} = T_y x,\ \sigma_z = \sqrt{\overline{w}^2}\,\frac{x}{\overline{u}} = T_z x \tag{2}$$

where: σ_x, σ_y, σ_z – atmospheric diffusion coefficients of Pasquille [m], $\overline{u}'^2, \overline{\upsilon}'^2, \overline{w}'^2$ –variances of wind velocity in direction x, y, z resulting from the existence of turbulent movements [m^2/s], $\overline{u}$ – mean wind velocity in considered layer [m/s], T_x, T_y, T_z – measures of intensivity of turbulence in directions x, y , (dimensionless quantities).

The diffusion coefficients given by Pasquille are depend on the distance x from the source of emission, it means on the time of pollution dislocation, which is expressed by the ratio $x/\overline{u}$. The numerical values of coefficients in directions y and z depend generally on atmosphere's turbulence structure, height above the surface of earth, roughness of terrain and its topography, time of concentration, distance from the source of emission and the state of atmosphere's equilibrium. Pasquille gave the key to determine the state of atmosphere's equilibrium, allowing the determination of coefficients σ_y i σ_z, for assumed distance from the source of emission.

For the purpose of simplifying the general solution of diffusion equation Pasquille introduced the following assumptions:

1. The field of concentration is determined in time: $\partial s/\partial \tau = 0$. To fulfil this condition, the intensity of emission must be constant in time, no shorter than the time of consideration of pollution movement from source to the point, where we determine the pollution concentration. Also, the meteorological conditions should be constant in this time.
2. The components of air movement velocity in direction y and z are equal to zero $\upsilon = w = 0$,
3. The air is treated as non-compressible fluid,
4. The atmospheric diffusion coefficients do not depend on height above the surface of earth.
5. There are not volumetric sources of emission, what means that $f = 0$.

Thanks to these assumptions, after applying the air turbulence $\sigma_i = \sqrt{2K_i \frac{x}{\overline{u}}}$ for the directions y and z, where $x/\overline{u}$ is the time of pollution movement τ, we obtain the differential equation:

$$\frac{\partial S}{\partial \tau} = \frac{d}{d\tau}\left(\frac{\sigma_y^{\ 2}}{2}\right)\frac{\partial^2 S}{\partial^2 y} + \frac{d}{d\tau}\left(\frac{\sigma_z^{\ 2}}{2}\right)\frac{\partial^2 S}{z^2} = 0 \tag{3}$$

Different from the starting equation we interprete the $\partial S/\partial \tau$, assuming that the point of reference is moving with velocity $\overline{u}$ and during this wander it is changing in time. The solution of equation (3) lead to the group of formulaes of Pasquille's type, obtaining different form, dependly on assumed conditions, i.e. by: $\tau \to 0$, $S \to \frac{E}{u}\delta(y)\delta(H-z)$ we obtain:

$$S = \frac{E}{2\pi\sigma_y\sigma_z\overline{u}}\exp\left(-\frac{y^2}{2\sigma_y^{\ 2}}\right)\left\{\exp\left[-\frac{(z-H)^2}{2\sigma_z^{\ 2}}\right] + f(u)\exp\left[-\frac{(z+H)^2}{2\sigma_z^{\ 2}}\right]\right\} \tag{4}$$

where: S – concentration of pollution in point of co-ordinates x, y, z, E – mass intensity od gas pollution emission, $\overline{u}$ – mean value of wind velocity in propagation layer, H – height of point location of emission source, $f(u)$ – function of „reflection" $f(u) = 1$ for wind above 7 m/s and $f(u) = u/7$ for winds below 7 m/s

From assumptions taken by Pasquille the limitations of application of his equation for open, flat suburban areas occur, when there is not inversion layer. These limitations caused some sort of modifications allowing enlargement of Pasquille's equation application (Juda and Chrosciel, [8])

Additional elements, which should be taken into consideration, applying the solution proposed by Pasquille, are decrease of pollution in atmosphere and changeability in time of emission intensity, occuring for unstable sources of pollution emission.

The point of start to diffusion equation calculation of dust concentration is identical as for gas. The differences, which occur during solving the equation may be as following:

The dust grains have an additional vertical falling velocity what for gas components may be ignored even for the biggest molecules.

There may be an assumption, that the dust grains after touching the surface of earth are completely or partially snatched away from aerosol flow (introduction of suitable edge condition for diffusion differential equation).

Because of the fact that the processes of spreading and decreasing of pollution are connected with diffusion and convection gas phenomenons, which are described by partial differential equations of parabolic type, the concept of solving these equations by variation methods with division of selected areas was presented by Ziemkiewicz (Chodorski and Pietrzyk, [6]). In the base of approach proposed by him, the group of solutions for warmth transport in solids was developped. Also, the works, which purpose is to adapt this solution to gas diffusion and convection problems, are undertaken, as well works over proposal of model in base of finite elements, allowing simulation of pollution spreading round the emission source.

The volumetric models are based on the mass balance, taking into consideration only carriage, without pollution diffusion. The Bringfelt model may be rated to the models of this type. The diffusion factor is not also directly taken into consideration in non-diffusive models, based on the formulaes obtained by mathematical statistics or probability theory. The stochastic models are based on the analysis of random character of pollution spreading. The regressive models are included to them, as they take into consideration the influence of various meteorological elements on the change of mean pollution coefficients values in certain area. It is very desirable to have the possibilty to interprete the form and coefficients of equation by the full physical, consistent with phenomenon's mechanism interpretation (Morawska-Horawska and Tumidajski, [9]).

The SO_2 concentration measurements, apart from applying it to air pollution evaluation, should be applied also in the SO_2 management by its delimitation (excluding of some objects) during crisis days and also to preventive purposes. To complete these tasks, the mathematical models of pollution forecasts are needed, which should allow to predict sufficiently precisely the values of concentrations and mainly the situations, when the allowed limits are exceeded. It is not necessary to apply the complicate diffusive models to this purpose (Juda and Chrosciel, [8]). Usually, the regressive models are efficient, which forms may have some theoretical reasons. More than once, the application of diffusive models, because of the necessity of having essential data to solve them (quantity of emission, circumstances of spreading as: air diffusion vertical and horizontal coefficients, topography of terrain), is even impossible. Good solution is application of stochastic models, which often give good prediction results, what makes possible the realisation of warning tasks.

To these models we may include (P(t)):

a) model based on determination of SO_2 concentration. During 24h the SO_2 concentration is the ratio between the mass of emitted SO_2 on certain area, mass of drifted SO_2 from neighbouring emitters and mass of SO_2, which was earlier in this area to the air volume, in which these masses are spreading.

Assuming that (for certain direction of air circulation) the mass of first two components depends on temperature (amount of combusted carbon) and chemical changes, connected with air humidity we may write that: $m = AW^aT^b$, where *A* is constant and indexes *a* and *b* characterise the influence of humidity on change of SO_2, dependly on temperature. The volume of air layer, where mixing occurs may be expressed by equation:

$V = BH^cv^d$, where *B* – constant, which characterise the width of mixing layer (constant for certain directions, *H* – height of mixing layer, *v* – wind velocity; *c*, *d* – indexes connected with the height or velocity corrections The quantities *H, T, W* are the functions of *t* variable.

If we are taking into consideration the aspect of autocorrelation of SO_2 concentrations, we may introduce the correction $kSO_2(t-1)+p$ into the model, which will correct actual concentration *P(t)*. So, we have:

$$\hat{P}(t) = \frac{AW^aT^b}{BH^cv^d} + kSO_2(t-1) + p \tag{5}$$

A similar model, which, however, does not take into consideration relative humidity and autocorrelation of SO_2 concentrations, was presented by Bringfelt (Bringfelt, [10]).

b) wien model. To forecast SO_2 concentrations in city centre of Wien, the following model is being applied [Bolzern, [11])]

$$\hat{P}(t) = a_1 P(t-1) + a_2[T(t) + a_3]^{-\alpha} + a_n[v(t) + a_5]^{-\beta} \tag{6}$$

The SO_2 concentration in day of number t is dependent on SO_2 concentration from the previous day, predicted mean temperature $T(t)$ and predicted mean wind velocity $v(t)$. The SO_2 concentration is to some extent connected (concentrations autocorrelation) with mass of pollution existing in the area at the end of (t-1)th day. Second expression takes into consideartion the increase of SO_2 emission, originated from the heating system, which is „produced" by falling of temperature, and the third expression describes the decrease of SO_2 concentration by the wind (eventually the drifting of neighbouring areas).

c) regressive models. In the range of air pollution concentration forecasting, usually the ARX models are being applied. These models are taking into consideartion concentrations autocorrelation (AR) (X – egzogenic points), not forgetting about the meteorological factors and their displacements in time. So, for SO_2 [Morawska-Horawska and Tumidajski, [9]; Finzi and Tebaldi, [12]; Morawska-Horawska and Kuros, [13]) we have:

$$\begin{aligned}\hat{P}(t) &= a_1 P(t-1) + \ldots + a_p P(t-p) + b_0 T(t) + b_1 T(t-1) + \ldots + b_k T(t-k) + \\ &+ c_0 v(t) + c_1 v(t-1) + \ldots + c_l v(t-l) + d_0 W(t) + d_1 W(t-1) + \ldots + d_r W(t-r) + e\end{aligned} \tag{7}$$

(the symbols for variables are the same as in previous models)

Usually p is smaller or equal to 2 and the values k, l, r do not exceed 1.

d) adaptive models. Because it is not always possible to transfer the autoregressive model from certain heating season to the next one, it is necessary to actualise the coefficients in base of actaully registered results. This method of modelling is called adaptive modelling and is being applied in neural networks (Rastrigin, [14]).

It is assumed, that the atmospheric pollution forecasting model is in the following form:

$$\hat{y} = f(\mathbf{X}, \mathbf{C}) = \sum_{j=1}^{k} c_j \varphi_j(\mathbf{X}) \tag{8}$$

where: X - vector of independent values, C – vector of coefficients, j = 1,...,k; N – number of experiments – groups of measurements data (x_{1i}, x_{2i}, ...,x_{ki}, y_i), i = 1,...,N; N ≥ k; $\varphi_j(X)$ – specified system of many variables, independent linearly

Let C be the vector of parameters values in the i-th stage of adaptive method. Let assume also, that we obtain a new group of data $I_{i+1} = (X_{i+1}, Y_{i+1})$. These data should help in replacing C_i by C_{i+1}, so will be the source of correction:

$$C_{i+1} = C_i + \Delta C_{i+1} \tag{9}$$

Now we will replace C_i by C_{i+1}. For the local discrepancy between value predicted by model and registered at the station we have:

$$q_{i+1}(C_i) = f(X_{i+1}, C_i) - y_{i+1} \tag{10}$$

the value ΔC_{i+1} should be such to decrease square of this difference. It is obtained by „antigradient" method, so::

$$\Delta C_{i+1} = -\alpha_{i+1} \nabla q^2{}_{i+1}(C_i) \tag{11}$$

where: α_{i+1} – positive coefficient, ∇ - nabla operator, $\nabla = \left(\frac{\partial q}{\partial c_1}, ..., \frac{\partial q}{\partial ck} \right)$

$$\nabla q^2(\mathbf{C}) = \left(\frac{\partial q^2(\mathbf{C})}{\partial c_1}, ..., \frac{\partial q^2(\mathbf{C})}{\partial c_k} \right) = 2q(\mathbf{C}) \left(\frac{\partial q(\mathbf{C})}{\partial c_1}, ..., \frac{\partial q(\mathbf{C})}{\partial c_k} \right) = 2q(\mathbf{C}) \nabla q(\mathbf{C}) \tag{12}$$

After transformations, for the function, given by equation (5) we obtain:

$$q = c_0 + c_1\varphi_1(X^{i+1}) + ... + c_k\varphi_k(X^{i+1}) - y_{i+1} \text{ oraz}$$

$$\nabla f(X,C) = [1, \varphi_1(X_1^{i+1}), ... \varphi_k(X_k^{i+1})]$$

so:

$$(c_0 - 2\alpha q \cdot 1) + (c_1 - 2\alpha q c_1 \varphi_1(\mathbf{X}^{i+1}) \cdot \varphi_1(\mathbf{X}_1^{i+1}) + ... + + (c_k - 2\alpha q c_k \varphi_k(\mathbf{X}^{i+1}) \cdot \varphi_k(\mathbf{X}_k^{i+1}) - y_{i+1} = 0$$

Solution gives an optimal value of α^*, for which the discrepancy $q(C_{i-1} + \Delta C_i)$ heads to 0.

$$\alpha^* = \frac{1}{2} \left[1 + \sum_{j=1}^{k} c_j \varphi_j^2(\mathbf{X}^{i+1}) \right]^{-1} \tag{13}$$

where: X^{i+1} - is a system of co-ordinates of start points vector X in the moment i+1.

These modelling methods were applied to the data of air pollution and meteorological conditions from the automatic measurement station in Katowice. These data were made available for us by Provincial Inspectorate of Environment Protection in Katowice.

3 Modelling results

According to the rules of ARX models determination, the significance of coefficients in equation (7) was checked by using STATISTICA program, with the displacements (for p, k, l, r = 0, 1, 2) for the data from measurement station in Katowice.

The model for heating season 1996/1997 (**R** = 0,8519; $\mathbf{s_r}$ = 27,66):

SO_2(t) = 55,52 – 10,02**v(t)** – 2,78**T(t-1)** + 0,59**SO_2(t-1)**

[6,69] [3,61] [0,42] [0,05]

(in square brackets – standard errors of coefficients, s_r – rest deviation)

The model for heating season 1997/1998 (**R** = 0,8055; $\mathbf{s_r}$ = 20,43):

SO_2(t) = 37,73 – 9,73**v(t)** – 1,79**T(t-1)** + 0,62**SO_2(t-1)**

[4,70] [2,65] [0,33] [0,05]

It occurs from the analysis of equations and their coefficients significance that the obtained regressive equations for the seasons of measurement station in Katowice are very significant and the estimation errors (mean rest deviations) are not large. There is clear difference between the influence of various factors on the SO_2(t) in individual seasons.

The obtained model for heating season 1996/1997 of measurement station in Katowice was the base to determination of coefficients in adaptive model for heating season 1997/1998. In the purpose of avoiding the strong influence of large fluctuations of individual variables, the additional cases were introduced to the adaptive modelling, which were the mean values of each following pairs of days. After calculations it occured, that the rest deviation for adaptive model amounted 14,81 $\mu g/m^3$ (calculated for real days) and applying the regressive model from the season 1996/1997 - 22,78 $\mu g/m^3$. Figure 3 presents course of conformity of SO_2 air pollution prediction in heating season 1997/1998 for adaptive model and for regressive model from season 1996/1997.

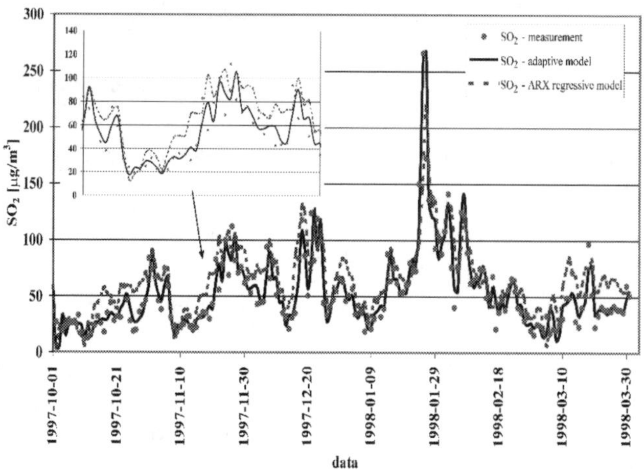

Figure 3: Course of conformity of SO2 air pollution prediction for adaptive regressive models.

4 Conclusions

The unfavourable conditions of ventilation occur very often during winter. They are the result of the chill of lower atmosphere's layers phenomenon, which lead to creation of temperature's inversion. It limits considerably the vertical exchange of air masses. In effect the pollution introduced to atmosphere from the low emission sources cumulate in its lower layer and the there is an increase of pollution concentration near the surface of earth. Furthermore, it is usually connected with weak winds. It is also the factor, which worsen the pollution's dispersion conditions, so it influences on the quality of air. The chill of the lower atmosphere's layer is condusive to water vapour condensation – fogs and mists occur very often. In connection with a large content of SO_2 and dusts in air it may lead even to creation of acid smog (winter smog).

The warnings about unfavourable conditions of air pollution are significant actions, because of its harmful influence on people's health state. So, it can be said, that the correct forecasting is crucial for preventive purposes.

Looking at the results presented above it seems to be correct to conduct these forecasts in the base of adaptive models. Thanks to them it is possible to adjust the model parameters to the change of the factors, which condition the air pollution state.

Acknowledgement

The paper is the effect of statutory work no. 11.11.100.238

References

[1] TEMIS – http://www.temis.nl.

[2] Szczepaniec-Cieciak E. & Koscielniak P., *Chemia srodowiska t.1*, Wyd. UJ, Krakow, pp. 155-215, 1999.

[3] Rutowski J., Moszczynski P., Dobrowolski J.W. & Krochmal D., *Immunological Effects of Environmental Exposure to SO_2*, Polish Journal of Environmental Studies, vol. 7, no 3, pp. 175-179, 1998.

[4] Carver J., *Respirable dust regulations in the United Kingdom*, Int. Mine Ventillation Congress, Johannesburg, South Africa, pp. 399-405, 1975.

[5] Walli R.A., *Mine dusts. Mine ventilation and air conditioning*, Chap.5, pp. 4-130, 1982.

[6] Chodorski M. & Pietrzyk M., *Propozycja zastosowania metody elementow skonczonych do symulacji rozprzestrzeniania się zanieczyszczen w atmosferze,* Ochrona powietrza i problemy odpadow, Wydawnictwo Naukowo-Techniczne EcoEdycja, year 3, pp. 90-93, 1997.

[7] Borysiewicz M. & Stankiewicz R., *Modelowanie procesów propagacji skażeń w atmosferze – podstawy modeli matematycznych i metod numerycznych*, Raport IAE-8/A, Instytut Energii Atomowej, Otwock-Swierk, 1994.

[8] Juda J. & Chrosciel S., *Ochrona powietrza atmosferycznego*, WNT, Warszawa, 1974.

[9] Morawska-Horawska M. & Tumidajski T., *Stochastyczne modele prognozy sredniego dobowego stezenia SO_2 dla Krakowa*. Wiadomosci IMGW, vol. 9, pp. 41-45, 1996.

[10] Bringfelt B.: *Important factors for the sulphur dioxide concentration in central Stockholm*. Atmosph. Envir. vol. 5, pp. 949-972, 1971.

[11] Bolzern P., Fronza G., Runce E. & Uberhuber C., *Statistical analysis of winter sulphur dioxide concentration data in Vienna*. Atmosph. Envir., vol 16, no 8, pp.. 1899-1906, 1982.

[12] Finzi G. & Tebaldi G., *A mathematical model for air pollution forecast and alarm in an urban area*. Atmosph. Envir., vol. 16, no 9, pp. 2055-2090, 1982.

[13] Morawska-Horawska M. & Kuros E., *Specyfika kształtowania się wielkosci emisji SO_2 na obszarze GOP i mozliwosci prognozowania srednich dobowych stezen SO_2*, Ochrona Powietrza i Problemy Odpadow, no 6, pp. 148-150, 1992.

[14] Rastrigin L. A., *Contemporary principles to control complex objects*, Mir Publishers, Moscow, 1983.

Section 13
Natural resources management

Sustainability of wetlands: nature conservation and agriculture in Baixo Vouga Lagunar

T. Andresen & M. J. Curado
Universidade do Porto, Faculdade de Ciências, Portugal

Abstract

In the central coastal area of Portugal an Environmental Impact Assessment Study of Infrastructures and Farmland Reallocation Project has taken place. The site – Lower Vouga Lagoon System – is a unique man-made landscape that is threatened by various factors, namely salinisation and abandonment. However, it is a place of significant interest for nature conservation.

The complexity of the site and of the Project, combined with the significant public attention that surrounded it, called for innovative approaches in terms of methodology and tools for the implementation of the recommendations that at the same time were technically credible and well understood by the public.

The Project offered various alternatives and after the Environmental Impact Assessment Study a solution was pointed out. Considering the environmental susceptibility the study pushed forward a set of recommendations towards the sustainability of this landscape that were translated into integrated monitoring plans for water, soil, and biodiversity and landscape diversity.

Keywords: wetlands, ecological corridors, landscape quality, biological diversity, farm reallocation, environmental impact assessment, impact assessment methodologies, monitoring plans.

1 Introduction

Based upon the Environmental Impact Assessment Study of Infrastructures and Farmland Reallocation Project of the Lower Vouga Lagoon System (EIA), the sustainability of wetlands through the conciliation of nature conservation objectives and optimization of intelligent farming practices of the past is discussed and confronted with today's practices of intensive farming. The recommendations arising from the EIA advocate that the sustainability of the

Lower Vouga Lagoon System *(Baixo Vouga Lagunar)* should involve an integrated monitoring strategy covering water, soil and biological and landscape diversity. The EIA was approved in 2003 and the project should start to be implemented in 2005 (Andresen, et al. [1]).

The Lower Vouga Lagoon System is an extremely vulnerable agro-ecosystem. Here, water and soil management are vital to ensure the maintenance of a system that was created by man on a land/water interface, where biological diversity is considerable and landscape quality is high. This man-made landscape of approximately 3000 ha, which is the support of significant habitats, is located in the central coastal area of Portugal, within the Aveiro lagoon. It is classified as a Special Protection Zone under the EU Natura 2000 project.

Water, soil and man are the reference trinomial of the vitality of the Lower Vouga Lagoon System, responsible for a landscape of singular characteristics with an exceptional added value from the point of view of the production of biomass and of biological diversity. However, water is the strategic element in the genesis and dynamics of the Lower Vouga Lagoon System. It is the permanent support of the earth's fertility and vitality. Water helped create the soil, which consists of relatively recent sedimentary material of predominantly fluvial origin deposited in an estuarine environment. Flooding is frequent and dramatic events are on record testifying to the loss of lives and crops and to the destruction of infrastructures. The salt water in the lagoon makes the agricultural land susceptible to salinisation. In summer, the scarcity of water is resolved by freshwater from rivers and streams with the use of hydraulic structures that are operated and maintained by the farmers. The water is also used by boats in the 'esteiros' that are wide walled ditches at the end parts of rivers and streams, a mode of transport that was extremely important in the past.

Local populations learned to adapt to the hydrological conditions and to develop their own culture. Insofar as possible, they shaped the physical landscape of the lagoon, controlling drainage and subduing the water to maintain the productivity of the land. The state of neglect reached by the Lower Vouga Lagoon System, particularly as a result of saline intrusion, the destruction and ageing of the infrastructures such as dykes, ditches and paths, and the reduced size and inaccessibility of the farm plots, called for a project to maintain an equilibrium adapted to modern ways of farming conciliating the promotion of biological and landscape diversity.

2 The Lower Vouga Lagoon System

There are three major landscape units in the Lower Vouga Lagoon System, interconnected by a compact network of corridors consisting of 'esteiros', ditches, hedges and paths: the "bocage" – the hedged landscape, the wetlands, and the open fields (Fig. 1). For the most part the nature of these units is the result of water quantity and quality which in turn determines the diverse textures of the soil, to which are linked the different uses of the soil and creation of habitats. Man's interaction with the mild characteristics of an Atlantic climate, the flat terrains of recent formation, soil fertility and the abundant water created the diversity and specificity of this agro-ecosystem, managed in accordance with objectives of production and economic sustainability, under permanent threat from flooding and saline intrusion.

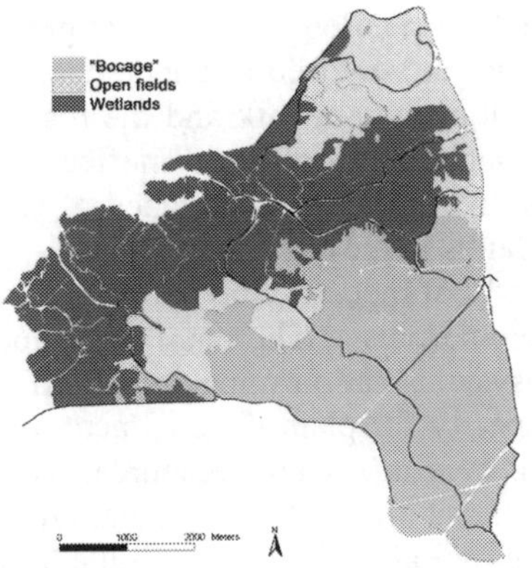

Figure 1: Landscape units.

The "bocage" is a rare habitat in Portugal. It is characterised by a large number of hedges and by small plots of land. It is therefore a priority in terms of preservation as well as being extremely important for the birds of the region, not to mention the mammals, amphibians and reptiles. It is a nesting area for many birds of prey. The wetlands are also highly important owing to their multi-functional nature. The composition and proportion of the different species of vegetation vary in accordance with the degree of salinity in the ditches, the distance to the river and the topography. Rush-beds and reeds predominate. The rush-bed, which today is cut on a small scale only, is undergoing a regressive process that endangers its existence as a result of decay and its natural replacement by other plants. Reeds appear where there is a greater proportion of freshwater. The wetlands are important particularly for migration and nesting and as winter quarters for a great number of bird species. The regression of the rice-paddies is also a negative factor given their importance as refuge, feeding and nesting grounds, namely of water birds. There are many amphibians in this area, as well as in the 'esteiros' and ditches, where one also notes a large number of fish. In the open fields there is a greater proportion of ploughed fields which gives this landscape unit great socio-economic importance. The predominant crops are maize, ryegrass and grazing fields.

The quality of the landscape of the Lower Vouga Lagoon System derives from a very intensive water/land relationship. It consists of very flat land where rivers converge and discharge their waters and where the flowing off into the lagoon is hindered by the effect of the tides. These natural conditions are enough in themselves to explain the drainage problems that have always existed in the area. The need to control the adversity of the river torrents during flood periods and to protect the soil against the salt water led to the application of specific hydraulic techniques such as dredging and cleaning of the vegetation in the main rivers, maintenance and upkeep of the dykes to prevent floods and salt water from entering the secondary irrigation and drainage networks. The defence system against the tides includes a network of dykes, embankments and summer sluices prevent polluted salt water entering from the lagoon upstream and to preserve the freshwater for irrigation purposes. At present the drainage systems have several problems such as very frequent and uncontrolled flooding – creating damage to the soil, the drainage network and the road network – difficulties in the flowing off into the lagoon as a result of ineffective working of the primary and secondary drainage system and the entrance of salt water in the 'esteiros' and ditches because of faults in the dykes and sluices.

Soils are predominantly of modern alluvial formation, sometimes undergoing hydromorphism and halomorphism. The main limitations of the soil relating to maintenance of the ecosystems and farming are linked to salinisation and water-logging limiting the capacity for plant development. Soil acidification is also a limitation. In short, soil here is a scarce resource, with high fertility potential, although very sensitive and at high risk of degradation.

The network of 'esteiros' and ditches constitute a particular heritage whose main function is to handle water in a permanent play for equilibrium. The network acts as the true support of the dynamics of the System. It consists of a relatively compact network without any coverings of any sort, designed, maintained and operated by farmers. It performs multiple functions which in itself symbolises the originality of the Lower Vouga Lagoon System. It serves as ground level and below ground level drainage and as water conduits for excess water to flow into the primary network. With the use of temporary sluices, the ditches also act as water reservoirs, as well as irrigation channels that convey water from the primary lines to the farmlands. The ditches also have other important functions: they serve as the dividing lines between rural properties, enabling the development of hedges that serves as fencing for animals and were once used as firewood. They support an aquatic biota of great fauna variety. Finally, the ditches are means of communication, acting as paths, in the case of the secondary ditches or for boats, in the case of the primary ditches, the so-called 'esteiros'. The responsibility for the maintenance and conservation of this collective network, which has continued to this day, was assumed by the communities of farmers who established rules and co-operative practices to sustain the System. The economic and social evolution of the last decades, however, has made its upkeep incompatible with human agricultural resources, particularly owing to the fact that it has been impossible to maintain the structures. The rise in the level of salt water in the lagoon during high tide has accelerated the decay of the traditional tide-defence structures, which has worsened the problem.

The water supply to the Lower Vouga Lagoon System aims at judicious management of freshwater during the summer to enable the soil to be suitably dampened – by irrigation of the crops and supplying the wetlands – and control of soil salinisation. The water is provided by River Vouga and River Antuã and from some small streams by means of inefficient temporary and artisanal dams. The water transport and distribution system for irrigation and nature conservation employs the same network of ditches as the drainage system. At the start of the summer season, the secondary drainage systems are shut off to conserve the freshwater and prevent the entrance and advance of salt water. This results in an extensive network of ditches whose aim is to convey and preserve freshwater, from which it is distributed to the plots. In the northern part there is also a traditional model for collective distribution of water managed fully by the farmers. The rice is grown here on the lower slopes of land where water can drain by gravity, irrigated by permanently submerged paddies. Maize and ryegrass are grown on higher fields using pumps from the ditches and irrigation from sprinklers. In the remaining part, particularly in the "bocage", underwater irrigation is used. This makes a very intelligent use of the drainage system to distribute water to the plots by controlling the groundwater level in an elevated position to dampen the soil by capillarity.

3 Impact assessment methodology and major conclusions

The main aim of the project is to defend the fields against the destructive effect of the floods and salinisation of the soils due to the progressive advance of the tides. On the agricultural land the aim is to implement a number of improvements in the irrigation, drainage and road infrastructures, and to carry out a process of farmland reallocation (IHERA, [2,3,4]).

The project submitted to environmental impact assessment presented various alternative solutions, which gave rise to a complex assessment methodology. The Lower Vouga Lagoon System already has a significantly diverse landscape and a particularly complex management system that has been virtually abandoned. The methodology was developed in response to a vast number of variables in an attempt to be comprehensive, supported on a hierarchical and selective impact procedure. Eleven environmental variables were considered, some of which were sub-divided: climate, air, noise, surface waters (quantity, quality, flooding), underground waters, soil, fauna ("bocage", wetlands, open fields, corridors and riparian galleries), flora ("bocage", wetlands, open fields, corridors and riparian galleries), landscape ("bocage", wetlands, open fields and landscape quality), cultural heritage, socio-economy (cultural occupation, market value of the land, farming income, farm employment and potential for diversification of activity).

The project was considered in its two phases – construction and operation – as well as its various alternatives. The project was considered as being made up of the following actions to build or re-build: tidal defence system, Vouga drainage system, Barbosa drainage system, Canelas drainage system, Antuã drainage system, road network, secondary drainage network, secondary irrigation network, main ecological corridors network, land reallocation and building sites. 16 parameters for impact assessment were identified in these actions:

CLASSIFICATION:	Indifferent; Positive; Negative
QUANTIFICATION:	Reduced; Moderate; High
PROBABILITY:	Very probable; Probable; Improbable
DURATION:	Temporary; Permanent
OCCURRENCE:	Immediate; Medium-term; Long-term
REVERSIBILITY:	Reversible; Irreversible.

The methodology was applied in four stages taking into consideration the project alternatives:

1st stage: Classification of impact (indifferent/positive/negative) of all actions per variable. Indifferent impacts eliminated.
2nd stage: Quantification of impact (reduced/moderate/high) by assessing the positive and negative impacts of all actions per variable. Reduced impacts eliminated.
3rd stage: Duration of impact (temporary/permanent) by assessing the average and high impacts of all actions per variable. Average and temporary impacts eliminated. Condition of reversibility (reversible/irreversible) by assessing the high impacts of all actions per variable. High reversible impacts eliminated.
4th stage: Identification of the positive and negative impacts simultaneously high, permanent and irreversible, of the actions per variable. Assessment of the probability and occurrence of the impacts.

After the 1st and 2nd stage the indifferent impacts, that is, those with no effect on the environment, and the reduced impacts, given their insignificance, were eliminated so that at the 3rd stage it was possible to concentrate the decision-making process on the moderate and high impacts. Assessment of the duration informed us about the time of occurrence of these impacts, distinguishing between temporary versus permanent. This enabled us to focus the assessment on the permanent impacts whilst the reversibility assessment highlighted the irreversible impacts. Finally, the 4th stage explained the positive and negative, high, permanent and irreversible impacts – i.e. the important ones that were definitely at stake – and were considered the decisive impacts for the decision process.

It was concluded that the impacts are all negative at the construction phase, being as they are linked to heavy mechanical work to implement the project. However, during the operation the variables that are most negatively affected are the fauna and flora. Following project implementation, and particularly with the tidal defence system, the "bocage" will tend to recover and increase in area. At this stage, too, the soil and socio-economy variables are those most positively affected. The impacts on landscape quality mostly reflect the efficiency of the management models in terms of the landscape units and respond to the principle of the added value of their diversity and also to the complementarities generated between them. It can be concluded that, in addition to the tidal defence system and the primary drainage systems, the remaining actions – road network, secondary ditch/drainage network, ecological corridors and land reallocation – are not as important as the former although the impacts introduced must be minimized and valorised.

4 Outline of the proposed intervention

The Project to be implemented after the environmental assessment of the alternatives is based on a set of tidal defence structures, four drainage basin systems (Vouga, Barbosa, Canelas and Antuã), two hierarchical networks of roads and ecological corridors and a farmland re-allocation plan (Fig.2).

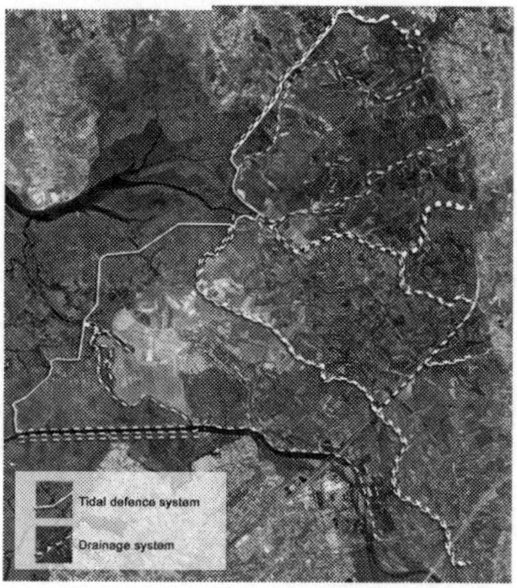

Figure 2: The project.

The aim of the tidal defence structures is to prevent the surface invasion of salt water into the fields and to establish a buffer zone acting as the interface between the farmland and the lagoon. The system will consist of three continuous dykes to establish a border line quite often built upon existing decaying structures. Hydraulic structures will help with the drainage flow from the rivers and control of the entrance of salt water into the 'esteiros'. Salt water will always be able to permeate the dyke floors. The aim of the primary drainage system is to reduce the frequency of the floods and minimise their disastrous effects. In the summer it is important that it helps to ensure the replenishment of the ground freshwater. The current beds of the rivers will be maintained without being lowered and they will only be widened along the stretches with greatly reduced flow capacity. Thus, the increased capacity is generally obtained by raising the banks reinforcing the existing dykes.

The project foresees the installation of a network of ecological corridors for compartmentalisation of the landscape consisting of hedges in public areas, that is, along the tide protection dykes, the primary and secondary rivers and the paths. The hedges will be located in such a way as to avoid casting shade over the crops. In addition to these hedges, it is intended to maintain and implement copse areas. The aim of the Project for the secondary irrigation and drainage and road networks is to improve working and farming conditions. The irrigation infrastructures envisaged will ensure that all areas that are traditionally irrigated will have access to water.

The farmland re-allocation plan basically is a proposition of possible ways to redesign properties, annexing ones that have been pulverised by progressive divisions due to inheritance. The aim is to reduce the number of owners in each perimeter, increase the contiguous farming lands and eliminate plots to which there was no access. The type of possible interventions are considerable but the understanding is that by improving the primary infrastructures reallocation will tend to happen depending on the farmers initiative and based upon a monitoring process. The heterogeneity of hedges is to be maintained and consolidated and the plots obtained will be irregularly shaped mostly following the organic development of the 'esteiros'.

5 Monitoring for a sustainable environment

The heightened environmental susceptibility of the Lower Vouga Lagoon System means that repairing and building the infrastructures envisaged will not in itself ensure fulfilment of the sustainability objectives. In terms of project operation an integrated monitoring programme must be implemented involving a water and soil management plan and a biological diversity and landscape quality management plan, both of course being inter-complementary.

The main aim of the water and soil management plan is to regulate the distribution of freshwater, bearing in mind the flow of the rivers and the demand during the drier periods among the areas of vegetable production, livestock and nature conservation. It is also important to monitor the saline intrusion in order to ensure that the quality of the water and the conservation of the soil are controlled, minimizing the risks of salinisation and acidification.

The water and soil management plan must be looked on as an instrument to fulfil the environmental objectives laid down in the Water Framework Directive (Directive 2000/60/EC). The plan comprises three components: 1) Monitoring Network – collecting site information through a network of observation posts, on the quantity and quality of the water and some soil parameters; data processing, information management and integration; experimenting with specific aspects of the ecosystems; 2) Operating Scheme – water distribution set out in a schedule for opening and regulating the flow control dams in response to the value of the variables of the state of the system (flows, demand for water for farming and for nature conservation); this scheme includes information on the quality of the water so that solutions are designed according to criteria of system sustainability; it also includes controlling the entry of salt water according to the needs of the wetlands. 3) Assessment – supervision, control and assessment of performance of the system and of the plan itself in order to adjust the rules applied during operation; the various agents involved in the system (farmers, environmentalists, State) should participate on a continuous basis in this component, to adjust the plan to evolution of the agro ecosystem throughout the duration of the project.

The biological diversity and landscape management plan covers fauna, flora, transformation of the landscape and recreational effects.

Monitoring flora and fauna foresees determining the variations in the abundance and specific wealth of the fish in the "esteiros", canals and ditches, the fauna in the "bocage" and the fauna in the areas subject to the tidal regimes, which will be limited by the protective structures to be built. As this is a Special Protection Zone, the evolution of the status of the species contained in Annex I of the Bird Directive should be monitored. Alterations to the flora must be carefully followed with studies on the evolution of the floristic succession in the wetlands inside the dykes; the appearance of invasive plants and their eradication on the banks of the canals, "esteiros" and ditches both in terms of diversity and density; the appearance of pests and others on the beds of the canals, "esteiros" and ditches. A control plan must be set up for the pests, for evolution of the floristic diversity of the "bocage" and for evolution of the population of *Campanula lusitanica*, given its status as a rare endemic Lusitanian species.

The monitoring programmes to assess evolution of the landscape and consequently redefine the respective management systems include the following: 1) Programme to identify the type and degree of transformation that may occur in the main cultural components of the landscape, in particular in the hedges and wetlands. The hedges must be characterised – floristic composition and linear metres – as must the wetlands – floristic composition and areas of occupation. These studies must be produced at regular intervals of time to act as temporal profiles of characterisation of the landscape. 2) Assessment programmes of the impact due to use for human recreational purposes. These studies should provide a demarcation of homogenous zones for use and the respective assessment of the negative impacts generated at the level of ecological value, management systems and visual quality of the landscape. The landscape monitoring programme must follow certain parameters: Characterisation of the system of hedges in terms of their size (width and linear development), density and floristic composition; characterisation of hedge maintenance and management practices, in particular as regards cutting and clearing of undergrowth and articulation with the management of the adjacent farmland; characterisation of the wetlands as regards their respective floristic composition; characterisation of the management practices in the wetlands as regards how regularly the vegetation is cut and its density; characterisation of the network of paths in particular as regards their conservation and density of use; characterisation of use for recreational purposes, namely in terms of counting visitors; assessing the state of the vegetation and soil compacting near the areas with a greater number of visitors and larger production of waste; and determination of the load capacity and its variation.

6 Conclusion

The Lower Vouga Lagoon System is in fact an extremely complex and fragile agro-ecosystem but one that has exceptional natural and cultural value. Water and soil management are vital for its sustainability both from an agronomic and a conservationist viewpoint. Although delicate, the intervention envisaged is also complex and demanding from the point of view of precision both concerning execution of the works and monitoring during the construction and operation phase. Hence the importance attributed to developing an environmental assessment methodology of hierarchical and selective characteristics and to the plans to monitor water and soil management and biological diversity and landscape quality management.

The EIA concluded that it was better to interfere in the system then letting it go to abandonment. A significant emphasis on the future of the system is placed on the monitoring plans. It is expected that they become a tool that is proficient and efficient in terms of the spatial and temporal interpretation of environmental variables as the support to defining the management problems of this ecosystem and finding the solutions. The success of these plans calls for many expertise and is demanding from the point of view of communication and dialogue. Indeed, an environment laboratory for wetlands is about to be installed.

Acknowledgements

The authors would like to thank the Ministry of Agriculture of Portugal and the Environmental Impact Assessment team.

References

[1] Andresen, Teresa et al (2001): Estudo de Impacte Ambiental do Projecto de Desenvolvimento Agrícola do Vouga: Bloco do Baixo Vouga Lagunar, Departamento de Ambiente e Ordenamento, Universidade de Aveiro, Portugal.
[2] IHERA (1996/7): Princípios e Orientações das Intervenções do MADRP nos Campos do Baixo Vouga Lagunar.
[3] IHERA (2000a): Anteprojecto dos Sistemas Primários de Defesa e Drenagem do Baixo Vouga Lagunar – Projecto de Desenvolvimento Agrícola do Vouga.
[4] IHERA (2000b): Contributo para o Estudo da Definição de uma Rede Principal de Compartimentação de Sebes no Baixo Vouga Lagunar.

Light control of the productivity of aquatic ecosystems

A. Cózar
Área de Ecología, Facultad de Ciencias del Mar, University of Cádiz, 11510 Puerto Real, Cádiz, Spain

Abstract

The role of nutrients in the control of productivity of aquatic ecosystems has been deeply studied in the past century. The role of light, however, remains less well understood despite the fact that light often becomes the main controlling factor of the aquatic ecosystems. The theoretical bias between nutrient and light control may have arisen due to the complexity in modelling the light environment of aquatic ecosystems (e.g., spatial-temporal variability of algal exposure, competing presence of optically active abiotic components, negative feedback of algal auto-shading). In the present work, we develop an ecosystem-specific model to determine the carrying capacity of algae from the light-biomass conversion efficiency. The feasibility of this method was demonstrated on two diverse ecosystems, the phytoplankton community of the Lake Victoria (East Africa) and the microphytobenthos community of the lacustrine system of the Ibera wetlands (South America). The relationship between maximum supportable algal biomass and light availability, mixing depth and background light attenuation was also determined. Such information has important implications on the investigation, modelling and management of the aquatic ecosystems

Keywords: aquatic productivity, photosynthesis, light control, euphotic depth, Lake Victoria, optical modelling.

1 Introduction

The role of nutrients in the control of algal biomass has been thoroughly researched in the past century. The role of light, however, remains less well understood despite the fact that light is often the controlling factor of algal biomass. In most benthic ecosystems or many eutrophic pelagic environments, the nutrient requirements of the algal populations are fully satisfied. In such situations, algal populations will grow until a steady state where light conditions are limiting. Therefore, a characteristic carrying capacity of algal biomass will correspond to a specific light availability just as a maximum supportable biomass may be calculated from a nutrient availability [1]. The theoretical bias towards light control may have arisen due to the complexity in modelling the light environment in aquatic ecosystems. The main challenges are the spatial-temporal variability of light within the water column, the competition for light with abiotic components and the negative feedback of algal auto-shading [2, 3]. Talling [4] and Reynolds [5] made the first attempts to calculate phytoplankton carrying capacity by using euphotic depth, the depth at which the downwelling solar irradiance falls to 1% of that just below the surface. In this way, however, the carrying capacity is independent of light supply. Recently, Huisman [6] developed a mechanistic approach based on the concept of critical light intensity, that is, the steady state light intensity that leaves the mixed layer [2]. However, this critical light intensity is invariably zero whenever the euphotic depth is smaller than the mixing depth, a common occurrence in light-limited ecosystems. We believe there is a fundamental need to model algal biomass by considering the spatial-temporal integration of the solar irradiance within a volume (or surface) in which the primary producers are distributed [7].

Existing theory focuses on mechanistic models to determine the light-controlled carrying capacity based upon the equilibrium between net photosynthetic gains and the net losses of the population [6, 8]. However, this dynamic equilibrium does not provide a workable basis on which to analyze real ecosystems. While in the laboratory, the photosynthetic response of algal populations to irradiance can be measured through photosynthesis-irradiance (P-I) curves. However, the integration of this function over space and time neglects the real situation of planktonic algae, which cannot maintain a constant position in space and are exposed to fluctuating levels of irradiance related to the exponential decay of the incident irradiance with depth [9]. Complex loss processes such as marine or lake “snow” formation or feces production by grazing also need to be considered [8]. Theoretical models derived from the production-losses balance agree qualitatively with real data and contribute significantly to the understanding of algal dynamics, but produce limited quantitative results [3]. Secondly, they require advanced computation techniques that hamper the expansion of these advances among the researcher and manager communities We develop a complementary ecosystem-specific approach where light-controlled carrying capacity is directly derived from an efficiency coefficient of light-biomass conversion.

2 Material and methods

2.1 Methodological development

Using different methodological approaches, Ryther [10] and Talling [4] reached the conclusion that, in nutrient replete conditions, aerial algal production is linearly related to the aerial biomass multiplied by a term linked to light availability (light extinction coefficient). More recently, this algorithm was used to estimate oceanic production from remote sensing data [11].

The total amount of photosynthetic available radiation (PAR) available in a water column (Q'_t) may be approximated by: [7]:

$$Q'_t = \frac{I_o}{c \cdot K}$$

where I_o is the incident PAR on the water surface, K is the vertical attenuation coefficient for PAR and c is the speed of the light in the medium. This expression considers that no light leaves the mixed layer. Using the Lambert-Beer's law to describe the vertical light gradient, the quantity of available light that exceeds the mixing depth (d) would be:

$$Q_d = \frac{I_o}{c \cdot K} \cdot e^{-K \cdot d}$$

Thus, the total amount of PAR available to the phytoplankton cells circulating within the mixed layer (Q_t) will be:

$$Q_t = \frac{I_o}{c \cdot K} \cdot \left(1 - e^{-K \cdot d}\right) \quad (1)$$

and the total amount of light available to a phytobenthic community (Q_{tb}) at a specific bottom depth (b) will be:

$$Q_{tb} = \frac{I_o}{c \cdot K} \cdot e^{-K \cdot b} \quad (2)$$

The aerial steady-state biomass of any phytoplankton community (W^*) will vary with Q_t depending on the light-biomass conversion efficiency (ψ) of the community as:

$$W^* = \psi \cdot Q_t - \psi \cdot Q_{\min} \quad (3)$$

where Q_{min} is the minimum light requirement to permit algal biomass. The conversion efficiency term (ψ, g-chl einstein^{-1}) considers the ratio of energy stored in the ecosystem as steady-state biomass to the solar energy available. The effects of the incident light intensity, light attenuation and mixing depth on the steady-state biomass of the phytoplankton community can be described as:

$$W^* = \frac{\psi \cdot I_o}{c \cdot K} \cdot \left(1 - e^{-K \cdot d}\right) - \psi \cdot Q_{\min} \tag{4}$$

From this equation, it would appear that W^* will increase unlimitedly with PAR availability (Q_t). However, increases in phytoplankton biomass will increase attenuation (K), thereby reducing Q_t. This negative feedback prevents unlimited phytoplankton growth. For the phytobenthos, the unlimited increase of biomass with Q_{tb} is inappropriate due to self-shading effects. The light-controlled carrying capacity for phytobenthos (W^*_b) reaches a plateau when the bottom is covered being described by a logarithmic function as:

$$W_b^* = \alpha \cdot \ln(Q_{tb}) - \alpha \cdot \ln(Q_{\min}) = \alpha \cdot \ln\left(\frac{I_o}{c \cdot K} \cdot e^{-K \cdot b}\right) - \alpha \cdot \ln(Q_{\min}) \tag{5}$$

where α is the logarithmic slope of the function. The value of light-biomass conversion efficiency for phytobenthos (ψ_b) must be estimated at low superficial densities, that is, in the absence of intra-specific competition. At these conditions, the slope of the logarithmic curve is maximal and equals to ψ_b.

The calculated carrying capacity for phytoplankton is useful for ecosystem analysis once measurements of K and biomass have been obtained. Using equation 4, it is possible to determine how far a phytoplankton community is from the condition of light-limitation. However, to model how variations in the concentrations of the optically active components will effect the algal carrying capacity, it is necessary to separate the total attenuation due to phytoplankton and non phytoplankton components as:

$$K = k \cdot w + K_{bg} \tag{6}$$

where k the specific light attenuation coefficient of the phytoplankton, w is the volumetric biomass of phytoplankton and K_{bg} is the total background turbidity. Substituting Eq. 6 into Eq. 4 and rearranging:

$$W^* = \frac{\psi \cdot I_o}{c \cdot \left(k \cdot \frac{W^*}{d} + K_{bg}\right)} - \frac{\psi \cdot I_o}{c \cdot \left(k \cdot \frac{W^*}{d} + K_{bg}\right)} \cdot e^{-\left(k \cdot W^* + K_{bg} \cdot d\right)} - \psi \cdot Q_{\min} \tag{7}$$

where biomass carrying capacity is a function of incident PAR, mixing depth, aerial phytoplankton biomass and the concentration of the non-phytoplankton water column components. This relation must be resolved iteratively due to the presence of W* in the exponent of Euler's number.

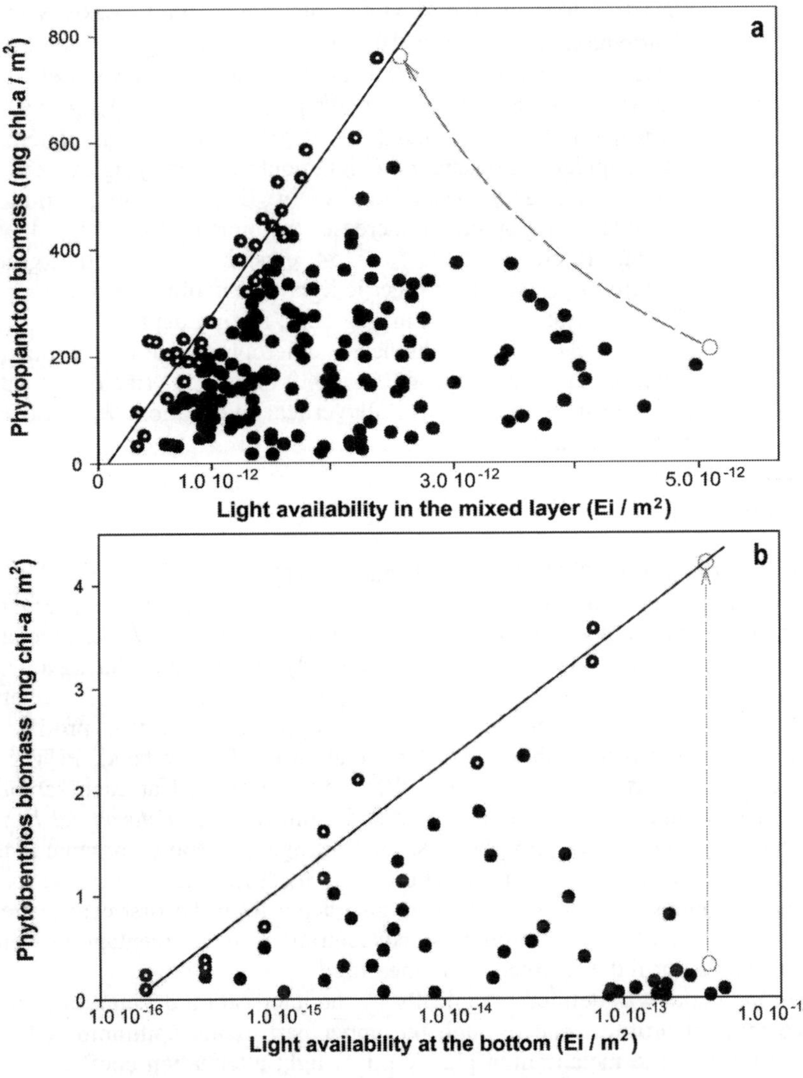

Figure 1: Relationship between the light availability and the aerial concentration of algal biomass in a set of 277 sampling sites in Lake Victoria inshore water (**a**) and a set of 54 samples in the bottom of lakes of *Esteros del Iberá* wetland (**b**). The lines were fitted by least-square regression to estimate of the light-biomass conversion efficiency (ψ) and the minimum light requirement to sustain the algal community (Q_{min}). Data points included in the regressions of this upper limit are marked with white center. All points non-included in the regressions were further than $2.5 \cdot 10^{-13}$ units from the phytoplanktonic upper limit and further than

$3.5 \cdot 10^{-13}$ units in the phytobenthic upper limit. Lake Victoria phytoplankton: $\psi = 0.29 \cdot 10^{12}$ g-chl einstein^{-1}, $Q_{min} = 6.42 \cdot 10^{-14}$ einstein m^{-2} and $R^2 = 0.9224$ ($P<0.001$). *Esteros del Iberá* microphytobenthos: $\psi_b = 1.19 \cdot 10^{12}$ g-chl einstein^{-1}, $Q_{min} = 0.02 \cdot 10^{-14}$ einstein m^{-2} and $R^2 = 0.9537$ ($P<0.001$). Displacement patterns of algal populations reaching the light-controlled carrying capacity are shown with grey dashed lines. In Lake Victoria, simulated phytoplankton population increases the biomass from 12 to 40 mg-chl m^{-3} (incident light, I_o = 54 einstein m^{-2} d^{-1}; background turbidity, K_{bg} = 0.3 m^{-1}; specific light attenuation coefficient of the phytoplankton, k = 0.019 m^2 mg-chl^{-1}; mixing depth, d = 20 m). In *Esteros del Iberá*, simulated microphytobenthos population increases the biomass from 0.3 to 4.2 mg-chl m^{-2} (incident light, I_o = 35 einstein m^{-2} d^{-1}; overall vertical attenuation, K = 1.0 m^{-1}; bottom depth, b = 1.5 m).

3 Sampling

Three surveys (2002-2004) were performed along the Ugandan and Kenyan coast (within 15 km from the coast) for a total of 277 sampling sites covering all major inshore areas types. In the lacustrine system of *Esteros del Iberá* wetland, 6 sites (mean depth, 2.0 m) were sampled regularly in nine dates during a whole seasonal cycle (1999-2000). Incident solar photosynthetic available radiation (PAR) was measured 3 m above the water surface. Vertical profiles of temperature (Hydrolab probe) and solar radiation (PAR waveband, PUV 514-Biospeherical Instrument) and Secchi depth were measured at each sampling site. Water samples were taken at 0.5 m and 2.0m (only in *Esteros del Iberá*). Chlorophyll-*a* (chl), total phosphorous, total nitrogen, dissolved organic matter and soluble reactive silicon concentrations were measured. In *Esteros del Iberá*, sediment samples (30 cm^2 x 1 cm) were also taken from the first centimetre of the bottom of the lakes. Chlorophyll-*a* concentrations and percentage in weight of organic matter in the sediment were measured.

Mixing depth was defined graphically by the intersection of trend lines fitted to the thermal profiles, one through the upper part of the epilimnion and the second through the metalimnion [12] Vertical light attenuation coefficient was determined using the irradiance profiles in Lake Victoria and indirectly-estimated from Secchi disk and chlorophyll-*a* concentration measurements [9] in *Esteros del Iberá*. Chlorophyll-*a* concentrations were measured using a calibrated portable fluorimeter (Turner) in Lake Victoria and using standard spectrophotometric methods [13] in *Esteros del Iberá.* In the sediment samples, chlorophyll analysis included centrifugation after the pigment extraction in acetone. Nutrient analysis (phosphorus, nitrogen and silicon) were performed through spectrophotometry following APHA standard methods (1992). Dissolved organic matter was estimated in the filtered samples (GV Millipore 22 μm filter) through the 272 nm-absorbance after gravimetric calibration [14].

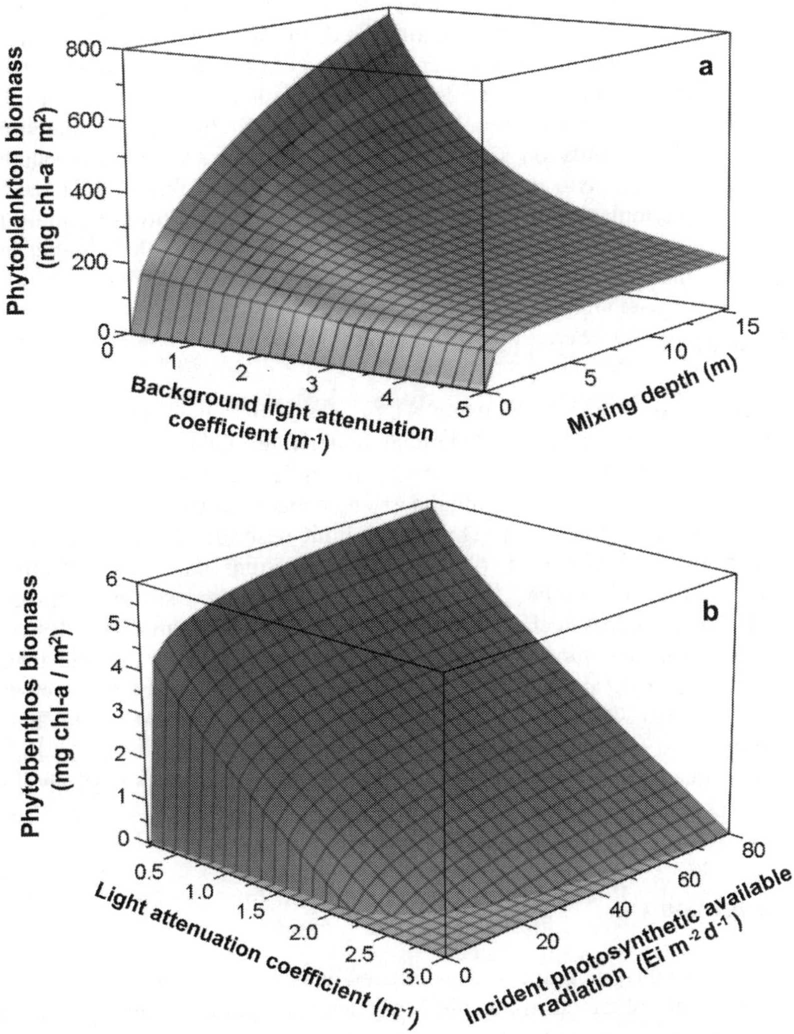

Figure 2: Effect of mixing depth (d) and background turbidity (Kbg) on the light-controlled carrying capacity of the phytoplankton community of the Lake Victoria inshore waters (a). Effect of depth (b) and vertical light attenuation coefficient (K) on the light-controlled carrying capacity of the microphytobenthos community of the lakes of Esteros del Iberá wetland (b). The solar flux densities in the tropical Lake Victoria vary slightly throughout the year with an averaged daily irradiance of 650 μEinstein s-1 m-2, while the monthly-averaged daily irradiance in Esteros del Iberá ranges from 200 to 800 μEinstein s-1 m-2. In Lake Victoria, K was empirically break down into the sum of Kbg and the attenuation due to the

phytoplankton (k·w) through a multiple regression (R2 = 0.73, P < 0.0001). Kbg was decomposed on a term depending on the dissolved organic matter concentration (DOM) and constant term due to other abiotic components. Wetlands fringing much of the Lake Victoria shoreline release considerable DOM, intervening significantly on K. The attenuation term due to the phytoplankton depend on the specific light attenuation coefficient of the phytoplankton (k) and the volumetric concentration of chlorophyll (w). The estimated value of k (0.019 m2 mg-chl-1) adequately matches within the k range observed in nature [7].

4 Results

The estimation of ψ was made using a large set of field measurements of algal biomass concentrations (W) and vertical underwater light profiles from each study area. In a scatter plot of W versus the underwater light availability (Q, *sensu* Kirk [7]), the light-limited algal carrying capacity corresponds to the upper limit of the dataset (Figure 1). This upper limit describes the maximum algal concentration possible at each Q. Algal concentrations that digress from this limit have either not reached their maximum light-limited steady state or are limited by other factors such as nutrients or grazing. The method was tested on the data set from the phytoplankton community of the Lake Victoria inshore waters (East Africa) and the microphytobenthos community of the lacustrine system of *Esteros del Iberá* (South America). For the tropical phytoplankton community, ψ was determined to be $0.29 \cdot 10^{12}$ g-chl einstein^{-1}, while for the subtropical microphytobenthos, ψ_b was $1.19 \cdot 10^{12}$ g-chl einstein^{-1}. Both ψ and Q_{min} demonstrated the higher efficiency and lower light requirement of benthic algae compared to pelagic algae [15].

5 Conclusion

While ψ is an ecosystem-specific parameter, it is easily determined from data that is commonly obtained in aquatic ecosystem investigations and can serve as the cornerstone in resolving the complex role of light in the control of algal biomass concentrations. With knowledge of the incident light flux, it is possible to determine the maximum supportable limit of biomass and the impact that changes in mixing depth and background light attenuation (due to non-phytoplankton components) may have on the steady-state concentrations of algae (Figure 2). The biomass supported by any ecosystem has to be within the envelopes simultaneously enclosed by both energy (light-controlled) and resource (nutrient-controlled) capacities [1]. Such information has important implications on the investigation, modelling and management of aquatic ecosystems.

References

[1] Reynolds, C.S., *Eutrophication and the management of planktonic algae: what Vollenweider couldn't tell us*. In Eutrophication: research and application to water supply. (Eds D.W. Sutcliffe & J.G. Jones), pp 4-29. Freshwater Biological Association, Ambleside, Cumbria 1992.

[2] Weissing F.J. & Huisman J., *Growth and competition in a light gradient*. J. theor. Biol. 168, 323-336, 1994

[3] Kunz, T.J., & Diehl S., *Phytoplankton, light, and nutrients in a gradient of mixing depths: a field test of producer-resource theory*. Freshwater Biology 48: 1050-1063, 2003.

[4] Talling, J. F. *The phytoplankton population as a compound photosynthetic system*. New Phytologist 56:133–149, 1957.

[5] Reynolds, C.S. *The Ecology of Freshwater Phytoplankton*. Cambridge University Press, Cambridge, 1984

[6] Huisman, J. *Population dynamics of light-limited phytoplankton: microcosm experiments*. Ecology 80: 202-210, 1999.

[7] Kirk, J. T. O. *Light and photosynthesis in aquatic ecosystems*. Second edition. Cambridge University Press, Cambridge, UK, 1994.

[8] Diehl, S.. *Phytoplankton, light, and nutrients in a gradient of mixing depths: theory*. Ecology 83:386-398.

[9] Scheffer, M., 1998. *Ecology of shallow lakes*. Chapman & Hall, London, 2002.

[10] Ryther, J. H. *Photosynthesis in the ocean as a function of light intensity*. Limnol. Oceanogr., 1, 61-70, 1956.

[11] Platt, T. *Primary production of the ocean water column as a function of surface light intensity: Algorithms for remote sensing*. Deep-Sea Res. I, 33: 149-163, 1986.

[12] Wetzel, R. G. *Limnology*. W.B. Saunders, 1975.

[13] Strickland, J. D., &. Parsons T. R. *A practical handbook of seawater analysis*. Bull. Fish. Res. Board Can. 167: 310, 1972.

[14] Bracchini L., Loiselle S.A.,. Dattilo A. M, Mazzuoli S., Cózar A., & Rossi C. *The spatial distribution of the optical properties in the UV and Visible in an aquatic ecosystem*. Photochem. Photobiol., 80(1) 139-149, 2004.

[15] Carrick, H.J., Aldridge, F.J. & Schelske C.L. *Wind influences phytoplankton biomass and composition in a shallow, productive lake*. Limnol. Oceanogr. 38: 1179-1192, 1993.

Self-regulation strategies and co-management of fisheries resources in the Amazon basin

C. E. C. Freitas[1], A. A. F. Rivas[1] & J. R. Kahn[2]
[1]*Center of Environmental Sciences, Federal University of Amazon, 69077-000, Manaus-Amazonas-Brazil*
[2]*Washington and Lee University, U.S.A.*

Abstract

Six kinds of fisheries were recently developed in the Amazon basin: subsistence, mono-specific commercial for exportation, multi-specific commercial for local market, ornamental, reservoir and recreative fishery. Some of them exploit the same stocks. These overlays generate conflicts between resources users, mainly between subsistence fisheries and commercial fisheries who harvest fish in floodplain areas. Self-regulation and co-management have recently shown good results as strategies to the conservation of natural stocks and to promote sustainable development. The settling of a pact between resource users has been the most frequently strategy used by the Brazilian government in the decentralization of fishery management. In this paper, we describe the users' conflicts in the Amazonian and analyze one case study of fisheries co-management in the Amazon basin, aiming to evaluate its feasibility as a strategy towards resource conservation and users welfare.
Keywords: fisheries.

1 Introduction

The fish exploitation at Amazon basin is a traditional activity and the pressure on the natural stocks changed in intensity since the start of European colonization [1]. Probably, demographic density is the main factor for changes, mainly the traditional establishing of towns, villages small and communities at margins of large rivers.

The complexity of Amazon fishing is very high. The predominance of small-scales procedures for school detection and catch is reflected by high diversity of

www.witpress.com, ISSN 1743-3541 (on-line)

fishing gears and commercialized species, uncommon in commercial fisheries [2]. Beside this, the complexity is increased by presence of different kinds of resource users, with distinct fishery strategies and different behavior in relation to resource conservation and environmental protection.

Six kinds of fisheries were recently developed in the Amazon basin: subsistence, mono-specific commercial for exportation, multi-specific commercial for local market, ornamental, reservoir and recreative fishery [3, 4, 5, 6]. Some of them exploit the same stocks and these overlays generate conflicts between resources users, mainly between subsistence fishers and commercial fishers who harvest fishes in floodplain areas.

Self-regulation strategies to management of fishery resources use for traditional populations, mainly those inhabitants of Amazonian floodplain lakes, exhibit different levels of success that result in general on organization degree of communities. These self-regulation strategies give right property to fishery resource [7], changing the status of common property of these resources [8].

The aim of this paper is to discuss the occurrence of user conflicts by use of fishery resources in the Amazon basin. After this, we analyze two case studies of fisheries co-management in the Amazon basin to evaluate its feasibility as strategy towards resources conservation and users welfare.

2 Fisheries and conflicts between users in the Amazon basin

The coexistence between fishing kinds are not homogeneous in the Amazon basin. Only commercial and subsistence fisheries coexisted in white river systems (Figure 1). The commercial fishermen in these environments are composed for two groups with strong interaction. One group exploit scale fish, mainly migratory characins as tambaqui *Colossoma macropomum*, jaraquis *Semaprochilodus* sp., matrinchãs *Brycon* and curimatãs *Prochilodus* sp. Other group exploit catfish as piramutaba *Brachyplatystoma vailantii*, surubim *P. filamentosum*, caparari *P. tigrinum*, dourada *B. rouseauxii* e piraíba *B. filamentosum*. The subsistence fisheries are developed for riverine people that exhibit a great dependence for fish as source of animal protein. Seasonally, factors as fish abundance, reduction in the agricultural activity and/or high values of fish in regional market can be incentive for subsistence fisherman to make sales your production, mainly species of high values.

In black river systems, four fisheries kinds are present (Figure 2). However, the ornamental species fishing exploits a specific stock and the competition with the other fisheries is weak. The sportive fishermen are an aloctone group, mainly composed by tourist. The competition with other fishermen are restricted for exploitation of tucunaré *Cichla* sp. stocks, the target species of sportive fisherman and a fish of high commercial value at the regional market. The competition between commercial and subsistence fisheries are smaller than in white river systems, because the lower demographic density and the lower fish abundance.

The intensity of users conflicts change as function of various factors as: user kinds at a specific region, demographic density, exploitation level of stocks, dependence degree for resource, cultural values, etc. However, the user conflicts for the use of natural resources demand the occurrence of one of two fundamental conditions: the resource scarcity or the spatial or temporal overlay of users with different strategies of exploitation and/or resource perception.

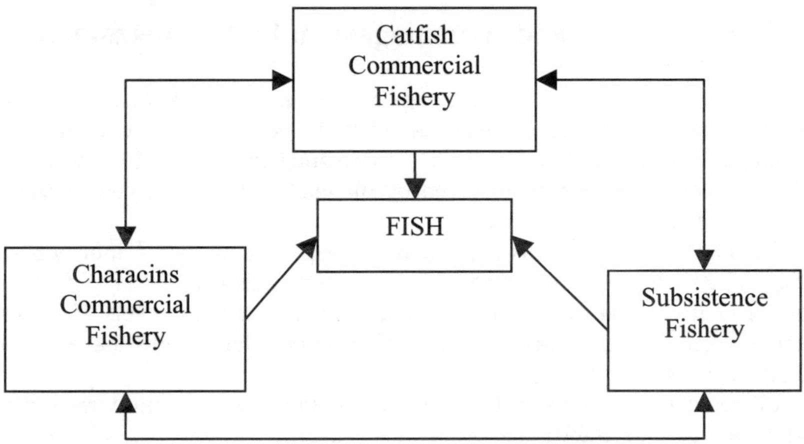

Figure 1: Fisheries and its interactions at white water environments.

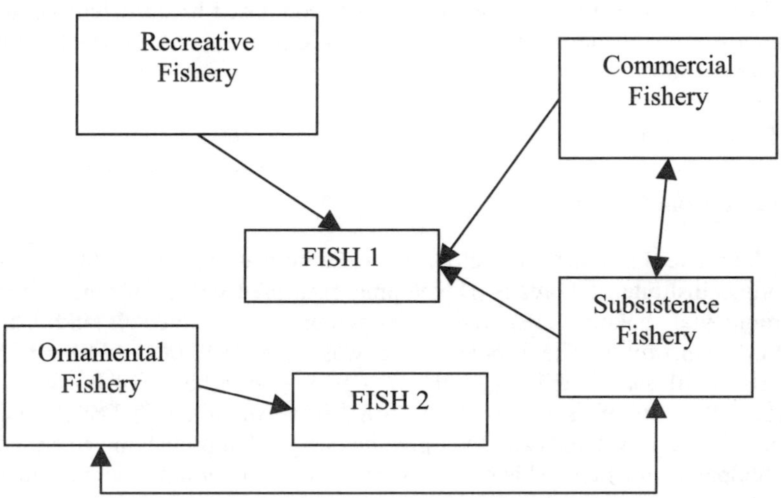

Figure 2: Fisheries and its interactions in black river systems.

Five kinds of conflicts between fisheries resources users were recently identified: (i) riverine versus riverine that result of demographic growth or local stocks depletion; (ii) riverine versus commercial fisherman that result of local stocks depletion or exploitation overlay; (iii) riverine versus sportive fisherman that result of exploitation overlay; (iv) commercial fisherman versus sportive fisherman that happen due exploitation overlay of a target specie; and (v) riverine versus land owner that happen due spatial overlay [9].

3 Self-regulation and co-management in the Amazonian

Proposals of include all users in the construction, implementation and monitoring of management planning of fisheries, that are nominated as co-management, communal management and participative management [10, 11] already been evaluated and, some times, validated by planned and non-planned experiences, mainly in small-scale fisheries [12].

Fishery co-management is defined as the responsibility and authority partition between government and users aim the management of a fishery. Co-management strategies can exhibit various compositions and levels of power and responsibility share, since a fully communal level until a centralized management [11].

Self-regulation proposals [12] to control the use of natural resources, in particular fish, to traditional Amazonian people exhibit several degrees of success. In general, these proposals give owner right to inhabitants [7] changing the status of common of these resources [8] and reduced the intensity of conflicts. However, the conflicts between riverine people and commercial fishermen were amplified when these proposals were a result of unilateral initiative. Nevertheless, some proposals were composed by an extensive debate between users and their preliminary analyses indicate that is a great factor to successful result.

4 Case studies

4.1 Mamirauá Reserve

The Mamirauá Sustainable Development Reserve was created in 1989 by IBDF (Brazilian Institute of Forestry Development), a predecessor of current federal environmental agency (IBAMA – Brazilian Environmental and Natural Resources Institute). The protected are was composed of 1.124 million ha comprising all the floodplains of the triangular region bordered by the Auatí-Paraná River, Solimões River and Japurá River. Mamirauá is Brazil's largest preserved area of wetlands and the only one designed to protect the ecosystem of the floodplains in Brazil. This reserve serves a very important function, since the floodplains represent from 60,000 to 100,000 km^2, or 5% of the whole Amazonian basin [13]. In addition to being important because of their role in the composition of the Amazonian basin, the floodplains comprise the principal habitat for the development of the life cycle of many species, including fish of great importance for the nourishment of the riverine and urban population in the region.

An interesting challenge, that has present since the creation of the reserve, is the necessity to conciliate the preservation of biodiversity with the sustainable development of the human population living within the reserve's area. This is a potentially difficult task, given the existence of 60 small riverside communities engaging in extractive and agricultural activities in the reserve. The success of the Mamirauá Sustainable Development Reserve is unique in rising to this challenge.

One of the unique aspects of the management model adopted in the Mamirauá Reserve is that all human inhabitants of the Reserve and the people living in the municipalities near to Reserve has been considered directly involved in decisive process. Thus, the local inhabitants are a resource in the preservation of biodiversity, providing the bulk of monitoring and enforcement activities in an effort to protect the reserve from outside exploitation of its natural resources. These people act as managers of the natural resources in the area, making resource management decisions, such as which lakes will be open for fishing, the length of fishing seasons, catch quotas and so forth. Before this, an active research programme support these resource management decisions. The scientists investigate ecological relationships, such as the life cycle of fish species and other information relevant to this type of decision-making. The local inhabitants also act as inspectors during the period of implementation of the measures, thus preventing this common property resource from suffering the degradation associated with open-access exploitation.

5 Final considerations

Local resource management systems are designed within the social, institutional, and economic context of the user communities. From the perspective of community-based conservation, local participation is the key to success. We believe that success is more likely when the value of conservation is realized first and foremost at the local level. While co-management of fish resources began as a response to threats against the subsistence base, the system has evolved as an adaptive strategy to improve the well fare. The strategy of self-regulation can be advanced by further research into adaptive utility of conservation programs developed within and for communities. Conservation has long been touted as a strategy for ensuring the long-term sustainability of natural ecosystems. Similarly, societies incorporating some manner of resource conservation and management into their socioeconomic organization will be better equipped to cope with the shrinking availability of natural resources in many areas of the world.

Acknowledgements

The authors would like to thank Federal University of Amazon and PIATAM Project (FINEP – PETROBRAS) for financial support.

References

[1] Freitas, C.E.C. & Rivas, A.A.F. Peixe: a sustentabilidade de um recurso comum na Amazônia. In: *Amazônia: Uma Perspectiva Interdisciplinar*. Org. A.A.F. Rivas e C.E.C. Freitas. Editora da Universidade do Amazonas, Manaus, 180-225, 2002.

[2] Freitas, C.E.C.; Batista, V.S. & Inhamuns, A.J. Strategies of the small-scale fisheries on the Central Amazon floodplain. *Acta Amazonica*, 32:1-7, 2002.

[3] Petrere Jr, M. River fisheries in Brazil: a review. *Regulated Rivers: research and management*, 4:1-16, 1989.

[4] Barthem, R.B. & Petrere Jr., M. Fisheries and population dynamics of *Brachyplatystoma vailantii* (Pimelodidae) in the Amazon Estuary. In: *Condition of the World's Aquatic Habitat. Proceedings of the World Fisheries Congress, Theme 1*. Ed. N.B. Armantrout, Oxford and IBH Publishing Co. Pvt., New Delhi. 329-340, 1995.

[5] Petrere Jr., M. (1996) Fisheries in large tropical reservoirs in South America. *Lakes & Reservoir: Research and Management*, 2:111-133.

[6] Leite, R.G. & Zuanon, J.A.S. Peixes ornamentais – aspectos da comercialização, ecologia, legislação e propostas de ações para um melhor aproveitamento. In: *Bases Científicas para Estratégias de Preservação e Desenvolvimento da Amazônia: Fatos e Perspectivas* Ed. Val, A. & Feldberg, E., 327-330, 1991.

[7] Pearse, P.H. Fishing rights and fishing policy: the development of property rights as instruments of fisheries management. In: *Proceedings of the World Fisheries. Theme 2: Fisheries Resource Utilization and Policy.* Ed.: R.M. Meyer; C. Zhang; M.L. Windsor; B.J. McCay; L.J. Hushak e R.M. Muth. New Delhi, Oxford & IBH Publishing Co. Pvt. Ltd., 10-25, 1996.

[8] Hardin, G. The tragedy of the commons. *Science*, 162:1243-1248, 1968.

[9] Ruffino, M.L. & Isaac,V.J. The fisheries of the lower Amazon: questions of management and development. *Acta Biologica Venezuelica*, 115(2): 37-46, 1994.

[10] McDaniel, J. Communal fisheries management in the Peruvian Amazon. *Human Organization*, 56(2): 147-152, 1997.

[11] Walters, C. *Adaptive Management of Renewable Resources.* MacMillan Publishing Company, New York, 372p. 1986.

[12] Achesson, J.M. & Wilson, J.A. Order out of chaos: the case for parametric fisheries management. *American Anthropologist*, 98:579-594, 1996.

[13] Pires, J.M. Tipos de vegetação na Amazônia. *Brasil Florestal*, 5(17):48-58, 1974.

Section 14
Recovery of damaged areas

Feasibility studies of utilizing domestic waste to refill a discarded open iron mine

W. Wu[1,2], K.-H. Lux[1], Z. Hou[1] & Q. Feng[3]
[1]*Institute for Waste Disposal and Geomechanics, Technical University of Clausthal, Erzstrasse 20, 38678 Claustha—Zellerfeld*
[2]*Institute of Rock & Soil Mechanics, the Chinese Academy of Sciences, 430071 Wuhan, People's Republic of China*
[3]*Institute of Environmental and Sanitary Design, 430022 Wuhan, People's Republic of China*

Abstract

The feasibility of utilizing Wuhan's domestic waste to refill the discarded Daye open iron mine is stated in the paper as follows: (1) the situation and existent of primary problems of municipal solid domestic waste (MSW) are analyzed; (2) the characteristics of the open iron mine and primary problems are investigated; (3) the feasibility of utilizing domestic waste to refill a more or less stable open mine and aspects of reconstruction of the landscape are presented in general; (4) the primary economic evaluations are performed. The results indicate that much money will be saved in the long term by cutting expenditure on Wuhan's domestic waste disposal and by recultivating land for the mine. In addition, environment surrounding the mine and Wuhan city will be improved and much land for landfills will be saved.
Keywords: waste disposal, discarded open mine reconstruction.

1 Introduction

In China, municipal solid domestic waste (MSW) amounted to 150.0 million tons in 2002. In the past few years, MSW has been dumped in the cities' surroundings, which has now resulted in more than 2/3 of the cities in China being besieged by MSW. The soil, water and atmosphere near the dumps of

MSW have been severely polluted and people's health has been also harmed. The situation is the same in Wuhan [1, 2].

On the other hand, a lot of discarded pits and shafts exist from the many years of mining in China. They will result in subsidence of the ground or sliding of slopes. All of these processes will have negative impacts on the environment and the safety of people living next to the mines; furthermore, the economic and social development in these areas will also be affected if the discarded mines or pits are not stabilized and reconstructed in time [5].

Daye open iron mine is one of the largest open mines in China and it is located next to Daye town in Hubei Province, 80 km from Wuhan, which is the capital of Hubei Province. The mined iron ores supply the Wuhan Steel Company with raw materials. The mine has been operated for more than 50 years up till now and will be closed in 2005. The volume of the mine is estimated to amount to more than 200 million m^3. The huge pit will give birth to many new negative impacts on the environment if it is not treated after closure.

In Wuhan, domestic waste generation amounts to annually 2.25 millions tons (in 2003), which has to be dumped in five uncontrolled landfills at present. Much land surrounding the city is taken up by the five landfills and the environment surrounding the landfills is also being polluted. Therefore, it may be an excellent idea to use Wuhan's domestic waste, after they have been treated, to refill the discarded Daye open mine. It has been calculated that the pit can be used to refill Wuhan's domestic for 87 years, taking into account an increase of 10% annually. It will be a good chance not only to dispose of Wuhan's domestic waste, but also to stabilize and reconstruct the discarded open mine.

This general idea has been the basis of some pre-investigation, the results of which are presented in this paper, titled "Feasibility of utilizing municipal solid domestic waste in Wuhan to refill open discarded iron ore mine of Daye with 200 million m^3 volume in China" [1].

2 Situation of MSW and the Mine

2.1 Situation of MSW in Wuhan

2.1.1 Waste management

Organizations of waste management are addressed as follows: Bureau of construction management of the city →Bureau of the District→Landfills (environmental and sanitary departments of the streets or companies).

(1) MSW Sources

Knowledge of the sources and the types of solid waste, along with data on the composition and rates of generation, is basic to the design and operation of the functional elements associated with the management of solid waste. There are, in general, five sources of MSW in Wuhan city, including industrial waste, commercial waste, institutional waste, hospital waste, and residential waste. In 2002, the highest fraction of MSW sources has been residential waste (56%), the second-highest, industrial waste (23%), and from the remaining 2% to 10% was constituted by hospital, commercial and institutional waste, respectively. Apart from hospital waste, the other types of waste are disposed in dumps or landfills.

(2) MSW Generation

From 1950 to 2003, MSW generation continued to increase sharply as an unfortunate concomitant result of several decades with development of sprawling urban area, the increase of its population and improvement of living standards in Wuhan City. For instance, in 1950, the population was about 1.08 million and MSW generated only 0.104 million tons of waste, but MSW generation has amounted to approximately 2.25 million tons and Wuhan's population was more than 7.0 million in 2003. MSW generation has been increased 16.5 times in 50 years.

(3) Components of MSW

In the 1970s, coal ashes and residual waste of households such as vegetables and skins of fruit constituted the largest portion of components of MSW at 60%, whereas residual foods of canteens, restaurants and hotels etc. were the second-largest portion (about 30%) and others such as waste paper, waste glass, porcelain and a small quantity of metals amounted to 10%. The food waste increased sharply from 12.94% in 1984 to 37.43% in 2003, and the coal ashes declined sharply from 74.70% in 1984 to 14.78% in 2003. The inorganic component reached at a level of 70% in 1984. But with improved living standards, such as the utilization of gas and electricity power for kitchens, the inorganic portion decreased drastically in MSW; meanwhile, the organic portion increased. It was determined that the inorganic portion took up 78.78%, 49.27%, 27.91% and 21.78% in 1984, 1994, 1996, and 2003 respectively; on the other hand, the organic portion took up 21.22%, 50.73%, 72.09% and 78.22% in 1984, 1994, 1996, and 2003, respectively.

(4) Collection and transportation of MSW

There are three principal collection modes for MSW in Wuhan (see Figure 1): (a) corridor collection. Corridors for MSW are installed along the aisles of some apartments; (b) container collection. Containers for MSW are installed some of the resident districts; (c) worker collection. In areas which have not corridors and containers, waste is collected by workers.

(a) (b) (c)

Figure 1: Collection modes for MSW. (a) corridor collection, (b) container collection and (c) worker collection.

Transportation of MSW has also three modes: (a) direct transportation - Waste are transported to the dump or the landfill from collecting places by vehicles; (b) indirect transportation - waste are first transported to the transferring station, then they are transported to the dump or landfill; (c) direct disposal - A small quantity of waste is disposed of directly onto sites. It was investigated that amounts of waste for indirect transportation took up the largest portion, comprising of 86.5% and the portion of direct transportation and others occupied 7.2 % and 6.3%, respectively in 1997.

(a) (b) (c) (d)

Figure 2: Some photographs of landfills in Wuhan city. (a) Baiyangqiao dump, (b) Liufang dump, (c) Daishan dump and (d) Jinkou sanitary landfill.

(5) Disposal

In Wuhan, the treatment method of MSW is only by depositing in landfills. MSW is not separated, and commingled MSW is also not pre-treated before they are transported to the dumps or landfills. There are now 4 uncontrolled landfills (dumps) and 1 simple sanitary landfill (see Figure 2). The facilities including the infrastructures of these landfills are at a very low technical level. This means that they don't have any facilities for leachate and gas collection, neither do they have good sealing systems. The dumps and the landfill were located next to the boundary of the city when they were built, but with the development of sprawling urban areas, the sites of the dumps are now situated in the residential center of districts. For instance, the international congress center and large resident apartment blocks were built surrounding the Jinkou landfill; other sites of the dumps will also become municipal development regions in the next future. The estimated available life span of the five landfill sites is only 1 to 3 years.

2.1.2 Problems of MSW disposal in Wuhan

The principal aspects of the problems associated with dumps are as follows:

- Dumps take up a lot of land, which takes up 275,000 m^2 annually if the total amount of WSM meets 2.25 million tons and the height of dumps comes up to 10 m. At present, 60-70% of the buildings in Hankou have been constructed on the old dumps.
- Facilities of waste disposal associated with infrastructures on the sites are at the very low technical level, particularly the collection and transportation system of waste and facilities of these dumps.
- The environment, especially the atmosphere, surrounding these dumps has been terribly polluted. Surveying results showed that the content of ammonia, sulphur hydrogen and small grains reached at 234—518mg/ m^3, 4.1—6.6 mg/ m^3 and 550-4640 mg/m^3 respectively in the atmosphere around the Guozikou dump in Hanyang district in 1997. All values exceeded limit values [2].
- Without good performance of the sealing systems and the leachate collection systems, the soil and water have been also severely polluted. Results indicated that the contents of heavy metals such as copper, lead, cadmium, chromium, arsenic and mercury as well as other hazardous substances exceeded limit values in the water and soil. [2]
- The facilities for the indirect transport systems of waste result in new polluting problems. Leachate and gas are produced during the process of transportation from waste collecting spots to the transferring stations because of poor performance of facilities associated with vehicles and transferring stations.

At present, the remaining life span of Wuhan city's 5 dumps amounts to only 1 to 3 years. New landfills must be sited and built in the near future.

2.2 Daye open iron mine

2.2.1 Introduction to Daye open iron mine

Daye open iron mine was designed in 1952 and its mining capacity has been 2.0 Mt/a; the ores of the mine are supplied to the Steel Corporation of Wuhan. They are still transported from the mine to Wuhan by train.

The railway, the road down to the bottom of the open mine and the drainage facilities at the bottom of the mine have been operating well.

(1) Mining parameters of the pit

The main mining parameters of the pit are indicated as follows: The length is 2.2km, the width, 1.1 km and the maximum and minimum depth reach, 520m and 100m; the estimated volume amounts to about 200 million m^3 and the inclinations of the working slopes reach at 41- 45°, as shown in Figure 3.

(2) The stratum and classification of rock mass

The stratum belongs to primary Triassic diorite which is a series of different rock formations; its lithology is classified commonly into diorite, tint diorite, strong corrode diorite with diopside, infirm diorite with diopside. The rock mass of the mine belongs to class I of the Chinese classification. This class contains hard and intact rock mass according to “the classification criteria of engineering rock mass” (GB50218-94 Chinese). The permeability of these rocks is very low.

(3) Structure properties of rock mass

(a) Large faults. The rock mass is crossed by few large faults, but they have enough load bearing capacity and good mechanical performance. There are six groups of faults, with an orientation in NNE, NE, NNW, NW, nearly SN, and NNW directions respectively. The dip of these faults range from 50° to $85\ ^{O}$. These faults are, normally, not harmful to slope stability of the mine.

(b) Little faults. There are 7 relatively small developed little fault systems. The principal direction is NNE, the others are NNW, SW, SN, and NWW, and the succession are NE and NW. Faults with azimuth/dip as N76°W/SW∠60°, N40°E/SE. NW∠75° and N51°W/SW∠82° are harmful to slope stability as shown in Figure 4.

(c) Joints and cracks. There are 7 or 8 joint groups in the district. Most of them are NE and NWW developed; NNE and NW are the second. In addition, many of the cracks were generated during operation, as shown in Figures 5 and 6.

Figure 3: The open mine.

Figure 4: The little faults.

Figure 5: The cracks.

Figure 6: The joints.

(4) Slope disaster—deformation and fracturing of the slopes.
The collapse of slopes has occurred twice in the open mine. Before sliding, that is before April 30, 1990, the displacement velocities of observation points in the parallel direction in neighbor rock bodies above ∇84m were lower than 1 mm/d, mostly 0.4 mm/d, from March 29 to April 27. After sliding, their displacement velocities increased sharply; the velocities of some points near to the sliding area even surpassed 15 mm/d, and this deformation process with its high deformation rates lasted for about 10 days. After this, the velocities decreased evidently to only 0.1 mm/d. The reason for this decrease is perhaps the unloading after sliding and the reduction of rainfall. From June 4 to June 16, the velocities increased to 3.5 mm/d with the increase of rainfall. Finally, the displacement velocities of the sliding bodies tended to be zero even after rainy season by reinforcement measures. [3,4]

The other sliding body called A1# started to slide in March 1991, and the displacement was up to 500 mm in a month. At that time, the stretching displacement of tensile cracks at ∇+72m platform in the east of this sliding body increased to 10 mm.

2.2.2 Main problems of the pit

Daye open mine will be closed in 2005. Up to now, the mine has not been reconstructed. The following problems may arise in general:

- Possibility of the large-scale collapse of slopes, which means severe threats to the life and estates of the people and to the environment surrounding the mine.
- No reuse of land in the order of a magnitude of 2.5 km^2 in the future.

3 Feasibility of utilizing domestic waste to refill the open mine

3.1 General remark

The pit will be boosted with enormous economic and social value if the MSW from Wuhan including Daye and Huangshi city near the mine is refilled into the mine. The operation time will exceed 87 years if a refilling amount of MSW of 2.0-3.0 Mt/a is taken into account. The main advantages by utilizing domestic waste to refill the open mine, which could be a new method for MSW utilization are as follows:

- Reduction of occupied land for landfills in Wuhan including Daye and Huangshi;
- Creating a new industry of MSW treatment and stabilization of the discarded mine.
- Renewing of lands at the surface of the refilled open mine;
- Improvement of environment around the city and the mine.
- Increasing chances of employment.

3.2 Feasibility of separated collection of MSW

MSW needs be separated in order to carry out the proposed treating method. In this context, the primary tasks for government, institutions and citizens at present are listed as follows:

- Constituting new regulations of integrated waste management including source reduction, recycling and disposal. At present, special items for integrated waste management are being investigated by some institutions of the government in Hubei Province;
- Public education for waste management such as newspaper releases, speeches, community calendar announcements, radios and TV. Citizens will understand that integrated waste management is essentially useful and significant;
- Techniques and criteria for a separated collection of MSW are being investigated by some institutions;
- Separated collection of MSW is being adopted in practice for some communities such as ShuiguoHu Community in Wuhan.

3.3 Feasibility of waste transferring and the transportation of the MSW to the mine

The MSW will at first be transported by vehicles from collecting waste containers to the transferring station. In order to transport the MSW to the mine, a waste pre-treatment at the transferring station will be necessary. This transferring station has to be set up in the Qingshan district near the Wuhan Steel Corporation. At the transferring station, the MSW will be separated, recycled, dehydrated, composted and packed. After pre-treatment in the transferring station, the waste will be transported to Daye open mine by train of a special railway. A special railway already exists from Wuhan Steel Corporation to the mine, and iron ores of several mines including some underground mines are transported by train from Daye region to the steel plant in Wuhan. But the trains have no loads to transport from Wuhan to Daye open mine. If MSW could be transported by the trains from Wuhan to Daye, the transporting income for Wuhan Steel Corporation will be increased; this means that the cost of transportation will be decreased.

3.4 Feasibility of reconstruction of the open mine.

3.4.1 Stability of the slopes in the mine

Daye open iron mine has been in operation for many decades. The slopes have been investigated and stabilization methods have been designed and constructed by the Institute of Rock Mechanics in Wuhan, Institute of Mining and Metallurgy in Changsha and Wuhan Steel Corporation. The research reports are listed in the references, [3, 4] and the conclusions have indicated that the main slopes are stable. One example for the existing main slopes in the Daye open mine is shown in Figure 7. The angle of the slopes are between 41° and 45°, the heights of the slopes are 60m, 72m, 91m, and the safety coefficients of the slopes are equal to 1.235 , 1.169 and 1.014 as respectively calculated by the Bishop's method for proof of slope stability. The slopes are stable at the moment because the calculated safety coefficients are more than 1.0.

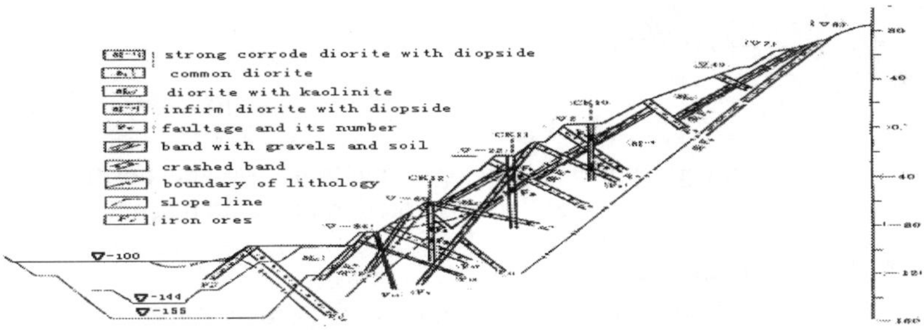

Figure 3: A typical calculation cross-section in Daye open mine.

However, long-term safety seems to be questionable with reference to the relatively low safety margins. It is possible that small-scale slopes will not be stable in the long term, taking into account effects such as rock corroding and weathering. A possible loss of stabilization could be monitored and prevented by appropriate reinforcement techniques such as anchors or anchor-ropes, resisting slide-piles, as well as injection and concrete etc. These measures were attested to be effective by deformation measurements during many years of mining.

3.4.2 Permeability of rock mass

Seepage is possible because of a great number of little faults and cracks around the bottom and the slopes in the pit. However, the problem of seepage can be overcome by technical measures. Concerned measures toward the permeable problems will focus on:

- Classification of the faults according to their permeability;
- Injection techniques to reduce permeability using clay or concrete that will be injected into the crashed rock mass in faults and cracks;
- Clay liners to be installed at the bottom and along the slopes;
- A synthetic liner to be installed at the bottom and along the slopes.

3.4.3 Drainage of leachate

There exists (1) a drainage tunnel with the dimensions of 2.0m*3.0m, length of 3.0km for transportation of waste water at the bottom of the mine to the outside of the mine and (2) a treatment facility for waste water, which has been operated well for many years shown in Figure 8. After the mine is closed, these facilities will be able to be used additionally for the transportation and treatment of seepage water from the deposited waste.

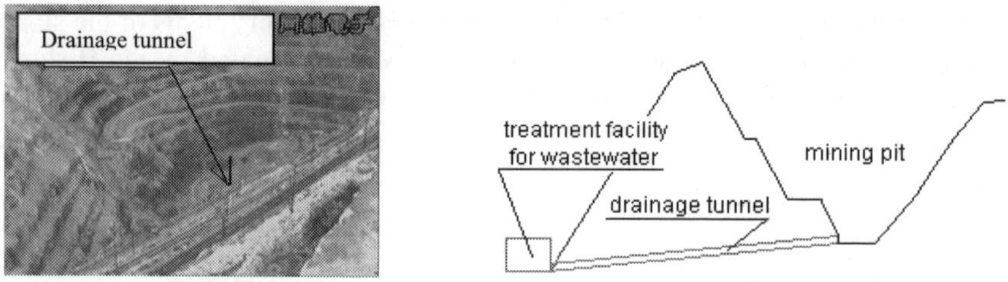

Figure 8: The drainage tunnel in the open pit mine. (a) the position of the drainage tunnel and (b) the cross-section of the drainage tunnel.

3.4.4 Refilling techniques

The principles of the refilling techniques will be taken as follows:

- The pit will be divided into different districts according to different waste types;
- The thickness of a layer of waste will be limited to 0.5—1.0m and every layer of waste will be compacted by a compactor in order to reduce the settlement of the waste. One must not forget that the organic waste will be pre-composted in the transferring station.
- The open pit volume has to be divided into sub-blocks and every sub-block should be handled like an individual landfill (monitoring, documentation);
- Leachate and gas production rates, as well as organic content, can be minimized by additional pre-treatment (offsite and site, and disposal techniques);
- A leachate collecting system will be integrated into the existing drainage system of the open mine;
- The pipes for gas collecting and transportation will be designed with a consideration of the deformation properties of the waste.

4 Economic analysis

Economic analyses are based on two scenarios as follows: (1) waste refilling into the open pit mine and (2) construction of a new landfill near Wuhan city. A description of the two scenarios is as follows:

(1) Scenario I utilizes Daye open mine for the disposal of waste: The distance between Wuhan and the mine is about 80 km, the area takes up 2.5 km^2 and its capacity will add up to about 150 million tons of waste. This means that the operation time will come to 87 years. Waste in Wuhan will be first transported to the transferring station by trucks with a compacting facility and afterwards, pre-treatment waste transported from the transferring station to the mine by train.

(2) Scenario II is siting and constructing a few new landfills near Wuhan city: The loaded waste distance is about 20—40 km from the city to the new landfills and the area of landfills (about 5 landfills) will take up 12.5 km^2

for 150 million tons of waste to disposed of (the height of the deposited waste amounts to about 20 m).

The investment calculation is based on the correlation data of the Erfeishan landfill which is a new landfill constructed next to Wuhan and financed by The Dutch and Chinese Government.

- *Construction investment*
  The construction investment adds up to 41 million Renmenbi Yuan (RMB) to scenario I, whereas scenario II reaches to 70 million RMB;
- *Equipment and materials investment*
  The equipment and materials investment of scenario I add up to 94 million RMB; ; that of scenario II will reach to 76 million RMB;
- *Other investments*
  (a) Land compensating cost: Land compensating cost will be zero to scenario I and will add up to 42 million RMB (3.4236 million RMB/km^2) in scenario II.
  (b) Other costs: These costs include managing cost, designing cost training cost and engineering insurance cost, etc. These costs are 11.3 million RMB for scenario I more than that for scenario II.
  (c) Transportation cost: The transportation cost of scenario I is 16 RMB/ton more than that of scenario II because there is train transportation which has to be taken into consideration in scenario I.

In summary, the total investment of scenario I will amount to 1.7 billion RMB and that of scenario II will amount to 3.0 billion RMB; this means that the investment of scenario I is in the order of a magnitude 1.3 billion RMB less than that of scenario II. Utilizing Wuhan's domestic waste to refill the discarded Daye open mine, will not only save much money and the landscape, but more jobs will also be created; furthermore, the environments of Wuhan and Daye city will be much improved.

5 Conclusion

Utilizing Wuhan's domestic waste to refill the discarded Daye open pit mine in the future will result in the fact that valuable lands occupied for landfills to date will be significantly reduced in Wuhan, including, in particular, Daye and Huangshi. The new landfills have to be built in the next few years because of the small number of years left for operation of Wuhan's landfills today. As part of the further consequences of the proposed waste management concept, the environment in Wuhan will be able to be significantly improved. By renewing the lands in the area of the open mine with waste backfill, the environment surrounding the mine will also be improved. Last but not least, the proposed method will reduce unemployment. The main conclusions are as follows:

- There are many problems associated with waste disposal in Wuhan and the discarded Daye open iron mine at present, which, essentially, have to be solved in the near future in order to improve the environment;
- It is feasible to utilize the waste from Wuhan to refill the discarded Daye open iron mine due to economy and environment factors, especially: (1) the

feasibility of classification and collection of MSW by constituting new laws, information of the public, education and making experiments; (2) the feasibility of waste transportation by vehicles to a transferring station with pre-treatment and then the transportation of pre-treated waste by trains to the open mine; (3) the feasibility of improving the stability of the open mine and the environment, as well as to use the existing facilities of the mine, especially the drainage tunnel and the waste water treatment plant;

- Investment for new landfills in Wuhan and for reconstruction measures in the mine will be saved.

Of course, many correlative items will essentially have to be researched in the near future because utilizing Wuhan's domestic waste to refill the discarded Daye open iron mine is a complex and highly disciplinary project.

Acknowledgements

The authors of the paper would like to express their sincere thanks to the sponsors of this pre-investigation, namely (1) the Bureau of Science and Technology of Hubei Province, and the Bureau of Construction of Wuhan City in China; (2) the Lower Saxony Government in Germany.

References

[1] Wen Wu et al (2002, in Chinese): Investigation report: environment integrated treatment by utilizing MSW in Wuhan to refill Daye open mine. Institute of Rock & Soil Mechanics, the Chinese Academy of Sciences, Wuhan.

[2] Wen Wu, Qiling Feng & Chunhe Yang (2003, in Chinese): *New method for waste disposal and renewing land of discarded mines*. Publishing House of Science and technology of Hubei.

[3] Xiurun Ge et al (1998. in Chinese): Investigation report: *Analysis on stabilities of slopes for Daye open mine*. Institute of Rock & Soil Mechanics, the Chinese Academy of Sciences, Wuhan.

[4] Xiurun Ge et al (1992, in Chinese): Investigation report: *Analysis on stabilities of slopes for Daye open mine and measures reinforcement of slopes in Daye iron open mine*. Institute of Rock & Soil Mechanics, the Chinese Academy of Sciences, Wuhan.

[5] Zhimeng Gu, Shiwei Bai (2000, in Chinese): *Suggestions of environment integrated treatment by utilizing MSW to fill discarded mines*. Technological progress and countermeasure, No.1, pp.1—4.

Geoplastics method as a tool for disturbed territories rehabilitation

A. Bolshakov
Irkutsk State Technical University

Abstract

Disturbed territory is a landscape disordered in such a way that it cannot be used by society before it is reclaimed. In landscaping, relief is of crucial importance. Relief directs the flows of materials in natural landscapes. The ordinary way of reclamation in Russia is based on a level relief. The author's experience shows that the folded surface is more effective for the reclamation. Creating of a folded relief with the purpose of the disturbed landscape restoration is a special method which I call the geoplastics. This method allows us to direct the landscape material flows and concentrate them in accumulative cells, to balance the relationship of the warmth, moisture, and fine grains of soil minerals. Thus, this method creates proper conditions for bioproductivity and biodiversity. A series of the author's projects confirm the reliability and effectiveness of the geoplastic method as a tool in fighting entropy of the landscapes disturbed by man.
Keywords: disturbed landscapes, folded restoration relief, control of the landscape material flows, order of the landscaping energy.

1 Introduction

Disturbed territories are a result of economic activity that has changed this territory in such a way that it can't be used by the society unless they are reclaimed. The disturbed landscapes have a negative impact on the environment. Disturbed territories and urban territories have the same area in Russia. In the former USSR, it was more than 7 million hectares [1]. The general feature of disturbed territories is that the correlations of the landscape's components such as rocks, waters, soils, and vegetation, are changed critically. The technology of disturbed territories reclamation consists of two steps. The technical step is vertical alignment of the disturbed surface. The biological step is formation of the soil-vegetation cover.

WIT Transactions on Ecology and the Environment, Vol 81, © 2005 WIT Press
www.witpress.com, ISSN 1743-3541 (on-line)

The restoration terrain design is the point of a special attention. The ordinary technology of reclamation is directed at the leveling of the terrain. It means filling up of quarries, as well as lowering and the alignment of the dump. The problem is that this approach is not based on the natural laws of landscaping. When the soil-vegetation cover is destroyed, the flat relief provokes dissipation of the landscaping energy and does not facilitate the restoration of the disturbed landscape. The author has studied the natural landscaping processes and has designed reclamation of a number of disturbed plots. As a result, the reclamation method was worked out. The method is based on that the folded relief is more effective for the landscape restoration than the leveled flat one. This method I call geoplastics. The folded terrain is also the dominant factor of natural landscaping.

2 Geoplastics as the natural landscaping factor

Relief is the basic factor of natural landscaping. First, relief directs the movement, deposition and development of the landscape material. Second, relief distributes the landscaping energy. There are two forms of relief: the mountains and plains. Each form has three elements or the sites: top, slope and lowland.

The character and the intensity of the landscaping processes are distributed to elemental sites in the following way. On the top, the landscape material (sediment, soil, moisture, seeds, living substance) is formed by local sources and due to the outer space. Part of the landscape material moves from the top to the lower site. This movement consists of water flows, creep, air down flow and is triggered by the gravity. This process is called eluvial one, and the top is an eluvial landscape, i.e. a donor. The slope is a transit landscape. This site produces its own landscape material, receives the material from the top and passes it through itself to the lower site. This is a deluvial process, and the landscape of the slope is a deluvial one. The lowland both accumulates the material coming from up and generates its own material. This is an accumulative process and the landscape is an accumulative one.

The correlation of the warmth, moisture, thickness of the sediment and the humus depends on the sites and the slope exposition. The optimum correlation of these components creates conditions for the enhancing of the general bioproductivity of the landscape. In nature we observe that more bioproductive landscapes occur in valleys and plains and in such lower parts of the slopes, which are favorably exposed. The general natural law stating that geochemical activity of the landscape depends on the sites of relief was described by the Russian scientist Polynov B.B. in 1915 [2]. So, the general natural law of bioproductivity (crop) distribution among the sites is that it increases from up down, from the top to the depression.

Thus, the relief controls the distribution and the development of the landscape material on the earth surface in nature because of it has a free energy due to gravity and different elevation of the sites, as well due to the fact that exposition of slopes differ in warmth and moisture.

3 Geoplastics as a method of the disturbed territories restoration in the author's projects

The author has designed a number of projects on reclamation in disturbed territories of the Baikal region, Russia. The general methodology of the design is the following. First, disturbance factors are revealed in the plot. Second, the direction of reclamation and further usage of the territory are defined. Third, the concept of geoplastics is worked out, i.e. the shape of the restoration relief that controls the movement and deposit of the landscape material in proper places and at a proper ratio. Fourth, the concept of the artistic image and design of the territory for its functional usage are worked out. Fifth, the biological stage of reclamation that adds to the geoplastic concept and meets the functional and aesthetical requirements of the territory is worked out. Let us consider concrete examples of geoplastics application in the author's projects carried out during the last ten years.

3.1 Reclamation of a dump in Bolshoye Goloustnoye

The dump in Bolshoye Goloustnoye is located on the coast of Lake Baikal 120 km southeast from the city of Irkutsk. In the 50-s in B.G. on the shoreline of Lake Baikal, timber industry storage was placed. It was used for timber-rafting. The logs were tied together and the rafts were towed by a tugboat to the consumers. For rafts, a channel was dug out on the coast. The mineral soil extracted from the channel was put in a dump on the coast. The original coastal landscape was meadow step, with a thick layer of humus. Under the dump, the topsoil was buried. The total area of the plot is 34 ha. The average thickness of the dump was two meters. Later, the surface was leveled and equipped with gantry cranes. The banks of the channel were fortified with the protection walls. In 1987, the timber enterprise was closed. In its place, the national park was established. The timber storage was abandoned.

In 1993, the author has worked out the reclamation project. The following disturbance factors were revealed. 1) Under the dump, the topsoil is buried. 2) The substratum of the dump is overcondenced, containing 70% of gravel and 30% of silt and sand. 3) The surface is not connected with the ground water. 4) There is no vegetation on the plot. 5) The visual image of the Baikal coast is roughly distorted by the shape of the dump. 6) The old building of the Orthodox Church that is situated close by is half-destroyed. Besides, the climate of the region is dry and windy.

In accordance with the master plan (Figure 1), the landscape park has been designed on the plot. The landscape park includes the church garden around Saint Nicolas Church, the harbor, the sport area, the landscape garden, the tourist camp, the children playground, and administrative area.

The geoplastic concept is the following. The dump is moved from the buried soil by detached parcel hollows rather than on the total area. The excavations form a network on the dump surface. The excavations should free the buried soil. The cut material is moved to the periphery of the excavations.

From this material, closed and partly opened screens are formed around the excavations. The micro-relief of the natural coastal landscape is a combination of hills, gullies, dunes and hollows. That is why the excavations are shaped as hollows; the banks are shaped as dunes. According to the general idea of the relief impact on the bioproductivity of the landscape, there are designed eluvial cells protecting the oases-hollows from the Aeolian deflation as well as slopes directing the moisture and sediments to the hollow and accumulative cells catching the fine mineral particles, seeds, snow and rain. Thus, for the purpose of reclamation of the dump in Bolshoye Goloustnoye, the dune-hollow restoration micro-relief is designed.

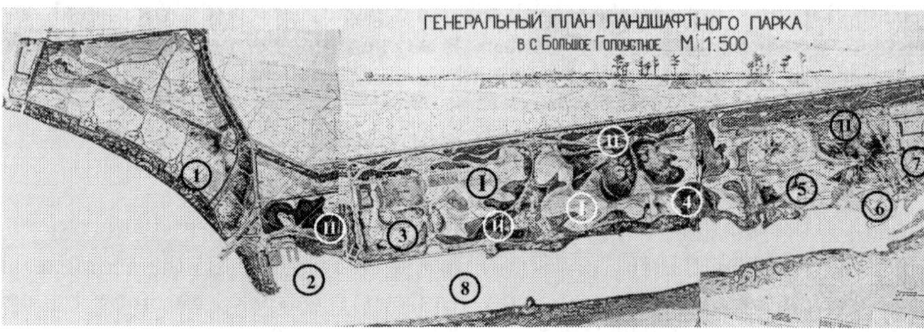

Figure 1: Master plan of Bolshoye Goloustnoye Park. Restoration relief: I banks; II – extractions. Functional zones: 1) Church garden, 2) Harbor, 3) Sport ground, 4) landscape garden, 5) Camping ground, 6) Children playground, 7) Administrative zone, 8) Channel.

Figure 2: State of plot before reclamation, 1994. 1) mark line of future relief, 2) moorage, 3) dyke, 4) channel, 5) inner damaged moorage, 6) Saint Nicolas Church, 7) plot of grass cover, 8) dump surface.

In 1994-1996, the first step of the project was carried out by a small enterprise under the guidance of the author. The results exceeded the expectations. The initial state of the plot is shown in Figure 2. The first step reclamation results are shown in Figure 3. In autumn 1994, the soil under the press of the gravel dump was freed with the help of hollows. It was already in spring 1995 that the opened surfaces got covered with grass. As soon as the buried soil was exposed to the sunlight, the rhizome and seeds which had stayed for forty years under the gravel dump started growing. In the wintertime, the snow is blown off the surface of the whole plain because of the strong winds. The only exceptions are the hollows of the park where the snow is trapped and accumulated through the winter till the spring start of the vegetation. In 1996, the recreation embankment was built on the coastal edge of the dump. Thus, the experimental results confirm the correctness of the geoplastics concept in the plot.

Figure 3: General view of park after the first step of reclamation, 1996.

3.2 The reclamation of the quarry project in the city Usolye Sibirskoye

The quarry for the sand-gravel soil is located on the border of the dwelling area and the chemical factory territory, 500 m from the Angara River bank, in the city of Usolye Sibirskoye. Nearby, there is a rubbish landfill. The disturbance factors are the following. The depth of the quarry is about 3 m. After the mining, because of the high water-table, the bottom of the quarry is going to be a few centimeters higher than the level of the underground water. This provides a sure forecast of a swamp formation in the quarry. The plot is a little higher than the flood plain. Inclination of the plot is 3 m in height per 500 m in length.

As the plot is situated on the green belt of the city and on the border of the Angara River water protection zone, the master plan defines the reclamation as water protection, nature protection and recreation. Figure 4. In order to avoid the swamp formation, to create the biodiversity of the landscape, including the water surfaces, meadows and tree plant, the concept of the geoplastics means shaping a special restoration relief that should meet the above aims. In order to create tree plant, the level of the topsoil should be elevated to a height above the water-table. Only the local resources should be used. The solution is the following. Over the bottom (and the water-table), the banks should be raised up to 1.6 m high. The material for the banks should be taken from the same bottom. For this purpose, the 50-80 m-wide and 1-1.5 m-deep channels are dug as drainage valleys. The underground water discharges to these valleys and moves along them directing to the drainage well in the lowest place of the plot. To improve water filtration the proper conditions are created in the well. The material extracted from the valleys is used to build banks-islands with the total area 18 ha. To elevate the islands, the rubbish from the city landfill is used as a filling material. Of course, this material should be isolated from the underground water by a clay cover. The soil taken from the channels is put above the rubbish, and then the original fertile soil is put on the top. According to the project, before mining quarry, the original topsoil is cut off and stored nearby.

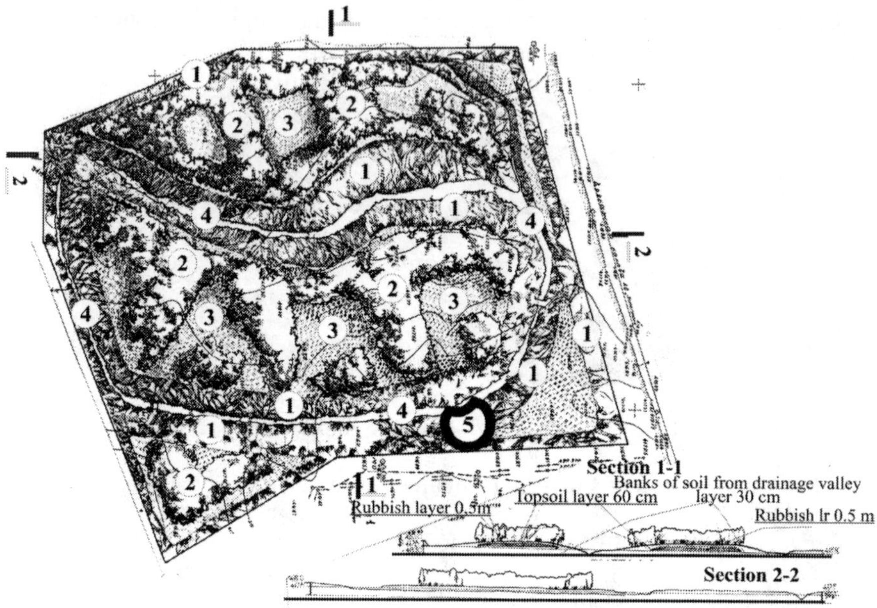

Figure 4: Master plan of quarry in Usolye Sibirskoye. 1) Slopes of islands – coasts of valley, 2) Birches plants, 3) Meadows, 4) Drainage channels, 5) Drainage well.

Thus, to the reclaim the quarry with a high water-table, a valley-island relief is used. In comparison with the surface used in the dump reclamation project in Bolshoye Goloustnoye, this surface is kind of turned inside out.

3.3 The quarry reclamation project in Angasolka

The granite quarry (23 ha) is located on the slope of the mountain valley. Here, granite is mined and broken up into the road-metal. This excavation is a terraced slope. The low terrace or the horizon is on the level 795 m, the high border is on the level 890 m. By the beginning of the design in 1998, it had six terraces 15 m high and up to several hundred meters wide. When the mining finishes, the shape of the quarry is going to change. The bottom is going to remain at the same height, but to become wider (from 4 ha to 12 ha). The number of terraces is going to decrease two times, their width decreasing to 10 m.

The disturbance factors are the following. 1) The natural slope is cut by an excavation with wide bottom (12 ha) and three terraces with the total height 75 m. 2) The bottom and terraces are covered by friable granite-dust soil (siftings) which do not retain moisture. 3) The surfaces are too open to winds. The deflation of the soil or the Aeolian movement is too active. 4) There is no vegetation on the terraces, although some of them are 30 years old.

At the bottom, we can see a different picture. It is overgrown with trees and bushes. The age of the bottom and low terrace is the same, however. The reason is the following. The bottom (4 ha) is closed by the walls of the quarry along almost the whole perimeter. There is no wind there. The water from the rock cracks discharges here. So, the bottom is an accumulative cell.

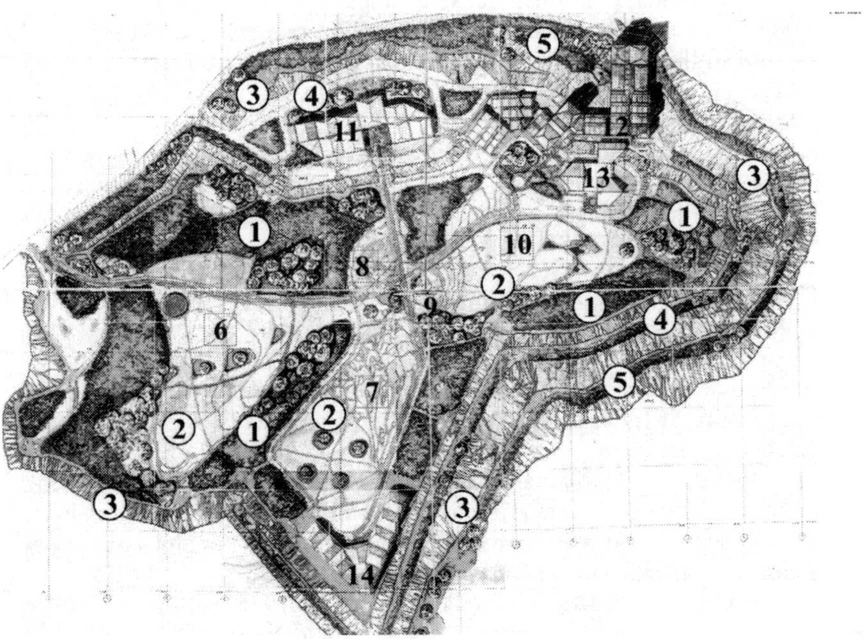

Figure 5: Master plan of Angasolka quarry reclamation. Geoplastic elements: 1) Wide banks – barriers, 2) Narrow banks, 3) Walls of Quarry, 4) Terrace of 810 m horizon, 5) Terrace of 840 m horizon; open spaces: 6) Parterre of Sun, 7) Parterre of Grass Roots, 8) Parterre of Tree, 9) Parterre of Man, 10) Parterre of Water; Buildings: 11) Health-care complex, 12) Hotel, 13) Multifunctional complex, 14) Technical building.

According to the master plan (Figure 5), after mining is finished a park and the tourist centre are designed. A health-care complex is designed on the terrace of the 810 m horizon that remains much wider than the mining project suggested. A big hotel is built on the slope of the quarry. The idea to build the tourist center arose because the place is a junction of three popular itineraries in the region.

The geoplastics concept is the following. The quarry surfaces and its siftings cover have a transit property that should be overcome. Stabilization of the deposition of the soil, the retaining of the soil moisture and the limitation of the soil Aeolian movement, are the main tasks of the landscape restoration. For these purposes, two types of the bank networks are created. The banks 20-30 m wide and 3 m high form the first network of the cells with the area about 4 ha. The barriers of this network enclose the open parterres of the same size as the overgrown old bottom. There is a network of the tectonic cracks of the granite body. The first type barriers repeat this crack network. The tree zones are created on the top of the barriers. Then, the big open parterres are covered by a network of narrow banks (2 m wide and 1 m high) with small cells (6-20 are). Due to their closed perimeters, the small cells accumulate the deposition and moisture. On the border of these cells the pioneer vegetation crops. It is confirmed by the observations in this quarry. The narrow banks network is also shaped as an art object. The design of the parterres creates the artistic images such as Grass Roots, Sun, Water, Tree, and Man.

In addition to the geoplastics, it is suggested that to create pioneer soil, compost is formed from the sawdust and the lignin that can be found in the settling tanks of the Baikalsk wood-and-pulp mill. More detailed information on the projects is presented in [3].

3.4 Architecture and ecology compensation project for a historical landscape, The Star Grove

The Star Grove is a historical green block (15 ha) on the riverside of the Angara River in the city of Irkutsk. In 1861, this plot of pine forest was allotted to the Eastern Siberia Governor-General as a dacha. Much earlier, in Paleolithic 7000 years ago, there was an early man site. The area is an archeological monument of a federal status. The green block is surrounded by a built-up area and is located on the third terrace of the Angara River. The terrain of the plot is an erosion valley with a very small stream named Star.

The disturbance factors are the following. In 1955, on the edge of the stream valley in the low third of it, a sewage station was built and across the stream, a sewage collector was laid. The stream was placed in a storm pipe. Two upper thirds of the deep valley was gradually filled up. The sewage collector crosses the valley inside the landfill. First, the "hot" point of disturbances is the contact place of the stream and sewage collector inside the soil banks. The leakage from the pipes causes the formation of a ravine in the dump. Every year the ravine is filled by the soil and rubbish, but it renews steadily. Second, the low third part of the stream valley that is 150 m long (up to the place where the stream flows into the Angara River), is the site of landslide processes. Third, the accidental sewage is poured out of station into the stream. Then the sewage gets into the Angara River, a national-status source of potable water.

The master plan (Figure 6) is the following. The plot is given to the State University of the Communications as a campus place. The landfill above the stream is chosen for the open sport and recreation facilities.

Figure 6: Master plan of the Star Grove Park. 1) Sport Palace. 2) Sport ground. 3) Building-bridge, 4) Anti-landslide frame, 5) Angara River embankment.

The recent landfill (50 years old) does not contain any archeological material. Construction is not banned there. The pedestrian boulevard along the stream leads to the embankment of the Angara River where the passengers' platform, recreational facilities and walkway are going to be. The monuments of architecture and history are protected. Instead of the ramshackle wooden houses along Gogol Street the Palace of sport is designed. A new green network is shaped, which corresponds to the landscape potential.

The geoplastics concept is the following. 1) A building-bridge is designed instead of the soil bank including the sewage and potable water pipes and the stream in the storm collector. The stream flows under the bridge, the sewage and the potable water (in the pipes) are placed on the technical floor of the building-bridge. The pedestrians go on the top of the bridge and along the stream under the bridge. So the flows are divided. The leakage from the pipes is under control. There is a ski pavilion on the first floor of the building. 2) An anti-landslide frame is designed to prevent the landslides in the low part of the stream valley. Retaining walls at the foot of the slopes are constructed. Then both walls are connected with transversal diaphragms. As a result, the pressure of one slope is counterbalanced by the pressure of the opposite one. 3) At the same time the anti-landslide frame is used as a bed for a pound–collector to treat the dirty water. Sand filters and biological treatment with the help of the swamp vegetation are suggested.

4 Conclusion: entropy and geoplastics method

Geoplastics is a method for restoring disturbed landscapes by means of controlling the movement and deposition of the landscape material. Restoration relief is a tool of control. Restoration relief directs the water and sediment movement, controls their deposition and accumulates these materials. The optimal combination of the sunlight, warmth, moisture, mineral and organic substratum give the positive effect – under these conditions, living substance develops and general bioproductivity and biodiversity of the landscape increases. Restoration relief creates a long-term unequal distribution of the free energy used for landscaping. The flows of energy are concentrated by the relief in proper directions and in proper cells chosen by a designer. This energy organization prevents its dissipation, i.e. entropy. Many kinds of the economy activity are accompanied by landscape deterioration and dissipation of the landscape energy. Geoplastics is a reliable tool that allows us to overcome these problems.

References

[1] Lazareva I.V. Охрана территориальных ресурсов градостроительства.- Киев: Будивельник, 1986.- 128 с., ил.

[2] Polynov B.B. Избранные труды. - Москва: Наука, 1956. - 751 с.

[3] Bolshakov A.G. Геопластика в архитектуре и планировке ландшафта.- Иркутск: Изд-во института географии СО РАН России, 2000.- 171 с.

Enhanced soil-washing treatment for soils which are highly contaminated with crude oil

L. G. Torres[1], A. L. Aguirre[1], A. Verdejo[2] & R. Iturbe[1]
[1]*Instituto de Ingeniería, Coordinación de Ingeniería Ambiental, Universidad Nacional Autónoma de México, Mexico*
[2]*Facultad de Química, UNAM, Mexico*

Abstract

Soil and water contamination due to hydrocarbon spills is a frequent problem worldwide. In the case of Mexico, even when programs oriented to the diminution of these undesirable events are in progress, in the year 2000 a total of 1,518 hydrocarbon spills (6,250 tons) were reported. Surfactant enhanced washing of soils is a remediation technology, which has been shown to be a high cost-effective process. The first step in the washing process development is the selection of suitable surfactants and doses. In this work, twelve anionic and nonionic surfactants and their mixtures were assessed in the remediation of highly contaminated crude oil soils. Moreover, the use of different amounts of NaCl and Na-silicate (10%), due to the high amount of Ca, Mg and Mn in the soils is shown and discussed. The studied soil was artificially contaminated with crude oil from the *El Batab* (Campeche, Mexico) perforation well in a concentration of 108,980 mgTPH/kg soil. SDS and E-600 surfactants at 1% concentration achieved higher TPH removal rates (20.4 and 32.9%, respectively). The surfactant-salt mixture that showed a TPH removal rate higher than those obtained with the best single surfactants was SDS+ EW600+Na_2SiO_3 10% (30.2%). Using a tensiometric technique, the SDS critical micelle concentration (CMC) was measured without any salt present and with 0.5, 1 and 2% of NaCl. These data were employed together with other surfactants CMC and HLB (hydrophilic-lypophilic balance) reported values in order to explain the surfactants performance during the soil washing assessments. In general, TPH removal values were higher when high HLB values-surfactants were employed.
Keywords: crude oil, hydrocarbon spills, ionic, nonionic, soil washing, surfactants.

1 Introduction

Soil and water contamination due to hydrocarbon spills is a frequent problem worldwide. For the case of Mexico, even when programs oriented to the diminution of these undesirable events are on progress, at year 2000 a total of 1,518 hydrocarbon spills were reported. The total amount of spilled hydrocarbons was around 6,250 tons. The main petroleum industry areas were those spills occurred were crude exploration and production, with 1,428 spills (1,097 tons), and crude refining, with 90 spills (5,155 tons)[1]. The main spills were in the refineries, pipelines and marine terminals. Among the soil remediation techniques applied to hydrocarbon contaminated samples, surfactant enhanced soil washing is one of the most promising. Surfactant enhanced washing of soils is a remediation technology, which has demonstrated being a high cost-effective process. The first step in the washing process development is the selection of the suitable surfactants and doses. In this work, twelve anionic and nonionic surfactants and their mixtures were assessed in the remediation of crude oil highly contaminated soils arising form a Mexican refinery.

2 Materials and methods

2.1 Soil

The sandy soil employed in this work was obtained form an old refinery located at North Mexico [2]. Soil was artificially contaminated with crude oil arising from *El Batab* perforation well (Campeche, Mexico). The crude-contaminated soil also was previously characterized [3]. Table 1 shows some oil-contaminated soil characteristics, regarding texture, metal contents, bulk density, porosity, and soil pH values. Note the high Ca+Mg+Mn/Na+K ratio value.

Table 1: Some oil-contaminated soil characteristics.

Parameter	Value	Unites	Parameter	Value	Unites
Porosity	0.37	-	Cd	1	mg/kg
Sand	92	%	Cr	10	mg/kg
Fines	7.9	%	Cu	23	mg/kg
Bulk density	1.82	mg/cm^3	Fe	9,085	mg/kg
pH, 1 M KCl	6.1	unites	Ni	12	mg/kg
Na	272	mg/kg	Pb	544	mg/kg
K	332	mg/kg	Zn	1,444	mg/kg
Ca	28,160	mg/kg	Na+K	605	-
Mg	996	mg/kg	Ca+Mg+Mn	29,246	-
Mn	90	mg/kg	Ca+Mg+Mn/Na+K	48.34	-

From [3]

2.2 Surfactants

Twelve commercial surfactants (nonionic and ionic, with different chemical nature, HLB and molecular weights spectrum) were assessed in the soil washing tests at 1% concentration Commercial surfactants employed along this work were, Emulgin 600, Emulgin 1000, Tween 20, Tween 60, Tween 80, Span 80, Texapon 40, Maranil lab, Brij 35, Brij 58 Brij 72 and SDS. The general properties of the surfactants are resumed at table 2. All solutions were prepared in distilled water and stored at 4°C until used. NaCl (0.5, 1, and 2%), and Na-silicate (10%) analytical grade were added in some assessments.

Table 2: Some surfactants characteristics.

Surfactant	Ionic nature	Chemical name	Mol weight (g/g mol)	HLB	CMC (mg/l)
SDS	Anionic	Sodium dodecyl sulphonate	288.4	40	400*
Texapon 40	Anionic	Sodium lauryl ether sulphate	442	NR	1,458 ***
Maranil Lab	Anionic	Sodium dodecyl-bencen sulphonate	348	NR	1,392
Emulgin 600	Non-ionic	Nonyl phenol (Poe 6)	483	11.0	45.06 **
Emulgin 1000	Non-ionic	Nonyl phenol (Poe 10)	NR	13.5	NR
Brij 35	Non-ionic	Lauric alcohol ether (Poe 23)	1,206	16.7	NR
Brij 58	Non-ionic	Stearilic alcohol ether (Poe 20)	1,122	5.6	NR
Brij 72	Non-ionic	Stearilic alcohol (Poe 2)	358	4.9	NR
Span 20	Non-ionic	Sorbitan monolaurate	214	8.6	NR
Tween 20	Non-ionic	Sorbitan monolaurate (Poe 20)	1,226	16.7	60.74 ***
Tween 60	Non-ionic	Sorbitan monostearate (Poe 20)	1,310	14.9	NR
Tween 80	Non-ionic	Sorbitan monoleate (Poe 20)	1,308	15.0	65.4**

*From this work, **from [5], ***from [6], NR, not reported.

2.3 SDS with and without NaCl-CMC measurement

Surfactant solutions were prepared with 0-2,000 mg/l of SDS in presence of 0, 0.5, 1 and 2% NaCl. Surface tensions ST were measured ten times in a Krüss automatic tensiometer (model K12). Measurements averages were plotted against surfactant concentration for every NaCl value. Deflection points, *i.e.*, where surface tension does not diminish anymore due to the increase in SDS concentration, are the CMC values for every NaCl concentration.

2.4 Soil washing efficiencies

Six grams of soil were put into 40 ml vials, and 20 ml of water, water, or a fixed concentration of a surfactant solution (with or without NaCl) was added. The assessed surfactant concentrations were 0.1, 0.5 and 1%. Assessed NaCl (JT Baker, USA) concentrations were 1, 2, and 3%. The flasks were kept at room temperature during 20 hours in reciprocating agitation. After this period, the flasks were allowed to sediment for 1 hour and samples were taken for TPH analysis. All assessments were carried out in duplicate and the average of the two tests was reported. Differences between duplicates were always less than 5%. After Soxhlet extraction, a gravimetric method was employed for TPH measurement.

3 Results and discussion

3.1 SDS CMCvalues

SDS solutions average ST values were plotted as shown in Figure 1, for every NaCl value. As mentioned in Materials and Methods section, CMC values are those where ST value did not diminish due to an augmentation in SDS concentration. CMC values for 0, 0.5, 1 and 2% NaCl resulted in values of 400, 300, 200 and 70 mg/l. For comparison the 1,586 mg/l value previously reported by Li-Zhong and Chiou [4] for CMC without any salt, was included.

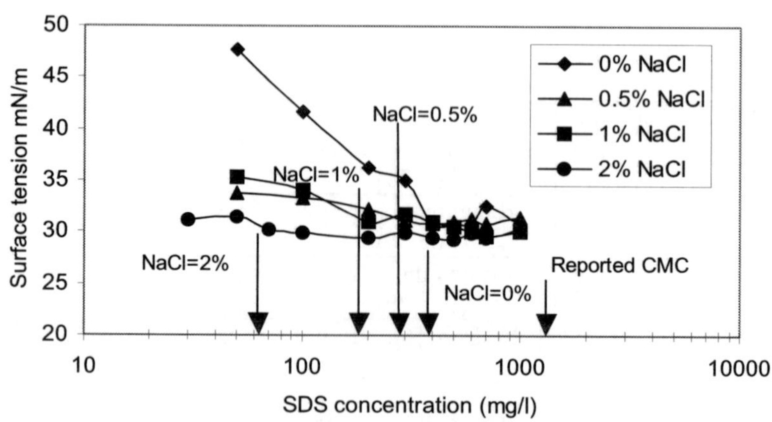

Figure 1: Surface tensions for the SDS solutions.

It is noteworthy when discussing the Na, K, Ca, Mg and Mn soil concentrations (table 1), that total monovalent cations are present in a total amount of about 600 mg/kg, while the correspondent divalent cations are present in more than 29,250 mg/kg. This value gave a Na+K/Ca+Mg+Mn of about 48. Some authors have reported the hardness tolerance of anionic surfactant solutions (*i.e.,* SDS), and underlined precipitation of these surfactants by the presence of divalent cations (Ca, Mg and Mn). It has been reported that hardness tolerance is increased by as much as a factor of 25 upon addition of 0.1M NaCl [7]. It was decide to use NaCl for enhancing the SDS performance and the SDS CMC values in the presence of 0, 0.5, 1, and 2% of NaCl was assessed. The CMC values were plotted ass a function of the NaCl concentration (%) at Figure 2. As observed they showed a lineal behaviour characterized by the equation (1):

$$CMC = 386 - 164\ [NaCl],\ \text{with}\ R^2 = 0.9859 \tag{1}$$

This trend was also observed by Stellner and Schamerhon [7], when studying precipitation of sodium dodecyl sulphonate by calcium.

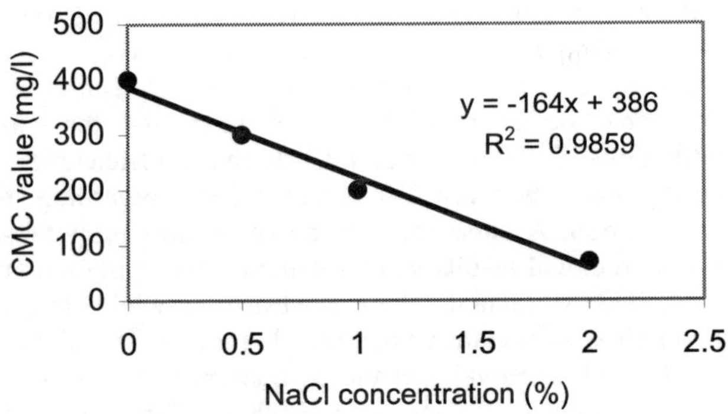

Figure 2: SDS CMC values as a function of NaCl concentration (%)

The equation found by these authors for describing that phenomenon is $\ln cmc_{DS} = -0.69832 \ln [Na^+]eq - 8.5134$, which is equivalent to results found in this work, employing a different Na concentration parameter. These authors reported that the Mg effect over the SD (the ionic SDS specie) CMC value is very similar. These values will be used in the next sections.

3.2 TPH removal values for single surfactants

The TPH removal for the blank test (water) gave a 3.52% value. Average results are reported. Standard deviations were lower than 5% of the total removals. As observed, values ranged from 0 to 32.9% for Brij 58 and Emulgin 600 (E-600), respectively. Other low TPH removal values were obtained for Brij 72, Texapon 40, and Span 20, with values of 0.4, 0.45, and 2.44%, respectively. Best results were obtained when using E-600 (32.9%), SDS (20.37), Brij 35 (16.86%), and Tween 80 (14.57%). Intermediate results were obtained when employing Emulgin 1000 (14.22%), Tween 20 (13.41%), Tween 60 (12.13%), and Maranil Lab (10.79%), see Figure 3. Note that regarding the initial TPH contaminated soil content of 108,980 mg/kg, these TPH removals correspond to high TPH values. For example, the E-600 32.9% value means that 32,905 mg TPH/kg soil was removed. The 20.37% removal achieved by SDS, means that 20,370 mg TPH/kg soil were removed. Even the lower values, means thousands of mg TPH removed per kg of soil. Torres *et al.* [5] reported the use of ethoxylated sorbitan monoleate and nonylphenol, and sodium lauryl ether sulphate for washing a soil contaminated with 20,00 mg/kg of TPH-diesel. They reached efficiencies between 41.9 and 88.2% when using doses between 0.5 and 300 x CMC for the products assessed. On the other hand, Lopez *et al.* [8] reported removal efficiencies between 16.1 and 69.4% when washing a soil contaminated with 17,200 mg/kg of PAHs and heavy petroleum fractions, using ethoxylated sorbitan monoleate, and nonylphenol, and sodium dodecyl sulphonate in concentrations between 0.1 and 1%. These authors reported the use of NaCl for SDS performance. Iturbe *et al.* [9], demonstrated that *in situ* flushing of soil contaminated with about 56,000 mg/kg of TPH (including some PAHs, gasoline, and diesel) was successful reaching a total removal of 98%. Polyethoxylated Sorbitan monoleate at a concentration of 0.5%. Finally, Iturbe *et al.* [10], reported that the same surfactant (TW80) was employed for washing soil contaminated with 3,800-17,200 mg/kg of TPH. Removal efficiencies with 0.5% surfactant solutions were between 50.3 and 92.8% regarding the initial contaminant concentration. A close look to the surfactants properties (table 1) shows that best TPH removal results were obtained when using a non-ionic (E-600) and an ionic (SDS) surfactant. There exist a trend when comparing TPH removal values and HLB surfactant values (see Figure 4). The higher the HLB value, the higher the TPH removal, but the correlation factor is not very high. Note that the highest point corresponds to E-600. Unfortunately there is no enough information for the set of surfactants regarding the CMC values. For the available values, including the CMC reported in this work, it seems that the lower the CMC value, the higher the TPH. A close look to the surfactants properties (Table 1) shows that best TPH removal results were obtained when using a non-ionic (E-600) and an ionic (SDS) surfactant. There exist a trend when comparing TPH removal values and HLB surfactant values. The higher the HLB value, the higher the TPH removal. Unfortunately there is no enough information for the set of surfactants regarding the CMC values. For the available values, it seem that the lower the CMC value, the higher the TPH removal (figure not shown). Due to the high divalent cation content of the soils (see Table 1) there is a detrimental effect over the ionic surfactants (SDS and Maranil Lab). There are different approaches to resolve this difficulty: 1) the use of NaCl, as suggested by Stellner and Scamerhon [7], 2) the use of a nonionic surfactant together with the ionic one, proposed by the previous authors and 3) the addition of divalent ions sequestrants like zeolites and phosphates (as in laundry detergents), or sodium silicate [11].

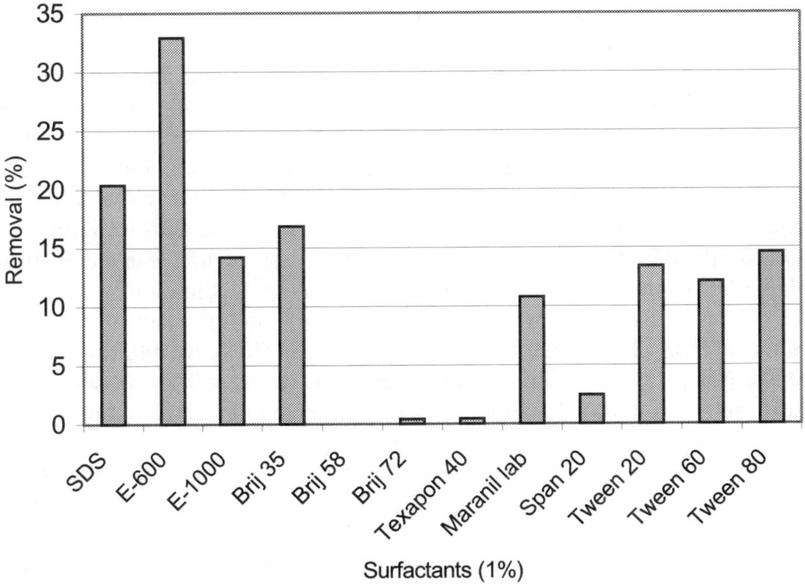

Figure 3: TPH removal values for the single surfactants assessments.

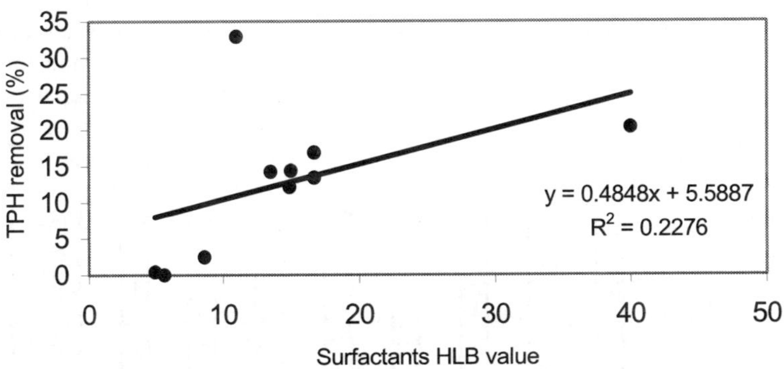

Figure 4: TPH removal (%) *versus* surfactant HLB values.

In this preliminary work, the three approaches were applied. SDS was selected between the two ionic surfactant employed because of its high initial TPH removal value. NaCl was added in amounts of 0.5, 1 and 2%. Besides, mixtures of SDS and a nonionic surfactant were assessed (always with a total surfactant concentration of 1%), *i.e.* SDS+ E-600, SDS+ TW80, SDS+ Brij35, and SDS+E1000. Sodium metasilicate analytic grade was employed as Ca sequestrants in a 10% concentration. Figure 5 shows the results of these assessments. It s remarkable that surfactant-surfactant and surfactant+salt assessments gave TPH removal efficiencies between 20 and 30%. In none of the assessments, TPH removal values higher than that found with E-600 at 1% was achieved. The addition of NaCl gave an increase in the TPH removal efficiency values of 21.97, 26.03 and 23.85% (for 0.5, 1 and 2% NaCl) in comparison with no salt (20.37%) assessments, since NaCl increases the SDS hardness tolerance and diminish the CMC value. This means 1.6, 5.66 and 3.48% of TPH removal enhancement due to NaCl addition. It seems that best choice is to add 1% NaCl addition. In the other hand, addition of 10% of Na-Silicate yielded in a TPH removal of 21.9%, in comparison with the SDS 1%, where 10.37% removal was achieved. At this point, results form the previous section can be helpful to explain this behaviour. Addition of NaCl promotes a diminution in the SDS CMC value. This effect was described before. An addition of 0.5% NaCl diminished SDS-CMC value from 400 to 300 mg/l (50%). An additional addition of 0.5% (up to 1%) yielded a CMC diminution from 300 to 200 mg/l (33%). Finally, an addition of a 1% more (up to 2%) yielded in a CMC value of 70 mg/l (a diminution of 65%). Since Na-silicate has been reported as a Ca sequestrants [11], but at the same time provides the Na^+ ion, both mechanisms *i.e.,* augmentation of SDS hardness tolerance and sequestration of Ca^{++} ions, are responsible by the enhancement in TPH removal. Regarding the SDS-nonionic assessments, it can be observed that all the combinations yielded TPH removal values higher than that found for SDS alone (all mixtures were prepared with a total of 1% surfactant, half and half). Differences were not quite enough high, but best results were obtained with the combination SDS+E-600. This fact is quite expectable, since both surfactants separately gave the best TPH removals. At this point it is important to remark the need of further experiments employing different surfactant doses (lower doses), and surfactant-surfactant proportions.

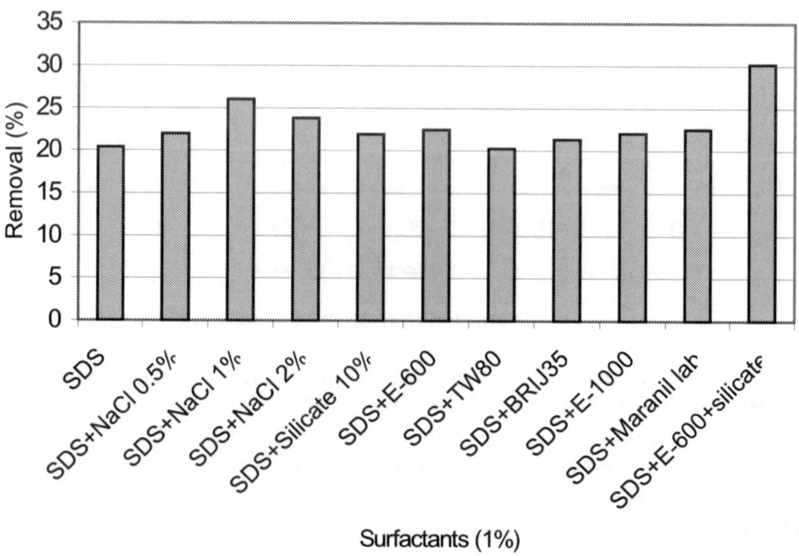

Figure 5: TPH removal values (%) for the mixed surfactant assessments.

The mixture SDS+Maranil lab is the only one anionic-anionic combination. It yielded a TPH removal of 22.57% higher than that obtained with only Maranil lab (10.79%) and SDS alone (20.37%), which indicates the existence of surfactants synergism. It is noteworthy that both products are very similar (dodecyl sulphonateand dodecyl-bencen sulphonate), except for the inclusion of the aromatic group.

At the end, the combination SDS-E1000+ Na-silicate yielded the best TPH removal value, *i.e.* 30.2%. It seems that Na-silicate augmented in a 7.7% the SDS+E-600 mixture performance (22.5%). It is very desirable to continue this work, employing different total surfactant doses and surfactant/surfactant/salt proportions. Since Na-silicate dose will impact the total washing process cost, it is necessary to evaluate the minimum amount required for the TPH removal enhancing.

4 Conclusions

Main conclusions of this work are the following:

1) It is possible to treat soils highly contaminated with crude oil (*c.a.* 109,000 mg/kg as TPH) employing surfactant-enhanced soils washing.
2) When washing with single surfactants (1%), best results were obtained with SDS, Brij 35 and E-600 (20.4, 16.8 and 32.9%, respectively).
3) Addition of NaCl to SDS solutions change the value of CMC, decreasing in a lineal proportion to the salt concentration in accord to the equation CMC = 386 – 164 [NaCl], with $R^2 = 0.9859$.
4) Mixtures of SDS+NaCl, SDS+nonionic surfactants and SDS-anionic surfactant (SDBS) gave better TPH removal rates that only SDS (for total surfactant concentrations of 1%). Best values were observed for SDS+NaCl 1% (26%), SDS+E-600 (22.5%), and SDS+Maranil lab (22.6%).
5) The mixture SDS+E-600+Na-silicate 10% gave the best TPH rate for the mixtures assessments, *i.e.* 30.2%.
6) These results are very promising, but more experimental work is necessary in order to optimise the surfactant and salt concentrations, and best TPH removal rate can be achieved with lower total surfactant and salts amounts.

Besides the surfactant and salts doses optimisation, evaluation of metal removals (Cu, Fe, Ni, Pb and Zn) is in progress.

Acknowledgements

Authors thank the technical support of Mr. G. Anaya (Facultad de Quimica/UNAM) in the measurement of surfactants surface tension and L. Fernandez (IMP) for the crude samples.

References

[1] PEMEX (2002). Annual technical report: www.PEMEX.com.mx

[2] Iturbe R,. Flores R.M, Flores C. and Torres L.G. TPH-contaminated Mexican-refinery soil: Health risk assessment and the first year of changes: Environmental Monitoring and Assessment. 2004. 91:237-255.

[3] Torres L.G., G. Urquiza, and Iturbe R. Characterization of soils contaminated with light, medium and heavy Mexican crude oils. Proceedings of the 1IMEBE Congress. Mexico City, Mexico. September 6-8, 2004.

[4] Li-Zhong Z and Chiou C.T. Water enhancements of pyrene solubility by single and mixed surfactant solutions. Journal of Environmental Sciences. 2001. 13(4):491-496.

[5] Torres L.G, Orantes J L and Iturbe R. Critical micellar concentrations for three surfactants and their diesel removal efficiencies in petroleum contaminated soils. Environmental Geosciences. 2003 10(1): 28-36.

[6] Krebs-Yuill B, Harwell JH, Sabatini DA, Quinton GE and Shoemaker SH. Economic study of surfactant-enhanced pump-and-treat remediation. WEFTEC 69th Annual Conference. October 5-9, 1996. Dallas, Texas, USA.

[7] Stellner KL and Scamerhorn JK. Hardness tolerance of anionic surfactant solutions. 2. Effect of added nonionic surfactant. Langmuir 1989. 5: 77-84.

[8] Lopez J, Torres LG and Iturbe R. Washing of soil contaminated with PAHs and heavy petroleum fractions using two anionic and one ionic surfactant: effect of salt addition. Journal of environmental Science and Health.Part A. 2004. Submitted.

[9] Iturbe R, Flores C, Chavez C, Ramírez A, and. Torres L.G. *In situ* flushing of petroleum hydrocarbon contaminated soils from a refinery: Laboratory and field assessments. Remediation Journal. Spring 2004: 141-151.

[10] Iturbe R, Flores C, Chavez C, Bautista G, and. Torres L.G. Remediation of contaminated oil using soil washing and biopile methodologies. Journal of Soils and Sediments. 2004. Published online DOI http://dx.doi.org/10.1065/jss2004.04.099

[11] De Lucas A, Rodriguez L, Sanchez P and Lobato J. Retention capacity of the builder δ–-$Na_2Si_2O_5$. Modelling the $Ca^{2+}/Mg^{2+}/Na^{+}$ equilibrium. J. Ind. Eng. Chem. Res. 2003.42:3257-3262.

Section 15
Remote sensing

Analysis of rapid land-use/land-cover change in North-eastern China using Landsat TM/ETM+ data

K. Okamoto[1], J. Shindo[1] & H. Kawashima[2]
[1]*National Institute for Agro-Environmental Sciences, Japan*
[2]*Graduate School of Agricultural and Life Sciences, University of Tokyo, Japan*

Abstract

The self-sufficiency of rice in China with the largest population in the world is 100% and Chinese people tend to prefer quality to quantity. The area of paddy field in the northeastern part of China has increased because the climatic conditions in this region are suitable for cultivating *Japonica* rice (short-grain rice). Large quantities of irrigation water are consumed for cultivating rice. Rainfed rice cropping is possible in places with sufficient precipitation, while rice cropping in regions with low precipitation is limited in places near sources of irrigation. Flatlands are advantageous to rice cropping because of their geographical and social conditions. The eastern Heilongjiang Province, China was selected as the test area. Land use/land cover was classified using the Landsat Thematic Mapper (TM) data of 1988 and the Enhanced Thematic Mapper Plus (ETM+) data of 2002. According to the statistics of the Heilongjiang Province, the area of paddy field has increased rapidly since 1995. Based on the 1988 land-use/land-cover classification map, places suitable for rice cropping were determined and compared with the distribution of paddy fields in 2002. Most of the paddy fields for 2002 were converted from dry arable land for 1988. Places suitable for rice cropping are places with easy access to water for irrigation.
Keywords: climatic impact, Landsat TM/ETM+, land-use/land-cover change, North-eastern China, paddy field, producer price, socioeconomic impact.

1 Introduction

The self-sufficiency of rice in Asian countries has reached nearly 100%. The self-sufficiency of rice in China with the largest population in the world is 100% and Chinese people tend to prefer quality (eating delicious rice) to quantity (eating heartily). Therefore, the production of good-tasting *Japonica* rice (short-grain rice) has increased compared with that of *Indica* rice (long-grain rice). The area of paddy field in the northeastern part of China, where the climatic conditions are suitable for cultivating *Japonica* rice, has increased. Heilongjiang is now a major granary in China. This province produces about 560 million metric tons *Japonica* rice per year, according to estimates from the statistics of FAO [1] and USDA [5]. The area of paddy field in Heilongjiang has increased from 2.2 x 10^3 km^2 to 16.5 x 10^3 km^2 (7.5 times) in the past 20 years, fig. 1. Large quantities of irrigation water are consumed for cultivating rice. Hydrological conditions change according to changes in water use in agriculture. Moreover, a paddy field is a source of methane which is one of greenhouse effect gases, [2]. It is also considered that a sharp change in land use/land cover and a rapid increase in the area of paddy field must negatively affect the ecosystems and environment.

In this study, part of Heilongjiang, China was selected as the test area and the satellite data acquired on different dates were analyzed. Changes in the area of paddy field were examined, and the geographical and social conditions of a location to be converted from dry cropland to paddy field were discussed.

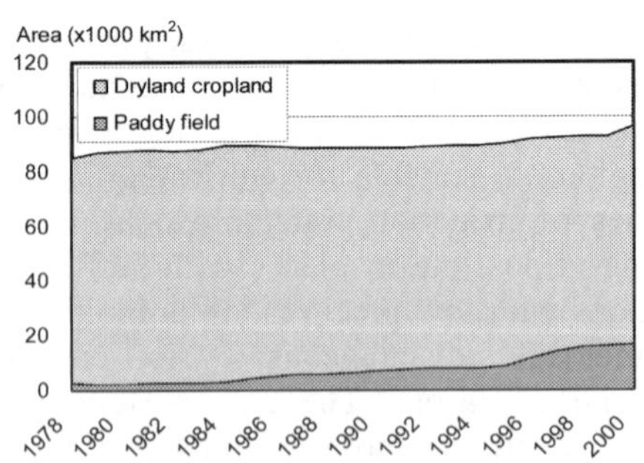

Figure 1: Changes in areas of paddy field and dry cropland in Heilongjiang, China.

2 Data and method

2.1 Test area

The land-use/land-cover change in the north-eastern part of China was analyzed using multitemporal Landsat data. The agricultural region (131° 35'-134° 33' E, 46° 29'-48° 24' N), which extends to the eastern Sanjiang Plain, Heilongjiang, China, and includes Fujin City, Tongjiang City, Fuyuan Prefecture and Raohe Prefecture, was selected as the test area, fig. 2. The Heilong Jiang (the River

Amur) flows north of this area, the Songhua Jiang flows west of this area into the Heilong Jiang, and the Wusuli Jiang flows east of this area. This area has 550-600 mm of annual precipitation and is located in a continental monsoon climatic zone. The highest temperature in summer reaches 22-27 °C.

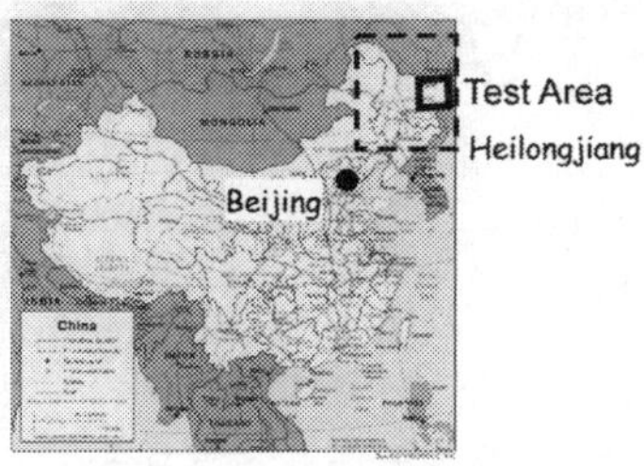

Figure 2: Test area: Eastern Sanjiang Plain, Heilongjiang Prov., China (Map is cited from UT Library Online [6] and is modified).

2.2 Data

The Landsat Thematic Mapper (TM) data acquired on 25th June 1988 and the Landsat Enhanced Thematic Mapper Plus (ETM+) data acquired on 24th June 2002 (Path-Row=114-27) were used for the land-use/land-cover classification. In the test area, rice seedlings are transplanted simultaneously within a short period from the end of May to the beginning of June. At the end of June, the rice plants are still small and the paddy fields are submerged. At this time, the crops planted on dry croplands are also small and the soil surfaces are exposed.

The 0.5-degree grid cell data of monthly mean air temperature from 1901 to 2000, [3], were used to examine the change in cumulative temperature for the rice-cropping season from June to September. The 1978-2000 statistics of the areas of paddy field and dry cropland derived from the yearbook of Heilongjiang, China, were used to examine the change in what area. The 1991-2001 statistics of the producer prices of rice, wheat and maize in China, [1], were used to analyze the impact of the change in the cultivated crop.

2.3 Method

The Landsat TM data acquired on 25th June 1988 and ETM+ data acquired on 24th June 2002 were given geographical coordinates using the Lambert Azimuthal Equal area projection (origin=110° E, 45° N), the spheroid WGS84 and the pixel size 30 m by 30 m. The TM/ETM+ data with bands 3 (red), 4 (near infrared), and 5 (middle infrared), in which the middle-infrared band was used in distinguishing submerged paddy fields, [4], were prepared for the land-use/land-cover classification. These data were classified by the unsupervised method ISODATA, in which 30 initial classes, 2σ class radius, and 98% convergence limit were used as parameters. The portions of misclassification in the land-cover maps for 1988 and 2002 were corrected by viewing interpretations of composite images, in which bands 5, 4 and 3 of TM/ETM+ data are shown in blue, green and red, respectively. Land-cover classes were reclassified into 12 classes, i.e., paddy field submerged, paddy field overgrown, bare dry cropland, dry cropland overgrown, bare ground, grassland, woodland, wetland, water, built-up, shade and shadow, and clouds.

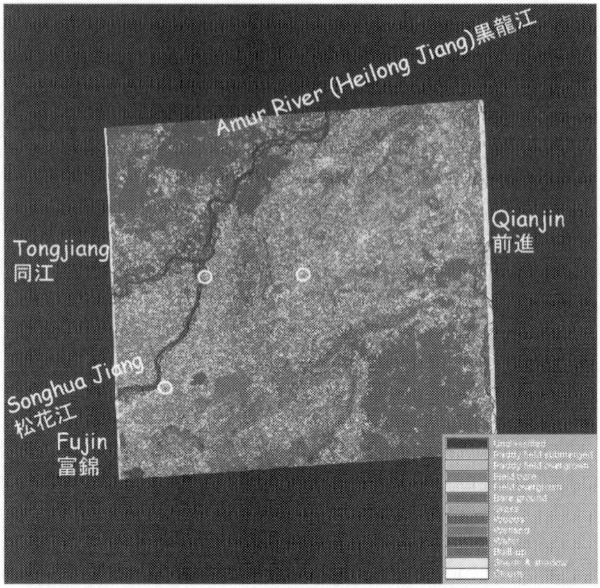

(a)

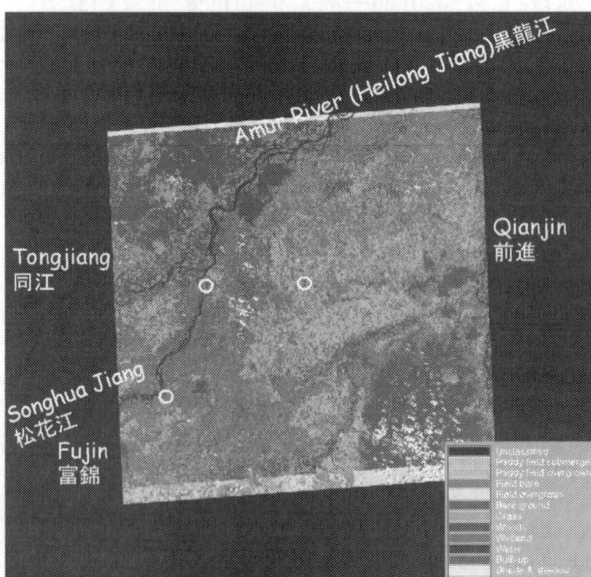

(b)

Figure 3: Land-use/land-cover maps; (a) 25 June 1988 and (b) 24 June 2002.

The land-use/land-cover changes between 1988 and 2002 were examined by overlapping the1988 and 2002 land-cover maps. Five-hundred- and 1,000-meter buffers around a water source were defined as the water availability for irrigation. Areas within 500 and 500-1,000 meters of water, which included classes of paddy field, wetland and water, were extracted. The land-use/land-cover changes between 1988 and 2002 were examined in terms of the distance to water.

Table 1: Areas of land-use/land-cover in 1988 and 2002.

(a) Changes in areas of land use/land cover between 1988 and 2002.

2002 \ 1988	C 1	C 3	C 4	C 6	C 7	C 8	C 9	Total
C 1: Paddy Field Submerged	97	1740	783	509	485	281	30	3925
C 3: Bare Dry Cropland	26	2565	1812	1480	1702	1304	98	8988
C 4: Dry Cropland Overgrown	0	0	0	0	0	0	0	0
C 5: Bare Ground	17	588	547	372	365	492	104	2485
C 6: Grassland	17	902	1540	2079	51	1097	155	5847
C 7: Woodland	0	0	0	0	7600	0	0	7600
C 8: Wetland	0	0	0	1	2	9	8	21
C 9: Water	4	0	0	0	41	0	580	626
C 10: Built-up	2	219	273	58	96	32	22	701
Total	166	6063	5002	4556	10718	3260	1014	81316

(b) Changes in areas of land use/land cover between 1988 and 2002 in terms of distance to water.

2002 \ 1988	C 1	C 3	C 4	C 6	C 7	C 8	C 9	C13	C14	C15	C16	Total
C 1	97	48	18	16	84	279	30	11	2	2650	690	3925
C 3	26	631	436	421	538	1293	98	285	91	2871	2298	8988
C 4	0	0	0	0	0	0	0	0	0	0	0	0
C 5	17	71	66	60	132	481	104	28	22	1057	448	2485
C 6	17	285	315	380	50	1014	155	0	269	2288	1066	5847
C 7	0	0	0	0	5436	0	0	454	112	1152	446	7600
C 8	0	0	0	0	1	8	8	0	1	3	0	21
C 9	4	0	0	0	14	0	580	0	0	27	1	626
C10	2	34	39	8	22	31	22	9	4	359	170	701
Total	166	1075	881	891	6601	3149	1014	793	509	10539	5164	81316

The classes "C2: paddy field overgrown" for 1988 and 2002, and "C5: bare ground" and"C10: built-up" for 1988 are 0 km^2 and thus are omitted. The class "C13" denotes isolated woodland, "C14" isolated dry cropland, grassland, bare ground and wetlands, "C15" regions within 500 meters to water, and "C16" regions within 500-1000 meters to water.

3 Results and discussion

3.1 Land-use/land-cover change

According to the statistics of Heilongjiang, the area of paddy field increased rapidly in both mid-1980s and mid-1990s, fig. 1. The land-use/land-cover maps are shown in fig. 3. According to the result from a comparison of the 2002 land-use/land-cover map with the 1988 one, the area of paddy field in the test area increased from 166 km^2 for 1988 to 3,925 km^2 for 2002, namely, it increased 23.6-fold, table 1(a), fig. 4. The area of dry cropland in the test area decreased from 11,065 km^2 for 1988 to 8,988 km^2 for 2002, namely, it decreased by 19%. However, the total area of arable land, which included paddy field and dry cropland, increased from 11,231 km^2 for 1988 to 12,913 km^2 for 2002. On the other hand, the area of wetland decreased from 3,260 km^2 for 1988 to 21 km^2 for 2002. The total area of woodland and grassland decreased from 15,274 km^2 for 1988 to 13,447 km^2 for 2002. Of the 3,925 km^2 of paddy field for 2002, 96.5 km^2 was also paddy field for 1988, but 2,523 km^2 was dry cropland for 1988, 509 km^2 grassland, 485 km^2 woodland, and 281 km^2 wetland. It was assumed that wetland had been easily converted to paddy field because of its proximity to rivers. However, only 9% of wetland in 1988 had been converted to paddy field in 2002, while 40% of wetland in 1988 had been converted to dry cropland in 2002. That is, the area converted from wetland to paddy field was smaller than that from wetland to dry cropland.

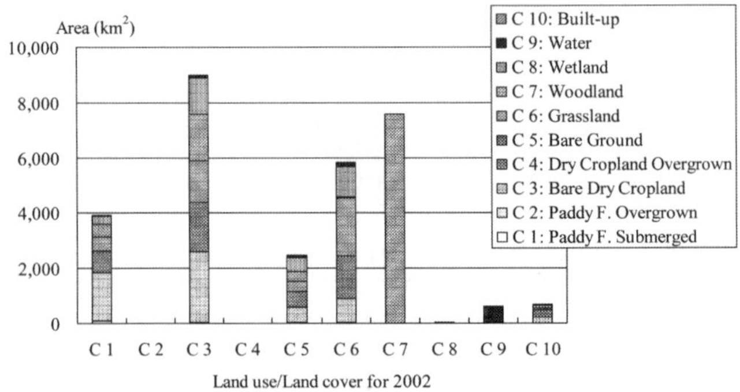

Figure 4: Changes in land-use/land-cover from 1988 to 2002.

The area of dry cropland, grassland and bare ground within 500 meters of a water source was 10,539 km^2 and that within 500-1,000 meters of a water source was 5,164 km^2, table 1(b), fig. 5. For 2002, 2,650 km^2 of paddy field was located within 500 meters of a water source, while 690 km^2 of paddy field was located within 500-1,000 meters of a water source.

These results suggest that most of the wetland in 1988 was reclaimed and converted to dry cropland in 2002, while part of the reclaimed wetland was converted to paddy field. It is possible that a sharp increase in the area of paddy field between 1988 and 2002 resulted from the conversion of dry cropland, which was favorably situated within easy access to the water, to paddy field.

The Landsat TM/ETM+ data, which were used in this study, for 1988 and 2002 were acquired on 25th June and 24th June, respectively. As Heilongjiang is a granary of spring wheat and maize, it was concluded that the land-cover class "dry cropland overgrown" was cultivated with spring wheat and the land-cover class "bare dry cropland" was cultivated with maize, referring to a cropping calendar. According to the land-use/land-cover maps, the area of bare dry cropland was 6,063 km^2 and that of dry cropland overgrown was 5,002 km^2 in 1988, while the area of bare dry cropland was 8,988 km^2 and that of dry cropland overgrown was 0 km^2 in 2002, table 1(a). These results suggest that farmers, who cultivated spring wheat in those croplands, stopped wheat cropping and converted their cropland from dry cropland to paddy field.

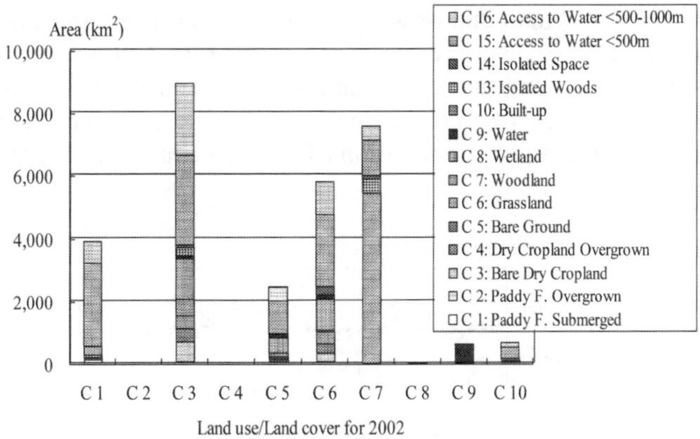

Figure 5: Changes in land-use/land-cover from 1988 to 2002 in terms of distance to water: Class "C14: isolated space" is a class of isolated dry cropland, grassland, bare ground and wetland.

3.2 Climatic impact and probable socioeconomic impact on land-use change

Temperature and precipitation are enumerated as natural factors that have an impact on cereal cropping. The cumulative temperatures of the rice-cropping season (June through September) in 1901-2000 are shown in fig. 6. All the cumulative temperatures at Harbin City, Jiamusi City and Qianjin Prefecture were just above the lower limit for cultivating *Japonica* rice and were nearly constant through the 21st century. On the other hand, the test area has geographically low and flat features. The level of groundwater is high and cropland in the test area is favorably situated within easy access to water. Consequently, it is surmised that climatic conditions, such as temperature and water, did not probably cause a sharp increase in the area of paddy field.

The producer price and consumer price related to cereal demand are enumerated as socioeconomic factors that have an impact on cereal cropping and land-use change. According to the statistics of Heilongjiang, the area of paddy field increased rapidly in both mid-1980s and mid-1990s, fig. 7. In particular, the area of paddy field in the middle of the 1990s increased markedly. The producer prices of rice, wheat and maize in China from 1991 to2001 are also shown in fig. 6. These 3 producer prices are not corrected according to inflation. A sharp increase in the area of paddy field from 1996 to 1998 followed a sudden increase in producer price. In 1994, the Chinese Government increased the purchase price of cereals by 40%, [7]. The prices shown in fig. 7 are the mean producer prices in China. The producer price of rice produced in Heilongjiang is higher than that of rice produced in other provinces because the price of *Japonica* rice produced in Heilongjiang is higher than that of *Indica* rice produced in southern provinces. The producer price of wheat produced in Heilongjiang is lower than that of wheat produced in other provinces because the quality of wheat produced in Heilongjiang is worse than that of wheat produced in other provinces. Therefore, the difference between the producer prices of rice and wheat produced in Heilongjiang is larger than that shown in fig. 7. Consequently, it is probable that the high producer price of rice, comparing with the producer prices of other cereals, is one of the strong motivations for converting dry cropland to paddy field.

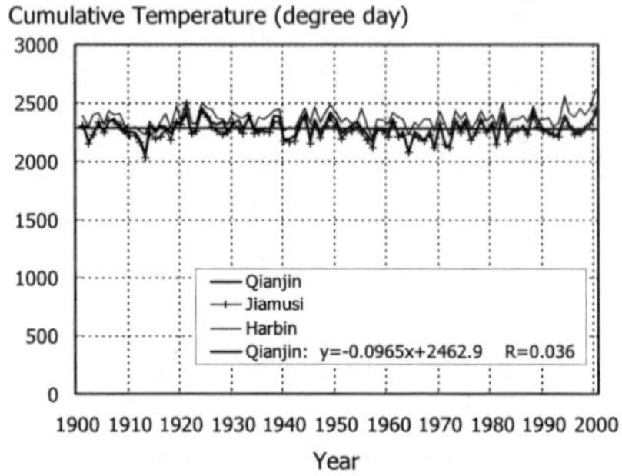

Figure 6: Cumulative temperature in Heilongjiang from 1901 to 2000.

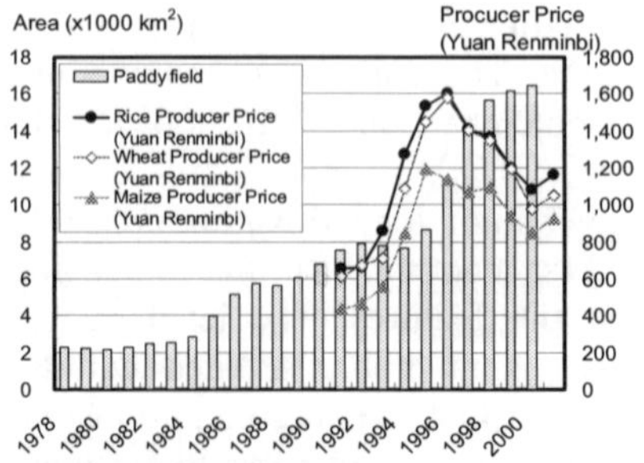

Figure 7: Changes in area of paddy field in Heilongjiang and producer prices of rice, wheat and maize in China.

4 Conclusions

The Landsat TM/ETM+ data collected over the northeastern part of Heilongjiang, acquired in 1988 and 2002, were classified and changes in the area of paddy field were examined. The area of paddy field increased from 166 km^2 for 1988 to 3,925 km^2 for 2002. The total area of arable land, which included paddy field and dry cropland, increased from 11,231 km^2 for 1988 to 12,913 km^2 for 2002. On the other hand, the area of wetland decreased from 3,260 km^2 for 1988 to 21 km^2 for 2002. Of 3,925 km^2 of the paddy field for 2002, 2,523 km^2 was dry cropland for 1988. It was assumed that wetland had been easily converted to paddy field because of its proximity to rivers. However, most of the wetland in 1988 was reclaimed and converted to dry cropland in 2002. It is possible that a sharp increase in the area of paddy field between 1988 and 2002 resulted from the conversion of dry cropland, which was favorably situated within easy access to water, to paddy field.

The cumulative temperatures of the rice-cropping season in 1901-2000 were just above the lower limit for cultivating *Japonica* rice and were nearly constant through the 21st century. Consequently, the temperature did not probably cause a sharp increase in the area of paddy field.

A sharp increase in the area of paddy field from 1996 to 1998 followed a sudden increase in producer prices. In 1994, the Chinese Government increased the purchase price of cereals by 40%. It is probable that the high producer price of rice, compared with the producer prices of other cereals, is one of the strong motivations for converting dry cropland to paddy field.

Hydrological conditions change according to changes in water use in agriculture. It is also considered that the sharp change in hydrogical conditions and land-use/land-cover negatively affects the ecosystems and environment.

References

[1] FAO (The Food and Agriculture Organization), FAOSTAT Home Page. apps.fao.org/, (Rome: FAO of the United Nations), 2004.

[2] IPCC (Intergovernmental Panel on Climate Change), *Climate Change 1995: The Science of Climate Change, edited by J. T. Houghton, L. G. Meira Filho, B. A. Callander, N. Harris, A. Kattenberg, & K. Maskell*, (Cambridge: Cambridge University Press), 1996.

[3] Mitchell, T. D., et al., A comprehensive set of climate scenarios for Europe and the globe, 2003 (in preparation).

[4] Okamoto, K., & Fukuhara, M., Estimation of paddy field area using the area ratio of categories in each mixel of Landsat TM. *International Journal of Remote Sensing*, **17**(9), pp. 1735-1750, 1996.

[5] USDA (United States Department of Agriculture), Chinese Rice Production. www.usda.gov/oce/waob/jawf/profiles/html/chi/chiric.html, (Washington: USDA), 1999.

[6] UT (University of Texas) Library Online, Perry-Castañeda Library Map Collection. www.lib.utexas.edu/maps/, (Austin: University of Texas), 2001.

[7] Chien, X., Personal communication, 22 November 2004, Researcher, Japan International Research Center for Agricultural Sciences, Tsukuba, Japan.

Space technology contribution for sustainable development in the Amazon floodplain

E. M. L. de Moraes Novo, J. L. Stech & C. C. F. Barbosa
Coordenação de Observação da Terra,
Instituto Nacional de Pesquisas Espaciais, Brazil

Abstract

This paper reports the results of using space technology, namely remote sensing and data collection platforms, to gather information on spatial and temporal variability in the Amazon Floodplain environment. Recent government policies caused an increased search for new frontiers for soybean plantations. To assess the impact of those new developments into the Amazon floodplain, since 2002 a project has been carried out in a floodplain lake, Curuai Lake, set near Santarém, Pará State. The first step in the project was to use a series of Landsat-TM images to seasonally monitor water exchanges of the Terra Firme Rivers and Amazon River and the floodplain lakes. Based on this study a suitable site was selected to install an automatic monitoring system, which allows for quasi-continuous in situ measurements of a pool of atmospheric and aquatic variables. The collected data is sent through a satellite link to researchers. These data are submitted to a series of analyses and stored in a database. As the program continues, there will be base line information against which environmental impacts can be checked and enforcement undertaken to guarantee a sustainable development for the region.
Keywords: space technology, remote sensing, automatic environmental monitoring system.

1 Introduction

The Amazon basin is the largest on Earth and is characterized by a dense drainage flowing into the Solimões/Amazon River (Amazon River). The Amazon River and its tributaries drain an area of around 7 million km^2 that receives an average annual precipitation of 2500 mm [1]. On the slopes of the Andes the precipitation can reach 5000 per year, whereas in the northern and southern borders it can drop to 1 500 mm [2]. Amazon River is around 6700 km long and has a very complex hydrology including inputs from snow melting from Andes as well intense tide effects at his mouth in the Atlantic Ocean. The ecological features of these floodplains are largely determined by the spatial and temporal variation of the inundation pattern, which in turn is determined by climatic variability. According to Richey et al, [3] oscillations in the Amazon hydrograph are coupled to the tropical Pacific climate cycle.

The Amazon basin, however, has been subjected to intense land cover changes since the 60´s of the twentieth century. Forest conversion to pasture in the 70´s and 80´s was responsible for an annual rate of deforestation around 20 000 km^2. At present the deforested area reached around 270,758 km^2 as the result of public policies to economically integrate the Amazon to the remaining country [4].

Recent policies are fostering the conversion of degraded pastureland into soybean plantation [5, 6]. The process of agricultural development in Santarém contributes to widespread smallholder displacement, illegal deforestation, water contamination and regional land-use change from smallholder farming to mechanized agriculture. Additionally, the political-economic framework supporting mechanized agriculture favors historically large landowners and incoming soybean farmers; promotes a process of development that excludes smallholder agriculture; and heightens smallholders' socio-economic insecurities. Agrochemicals used to combat diseases; insects and weeds in soybean cultivation can have impacts on the environment, particularly in the Santarém region at the Tapajós River and the Amazon River junction. In this area there are large floodplain lake systems, which during the low Amazon water level are fed partially by overland flow from the Terra Firme region around Santarém and partially by the Tapajós water. Those water sources to the floodplain lakes up to know are responsible for improving the light environment and keeping the phytoplankton productivity. It is expected that with soybean occupation, the runoff of chemical will disrupt the natural balance of the floodplain and affect fishery as well as population health.

So, it is expected large water quality changes in lake as soybean plantation increases. In order to monitor this impact and document those changes, however, it is mandatory to set up a long-term-high-frequency water quality monitoring system. Long term environmental time series of continuously collected data are fundamental to perform the identification and classification of pulses and determine its role in the aquatic systems. Boundary condition variables for the functioning of aquatic systems [7] such as climatic (e.g., temperature and wind), hydrological (e.g., outflow) needs also to be monitored. On the other hand it is also important to have a data base of land cover changes in the floodplain region. In this respect, the remote sensing data analyses enables the monitoring of annual changes in land cover which can be related to water quality changes. The objective of this paper is to present preliminary results of a research project carried out to monitor limnological variables at Curuai Lake using space technology tools.

2 Materials and methods

2.1 Study area

The study area is comprised by a set of lakes which at the high water coalesce into the locally known Lago Grande de Curuai. It is located along the Amazon River, 900 km upstream from the river mouth at the Atlantic Ocean (Figure 1). The lake functioning is highly modulated by the Amazon water level fluctuation at Óbidos.

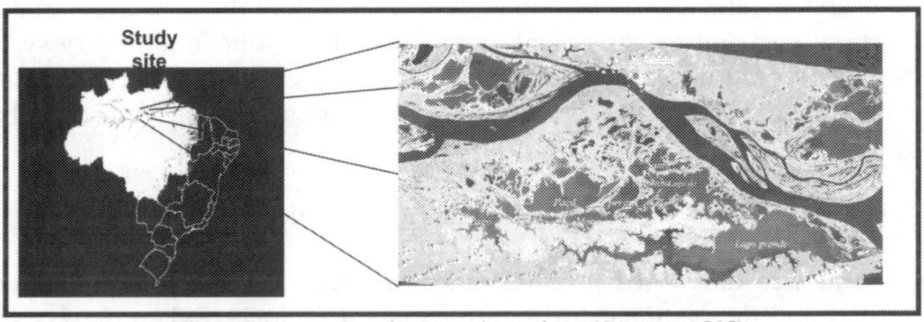

Figure 1: Study area location (Source: [8]).

Table 1: Limnological variables measured at Curuai Lake at 4 different Amazon River stage: rising water, high water, falling water and low water level.

Variable	Measurement method
Chlorophyll concentration	Nush [10]
Dissolved Organic Carbon	APHA [11]
Dissolved Inorganic Carbon	APHA [11]
Total Suspended Matter	Wetzel & Likens [12]
Total Suspend Inorganic Matter	Wetzel & Likens [12]
Total Suspended Organic Matter	Wetzel & Likens [12]
Turbidity	Horiba Water Quality Checker U-10 (HWQC U-10)
Dissolved Oxygen	(HWQC U-10)
pH	(HWQC U-10)
Conductivity	(HWQC U-10)
Temperature	(HWQC U-10)
Secch Depth	Secch Disk
Lake Depth	Ecosounder

2.2 Procedures

The first step in setting up an automatic monitoring system in the region was to determine which water quality changes were naturally induced by the functioning of the system. For that, a research was carried out in the lake [8] in order to study the water quality changes in response to water level fluctuation. Limnological data were collected in four water level stages in 70 different sampling stations (Table 1). The second step was to identify a site at the lake which would not dry during the low water period and would probe water quality changes related to land use. The selected site to place the Automatic Environmental Monitoring System (SIMA) was defined using a set o multi-date Landsat-TM images acquired in different Amazon River level. The method is described in [9]. The third step was to define the final SIMA configuration including monitoring frequency needed to uncover changes beyond the system baseline and parameters to be monitored. Those definitions were a trade-off between the cost and technological maturity of the available telemetry systems and the monitoring needs. The sensors to be used were also defined in terms of need of maintenance, calibration as well robustness to cope with very harsh environmental conditions.

2.3 The integrated system for environmental monitoring (SIMA)

The system was developed in cooperation between Paraíba Valley University (UNIVAP) and the National Institute of Space Research (INPE). It is a set of hardware and software projected for data acquisition and real time monitoring of hydrological systems [13]. The system comprises independent subsystems: an anchored buoy, a payload rack to support the sensors, the data storage subsystem, a transmission antenna and a solar panel. All the subsystems are fixed in the buoy as seen in Figure 2.

Figure 2: Configuration of the SIMA placed at Curuai Lake.

The data are collected in preprogrammed time interval and are transmitted by satellite in quasi-real time for any user in a range of 2500 km from the acquisition point. Table 2 shows the parameters measured by the system. The data have been continuously transmitted to the National Institute of Space Research, where they are continuously submitted to quality control and storage in a numerical database since April 2004.

Table 2: Environmental parameters measured by the system.

Limnological	Climatic
Chlorophyll-a	Incoming Solar Radiation
Water Temperature (4 depths	Reflected Solar Radiation
pH	Wind Direction and Intensity
Turbidity	Atmospheric Pressure
Dissolved O2 Concentration	Relative Humidity
Electric Conductivity	Air Temperature

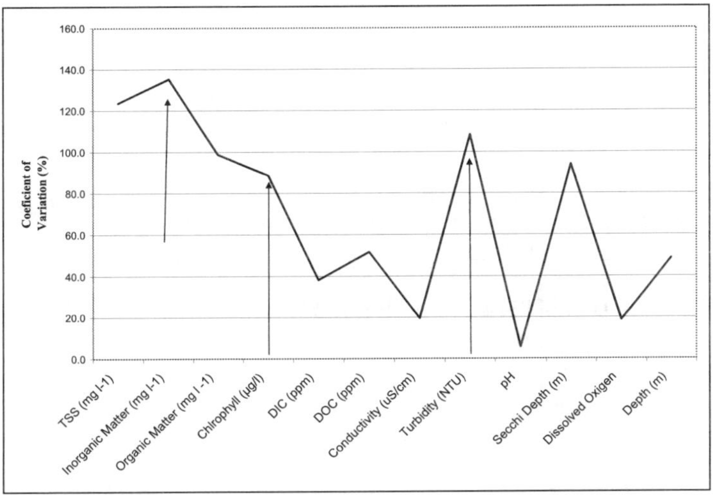

Figure 3: Coefficient of variation of the various limnological variables measured in four Amazon River stages at Curuaí Lake.

3 Preliminary results

3.1. Natural changes in water quality

Figure 3 shows the coefficient of variation (%) of the limnological variables measured during the four ground missions at Curuai Lake. It can be observed that they present huge time variability mainly those responding directly to the Amazon flood pulse. Chemical variables, however, such as conductivity, dissolved oxygen and pH are less affected by seasonal variation, presenting a more conservative behavior. Those variables, however, can be affected by local changes. The assessment of those local changes can only be carried out by continuous monitoring since they respond to factors such as local precipitation, winds and human action (land use conversion).

Figure 4 shows the short term variability of the Chlorophyll concentration measured by the SIMA. The time change in concentration is very large. Daily changes in Chlorophyll concentration are very large and are not captured at seasonal scale. Figure 5 shows the short term variability of pH which is also large and not detected at seasonal scale.

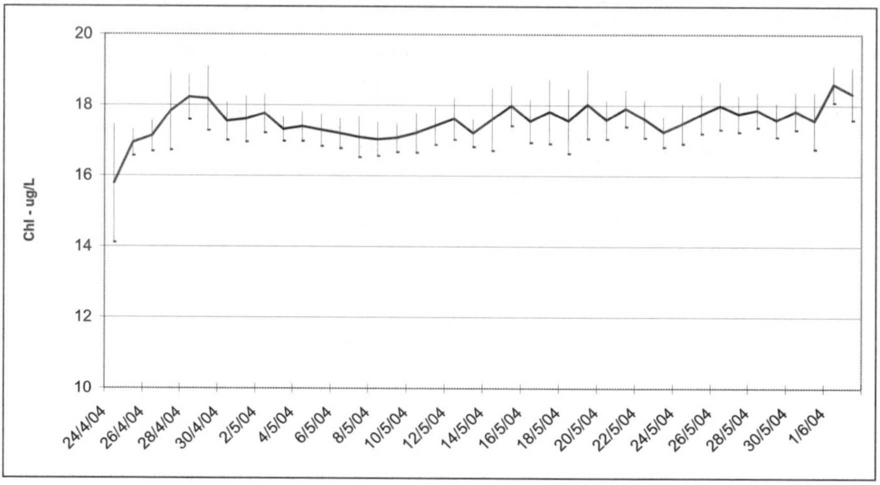

Figure 4: Daily changes in Chlorophyll concentration at Curuai Lake, measured by SIMA.

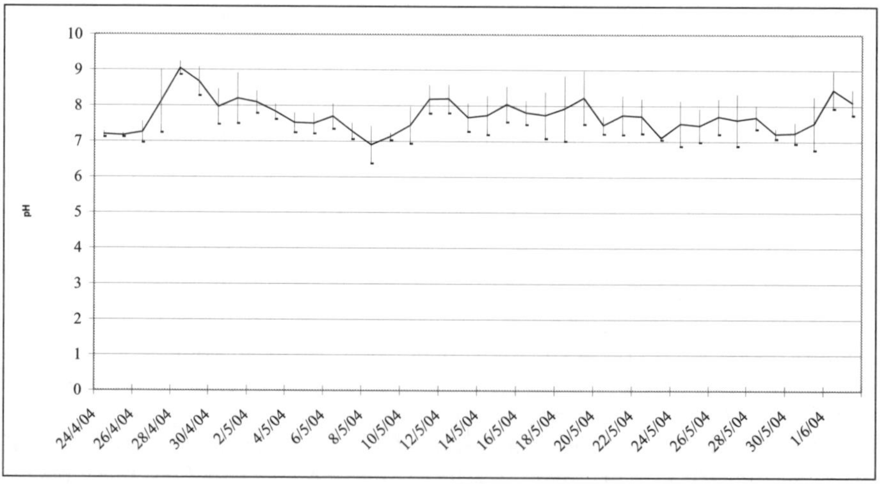

Figure 5: Daily change in pH at Curuai Lake, measured by SIMA.

Those preliminary results show that the integrated use of space technology is fundamental for environmental monitoring. Episodic surveys are not able to grasp short term changes in the environment whose cumulative effect will only be captured when the environmental balance is disrupted.

5 Conclusion

The results support the importance of space technology for environmental monitoring. Remote sensing data proved to be useful to identify key regions of the lake to be monitored at high frequency. This area is less subjected to seasonal changes modulated by the Amazon flood pulse. Then, the SIMA system can depict the effects of short term variables on lake functioning.

Acknowledgements

The authors acknowledge the support given by the Fundação de Amparo à Pesquisa do Estado de São Paulo (FAPESP), Grants no 02/09922-1, 2003/00785-3 and Conselho Nacional de Pesquisa e Desenvolvimento Tecnológico (CNPq), Grant no CTHIDRO – 55.0301/02-0.

References

[1] Wissmar, R. C.; Richey, J. E.; Stallard, R. F.; Edmond, J.M. Plankton metabolism and carbon processes in the Amazon River, its tributaries and floodplain waters, Peru-Brazil, May-June 1977. Ecology 62: 1622-1633, 1981.

[2] Piedade, M.T.F; Junk, W.J.; Mello, J. A. N. A floodplain grassland of the central Amazon. (Chapter 5). Primary Productivity of Grass Ecosystems of the Tropics and Suptropics. Long, S.P.; Jones, B.J. & Roberts, M.J. (eds) .Chapman & May/UNEP, 1992.

[3] Richey, J. E.; Nobre, C.; Deser, C. Amazon river discharge: 1903 -1985. Science, 246: 101-103.

[4] http://www.obt.inpe.br/prodes/prodes_1988_2003.htm.

[5] Fearnside, P.M. Avança Brasil: Environmental and Social Consequences of Brazil's Planned Infrastructure in Amazônia Environmental Management Vol. 30, No. 6, pp. 735–747, 2002

[6] Steward, C. The Prospect of Soybean Cultivation in the Brazilian Amazon: Mapping the social, economic and ecological factors in southern Amazonia, Master Dissertation Project. Yale School of Forestry and Environmental Studies, Tropical Resources Institute, 2004

[7] Tundisi, J.G., 1999: Reservatórios como sistemas complexos: Teoria, aplicações e perspectivas de usos múltiplos. - In: Henry, R. ed. Ecologia de reservatórios: estrutura, função e aspectos Sociais: FUNDIBIOFAPESP: 29-38.

[8] Barbosa, C.C.F. Estudo da dinâmica de circulação da água entre sistemas lóticos, lênticos, e a planície de inundação amazônica. Tese de Doutoramento em Sensoriamento Remoto, em andamento, INPE, São José dos Campos, 2004.

[9] Lima, I.B.T.; C.C. Barbosa; E.M.L.M. Novo, J.C. Carvalho; J.L. Stech Localização de áreas de monitoramento telemétrico em ambientes aquáticos da Amazônia (in press) Acta Amazônica, 2005.

[10] Nush, E. A. Comparison of different methods for chlorophyll and phaeopigment determination. Arch. Hydrobiol. Beih. Stuttgart, p. 14-39, 1980.
[11] APHA Standard methods for the examination of water and wastewater. 20 ed., Washington, American Public Health Association. 874 pp, 1998.
[12] Wetzel, R. G. e Likens, G. E. Limnological Analyses", 2nd Ed., Springer-Verlag, New York, 1991.
[13] Stevenson, M.R.; Lorenzzetti, J.A.; Stech, J.L.; Arlino, P.R.A., SIMA - An integrated environmental monitoring system. - Anais do VII Simpósio Brasileiro de Sensoriamento Remoto, Curitiba, Brazil 4: 300-310, 1993

Investigation and design of a classification and mapping system for landscape scenic quality, using digital photographs, GIS and GPS

A. Tsouchlaraki
National Technical University of Athens, Greece

Abstract

This paper proposes the concept of an integrated classification and mapping system for landscape scenic quality, which will make use of digital ground photographs as the landscape's evaluation means, texture measurement indices for the automated classification of the landscape's scenic quality, a GPS receiver for defining the co-ordinates of the shooting points of the photographs, and a GIS for the analysis and the mapping of the results. The basic advantages of the system proposed are: the evaluation of the view offered in an area, taking into account the perspective conditions of observation and not the plan view conditions as depicted on maps, aerial photographs and telescopic representations; the use of a simple and economical mechanical equipment for on-site data acquisition; the automated classification of the scenic quality depicted on the photographs; and the use of simple mapping methods with a Geographical Information System. The paper examines basic issues regarding the design of the system proposed and its implementation. When completed, the system will facilitate the creation of landscape maps, with many applications in environmental planning.
Keywords: landscape scenic quality, landscape classification and mapping system, digital ground photographs, GIS, GPS.

1 Introduction

Landscape is the combined result of physiography, geological formations, vegetation, waters and the various cultural interventions that occur in a given area. This combination attributes shape, line, colour and texture to a landscape, while the aesthetic result is considered on the basis of the variety or the uniqueness offered and is usually classified into three main classes: 1) indistinctive, 2) common, 3) distinctive [1,2,3]. This classification determines those landscapes which are most important and those which are of lesser value from the standpoint of scenic quality. The classification is based on the premise that all landscapes have some scenic value, but those with the most variety or diversity has the greatest potential for high scenic value. A frame of reference is developed by which to judge the physical features of an area as indistinctive, common or distinctive [2,3]. Features such as landforms, water forms, rock formations, and vegetative patterns are compared singularly or in combination. Through this comparison an area's overall degree of scenic quality and resultant variety class rating is determined.

The combinations of the variables mentioned above are indefinite in number and it is therefore obvious that the more the characteristics under examination increase, the more complex the landscape's evaluation becomes. Besides, there are many divergent views even among experts. This justifies the demand for creating a conventional and common method for evaluating and classifying a landscape's visual quality.

The registration means that are usually used in landscape analysis and management are thematic maps (topographic, vegetation, land uses, etc.), satellite photographs, ground photographs, aerial photographs and nowadays video recordings. Other techniques and means that are used in landscape evaluation include simulation and image processing techniques, as well as reverse photogrammetry techniques [1]. More specifically, the use of ground photographs in the evaluation of a landscape's scenic quality offers many advantages, bearing in mind that aerial photographs and telescopic representations do not depict what the human eye perceives inside a landscape. Issues of perspective, relative position, direction, lighting conditions, seasonality are depicted on a ground photograph and help at interpreting perception. Further to this, photographs are the most familiar and economical means for the landscape's analysis and presentation [4].

In practice, however, only few of the aforementioned possibilities are being used. The experience at least in Greece shows that the studies carried out with regard to the visual analysis of a landscape's quality are isolated, occasional and are usually limited to environmental impact studies, on the occasion of a technical project or a development initiative. These studies often use descriptive approaches, mainly characterised by the researcher's subjectivity. This is an issue that impedes the monitoring of the quality of a visual environment and constitutes another reason for creating a practical and commonly acceptable system for the evaluation and classification of a landscape's scenic quality.

This paper proposes the concept of an integrated classification and mapping system for landscape scenic quality, which will make use of digital ground photographs as the landscape's evaluation means, texture measurement indices for the automated classification of the landscape's scenic quality, a GPS receiver for determining the co-ordinates of the shooting points of the photographs, and a GIS for the analysis and the mapping of the results. Such a system will evaluate and classify the landscape of an area, taking into account the observation perspective conditions of each position, and will provide an automated classification of the landscape's scenic quality, leaving aside the subjective estimations of the researchers. The possibility to create maps for an area's view shall provide at the same time a possibility for a diachronic monitoring of the visual environment, with many applications in various issues. In order to complete such a system, many individual aspects should be previously examined, such as the number and the density of the ground points from which photograph shootings took place, the number of the photographic shootings that must be effected around each observation position, in order to depict the overall viewshed of the observation post, the selection of the texture measurement indices to be used in the classification of the landscape's scenic quality that will be offered by each observation post, and the method to be used in order to map the results and to create a landscape map. These issues regarding the design of the system proposed and its implementation are presented in detail below.

2 Methodology

2.1 Photo shooting and ground co-ordinate acquisition

When we need to examine a certain area, the ground photographs to be shot must sufficiently cover the area in question. Two basic issues are then presented: 1) how dense should the shooting points of the photographs be, in order to cover the whole area under examination; and 2) how many shootings should be effected around the shooting point, in order to cover the entire viewshed offered by each position.

With regard to the first issue, two solutions are proposed. The first one is based on the fact that the very close viewing zone, which is placed by many scientists at the first 400m, is not examined in landscape analysis and evaluation, because it is regarded as a general threshold for the convenient stereoscopic observation of the objects [1]. Therefore, a systematic sampling of the points of the area under examination may be carried out at regular intervals of approximately 400m. Theoretically, there is no point examining a shorter distance than the one of 400m, however a longer distance may be used depending on the needs of each application, up to 1000m, which according to scientists constitutes the close viewing zone [1]. The close viewing zone is characterised by great details in the texture and the colours of the elements. The elements in this zone are compared in a scale to the observer's size. The most important zone in landscape analysis is the middle zone, which extends from 1 to 5km, because it gives a complete perception of the shapes, the forms and the templates of the elements [1]. This is the reason for which we propose in this paper the 1000m as the upper limit for shooting ground photographs, in order to have the possibility to monitor any changes in the middle zone. Based on these regular intervals a coarse template will be created from the peaks of which shootings will take place. Due to the fact that the physical relief affects directly the alteration rate of the view, and in order to further document the issue of the shootings density, an investigation in mountainous, hilly and plain areas is proposed, where shootings will be carried out at regular intervals so as to evaluate the differentiations in the results and to draw some conclusions on the view's alteration rate. Perhaps, this investigation will give us the optimum interval that will cover all cases. However, the final selection of the regular intervals from which shootings will take place, shall depend on the needs of the application and the accuracy requirement.

A possible problem that can arise is that there are difficult-to-access areas, due either to the rough relief, or to the existence of waters and other physical obstacles, which cannot be approached for shooting ground photographs. The second solution proposed relates to cases, in which shootings may be carried out from various points of population concentration in the area, such as rural roads, parks, churches, archeological sites or tourist centres.

In mixed cases, where some parts of the area examined are accessible and others not, a combination of the previous proposed solutions may be applied.

There are, however, cases of natural landscapes, to which there is no access, in order to shoot ground photographs. In these cases, we can use image representations of the landscape, which will be created by combining a DTM and aerial photographs.

Shootings can be effected with the use of a simple digital camera. There are no particular specifications with regard to data resolution and to the number of colours. Besides, all modern digital cameras offer millions of colours. The shooting axis should be horizontal, something that can be easily achieved by using a tripod and a bubble level. The shooting orientation could be determined with the use of a compass.

In order to depict the overall viewshed around an observation post, and taking into account that wide-angle lenses are usually used, at least four shootings must be effected for each position, one for each main orientation, i.e. north, south, east and west. In this way, we can have later a combination of successive photographs that will depict the entire viewshed offered by an observation post. Alternatively, we propose the video-recording of the entire viewshed, 360° around each observation post. However, this selection will obviously increase the cost of the system and the processing time. An investigation that can be proposed in this point is to video-record the viewshed of certain observation posts and at the same time to effect four shootings for each main orientation around each observation post, in order to be able to compare later the results and to find out whether the video-recording justifies the increase of the cost and the processing time.

Finally, for each observation post the ground co-ordinates must be taken into account, in order to map at a later stage the results. For this purpose, we can use a simple portable GPS receiver. The accuracy of such an instrument on site for the identification of the position is 3m, which is however more than enough, taking into consideration that the view within 3m is not considered to change, as mentioned above.

2.2 Method for evaluating and classifying a landscape's scenic quality

In May 2002 the Laboratory of Physical Geography and Environmental Impact of the National Technical University (NTUA) completed a pilot research programme entitled "SCAPEVIEWER" [5, 6]. The main objective of this programme was the design of a user friendly and mainly computerised instrument, which would not require specialised knowledge from the user. The methodology pursued was based on the theoretically proven characteristics of the landscape, which were quantified empirically, on the basis of the scientific opinion of a seven-member group, and were applied to a sample of ground photographs, while the results of the quantification constituted the input and training data for a neural network.

In the above mentioned research programme, the selected indices were evaluated empirically. An empirical evaluation often includes a sub-optimal dependence on the experience of the evaluator, a time-consuming examination of the large number of attributes and interactions, and the increasing complexity of landscape evaluation as the number of estimated landscape attributes increases. Further to this, a post-doctoral research was carried out in the Department of Rural and Surveying Engineering of the NTUA, which investigated the possibility for an automated classification of landscape scenic quality, using texture indices that are developed for landscape standards analysis [7]. The methodology proposed in this paper with regard to the classification and evaluation of a landscape's scenic quality is based on the results of the post-doctoral research. These results are presented in brief below.

For the purposes of this research, we used the sample of ground photographs that was also used in the research programme "SCAPEVIEWER". The sample of the 108 photographs was available in the form of slides and it was digitised using the KODAK RFS3570 slides scanner. The resolution was 96 ppi (pixels per inch), and 16 million colours were used.

Given that the processing and management of 16 million colours is a hard task, the colour palette should be reduced to a maximum of 256 categories. This reduction would facilitate a further data processing and the calculation of the texture indices, while at the same time in terms of visual perception, does not cause an essential problem, taking into account that humans can perceive and assess the quality of a landscape, even based on black and white photographs [1]. Moreover, since measurement indices are created from scratch in this research, their application conditions are defined empirically in the most convenient way. From the available colour generalisation choices, the generalisation and standardisation selected was in 216 colour (6x6x6), using 6 levels for each of the basic colours/channels Red-Green-Blue. In this way, the colour category, whose value ranges from 0 to 215, constitutes information that is directly comparable to all photographs and is the arithmetic value "z" of each pixel. The generalisation was effected using the corresponding algorithm availed by the Idrisi GIS. The number of pixels is similar for all photographs, approximately 927X627 pixels.

The indices investigated in the post-doctoral research are the most essential that prevail in landscape standards analysis. These are the richness, fragmentation, diversity, dominance, contagion and complexity indices [8,9,10,11,12,13,14,15]. The Idrisi GIS package was used for the calculation of the values of the indices, and in the absence of relative algorithms, these were programmed. It should be noted that these indices examine the heterogeneity that appears in each landscape photograph, by the colour categories that exist each time. Each photograph is regarded as a spatial unit of landscape and the indices are calculated from the total number of pixels that exist in each photograph. Table 1 presents the texture indices investigated and their calculation formula.

Table 1: Textural measurements.

Index	Mathematical relation	Explanation of symbols
Richness (n)	n=m	m = the number of colour categories appearing in the photograph
Diversity (h)	$h = -\sum_{k=1}^{m} (P_k)\ ln(P_k)$	P_k = the percentage of the pixels belonging to colour category *"k"* m = the number of the appearing colour categories
Dominance (d)	$d = H_{max} + \sum_{k=1}^{m} (P_k)\ ln(P_k)$	$H_{max} = ln(m)$ P_k = the percentage of the pixels belonging to colour category *"k"* m = the number of the appearing colour categories
Fragmentation (f)	f=g	*g= number of appearing groups*
Contagion (c)	$C = -\sum_{i=1}^{m}\sum_{j=1}^{m} (Q_{i,j})\ ln(Q_{i,j})$	$Q_{i,j}$ = the percentage of category "i" neighbouring with category "j" m = the number of the appearing colour categories
Complexity (dfm)	$df_I = 2 \cdot ln\ (P_i / 4) / ln\ (A_i)$ $Dfm = (\sum_{i=1}^{g} (dfi))/g$	Ai = the surface area of a group Pi = the perimeter of a group *g= the number of the appearing groups*

The basic issue examined was whether and to what extent these measurement indices could be utilised, and in the case of ground photographs, for classifying the landscape's scenic quality. The landscape's scenic quality depicted in each photograph was already classified qualitatively and empirically in three classes (C1: Indistinctive, C2: Common, C3: Distinctive) within the framework of the «SCAPEVIEWER» research programme, by a seven-member group of the NTUA's Laboratory of Physical Geography and Environmental Impact. These persons had a basic theoretical background in terms of landscape visual analysis. Figure 1 shows an example of landscape for each of these categories.

Further to this, the classification of the photographs was carried out, using texture measurement indices and applying the linear discrimination method. The results from this investigation showed that there are texture indices, such as the fragmentation and complexity indices, that can correctly classify on their own approximately 55% of the observations. The richness, entropy and dominance indices classified in combination 57.41% of the cases, while the major percentage of successful classification achieved was 62.04% when using all texture measurement indices.

(a) (b) (c)

Figure 1: Example of: a) indistinctive category of landscape, b) common category of landscape, c) distinctive category of landscape.

Therefore, the results from this investigation were positive and encouraging enough in order to pursue research. The texture measurement indices seem to be sensitized in general in the landscape's scenic quality and can be used for its classification [7]. However, in order to be able to develop a reliable model for view classification, the sample of photographs must be further enriched and the research pursued.

2.3 Mapping methodology

The mapping of the results depends on the way data acquisition is carried out. With regard to each point for which a shooting was effected, the decision on which landscape category –indistinctive, common, distinctive- it belongs to will be made on the basis of the classification process. The shootings may be focal, however they represent specific surfaces of the area examined. Therefore, in case the shootings are effected at intervals e.g. of 400m, each shooting will be regarded as representing a quadrangle of 400mX400m. The co-ordinates of the shooting point will be in the centre of the quandrangle, and the results will take in this way a pixel form and can be easily mapped with the use of a GIS.

A mapping problem arises in case of mixed situations, in which shootings are effected sometimes at regular intervals and other times from points of population concentration. In these cases, it is proposed to use the pixel form for the data, depending on the interval selected for the photo shooting, and to leave blank the pixels without shooting data. We could propose intervention methods so that blank pixels acquire an estimation of the view category. The intervention methods may indeed be useful in certain cases, but in order to suggest this, the investigation proposed in paragraph 2.1 (with regard to the alteration rate of the view category) must be completed in advance.

A second solution is for empty pixels to acquire an estimation of the view category, using, instead of photographs, image representations of the landscape that would have resulted from the combination of a digital terrain model and an aerial photograph. In this case, however, in order to avoid the confusion of the two methods, that obviously give a different accuracy to the results, the quality categories of the view that derived from the shootings must be distinguished on the map from the one that derived from image representations.

Another possibility is to create four different maps of view for each orientation, with the proviso that there are photo shootings for each of the main orientations, North, South, East, West. This possibility may probably be very useful for certain applications in environmental planning.

3 Discussion

This paper aimed at presenting in detail the concept of a classification and mapping system for landscape scenic quality. The basic advantages of the system proposed are: the evaluation of the view offered in an area, taking into account the perspective conditions of the observation and not the plan view conditions of the landscape as depicted on maps, aerial photographs and telescopic representations; the use of a simple and economical mechanical equipment for on-site data acquisition (digital camera, portable GPS device); the automated classification of the view quality depicted on photographs; and the use of simple mapping methods with a Geographical Information System.

Several individual investigations have been proposed in the previous paragraphs, in order to complete such a system. Some of them have already started and are in progress. The final aim of these investigations is to create a fully automated system for the classification and mapping of an area's scenic quality, which would be addressed to the general public and would not require specialised knowledge by the user. Our effort continues in this direction.

When completed, the system shall facilitate the creation of landscape maps and the on-going monitoring of the quality of the visual environment, with many applications in environmental planning. For example, the view offered by an observation post, which changes over time, as the prevailing land uses change, affects the area's value. In addition to this, the spatial arrangement of many activities, such as tourist centres and businesses depends on the view offered by the area. The spatial arrangement of various technical works, such as open mines, inert material mining sites, SLS, road works, etc. alter the landscape of an area and cause visual effects. The system proposed would be very useful in environmental planning and in the investigation and monitoring of the visual impact caused by the spatial arrangement of various technical works; this system would classify and map the landscape's scenic quality viewed in an area. For these reasons, it is our belief that when completed, the proposed system would be broadly implemented and have a great appeal to the research community.

References

[1] Smardon R., Palmer J., Felleman P.J., *Foundations for Visual Project Analysis*, John Willey & Sons, N.Y. 1986.

[2] USDA Forest Service, *National Forest Landscape Management,* Government Printing Office, Ag. Handbook 434, Washington 1974.

[3] USDA Forest Service, *Landscape Aesthetics*, Government Printing Office, Ag. Handbook 701, Washington 1995.

[4] Shuttleworth S., The use of Photographs as an Environmental Presentation Medium in Landscape Studies, *Journal of Environmental Management*, 11:61-76, 1980

[5] Mougiakakou S.G., Tsouchlaraki A., Cassios C., Matsopoulos G., Nikita K.S., Uzunoglou N., "SCAPEVIEWER: Preliminary Results of a Landscape Quality Classification System", SFB 565 *International Conference: "Disturbed Landscapes: Theory and Models"*, Brandenburg University of Technology, Cottbus, September 24-27, 2002.

[6] Mougiakakou S.G., Tsouchlaraki A., Cassios C., Matsopoulos G., Nikita K.S., Matsopoulos G.. Uzunoglou N., Leka A., "SCAPEVIEWER: A Semi-Automatic System for Landscape Quality Classification and Landscape Indices Selection", *Proceedings of the Inter. Conf. on Sustainable Development Indicators in the Mineral Industries (SDIMI 2003)*, Milos, Greece, 2003, pp. 335-340.

[7] Tsouchlaraki A., *Investigation and Design of Measurement Indices for the evaluation and classification of the landscape's quality based on digital ground photographs*, Post-doctoral Research, Dept. of Rural and Civil Eng., NTUA, Athens 2003.

[8] Frohn R., Remote Sensing for Landscape Ecology: New Measurement Indicators for Monitoring, *Modeling, and Assessment of Ecosystems*, Lewis Publishers, USA 1998.

[9] Hulse D., Melnick R., "GIS as an Aid to Rural Landscape protection", *L.A.Computer News/LaLUP, ASLA Open Committee(s) on Computers/Landscape and Land use Planning, LACN* vol. 4 no. 2, LaLUP no. 19, Summer 1991.

[10] Milne B., "Lessons from Applying Fractal Models to Landscape Patterns", Quantitative *Methods in Landscape Ecology*, Edited by Turner M., Gardner R., Springer Verlag, 1990.

[11] O'Neill R. et al., "Indices of landscape pattern", *Landscape Ecology,* SPB Academic Publishing bv, The Hague, vol. 4, no.1, 1990.

[12] Olsen E., Ramsey R., Winn D., "A modified fractal dimension as a measure of landscape diversity", *Photogrammetric Engineering & Remote Sensing,* Vol. 59, No. 10, October 1993.

[13] Turner M., O'Neill R, Gardner R., Milne B., "Effects of changing spatial scale on the analysis of landscape pattern", *Landscape Ecology*, SPB Academic Publishing bv, The Hague, vol. 3, nos.3/4,1989.

[14] Turner M., "Quantitative Methods in Landscape Ecology: An Introduction", *Quantitative Methods in Landscape Ecology*, Edited by Turner M., Gardner R., Springer Verlag, 1990a.

[15] Turner M., "Spatial and temporal analysis of landscape patterns", *Landscape Ecology*, SPB Academic Publishing bv, The Hague, vol. 4, no.1, 1990b.

Section 16
Landscapes and forestation issues

Urban landscape ecology in the Delta Metropolis, a modern chaos?

W. Timmermans, R. P. H. Snep & V. Kuypers
Wageningen University & Research Centre, Wageningen, The Netherlands

Abstract

Within a special issue of Archis, a Dutch journal on architecture, different authors discussed the relation between architecture and ecology (Archis, 1999). The editors stated that it is necessary to "investigate ecology as a vital dimension of tomorrow's building task", but that "as long as ecology remains the preserve of moralisers and environmentalists, its capacity to influence society will be slight and consumers culture will continue as before". In this paper we will discuss the relation between nature and the city. In our research we apply principles from landscape ecology and spatial planning in urban ecological studies. This specific approach of urban ecology is called 'urban landscape ecology'. The paper starts with an introduction to the national nature policy of the Netherlands. Than the concept of urban landscape ecology is introduced and the Dutch Delta Metropolis is described. We describe six case-studies, combining urban landscape ecology, spatial planning and architecture into new concepts on urban green for nature, human and economy. Finally some remarks will be made about these approaches from the point of view of modernism and complexity.

1 National nature policy in the Netherlands

The Netherlands have been completely man made (Koh, [7]). This fact has among others determined the culture of spatial planning: its tradition is very modernistic. Also the National Nature Policy has highly been influenced by modernism. It outlines exactly which area of the country has to be conserved as or transformed into a natural area. More than a 130 specific types of nature have been exactly defined and described.

WIT Transactions on Ecology and the Environment, Vol 81, © 2005 WIT Press
www.witpress.com, ISSN 1743-3541 (on-line)

This approach of planning, developing and managing 'nature', as part of their technocratic tradition, has grown to a somehow bizarre system of policy, regulations and funding. Every inch of the Netherlands has been carefully researched and designated for a certain land use. Within the land use 'nature' hundreds of types of different target vegetation can be distinguished, as described by the Ministry of Agriculture, Nature and Food Quality (Bal et al, [2]). Both farmers and land owners get funding to create or conserve those target vegetation and especially for the National Forest Service and other land use owners with nature conservation aims those funding form a vital part of their overall financing. The 'production' of specific nature thereby has become generally accepted way to earn money. It also created a fixed culture in which 'nature' is linked with 'planned vegetation', and spontaneous vegetation and colonisation of pioneer species like the Natterjack Toad (Bufo calamita) cause serious troubles for both ecologists and planning- and decision-makers.

The national network of existing and new nature areas must have been established in 2018. Nature conservation and development, including the supporting research, is highly characterised by a technocratic, approach. Koh [7] argues that this nature policy is control based. Moreover the nature which has to be established does not consist of extreme and potentially dangerous processes like floods, but on certain combinations of habitat, animals and vegetation.

The modernistic nature policy plan has been established in a period of time when spatial policy was more or less seen as a linear process. The Ministry of Agriculture, Nature and Fisheries combined spatial nature planning with major accompanying financial investments. It had had a leading responsibility for planning and investment in the rural areas. Together with the farmers and their organisations and with nature conservation organisations it could implement its policy. But complexity became larger and larger. The sharp difference between town and country is more and more disappearing (Timmermans et al, [17]). On the one hand globalization disrupted traditional farm related networks, on the other hand rich city people colonised the countryside more and more. The Ministry appeared no longer to be the only or even the major player in the (rural) field. The Delta Metropolis is a highly dynamic area. This fact has big consequences for nature and nature policy. A growing lack of space asks more and more for multiple land use. Nature will have to be combined with other functions. Policy and research have to change from modernistic and linear into complexity based.

2 Urban landscape ecology

Considering the description of the rural-based term 'landscape' the urban landscape stands alone (Luck and Wu, [9]). Cities both have the size and internal heterogeneity which distinguish them from other landscapes. Besides, the characteristics, configuration and mutual relations of the accompanying landscape elements differ much from the adjacent areas. The urban landscape has its own collection of underlying patterns and processes, which provides the conditions for a self-supporting ecosystem: the urban ecosystem (Niemelä, [11]). Inside this ecosystem terrestrial ecological, physical, and socio-economic components of metropolitan areas are linked (Yen and Nyuk Hien, [20]; Smardon, [13]; Van Druff et al., [19]; Clergeau, et al, [3]; Gobster, [5]; Roovers, et al., [12]).

Urban ecology, the study of urban plant and animal species and their environment, has developed as a new but fast-growing field of scientific research. Most urban ecology studies that have been conducted in the past decades were however descriptions of very local situations, not experimental applications nor spatially explicit studies on the distribution of species through the urban landscape. As we define 'urban landscape ecology' as the study of urban plant and animal species in a spatial, highly dynamic, environment, it is obvious that those traditional, more descriptive 'site-studies' are not equipped to deal with the request from local governments for ecological information to be implemented in planning and urban development. This is because they are time-consuming in describing local situations in detail, thereby always been overtaken by (urban) developments. For example, the recent colonisation of flat roofs in the Netherlands by shore birds has not been studied in detail, whereas urban developers now ask for information how to include plant and animal ecology in their development projects. With the term 'urban landscape ecology' not only fundamental but also more applied research is indicated, thereby including opportunities to experiment with combinations of urban development and nature conservation.

3 Urban landscape ecology in the Dutch Delta Metropolis

With the exception of the three northern provinces, the Netherlands can be considered as a new type of city, the Delta Metropolis. This metropolis is situated in the delta of the European rivers Rhine, Meuse and Schelde and stretches out over the Dutch Randstad, the German industrial Ruhr district and Belgian Flanders. It is a 'spacious metropolis with villages, urban centres, suburbs, industrial estates, harbours, airports, forests, woods, lakes, beaches, reserves, pasture land, fields, roads, canals, railways and the monocultures of the high-tech areas of agricultural land' (Geuze and Breugem [4]). Their spatial, economic, social and cultural interrelationship is strong. Practically all of the components that make up the spacious metropolis fulfil more than one function.

This metropolis landscape was developed due to a high level of urbanisation during the last decades and this rapid urbanisation process is still on-going. It appears to result in a lack of space for both the Dutch inhabitants and the Dutch nature. Research and practice in the field of urban landscape ecology can sometimes hardly be disconnected. In this battle for space and attention much creativity and flexible perspectives are required from researchers and policy makers on urban landscape ecology. We will give some examples, some of which are still in progress.

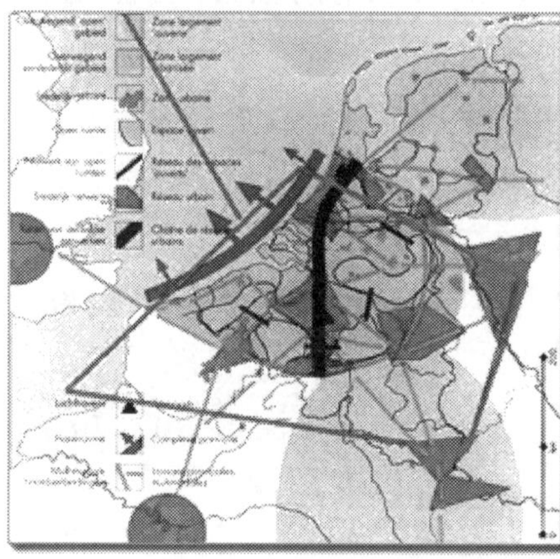

4 Hoogvliet, Rotterdam: peri-urban nature increases inner city nature perception

In many Dutch cities, the amount and quality of urban green space has decreased in the course of time as a result of 'reduction' (e.g. replace a city garden with parking places or houses) and intensive utilisation of the public green space by their citizens. The question is whether a clever configuration of urban green space together with some form of nature development on the edges of town (the peri-urban area) is a promising solution for keeping up the best possible quality of urban nature. In the Rotterdam borough Hoogvliet a pilot research project was carried out. A movement model, SmallSteps, was used to calculate several spatial scenarios whereby butterflies could colonise the built-up area from source populations in the surrounding green areas. The model has been built up using data on habitats and behaviour of the butterflies in the rural natural areas; it was adapted for urban use. The results of the modelling were discussed with different butterfly experts. The study produced clear results as to the positive contribution that peri-urban nature can make to improving the quality of nature in the city itself. Also it was found that the model, after adaptation, can be useful in urban circumstances. However the results have not been used in the local policy of the borough. The new management was not interested in ecological aspects of their work anymore; also they cancelled a planned research project to investigate the specific wishes of the people on urban green.

4.1 Almere: Multi functional wildlife overpasses

As described in more detail by Timmermans and Snep [18]), Alterra studied the ecological preconditions that a multi functional wildlife passage must meet. This is a structure over a motor way which incorporates buildings (office space) as well as nature (wildlife corridor). This construction would have to comprise a building of one or more floors with a roof designed in such a way that it can function as an ecological corridor zone. The challenge here is to make a design that is so sophisticated that all functions (infrastructure, building and ecology) can function to the highest level of perfection. For ecology purposes, it is important here to create an attractive environment for all sorts of fauna groups, keeping disruptive elements such as light, sound and human presence to a minimum.

This concept, the ‘office duct’, has been worked out as part of a spatial development plan for the municipality of Almere. The ambition of Almere was to have some kind of land mark at the edge of the town that symbolised the importance and quality of the green surroundings and the parks of the new town. The plan has been made together with a building company. However it will never been built: the political agenda of Almere changed after local elections, the deputy who was responsible for the idea left and the project leader moved to another job elsewhere. The concept of the office duct however got a lot of attention. It was felt ‘sexy nature’. Probably it will be realised somewhere else.

5 Port of Rotterdam: combining industry and ecology

The Port of Rotterdam, the world largest harbour measuring more than 35 km in length, has many values and opportunities for nature alongside industry. Alterra used the LARCH spatial expert system to study which nature values derelict land and pipeline verges could have in various design and management scenarios (Snep et al [14]). This spatial analysis showed that derelict land has good potential for thicket birds in particular if their management is left unchanged. It was also found that pipeline verges play a potentially important role as an ecological corridor for butterflies through the harbour area. The nature value of industrial estates can improve significantly if the design and management of the existing green space is geared better to nature. The results of the research appeared to be eye openers to many planners. At the moment Alterra is involved in several studies to realise nature as part of the planning of business areas.

6 Amsterdam, De Loodsen: Architecture supports abundance of plants and animals

Construction of housing and office buildings can create opportunities for nature development. Alterra was partner in an architecture contest and worked out the idea that houses can provide a habitat for numerous organisms. The original plan included shingled roofs as a breeding habitat for common terns; niches and grooves as nesting places for Peregrines (Falco peregrinus), walls where wall plants can shoot their roots, roofs like Babylonian gardens, etc. The contest was won and the house will be built. Design and building process is still going on. Part of the nature will be realised, although economy is not as strong as it was. In the meantime more ideas about ecology inclusive building are coming up. The idea of a typical urban nature, mostly not being insects, is of great interest for part of the cultural elite in the cities.

7 Wassenaar: New estate development

The edge of the dunes near the coastal zone of the Duct city of Wassenaar is one of the most exclusive places to live in the Netherlands. It is also one of the most vulnerable areas from an ecological point of view. The question is whether and if so how new houses can be developed in the area. So far top down planning traditions inhibited new developments. However the national, planning policy in the Netherlands is changing dramatically. Top down planning policy is changed into an approach where bottom up initiatives on the basis of pronounced ambitions are stimulated.

Alterra proposed a new planning methodology of sustainable development. It starts with the ecosystem: initiatives in ecologically vulnerable areas should be adapted to it. New housing must eco-inclusive and strengthen the vulnerable forest and hydrological system, more or less ‘emerging from the ecosystem’. In a next step the plans should be adapted to the existing cultural heritage in the region: large houses in the middle of large privately owned parks. Then new houses should strengthen the existing water and traffic infrastructure networks. Rain water must infiltrate, existing roads will not be extended. Finally as all the others in the neighbourhood the new houses should be built under actual high quality architecture.

The methodology is trying to define sustainable conditions for bottom up building initiatives with sustainable ambitions. Shortly after the research was established, the national policy really changed from a top down to a bottom up planning policy. The search for new methods just started.

7.1 Biennial of architecture: mobile nature reserve

In the year 2003 an International Biennial of Architecture, with the theme Mobility, was organised in Rotterdam. Alterra joined an initiative by MattonOffice from Wenndorf, Germany to establish a 'moving nature reserve'. First of all the mobile nature reserve was meant to be an object of art. the interior of a public transport has been transformed into a forest.

During the exhibition it was transporting people between the different locations of the Biennial. Second the mobile nature reserve forced people to think about nature and about the parks and green areas in and around their town. Third the reserve was used for excursions and debates between ecologists and architects, between world historians and philosophers. Finally the reserve was used to reframe the thoughts of management and many researchers of the different departments of Alterra. Actually, only after the Queen of the Netherlands visited the moving nature reserve, or junglebus, and after all the national newspapers wrote articles about it, the project was taken seriously. Main conclusion of the project is that while citizens were very enthusiastic about the mobile reserve and started to enjoy, researchers and also many policy makers could not "imagine that this is nature".

8 Nature policy in a highly dynamic Delta Metropolis

What can we learn from the given examples on nature development and nature policy in the context of the Delta Metropolis?

In the Delta Metropolis with its highly dynamic battle for space, the concept of nature appears to become in some way more 'fluid'. Dangerous, flammable kerosene pipeline verges can to be outstanding ecological corridors. It seems possible to establish a wildlife overpass on the roof of an office and to build houses in very vulnerable ecological areas with positive effects on nature. Many 'ordinary people' are not interested in the difference between a 'mobile nature reserve' and a traditional nature reserve. On the other hand it can happen that a policy directed on realisation of new nature in or around the city can suddenly completely change. What is going on?

First of all we have to answer the question 'what is nature' in a different way than approximately 15 years ago, when the Ministry was the one and only responsible policy maker for nature. At that time the discussion about 'what is nature' could be answered relatively easy. The Ministry should be convinced. When the Ministry was convinced about the modernistic approach, most of the research money was spend to support the policy with knowledge. However the Ministry has lost its monopoly. It has to realise projects together with many municipalities and building companies, with deputies, architects, housing developers and for rich and poor people who want to recreate, party or just relax.

They all have their own ideas about what nature is. Policy and research will have to deal with that.

The second question will be ‘what do all the new stakeholders want’. Research is necessary to understand why a nature developing policy at the local level suddenly stops. How interesting is technocratic nature for the people in the city and for the policy makers? Architects and artists have to be seduced by new, sexy concepts of nature, which can be combined with splendid architecture (Koh [7]). (foto’s gebouw) How difficult this will be came up during the debate between ecologist Jelle Reumer and architect Ton Salman in the junglebus (Matton et. al., [10]). Reumer stated: “The Knotgrass and the Indian Lovegrass that sprouts unregarded between the basalt blocks of the Westzeedijk in the vicinity Rem Koolhaas’ Kunsthal is what I consider nature. You need architecture to make the city and nature reacts on it”. Salman Replied: “A question that occupies me is how I can plan for nature. I depend on receiving ecological information, such as detailed habitat requirements in order to make design decisions. How big does a nesting site have to be. Could it be made of glass? What is the minimum permissible distance between a nesting box and the rails for the window washing installation on the roof? Can I put the box between the rails? Will a blue colour attract or repel a certain kind of bird?”

It is a fascinating world, but a traditional modernistic approach of nature development and nature policy will not bring good results in highly dynamic area with continuously changing public opinion. There is a need for a more pragmatic approach, based on a combination of facts, expertise and intuition. The role of the ecological researcher changes dramatically. From the starting point of at least the knowledge on the habitat and behaviour of animals and vegetation he or she has to develop many different and always changing ideas about nature as part of many multiple land use plans. It should be a fascinating world.

References

[1] Archis, 1999: Architecture and ecology. Archis, volume 2. Pp 98. NAi & Elsevier. Rotterdam.

[2] Bal, D., H.M. Beije, Y.R. Hoogeveen, S.R.J. Jansen & P.J. van der Reest 1995. Handboek natuurdoeltypen in Nederland (Handbook nature target types in the Netherlands). IKC Nature Management. Report 11. 293 p.

[3] Clergeau, P., G. Mennechez, et al. (2001). Human perception and appreciation of birds: A motivation for wildlife conservation in urban environments of France. Avian ecology and conservation in an urbanizing world. J. M. Marzluff, R. Bowman and R. Donnelly. Norwell, Massachusetts, Kluwer Academic Publishers: 69-87.

[4] Geuze, A. & I. Breugem 1995. There's a house in Holland (in Dutch) Rotterdam, Nai. 156 p.

[5] Gobster, P. H. (2001). "Visions of nature: conflict and compatibility in urban park restoration." Landscape & Urban Planning 56(1-2): 35-51.

[6] Interheem projectontwikkeling , Moes bouwbedrijf, Woningbedrijf Amsterdam, Köther en Salman architecten, Instituut voor Bos- en Natuuronderzoek, Stichting Nederlands Telewerk Forum & Adviesbureau Peutz & Associés BV, 1999: Homework, een visie op wonen en werken aan het IJ.

[7] Koh, 2004

[8] Kuypers, V., J. Jonkhof & J. Bervaes, 2004: Wonen op de strandwal in Wassenaar. Alterra. Wageningen.

[9] Luck, M. and J. G. Wu (2002). "A gradient analysis of urban landscape pattern: a case study from the Phoenix metropolitan region, Arizona, USA." Landscape Ecology 17(4): 327-339.

[10] Matton, T., V. Kuypers & W. Timmermans, 2004: BosBus, mobile nature reserve. Episode. Rotterdam.

[11] Niemela, J. (1999). "Is there a need for a theory of urban ecology?" Urban Ecosystems 3: 57-65

[12] Roovers, P., M. Hermy & H.Gulnick (2002). "Visitor profile, perceptions and expectations in forests from a gradient of increasing urbanisation in central Belgium." Landscape and Urban Planning 59: 129-145.

[13] Smardon, R. C. (1988). "Perception and aesthetics of the urban environment: Review of the role of vegetation." Landscape and Urban Planning 15(1-2): 85-106.

[14] Snep, R.P.H., R.G.M. Kwak, H. Timmermans & W. Timmermans 2001. Landscape ecological analysis in the Port of Rotterdam: LARCH-scenario

studies on the potential for nature of derelict land and industrial verges [in Dutch]. Alterra, Wageningen UR. Alterra-report 231.
[15] Snep, R.P.H., P.F.M. Opdam, J.M. Baveco, M. WallisDeVries, W. Timmermans, R.G.M. Kwak and V. Kuypers (in prep). How peri-urban design can improve nature quality within cities: a modeling approach. Biological Conservation.
[16] Timmermans, W. & R.P.H. Snep, 2001: Ecological models and urban wildlife. In: Y. Villacampa, C.A. Brebbia & J.L. Uso, 2001: Ecosystems and sustainable development III. WIT Press. Southampton. Boston.
[17] Timmermans, W., L. van den Berg, J. Luttik, 2002: New housing schemes: urbanisation that incorporates nature. In: Brebbia, C.A., J.F. Martin-Duque & L. Wadhwa, 2002: The sustainable city II. Advances in Architecture. WIT-press, Southampton, Boston. Pp 259 – 271.
[18] Timmermans, W. & R.P.H. Snep 2003. Combining urban development and wildlife overpasses together in one multifunctional and multilevel building across highways. Innovative nature concepts in highly urbanized areas. In: E. Tiezza, C.A. Brebbia & J.L. Usó (eds.), Ecosystems and sustainable development IV. (Proceedings ECOSUD conference Siena). Southampton, WIT, 2003. Adv. ecol. Sci. 18, pp. 501-508.
[19] VanDruff, L. W., D. L. Leedy, et al. (1995). Urban wildlife and human well-being. Urban Ecology as the Basis for Urban Planning. M. N. H. Sukopp, A. Huber. The Hague, SPB Academic Publishing.
[20] Yuen, B. and W. Nyuk Hien (in press) "Resident perceptions and expectations of rooftop gardens in Singapore." Landscape and Urban Planning..

Dynamics and evolution of urban patterns: the evidence of the Mobile Landscape project

R. M. Pulselli[1], F. M. Pulselli[1], C. Ratti[2] & E. Tiezzi[1]
[1]Department of Chemical and Biosystems Sciences, University of Siena, Italy
[2]SENSEable City Laboratory, M.I.T, Cambridge, U.S.A.

Abstract

This research is focussed on cities and it develops innovative approaches for urban studies. In particular, the novelty comes from the theories of evolutionary physics and biosystems sciences applied to urban systems; the expected issue is concerned with the definition of an interdisciplinary theoretical viewpoint.

A new method for monitoring urban mobility, named Mobile Landscapes, is finally shown as evidence of the complex behaviour of cities. This project uses location data from cell phones in order to study locations and intensities of urban activities and also to analyse people densities and their movements through urban regions. Briefly, the Mobile Landscapes project focuses on cities and aims to investigate their dynamics. Therefore, enhancing the importance of dissipative self-adaptive behaviours of cities, the outcomes, in the form of maps of urban activity, can also reveal how a city organises itself as a living organism. Focusing on flows and dynamic patterns generated by people and goods mobility, this project can also be a valuable method to highlight the role of time and to direct the practices of urban management and planning by way of an evolutionary approach. The case study described in this paper uses data on the activities of cell phone antennae in the metropolitan area of Milan, Italy.

1 Introduction

Interactions between groups of agents take place in cities. Their changeable relations, intensities and locations, even supported by stationary urban infrastructures and built environments, generate complex behaviours; evolutionary trends, unexpected events and dynamic patterns, made of fluxes

WIT Transactions on Ecology and the Environment, Vol 81, © 2005 WIT Press
www.witpress.com, ISSN 1743-3541 (on-line)

flowing through and within the boundaries of cities, call for new practices in urban studies and management. Topics like the rising of people and goods mobility, transports and other phenomena due to the growth of the global market, the deployment of communication technologies and the internet, the request for information and constant connectivity, are emergencies that have to be taken into account investigating urban dynamics. For instance, the huge deployment of mobile communications has a significant impact on social dynamics. In the last few years, people have changed their behaviour, their social life and their way to work due to the rise of this kind of services. The main result is the ability to act with few constraints and to achieve high levels of flexibility and freedom in mobility. As a consequence, the dynamics of any social system became more complex and new information are required to understand their evolutionary trends. Therefore, on one hand, the mobile technologies cause an increase of complexity and indeed of uncertainty in investigating urban dynamics; on the other hand, they can be a valuable and accurate source of information.

According to these emerging landscapes, the perception of cities has changed. The city behaves like an open system whose dynamics are those of a living eco-system, an evolutionary organism or, at least, a dissipative structure. “Town is like an artificial ecosystem where there is a continuous exchange between living organisms and the physical anthropic environment where they live” [1]. The stationary structure made of buildings, streets, infrastructures and other settings is just the basement for a multiplicity of activities, dynamic phenomena and coevolutionary processes. “It is not to look at the city as the lifeless inert structure that supports life just like the sum of buildings, technologies and distinct isolated elements. On the contrary, it is to look at the city as an evolutionary organism that constantly interacts with man; it is customized by man and it works to customize human behaviour” [2].

Life of human systems is actually the focus of our investigation and, consequently, the scale of observation is that of broad urban regions. It is a macro-scale with the meaning that the behaviour of urban systems is studied as a whole where many interactions have been investigated in the aggregated form. Dealing with evolution and design, Erich Jantsch says: “human life is movement. It is movement not by and for itself, but within a dynamic world, within movements of higher order. On the one hand, these higher-order movements constitute the life of human systems – of relations, organizations, communities, institutions, nations and cultures of the entire human world [3].

2 The eco-dynamic approach: keynotes

The Theory of non equilibrium thermodynamics by Ilya Prigogine, Nobel Prize for Chemicals in 1977, as well as the general theory of Chaos applied on self adapting systems, represents an authentic change of route in studying natural and anthropic systems and their dynamics. The novelty is that “physics leaves its ivory tower of useless purity and comes to grip with nature, society, the bios and the oikos, the complexity of the true problems of humanity and our planet, without compromising its rigour and scientific character” [4]. The Prigogine’s idea is that living systems behave like dissipative structures. “Living dissipative structures actually behave like open systems in a steady state (dynamicity, diversity, life) that maintain themselves in life (at high levels of order and complexity) by self-organizing due to material and energetic fluxes received from outside and from systems with different conditions of temperature and energy” [5].

The observation of evolutionary and narrative elements is a starting point as the Nobel Prise underlines: “at all levels of nature we see the emergence of ‘narrative elements’. [...] At all levels we observe events associated with emergence of novelties, which we may associate with the creative power of nature. These narrative historical aspects are part of complexity” [6]. Reality is plunged into the flowing time whose irreversibility makes the difference between abstract deterministic models and real systems. The existence of the arrow of time is demonstrated by the irreversibility of processes in nature; time has a scientific relevance and that is why evolutionary physics definitely exceeds the heritage of deterministic approaches based on relativity of time in investigating real phenomena. Consequently, irreversibility of time avoids any theoretical model to be exhaustive and any prevision to be reliable if applied on animated subjects.

Time plays its unconditioned role especially determining the form of a city, as well as its aesthetic. The configuration of a system is the expression of its organization and the outcomes (temporary) have been achieved by processes of adaptation and selection. “Organization emerges on a macroscopic space-time scale, that is many times bigger of microscopic interactions between the elements” [7]. Therefore, the organization of a system emerges spontaneously as an additional information value that is not visible just observing single parts. “Atoms go toward a slightest energy state constituting chemical links and ordering themselves into molecules. Organisms continuously adapt each other by their co-evolution processes and constituting an ecosystem. These are examples where groups of agents, looking for their own consistence and reciprocal adapting, can transcend themselves and acquire collective properties, that do not exist individually, like the life and the thought” [8]. It is obvious that “the whole is greater than the sum of its parts” [9].

So, organization and self-organization processes in complex dissipative systems concern with both the micro and macro dimensions. The organization chosen by a system at once is the one that harmonizes the interactions between the elements according to the suggestions coming from the environment. That is why selection works on a macroscopic level. At the same time, interactions between the constitutive elements let them adapt each other and a microscopic fluctuation caused by a local perturbation can be amplified until it pervades all the system, creating an ordered structure. “In a complex system non linearity can reinforce a local action to generate a chain of effects extended to the all system” [10]. In conclusion, no-linearity amplifies not only from local to global levels, but even, on the inverse, from global to local [11]. The direction of information is both from up to bottom and from bottom to up that means from the global to the local level and from the local to the global.

Accordingly to this analysis on complex systems general behaviour, also the investigation has to be addressed on different scales of observation, that means information should be collected at different levels, both a detailed level on individual elements and a dilated level on the whole system and its comprehensive structure. "The idea is that knowledge of nature must come from a global, systemic view of events and from study of the network of information joining the various forms of matter, energy and life in time and space" [12].

Complex behaviours and evolutionary frameworks became the subjects of urban studies. "In a town, the natural cycles are almost completely replaced by artificial cycles. The results let us consider the concept of ecosystem in more abstract terms. The ecosystem may be a set of interactive conditions rather than a physical system" [13]. People moving through buildings and infrastructures, flowing fluxes of energies and matters or changes of information through communication technologies are the practical examined issues. The definition of a scientifically rigorous approach is aimed to handle these multiple factors of complexity and to make information on cities more and more available: "[…] we are more likely to choose the best measurements if we can see them, appraise them with outstretched hands, not merely imagine them" [14].

3 Mobile Landscapes

Generated patterns of urban dynamics do have their own geographies and their changeable evolutionary nature is the evidence of cities complex dissipative behaviour. For this reason, the analysis on urban mobility starts from their visualization in the form of maps and temporal sequences of maps that is in the form of geographies and mobile geographies.

With regard to this theoretical statement and the need of concrete tools, a joint research project, named Mobile Landscapes, has been recently developed at the MIT SENSEable City Laboratory in Cambridge, UK, in collaboration with the Department of Chemicals and Biosystems Sciences of the University of Siena, Italy.

The Mobile Landscapes project uses the technology for determining the geographic locations of cell phones to analyse mobility fluxes in urban regions. Data based on the location of mobile devices have been collected and processed in an aggregated and anonymous form and finally plotted onto a sequence of maps. The results enable a graphic representation of the intensity of urban activities and their evolution through space and time. Different ranges of time can be analysed from the 24 hours of the day to long periods like seasons and years. Furthermore, it is also reliable assuming the intensity of cell phone activity is a statistically relevant information about the real time human density in urban areas. Therefore, the outcomes are in the form of mobile geographies that reveal how people move through the city.

The expected issue deals with the real behaviour of urban systems more than with their structure; it appraises the real way people use spaces relating to time that is much more than providing any conventional description of land uses. For this reason, it seems the Mobile Landscapes project definitely opens the way to a new approach on urban systems and probably belongs a new urban paradigm.

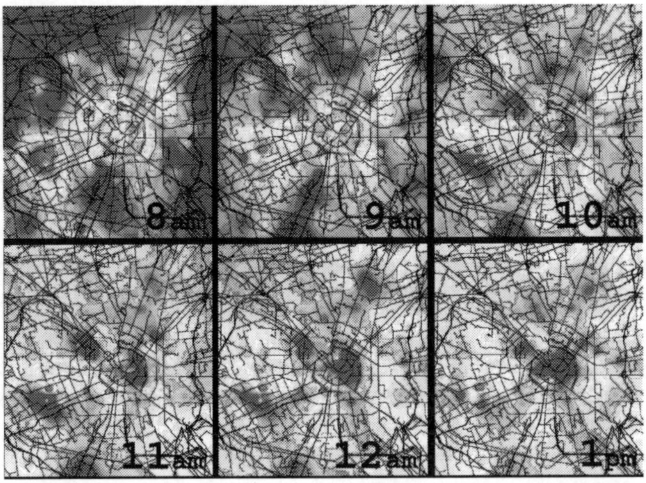

Figure 1: Mobile Landscapes Project: an application on Milan Metropolitan Area from 8am to 1pm.

Evolutionary and stochastic patterns in human settlement are finally revealed as added values. "The contemporary embodiment of general system theory is complexity theory. But there has been a sea change. Dynamics has become significantly more important than structures in providing the essential drivers [...]. The idea that systems can be 'explained' in static terms now seems nonsensical" [15].

Monitoring urban activities and people movements in real time, many information can be provided about how the system reacts to local perturbations and external actions. For instance, a folk event, a concert or a soccer match, the lock of a street for road-works, the opening of a new building with a certain urban function, the development of new facilities as those provided by communication technologies (that actually are in constant evolution like, for instance, wireless networks), any new plan of public transport, and many others, are examples of perturbations in the system that let it react and self-organise in a new pattern.

The provision of real time location-based maps, can detect systems highlighting critical points as nodes and areas with high levels of activity during the time and also conditions and causes of congestions can be revealed and handled. So, on the one hand, the analysis of the maps can provide feedbacks to correct or better organise any urban pattern pursuing very practical issues in anyone of the cases described above. On the other hand, the Mobile Landscapes project would also reveal some unexpected phenomena occurring in the macro-scale of the city just caused by a simple event like the opening of a new cafeteria with a very good ice-cream. "It offers an opportunity to understand the mutating complexity of the contemporary city. Its focus on temporal, rather than spatial patterns, refers to a new paradigm for urban analysis" [16]. Furthermore, it has the ambition to visualize trends and behaviours, to reveal the *fractal geometry* of cities and the interactions between elements at different scales. "Dynamics of course represent the key to all of this. As architects and planners and urban theorists, we delight in approaching the city in terms of its morphology but morphology is not enough. It must be unpacked and the only way to unpack it is through dynamics" [15].

4 Conclusions

The effects of any human activity, according to the theory of chaos, cannot be completely determined or predicted. The organization of complex systems depends on a multiplicity of agents and positive feedbacks can take place in cities, amplifying local fluctuations and generating new and surprising structures. Dynamic patterns of urban mobility have self-adapting properties that let us look at the city as an organism, as a living dissipative structure, where motions and interactions are continually taking place.

The Mobile Landscape project is applied to urban regions and broad areas and it is aimed to appraise, quantitatively and qualitatively, fluxes of mobility and their dynamics; their mobile geographies are revealed in order to understand (and try to handle) the complexity of urban systems. Dynamics cannot be predicted of course but they can be observed and the observation on urban dynamics through space and time adds value to any potential strategy with the obvious consciousness that urban eco-systems are driven by human choices as well as by chance.

Urban studies call for flexible techniques that can reveal complex behaviours and ordering principles without denying the existence of stochastic unpredictable processes. Consequently, on our belief, a new evolutionary approach is the starting point to reload criteria and targets in urban studies even based on a scientifically relevant observation. This idea is the beginning of a research dealing with contemporary cities aimed to open new perspectives and to direct next generation choices of urban planners and designers.

References

[1] Scandurra E., 1994, Il progetto della città ecologica; Etas-Libri.

[2] Vernetti G., 1990, La città come ecosistema territoriale; in Magnaghi A., 1990, Il territorio dell'abitare; Franco Angeli.

[3] Jantsch E., 1975, Design for Evolution: Self-organization and Planning in the Life of Human Systems; George Braziller, New York.

[4] Tiezzi E., 2003, The Essence of Time; WITpress, Southampton, UK.

[5] Pulselli R.M., Magnoli G.C., Marchettini N., e Tiezzi E., 2004, Dissipative structures, complexity and strange attractors: keynotes for a new eco aesthetics; Second International Conference: Comparing Design in Nature with Science and Engineering "DESIGN & NATURE II", Rhodes, Greece, WIT PRESS, Southampton, UK, 381-387.
[6] Prigogine I., 2003, From a space to a time culture; in Foreword of Tiezzi E., 2003, the Essence of Time; WITpress, Southampton, UK.
[7] Nicolis G., 1989, Physics of Far–From-Equilibrium Systems and Self-organization; In Davies P., 1989, The New Physics; Cambridge University Press: New York.
[8] Lucchi Basili L., 1997, La geometria frattale dell'organizzazione urbana: oltre la crisi dell'ordine spontaneo; In Bertuglia C. S. e Vaio F., 1997, La città e le sue scienze, volume 1, La città come entità altamente complessa; Franco Angeli: Milano, pp. 205-238.
[9] Von Bertalanffy L., 1972, General System Theory; Penguin Books, Harmondsworth.
[10] Pulselli R.M., Bastianoni S. e Tiezzi E., 2002, Self-organization as a resource for a sustainable city planning; Second International Conference on Urban regeneration and sustainability 'the sustainable city II', Segovia, Spain, WITpress, Southampton, UK, 103-113
[11] Bertuglia C.S. e Staricco L., 2000, Complessità Autorganizzazione Città; Franco Angeli, Milano.
[12] Tiezzi E., 2004, Beauty and Science; WITpress, Southampton, UK.
[13] Rossi L., 1991, A study of the energy flux of Rome urban ecosystem and impact sensitivity of bioindicators in river Tevere; Proceedings of. the MAB-UNESCO International Symposium, Rome.
[14] LeCorbusier, 1968, Modulor; MIT Press, Cambridge, US
[15] Batty M., 2000, Less is more, more is different: complexity, morphology, cities, and emergence; in Environment and Planning B: planning and design; Vol.27
[16] Ratti C., Pulselli R.M., Williams S., Frenchman D., 2004, Mobile Landscapes: using location data from cell phones for urban analysis; in Environment and Planning B: planning and design, (submitted).

Urban forest ecosystem structure and the function of the gulf coastal communities in the United States

K. K. Abdollahi[1], Z. H. Ning[1] & M. Stubblefield[2]
[1]*Urban Forestry Program & NASA Center for Coastal Zone Assessment and Remote Sensing, SU, U.S.A.*
[2]*Center for Energy and Environmental Studies, SU, U.S.A.*

Abstract

In the United States it is estimated that 90 percent of the entire population now lives within the boundaries of what is defined as urban forest. Additionally, the total yearly economic value of urban forest services is more than $400 billion. To achieve sustainability of our rapidly expanding urban ecosystems and deliver the maximum level of benefits to the inhabitants, the urban forest must have healthy tree resources, comprehensive management and community-wide support. This paper presents the results of a collaborative study among SU, USDA-FS, NASA and The Gulf Coast Chamber of Commerce pertaining to the sustainability of the urban forests of the Gulf Coastal areas in the United States. The urban forest ecosystem analysis of the Gulfport, Mississippi indicated a 30% tree canopy cover and nearly 25% green space in 2001. This represents 20% urban forest canopy loss since 1990. The current health of this urban forest is under pressure from urban sprawl and soil compaction. Urban forest ecosystem models and geographic information system (GIS) are being utilized to study the urban land use, urban forest health and urban sprawl in the Gulf Coast.
Keywords: urban forest ecosystem, gulf coast, sustainable ecosystem, urban ecosystem, urban forest health, urban ecosystem analysis, urban sprawl

1 Introduction

The urban forest covers a large and expanding area. Approximately 3.5% of the United States is currently classified as urban (urban areas). Nearly 25% is either located in or functionally tied to urban areas (i.e., greater metropolitan areas,

Nowak et al [2]). Urban and metropolitan areas have grown tremendously, with urban sprawl being a significant environmental concern of the 21st century. Between 1950 and 1990, metropolitan areas increased threefold, while between 1969 and 1994, urban areas doubled in size (Dwyer et al [1]). Substantial population growth outside urban and metropolitan areas continues to extend urban influences to forest resources across the landscape, particularly in places with considerable scenic and recreational value. Urban and metropolitan areas include substantial forest resources that have the potential for significantly improving the quality of the urban environment and the well-being of its residents. Across the United States, tree canopy cover in urban and metropolitan areas averages 27% and 33%, respectively, approaching the national average tree cover of 33%. With approximately 74.4 billion trees in metropolitan areas and 3.8 billion trees in urban areas, the magnitude of the urban forest resource should not be ignored (Dwyer et al [1]). Urban forests can make a considerable difference in quality of life by directly influencing the daily lives of nearly 80% of the U.S. population. Further, what happens in urban areas can have a profound impact on urban forests and the extended exurban landscape. Considering the significance of the resource, urbanization and urban forests are likely to be especially significant in the 21st century (Dwyer et al [1]). The increasing significance of urban influences across the United States calls for resource policy makers, planners, and managers at the national, regional, and local levels to bring cooperative attention to planning and management efforts to sustain urban forests.

1.1 Coastal communities and the urban forest

In 2001, more than half of the U.S. population lived along the coast, an area that represents only one fourth of the U.S. land mass. As a consequence, areas of the coastal zone are densely populated, ranging from 422 people per square mile in 2001 along the Atlantic Coast and 232 people per square mile in the coastal counties of the Great Lakes to 149.3 people per square mile along the Gulf Coast and 71.6 people per square mile along the Pacific Coast. In contrast, population density in the non-coastal portion of the United States was 48.1 people per square mile in 1998. From Texas to Florida, the Gulf coast region is rich with ecological resources that support the region's economic wealth. Over time, human activities from dam construction to shoreline development have dramatically altered natural landscapes, waterways, and ecological processes. Pressures from human activities remain the most important agents of ecological change in the region today. Over the century ahead, land-use changes are likely to increase as rapid population growth continues. As the Mississippi Gulf Coast caught the national headlines with its economic recovery in the 1990's, the three-county Gulf Coast region of Hancock, Harrison, and Jackson counties has often been cited as heralded as the economic "engine" of this change. Historically driven by the seafood, timber and tourism industries, the Coast economy today now runs the gamut from chemicals to computers, apparel to aerospace. Since 1992, the Mississippi Coast has experienced over $3.5 billion in new commercial and industrial development, added over 38,484 new jobs to the economy, and had its largest influx of residents in 20 years. The Coast now is home to over 12,000 businesses, the second highest concentration of businesses in the state, and is home to three of Mississippi's top five employers. The Coast's strategic location between the cities of New Orleans, Louisiana and Mobile, Alabama is unique – making it, simultaneously, an employment center, suburb, vacation destination, and transportation corridor. Covering a land area of nearly 1,800 square miles, the region is highlighted by more than 26 miles of white sand beaches along the Gulf of Mexico. Well-developed air, land, sea, and rail arteries provide access to nearly 75% of the United States population, as well as emerging Mexican and Latin America markets. With an estimated 11 million annual visits and over $3 billion in travel-related expenditures, the region has skyrocketed into the nation's third gaming destination with over $1.1 billion in gross gaming revenues in 2001.

2 Urban forest ecosystem of the Gulf Coast

2.1 Study site

The following 15 aerial image tiles (Table 1) of the City of Gulfport (Fig 1 and 2) were randomly selected. A random number generator was used to select from approximately 430 images. Due to over lap in the photography a re-selection was made when two adjacent tiles were selected. A re-selection was also made when the tile did not reside in the current City of Gulfport City limits. Each tile, taken at 3650 ft altitude, covers an area approximately 4015 ft by 4015 ft (or 3521 x 3521 pixels) and encompasses approximately 370 acres. The pixel resolution is 1.14 ft.

Table 1: Study area image tiles.

Rev B			Latitude (N)			Longitude (W)	
	Tile Number	Date	Deg	Min		Deg	Min
	1	4/2/2001	30	24.349		89	0.100
	2	4/2/2001	30	28.946		89	5.429
	3	4/2/2001	30	27.074		89	3.292
	4	4/2/2001	30	23.428		89	3.806
	5	4/2/2001	30	24.367		89	5.424
	6	4/2/2001	30	26.633		89	5.425
	7	4/2/2001	30	24.336		89	6.490
	8	4/2/2001	30	22.065		89	6.488
	9	4/26/2001	30	25.245		89	7.579
	10	4/26/2001	30	22.925		89	2.793
	11	4/2/2001	30	22.551		89	4.356
	12	4/2/2001	30	21.564		89	7.031
	13	4/2/2001	30	28.513		89	1.688
	14	4/2/2001	30	23.396		89	1.689
	15	4/2/2001	30	23.412		89	0.634

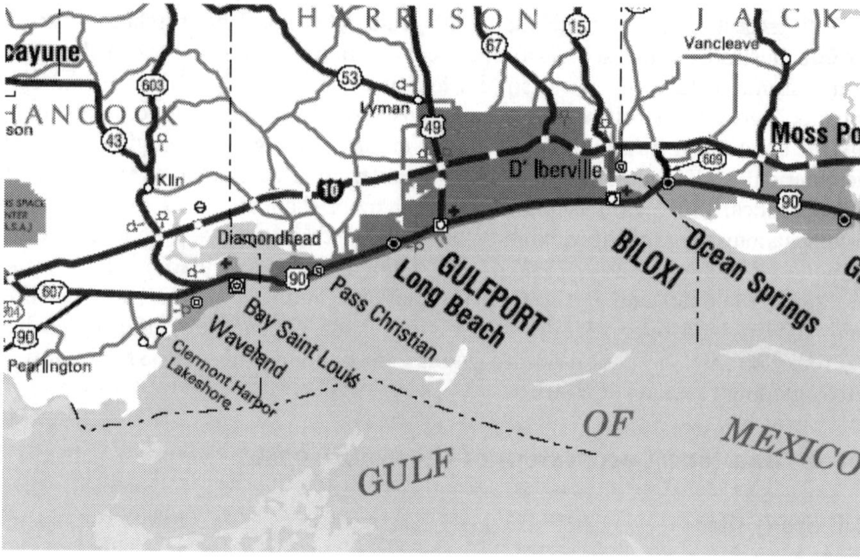

Figure 1: Mississippi Gulf Coast.

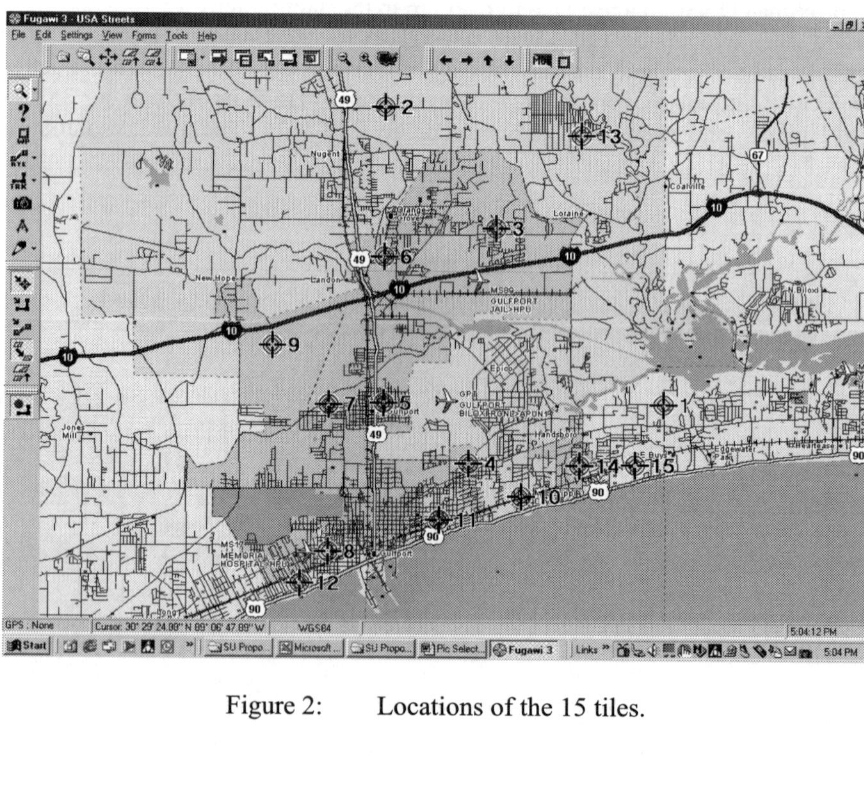

Figure 2: Locations of the 15 tiles.

Each individual tile (Fig 3) was approximately 4015 ft x 4015 ft. A random number generator was used to select fourteen one acre plots within the tile. The Figure shown below is a representation of a single tile divided into a 17 x 17 matrix (289 polygons) with the fourteen 1 acre plots selected and shown as shaded areas. The plots were planned to be circular; however, software limitations dictated using square plots. The plot that is crosshatched is the center of the tile with the Latitude and Longitude position indicated in Table 1. The plots were named according to their location along the X and Y axis.

Figure 3: An urban forest tile.

2.2 Principal component analysis

The following describes the Principal Component Analysis (PCA) technique as used on Tiles 1-15. The Principal Component Analysis is an image transformation method that is used for a variety of purposes in Remote Sensing and GIS applications including data compression and change detection. In general the bands of a multi-spectral image usually do not contain completely independent information. More likely, there will be some degree of correlation between bands, indicating they share common elements of information. If the reflectance levels for a set of pixels for two bands of interest are plotted, in what is commonly referred to as "band space" the following plot is obtained. Each of the axes represents reflectance in the spectral band. In our case, for our photography and analysis needs, band 1 is brightness and band 2 is green. Each image pixel was plotted by placing its location at the intersection of its value on each band. This reveals a high level of correlation between the bands. (i.e. if a pixel has a high value on band 1 it is likely to have a high value on band 2). Since the bands are correlated they do not carry independent information. One can predict the reflectance of a pixel on one band from the reflectance value on the other. This confirms there is some degree of redundancy in the information they carry. It is this redundancy that the principal components seek to remove when it is used for the purpose of data compression. The principal components transformation is a linear transformation that can be described as a weighted linear combination. It produces a new set of bands (called components) by multiplying each of the bands by a weight and adding the results.

e.g. C= w1B1 +w2B2 + w3B3….wnBn

The weights in the transformations are the eigenvectors. The results of the principal components transformation process can be thought of as a mathematical determination of a new set of axis in band space such that the resulting images are: 1) uncorrelated with one another and 2) ordered in term of their explanatory power. Usually component 1 (CI) is oriented along the axis of the largest variation and component 2 (CII) is by definition perpendicular to component I and is oriented in the direction of lesser variation. For this analysis a PCA was used to assist in finding the classes of data that had a very bright reflectance in the green band. For this analysis principal component one is brightness and principal component is the green band.

2.2.1 Script files sequence

All PCA and supervised classification processing were accomplished using the ELAS program and script files. The following describes the script files sequence used to process the images. First, the area of the tile selected for analysis was determined. In developing the prints and in the negative scanning processing some edge effects were apparent. These were trimmed from the electronic image before processing. Next, the raw data was converted to principal components as discussed above and a principal component plot was generated. From this plot the classes exhibiting the greatest variation were easily identified. The ELAS software was then used to identify and number 50 plus classes of pixels. The exact number of classes varied with each tile. A tabulation of the number of pixels per class, percent, cum percent, mean, median and standard deviation was generated. Next, the statistics were obtained. The statistic file was rearranged to obtain the decreasing means for Band 2 (green). Then a maximum likelihood classifier was performed and 2-space color plots (band 1 = brightness verses band 2 = green) and were generated. Next, the means of each class and number of samples in each signature were tabulated and then the means, standard deviation and number of samples (pixel by pixel) were tabulated. Finally, the frequency distribution of classes was tabulated. Once the PCA was performed, a supervised classification (with ground truthing) was used to determine the classes of interest, i.e. oaks, thin oaks, other trees, grass, water, inert shadow and beach. The classes determined in the Principal Component Analysis were group into major classes. This was accomplished by reviewing the photography and comparing it to the PCA class. Each PCA class was identified by type (i.e. bare soil, mowed grass, thin oaks, tin roof, roads, shadow, etc.). Similar types of ground features were grouped together and then these groups were reduced to 7 major classes. The frequency distribution of the 50 plus classes, the reduction down to 7 classes, and the surface cover classification details were documented (e.g. Table 2 and 3).

Table 2: Major classes for tile 4.

Tile 4 – Table of Major Classes, Type, Color Assignment & Coverage Area					
Major Class	**Type**	**Color Assignment**	**PCA Class**	**% coverage entire tile**	**Acres**
1	Oaks	Red	9,29,30,33,35	10.58%	39.70
2	Thin Oaks	Green	18,19	4.82%	18.09
3	Other Trees	Cyan	1,2,5,7,8	12.26%	45.99
4	Grass	Yellow	6,11,13,14,17	27.31%	102.46
5	Water	Blue	31,56	33.26%	12.48
6	Inert / Shadow/ Beach	Gray	3,4,10,12,15,16,20-28,32,34,36-46,49-55,57	41.71%	156.51

Table 3: Analysis of tile by plots.

Tile 4 – One Acre Plot Coverage (Percent)							
		Oaks	**Thin Oaks**	**Other Trees**	**Grass**	**Water**	**Inert/Shadow**
		Red	**Green**	**Cyan**	**Yellow**	**Blue**	**Grey/Beach**
Plot	**Number**	**1**	**2**	**3**	**4**	**5**	**6**
1	X3Y3	9.104%	8.200%	11.879%	44.128%	3.965%	22.724%
2	X2Y7	6.295%	4.628%	8.268%	31.921%	2.828%	46.060%
3	X4Y10	25.686%	9.448%	33.542%	16.423%	4.781%	10.120%
4	X4Y15	2.864%	1.347%	0.218%	4.676%	1.487%	89.408%
5	X5Y6	1.209%	2.114%	3.183%	80.313%	0.887%	12.294%
6	X7Y3	9.800%	9.546%	69.581%	10.350%	0.185%	0.537%
7	X9Y5	15.611%	5.366%	50.393%	24.208%	1.218%	3.204%
8	X9Y15	20.538%	14.037%	3.473%	17.537%	15.345%	29.069%
9	X11Y12	0.317%	0.128%	0.376%	13.643%	0.084%	85.452%
10	X13Y16	15.301%	7.704%	2.090%	15.644%	8.194%	51.068%
11	X14Y9	0.152%	0.546%	1.200%	8.651%	0.358%	89.092%
12	X14Y12	9.233%	2.395%	12.225%	30.885%	2.156%	43.107%
13	X15Y7	0.331%	0.570%	0.755%	12.801%	0.570%	84.971%
14	X17Y14	16.546%	8.400%	17.866%	27.726%	4.151%	25.313%

2.3 Determining the urban forest canopy cover

Fifteen tiles each covering approximately 0.58 square miles were randomly selected from the 2001 70mm aerial photographs. A Principal Component Analysis (PCA) technique was performed on each of the fifteen tiles to group like pixels into approximately 50 plus classes. Next a supervised classification technique was used to group the 50 plus classes into the following 7 classes of interest, oak trees, thinning oaks, other trees, grass, water, inert/shadow, and beach. Next fourteen one-acre plots were randomly selected on each tile and the surface classification results were tabulated. The original imagery tile, PCA classes and the supervised classification plots were georeferenced and formatted to be used in ESRI ArcView GIS Version 3.0. Plots, including enlarged plots contained in this report were exported using the export feature of ArcView. The selected approach of using a PCA to reduce classes, followed by a supervised classification, was necessary due to the diversity of surface features in the urban environment of the City of Gulfport and the desire to isolate and identify Live oak trees. The selection of 15 tiles from an available 430 tiles was semi-randomly accomplished. When adjacent tiles were randomly selected they were eliminated. This was done to prevent duplication of information, since the aerial photography contains approximately 30 % overlap. In addition some ground truthing was required. It was also practical to perform a PCA and subsequent surface cover classification on the entire tile (370 acres – total of 5550 acres) prior to selecting the one acre plots. The one acre plots were created by sub dividing the tile into a 17 x 17 matrix and using a random number generator to select 14 one acre plots. Thus a total of 210 one acre plots were selected in the City of Gulfport. The results were then tabulated to identify up to 7 major classes of interest. Since the City of Gulfport is about 120 square miles approximately 7 percent of the surface will be classified. In addition, 210 random one acre plots will have been established. The plots in this report are exported from the GIS software ArcView. Where possible, the data user or reader is encouraged to utilize the GIS software and data files to study particular areas of interest. Plotted information, such as contained herein, is useful but does have viewing limitation.

Table 4: Urban forest coverage.

Summary of Coverage by Tile (percent)						
	Oaks	**Thin Oaks**	**Other Trees**	**Grass**	**water**	**Inert/Shadow**
	Red	**Green**	**Cyan**	**Yellow**	**Blue**	**Grey**
Tile	**1**	**2**	**3**	**4**	**5**	**6**
1	17.25%	6.29%	3.57%	24.53%	13.04%	35.32%
2	21.10%	22.38%	5.75%	29.80%	9.30%	11.69%
3	12.49%	6.19%	2.35%	34.63%	14.06%	30.28%
4	10.58%	4.82%	12.26%	27.31%	33.26%	41.71%
5	16.04%	6.06%	3.07%	29.32%	7.57%	37.95%
6	10.35%	4.60%	7.44%	23.32%	1.80%	52.49%
7	12.02%	8.78%	6.08%	45.96%	0.00%	27.16%
8	15.14%	8.40%	5.18%	21.03%	3.75%	46.50%
9	0.00%	0.00%	10.61%	23.04%	0.20%	66.16%
10	12.04%	10.89%	16.38%	15.98%	9.21%	35.51%
11	18.43%	12.85%	12.84%	10.91%	15.44%	29.53%
12	6.13%	9.85%	6.37%	8.40%	23.71%	45.55%
13	13.38%	6.33%	20.11%	26.79%	12.77%	20.62%
14	26.66%	7.18%	20.02%	15.49%	9.33%	21.32%
15	5.84%	0.00%	1.48%	38.26%	8.23%	46.18%
Average	**13.16%**	**7.64%**	**8.90%**	**24.98%**	**10.78%**	**36.53%**

The urban forest ecosystem analysis of the Gulfport, Mississippi indicated a 30% tree canopy cover and nearly 25% green space in 2001 (Table 4). This represents 20% urban forest canopy loss since 1990. The current health of this urban forest is under pressure from urban sprawl and soil compaction.

Table 5: Declining (Thin) oaks.

Table - Oak and Thin Oaks as percent of total tree coverage					
Tile	Total Trees as % of Tile	Oaks	Thin Oaks	Total Oaks	Other Trees
		(as percent of total tree coverage)			
9	10.61%	0.00%	0.00%	0.00%	100.00%
15	7.32%	79.77%	0.00%	79.77%	20.23%
14	53.87%	49.50%	13.33%	62.83%	37.17%
13	39.82%	33.59%	15.90%	49.49%	50.51%
4	27.66%	38.26%	17.43%	55.69%	44.31%
6	22.39%	46.21%	20.56%	66.77%	33.23%
1	27.10%	63.64%	23.20%	86.84%	13.16%
5	25.16%	63.73%	24.08%	87.81%	12.19%
10	39.31%	30.62%	27.70%	58.32%	41.68%
11	44.12%	41.78%	29.13%	70.91%	29.09%
8	28.72%	52.72%	29.24%	81.97%	18.03%
3	21.03%	59.37%	29.44%	88.81%	11.19%
7	26.88%	44.70%	32.68%	77.38%	22.62%
12	22.35%	27.43%	44.07%	71.50%	28.50%
2	49.40%	42.71%	45.65%	88.35%	11.65%
	Avg	**44.94%**	**23.49%**	**68.43%**	**31.57%**

3 Conclusion

Across the United States, tree canopy cover in urban and metropolitan areas averages 27 percent and 33 percent, respectively, approaching the national average tree cover over all lands of 33 percent. This case study of the Gulfport, Mississippi representing the Gulf Coastal communities of the United States indicates average tree canopy cover of 30%. However, this represents a 20% tree canopy loss since 1990. Tree inventory and urban forest ecosystem analysis reveals possible impacts from urban sprawl and soil compaction. The impacts of other environmental factors such as drought and extreme climatic events in the coastal areas should not be ignored. The magnitude of the urban forest resource in the Gulf Coastal region of the United States is substantial. Urban forests can make a considerable difference in the quality of life of these communities. What happens in Gulf Coastal urban areas can have a profound impact on forests and forestry across the urban to wilderness landscape. The increasing extent and significance of urban influence in the Gulf Coastal and other communities of the United States call for resource policymakers, planners, and managers at national, regional, and local levels to focus their attention on forest resources in urban settings. The Gulf Coastal urban forests can undergo significant change with the growth, development, and succession of their biological components over time.

Urban forest management practices need to be applied urgently to reduce the impacts of urban sprawl and human induced pressure. To sustain the growth and development of urban forest resources much more powerful and swift human-induced factors need to be considered. Coupled with the relatively slow rate of tree growth and plant succession, the swift human forces for change make the dynamics of the urban forest particularly challenging for managers and users. The expansion and development of urban areas in the Gulf Coastal areas could bring important changes in urban vegetation and other urban resources. Alterations to the distribution of land uses, intensity of urbanization, and population characteristics in these urban areas result in different combinations of ground cover, increased or decreased opportunities for tree establishment and growth, changing environmental conditions, and general urban forest health.

References

[1] Dwyer, J.F., D.J. Nowak, M.H. Noble, and S.M. Sisinni. 2000. *Connecting people with ecosystems in the 21" century: an assessment of our nation's urban forests.* General Technical Report PNW-GTR-490, U.S. Department of Agriculture, Forest Service, Pacific Northwest Research Station, Portland, OR.

[2] Nowak, D.J., M.H. Noble, S.M. Sisinni, and J.F. Dwyer. 2001a. Assessing the U.S. urban forest resource. *Journal of Forestry.* 99(3): 37-42.

Amazon River Basin: characterization and environmental impacts due to deforestation

R. Barthem[1], M. Marques[2], P. Charvet-Almeida[1]
& L. F. A. Montag[1]
[1]*Emilio Goeldi Museum (MEG), Belém, Brazil*
[2]*Rio de Janeiro State University (UERJ), Rio de Janeiro, Brazil*

Abstract

The Amazon River basin is the largest basin of the planet and contributes about 15% of the total freshwater discharge in the world. Among the environmental concerns, habitat modification is considered the most relevant, since the integrity of the aquatic ecosystems and associated coastal/marine ecosystems are strongly dependent on the preservation of the terrestrial ecosystems. In the Amazon basin, deforestation has changed patterns during recent years; besides the "deforestation arc" embracing the south-eastern and eastern borders of the basin, new projects are now dissecting the heart of the basin. At the present deforestation rate, the main biomes - Amazon Rainforest and Cerrado - are expected to disappear in less than 100 years, leading to regional climate changes. Effective policies to preserve the integrity of terrestrial and aquatic ecosystems must focus on the root causes for the ongoing land conversion process.
Keywords: Amazon River basin, hydrological aspects, environmental impacts.

1 Introduction

The Amazon River basin, with a total area of 6,869,000 km^2 (table 1) is the largest basin of the planet and a major heat source in the general atmospheric circulation system [1]. It is totally situated in the tropics, between 5°N and 17°S and occupies more than one-third of the South America continent. Seven countries (Brazil, Bolivia, Peru, Colombia, Ecuador, Venezuela and Guyana) share the basin. The main headwaters are located in the Andes Cordillera, in Bolivian, Peruvian, Ecuadorian and Colombian territories. Headwaters of important tributaries are located in the Guyana and Brazilian Shields, an ancient

Precambrian crystalline basement along the north and south border of the basin. The headwaters of the north are shared by Venezuela, Guyana and Brazil, and the headwaters of the south are in the Brazilian territory.

Table 1: Areas by country that form the Amazon River basin.

	Amazon River Basin	Brazil	Peru	Bolivia
(km^2)	6,869,000	4,746,479	783,066	734,983
%	100	69.1	11.4	10.7
	Colombia	Ecuador	Guyana	Venezuela
(km^2)	405,271	137,380	6,869	54,952
%	5.9	2.0	0.1	0.8

The Amazon River arises in the oriental slope of the Mountain Andes and reaches the sedimentary lands of low declivity in the Peruvian lands, before crossing the frontier with Colombia and Brazil. Although the headwaters of the Amazon are approximately 100 km of the Pacific Ocean, the water runs 6,400-6,800 km towards the opposite direction to reach the Atlantic Ocean. The lack of precision in its length is due to: (i) the uncertainty as to where its main headwater is located and (ii) the difficulty in measuring the extension of long meandering rivers [2]. Most of the Amazon basin altitude is below 250 m and the main humid zones are identified below 100 m. The Amazon River flow (220,800 m^3/s) represents 15% of the total discharge of the rivers in the world [2]. Amazon transports annually 1.2 billion tons of sediments (less than Yangtze River in China and Ganges-Brahmaputra River in India-Bangladesh) [3]. The mouth of the Amazon River is in the Brazilian territory. The discharge of the Amazon River creates in the NE South America coast a large freshwater and salt-water mixture zone with 1,700-mile stretch of low-lying, muddy, and mangrove-fringed. This environment extends from the Orinoco Delta in Venezuela into the Brazilian State of Maranhão and hosts a large number of endemic species, genera and sub-families of fishes [4]. About 15 tributaries of Amazon River have more than 1,000 km and three have more than 3,000 km of extension [2]. Eight are formed by transboundary basins (basins shared by two or more countries) and six (five Brazilian and one Peruvian) are national rivers.

The main geological units of the Amazon basin include high mountains (Andes), old plateaus (Brazilian Central Shield and Guyana Shield) and the extensive lowlands (Central Amazonian Lowlands-Amazon Plain) (fig. 1). These geological structures are of high importance for the chemical characteristics of the water and the aquatic biodiversity. The Amazonian waters are classified as [5]: (i) white, (ii) clear and (iii) black (fig. 2). The high turbidity of the *white-water* rivers reflects a great amount of suspended matter, which lowers the visibility to around 20 cm depth. These rivers (Amazon, Napo, Marañón, Tiger, Juruá, Purus and Madeira) arise from the Andean slopes. The conductivity is high (above 60 micromho/cm), and the pH is 6.5 to 7.

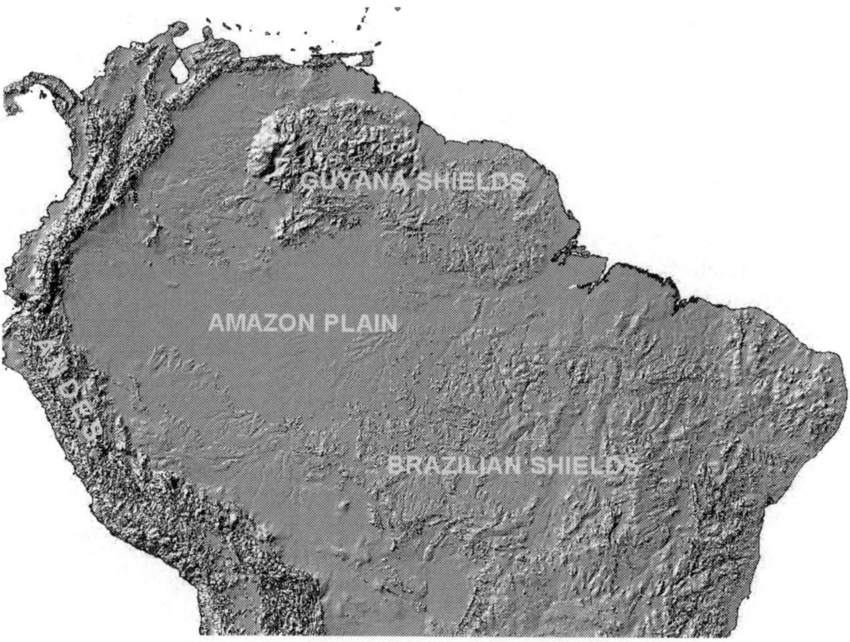

Figure 1: Geological landscapes of Amazon River basin.

Figure 2: Negro (black-waters) and Solimões rivers (white-waters) meet nearby Manaus city in Brazil. The waters flow side by side for 6 km before mixing.

Transparency is a characteristic of the *clear-water* tributaries. The visibility reaches almost 5 m depth for Tapajós, Xingú and Trombetas rivers. They are originated in the crystalline Shields of Guyana and Central Brazil that undergo erosion processes, with few suspended particles to be transported by the water. As a result, these waters are chemically poor, with low conductivity (6 to 5 micromho/cm) and pH 5-6 [5].

A great amount of humic acid in the colloidal form is a characteristic of *black water* rivers, such as Negro (fig. 2) and Urubu. The chemical properties of these waters originate from a sandy soil associated to a type of vegetation known as Campina and Campinarana. Soil porosity allows for high amounts of humic acid colloids to be carried by the river, acidifying the water (pH 4-5.5) and generating the dark appearance. Despite the elevated concentration of organic matter, these waters are chemically purer than white-waters. The conductivity is about 8 micromho/cm [6].

2 Climatic and hydrological characteristics

The Amazon River basin, in spite of its extension, is relatively homogeneous with regards to climatic parameters, such as temperature. This is probably due to small topographical variations, the abundance of the Tropical Rainforest as the main biome, and its position that occupies the north and centre of South America. However, important temporal/spatial variations are observed in relation to other climatic parameters. The area, according to the classification of Köeppen, is characterized by the several climate types: type *Afi* (relatively abundant rains throughout the year, total precipitation in the driest month exceeding 60 mm); type *Ami* (relatively dry season, elevated total annual pluviometric index); type *Awi* (relatively elevated annual pluviometric index, and clearly defined dry season) [7]. The annual rainfall presents great spatial variation (1,000-3,600 mm), exceeding 8,000 mm in the Andean coast [2]. In the Amazon River mouth, the annual rainfall exceeds 3,000 mm, while in the less rainy corridor (from Roraima state through Middle Amazon to Góias state in Brazil) with annual precipitation from 1,500 to 1,700 mm [8]. There are also different patterns of rainfall distribution along the year. As to the thermal regime, the climate is hot, with average temperature varying from 24-26ºC, practically for the entire basin. In the mountainous areas, the average temperatures are below 24ºC and along the Lower and Middle Amazon the averages surpass 26ºC [6]. Annual average evapotranspiration varies from 1,000 mm/yr, in the proximities of the Juruá and Purus rivers, to more than 2,600 mm/yr, close to Amazon River mouth, where the radiation is higher in relation to the lowest cloudiness (presence of winds) and to the lower latitude (line of Ecuador).

3 Main biomes in Amazon River basin

The limits of the Amazon Rainforest Biome extend far from the area of the Amazon River Basin and cover a great part of Suriname and French Guyana to the north. Beyond the limits of the Amazon Forest, the Amazon basin is covered by an extensive area of *Cerrado* and Savannah in the headwaters of the Brazilian and Guyana Shields [9] (fig. 3). The biodiversity for the Cerrado Biome, including all its physiognomic forms, is estimated at 160,000 species of plants, animals, and fungi. Endemic higher plants have recently been estimated as 4,400 species, 1.5% of the world's total vascular plant species. Endemic vertebrates range from 3% (birds) to 28% (amphibians) of the species recorded [10].

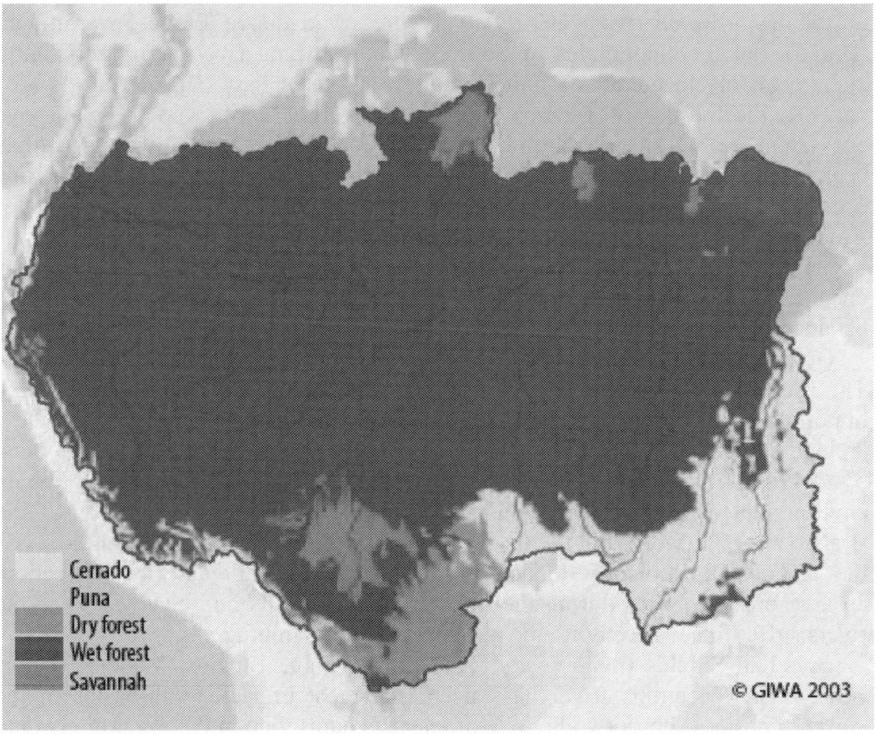

Figure 3: The main habitats of Amazon River basin [11].

The cloud forest is a special type of vegetation that grows between 1,500 m and 3,000 m on the slopes of the Andes and is exposed to constant moisture-laden winds. The vegetation changes abruptly at altitudes above 3,000 m, the climate becomes dry and cold with predomination of a vegetation type known as *Puna* composed mainly of grasses and bushes [2].

4 Main tributaries of Amazon basin and associated impacts

Amazon Plain (main rivers: Solimões, Purus, Tapajós, Xingú): One of the most important environments of Amazon Lowlands is the floodplains named *várzea* and *igapó)*. These areas extend along the rivers and are almost entirely flooded during the rainy season. This environment shelters endemic species of several taxonomic groups and also maintains a great biomass of fish species [6, 11]. It is difficult to determine accurately the areas that are periodically flooded because of the complexity of the flooding regime, which is influenced by local rainfalls, river overflow and tides [2]. It is estimated that in Brazil, there are 70,000 to 100,000 km^2 of floodplains and more than 100,000 km^2 of lakes and swamps [2]. In Bolivia, flooded areas occupy 100,000 to 150,000 km^2 [12]. The floodplains of the *white-water* rivers are relatively preserved above Purus River mouth (Brazil), but the floodplains of Solimões and Amazon rivers are significantly altered, mainly in the area around Santarém, State of Pará (Brazil). In the area between the mouths of Tapajós and Xingú rivers (Brazil), and the mangrove ecosystem, *várzea* of tides are observed. In spite of the fact that mangrove has been intensely exploited by logging companies and small farmers [13, 14], this ecosystem is still preserved in the Breves channels as well as in the inner delta of Amazon River. Fields flooded by the rain are quite typical in the bigger islands of the Amazon mouth as well as in the coastal area of Amapá and Pará states, one of the most threatened areas of the entire Amazon plain due to human occupation, dams, channels, cattle and agriculture expansion [15].

Guyana Shields (main rivers: Negro, Branco, Trombetas, Jari and Araguari): The Negro River is the largest one that drains the Guyana Shields. Some important floodplains are the Anavilhanas Archipelago and the nameless archipelago between Padauari/Demini and Branco rivers. These areas are flooded by Negro River overflow. The forest periodically flooded by rainfall forms an environment with great contiguous areas close to the margins of the Negro and Branco rivers as well as in the headwaters of its tributaries. In the Branco River, the Savannah periodically flooded by rainfall favours cattle and rice cultivation, an area prone to fires during the dry periods. The falls and headwaters of the rivers suffer of severe environmental impacts due to mining.

Brazilian Shields (main rivers: Tocantins, Xingú, Tapajós, Madeira, Purus, Juruá): The Tocantins River has one of the most impacted sub-basins of the Amazon basin. It hosts two large hydroelectric dams, one in the Tucuruí city and the other in Lageado city. The ichthyofauna of the Xingu River upper the waterfall of Altamira dam is completely different from the lower. Although the fauna is not well-known, the main impacts are related to mining and agriculture in its headwaters. Tapajós River is the most impacted one by mining activities in its headwaters as well as by dredging but the ecology is not sufficiently known to evaluate the severity of the impacts. Madeira River (one of the most studied tributaries) has headwaters located in the Andean slopes but sub-basins that drain the Brazilian Shield. The impacts are due to: (i) mining, (ii) construction of Samuel's hydroelectric dam in the Jamari River, and (iii) agricultural activity in its headwaters. The impacts of mercury contamination and mining dredges on the migration of catfishes have not been properly assessed. The Purus and Juruá (state of Acre), are *white-water* rivers, with headwaters below 500 m of altitude. In the past they were connected with the Andes. The drainage changed in the geological past and now those rivers are draining a landscape formed by an older alluvium deposit. The rivers carry large loads of suspended solids and have one of the largest floodplain areas of the Amazon, explored by professional fishermen in Manaus city [16]. Indians/local communities have been the main reason for creating protected areas for extractive activity and preservation of ethnic groups [2].

Andes (main rivers: Madeira, Marañón, Putumayo-Içа, Caqueta-Japura, Ucayali): The Madeira River is formed by Mamoré, Beni and Madre de Dios rivers and it is the main source of sediments of the Amazon basin. Madre de Dios River is one of the biggest alluvial gold sources in Amazon basin [17]. The foothills of the Andes are formed by a sequence of habitats, which change from the snowfall streams to the large rivers in the base of the mountains. The biodiversity increase downstream, but chemical processes and endemic species make the high portion an important area. The confluence of the rivers from the Andes and the Brazilian Shield is observed along a succession of rapids and falls located above the Porto Velho city. Below this point, the river is calm and navigable. The largest floodplain areas are located in the Bolivia territory, in the flooded Savannah. These areas are flooded by rivers and by local rainfall [2]. The Andean rivers Putumayo-Iça and Caqueta-Japura are the most preserved sub-basins of the entire Amazon basin having mainly indigenous inhabitants. However, the Andean zone has a similar history of the Madeira, Ucayali and Marañón rivers: the foothill region is an impacted area with the presence of colonization by the road. The area is a major coca-growing region, which has caused deforestation of large areas. Fishing is an important activity in the lower river. Gold exploitation occurs at the Colombian and Brazilian borders [2, 18].

5 The main cause of habitat modification: deforestation

Among others, (i) large extensions affected, (ii) the unknown degree of the severity of the impacts and (iii) the irreversibility nature of habitat destruction due to deforestation are the main reasons for considering this a priority concern in Amazon River basin. The economic pressures on the Amazon River basin [19] has been expressed by modifications of large extensions where terrestrial ecosystems, mainly the Amazon Rainforest and Cerrado have been substituted by agricultural and cattle grazing fields, which in turn, is likely to have a significant impacts on aquatic ecosystems. Unfortunately these impacts have not been fully-accessed. Since the 1960s, large-scale deforestation has been concentrated in the eastern and southern portions of the Amazon River basin inside Brazil, along the "arc of deforestation", as well as along the main rivers. However, during recent years, the heart of the basin has been dissected by new highways and power lines that provide access to previously remote areas [20]. In the 1990s and 2000s, forest fires have ravished the Amazon. Many of these fires, which are set by land clearers to expand the agriculture frontier, spread accidentally into the virgin rainforest. Moreover, the severe drought provoked by the 1997-1998 El Niño threatened to increase the flammability of the forest adjacent to the agricultural areas of the eastern-southern regions of the basin, creating the potential for massive ecological losses through accidental fires.

During 20-year period (1978-1998) the mean rate of gross deforestation in the Brazilian portion of Amazon Rainforest was 0.66%/year, representing 13.2% of the Brazilian primary forest converted to agriculture and pasture [21]. Colombia, Venezuela, Ecuador and Bolivia have also registered high rates of deforestation [22]. In recent years (2001-2003), the Brazilian Rainforest experienced the highest annual rates of deforestation observed during a 15-year period (1988-2003), excluding the record of 1994-1995, when 29,059 km^2 of the original Rainforest were destroyed (fig. 4). At the present rate, the Rainforest is expected to disappear in less than 100 years [23]. Additionally, climate changes are foreseen as a result of deforestation.

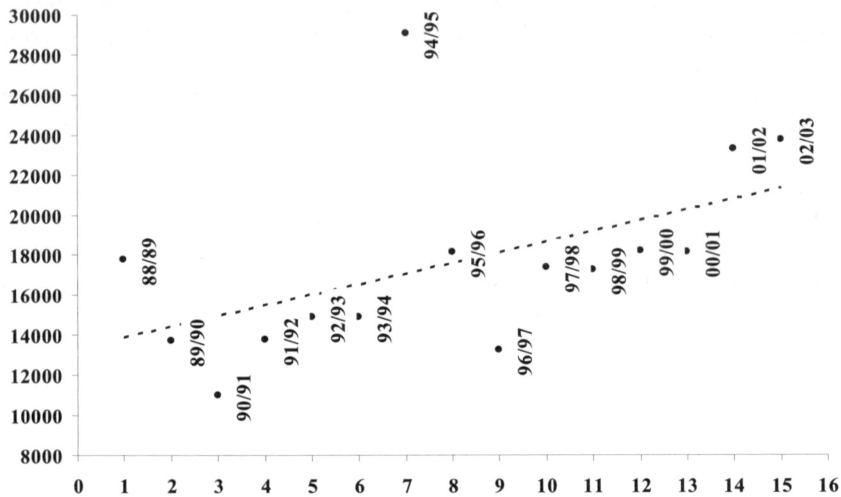

Figure 4: Mean rate gross deforestation in Amazon (km^2/yr) during a 16 year period obtained from satellite data [21].

Based on atmospheric general circulation model (AGCM) simulations, higher surface temperatures and lower evapotranspiration rates are two major effects of complete Amazon deforestation [22]. Cloud cover comparisons of deforested and forested areas suggest that a regional climate change is already underway in the most deforested part [1].

Differently from the Amazon Rainforest, very little international attention has been given to the Cerrado, despite the fact that it is the 2nd biome in importance for the Amazon River basin, one of the most threatened in South America that covers 22% of the Brazil's surface area (2 million km^2). The pressure over this biome is expressed by the fact that the Cerrado spatial distribution (fig. 3) is almost coincident with the "deforestation arc". Nearly 50% of the Cerrado is currently under direct human use, and about 35% of its total natural cover has already been converted into planted pastures and crops [10]. The average annual rate of land clearing in the Cerrado during 1970-1975 was nearly twice the estimated rate for the Amazon Rainforest during 1978-1988 [10].

6 Conclusions

The Rainforest and the water cycle are known to be closely linked together. The conservation of terrestrial habitats is therefore indicated as a priority action in order to guarantee aquatic ecosystem integrity and control of the foreseen climate changes. Unless a significant reduction in the current deforestation rate in both Amazon Rainforest and Cerrado Biomes occurs, the Amazon River basin is likely to loose most of its original cover in less than 100 year period, representing large portion of the world biodiversity. The regional and global climate consequences are not fully addressed. Regardless all research initiatives carried out in the basin, the severity of the impacts is not clearly known. However, due to the basin extension and complexity, more important and urgent than conducting a comprehensive assessment of the environmental impacts due to deforestation - a necessary but time and resource-consuming effort - is the identification of the main socio-economic factors and driving forces that have increased deforestation during recent years [18], regardless all efforts to promote environmental laws compliance. A clear understanding of these factors must precede the decision-making process to be carried out by those countries sharing the basin, in order to achieve an alternative and less-destructive model for the economic development of the region.

References

[1] Durieux, D., Machado, L.A.T. & Laurent, H. The impact of deforestation on cloud-cover over Amazon arc of deforestation. *Remote Sensing of Environment*, **86**, pp. 132-140, 2003.

[2] Goulding, M., Barthem, R.B. & Ferreira, E., *The Smithsonian Atlas of the Amazon*, Smithsonian Books: Washington, 2003.

[3] Meade, R.H., Nordin, C.F.Jr., Curtis, W.F., Rodrigues, F.M.C., Vale, C.M. & Edmond, J.M., Sediments Loads in Amazon River, *Nature*, **278**, pp. 162-164. 1979.

[4] Myers, G.S., The genera and ecological geography of the South America banjo catfishes, Famiy Aspredinidae, *Stanford Ichth. Bulletin*, **7**, pp. 132-139. 1960.

[5] Sioli, H., Amazon Tributaries and Drainage Basins (Chapter), *Coupling of Land and Water System*. pp. 199-213. ed. A.D. Hasler, Springer-Verlag: Berlin, 1975.

[6] Junk, W.J., *The Central Amazon Floodplain*, Springer-Verlag: Berlin Heidelberg, New York. 1997.

[7] Day, J.A. & Davies, B.R., *The Ecology of River System*, ed. Dr. W. Junk Publishers: Dordrecht, Netherlands, pp. 289-318. 1986.

[8] Capobianco, J.P.R., Verísimo, A., Moreira, A., Sawyer, D., Santos, I. & Pinto, L.P., *Biodiversidade na Amazônia Brasileira*, ed. Câmara do Livro: São Paulo, Brasil. 2001.

[9] Bartem, R.B., Charvet-Almeida, P., Montag, L.F.A. & Lanna, A.E., *Amazon Basin, GIWA Regional Assessment 40a*. United Nations Environmental Programme-UNEP, University of Kalmar: Sweden, 2003.

[10] Oliveira, P.S. & Marquis, R.J., *The Cerrados of Brazil: Ecology and Natural History of a Neotropical Savanna*, Columbia Univ. Press: New York. 2004.

[11] Barthem, R.B., Guerra, H. & Valderrama, M., *Diagnóstico de Los Recursos Hidrobiologicos de la Amazonia*, Secretaria Pro Tempore, Tratado de Cooperación Amazonica: Lima, Peru. 1995.

[12] Barthem, R.B., Componente Biota Aquática, *Biodiversidade na Amazônia Brasileira*, eds. J.P.R. Capobianco, A. Veríssimo, A. Moreira, D. Sawyer, I. Santos & L. P. Pinto. Câmara do Livro: São Paulo, Brasil pp. 60-78. 2001.

[13] Barros, A.C. & Uhl, C., The economic and social significance of logging operations on the floodplains of the Amazon Estuary and prospects for ecological sustainability, *Várzea: diversity, development and conservation of Amazon's white water floodplains*. eds. C. Padoch, J.M. Ayers, M. Pinedo-Vasquez & A. Henderson, The New York Botanical Garden Press: New York, pp. 153-168. 1999.

[14] Smith, N.J.H., *Amazon sweet sea: land, life and water at the river's mouth*. University of Texas Press: Texas, USA. 2002.

[15] Leite, R. de A.N. & Bittencourt, M.M., Impacto das hidrelétricas sobre a ictiofauna da Amazônia: O exemplo de Tucuruí, *Bases científicas para estratégias de preservação e desenvolvimento da Amazônia: Fatos e perspectivas*. Eds. A.L. Val, R. Figliulo & E. Feldberg. INPA: Manaus, pp. 85-104. 1991.

[16] Núñez-Barriga, A. & Castañeda-Hurtado, I., Environmental Management in a Heterogeneous Mining Industry: The Case of Peru (Chapter 4), *Mining and the Environment: Case Studies from the Americas*, International Development Research Centre-IDRC, 1999.

[17] Férnandez, C.A.R., Bagres, Malleros y Cuerderos en el Bajo Rio Caqueta, *Estudios en la Amazonia Colombiana*, eds. J.G. Saldarriaga & T.V. der Hammen, Tropenbos, Colombia, pp. 2-152. 1991.

[18] Marques, M., Barthem, R., Charvet-Almeida, P. & Montag, L.F.A. Amazon River Basin: Socio-economic issues and pressures behind deforestation, *Transactions on Ecology & the Environment,* V. 80, eds. E. Tiezzi & C.A. Brebbia, WIT: UK. 2005.

[19] Fearnside, P.M., Agroforestry in Brazil's Amazonian development policy: The role and limits of a potential use for degraded lands, *Brazilian perspectives on sustainable development of Amazon Region*, ed. Clusener-Godt & I. Sachs, The Panteon Pub., Unesco: Paris, pp. 125-148, 1995.

[20] Laurance, W.F., Cochrane, M.A. Bergen, S., Fearnside, P.M., Delamônica, P., Barber, C., D'Angelo, S. & Fernandes, T., The Future of the Brazilian Amazon, *Science*, **291** (5503), pp. 438-439. 2001.
[21] Instituto Nacional de Pesquisas Espaciais, http://satelite.cptec.inpe.br/
[22] Costa, M.H. & Foley, J.A., Combined effects of deforestation and doubled atmospheric CO_2 concentrations on the climate of Amazon. *Journal of Climate*, **13**, pp. 18-34. 2000.
[23] Nobre, C.A., Sellers, P.J. & Shukla, J., Amazonian deforestation and regional climate change. *Journal of Climate,* **4**, pp. 957-988. 1991.

Landform characteristics and the impact of human structures on the coastal area of Pozzallo (South Sicily, Italy)

V. Liguori[1], G. Anfuso[2], J. A. Martínez [2] & J. Benavente[2]
[1]*Dipartimento Ingegneria Strutturale e Geotecnica, Università di Palermo, Facoltà di Ingegneria Viale delle Scienze, Palermo, Sicilia, Italy*
[2]*Department of Geology, Faculty of Marine and Environmental Sciences, University of Cadiz, Polígono Río San Pedro s/n, 11510 Puerto Real, Cádiz. Spain*

Abstract

A geomorphologic approach, combined with GIS tools, was used to investigate a 26 Km long coastal sector in South Sicily, Italy, affected by important erosive processes. The applied methodology allowed for a database to be obtained involving all coastal characteristics, providing helpful information on coastal processes and general sediment circulation patterns. Coastal erosion, mainly linked to the construction of a port, was locally contrasted by the construction of hard structures, especially rip-rap revetments and breakwaters, generating environmental stress in the downdrift area. Nowadays a nourishment project has been planned to solve existing erosive problems, but there is still the lack of a general erosion management plan that should be principally based on the installation of a by-passing system.
Keywords: erosion, port, Pozzallo, Sicily.

1 Introduction

Coastal retreat is the landward displacement of shoreline because of marine erosion or flooding [1]. Usually, it is contrasted by protection works constructed on very specific sites, to solve concrete and urgent problems. Most of them constitute a temporary remedial without a general erosion management plan [2 and 3]. According to [4, 5 and 6], coastal erosion management must be organized at fully scales (i.e. at a large, regional scale) in which the dynamics of the whole coastal system is represented. In this sense, [7, 6, 8 and 9], affirm that for a deeply understood of coastal erosion problems it is important to know the areas of inputs, transfers, storage and outputs of sediments.

This paper would like to be a "first step" in the direction of improving the general knowledge of erosion problems and sediment circulation patterns within a 26 Km long coastal sector in South Sicily (Italy). Obtained results are useful information to develop an integrated coastal erosion management program aimed to partially solve erosion problems and review location of human activities and arrangements.

2 Study zone

Administratively, the study littoral belongs to different municipalities within the Ragusa Province, South of Sicily, Italy (figure 1). Coastal zone, E-W elongated and Southward exposed, is composed by sandy beaches of different width, rich in quartz (≅ 65%), carbonates (≅ 30%), containing also feldspars and heavy minerals [10 and 11].

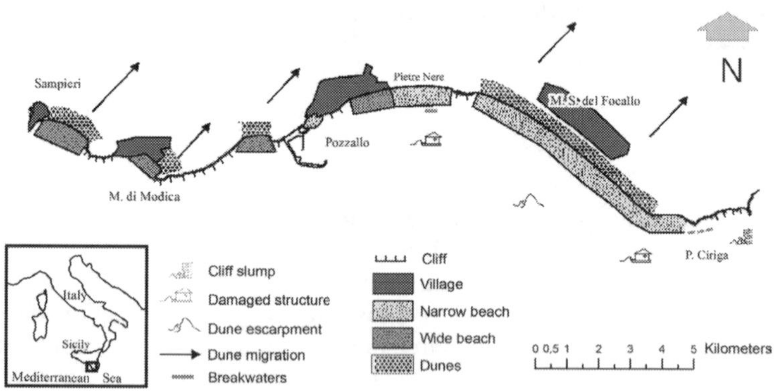

Figure 1: Landforms and human occupation along the study area.

Beaches are backed by dune ridges and cliffs, cut in sandstones, marls and limestones, dividing littoral in morphological cells [5]. No significant sedimentary inputs derive from cliff retreat because eroded sediments are generally too fine, being rapidly winnowed by waves and currents. Fluvial inputs [10 and 11] are not significant because many of the rivers are predominantly derived from chalk catchments. Additionally, sediment supply, important at an historical scale, was greatly restricted because of weirs and dams that favour rivers silting up during summer periods and, in last decade, because the artificial canalization of rivers and streams to avoid the flooding of urbanized areas.

Dealing with marine climate, the zone is a "microtidal environment" [12], principally affected by winds blowing from the second and third quadrants.

According to KNMI data (Leo observations), most important storms hit the coast preferentially from the third quadrant, with deep water values of significant wave height (H_s) of 8 m and 11 sec. associated period (T). Less important storms approach from the second quadrant with H_s = 5.5 m and T = 10.5 sec. Due to coastal orientation, the studied sector is stricken by storms approaching from East and West directions that give rise to important longshore currents, and from south approaching directions, that form a predominantly cross-shore transport.

During the last decades, the study area has recorded a great increase of human activities, constituting an important economic resource for the hinterland. Nowadays, many man-made structures or recreational activities are threatened by coastal retreat. In order to counteract this process, breakwaters and several rip-rap revetments were built when destruction of property was imminent, without any adequate plan or consideration of their long term side-effects.

3 Methods

According to [13, 14, 15 and 16], landforms characteristics and land use activities of the study area were obtained through several field observations and the analysis of recent aerial photographs and topographic maps. Following [17, 18, 19, 20 and 21], aerial photographs were scanned, geo-referenced and computer rectified to solve scale and distortion problems [22, 14 and 23]. Two data sets were used: the aerial photographs of 1977, at an original scale of 1:16,000, and the one, geo-referenced, of 1999 at scale 1:12,500, both realized by the Sicilian Regional Administration. In a further steep, beach dimensions were measured with GIS tools on the geo-referenced aerial photos, and coastline evolution was reconstructed. Ground Control Points (GCP^s) for the 1977 photo registration were obtained from the 1999 ones. Taking into account the smooth topography of the study area, an affine transformation (1ST order) was applied in the registration process [24]. The number of GCP^s used varied from one photograph to another, ranging form 10 to 14 units. Their position was located in unequivocal places such as groins and building corners according to [25]. The error in the geo-referenced photographs was controlled with the RMSE (Root Mean Square Error).

Shoreline position, which can be identified with seaward vegetation limit, dune foot, etc. [15 and 26], in this work was defined as "the water line at the time of the photo".

4 Results

4.1 Landform units

A schematic distribution of landforms, human occupation and coastal structures are presented in figure 1.

4.1.1 Beaches

Littoral is mainly composed of open and pocket fine-sand beaches of different dimensions, from hundreds of meters to several kilometres. The longest beach is

Santa Maria del Focallo, extended 11.2 Km, and the smallest one is close to Point Ciriga.

The dry beach width is about 30 m, with wider beaches observed updrift, or in correspondence, of human structures or natural headlands (figure 1). Morphological seasonal changes are on the scale of tens of meters, being wider beaches observed during summer time, i.e. from June to August [27].

Beach face slopes are usually very smooth and consist of fine sands. Field observations show that the nearshore zones present smooth slopes (1-2%) characterized by large surf zones with spilling breakers, typical of dissipative beach states [9 and 28]. One or more longshore bars are often observed and control breaking wave processes. Finally, the gentle nearshore slope favours wave refraction processes and wave fronts usually arrive at the shoreline with a small approaching angle.

4.1.2 Dunes

Their morphodynamic is related to the action of dominant winds that blow from the third quadrant, giving rise to generally small W-E elongated incipient foredunes and single dune ridges, parallel to shoreline. Ridges (2 to 6 m in height) are developed especially at Santa Maria del Focallo beach (figure 1), where they present a degraded vegetal cover composed by Mediterranean bushes. In other areas vegetal cover consists of pioneer plants. In the area of study, there are only few sedimentary supplies also during fair weather condition. The foredunes have almost disappeared and dune ridges suffer periodical erosion during winter periods in the most part of littoral. By the other way, great quantities of sediments are landward transported because of aeolian processes, being definitely lost to sedimentary budget.

4.1.3 Cliffs

Cliffs and promontories, 6-7 m in height, are a quite common morphology along the Ragusa Province littoral. Rocks with a low degree of resistance are constituted by the sandstones of the Pleistocene marine terraces and the Low Miocene marls that outcrop at Pietre Nere and at Point Ciriga (figure 1). These "weak" rocks are mainly affected by landslide rock falls types due to wave erosion at the foot of the cliff. The presence of rock blocks at cliff foot, remnant of previous falls, should have the function of reduce cliff erosion but, during heavy storms, sea waves overpass them and reactivate erosive processes.

4.2 Human constructions and interventions

4.2.1 Coastal occupation

Dealing with urban development in the study littoral, it was greatly increasing during the last decades, as in other Mediterranean areas. Small, pre-existing villages, with fishing or agricultural activities as a primary source of life, recorded a great expansion, and essentially linked to the construction of summer houses vacated to the local tourist demand. The table 1 show the changes of numbers of inhabitants in winter and summer time for the most important villages present along the study littoral.

Table 1: Population of most important villages along the littoral.

Village	Winter population	Increment during summer time	Total population in summer time
Sampieri	1,000	18,000	19,000
Marina di Modica	3,000	25,000	28,000
Pozzallo	17,500	5,000	22,500
Santa Maria del Focallo	0	8,000	8,000

4.2.2 Ports and harbours

Small marinas and pier rope haulages exist at several places, such as Marina di Modica, Sampieri and Pozzallo. These areas, initially used for traditional fishing purposes, nowadays host small pleasure boats.

Pozzallo port, the biggest one in the Province, presents an 1864 m long, N-S oriented, main dock, and a maximum depth of 15 m. It was constructed in the seventies to support the industrial activities developing in the hinterland. This structure, still underused, is devoted to pleasure and fishing boats and cargo ships. The port blocked longshore sediment transport, with sand accumulation at East side, close to the structure. As a consequence, beach facilities and recreational structures have been greatly implemented during last years on this enlarged beach (figure 2).

Figure 2: Accretion recorded East of Pozzallo port.

Figure 3: Breakwaters at Punta Ciriga retaining large quantities of sand.

4.2.3 Protective structures

Among the defensive structures, detached breakwaters of calcareous blocks were built along the littoral to stop more than to prevent coastal retreat, resulting in the downdrift shifting of erosive problems. Nowadays, the great majority of them are connected to the shoreline by tombolos (figures 1 and 3).

Sea walls and rip-rap revetments are also present in very narrow coastal sectors, usually to preserve summer houses. Location and characteristics of protective works are presented in Table 2.

Table 2: Characteristics of most important protective structures.

Location	Type	Material	Number	Unitary length (m)
Pietre Nere beach	breakwater	rocky blocks	1	140
St M. Focallo beach	Rip-rap revet	Concr. blocks	1	100
Point Ciriga	breakwater	rocky blocks	4	75

A nourishment project was designed for Santa Maria del Focallo beach to stop erosive processes linked to the Pozzallo port and the breakwaters at Point Ciriga. This project is not still founded because considered too expensive (11,000,000 €), for the high cost of the borrow sand.

5 Discussion

Study littoral is divided in several cells of different dimensions, within which sediments circulate. Effects of coastal embaymentisation, because of natural and artificial structures, are quite evident on beach plan form and surf zone circulation.

Concerning cell boundaries, these are places characterized by discontinuities in rate or direction of sediment transport: they can be "fixed", if stabile, or "transient" or "free", if their position changes with time [5 and 7].

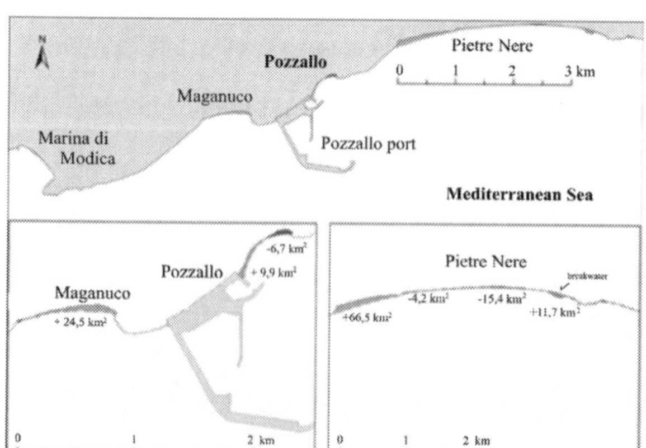

Figure 4: Surfaces of beach erosion and accretion (km^2) calculated around Pozzallo area comparing the 1977 and the 1999 aerial photographs.

In study littoral the former are essentially associated to engineering structures, the latter are not necessary associated with any morphological. This way, small headlands and cliffs observed along the study littoral allow periodic bi-directional transport that, according to field observations, takes place along narrow zones parallel to shoreline, extended to a variable depth, depending on wave conditions and bottom morphology. Furthermore, headlands bypass takes easily place because of sand transport on the top of longshore bars. Bypass processes occur frequently in correspondence of small headlands, while in correspondence of most important ones (Sampieri and Marina di Modica), sediments trespassing is more difficult and takes place during important storms.

By the other way, Pozzallo port causes artificial compartmentalisation, more important than natural one. It constitutes an artificial, fixed and absolute limit, that block littoral transport giving rise to important accretion updrift and huge depletion downdrift.

In order to have a first, broad idea of recent littoral evolution and predominant littoral transport effects, main zones of accretion, erosion or stability, were determined taking into account aerial photographs of 1977 and 1999 (figure 4).

At the origin, Pozzallo port was composed by an offshore dock enlacing with land by a piper that not greatly affected littoral drift. In the eighties, the original structure was modified by the construction of a new East pier in order to protect the port from the waves coming from the third quadrant.

As can be observed in figure 4, shoreline advancements were recorded in different areas: in Maganuco, and immediately East of the port (figure 2) and, especially, in Pietre Nere (66,000 km^2). A small accretion was also observed in correspondence of the breakwater constructed in Pietre Nere and diffuse erosion took place west of the structure. Santa Maria del Focallo and Point Ciriga beaches recorded general erosion too.

Previous results seem to be related with the action of waves and currents from the second and third quadrants that generate opposite transports, both affected by the presence of the structure (figure 4).

By one way, waves and currents approaching from the East accumulate sediments in Maganuco that is protected by the second quadrant approaching waves because of the port.

By the other way, the prevalence of waves and associated currents from the second quadrant accumulate sediments close to the East side of the port where they can not be removed by waves from the third quadrant, because in the port lee side. The consequent erosion is recorded at east of the port, in Pietre Nere, where a summer house was protected a breakwater, and in Santa Maria del Focallo beaches, where the littoral road, greatly damaged by erosive processes, was protected by concrete blocks.

Important sediment sinks are also related to wind processes, especially to the ones from western directions that favour eastward dune migration. Examples of this process are quite common at Marina di Modica (figure 5) and Santa Maria del Focallo. In these places, small incipient foredunes and well developed, unvegetated dunes migrate landwards with a consequent loss of sediments. Sand is transported inland, sometimes covering coastal roads that need periodic maintenance. Recollected sediments are not injected in beach system and are accumulated in city dumps.

Figure 5: The rapidly landward migrating avalanche face of a well developed dune at Marina di Modica.

Other, significant sediment sinks are related to different measures and modalities used by local Administrations in port dredging works or beach cleaning processes. Sediments and algae are periodically dredged in Pozzallo port (Table 3) and in correspondence of other smaller structures, being these works always carried out under remedial and urgent conditions, without any kind of management plan. This way, great quantities of sands were in the past accumulated in dumps or injected offshore, in deep water, subtracting them to the sedimentary budget.

Table 3: Volumes of dredged sediments.

Location	Period	Dredged volumes (m^3)	Destination of dredged sand
Pozzallo port	1982-1995	1,150,000	3,700 Km offshore
Pozzallo port	2000	unknown	Pietre Nere beach

Furthermore, modalities of beach cleaning and maintenance, based on the removing of large quantities of leafs of *posidonia oceanica* or other marine phanerogams, usually accumulated on beaches during summer and autumn periods, produce the abstraction of large quantities of sediments and favour beach erosion.

6 Considerations

In studied littoral, coastal erosion was contrasted by the construction of hard structures generating important environmental stress in downdrift areas. Nowadays a nourishment project has been planned to solve existing, local erosive problems, keeping in mind that a healthy beach is the best form of coastal defence and has a maximum recreational benefit.

Moreover, there is still the lack of a general erosion management plan that should be principally based on:
i) the installation of a port by-passing system,
ii) the dismissal of actual beach cleaning and port maintenance procedures that substrate a great quantity of sediments and
iii) the control of inland wind transport.

The realization of these objectives and actuations requires further studies to identify small, independent shoreline management units, and quantify littoral sedimentary budget within each unit and the whole littoral.

References

[1] Bird, E.C., Submerging coasts. J. Wiley & Sons. 184 p., 1993.

[2] Hooke, J., Coastal defense and earth science conservation. The Geological Society, 270 p., 1998.

[3] Pethick, J., Coastal management and sea level rise. Catena. 42 (2-4): 307-322, 2001.

[4] Fischer, D., Responses to coastal threats: toward an integrated strategy. Jour. Coastal. Res., 1(4): 383-388, 1985.

[5] Carter, R.W.G., Coastal environments. Academic Press, 617 pp.

[6] Bray, M., Carter, D. and Hooke, J. (1995). Littoral cell definition and budgets for central southern England. Jour. Coastal Res., 11 (2): 381 – 400, 1988.

[7] Bray, M. and Hooke, J., Strategy for conserving dynamic coastal landforms. In: Healy M. G. and Doody J.D. (edrs.) Directions in European Coastal Management, 275-290, 1995.

[8] Komar, P.D., Beach processes and sedimentation. Prentice-Hall. 544 p., 1998.

[9] Short, A. D., Beach and Shoreface morphodynamics. J. Wiley & Sons, 379 p., 1999.

[10] Randazzo G., Dinamica del litorale e caratteristiche tessiturali dei sedimenti della fascia costiera compresa tra Cava d'Aliga e la Foce del fiume Dirillo – Acate. Degree Thesis, Univ. of Catania, unpublished, 1985.

[11] Anfuso, G., Il litorale ragusano compreso tra Cava d'Aliga e la foce del fiume Dirillo. Bollettino Accademia Gioena Scienze Naturali, 31 (355): 287-301, 1999.

[12] Davies, J. L., A morphogenetic approach to world shorelines. Zeit. für Geomorph., 8:127-142, 1964.

[13] Dickson, S. M., Coastal sand dune map: Hills beach. Maine geological survey, Augusta, ME, USA, 1:4800, 1990.

[14] Crowell, M., Leatherman, S.P. and Buckley, M., Historical shoreline change: error analysis and mapping accuracy. Jour. Coastal Res., 7 (3): 839-852, 1991.

[15] Crowell, M., Leatherman, S.P. and Buckley, M., Shore-line change rate analysis: long term versus short term data. Shore and Beach, 61 (2): 13-20, 1993.

[16] Gorman, L., Morang, A. and Larson, R., Monitoring the coastal environment; part IV: mapping, shoreline changes and bathymetric analysis. Jour. Coastal Res., 14 (1): 61-92, 1998.

[17] Dolan, R., Fester, M.S. and Holme, S.J., Temporal analysis of shoreline recession and accretion. Jour. Coastal Res., 7 (3): 723-744, 1991.

[18] Dolan, R., Hayden, B., May, P. and Suzette, R., The reliability of shoreline change measurements from aerial photographs. Shore and Beach, 48: 22-29, 1980.
[19] Leatherman, S., Shoreline mapping: a comparison of techniques. Shore and Beach, 51: 28-33, 1983.
[20] Jiménez, J., Sánchez-Arcilla, A., Bou, J. and Ortiz, M., Analysing Short-term shoreline changes along the Ebro delta (Spain) using aerial photographs. Jour. Coastal Res., 13 (4): 1256-1266, 1997.
[21] Pajak, M.J. and Leatherman, S., The high water line as shoreline indicator. Jour. Coastal Res., 18 (2): 329-337, 2002.
[22] Lillesand, T., and Kiefer, R., Remote sensing and image interpretation. 2nd edition. New York, Wiley, 1987.
[23] Moore, L., Shoreline mapping techniques. Jour. Coastal Res., 16 (1): 111-124, 2000.
[24] Chuvieco, E., Fundamentos de Teledetección Espacial. Rialp Ed., 567 p., 2000.
[25] Thieler, E. and Danforth, W., Historical shoreline mapping: Improving techniques and reducing positioning errors. Jour. Coastal Res., 10 (3): 549-563, 1994.
[26] Fisher, J. and Overton, M., Interpretation of shoreline position from aerial photographs. Proc. 24th Coastal Engineering Conference, (ASCE), 1998-2003, 1994.
[27] Anfuso G., Evoluzione temporale e caratteristiche tessiturali dei sedimenti della fascia costiera tra Punta d'Aliga e la foce del fiume Dirillo-Acate. Degree Thesis, Univ. of Catania. 178 pp., unpublished, 1993.
[28] Wright, L.D. and Short, A.D., Morphodynamic variability of surf zones and beaches: a synthesis. Marine Geology, 56: 93-118, 1984.

Wetland impacts on the optical characteristics of the inshore bays of Lake Victoria, East Africa

C. Rossi[1], A. Cózar[2], L. Bracchini[1], S. Focardi[1] & S Loiselle[1]
[1]*Department of Chemical and Biosystem Sciences, University of Siena, Siena, Italy*
[2]*Área de Ecología, Facultad de Ciencias del Mar, University of Cádiz, 11510 Puerto Real, Cádiz, Spain*

Abstract

Lake Victoria is the largest tropical lake in the world and has the most densely populated lake catchment in the tropics, with major cites from three nations that lie on its shores. The lake provides resources that are fundamental for the local population and national economies. Inshore areas are particularly sensitive to changes in land use, wetland management and wetland vegetation. The highly heterogeneous inshore waters of Lake Victoria present a wide range of optical environments, from strongly humic environments to highly turbid areas and to areas of massive algal blooms. In the present study, the spatial analysis of the light field along the Ugandan and Kenyan coast was analysed using a series of spectroradiometers, simultaneously with chemical and biological measurements. By combining both the high spatial resolution data from the water column, with the satellite derived spatially explicit information about the coastline characteristics, it was possible to examine the relation between wetland coverage and water quality. The extinction coefficients in the visible wavelengths showed higher extinction in wetland-bordered areas for wavebands necessary for chlorophyll photosynthesis, reducing the euphotic depth available for phytoplankton growth.
Keywords: Lake Victoria, Africa, DOM, PAR, water quality, wetlands, Great Lakes.

1 Introduction

The absorption of solar electromagnetic radiation and the biological conversion of this available energy to chemical bonds in the form of organic molecules is the basis for all ecosystem productivity. Approximately 40% of the Earth's photosynthesis occurs in aquatic environments [1]. It is therefore important to understand how the variation in the optical conditions of a water body may change the availability of energy for the photosynthetic process. The optical properties of a particular water medium depend largely upon the characteristics of the dissolved and particulate matter of the medium. As both influence the absorption and scattering of the incoming radiation, seasonal and spatial variations in their concentration will influence the available energy within the water medium. When considering this loss along the water column, the radiant flux will diminish in an approximately exponential manner, according to the Lambert Beer Bouguer-law.

$$K_d = - d\,(\ln I_d)/dz \quad (1)$$

where I_d is the downward irradiance, K_d is the vertical attenuation coefficient and z is the depth. This coefficient considers both the absorptive and scattering properties of the medium in the direct measure of the diminution of the available radiation with depth. The determination of the vertical attenuation coefficient is therefore a method for characterising the optical properties of a water column. K_d is expected to remain the same if the conditions of the medium do not change, increase or decrease according to the changes in the water quality.

The release of organic matter into lakes from the surrounding catchment and littoral areas can play a fundamental role in the ecological and physical functioning of the inshore ecosystem. In many tropical lakes, extensive littoral wetland areas release significant quantities of dissolved organic matter and in doing so create optical conditions that are significantly different than adjacent open lake areas. In the African Great Lakes, much of the coastline is dominated by floating papyrus wetlands which extend for tens of kilometres. These wetlands receive waters (and inorganic nutrients) from catchment areas and population centres and release dissolved organic material (and organic nutrients) into the lake.

Allochthonous coloured dissolved organic matter (CDOM) can impact freshwater ecosystem functioning on several levels. For example, microbial activity is strongly tied to CDOM concentrations. Complexation of trace metals and pH buffering by CDOM can also be significant. Important impacts on the optical environment of the water column are also evident. From the point of view of the aquatic light environment, the release of high molecular weight organic matter from the degraded wetland biomass into the water column can limit the availability of PAR in the upper water column. Likewise, CDOM attenuates incident radiation in the UVA and UVB wavelengths, thereby reducing reduce the negative impacts of shortwave radiation (in particular UVB) on the aquatic organisms that circulate in the water column. High doses of UV radiation may cause chlorophyll photobleaching, modification of the DNA structure, cellular damages and the inhibition of motility in plankton [4,5,6].

In the present paper, we describe the optical characteristics of the inshore waters of Lake Victoria, based on an extensive sampling performed along the Ugandan and Kenyan coastlines. We determine the spatial distribution of these optical properties with respect to the inshore coastline characteristics.

2 Experimental

During the last 50 years, Lake Victoria and many of the East African Great Lakes have undergone major changes, both in trophic structure as well as in water quality. Phytoplankton abundance and composition have changed [8], demonstrating an increasing eutrophication [9] which has led to anoxia and a loss of fish habitat [10]. The combined reduction of the water quality and trophic complexity has led to a potentially catastrophic simplification of the energy transfer within the ecosystem. The cascading effect on the trophic chain is yet to be clearly identified and the driving forces that have led to the present state have yet to be completely addressed. These include the increasing nutrient load, further evolution in the aquatic trophic web, climate change and a reduction in the extension and functional capacity of the Lake's wetland borders [11,12,13]. In the present condition of the East African Great Lake ecosystems, where the pressure of a growing population will most likely increase, the aquatic resources have a vital importance in the health and well being of over 30 million persons [14].

To contribute to this important area, a European Union (EU) sponsored international research project was initiated with the objective of determining the role that wetlands have in maintaining the aquatic resource quality. Three measurement campaigns were performed along the Uganda and Kenyan inshore areas of Lake Victoria in 2002 – 2004. The first measurement campaign was performed in November 2002, in which both inner and outer Katonga Bay were sampled for a total of 40 sampling sites obtained over a 2 day period. The second measurement campaign was performed in June 2003 and repeated the measurements in the same sampling location in Katonga Bay (n=20) as well as sampling several other bays, with different degrees of wetland coverage along the Ugandan coast. The final campaign was performed along the Kenyan coastline in March 2004. In this paper, the optical data from the three measurement campaigns is presented and compared to the limited historical data available. In each site, the vertical profile of the photosynthetically available radiation (PAR) and water temperature, Secchi depth, chlorophyll *a* fluorescence and dissolved organic matter were measured simultaneously.

The profile of the photosynthetically available radiation (PAR) in the water column in each measurement site was measured using a PUV541 spectroradiometer (Biospherical Corp.). The instrument was calibrated in July 2001 by comparing the measured irradiances of the instrument with a second spectroradiometer. The PUV541 was connected to a battery and a portable computer with a specific programme to collect the irradiance data. The instrument is lowered into the water column and measurements of PAR irradiance in μEm $^{-2}$s $^{-1}$, water temperature and water depth were acquired simultaneously every 0.3 seconds. The measurement considers the total flux of radiation in the waveband between 400 – 700 nm. The background measurement with the sensor covered (dark current) was on the order of 3 μEm $^{-2}$s $^{-1}$.

Measurements were made between 10:30 and 15:30 in all campaigns, under similar weather conditions, limited cloudiness and low wind. The geographical location of each sampling point was recorded using a GPS (Garmin). The PUV541 was positioned below the water line (-2 cm) and measurements were recorded while the instrument was lowered to the lake bottom as well as during the raising of the instrument to just below the water surface. Each profile of irradiances was repeated directly after the first profile was obtained. On average, around 130 measurements (irradiances, temperature and water depth) were obtained along the water column in each profile. Water column depth ranged from 0.5 to 8 meters.

The resulting radiation profile was corrected by removing the instrument dark current and plotted against water depth. As the PUV541 has cosine corrected flat collector, there is no dependence on the illumination angle. The downward irradiance diminishes in an approximately exponential manner with depth. The coefficient of attenuation (K_d) was calculated by fitting the best exponential curve to the profile data, according to equation 2.

$$K_d = - (z-z_0)^{-1} \ln (I_z/I_{z0}) \qquad (2)$$

where z is water depth, z_0 is 0.02 m, I_z is the measured irradiance at depth z, I_{z0} is the measured irradiance at depth z_0 (0.02 m). All profiles in which the R^2 of the exponential fitting was less than 0.90, were discarded.

Samples were obtained at a depth of 25 cm for the measurement in laboratory of dissolved organic matter (DOM). Dissolved organic matter is an important component of the water column, contributing to the attenuation of solar radiation [15] as well as providing organic matter for secondary production [16,17]. The DOM present in the inner bays of Lake Victoria appear to have its origin in the decaying vegetation in the floating papyrus stands that cover much of the shoreline. At each site a sample of 20 ml was obtained, filtered (0.22 μm, Millipore filter) on site and stored in hermetic containers in the dark at 4°C. The filtered samples were analysed without further modification by UV/VIS spectroscopy (Pharmacia Biotech Ultrospec 2000® UV/VIS Spectrophotometer, spectral bandwidth 3nm) in 0.01 m path length quartz curvettes [18].

The absorbance of high molecular weight DOM in the UV/VIS spectral region decreases with increasing wavelengths. This phenomenon is linked to the aromatic ring structure that constitutes a major part of the function groups of the humic and fulvic substances formed from the degradation of lignin-cellulose materials. The responsible electronic transition is of the type $\pi \rightarrow \pi^*$ and occurs in the wavelength region between about 270 and 280 nm for benzoic acids, aniline derivates, polyenes and polycyclic aromatic hydrocarbons with two or more rings. A number of wavelengths have been used to measure DOM [19].

The wavelength 272 nm was selected as it permits an estimation of all the dissolved organic matter present in the water sample, comprising not only humic and fulvic acids, but also decomposition products of semi-stable organic materials in solution.

The concentration of chlorophyll a was estimated by using a temperature corrected and calibrated portable fluorometer (Turner Instruments SCUFA II). The fluorometer uses an excitation light source at 465 nm and silicon photodiode to measure fluorescence of chlorophyll a at 685 nm. The detection of in vivo fluorescence is a qualitative measurement. Numerous physiological and environmental factors can influence the measurement. Fluorescence yields vary from phytoplankton species to species as well as depend upon the history of exposure of each cell. Over a single lake, with few dominating phytoplankton species, it is possible to assume that higher phytoplankton chlorophyll concentrations will lead to higher fluorescence. Before each campaign the fluorometer was calibrated by comparing the measured fluorescence to actual chlorophyll a concentrations measured by standard spectrophotometric methods. The resultant calibration curve (R^2 = 0.85, $p<0.05$) was used to estimate chlorophyll a concentrations from the measured fluorescence.

3 Results and discussion

The irradiance profile was analysed and an attenuation coefficient was calculated for each site. A wide range of values was observed in each measurement campaign, linked to the spatial variation was noticed within the lake. To examine these spatial patterns in relation to the lake morphology, maps of the spatial distribution of the K_d were made using a Kriging interpolation method in the Surfer (7.0) software package. The map for Katonga and Bunjako bays are presented in Figure 1 below.

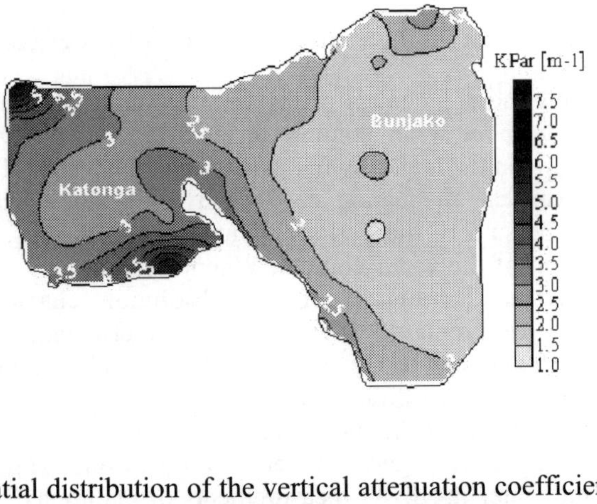

Figure 1: Spatial distribution of the vertical attenuation coefficient of PAR in Katonga and Bunjako Bays, Uganda in November 2002.

To determine the total adjoining wetland area of each of the study bays, a series of multispectral satellite images from the SAC-C satellite system (MMRS sensor) were used. Satellite measured radiances were converted to surface reflectances by estimating atmospheric path irradiance according to Chavez [20]. A semi-supervised classification of the littoral areas of each inshore bay was performed from on site observations and available maps. The estimated wetland coverage and relative littoral area covered by wetland is reported in the following table (Table 1). The coastline of both Katonga and Nsonga Bays are dominated (>50%) by wetlands (papyrus) while Bunjako and Tende have very low percentages of wetland coverage (<7%). Winam Bay in Kenya presents an intermediate situation.

Table 1: Wetland coverage for the inshore areas studied, obtained by satellite image analysis.

Inshore area	Open water area (km^2)	Adjoining wetland area (km^2)	Percent wetland coastline (%)
Katonga Bay	11.0	10.3	82
Bunjako Bay	43.9	5.7	6
Nsonga Bay	15.5	25.2	59
Tende Bay	5.7	0.5	7
Winam Bay	1392.0	74.4	13

A clear relationship was observed between wetland coverage of each bay and the measured optical properties of the water. In fact, bays with significant wetlands (Katonga, Nsonga) have consistently higher [CDOM]. Likewise these bays are characterised by a high variance in K_d and generally increased overall attenuation. [CHLa] does not show any significant difference between bays in the same measurement campaign.

3.1 Controlling factors in light attenuation in the water column

To examine how the compounds of the water column influence the availability of PAR in the inshore water column, an analysis was made to determine the relationship between the major light attenuating components of the water column and K_d. The vertical attenuation coefficient for a single wavelength can be considered as the sum of the partial attenuation coefficients, each related to a single component of the water column. When considering a waveband, such as PAR, the spectral distribution of the absorption characteristics of each component are different. However, as an approximate relationship, the attenuation coefficient can be considered as the sum of the concentration of each component times its specific vertical attenuation coefficient. The main attenuating components of the water column are the photosynthetic pigments in phytoplankton, dissolved organic matter (CDOM), tripton (nonliving particulate matter) and the water itself. As measurements of chlorophyll a (most common phytosynthetic pigment in phytoplankton) and CDOM were made in each of these bays, a multiple regression analysis was made for each inshore area, comparing Kd and the measured concentrations of CDOM and Chlorophyll a. The resulting equations describe the role of each water column component in the attenuation of the total solar radiation available.

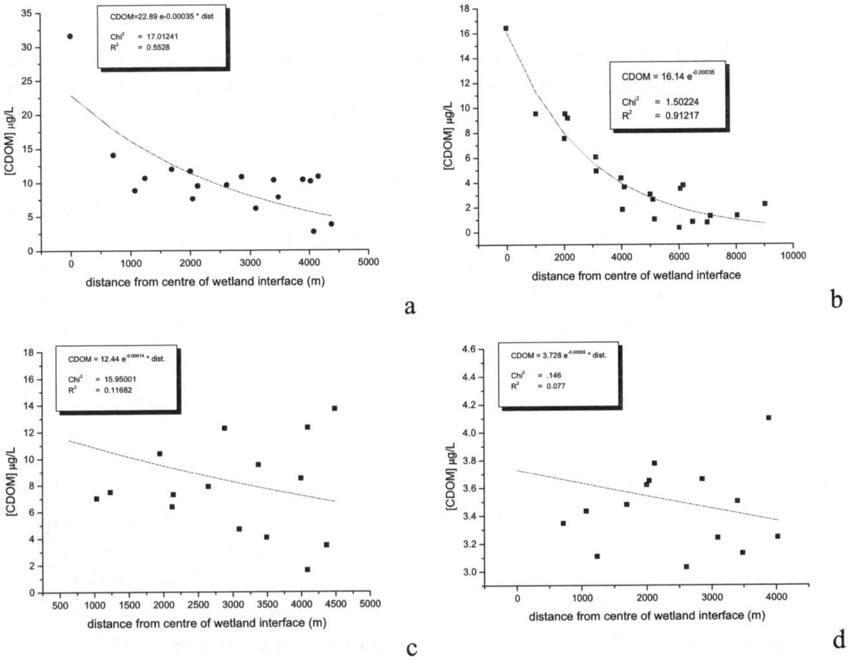

Figure 2: Spatial relationships between wetland areas and [CDOM] measured in three Bays during two sampling campaigns, a) Katonga, June 2003, b)Nsonga June 2003, c) Katonga November 2002, d) Tende June 2003.

These equations demonstrate the relationship between the attenuating components and the vertical attenuation of the PAR. All equations, with the exception of Bunjako Bay have P-values in the ANOVA table of less than 0.05 meaning that there is a statistically significant relationship between the variables at the 95% confidence level. The statistically significant algorithms were found to explain between 40 and 88 % of the variance in the KPAR measurements. The P-value of the independent variables show the significance of the variables within the equation. In the second Katonga campaign, Nsonga Bay and Winam Bay, the CDOM concentration is highly significant. The [CHLa] is significant only in the first Katonga campaign, as well as in Tende and Winam bays. By comparing the average concentration of CHLa and CDOM with the specific parameters of each algorithm, it is possible to determine that [CHLa] is the dominating attenuation coefficient in the first measurement campaign (Katonga and Bunjako, November 2002), while [CDOM] dominates the attenuation in all other campaigns.

Measurement campaigns concentrated on obtaining spatially explicit data, and are not aimed at examining the seasonal variability. Only the Katonga Bay sample was repeated and significant differences were observed between the two sampling campaigns. In the first campaign, [CHLa] was significantly higher with respect to the second campaign ($p = 0.008$). This may be the result of an increase of nutrients from the catchment area in relation to the heavy rain season. Both measurement campaigns were performed after the seasonal rainy season. However, strongest rainy season occurs in April and May.

The spatial analysis of the measured parameters reveals further information about the role of the wetlands in the optical properties of the water column. By analysing the variations in the concentrations of the attenuating components with respect to distance from the centre of the wetland area, a clear relation can be seen between [CDOM] and the distance from the wetland in those bays (Nsonga, Katonga-June 2003) were wetlands dominate. In those bays where wetlands do not have a significant impact (Tende, Katonga- November 2002), there is no significant correlation between distance from the wetland and [CDOM].

4 Conclusion

In the inshore area of freshwater lakes, the presence of floating wetlands can have a significant impact on the light environment. Spatial and temporal variations in the light environment have an important influence on the aquatic productivity. As a property of the water column, K_d is both influenced by, as well as influences, the chemical and biological conditions of the water body. In the comparison with other lakes [19], the present K_d measurements in the inshore areas of Lake Victoria fall are higher than the values that are usually reported for inland waters in temperate environments. The high spatial resolution used in the present study made it possible to determine potential causes of the spatial variation in the Lake water's optical conditions. As evidenced in the comparison of the two measurements in Katonga Bay, seasonal changes in the hydrological regime of the catchment will have important consequences on the underwater light conditions. Likewise, changes in the land use within the watershed could effect the presence of CDOM and nutrients in the water. Further investigation regarding the estimation of nutrient loads from satellite determined land use classification is presently underway. However, the release of CDOM from extensive littoral wetlands is a dominating factor in the control and modification of the availability of solar radiation in the water column and was clearly demonstrated in the present paper.

Acknowledgements

This project is supported through the European Commission RTD INCO programme (ICA4CT2001-10036). We would like to thank our colleagues at the Department of Water Resources in Entebbe Uganda and the Kenyan Marine

Fisheries Research Institute for their collaboration in data gathering and analysis. The authors would like to thank the Argentine Space Agency (CONAE) for their collaboration in obtaining satellite images of the study area. The research was supported by the Italian Interuniversity Consortium CSGI.

References

[1] P.G. Falkowski,. *Photosynthesis Research* 13: 21 (1994).
[2] R.C. Smith, *Limnol. Oceanogr.* 13: 423 (1968).
[3] J.T.O. Kirk, *Aust. L. Mar. Freshwater Res.* 28: 9-211977.
[4] S. A. Wängberg, J.S Selmer In Häder DP eds, *The effects of ozone depletion on aquatic ecosystems*. Academic Press 199 (1997).
[5] D. P. Häder, S.M. Liu. *Current Microbiology*, 21, 161(1990).
[6] W. Nultsch, G. Agel, *Archives of Microbiology*, 144, 268 (1986).
[7] J.S. Balirwa, *Lake Victoria wetlands and the ecology of the Nile Tilapia, Oreochromis Niloticus* ISBN: 90 5410 411 2 IHE Dissertation 13 (1998).
[8] R. Mugidde *Verhandlungen der Internationale Vereinigung für Llimnologie 25*: 846 (1993).
[9] P.B.O. Ochumba, In T.J. Pitcher and P.B. Hart (Editors), The Impact of Species Change in African Lakes, Chapman & Hall, pp. 33. (1995).
[10] L. Kaufman. *Bioscience* 42:846 (1992).
[11] R. Ogutu-Ohwayo, *Environ. Biol. Fish. 27*: 81 (1990).
[12] R.E. Hecky, *Verhandlungen der Internationale Vereinigung für Llimnologie 25*: 39 (1993).
[13] H.Lung'ayia, L.Sitoki and M.Kenyanya, *Hydrobiologia 458*: 75. (2001).
[14] F.W.B. Bugenyi,.. *Hydrobiologia 458*: 33. 2001.
[15] D.W., Schindler, P.J. Curtis B.R. Parker, and M.P. Stainton,. *Nature* 379: 705-707 (1996).
[16] L.J. Tranvik, *Microb. Ecol.* 16:311 (1988).
[17] G.K Nürnberg and M. Shaw, *Hydrobiologia* 382: 97 (1999).
[18] K. Hautala, J. Peuravuori, and K. Pihlaja,. *Wat. Res.* 34: 246 (2000).
[19] J.T.O. Kirk, *Light and Photosynthesis in Aquatic Ecosystems*. Cambridge Press, Cambridge: 401 pp. (1994).
[20] P.S. Chavez Jr., *Photogramm. Eng. Rem.* S. 629, 1025 (1996).

Section 17
Soil and agricultural issues

Environmental and socio-economic contributions of palm-leaf geotextiles to sustainable development and soil conservation

C. A. Booth, K. Davies & M. A. Fullen
Environmental & Analytical Sciences Division, Research Institute in Advanced Technologies (RIATec), The University of Wolverhampton, UK

Abstract

Geotextiles are employed in civil engineering and construction applications to efficiently and economically conserve soil. Palm-leaf geotextiles offer considerable potential to contribute to sustainable development and soil conservation. Their use can promote sustainable and environmentally-friendly palm agriculture, labour-intensive employment and earn hard currency. Ongoing field and laboratory research is investigating geotextile mats manufactured from palm-leaves to evaluate their long-term effectiveness in controlling soil erosion and assess their sustainability and economic viability. Palm-leaf geotextiles are novel and offer new bioengineering solutions to environmental problems. This is achieved through:

(i) Promotion of sustainable and environmentally-friendly palm agriculture to discourage deforestation, promote both reforestation and agroforestry and offer a potential for commercial development.
(ii) Construction of palm geotextiles to develop into a rural based labour-intensive industry, particularly encouraging employment of socially disadvantaged groups. In turn, this contributes to the stabilization of rural populations, thus decreasing migration to urban areas.
(iii) Export of completed palm geotextiles to industrialized countries earns hard currency for rural developing economies, based on the principles of fair trade.
(iv) Application of palm geotextiles are especially beneficial for complex engineering problems, as temporary application of geotextiles allows sufficient time for plant communities to stabilize engineered slopes.

Investigations suggest palm geotextiles are an effective, cheap and economically-viable soil conservation method, with tremendous potential. Palm geotextiles offer enormous multi-faceted environmental benefits, which include technologies for sustainable plant production, promoting sustainable use of indigenous plants, improved ecosystem management, decreasing deforestation, improved agroforestry and successful and cost-effective geotextile applications in diverse environments. Palm geotextiles improve socio-economic foundations for sustainable development and the benefits for developing countries include poverty alleviation, engagement of disadvantaged groups as stakeholders, employment for disadvantaged groups, SME (small and medium enterprise) development, earning hard currency, environmental education and local community involvement in reclamation and environmental-improvement programmes.

Keywords: soil erosion, runoff plots, geotextile, Borassus aethiopum.

1 Introduction

Water erosion is a major issue; responsible for 56% of global land degradation [1]. Loss of valuable productive topsoil impacts food production and threatens security, particularly in the developing world. The 'United Nations Environment Programme' [2] forecast that, by 2025, 83% of the world's estimated 8.5 billion population will be living in the developing world. There is uncertainty whether available resources and technology will satisfy food demands, particularly where population demands place severe pressures on soil resources.

Recent improvements have been made in soil conservation technology and over the last three decades, significant advances have been made in our understanding of soil erosion mechanisms and rates under different environmental conditions. However, there have been few advances in developing innovative soil conservation techniques. Moreover, relatively little research has been conducted at the interface between soil technology and socio-economic issues, such as sustainable development, poverty alleviation and rural employment. One technique for soil conservation is geotextiles, which can create stable, non-eroding environments that provide the time necessary for vegetation to establish and grow. If constructed from indigenous materials, geotextiles can be effective, affordable and compatible with sustainable land management strategies.

2 An appropriate strategy for soil conservation

Despite synthetic geotextiles dominating the commercial market, geotextiles constructed from organic materials are highly effective in erosion control and vegetation establishment [3,4,5]. Jute is the market leader in organic geotextiles. However, other natural fibres, such as coir, sisal and ramie, also have geotechnical applications [6]. Recent studies have shown natural fibres are more effective than synthetic in controlling erosion [3] and were the preferred method in a wildlife refuge, because of their 100% biodegradability and better adherence to the soil [4]. Moreover, in developing regions, commercially marketed materials are usually too expensive [7].

Palmae have been used extensively for over 6,000 years, providing some 800 resources for human use [8]. However, extensive reviews suggest palm-leaf is not currently used in the geotextile soil erosion control industry and, to date, studies have not quantified the effects of palm-mat geotextiles on water and wind erosion rates. In this pilot project, the feasibility of employing palm-mat geotextiles as a potential soil conservation technique is investigated.

3 Socio-economic impact of palm-mat geotextiles

Preliminary investigations suggest palm-mat geotextiles could be an effective and cheap soil conservation method, with enormous global potential. A 'time and motion' study was conducted during the construction of the mats, to assess the economic viability of utilizing palm-leaves as a geotextile. Initial results are very favourable, showing the mats can be constructed at an economically viable price of $0.35-0.60 (USD) per square metre, which is comparable to other geotextiles (Table 1).

Table 1: Guide to geotextile prices [9].

Application	Product	Price US $ per sq metre
Erosion Control	Synthetic	1.00 - 3.00
	Woodfibre/Straw	0.55 - 1.10
	Jute	0.30 - 1.00
	Coir	0.90 - 2.20
Agro-mulching	Plastic-film	0.10 - 0.25
Unpaved roads/separators	Synthetic	3.00 - 5.00
	Jute	0.60 - 1.00
	Coir	0.90 - 2.20

The strategic impact of palm-leaf geotextiles involves the promotion of sustainable and environmentally friendly palm-agriculture, which will discourage deforestation, promote both reforestation and agroforestry and offer a potentially profitable technique to augment the income of financially deprived farmers. Thus, construction of palm geotextiles could develop into a rural, labour-intensive industry, particularly encouraging the employment of socially-disadvantaged groups, such as women, disabled and elderly people (i.e. hand-work performed sitting down). In turn, this will contribute to rural population stabilization, thus decreasing migration to urban areas. Moreover, export of completed palm geotextiles will earn hard currency and promote development, based on the principles of fair trade.

Palm-leaf geotextiles can improve the socio-economic foundation for sustainable development in developing countries. Potential benefits include poverty alleviation, engagement of disadvantaged groups as stakeholders, employment for disadvantaged groups, SME development, export of geotextiles earning hard currency, environmental education and local community involvement in reclamation and environmental-improvement programmes. Education programmes are necessary to actively inform the public of the importance of soil as an essential resource. These schemes should particularly encourage 'land literacy' among participants so that society recognizes broader benefits of effective soil conservation, such as its potential contribution to habitat creation, biodiversity and carbon sequestration.

4 An environmental assessment of palm-mat geotextiles

4.1 Palm-mat geotextile manufacture

Geotextile mats were constructed from the leaf of *Borassus aethiopum*. The genus Borassus is one of the most widely distributed of the Palmae, with a range extending from West Africa to eastern Indonesia. Literature on Borassus palms tends to be limited to botany. As Borassus palms are of significant value to local populations, attention has been drawn to them because of global assessments of the potential of underdeveloped tropical plant resources. Sustainability studies in India and Indonesia stress the need for conservation measures [10,11,12]. If harvested correctly, Borassus palm is highly sustainable. Allowed to grow to maturity, they are estimated to have 100 years longevity [8] and grow to 25-30 m height with ~30-40 palmate fronds. One leaf is produced per month and they naturally shed 12-14 fronds annually [13].

(a)

(b)

Plate 1: (a) Cottage industry geotextile production in The Gambia, and (b) A completed palm-mat geotextile (50 x 50 cm).

A small cottage workshop was established in The Gambia, West Africa, in May 2001, to harvest and manufacture the mats (Plate 1a). The fronds were cut and sun-dried over four weeks. The thick central spines, which give the leaf their fan-like appearance, were stripped and the vegetation cut into lengths ranging from 1-1.5 m length and 2 cm width. These were then soaked in water to make the material pliable and then using a 2,500 cm^2 wooden template, woven into 50 x 50 cm (2,500 cm^2) squares, where the outer edge of the mat was sewn using fibre from the leaf waste. Strips were then woven into a grid pattern, vertically and horizontally, using a slipknot at 5-7 cm intervals. Then every strip was wrapped around, working from one edge to the other, using the prepared material. It took approximately one frond to construct one 2,500 cm^2 mat, weighing ~200 g (Plate 1b).

4.2 Experimental field design and plot trials

A preliminary study is in progress evaluating palm-mat effects on runoff and erosion rates from established runoff plots, based at the University of Wolverhampton's Hilton Field Experimental Site, in east Shropshire, U.K. (52°033'5.7''N, 2°19'18.3''W; NGR SO778952) (Figure 1).

The Hilton Experimental Site has been used extensively since 1976 [14] and covers 0.52 hectares with an upper elevation of 67.46 m, where a meteorological station is positioned (Figure 1). The region experiences a temperate climate with a mean annual precipitation of 648.3 mm [15]. The soil is Bridgnorth series loamy sand with a typical Ap horizon texture of 79.8% sand, 14.8% silt and 5.4% clay and 1.9% organic matter content [16].

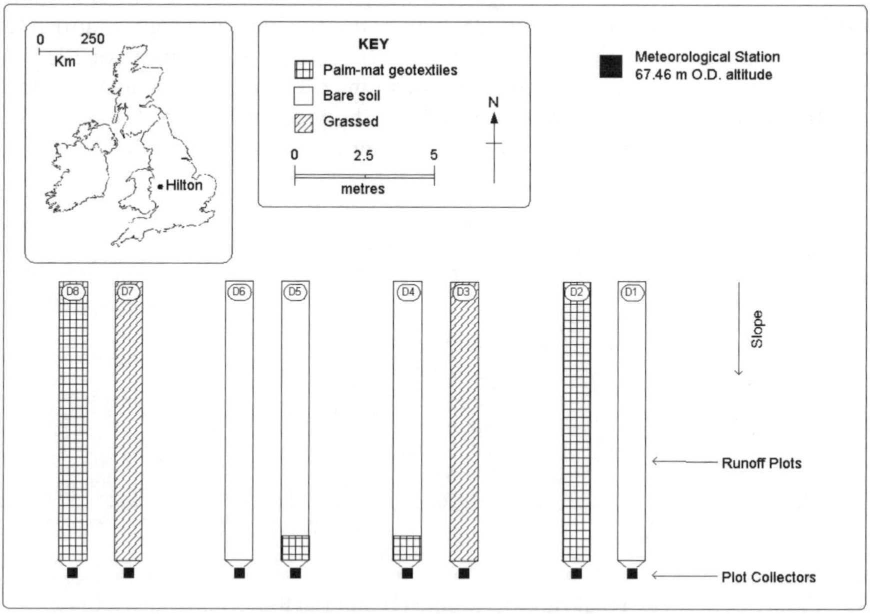

Figure 1: Plan of the runoff plots at the Hilton Experimental Site, U.K.

Eight runoff plots, situated on a 15° south-west facing slope, numbered D1-D8 and measuring 10 x 1 m, are being used for the field study (Figure 1). Prior to observations, bare (control) and treated plots were motivated to ~20 cm depth and treated with *Roundup* herbicide to remove vegetation. Plots were bordered with black plastic lawn-trim, with 10 cm intruding into the soil and 10 cm protruding above the soil.

Observations began on 14 January 2002, with a calibration period until 25 March 2002, when the plots were treated, and continued until 09 February 2004. Using random selection, plots D2 and D8 were completely covered with palm-mats, D4 and D5 had 1 m buffer zones of palm-mats at the plot lower end, D1 and D6 are the bare soil (control) plots and D3 and D7 are grassed plots. All palm-mat and bare plots were periodically sprayed with *Roundup* herbicide to prevent vegetation growth. Runoff was measured to the nearest ml, while the sediment yield was measured by weighing containers, oven-drying the runoff overnight at 40°C, then reweighing the containers. This was performed regularly, usually every two weeks or after erosive storms.

4.3 Experimental results and discussion

The runoff investigation consisted of 35 observations over 98 weeks, with the first six observations used as a calibration period (showing reasonable bare soil comparability: data not presented). Total plot data for the period 25/03/2002–09/02/2004 (precipitation total 1118.4 mm) is shown in Figures 2a and 2b. Combined plot data are presented in Table 2. Runoff volumes from both grassed plots were similar (e.g. D3 = 20,935 ml; D7 = 27,855 ml). In contrast, runoff volume from the buffer zone plots and geotextile plots show noticeable differences (e.g. D4 = 12,750 ml; D8 = 56,580 ml). Comparatively, runoff from the geotextile covered plots was higher than the bare plots by a mean of 121.2%, while runoff from the buffer zone plots was lower than the bare plots by a mean of 60.5% (Table 3a). Total runoff as a % of the precipitation for the bare plots (0.59) was notably higher than both the grassed (0.44) and buffer (0.36) treatments, but not the geotextile-covered plots (0.71).

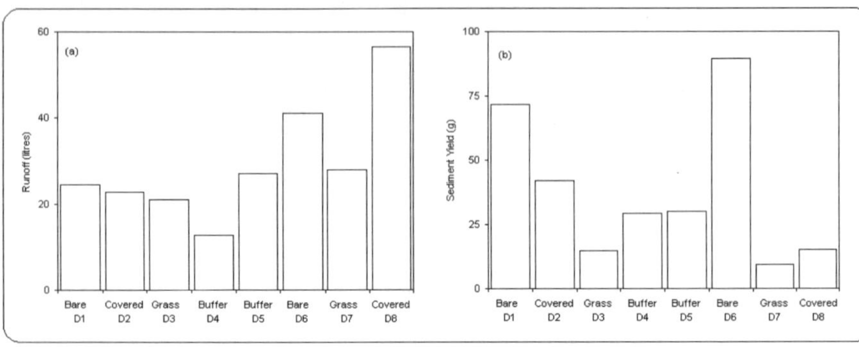

Figure 2: (a) Total runoff volume (l) and (b) total sediment yield (g).

Erosion from the treated plots was noticeably lower than from the bare plots during the same period. Sediment yields from the buffer zone plots were similar (e.g. D4 = 29.38 g; D5 = 30.20 g). In contrast, there are notable differences in sediment yields from the bare, grassed, geotextile-covered and buffer zone plots (e.g. D6 = 89.63 g; D7 = 9.38 g). This is reflected in the percentage difference in sediment yield when comparing the bare and treated plots (Tables 2 and 3b). Thus, mean total soil loss equates to 0.81 t ha^{-1} from the bare plots, 0.30 t ha^{-1} from both the covered plots, 0.29 t ha^{-1} from the buffer zone plots and 0.12 t ha^{-1} from the grass plots. Since erosion from buffer strip plots approximately equals those from mat-covered plots, this indicates buffer strips are very effective in reducing erosion.

Preliminary data suggest palm-mat geotextiles are effective in reducing runoff when used as a buffer zone. However, mats are not effective in reducing runoff compared to bare soil. Other studies support these findings. For instance, an investigation on the effectiveness of geotextiles on runoff and sediment yield at Hilton, revealed runoff from plots covered with jute geotextile was 146.8% greater than from bare soil [15]. One of the factors that appear affect the ability of geotextiles to reduce runoff is the effects of the manufacturing process on their retention capacity [17], which may have been an influence in this study. Palm-mats in the covered plots and buffer zones were effective in reducing erosion compared to bare soil. As the erosion rate from the buffer strip plots is almost equal to the rate from the mat-covered plots, this indicates buffer strips are very effective in conserving soil. Therefore, targeting buffer strips on vulnerable segments of the landscape (e.g. convex slopes, erodible soils and riparian zones) may be a valuable application of geotextile mats. Geotextiles have proved effective in reducing soil erosion compared to bare soil [3,4]. Recent field experiments at Hilton, comparing the effects of different treatments on erosion rates, showed that jute-net had 1.4% of the sediment yield from bare plots, while jute-mat had 1.1% [15].

Table 2: Summary field data, with S.D. (*in parentheses*) values, for runoff and erosion of the plots at the Hilton Experimental Site (n = 29 measuring periods).

	Bare (D1+D6)	Grass (D3+D7)	Buffer (D4+D5)	Covered (D2+D8)
Total runoff (litres)	65.84 (1.14)	48.94 (0.99)	39.81 (0.76)	79.79 (1.62)
Total runoff (mm depth)	6.58 (0.11)	4.89 (0.10)	3.98 (0.08)	7.98 (0.16)
Total runoff as a % of precipitation	0.59 (0.11)	0.44 (0.10)	0.36 (0.08)	0.71 (0.16)
Total sediment yield (g)	161.49 (4.52)	24.33 (0.41)	59.58 (1.31)	57.04 (1.36)
Total soil loss equivalent (t ha^{-1})	1.61 (0.45)	0.24 (0.04)	0.60 (0.13)	0.57 (0.14)

Table 3: Combined plot data and percentage of bare (control) for (a) Runoff volume and (b) Sediment yield.

(a)	Bare (D1+D6)	Grass (D3+D7)	Buffer (D4+D5)	Covered (D2+D8)
Mean runoff volume (L)	1.18	0.87	0.71	1.42
Percentage of bare (control)		74.34	60.47	121.19
(b)	Bare (D1+D6)	Grass (D3+D7)	Buffer (D4+D5)	Covered (D2+D8)
Mean sediment yield (g)	2.88	0.43	1.06	1.02
Percentage of bare (control)		15.07	36.89	35.32

4.4 Ongoing and proposed further work

A research team, based in Europe, Africa, South-East Asia and South America, funded by the EU for three-years (Project 'BORASSUS': Contract Number

510745), has recently commenced the first complete scientific and socio-economic evaluation of the potential of palm-leaf geotextiles. Full geotechnical evaluations of these geotextiles are an integral part of the work. Therefore, as part of the established information dissemination strategy, the team will publish manufacturing and production protocols and standards. These will be broadly disseminated and thus available for SMEs to adopt and adapt. These standards will contribute to the global production of high-quality palm-mat geotextiles suitable for multiple and complex applications.

Design methodology and rationale for the geotextiles will be based on current European national design standards. However, if palm-leaf geotextiles are to be accepted and successfully utilized for land management programmes, their engineering and environmental properties and capabilities need to be thoroughly investigated to find the force needed to maintain slope stability within specified 'Factors of Safety'. Fortunately, besides socio-economic evaluations, this work addresses issues of geotextile quality, production, durability and performance in both field and laboratory environments, as a fundamental study of the shearing interaction and synergy between geotextiles and different soil types and climates. Thus, the study will enable a comprehensive evaluation of palm-leaf geotextiles to satisfy the scrutiny of national, European and international standards.

5 Conclusions

Geotextiles constructed from the leaf of *Borassus aethiopum* have potential as a biotechnical soil conservation method. The results from almost two years of investigation indicate geotextiles constructed from palm-leaf effectively reduced soil erosion. If harvested correctly, the *Borassus* leaf is highly sustainable and readily available in most semi-arid and sub-humid bioclimatic regions. They are biodegradable, providing organic content matter to stabilize the soil and their permeability makes them suitable for use with cohesive soils. There are no high-energy production procedures in the manufacturing process and, when used in their natural environment, they may provide a cost-effective method of conserving soil in developing countries, where farming techniques are scaled to low levels of disposable income.

Acknowledgements

This work is dedicated to the memory of the doctoral research student, Kathy Davies, to whom we acknowledge as the initiator and inspiration for palm-leaf geotextile research. We gratefully thank the technical assistance of Andrew Black, David Luckhurst, Keith Thompson and David Townrow of the School of Applied Sciences at the University of Wolverhampton.

References

[1] United Nations Environment Programme, *Global Environment Outlook*, Earthscan, London, U.K., 2002.

[2] United Nations Environment Programme, *Report of the UN Conference on the Environment and Development*, Rio de Janeiro, Section 11(14.1), 1992.

[3] Sutherland, R.A. & Ziegler, A.D., Geotextile effectiveness in reducing interill runoff and sediment flux, In: *International Erosion Control Association Proceedings of Conference* XXVI, 1995, Atlanta, (USA), pp. 359-370, 1996.

[4] Langford, R.L. & Coleman, M.J., Biodegradable erosion control blankets prove effective on Iowa wildlife refuge, in: *International Erosion Control Association Proceedings of Conference XXVII*, Seattle, (USA), pp. 13-20, 1996.

[5] Ogbobe, O., Essien, K.S. & Adebayo, A., A study of biodegradable geotextiles used for erosion control. *Geosynthetics International*, **5**, pp. 545-553, 1998.

[6] Ranganathan, S.R., Jute geotextiles in soil erosion control, In: *International Erosion Control Association Proceedings of Conference XX111*, Indianapolis, (USA), pp. 343-351, 1992.

[7] Gumaa, Y.T., Haffar, I. & Al-Afifi, M.A., Financial appraisal of date-frond mat fence systems for wind erosion control and dune stabilisation in the arid regions of the United Arab Emirates. *Journal of Arid Environments*, **39**, pp. 549-557, 1998.

[8] Davis, T.A. & Johnson, D.V., Current utilisation and further development of the Palmyra Palm (*Borassus flabellifer* L., Arecaceae) in Tamil Nadu State, India. *Economic Botany*, **41**, pp. 247-266, 1987.

[9] Smith, R., The potential market for sisal and henequen geotextiles. In: Food and Agricultural Organisation and Common Fund for Commodities *Proceedings of Seminar,* Rome, Technical Paper 14, 2001.

[10] Paulas, D., Research for exploitation of Palmyra. In *Food and Agriculture Organisation of the United Nation/DANDIDA Proceedings*. Workshop at Jaffina: Sri Lanka, 1983.

[11] Koovor, A., The Palmyra palm: potential and perspectives. In Plant Production and Protection, *Proceedings by the Food and Agriculture Organisation of the United Nations*, Rome: Italy, 1983.

[12] Davies, K., *An evaluation of the effectiveness of palm-mat geotextiles on the conservation of loamy soils of the Bridgnorth series*. Unpublished B.Sc. dissertation, The University of Wolverhampton, U.K., 2000.

[13] Davis, T.A. & Arulpragasam, P., Palmyra - the state tree of Tamil Nadu. *Economic Botany*, **43**, pp. 95-106, 1986.

[14] Fullen, M.A. & Reed, A.H., Rainfall, runoff and erosion on bare arable soils in East Shropshire, England. *Earth Surface Processes and Landforms*, **11**, pp. 413-425, 1986.

[15] Mitchell, D.J., Barton, A.P., Fullen, M.A., Hocking, T.J., Lu Liguang, Wu Bo Zhi, Zheng Yi., Effects of jute geotextiles on runoff and sediment yield: field experiments in the UK. *Soil Use and Management*, **19**, pp. 182-184, 2002.

[16] Fullen, M.A. & Brandsma, R.T., Property changes by erosion of loamy sand soils in east Shropshire, U.K. *Soil Technology*, **8**, pp. 1-15, 1995.
[17] Palmeira, E.M., Fannin, R.J. & Vaid, V.P., A study on the behaviour of soil-geotextile systems in filtration tests. *Canadian Geotechnical Journal*, **33**, pp. 899-912, 1996.

Sustainable agriculture in the West African savannah: considerations for modern crop promotion in traditional farming systems

B. Polidoro[1] & E. H. Franz[2]
[1]*Centro Agronómico Tropical de Investigación y Enseñanza (CATIE), Costa Rica and University of Idaho, U.S.A.*
[2]*Washington State University, U.S.A.*

Abstract

Sustainable agriculture techniques in West Africa are largely based on the planting of modern crop varieties of nitrogen-fixing legumes to improve soil fertility and increase harvest yields for the subsistence or smallholder farmer. In the northern savannah of Togo, native crop varieties, or landraces, of intercropped sorghum and cowpea were grown in a demonstration field for comparison with internationally promoted monocropped soybean and the cover crop mucuna. After two growing seasons, no significant changes in soil chemistry were observed. However, harvested yields of the native crops were double those of the promoted modern crops. Several biological and practical reasons account for the failure of soybeans or mucuna to improve soil fertility over the two-year period. Similarly, the genetic and cultural benefits of traditionally intercropped sorghum and cowpea may further hinder local farmer adoption of soybean or mucuna. These observations suggest that the widespread promotion of soybean and mucuna to improve soil fertility may not be appropriate within the context of specific environmental conditions and cultural practices. Sustainable agriculture initiatives might be better achieved if based on increased research of native crops, trees and forages for use within tailored 'in situ' soil conservation projects that incorporate indigenous farmer knowledge and local cultural values. For this aim, appropriate sustainable agriculture projects require adaptive interdisciplinary approaches that integrate farmer participation with both socioeconomic and biophysical research.
Keywords: soil fertility, harvest yield, landraces, West Africa, nitrogen fixation, cover crops, indigenous knowledge, sustainable agriculture.

1 Introduction

Farming practices in West Africa are historically based on shifting cultivation to maintain soil fertility. In the past, when land was abundant, traditional slash and burn systems allowed farmers to cultivate land for two to five years and then abandon it for up to 10, sometimes 25, years for fallow before cultivating again [1]. However, rapid increases in human and livestock populations no longer allow such long fallow cycles; marginal lands have been brought into cultivation, and farmers have been forced to change from extensive to intensive cultivation of the land [2, 3]. This intensification of cultivation has contributed to widespread deforestation and desertification, soil acidification, invasion by noxious weeds, and a marked decline in soil fertility and harvest yields [3, 4]. At present, only 24% of West African soils are fertile enough to support crops, while the remaining 76% are characterized as poor with severe deficiencies in nitrogen and/or phosphorus, requiring the liberal use of fertilizers, organic-matter management, and erosion control [4]. With increased population growth and the agriculture sector currently responsible for one-third of the continent's gross domestic products, agricultural development in Africa to sustain and improve food, animal feed, fuel wood and fiber productivity, is as critical to economic growth as it is to the continent's food security and to population health.

According to the Food and Agricultural Organization, approximately 70% of the African population lives in rural areas as subsistence or smallholder farmers. Accordingly, development organizations, government agencies and research institutions currently working in West Africa to improve agricultural productivity are largely focused on sustainable agriculture technologies for the individual smallholder or household farmer. As most rural African farmers cannot afford the purchase of inorganic fertilizers, the majority of these technologies are based on the use of organic amendments and biological nitrogen fixation as a means to improve soil fertility and increase harvest yields [2, 5, 6]. Although the nutrient benefits of the lost fallow system are not easily replaced by changes in soil tillage or cropping practices [7], current soil improvement technologies represent "low-tech" but knowledge intensive practices and include agroforestry systems and alley cropping with leguminous trees; crop and shrub residue mulching; and the planting of non-traditional or introduced "modern" leguminous and green manure crops [2, 3]. In Togo and in many other parts of West Africa, soybeans (*Glycine max*), and the cover crop mucuna (*Mucuna pruriens*), are often promoted for rotation with, or as companion crops to, the traditional sorghum/cowpea (*Sorghum bicolor* and *Vigna unguiculata*) intercrop to improve soil fertility and augment harvest yields, as well as to provide supplemental nutritional choices and income-generating activities.

A native crop of Asia, soybeans were introduced in Nigeria roughly 20 years ago, but were not actively promoted until 1987 when the International Institute for Tropical Agriculture (IITA) launched an ambitious effort to combat widespread malnutrition. According to the IITA, soybeans have an average protein content of 40%, which is more than any other common vegetable or animal food source found in Africa. Since 1987, over 150 different soy food products have been developed in Nigeria, which now produces over 500,000 tons of soybeans worth $85 million annually for use in more than 65 soybean-processing industries [8]. The large-scale adoption of soybeans in Nigeria as a successful cash crop and protein source, in addition its nitrogen-fixing capabilities, has led to its promotion by national governments and development agencies in other West African countries such as Togo for incorporation into malnutrition and soil fertility initiatives. Eaglesham and Ayanaba [9] estimated that soybean rotations in Nigeria contribute anywhere from 15 to 125 kg/ha of residual soil nitrate while native cowpeas contribute an average of 122 kg/ha [2]. In South Africa, Bloem [10] found that maize yields increased by 27% and 51% after rotation with cowpea and soybean respectively and suggested that soybeans may also contribute to beneficial soil microbial activity or excrete growth-promoting substances.

The origins of the leguminous cover crop mucuna or velvet bean are not well-known, although it is thought to be indigenous to Asia or Central America. Mucuna for cultivation was first introduced to West Africa in the late 1980's by the National Institute of Agricultural Research in Cotonou, Benin, and later by other national and international extension services. As a nitrogen-fixing legume, mucuna has been widely promoted as a green manure cover crop to improve soil fertility, suppress weeds and control erosion [11, 12, 13]. Although mucuna has also been shown to increase soil porosity and infiltration rates [14], the main nutrient advantage in mucuna is from the mineralization of crop biomass. Mucuna grown in humid regions can provide as much as 12 ton/ha in aboveground dry matter biomass [12] and can contribute as much as 100 kg/ha of nitrogen to the following crop [15]. In field tests in Benin, maize crops following one-year mucuna fallows resulted in increased seed yields of approximately 500 kg/ha for local maize varieties and 800 kg/ha for improved varieties [13, 16]. Several different varieties of mucuna are distributed by development and extension agencies in Togo to farmers for use as a sole cover crop planted as a short fallow for severely degraded soils, or as a sorghum or maize intercrop for fields requiring less rehabilitation.

2 Case Study: Tamberma Valley, northern Togo

The Tamberma Valley is located in the north eastern Kara region of Togo. With less than 1000mm of annual rainfall and 180 days in the growing season, the area is considered a tree and shrub savannah within the Sudano-Guinean ecological zone. The Tamberma people are both geographically and culturally isolated from the other 40 different ethnic groups in Togo, and as a result, have retained much of their traditional cultural and farming practices. In general, the Tamberma are subsistence farmers that practice a diversified system of agricultural production based on non-irrigated crop rotation, with some fallow seasons if resources permit, combined with the raising of a variety of livestock. The traditional staple crops are millet, sorghum, cowpeas, groundnuts, chickpeas, and fonio (*Digitaria exilis*). As is typical of most West African farming systems in semi-arid zones, sorghum and millet in Tamberma Valley are almost exclusively intercropped with cowpea. The Tamberma people are thought to have migrated to northern Togo and Benin from the Fada-N'Gourma region of Burkina Faso approximately 500 years ago, suggesting that growing conditions at this time may have been more favourable. According to oral accounts and limited rainfall data, this region had more forested land and a longer growing season in the recent past. However, deforestation, annual bush fires, and increasingly intensive cultivation combined with a growing population have contributed to soil degradation and less opportunity for fallow seasons. The alfisols of the Tamberma Valley are currently among the poorest and most highly degraded soils in Togo [17], primarily due to low fertility and severe wind and water erosion [18].

For these reasons, a soil improvement demonstration field was established in the Tamberma village of Warengo under the direction of local and international development organizations and regional government agencies. The objective of the 1600m^2 demonstration field was to introduce local farmers to soybean and mucuna rotation and compare them to the traditional sorghum and cowpea intercrop through direct observation and participation. Using a standard spacing of 0.25m between all plants, local sorghum seed was intercropped with local cowpea seed the first year in two plots in the southern half of the field, while modern varieties of soybean and mucuna were separately monocropped in two plots on the northern half of the field. Using the same spacing, the plots were rotated the second year in order to follow the local tradition of annual crop rotation, as well as to observe any increase in subsequent sorghum seed yield as a result of previous soybean or mucuna cultivation. Seed yield data for each crop was collected after each year's harvest. Composite topsoil samples were taken at 10cm below the soil surface from 10 randomly selected sites within each of the four planted plots as well as from the surrounding natural *Andropodon* grass fallow. Soil samples were taken at the beginning of each planting season (June 2000 and 2001), the end of each harvest (November 2000 and 2001), and once during the dry season (March 2001). The soil samples were sieved to the 2mm fraction and analyzed at the National Institute for Agronomic Research (ITRA) in Lomé, Togo. ITRA used flame photometry and atomic absorption spectrometry to determine soil sodium, potassium, calcium and magnesium, colorimetry using the Olsen method for available phosphorus, spectro-photocolorimetry using potassium dichromate and sulphuric acid for carbon and organic matter, and titration using the Kjeldahl method for nitrogen.

The results for harvest yield (Table 1) show a large difference between the traditional intercropped cowpea/sorghum and the monocropped soybean and mucuna. As cowpea and sorghum are intercropped as companion crops on the same area of land, their net harvests must be added together to provide a total of 1213 kg/ha of seed for the year 2000 harvest and 1143 kg/ha of seed for the year 2001 harvest. Thus, the total yield of food per unit of land for monocropped soybean and mucuna was less than half of what was harvested for the traditional sorghum/cowpea intercrop. Additionally, soil nutrient measurements across all plots did not show any significant changes in soil nutrients over the two-year period (Table 2). Even though the demonstration plots were not successfully replicated for further statistical analysis, the attempt to demonstrate to farmers the effects of soybean and mucuna rotation on soil fertility and harvest yield was not successful over the two-year study period. With this experience, several potential biological and practical explanations arose as "lessons learned" for subsequent project development.

Table 1: Harvest yield.

	Crop	Area (ha)	Harvest (kg)	Net (kg/ha)
Year 2000	Cowpea	0.104	66	635
	Sorghum	0.104	60	578
	Soybean	0.035	21	605
	Mucuna	0.025	15	595
Year 2001	Cowpea	0.094	60	635
	Sorghum	0.094	48	508
	Soybean	0.045	24	532
	Mucuna	0.026	15	564

Table 2: Measured soil chemistry averages.

Measurement	Mean	n	s.d.	Measurement	Mean	n	s.d.
% OM	4.32	25	1.04	Ca (cmol/kg)	6.69	20	3.9
% C	2.52	25	0.59	Mg (cmol/kg)	1.3	20	0.35
% N	0.14	25	0.02	K (cmol/kg)	0.272	25	0.15
C/N Ratio	16.99	25	3.62	Na (cmol/kg)	0.071	25	0.09
P (ppm)	19.01	25	5.92	pH (H_20)	6.16	25	0.23

3 Biological constraints

In the low fertility soils of the West African arid zones, there is an inherent limitation of leguminous crops to produce sufficient biomass to significantly alter soil fertility characteristics over a two-year study period. The maximum potential nitrogen contribution can be calculated using aboveground dry matter averages for the crops in the semi-arid savannah zone and their corresponding inorganic nitrogen content discussed in previous studies. Using this method, the cowpea crop is estimated to have produced 2.5 t/ha of dry matter [12], not including harvested seeds, and with an average of 10 kg nitrate N per t/ha biomass [10], therefore could have potentially contributed 25 kg/ha of nitrate nitrogen to the field. Soybeans can potentially contribute 10 kg nitrate N per t/ha of soybean seed yield [10]. Based on the 2-year average soybean seed yield of 0.568 t/ha, the soybean crop is estimated to have contributed 5.7 kg/ha of nitrate N. Finally, the mucuna crop is estimated to have produced 4.7 t/ha of aboveground biomass, including unharvested seed [12], and with approximately 10.7 g of inorganic N per kg of aboveground biomass [19], could potentially have contributed 50 kg/ha of inorganic N. Thus, the maximum contribution of inorganic nitrogen from the combined aboveground biomass of cowpea, soybean and mucuna in the demonstration field was estimated to be approximately 81 kg N/ha. Using the standard average of 2.2 million kg of soil per hectare, the average nitrogen content of 0.14% found in this study of Tamberma soils represents 3080 kg of total nitrogen per hectare. The maximum potential inorganic nitrogen contribution of 81 kg/ha from the calculated and combined aboveground biomass production of cowpea, soybeans, and mucuna represents only 2.6% of the present total nitrogen content and would therefore only provide a very small (0.003%) overall increase in soil nitrogen content. As a result, this potential maximum contribution of 0.003% annual increase in nitrogen content is too small to be recognized within the less than 0.1% variation in soil nitrogen content measured over the two-year study period.

Low fertility soils can not only limit initial biomass production, but can also affect other physiological processes that influence biomass nutrient content and nitrogen fixing capabilities. Research in Benin by Houngnandan [20] showed that mucuna biomass nutrient composition decreased by 69% for nitrogen and 33% for phosphorus when these nutrients were absent from the growing medium. The capacity for root nodulation and nitrogen-fixation capability is also inherently limited by soil phosphorus content for soybean [21], and soil nitrogen for mucuna [22, 23]. Specific rhizobial populations must also be present in the soil to promote nodulation. As introduced crops, native rhizobial bacteria populations necessary for root nodulation of mucuna and soybean are generally lower or nonexistent in West African soils [20, 22]. Thus, without improved varieties, a stable supply of inoculant, or other soil nutrient amendments, the soil nitrogen contribution from mucuna and soybean in this region would be expected to be lower than that for the native cowpea.

4 Practical constraints

The IITA in Nigeria has developed improved varieties of soybean that fix more nitrogen without rhizobial inoculation and have lower phosphorus requirements. However, the problem remains as to how to maintain a consistent supply of these improved varieties to farmers. In Togo, soybeans for cultivation are bought in local markets, including many of those distributed by development organizations, without knowledge of where the seeds came from or how far removed they are from the original variety. Even if select farmers were given an original strain, the widespread practice of saving out harvested seed for the next year's planting would quickly lead to hybridization. By contrast, mucuna seeds are not currently found in local markets in Togo, but are mainly distributed by local and international non-profit organizations and agricultural development agencies. As a result, farmers' exposure to mucuna varieties depends entirely on consistent access to a mucuna promoting organization in the area.

The effect of the long dry season in the West African savannah and sahel regions cannot be underestimated. Nutrient rich biomass to be incorporated back into the soil for the benefit of the next growing season must be protected during the dry season from post-harvest bushfires, free-range grazing animals and erosion from the scouring Harmattan winds. In coastal areas with bimodal rainfall and longer growing seasons, soybean and mucuna are promoted as companion or intercrops to maize, millet or sorghum. Like the cowpea in sorghum intercropping, intercropped soybean or mucuna must be planted 30 to 45 days after the cereal crop in order to prevent initial crop competition for nutrients. However, due to lower rainfall conditions, a shorter growing season, slower growth, and nutrient competition, soybean and mucuna can generally only be planted as monocrops in semi-arid savannah. Monocropping can be very labour intensive and is often an inefficient use of land. For example, cowpea intercropped with sorghum, grows to cover the spaces between sorghum plants and therefore, requires little weeding. As a cover crop, mucuna also requires little weeding during the growing season, however, incorporation of crop residues at the end of the harvest is often extremely difficult in the already dry soils. With their more shrub-like growth, soybeans are more labour intensive as they often require multiple weedings per growing season.

5 Compatibility with indigenous knowledge and practices

Hundreds of years of accumulated knowledge and experience provide farmers with a variety of details and improved methods for native seed selection, storage, and crop harvesting, planting and weeding. For example, Tamberma farmers can identify and select for market or for sowing different sorghum and cowpea varieties by their color, taste, size, hardness and plant growth characteristics. With newly introduced modern crops, farmers do not have this advantage of time-tested knowledge. Similarly, little local knowledge exists for the integration of soybean and mucuna into traditional farming systems. No local knowledge exists for selecting the type of land, such as lowland, riparian, or hillside sites, as well as proximity to specific animal predators, which will best accommodate soybean or mucuna cultivation. Farmers have no experience with identifying soybean or mucuna crop diseases or signs of nutrient deficiencies. Additionally, farmers do not have the experience or precedence necessary to place soybean or mucuna into their crop rotation or intercropping systems. Instead they must rely on outside organizations for information, which for an illiterate population, can only be successfully retained by numerous trainings and actual hands-on experience.

Mucuna in general is not a readily accepted food crop due to unfamiliarity with preparation and cooking requirements necessary to remove the high levels of L-Dopa toxin. In light of a growing population, decreasing fallow opportunities and smaller household farms, most subsistence farmers may not be able to risk cultivating a portion of their land with an unfamiliar crop without the benefit of income-generation or an edible seed harvest. As a recognizable food crop with commercial value [8], soybeans have been more accepted than mucuna for cultivation. However, an underlying problem with soybean adoption in more isolated regions such as in the Tamberma Valley is related to strict gender roles in the community, which are common to many societies in West Africa. In the Tamberma Valley, women cultivate the bean crops, while men cultivate the cereals. As a result, soybeans are generally only promoted to women and remain an unfamiliar and unimportant crop to men, which can create difficulties for women in obtaining household land for soybean cultivation.

As traditional crops, cowpeas and sorghum also have important cultural and economic roles. In the Tamberma Valley, bean cakes made from cowpeas are used in important rain ceremonies and coming-of-age initiations while the preparation of sorghum-beer is the main income-generating activity for many West African women. Dry sorghum stalks are cut in half at the end of the harvest for use as fuelwood and for construction of doors and animal pens, while the remaining lower half of the stalks are left standing in fields to camouflage household chickens and guinea fowl from hawks and other bird predators. It is nearly impossible for newly introduced modern crops such as soybean and mucuna to fill the numerous integrated cultural and practical roles of native crops in traditional farming systems.

6 Inherent benefits of the cowpea/sorghum intercrop

From a production perspective, the main value of native crop varieties appears to be their contribution to genetic diversity and their adaptation to local growing conditions [24, 25]. Modern crop varieties are generally introduced and developed to provide relatively high yields under optimal growing conditions for a broad geographic region. In marginal environments such as the semi-arid savannah zones, varieties of modern crops such as soybean or mucuna often need relatively high levels of inputs in order to reach the optimum yields and benefits for which they are promoted [24]. Genetically adapted native crop varieties are less sensitive to minor fluctuations in local environmental conditions, resulting in more consistent and sustainable harvest yields over time, which is often more important to subsistence farmers than the promise of simply higher yields. Native crop varieties may have lower mean yields in optimal environments compared with other varieties, but often have higher mean yields in the marginal environments to which they are adapted [24]. For example, the cowpea varieties grown in Tamberma Valley may represent the result of numerous genetic adaptations to the local conditions, as the approximately 600 kg/ha average cowpea yield in this area is well above the 300 kg/ha average cowpea yield reported for all of Africa [8].

The majority of cultivated area in West Africa is under a mixed cereal/legume cropping system, yet there has been relatively little biological or genetic research on these intercropped systems. In low nutrient soils, cowpea roots may excrete nitrogen for the benefit of the companion crop [26]. Cowpeas have also been shown to increase pH and available phosphorus in the rhizoplane [27]. Aboveground cowpea litter or dry matter, soluble leaf nitrogen and nitrogen from decaying root nodules may also account for the nitrogen transferred to the cereal [28]. Intercropping legumes and cereals also is beneficial because it reduces the risk of total crop failure from selective pathogens, makes efficient use of land and labour, and provides farmers with a balanced diet. Cowpea grown with sorghum can also be a sound soil-conservation strategy as it provides a complementary ground cover that reduces weeding and soil erosion, while maintaining soil moisture.

7 Conclusions

Selected farmers in West Africa have indeed benefited from the cultivation of recently introduced modern crops. In parts of Nigeria, soybeans have already developed an economic niche and are quickly becoming an important cash crop, providing a much needed income to families. As a green manure crop, mucuna has helped some farmers in the more humid regions of Benin, Togo and Ghana to recover fields previously abandoned to weeds and to increase maize yields. These successes, however, are not only dependent on consistent farmer access to development organizations for seed, inoculant, and knowledge, but also on specific environmental and cultural conditions necessary for optimal soybean or mucuna growth and subsequent soil enhancement. The farther traditional farming systems are from these optimal environmental and cultural conditions required for modern crop varieties to succeed, the more sustainable agriculture projects need to rely on the existing adaptations and benefits of native crop varieties to address soil fertility problems.

The promotion of modern crop varieties that overlooks the specific cultural, economic, and practical roles of native crops and traditional farming systems, increases the risk of losing traditional knowledge and local crop genetic diversity. To more appropriately match sustainable agriculture technologies to local farming systems, sustainable agriculture projects might be better developed initially “in situ,” relying on local resources and emphasizing the preservation of native seed genetic diversity, farmer knowledge and crop stability. "In situ" research and development projects would require an increased understanding of the local farming system and more research on the available native crops, forages and tree species for use within a specific environmental and cultural context. These integrated projects would rely on a combination of socioeconomic and biophysical research integrated with local farmer participation. For this to be achieved, interdisciplinary and interagency collaboration is essential.

Many development organizations and research institutions are already using more participatory techniques to create and implement "in-situ" soil improvement and sustainable agriculture projects. These participatory research approaches give greater attention to local farming practices, farmer needs and farmer knowledge by involving local community members in each of the diagnostic, design, implementation and evaluation phases of a development project [29]. The challenge remains as to how to integrate identified local knowledge and farmer priorities with scientific knowledge and interdisciplinary research activities. Researchers and development agencies need adaptive interdisciplinary tools to strengthen communication and understanding between disciplines, institutions and project beneficiaries. For this aim, development organizations, research institutions and government agencies are encouraged to share resources and seek more opportunities for collaborative partnerships and interdisciplinary research.

References

[1] Tarawali, G., Manyong, V.M., Carsky, R.J., Vissoh, P.V., Osei-Bonsu, P. & Galiba, M., Adoption of improved fallows in West Africa: lessons from mucuna and stylo case studies. Agroforestry Systems, 47, pp. 93-122, 1999.

[2] Sanginga, N., Role of biological nitrogen fixation in legume based cropping systems; a case study of West Africa farming systems. Plant and Soil, 252, pp. 25-39, 2003.

[3] Bationo, A., Lompo, F. & Koala, S., Research on nutrient flows and balances in West Africa: state-of-the-art. Agriculture, Ecosystems and Environment, 71, pp. 19-35, 1998.

[4] Manyong, V.M., Smith, J., Weber, G.K., Jagtap, S.S. & Oyewole, B., Macrocharacterization of Agricultural Systems in West Africa: An Overview. Resource and Crop Management Research Monograph No. 21, International Institute of Tropical Agriculture: Ibadan, 1996.

[5] Breman, H., Soil Fertility Improvement in Africa, a Tool for or a By-Product of Sustainable Production? IFDC-Africa, Lomé, 1999.

[6] Bofana, B., Breman, H., Carsky, R.J., Van Reuler, H., Tamelokpo, A.F. & Gnakpenou, K.D., Using mucuna and P fertilizer to increase maize grain yield and N fertilizer use efficiency in the coastal savanna of Togo. Nutrient Cycling in Agroecosystems, 68, pp. 213-222, 2004.

[7] Franz, E.H., Potential influence of climatic change on soil organic matter and tropical agroforestry. Soils on a Warmer Earth: Effects of Expected Climate Change on Soil Processes, eds. H.W. Scharpenseel, M. Schomaker, & A. Ayoub, Elsevier Science Publishers: The Netherlands, 1990.

[8] IITA, www.iita.org/crop/soybean.htm

[9] Eaglesham, A.R.J. & Ayanaba, A., Tropical stress ecology of rhizobia, root nodulation and legume nitrogen fixation. Selected Topics in Biological Nitrogen Fixation, ed. N.S. Subba Rao, Oxford/IBH Publishing: New Delhi, 1984.

[10] Bloem, A.A., Effect of annual legumes on soil nitrogen and on the subsequent yield of maize and seed sorghum. South African Journal of Plant and Soil, 2, pp. 56-61, 2001.

[11] Chikoye, D. & Ekeleme, F., Response of Imperata cylindrical to smothering by different mucuna accessions. Cover Crops for Integrated Natural Resource Management in West Africa, ed. R.J. Carsky, International Institute of Tropical Agriculture: Ibadan, 2000.

[12] Carsky, J.R. & Ndikawa, R., Identification of cover crops for the semi-arid savanna zone of West Africa. Cover Crops in West Africa: Contributing to Sustainable Agriculture, ed. D. Buckles, IDRC/IITA/SG: Ottowa, 1998.

[13] Versteeg, M.V. & Koudokpon, V., Mucuna helps control Imperata in southern Benin. West Africa Farming Systems Research Network Bulletin, 7, pp. 7–8, 1990.

[14] Hulugalle, N.R., Lal, R. & Ter Kuile, C.H.H., Amelioration of soil physical properties by mucuna after mechanized land clearing of a tropical rain forest. Soil Science, 141, pp. 219-224, 1986.

[15] Osei-Bonsu, P. & Buckles, D., Controlling weeds and improving soil fertility through the use of cover crops: experience with Mucuna spp in Benin and Ghana. West African Farming Systems Research Network Bulletin, 14, pp. 2-7, 1993.

[16] Versteeg, M.V. & Koudokpon. V., Participative farmer testing of four low external input technologies to address soil fertility decline in Mono province (Benin). Agricultural System, 42, pp. 265–276, 1993.

[17] Brabant P., Darracq, S., Eque, K. & Simmonneaux, V., Togo Human-Induced Land Degradation Status, Collection Notice Explicative No. 112, ORSTROM Institute: Paris, 1996.

[18] Poss, R., Etude Morphopedologique du Nord du Togo a 1/500,000, Collection Notice Explicative No. 109, ORSTROM Institute: Paris, 1996.

[19] Ibewiro B., Sanginga, N., Vanlauwe, B. & Merckx, R., Transformations and recovery of residue and fertilizer nitrogen-15 in a sandy Lixisol of West Africa. Biology and Fertility of Soils, 31, pp. 261-269, 2000.

[20] Houngnandan, P., Sanginga, N., Okogun, A., Vanlauwe, B., Merckx, R. & Van Cleemput, O., Assessment of soil factors limiting growth and establishment of mucuna in farmers' fields in the derived savanna of the Benin Republic. Biology and Fertility of Soils, 33, pp. 416-422, 2001.

[21] Olufajo, O.O. & Adu, J.K., Response of soybean to inoculation with Bradyrhizobuim japonicum in the northern Guinea savanna of Nigeria. Biological Nitrogen Fixation and Sustainability of Tropical Agriculture, eds K. Mulongoy, M. Gueye and D.S.C. Spencer, Sayce Publishing: UK, 1990.

[22] Dogbe, W., Fening, J.O. & Danso, S.K.A., Nodulation of legumes in inland valley soils of Ghana. Symbiosis, 28, pp. 77-92, 2000.

[23] Houngnandan P., Sanginga, N., Woomer, P., Vanlauwe, B. & Van Cleemput, O., Response of Mucuna pruriens to symbiotic nitrogen fixation by rhizobia following inoculation in farmers' fields in the derived savanna of Benin. Biology and Fertility of Soils, 30, pp. 558-565, 2000.

[24] Cleveland, D., Soleri, D. & Smith, S., Do folk crop varieties have a role in sustainable agriculture? BioScience, 44, pp. 740-751, 1994.

[25] Jarvis, D.I., Myer, L., Klemick, H., Guarino, L., Smale, M., Brown, A.H.D., Sadiki, M., Sthapit, B. & Hodgkin, T., A Training Guide for In Situ Conservation On-Farm, International Plant Genetic Resources Institute: Rome, 2000.

[26] Eaglesham, A.R.J., Improving the nitrogen nutrition of maize by intercropping with cowpea. Soil Biology and Biochemistry, 13, pp. 169-171, 1981.

[27] Bagayoko, M., Alvey, S., Neumann, G. & Buerkert, A., Root-induced increases in soil pH and nutrient availability to field-grown cereals and legumes on acid sandy soils of Sudano-Sahelian West Africa. Plant and Soil 225, pp. 117-127, 2000.

[28] Remison, S.U., Neighbor effects between maize and cowpea at various levels of N and P. Experimental Agriculture, 14, pp. 205-212, 1978.
[29] Chambers, R., Recent Developments in Rural Appraisal: from Rapid to Relaxed and Participatory, Aga Khan Foundation: Ottawa, 1995.

Adaptation of life cycle assessment (LCA) to agricultural production on a regional scale in Japan

S. Mishima, S. Taniguchi & M. Komada
National Institute for Agro-Environmental Sciences, Japan

Abstract

LCA was applied to paddy rice farming with a relatively low livestock production area on a mid-river basin scale in Japan. Conventional farming, standard application of chemical fertilizer and manure, and low chemical fertilizer input and forage production scenarios were tested. The aquatic eutrophication potential and the global warming potential per unit of crude protein production were lower for low chemical fertilizer input and forage production than for conventional farming, although terrestrial eutrophication was not reduced. These results indicated that reduced input would be effective in areas with contamination of ground and surface water and regulation of nutrient input would be reasonable. Abiotic resource use was also lower for low chemical fertilizer input and forage production than for conventional farming. Recycling of livestock excreta would be viable in non-intensive livestock production areas.
Keywords: agriculture, fertilizer, life cycle assessment, livestock, region.

1 Introduction

Life cycle assessment (LCA) is a method that integrates various environmental impacts at each production step into simple indices to indicate what and where are the hot spots of environmental load on production. Brentrup et al. [1] devised theoretical steps to adapt agricultural production to LCA and evaluated environmental impact on wheat and beet production [2, 3]. Despite several trial calculations for effective nitrogen (N) management for low impact agriculture at regional and river basin scales [4, 5], LCA has not been applied to these scales. In this study, we tried to apply the LCA method to agriculture to a mid-scale river basin and evaluate how recommended practice would reduce environmental impacts caused by N and phosphate (P2O5) deriving from fertilizer and feed use.

2 Methods

2.1 Site description and data source

We chose the Omoigawa river basin in Tochigi prefecture in Japan as a typical paddy rice farming area. For data availability, old 36 districts were selected as the basin that could identify the shape of basin. An overview of this river basin and agricultural statistics are shown in Table 1 and compared with the Japanese average. These data were taken up from 2000 Agricultural Census [6] and agricultural statistics [7].

Table 1: Basic statistics of Omoigawa basin.

	Area (ha)	Occupation	Japanese average
Total area	92,800		
Total farmland	19,030	100.0%	100.0%
Total planted are:	16,048	84.3%	88.9%
Paddy field	11,289	59.3%	39.3%
Upland field	4,122	21.7%	23.4%
Orchard	432	2.3%	7.0%
Forage	205	1.1%	19.2%
No cultivation	3,187	16.7%	11.1%

Livestock	Head number	Density (head ha^{-1})	(Japanese average)
Daily cattle	5,737	0.33	0.38
Beef cattle	14,808	0.86	0.58
Pig	37,654	2.18	2.00
Layer	1,665	0.10	38.67
Broilar	2,825	0.16	119.08

2.2 Goal and scope definition

We defined the goal and scope of this analysis as estimation of environmental impacts caused by N and P2O5 use on crop and livestock production in a mid-scale river basin and estimation how environmental impacts will be reduced by different management practices.

The crop and livestock management systems were analyzed under conventional farming (CONV), standard farming (STD) and low input and forage production farming (LIFP). On CONV, chemical N and P2O5 fertilizers and manure use was according to the results of a questionnaire administrated by the Ministry of Agriculture, Forestry and Fisheries (MAFF) in 1998 and Tochigi prefecture. On STD, chemical fertilizer was applied according to the prefecture's recommendations [8]. Manure application to each kind of farmland was according to Shiga [9]. On low input and forage production (LIFP), chemical fertilizer application was reduced by slow release fertilizer [10]. Some of the chemical fertilizer for paddy rice was replaced with chicken manure [11], While some part of purchased forage from outside was self-stuffed on non-cultivated farmland by recommended amount of manure, urine and chemical fertilizer.

The system boundary was set as shown in Figure 1 to encompass the Omoigawa river basin geographically. A recycling pathway was included in this system as an original framework. Abiotic resource use accompanying fertilizer use and forage production and emissions from each process are also indicated in Figure 1.

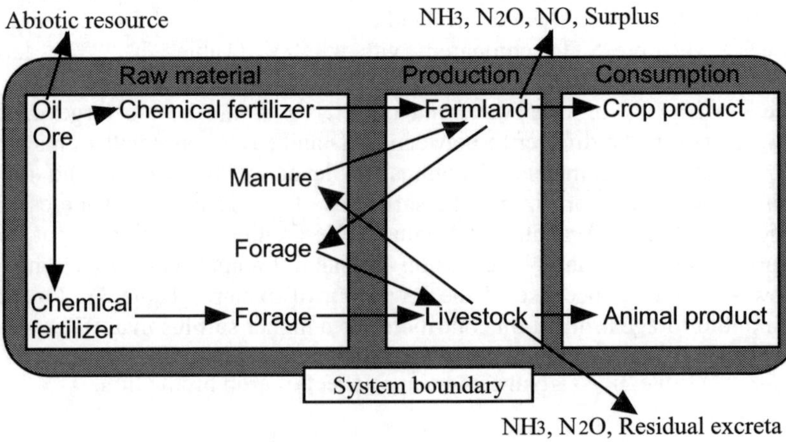

Figure 1: Framework of this study.

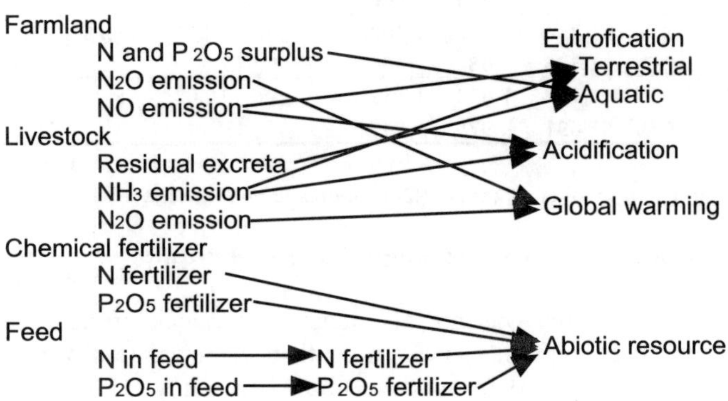

Figure 2: Impact categories.

2.3 Life cycle inventory and life cycle impact assessment

Abiotic resource use and impacts on the environment in each process are shown in Figure 2. Emission factors for each process were based on past studies [12, 13, 14, 15, 16]. Normalization values that aggregate various impacts into simple ones were according Brentrup et al [1].

Crude protein (CP) was set as the functional unit, because protein is contained in all crops and livestock products and is considered to be an important nutrient.

3 Results and discussions

3.1 Lifecycle inventories

Crop production was the highest on LIFP, because of the increase of forage production from non-cultivated farmland (Table 2). Chemical fertilizer use was reduced >30% on STD compared with CONV (Table 2). The largest contributors were paddy and upland fields where chemical fertilizer input was reduced to 25-50% of CONV. Input on CONV would be too large in these fields. However, the difference between STD and LIFP was small. This would indicate that the recommended application level is low enough and a little margin to reduce the fertilizer. The surpluses of N and P_2O_5 that indicated by chemical fertilizer and manure and natural (N_2-fixation, irrigation) input minus crop production, N_2O and NO emission and natural output (denitrification) were the lowest for STD, because of the low input of manure (Table 3). On LIFP, high input to forage production contributed to a higher surplus than STD.

Table 2: Nutrient balance sheet of crop production.

Scenario		Chemical fertilizer	Manure	Product	Natural in and out*	N_2O emission	NO emission	Surplus
CONV	N	1,817	492	1,009	-1	9.87	143.17	1,147
	P_2O_5	2,659	535	466				2,728
STD	N	1,234	508	1,009	-1	7.71	111.78	627
	P_2O_5	1,825	682	466				2,041
LIFP	N	1,142	1,073	1,139	-1	6.62	95.97	972
	P_2O_5	1,691	975	547				2,118

Unit : Mg

*:Aggrigated value of irrigation, N2-fixation and denitrification.

3.2 Feed consumption, livestock manure use and dispose

Although this study area was not an intensive livestock production area, the amount of feed consumption N was larger than chemical fertilizer N and feed was mostly imported from outside of the study area. Only 1/4 to 1/3 of nutrients were utilized as products except poultry, therefore livestock excreta would have significant effect for environmental load (Table 3) and it can be said the excreta

www.witpress.com, ISSN 1743-3541 (on-line)

came from outside of study area. About 40% of the excreta N volatilized as NH3 and N2O during the composting and storage of dung and urine. More than half of the excreta was utilized and the other was disposed (Table 4).

While this condition would be improved under STD that aimed to maintain soil fertility, forage production (LIFP) was needed to consume all livestock excreta (Table 4).

Table 3: Nutrient balance sheet of livestock production.

		Feed	Product	Excreta		Manure	Emission	
				Dung	Urine		NH_3	N_2O
Bovine	N	1,621	373	630	617	711	536	0.388
	P_2O_5	805	231	559	14	574		
Swaine	N	645	152	118	375	292	201	0.073
	P_2O_5	437	142	215	80	295		
Poultry	N	241	121	120	0	49	71	0.026
	P_2O_5	121	24	97	0	97		

Unit : Mg

Table 4: Fate of livestock excreta.

Scenario		Use		Dispose	
		N	P_2O_5	N	P_2O_5
CONV	Bovine	337	359	374	215
	Swaine	121	165	171	130
	Poultry	0	0	49	97
	Total	458	524	594	442
STD	Bovine	424	559	287	14
	Swaine	68	125	224	171
	Poultry	0	0	49	97
	Total	492	684	560	282
LIFP	Bovine	711	574	0	0
	Swaine	292	295	0	0
	Poultry	49	97	0	0
	Total	1,052	966	0	0

Unit : Mg

3.3 Abiotic resource use

Abiotic resource use was reduced in STD and LIFP in conjunction with reduction of chemical fertilizer use and recycling of manure as fertilizer (Table 5) without reduce crop production (Table 2).

Table 5: Abiotic resource use.

			CONV	STD	LIFP
Chemical fertilizer	N	Oil	994	677	587
	P_2O_5	Ore	3,982	2,786	2,677
		Oil	1,007	704	677
Chemical fertilizer for foage production	N	Oil	1,994	1,994	1,762
	P_2O_5	Ore	7,578	7,578	6,740
		Oil	1,916	1,916	1,704

(Mg)

Table 6: Environmental impacts by agricultural production.

	Unit	CONV	STD	LIFP
Impacts				
Aquatic eutrophication potential	Mg PO4eq.	483	350	324
Terrestrial eutoriphication	Mg NOxeq.	0.353	0.350	0.357
Acidification	Mg SO2eq.	0.019	0.018	0.018
Global warming potential	Mg CO2eq.	0.311	0.246	0.220
Abiotic resource use	-	257,052	230,130	205,760
Function unit	Mg CP	10,317	10,317	10,317
Normalized value				
Aquatic eutrophication potential	kg Mg^{-1}	46.77	33.92	31.36
Terrestrial eutoriphication	g Mg^{-1}	34.24	33.88	34.65
Acidification	g Mg^{-1}	1.89	1.74	1.71
Global warming potential	g Mg^{-1}	30.17	23.87	21.28
Abiotic resource use	Mg^{-1}	24.91	22.31	19.94

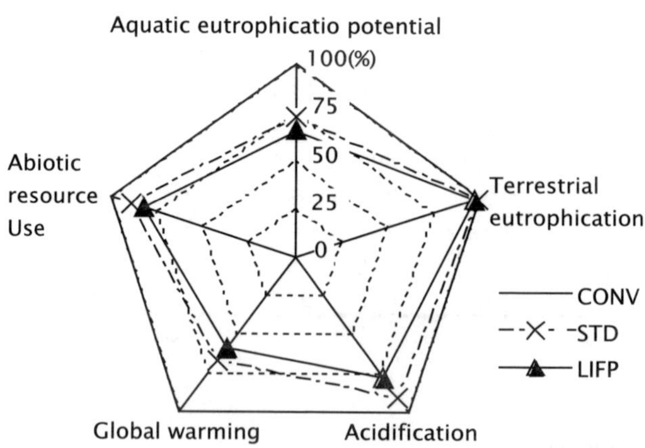

Figure 3: Relative environmental impact. (CONV was set as 100%.)

3.4 Environmental impacts

Environmental impacts (aggregation of each emission and resource use with characterization factor) were indicated in Table 6. Environmental impacts were the highest in CONV and the lowest in LIFP and LIFP was the lowest in all impacts. This indicates LIFP was the best management practices for this study area. However, the degree of reduction was different for each impact (Fig. 3). The rate of reduction of aquatic eutrophication potential, global warming and abiotic resource use were relatively larger than terrestrial eutrophication and acidification.

4 Conclusion

In this study, weighting was not done, because our purpose was to evaluate the degree of reduction of environmental load by different management practices. Mishima [5] indicated that residual N could be reduced by low input of chemical fertilizer and recycling of livestock excreta. This study indicated that P_2O_5 could also be reduced. Reduction of N and P_2O_5 input would reduce eutrophication and global warming that are important impacts from agro-environment. This study showed that these impacts could be reduced easily by changing fertilizer application.

Recently, local governments have recommend low inputs of chemical fertilizers, especially for paddy rice, and have attempted to shift production techniques from CONV to STD. Limiting chemical fertilizer and manure application could reasonable actions in water-contaminated areas, although it might be difficult to feel low contribution to global warming. However, this area has enough abundant farmland that could be converted to forage fields with a higher capacity to utilize and recycle manure and urine. These factors are capable of mitigating environmental impacts. The reduction of abiotic resource use has advantages in low input and forage production. However, these techniques are only effective in low livestock production areas. Mishima [17] indicated there might be no mitigation method for heavy livestock production areas. LCA should be done in such areas to formulate better management practices.

References

[1] Brentrup F., Küsters, J., Kuhlmann H., & Lammel J. Environmental impact assessment of agricultural production systems using the life cycle assessment methodology: I. Theoretical concept of a LCA method tailored to crop production. European Journal of Agronomy, 20(3), pp. 247-264, 2004

[2] Brentrup, F. Kusters, J. Kuhlmann, H. & Lammel, J. Application of life cycle assessment methodology to agricultural production: an example of sugar beet production with different forms of nitrogen fertilizers. European Journal or Agronomy. 14 pp. 221-233, 2001

[3] Brentrup, F. and Kusters, J. Lammel, J., Barracluough, P. & Kuhlmann, H. Environmental impact assessment of agricultural production systems using the life cycle assessment (LCA) methodology II. The application to N fertilizer use in winter wheat production systems. European Journal of Agronomy. 20, pp. 265-279, 2004

[4] Zebarth, B.J., Hii, B., Leibscher, H. Chipperfield, K. Paul, J.W. Grove, G. and Szeto, S.Y. Agricultural land use practices and nitrate contamination in the Abbotsford aquifer, British Columbia, Canada. Agriculture, Ecosystems and Environment. 69, pp. 99-112, 1998

[5] Mishima, S. Recent trend of nitrogen flow associated with agricultural production in Japan. Soil Science and Plant Nutrition. 47(1), pp. 157-166, 2001

[6] Ministry of Agriculture, Forestry and Fisheries (MAFF) (eds.) Agricultural Census 2000, MAFF: Tokyo, 2001.

[7] MAFF The 77th Statistical Yearbook of MAFF Japan 2000-2001, MAFF: Tokyo, 2002

[8] Tochigi prefecture Fertilization Standard, Tochigi prefecture: Utsunomiya, pp. 5-60, 2004

[9] Shiga, H., Capacity of organic resources application to farmland and livestock wastes, Research centre for daily farming: Sapporo, pp. 25-44, 1994.

[10] Ibaraki prefecture, Guideline for sustainable agricultural production, Ibaraki prefecture: Mito, pp. 95, 1995.

[11] Iwate prefecture, Report of advanced utilization farming method of livestock feces, Iwate prefecture: Morioka, pp. 11-19, 1997.

[12] Kobayashi, H. & Sato, R. A study on life cycle assessment of energy consumption and CO2 emissions in the manufacturing and transportation processes of nitrogen and phosphate fertilizers. Japanese Journal of Farm Work Research. 36(3), pp.141-151, 2001

[13] Akiyama, H., Tsuruta, H. & Watanabe, T. N2Oand NO emissions from soils after the application of different chemical fertilizers. Chemosphere, 2, pp. 313-320, 2000

[14] Yasuo, H., Quality of livestock excreta (Chapter 8) Livestock Production Part, Encyclopedia of Agricultural Technologies, ed Nosangyosonnbunka Association, Nosangyosonnbunka Association: Tokyo, pp.1-6, 1999

[15] Japan Soil Association, Report about global warming gas emission from soil, Tokyo, pp. 24,1995.

[16] Haga, K. & Waki, M., LCA of composting method of beef cattle, Norinsuisan Research Journal, 22(10), pp. 33-36, 1999

[17] Mishima, S. Quantitative evaluation of environmental risk associated with nitrogen flow in agricultural production and mitigation plan for 2 typical prefectures in Japan, Soil Science and Plan Nutrition, 47(3), pp. 511-518, 2001.

Section 18
Water resources

Clean technology for alternative irrigation systems

A. de Miranda
School of Oriental and African Studies, London, U.K.

Abstract

In many countries of the Mediterranean basin, Near and East Asia, as well as in some parts of Central and South America, the so-called "hydraulic noria", one of the categories of water-wheels, has represented a significant ecological system which has played a leading role in solving the main problem of supplying and carrying water for irrigation. This typology, based on the best employment of the power of the river, is a clean technology for the environment with easy and low-cost maintenance requirements.

This paper analyses some different and significant typologies still in use in Syria, East Asia and Central America, focusing on their architectural aspects, ecological characteristics and identifying differences, advantages and disadvantages, by examining the shape and design of the wheels.
Keywords: Irrigation systems, landscape, mechanical devices, hydraulic noria.

1 Introduction

The "hydraulic noria" represents the most elegant of hydraulic devices. It is an installation which, using the power of the river, raises water to irrigate fields which are usually at a higher level than the level of the water (Figure 1). The system is composed of two main parts, the wheel and the aqueduct. The wheel is mobile and is placed beside the aqueduct, on the bank of a stream, in a vertical position. The wheel is usually made of wood and is built by local craftsmen. The main structure of these water-wheels consists of two pairs of continuous parallel beams perpendicular to each other. They are the main spokes of the structure and are pivoted around a central axis supported at each end by stone walls or poles made of wood. The secondary beams stabilise the structure. The base of the wheel is submerged in the river and turns because of the current. Water is

transported through compartments or pots placed on the periphery of the rim, and is carried into the channel on the top of the aqueduct, and is directed to irrigate fields and gardens.
In the past the device was widespread in many parts of the Mediterranean basin, in Asia and America, while nowadays it is still in use in some areas of Syria, East Asia and Central America where the favourable characteristics of certain rivers have allowed the construction of these devices.

Although nowadays many examples have disappeared and have been replaced by motor pumps, there are still some countries where this typology is employed for its environmental and functional advantages. It is economical, requiring no petrol or oil, but exploiting the power of nature. The device has a simple mechanism and a continuous movement always in the same direction. Since water wheels operate continuously, they typically require partial restoration of the worn wood each year. The wheels are also well integrated into the landscape, using materials found in the area, and a light structure which makes them appear part of the natural environment. In fact the best wood for building different elements of the wheels is easily available near the rivers.

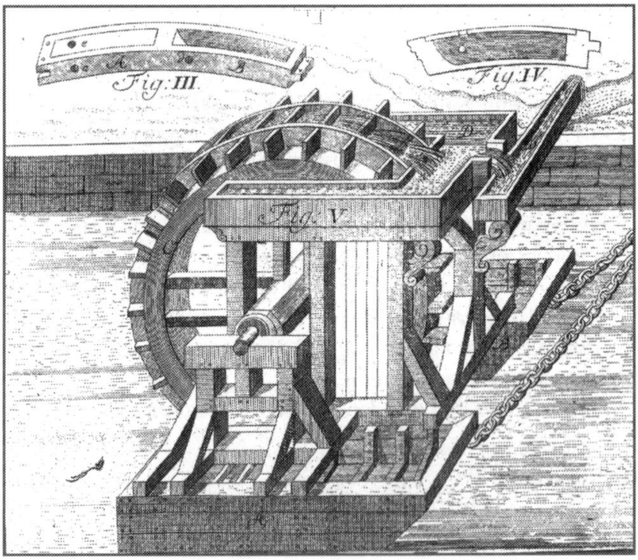

Figure 1: Scheme of the system for raising water.

3 Syrian examples

Syrian hydraulic norias are numerous on the Oronte river (Figures 2 and 3). The technique for their construction was originally imported by the Romans at least in the 3rd century A.D.. The installations are not used for irrigation any longer, but are kept in working order as part of Syria's architectural heritage. The construction and use of these devices is allowed by favourable morphological conditions, that is a constant speed of the river, a gradual slope of the ground and the absence of floods. In particular the constant speed of the water enables the hydraulic norias to move continuously.

These installations include wheels which can reach a diameter of more than 20 metres and also include secondary works made of masonry which improve the function of the wheel: the dam, which maintains a sufficient level of water, the derivation channels and the barrages which regulate the level of the water during periods of plenty or scarcity, the channel which conveys water to the wheel and increases the flow of water under it and the triangular wall which supports the wheel through a horizontal shaft (the other end of the shaft is placed on the sill of the fronton of the aqueduct).

The rotation velocity of the wheel increases with the velocity of the flowing water. Thus, the most appropriate locations to install these wheels are where the water stream is narrowest and reaches its highest velocity.

These hydraulic norias show unique characteristics in terms of material and typology. In fact the river water, the wood and the natural stone easily available in the area, allow a close integration of these installations into the ecological system of the landscape. In fact the best wood for building different elements of the wheels is durable, flexible and easily available near the Oronte. Poplar plantations can provide timber up to 15 metres long to make the spokes for the large wheels, and wood which is easy to work to make the small parts. Mulberry is the ideal material for the load-bearing axis of the wheel. It can last up to 25 years. The limestone employed to make the masonry works may not at first seem ideal because of its permeability. However, because the water of the Oronte is rich in calcium, it tends to deposit a thin layer on the limestone walls making them water-proof.

Figure 2: Syrian installations on the Oronte river. Scheme of the device (left) and the *Dawwar* installation outside Hama (right). Every wheel is connected to a separate aqueduct.

Another unique characteristic of these installations is the fact that, when it is necessary to supply a large amount of water and to raise it to different levels, they can be arranged in groups of four or more wheels, where every wheel is connected to a separate aqueduct.

Figure 3: Syrian installations on the Oronte river. The *Utmaniyyatani* group (left) and the *Ja'bariyya* and *Sihyuniyya* group (right) in the city of Hama.

Figure 4: Example of Chinese installation (left) and drawing of a hydraulic noria from a 17th century Chinese manuscript (right).

4 Asian examples

A unique typology of hydraulic noria with pots is still in use in East Asia, particularly in the regions of South and West China, in Indonesia, Cambodia, Thailand and Sri Lanka (Figures 4, 5 and 6). It is characterised by a very light and flexible structure made of bamboo, material easily available in these areas.

As in Central America they do not have masonry works for the canalisations and to support the wheel, but are fixed to the bed and to the banks of the river by poles. The structure consists of two parallel rims connected to each other by parallel bars and by radial spokes. Pots, made of bamboo like the other parts, are tied to the rims. During the circular motion they gradually change position depending on the volume of water carried in the pot. Bamboo is an excellent material. In fact it is easy to split and still strong. Some installations in Thailand and Sri Lanka show a structure characterised by several paddles also made of bamboo and by pots placed around, instead of perpendicular to, the rims. While in East Asia they are characterised by this unique bamboo device, in some regions of China, like in the Yunnan or in the Gansu on the Yellow River, they are entirely made of wood and show a typology similar to the Syrian ones.

Figure 5: Installations in South East Asia: at Chiang Mai in Thailand (left) and in Cambodia on the Siem Reap river (right).

Figure 6: Two type of Chinese installations. Installations with compartments and paddles at Lanzhou on the Gansu province (left) and installations near Sanjiang on the Guangxi province (right).

5 Mexican examples

The hydraulic noria was also used in Central America, where it was introduced by the Spanish colonisation during the early 16th century, in particular in the northern Mexican states of Aguascalientes, Zacatecas, San Louis Potosì, in the Yucatan Peninsula and in Jamaica. Although some examples are still in existence, like the wheel at Jalcomulco on the Huitzilapan River or that at Falmouth in Jamaica, none are in operation, due to the high cost of maintenance for moving the wheels during the annual flood, i.e. dissembling and reassembling the machines. Nowadays in Central America, as in Syria, these installations have been replaced by motor pumps as a means of raising water from the river.

The Jalcomulco wheel, which is a recent construction still in existence, is typical of Mexican installations. It has a diameter of 10m and a width of 1m and is characterized by paddles which convert the force of the stream into water-lifting energy. It is mainly made of wood. Attached to both ends of the paddles, instead of pots made of wood, which probably have characterised the old examples of this typology, there are plastic buckets which are more practical and economical. The channel which carries water to a field that lies at an elevation approximately 5 metres higher than the river level, is, as in the Asian installations, made of PVC and supported by poles driven into the stream bed. The movable structure which supports the PVC channel enables the channel itself to change direction towards the fields which need to be irrigated. As in the Asian examples, the wheel is fixed to the river bed by a system of poles. Mexican installations are able to work properly in favourable conditions, but they can also be easily destroyed by floods and an excessive speed of the river (Figure 7).

Figure 7: Installation in Mexico at Jalcomulco with the detail (right) of the buckets pouring water into the channel.

6 Comparisons

It is opportune to note that, although the hydraulic norias from East Asia and from Central America have the same function and mechanism as those in Syria, the structures are clearly different. Unlike the Syrian installations, where the wheels are inserted into a canal which increases the speed of water, in Central America and East Asia the wheels are along the river banks, without the possibility of modifying the flow of the water to guarantee a constant rotation of the machine. The lack of a stone support and aqueduct on the sides of the wheel could be a disadvantage compared to Syrian machines where they guarantee protection and stability to the wheel, even during periods of plenty. But some of these installations, such as the Asian examples, are often easily replaced due to their extremely easy assembly and lightness. For this reason, nowadays they are the only devices still employed as systems for raising water, while the Syrian examples are mainly considered as historical constructions not in use but kept in working order. Another difference between the Syrian and the other installations concerns the proportions of the wheels. The Asian and American ones have a diameter which is approximately ten times the width, while in the Syrian ones the width is always 50 centimetres, for large and small wheels.

7 Conclusions

Due to the introduction of new technologies based on oil or electricity, this device could disappear as a viable technology. However, due to its simplicity, efficiency and low operation and maintenance costs, this device deserves further attention and consideration.

In particular in the Syrian city of Hama, although the installations are in use but not employed for irrigation, the Governorate is preserving them through constant inspections and careful restorations, in order to re-evaluate a device which, in some cases, could still be fully employed for its original purpose and which has not changed its technology despite the progress of the 19th and 20th centuries.

References

[1] Baroja C. J., "Norias, azudas, aceñas". Revista de dialectologia y tradiciones populares X, pp. 26-160, 1954.

[2] Barrès, M., Un jardin sur l'Oronte. Plon: Paris, 1922.

[3] Bonnin, J., L'eau dans l'antiquité – L'hydraulique avant notre ère. Eyrolles: Paris, 1984.

[4] Carle, G., "L'hydraulique agricole et industrielle en Syrie". La géographie 39/5, pp. 564-602, 1923.

[5] Colin, G. S., "La noria marocaine et les machines hydrauliques dans le monde arabe". Hesperis XIV, pp. 22-60, 1932.

[6] Cuneo, P., "Noria. Utilitas, firmitas, venustas nell'architettura dei dispositivi idraulici a ruota elevatoria". Il teatro delle acque, ed. D. Jones, Edizioni dell'Elefante: Roma, pp. 51-68, 1992.
[7] Delpech, A., Les norias de l'Oronte: analyse technologique d'un element du patrimone syrien. Institut français de Damas: Damascus, 1997.
[8] De Miranda, A., "Aesthetic tradition and ancient technology: a case study of the water-wheel". Design and Nature II. Comparing Design and Nature with Science and Engineering, eds. by M. W. Collins and C.A. Brebbia, WIT Press, Southampton, pp.105-114, 2004
[9] De Miranda, A., "Traditional craftsmanships in Mediterranean lands". Mediterranean Architecture, Msr International University: Cairo, pp. 81-89, 2004.
[10] Dias, J., Aparelhos de elevar a água de rega. Don Quixote: Lisbon, 1986.
[11] Doolittle, W.E., "Against the Current and Against the Odds: Noria Technology in Mexico". Bulletin of the International Molinological Society, International Molinology, 59, pp. 8-13, 1999.
[12] Fiorillo C., & Vercueil J. (eds.), Syrian agriculture at the crossroads. Food and Agriculture Organisation of the United Nations: Rome, 2003.
[13] Fitchett, J. & Deford, M., "A river called Rebel". Aramco World Magazine, vol. 24, 3, pp. 12-21, 1973.
[14] Forbes, R. J., Studies in ancient technology. Vols. 1 and 2, E. J. Brill: Leiden, 1955.
[15] Hill, D., "Traditional Islamic Technology: Water Power". UR 2/3, pp. 89-92, 1982.
[16] Landels, J. G., Engineering in the Ancient World. Chatto and Windus: London, 1978.
[17] Needham, J. & Ling, L., Science and Civilisation in China. Vol. 4, part 2, Cambridge University Press: Cambridge, pp. 330-362, 1965.
[18] Oleson, J. P., "Water-Lifting". Handbook of Ancient Water Technology, ed. by O. Wikander, E. J. Brill: Leiden-Boston-Köln, pp. 217-302, 2000.
[19] Reynolds, T. S., Stronger than a hundred men: a history of a vertical water-wheel. Johns Hopkins University Press: Baltimore, 1983.
[20] Rudofsky, B., Architecture Without Architects. A short Introduction to Non-Pedigreed Architecture. The Museum of Modern Art: New York, 1965.
[21] Schiøler, Th., Roman and Islamic Water – Lifting Wheels. Acta Historica Scientiarum Naturalium at Medicinalium, edidit Bibliotheca Universitatis Haunensis, 28, Odense University Press: Odense, 1973.
[22] Weulersse, J., L'Oronte, étude d'une fleuve. Arrault: Tours, 1940.
[23] Zaqzouq, A., "Les norias. Anciens moyens d'irrigation les plus importants dans la région de Hama". Techniques et pratiques hydro-agricoles traditionnelles en domaine irrigué, ed. by B. Geyer, Librairie orientaliste Paul Geuthner: Paris, pp. 337-382, 1990.

Methods for biomass amount and sorption capacity estimation

V. Racys & I. Valunas
Department of Environmental Engineering,
Kaunas University of Technology, Lithuania

Abstract

Rising environmental standards for treated wastewater necessitate the improvement of current wastewater treatment methods or the need to look for new ones. Often this task is rather difficult because new or modified methods have to be investigated thoroughly and the main parameters for process modelling and effectiveness estimation have to be set. For instance, biomass concentration in the biosorption method is an important technological parameter although there is no accurate technique for its estimation. A thermal dissociation technique to determine biomass concentration was developed as an alternative to the standard volatile suspended solids (VSS) method.

Another important technological parameter in adsorption or biosorption processes is the sorption capacity of the sorbent. A simple technique was developed for the estimation of this parameter. The sorption capacity of the sorbent can be estimated using red formazane – a large-sized molecule compound–spirit solution. The results obtained show that this technique was quicker, simpler and more accurate than the standard procedure.
Keywords: biosorption, stable organic compounds, biomass, sorption capacity, technological control.

1 Introduction

One of the main technological parameters for the biological waste water treatment process control is the biomass amount variation during process time span. Biomass concentration is important for the technological calculations of the system, estimation of the oxidation potential and for the evaluation of biomass growth in accordance to decomposed pollutants, etc. Media of different types used in complex biological waste water treatment processes films over with biomass and it becomes difficult to estimate biomass content and present it using identifiable units. The agglomerate media - biomass (active sludge) makes it impossible to use common method for the biomass estimation. The problem is that the biomass cannot be properly separated from the media. Also small particles of the media in the sample of active sludge would determine substantial analysis errors.

In the scientific literature usually methods for approximate biomass estimation can be found. The fluorescence of a fermentation culture was studied for its application as an estimator of biomass concentration [1]. But it is difficult to estimate biomass concentration in identifiable units, like g/l. Many factors have influence to exactitude of the analysis: temperature, pH, medium chemical composition and cell activity. Other authors [2] developed technique to determine biomass concentration as chemical oxygen demand (COD) as an alternative to the standard volatile suspended solid (VSS) method. But even using very small amounts of sorbent for COD analysis, COD values are very high. That is why this method can not be used for control of biosorption process. The modified micro-Kjeldahl and Lawry method [3] is designed for estimating amounts of organic nitrogen and proteins in the sample. These two components are the main components in the living cell, so it is possible to estimate biomass concentration from the results of this method. However, this technique has following limitations: (1) total organic nitrogen is measured, not only that in the cells; (2) the method requires careful standardization for any particular application; (3) the colour is not strictly proportional to the concentration. German scientists try to work out this problem. A very promising way appears to be the impedance spectroscopy which enables a fast determination of the biomass concentration even at high optical densities [4]. It utilizes the properties of the membranes of living cells which exhibit a high polarization and contribute a significant amount of capacitance to the impedance. The different polarization states of the cell yields a characteristic curve of permittivity from which the cell concentration can be derived. However this technology is in the initial stage yet and unique equipment is used. That is why another solution to solve this problem must be found.

Sorption capacity of the sorbent is another important parameter for technological control. Usually this analysis is performed using oil products. After the sorption period unabsorbed oil products are estimated according to ISO 9377- 2:2000 (E). However, quantitative determination of oil products is quite complicated, expensive, time consuming, analysis errors are determined by intermediates of biochemical petroleum degradation. Therefore it would be convenient to find another way to evaluate sorption capacity. We decided to use chromatic compound (red formazane) that would have molecular size close to the compounds of interest, fig. 1. In this way analysis would be less time consuming and more accurate.

This research covered two areas. The objective of our research was to develop and verify in practice accurate methodology for the determination of the biomass amount in the biosorption system, using fairly simple devices and to develop the technique for the estimation of sorption capacity of the sorbent.

The biomass amount and sorption capacity in AC (active carbon) and AS (active sludge) agglomerate - biologically activated system (BAS) - are the objects of this research.

Figure 1: Molecular structure of red formazane.

Biomass amount research tasks are: 1) to determine thermal dissociation dynamics for active carbon A in chosen temperature interval; 2) to determine thermal dissociation dynamics for active sludge in the same temperature interval; 3) to determine temperature points/intervals, when the mass of both components is unvarying; 4) to verify methodology in practice.

Sorption capacity research tasks are: 1) to select stable chromatic organic compound; 2) to make its standard curve; 3) to carry out the experiments with chosen sorbent.

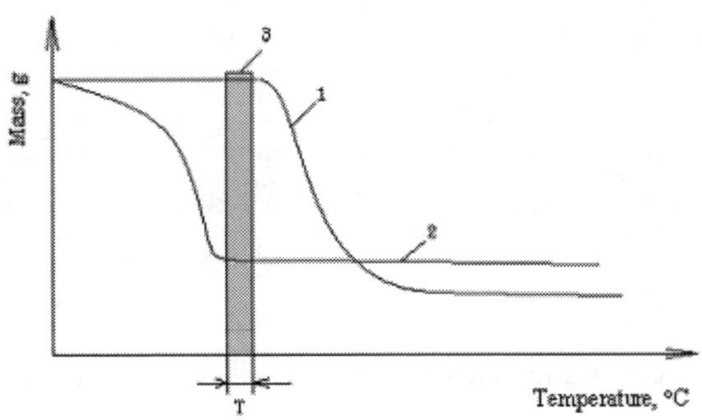

Figure 2: Theoretical thermograms: 1) thermogram of AC; 2) thermogram of AS; 3) the temperature range acceptable for agglomerate heating.

2 Research methodologies

2.1 Biomass content estimation

The equipment needed for the experiment is muffle furnace, analytical scale, ceramic melting pots, desiccator. AC sample is dried for 1 hour at temperature 105 °C until the stable mass. Then AC is heated at: 200, 300, 400, 500, 600, 700, 800 and 900 °C temperatures. As too big mass changes were observed in temperature intervals 300-400 and 400-500 °C, these intervals were divided into smaller intervals and the temperature sequence for experiments was chosen: 200, 300, 350, 400, 430, 460, 500, 600, 700, 800 and 900 °C.

WIT Transactions on Ecology and the Environment, Vol 81, © 2005 WIT Press
www.witpress.com, ISSN 1743-3541 (on-line)

At each temperature AC is heated till stable weight is reached. Preparation and analysis of AS is analogous to AC.

Theoretical thermograms of activated carbon and active sludge are represented in fig. 2. Their character was predicted before the experiment, i.e. it was premised that the curves would have three regions. These regions would represent temperature intervals when dissociation of both components does not take place, when dissociation takes place for both components and when both components are completely dissociated.

2.2 Sorption capacity estimation

The equipment needed for experiment is spirituous solution of red formazane, centrifuge with proper test tubes, photoelectrical colorimeter, tube shaker, transparent tubes, flasks of 50 ml and 250 ml.

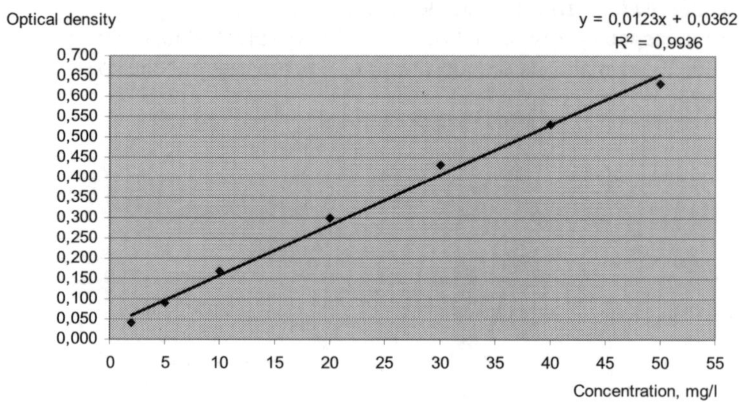

Figure 3: Calibration curve for red formazane spirituous solutions.

2.2.1 Standardization (calibration) curve

Series of standard solutions are prepared. Red formazane concentration in these solutions is 50, 40, 30, 20, 10, 5 and 2 mg/l respectively. Optical density of the solutions is measured using photoelectrical colorimeter at wavelength 490 nm. We obtained calibration curve with correlation coefficient R^2 = 0, 9936, fig. 3. This means that the curve can be used for estimation of red formazane concentration in spirituous solutions without noticeable errors.

During the experiments sorption capacity was estimated for two biologically activated systems – BAS-A and BAS-B and for two active carbons A and B. Sorption capacity tests are performed for: active carbons A and B, at 105°C dried BAS-A and BAS-B, not dried BAS-A and BAS-B. For these tests samples are transferred into test tubes, then 5 ml of operating solution is added and tubes are shaken for 30 minutes. Solution is separated by centrifuging. Optical density is measured. Five replicates for each sample were analyzed.

3 Results and discussions

3.1 Biomass content research results

The characters of plotted experimental data were analogous with the character of theoretical curves, fig. 4.

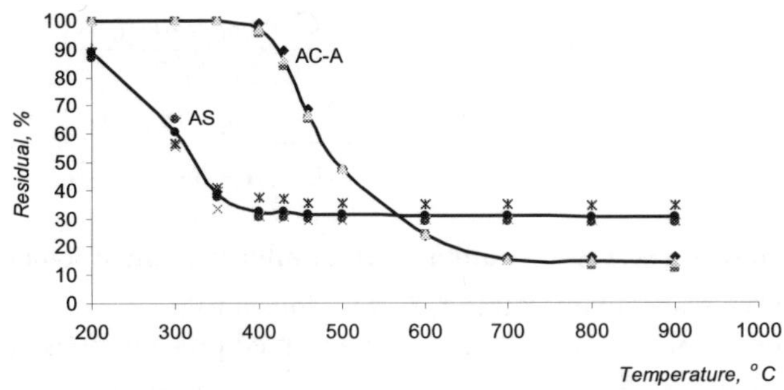

Figure 4: Experimental thermograms of AC-A and AS.

The equation for the first region of curve of AC is:

$$y_1 = 3 \cdot 10^{-7} t^2 - 0.0002t + 100 \quad (1)$$

where y_1 – residual of activated carbon, %, in temperature range 100-400 °C; t – temperature, °C.

The correlation coefficient for this equation is $R_1^2 = 0.98$. The equation for the third region of curve of AS is:

$$y_2 = 2 \cdot 10^{-6} t^2 - 0.0045t + 31.93 \quad (2)$$

where y_2 – residual of active sludge, %, in temperature range 350-900 °C; t – temperature, °C.

The correlation coefficient for this equation is $R_2^2 = 0.96$.

The percentage weight loss at various temperatures for the same type of active carbon is similar. This allows to presume that ratios of samples weight between m_{350}^{AC} and m_{900}^{AC}, m_{105}^{AC} and m_{900}^{AC} after heating at temperatures 105, 350 and 900 °C are constant. At the temperature 350 °C volatile organic part of active sludge almost completely dissociates and further rise of temperature has no effect on weight loss. Here we presume that ratio of residues weight after heating at 350 and 900 °C for the same type of active sludge is also similar. The results of these presumptions are the following formulas which enable to calculate organic part of biomass in the sample:

$$m_{org} = m_{105}^{AS} - \alpha \cdot m_{900}^{AS} \tag{3}$$

where m_{org} – organic part of biomass, g; m_{105}^{AS} - organic part of biomass in a sample after drying at 105 °C temperature, g; m_{900}^{AS} - residual of biomass (mineral part), after sample heating at 900 °C temperature, g; α - constant.

$$m_{105}^{AS} = m_{105} - D \times \frac{C \cdot m_{900} - m_{350}}{A - B \cdot C} \tag{4}$$

$$m_{900}^{AS} = \frac{m_{350}}{C} - \frac{B(C \cdot m_{900} - m_{350})}{C^2 (A - B \cdot C)} \tag{5}$$

where $m_{105}, m_{350}, m_{900}$ - sample weight after heating at temperatures 105, 350 and 900 °C, respectively, g; *A, B, C, D* – constants.

By means of eqn (1) and (2) under accepted presumptions constants *A*, *C* and α can be calculated:

$$m_{105}^{AC} / m_{350}^{AC} = \frac{3 \cdot 10^{-7} \cdot 105^2 - 0{,}0002 \cdot 105 + 100}{3 \cdot 10^{-7} \cdot 350^2 - 0{,}0002 \cdot 350 + 100} = 1{,}002 \approx 1 = const.A \tag{6}$$

$$m_{350}^{AS} / m_{900}^{AS} = \frac{2 \cdot 10^{-6} \cdot 350^2 - 0{,}0045 \cdot 350 + 31{,}93}{2 \cdot 10^{-6} \cdot 900^2 - 0{,}0045 \cdot 900 + 31{,}93} = 1{,}037 = const.C, \tag{7}$$

$$\alpha = \frac{m_{600}^{AS}}{m_{900}^{AS}} = \frac{2 \cdot 10^{-6} \cdot 600^2 - 0{,}0045 \cdot 600 + 31{,}93}{2 \cdot 10^{-6} \cdot 900^2 - 0{,}0045 \cdot 900 + 31{,}93} = 1{,}015 = const. \tag{8}$$

Constant *B* can be calculated using experimental data referring to presumptions mentioned above:

$$m_{105}^{AC} / m_{900}^{AC} = 6{,}580 = const.B \tag{9}$$

Equation for constant *D* is derived from eqn (4):

$$D = \frac{A \cdot B}{C} \tag{10}$$

It must be stressed that the values of all constants are the same only for the same type of active carbon and active sludge.

The temperature range for thermal separation of AS and AC composite (BAS) can be apparently seen in averaged values thermogram of active carbon and active sludge, fig. 5. The first region of the curve (100-350°C) goes down because of dissociation of active sludge. The third region of the curve represents thermal dissociation of active carbon. The median horizontal region (350-400 °C) represents the range of temperature when the amounts of both components do not change, i.e. active sludge is dissociated already and thermal dissociation of active carbon has not begun yet.

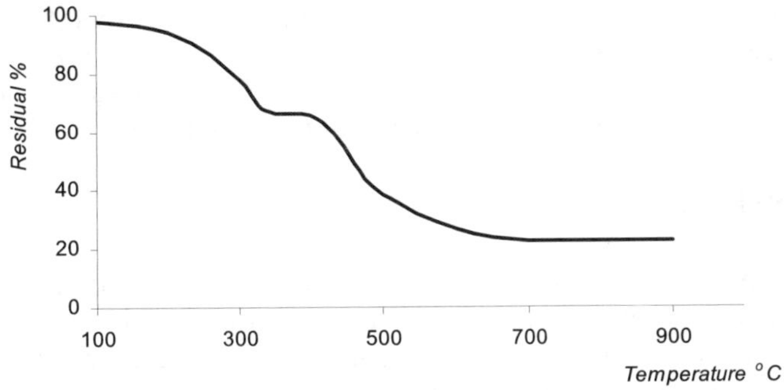

Figure 5: Averaged values thermogram of AC-A and AS.

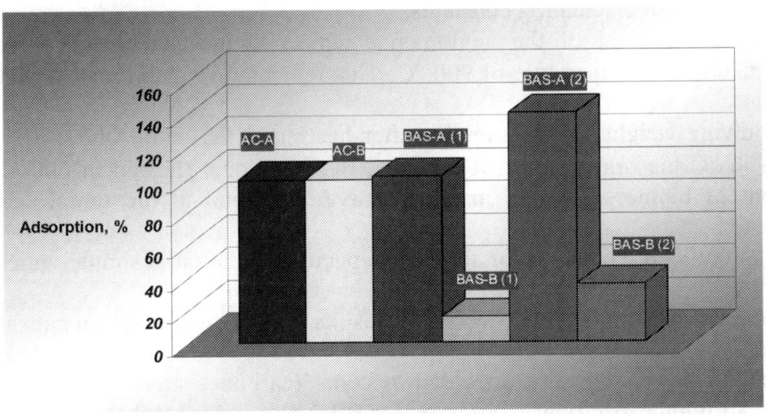

Figure 6: Sorption capacity research results.

3.2 Sorption capacity research results

The results from the experiments are shown in fig. 6.

Two ACs and two BASs were tested during the research of sorption capacity: AC-A and AC-B, BAS-A and BAS-B. Sorption capacity of ACs samples was equated to 100%, fig. 6. (AC-A, AC-B). It was estimated that sorption capacity of AC-A and AC-B was $4.24*10^{-3}$ and $6.1*10^{-3}$ g/g of red formazane respectively. Initial sorption capacity of AC-B was 30.5 % higher than that of AC-A. Test results of dried BAS-A and BAS-B samples show that sorption capacity of BAS-A sample stayed almost at the same level as the initial sorption capacity of AC-A. However sample BAS-B adsorption decreased 84%, fig. 6. (BAS-A (1), BAS-B (1)). During the experiment with not dried samples, sorption capacity of BAS-A increased 40%, according to initial sorption capacity. Sorption capacity of BAS-B makes only 30% of initial sorption capacity, fig. 6. (BAS-A (2), BAS-B (2)).

These results show that during the biosorption process BAS-A is regenerated by biomass. Sorbent BAS-B during the process is not regenerated, the stoppage of pores occurs and in the agglomerate of AS - AC only one active component – biomass stays and sorption characteristics of the system are lost.

4 Conclusions

1) It is experimentally proved that the heating process proceeds regularly. The relation between temperature and burnt out part of activated carbon at the temperature range 200-400 °C is strong and correlation coefficient is $R_1^2 = 0.98$. The relation between temperature and volatile organic part of active sludge at the temperature range 350 – 900 °C is strong and correlation coefficient is $R_2^2 = 0.96$.
2) The experimental research confirmed that organic volatile part of active sludge can be estimated after heating sample at the temperature of 350 °C. This value is used for calculating constants.
3) The ash content of the agglomerate active sludge - activated carbon is estimated at the temperature of 900 °C. This temperature is the final for heating samples.
4) Knowing weights of the samples after heating at the temperatures 105, 350 and 900 °C the organic part of biomass, the traditional (heated in 600°C) ash content of biomass and the mass of activated carbon in the sample can be estimated.
5) The modified technique for sorption capacity estimation is simple, quick and accurate.
6) Sorption capacity analysis with ACs results show higher sorption capacity of AC-B.
7) Examining biologically activated systems (carbon - alive biomass) much higher sorption capacity was observed for BAS-A than for BAS-B.
8) The method was verified on different BASs. It enables to evaluate the regeneration degree of sorption capacity of BAS.

References

[1] Zabriskie, D.W. & Humphrey, A.E., Estimation of fermentation biomass concentration by measuring culture fluorescence. *Applied and environmental microbiology*, **35(2)**, pp. 337-343, 1978.

[2] Contreras, E.M., Bertola, N.C., Giannuzzi, L. & Zaritzky, N.E., A modified method to determine biomass concentration as COD in pure cultures and in activated sludge systems. *Water SA*, **28(4)**, pp. 463-467, 2002.
[3] Sapan, C.V., Lundblad, R.L. & Price, N.C., Colorimetric protein assay techniques. *Biotechnology and applied biochemistry,* **29**, pp. 99-108, 1999.
[4] Hamburg – Harburg University of Technology (TUHH). Micro Systems Technology (former Semiconductor Technology) Web Site, Germany, http://www.tu-harburg.de/mst/english/forschung/muel_10.shtml

Evaluation of a parking lot bioretention cell for removal of stormwater pollutants

C. Glass & S. Bissouma
Department of Civil Engineering, Howard University, Washington D.C., U.S.A.

Abstract

Bioretention is used to retain and treat urban stormwater, which has been identified by the United States Environmental Protection Agency as one of the most significant forms of water pollution. In this study, the efficiency of a bioretention facility in terms of temperature, pH, dissolved oxygen, nutrients, and heavy metals removal over a period of 15 rain events was evaluated. This was performed by collecting representative samples of the stormwater runoff for laboratory analysis of both the influent to and the effluent from the bioretention cell. The bioretention was efficient in terms of pollutant removal in the following order: TSS (~ 98%) > Zn (~ 80%) > Cu (~ 75%) > Pb (~ 71%) > Cd (~ 70%) > NH_3-N (~65%) > Fe (~ 51%) > Cr (~ 42%) > NO^-_2-N (~ 27%) > Al (~ 17%) > PO^{3-}_4-P (~3%). From the field results Cu (II), Zn (II) and Pb (II) were removed significantly at 81%, 79% and 75%. The field results indicate that bioretention facilities can be effective for the removal of heavy metals in the following order: Cu > Zn > Pb > Cd > Fe > Cr > Al. Although the removal efficiency for this actual field bioretention cell was not has high as previously reported laboratory and field evaluations, removal of pollutants was significant. Organic matter and plants were believed to be the dominant bioretention elements for the removal of heavy metals.
Keywords: bioretention, stormwater, heavy metals, adsorption.

1 Introduction

Combined sewer overflows (CSO) continue to occur throughout major cities in the Northeast, Great Lakes, and Northwest regions of the U.S., primarily as a result of rainwater that is diverted from roads, parking lots, and the roofs of buildings during storm events [1]. The rapid transport of water away from the built environment to natural water bodies has dominated engineering for the past 130 years, since the recognition that pathogens in wastewater caused several human diseases. In older cities with combined sewers the continued replacement of natural surfaces with impervious ones leads to greater amounts of stormwater runoff. The contamination of natural water bodies leads to the destruction of habitat potentially leading to negative human health impacts (Griesel and Jagals [2]). Developing best management practices to prevent rain water contamination, remove pollutants before the runoff enters the combined sewer system, and retain or detain the movement of water in a decentralized fashion can potentially mitigate CSO events.

Urbanization creates impervious surfaces such as roads, sidewalks, highways, rooftops, and parking lots that result in an increase of stormwater runoff at the expense of infiltration. The stormwater runoff quickly flows over those impermeable surfaces and accumulates toxic pollutants such as heavy metals [3, 4, 5] generated by automobile use, weathering of building materials and atmospheric deposition (Davis *et al* [6]). A nationwide U.S. urban study showed that heavy metals were by far the most prevalent pollutant constituents of urban stormwater runoff (Cole *et al* [7]). Due to its toxic content, the storm water runoff when discharged to a stream, severely impacts the quality of natural water systems by causing a threat to aquatic life and human health, and also flooding and erosion. As a result, urban stormwater runoff has been identified as one of the most significant water pollution problems in the United States (Wiginton *et al* [8]).

To address the problem of surface water pollution from urban stormwater runoff, a number of engineered and managed natural systems have evolved and are being offered as “best management practices” (BMPs) for low impact development. They are part of the United States Environmental Protection Agency’s (USEPA) effort to regulate the release of pollutants into natural aquatic environments through water quality standards set forth by the National Pollutant Discharge Elimination System (NPDES). A stormwater BMP is a device, practice, or method used to remove, reduce, retard, or prevent targeted stormwater runoff pollutants from reaching receiving waters in the most cost-effective manner.

In the early 1990s, Prince George’s County, Maryland began developing and promoting a natural-based stormwater BMP system known as bioretention (or rain garden) [9]. Bioretention is a simple but effective way to improve the quality of stormwater runoff from developed areas such as parking lots, in order to minimize surface water impacts. Bioretention is a porous sand/soil media, supporting a vegetative layer, with a topping layer of hardwood mulch. Water quality enhancement occurs through the bioretention facility via biological, chemical and physical processes including phytoremediation, precipitation, adsorption, complexation, microbial activity, decomposition, sedimentation, filtration, and volatilization. In urban environments these systems are typically designed by filling a concrete box with gravel, sand, planting soil, a top layer of mulch, and various species of water loving plants. Currently little is known with regard to the field performance of bioretention cells. Few researchers have evaluated the performance of best management practices with actual stormwater runoff (Davis *et al* [10]).

The objective of this study was to evaluate the efficiency of a bioretention facility located at a parking lot of the Navy Yard, Washington, DC in terms of stormwater pollutants, with an emphasis on heavy metal removal due to their toxicity. Representative samples of the "first-flush" of stormwater runoff were collected at the inlet and outlet points of the bioretention cell and transported directly to the laboratory for analysis. Heavy metals were of particular concern due to their toxicity, possible accumulation in the bioretention facility, long-term fate, and persistence. Data was collected on the amount of rainfall and concentrations of heavy metals present in the influent and effluent runoff.

2 Materials and methods

Samples were collected from March 21, 2003 to June 20, 2003 (15 storm events), in accordance with the procedures outlined in Standard Methods for the Examination of Water and Wastewater, 20th Edition, section 1060 [11]. To monitor water quality and assess the efficiency of this bioretention facility to remove pollutants, composite samples were collected at the inlet and outlet points using two automatic samplers (3710 compact composite sampler, ISCO, Inc., NE), placed in protective shelters, and a rain gauge (674 rain gauge, ISCO, Inc., NE), placed on top of the inlet protective equipment shelter (Figure 1). The rain gauge initiates monitoring activity when there is a sufficient amount of rainfall.

At the inlet point, the sampler periodically collected the samples from the inflow stream into a collector plastic box placed at the end of the paved surface entrance. The sampler controller was programmed to initiate each collection sequence and to regulate the amount collected. The sequential composite samples were collected after a set volume of stormwater (volume needed to do the laboratory analysis, approximately 1.5 L) passed the monitoring point and by using continuous, constant sample pumping. The rain gauge's rain collecting mechanism is triggered when the amount of rainfall reaches approximately 0.5 inches over 6 hours. At this point, a signal is then sent to the sampler.

The interest of the stormwater sampling at this site was to collect "first-flush" samples, typically during the first 30 minutes of a storm event. At the outlet point, depending on the intensity and the duration of the rain and also due to time the water takes to be infiltrated through the media (approximately 12 to 48 hours), the samples were collected by a manual activation of the sampler. No effluent was collected from the fifth storm event because of the low volume of the storm and the dry period that preceded it. During the eleventh storm event the collection devise was tampered with resulting in no data collection for the influent.

2.1 Site characterization

The field site in this study was a 30-acre paved parking lot located at the Navy Yard, Washington, DC. Engineers of the Water Quality Division, D.C.

Department of Health, and experts at the Low Impact Development Center, MD, along with the authors selected this site because of its convenient location and its affinity to the monitoring equipment.

Figure 1: Bioretention cell.

The field study was conducted at a facility designed and constructed in 2001 by the Low Impact Development Center, MD. This facility is a 292-square-foot bioretention cell (Figure 1), part of a 0.27-acre watershed (area of the parking lot that drains along the stream to the outlet point). Curb cuts were placed around the cell to direct the stormwater runoff into the facility at the inlet entrance.

The bioretention media is a mixture of construction sand (50%), rocks and topsoil (30%) (with a modified clay content (≈10%) and organic content (≈20%)) hardwood mulch and plants (20%). The facility surface is dominated by approximately 6 cm of mulch, some selected plants such as *cephlantus occidentalis* and *aronia arbutifolia red chokeberry* and a few shrubs. A 6-inch (inside diameter) perforated PVC pipe, located at a depth of 30 inches, collected the infiltrated runoff. The outlet of this pipe opens into a 24-inch manhole, which feeds into a 12-inch storm sewer pipe. The outlet consisted of a concrete box with a rectangular opening in the side, set as an overflow for a water level exceeding the design ponding depth, with access to the effluent through a manhole cover.

2.2 Analytical methodology

Prior to metals analysis, the stored samples were filtered through 0.2 µm non-sterile syringe filters (Millipore millex, Fisher Scientific, Pittsburgh, PA) and placed into 2 mL plastic vials (Perkin-Elmer Corporation, Norwalk, CT). Heavy metal analysis was performed using an atomic absorption spectrometer (AAS) via the furnace module (800AAnalyst, Perkin-Elmer Corporation, Norwalk, CT) following Standard Methods [11]. The collected filtrates were analyzed for the following dissolved heavy metals: Al, Cd, Cr, Cu, Fe, As, Pb, and Zn. Quality assurance and quality control procedures included triplicate and spiked samples for accuracy and confidence measurement.

Ammonia was analyzed using an ammonium selective electrode (Thermo Orion model 9318, Beverly, MA) with a detection limit of 0.07 mg/L NH_3, using a detection meter (Thermo Orion Model 920 A+). Nitrate, nitrite, and phosphate concentrations were determined using an ion chromatograph (Dionex, Model DX-120) equipped with a guard column (AG-14A) and separation column (AS-14A). Temperature and pH were determined using a portable dissolved oxygen meter with a thermocouple (Oakton, DO 100 Series 35640). Total Suspended Solids were determined following Standard Methods [11]. pH was measured using an Accumet pH probe and Accumet Research meter (AR20 pH/conductivity meter, Fisher Scientific).

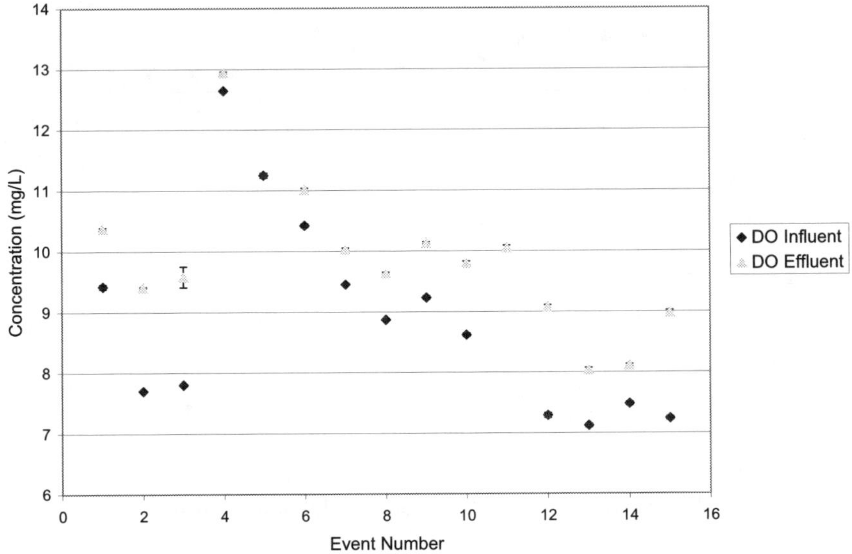

Figure 2: Dissolved oxygen concentration for 15 storm events.

3 Results

This field study was conducted in order to evaluate the efficiency of the Navy Yard bioretention in terms of dissolved oxygen, temperature, pH, and heavy metals removal. In Figure 2 the dissolved oxygen concentration of influent and effluent to and from the bioretention are presented. Given the low temperature of the rain events 4-6, that marked the end of winter, the dissolved oxygen concentration was supersaturated leading to high dissolved oxygen concentrations. Even at supersaturated concentrations, the dissolved oxygen concentration was higher as the stormwater left the bioretention cell for all of the storm events

The pH of rain water, influent, and effluent stormwater are presented in Figure 3. In Figure 3 the slightly acidic nature of rainfall in the Washington D.C. area can be seen with an average pH of 5.4 ± 0.2. The area of this study is known to have acid rain with a pH range as low as 4.2-4.4 [12]. Nevertheless the pH of the rain water increased as it created runoff into the system with an average pH of 7.5 ± 0.5 and did not significantly change as the stormwater passed through the system resulting in an effluent pH of 7.4 ± 0.4.

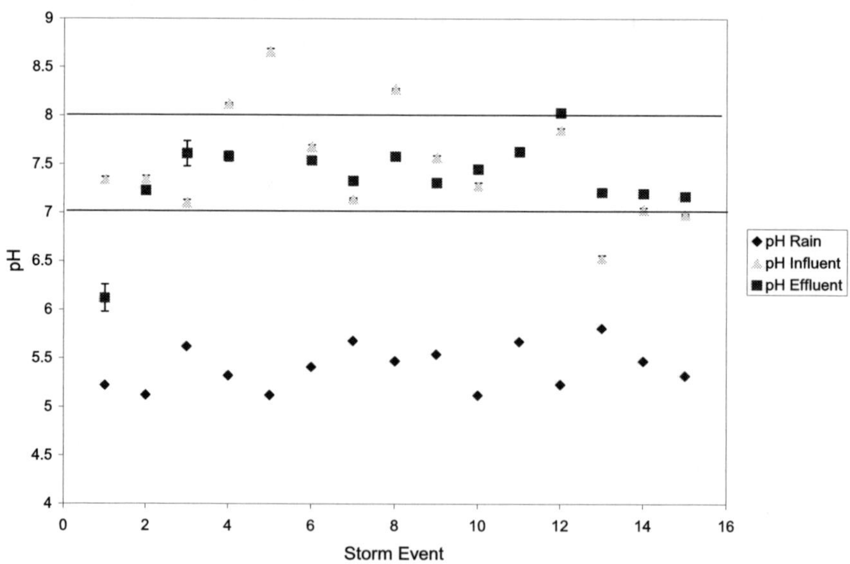

Figure 3: pH of rain water, influent and effluent.

3.1 Heavy metals removal

The summary of results for the average concentrations of heavy metals in the influent and effluent are presented in the Table 1. In addition, in Table 1 the drinking water maximum contaminant level required by the USEPA is listed as a reference for which parameter exceeded this regulated value. In this study only lead and cadmium concentrations in the influent exceeded the drinking water standard for these parameters. Nevertheless, the effluent metal concentrations were observed to be below the influent concentrations for all of the heavy metals displaying the successful adsorption of these compounds in the bioretention cell.

Table 1: Summary of heavy metal concentrations.

	Cu	Cd	Zn	Cr	Pb	Al	As	Fe
C_{in} (μg/L)	56.8	5.6	98.3	7.6	41.4	3.5	2	26.8
C_{ef} (μg/L)	10.9	1.9	20.6	3.6	10.2	2.9	1.7	12.6
Removal %	81	66	79	53	75	17	11	53
Maximum Contaminant Level (μg/L)	1000	5	500	100	15	200	50	300
Detection limit (μg/L)	0.85	0.065	0.05	0.35	1.5	1.55	2	0.6

In Figure 4 the removal of cadmium is depicted for the 15 storm events evaluated in this investigation. The bioretention performed well, removing cadmium to below the drinking water maximum contaminant level in all but two storm events, which happened to correspond to the events with the highest concentrations of cadmium. The percentage removal of cadmium based on concentration was 66% and 62% based on the load to the system. Figure 4 shows the drastic variation in the influent concentration in to the bioretention from storm to storm. This is largely dependent on the varying amounts of deposition in between storm events and was true for all of the heavy metals monitored in this study.

Lead was the only other heavy metal consistently present at influent concentrations that exceeded the drinking water maximum contaminant level. All of the storm events contained concentrations of lead in excess of the drinking water standard. The bioretention cell removed lead to concentrations below the drinking water standard for all storm events with an average removal rate of 75%.

Copper, zinc, iron, chromium, aluminium, and arsenic were removed from the stormwater at average percentage removal rates of 81%, 79%, 53%, 53%, 17%, and 11%, respectively. Due to space limitations the graphs that show the influent and effluent concentrations to and from the bioretention for all of these metals are not shown, but there was a wide variation in the concentrations due to the nature of this field monitoring study. In addition, the concentrations vary based on the time period and the activity of the parking lot between storm events.

According to the field results, the bioretention is efficient in terms of heavy metal removal in the following order: Cu > Zn> Pb > Cd > Fe > Cr > Al > As.

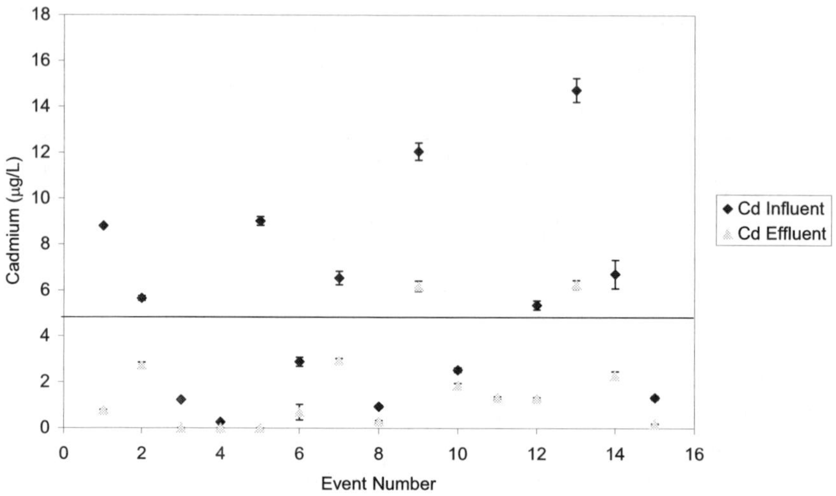

Figure 4: Cadmium concentration for 15 storm events.

Nutrient removal in the field study showed successful removal of nitrate, nitrite, ammonia, however none of these parameters were ever present at concentrations exceeding 1 mg/L. Soluble phosphorus as phosphate was never detected in the influent or effluent from the bioretention cell, with a detection limit of 0.1 mg/L. Ammonia was present in the influent at an average concentration of 0.5 mg/L and was never detected in the effluent. Nitrate was not detected in 8 of the 15 storm events and was only detected in the effluent of 4 events. Nutrients were not present at elevated concentrations in this parking lot.

4 Discussion

The metal removal efficiency results were less than those found in the literature for laboratory studies by Davis *et al* [6]. This is certainly due to the lack of maintenance of the bioretention mulch layer, which should retain metals at efficiencies from 88-99%. Laboratory and pilot studies have shown that the surface mulch layer is the most important component of the bioretention system for metal removal. In this study no special changes were made from the normal maintenance and operation of the bioretention area studied. During the early spring/late winter timeframe of this study the bioretention area contained a low growth of plants and had not received new mulch. The facility was two years old and had not been replanted in that time prior to the study. The plant roots should have improved metal removal and the bioretention age should have provided more efficient metal uptake. However, in many of the prior studies a constant concentration higher concentration of synthetic water was utilized instead of the changing concentrations of actual stormwater.

5 Conclusions

In Washington D.C. approximately 1/3 (12,640 acres) of the city is served by a combined sewer system. Annually the 50 combined sewers expel over 3 billion gallons of combined sanitary wastewater and stormwater in an average year [13]. The majority of this water, approximately 2 billion gallons, enters into the Anacostia River which continues to be one of the most polluted rivers in the U.S. [14]. As a result of the continued CSO events in June 2003 a settlement was reached between the E.P.A. and the District of Columbia Water and Sewer Authority (WASA) to pay a fine of $250,000 and to provide $2 million to stormwater pollution prevention. A portion of the $2 million is to be used to promote Low Impact Development (LID) in the watersheds with CSO's (E.P.A. 2003).

Although WASA established a long-term control plan in 2001, the cost to date, estimated at over $1 billion has been prohibitive to the initiation of the project. A more aggressive approach in the use of LID processes could yield important benefits. Of the many small drainage areas that lead to CSO's in Washington D.C. the majority of them have a minimum rainfall of less than 1 inch to cause an overflow. Eighteen of the CSO's overflow with less that ½ inch of rainfall. Although hundreds of rain barrels, bioretention cells, roof gardens, down spout disconnections, and other decentralized controls would have to be implemented to reduce the number of CSO events to zero, doubling or tripling the amount of rainfall required for an event would decrease the number of events significantly in a region that generally receives multiple small storms. The purpose of this project was to confirm the capability of bioretention cells to remove pollutants from stormwater lowering the load on the combined sewer system and the Anacostia River. Others have shown the capability of bioretention cells in the laboratory and with synthetic storm water in the field, but there are few studies that have evaluated the performance of bioretention cells with actual stormwater in a maintained field study.

The bioretention removed pollutants in the following order: TSS (~ 98%) > Zn (~ 80%) > Cu (~ 75%) > Pb (~ 71%) > Cd (~ 70%) > NH_3-N (~65%) > Fe (~ 51%) > Cr (~ 42%) > NO^-_2-N (~ 27%) > Al (~ 17%) > PO^{3-}_4-P (~3%). From the field results Cu (II), Zn (II) and Pb (II) were removed significantly at 81 ± 29%, 79 ± 14% and 75 ± 19%. The field results indicate that bioretention facilities can be effective for the removal of heavy metals, nutrients, and increase the dissolved oxygen content. In order to ensure removal of heavy metals to 90% the soil organic matter must be kept high and plants must be well maintained.

References

[1] Experts Workshop on Public Health Impacts of Sewer Overflows, United States Environmental Protection Agency. Summary of the August 14-15, 2002, Washington, DC. EPA No. 833-R-02-002, 2002.

[2] Griesel, M., & Jagals, P., Faecal indicator organisms in the Renoster Spruit system of Modder-Riet River catchment and implications for human users of the water. *Water SA*, **28**(2), pp. 227-234, 2002.

[3] Sansalone, J.J., & Buchberger, S.G., Partitioning and first flush of metals in urban storm water. *Journal of Environmental Engineering*, pp. 134-143, February, 1997.

[4] Barrett, M.E., Irish, L.B., Malina, J.F, & Charbeneau, R.J., Characterization of highway runoff in Austin, Texas. *Journal of Environmental Engineering*, pp. 131-137, February, 1998.

[5] Wu, J.S., Allan, C.J. and Evett, J.B., Characterization and pollutant loading estimation for highway runoff. *Journal of Environmental Engineering*, pp. 584-592, July, 1998.

[6] Davis, A.P., Shokouhian, M., Sharma, H. and Minami, C, Laboratory study of bioretention for urban stormwater management. *Water Environment Research*, **(73)**, pp. 5-14, 2001.

[7] Cole, R.H., Frederick, R.E., Healy, R.P., & Rolan, R.G., Preliminary findings of the priority pollutant monitoring project of the nation wide urban runoff program. *Journal of the Water Pollution Control Federation*, **(56)** 7, pp. 898-908, 1984.

[8] Wigington, Jr., P.J., Randall, C.W., & Grizzard, T.J., Accumulation of selected trace metals in soils of urban runoff swale drains. *Water Resource Bulletin*, **(22)** 1, pp. 73-79, 1986.

[9] Low Impact Development Design Manual, Department of Environmental Resources, Prince George's County (Maryland, U.S.) Government. Department of Environmental Resources, 1997.

[10] Davis, A.P., Shokouhian, M., Sharma, H., Minami, C, & Winogradoff, D., Water quality improvement through bioretention: lead, copper, and zinc removal. *Water Environment Research*, **(75)**, 1 pp. 73-82, 2003.

[11] American Public Health Association; American Water Works Association; & Water Pollution Control Federation (20th Edition), Standard Methods for the Examination of Water and Wastewater.

[12] United States Geological Survey, http://pubs.usgs.gov/gip/acidrain/2.html

[13] District of Columbia Water and Sewer Authority, Long-Term Control Plan, http://www.dcwasa.com/education/css/longtermcontrolplan.cfm

[14] National Resources Defense Council, Cleaning Up the Anacostia River, http://www.nrdc.org/water/pollution/fanacost.asp

Status of the Barra das Jangadas estuary (North-eastern Brazil): an ecological approach

S. J. Macedo[1], S. Neumann-Leitão[1], M. L. Koening[1], M. Araújo Filho[1], R. Schwamborn[2], F. A. N. Feitosa[1], K. Muniz[1], S. R. Lacerda[3] & M. J. Flores Montes[1]
[1]*Department of Oceanography, Federal University of Pernambuco, Brazil*
[2]*Department of Zoology, Federal University of Pernambuco, Brazil*
[3]*Department of Biology, State University of Cariri, Crato, Ceará, Brazil*

Abstract

The basic hydrological and planktonic characteristics of the Barra das Jangadas estuary were monitored to assess the water quality and the abiotic factors influencing the plankton populations. An intensive seven day sampling program was conducted at a fixed station, during the dry (January/2001) and the rainy (July/2001) seasons. Phytoplankton, zooplankton and the water physico-chemical parameters were sampled in different tides, totaling 56 sampling procedures during the 168-hours-program, in each season. The dissolved oxygen was under saturation at low tide in both seasons, indicating a polluted area; and saturated during high tide due to marine influence. High overall nutrient concentrations indicated an eutrophic environment. Chlorophyll-a was high (~25 $mg.m^{-3}$). The marine eurihaline plankton dominated the area. Phytoplankton presented 266 species, however only six were abundant and frequent; density varied from 95.10^3 $cel.L^{-1}$ to $7,830.10^3$ both in the rainy season, and cyanobacterial blooms usually occurred in the estuary unbalancing the system. The zooplankton presented 87 taxa and varied from 1,300 to 18,500 $ind.m^{-3}$. The plankton diversity was low, mostly composed of r-strategists. The main pattern observed was marine eurihaline species in the dry season during high tide and limnetic species in the rainy season, low tide. During the neap tide in both seasons the water renovation was very poor, increasing the pollution load residence time.

Keywords: estuary, water quality, nutrients, phytoplankton, zooplankton.

1 Introduction

An estuary, due to its condition as boundary between marine and freshwater systems, is characterized by extreme environmental gradients. Thus, the estuarine communities present a variability pattern that is a function of its geographic distribution. Nevertheless, that natural variability is often hidden under other much more erratic variability associated with anthropogenic activity, both urban-industrial and agricultural [1, 2].

The widespread human population cause nutrient enrichment of estuarine ecosystem and this trend is predicted to increase further in the present decade [3]. High rates of nutrient loading to coastal environments frequently enhance phytoplankton growth and biomass, and increase the rate of organic matter loading, ultimately resulting in eutrophication [3, 4]. Change in nutrient loading, can alter the species composition of primary producers [5]. Such shifts in the primary producer community are likely to cascade through the food web, altering consumer food web dynamics, and thus the flow of carbon through a system. It is therefore critical to understand the ecosystem response to nutrient loading.

The Barra das Jangadas tropical estuary, formed by the confluence of the perennial Jaboatão and Pirapama rivers, is under intense anthropogenic impacts since the sixties. Earlier surveys in this estuary [6] showed already an impacted ecosystem, as the water quality was degraded by the discharge of domestic sewage and sugar cane residuals. At that time, Eskinazi [7] showed already, that the phytoplankton community indicated an euthrophic system with intense diatoms blooms. For nearly 4 decades very few studies on the water quality were conducted in the estuarine area, most of them carried out in the last four years as impacts reports, dissertations or thesis (see [8, 9]).

The purpose of this study was to assess the status of the Barra das Jangadas estuary through the structural and functional aspects of the plankton communities and their relationship with the organic enrichment and nutrient gradients.

2 Material and methods

2.1 Study area

The Barrra das Jangadas estuarine system is located in Northeastern Brazil in Pernambuco State (8°12'30"- 8°15'20"S and 34°55'00"- 34°57'30"W), and is formed by the Pirapama and Jaboatão rivers and their tributaries. It has a long "S" shape with 200-250m wide and 1 Km long [10]. These rivers drain together a 1,002.3 Km^2 area into the Atlantic Ocean, fig. 1. Tides at Barra das Jangadas are semidiurnal with a mean range of 1.3 m at neap tide and 2.2 m at spring tide.

The annual mean temperature is approximately 26$\pm$2.8°C. The regional year can be divided in two different periods: the rainy season (March to August) with frequent rain (>400 mm) and the summer dry season (September to February), with lower amounts of rain (<100 mm) [10].

The Jaboatão is a shallow (1-4 m deep), 75 Km long tropical river. Its tributaries drain a basin of 413 Km^2 including small areas covered by the original Atlantic forest. It receives a high load of domestic and industrial wastes as well as a seasonal input of high levels of organic matter from the sugar-cane industries in its middle course; its lower course is bordered by relatively well preserved mangrove swamps [10].

The Pirapama River is located in the southern part of the Atlantic forest. Its springs and tributaries are used as water supplies. There is an industrial zone on its banks comprising mostly rum distilleries and sugar factories [10].

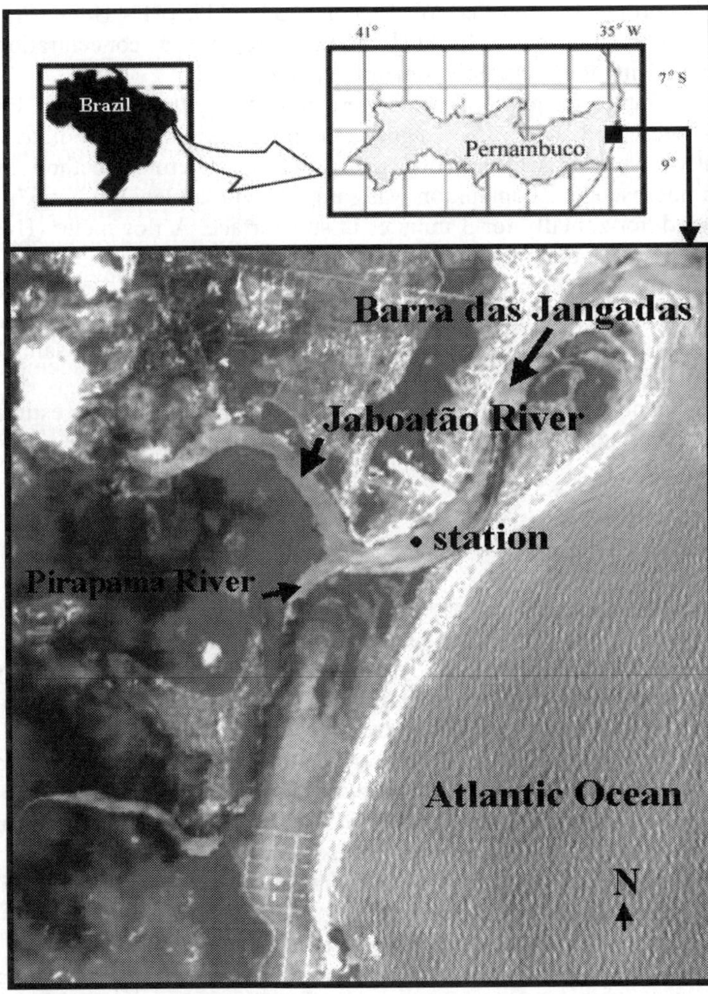

Figure 1: Barra das Jangadas area and sampling station, Pernambuco, Brazil.

2.2 Sampling and sample processing

Intensive seven days sampling was conducted at one fixed station located at the Barra das Jangadas estuary, fig. 1, from a spring to a neap tide, in different tide levels (high, low, ebb, flood) nearly 3 hours intervals, during the dry (January/2001) and the rainy (July/2001) seasons, totaling 168 hours sampling program in each season. Since the aim of this study was directed towards impacts of the Barra das Jangadas loading on plankton abundances, sampling was restricted to the surface layer. Water for abiotic factors data were collected at surface with a Nansen bottle. The following variables were measured: temperature – digital thermometer; salinity (Mohr-Knudsen method); dissolved oxygen according to modified Winkler method [11]; pH - Hanna Instrument 8417 pHmeter; nutrients [12, 13], and chlorophyll **a** concentrations were determined using the spectrophotometric technique [14].

Water samples for phytoplankton were collected with a Van Dorn bottle and samples preserved with 1% Lugol's iodine solution. In laboratory quali-quantitative analysis were carried out using the Ütermol method under an inverted microscope. Zooplankton was sampled with a plankton net 65µm mesh size, hauled horizontally for 3 minutes at sub-surface. A flowmeter (Hydrobios, Kiel) was fitted on the opening of the net used. Samples were preserved in a 4% buffered formaldehyde/seawater solution. Zooplankton species were identified until the lowest taxonomic unit possible and taxon abundance (per cubic meter) counted under a compound microscope (1ml subsample). These samples were taken with a Stempel-pipette of each the entire sample (250 ml).

The Shannon diversity index (H') [15] was applied for the estimation of plankton community diversity based on $\log_2$, and the evenness according to Pielou [16].

3 Results

3.1 Abiotic parameters

The most characteristic physical feature of Barra das Jangadas estuary is the shallow water column, often well mixed. The circulation pattern is mainly dominated by tidal currents. The current velocity varied from 0 to 1.10 m.s-1. Water transparence, varied from 0.4 m (rainy season) to 1.41 m (dry season), and higher values were registered during the dry season spring high tide. The studied estuary presents a warm temperature with slight daily variation with a minimum of 25.2°C in the rainy season and a maximum of 29.7°C in the dry season. Average temperature was 26.61$\pm$0.75°C (rainy season) and 28.11$\pm$0.77°C (dry season). The minimum (6.12) and maximum (8.76) pH values were registered in the rainy season. General average for both seasons was 7.47+0.61.

Salinity varied largely between tides and with season, fig. 2. The smallest salinity values (PSU) were 0.27 (rainy season, flood, neap tide) and the highest was 34.76 (dry season, high tide, spring tide) with an average value of 9.43$\pm$11.61 (rainy season) and 19.16$\pm$11.91 (dry season), table 1. These results show that the salinity regime in the area varies from oligohaline to euhaline in the dry summer season, and from limnetic to euhaline during the rainy season.

Dissolved oxygen also varied significantly ($p<0.05$) from 0.13 $ml.L^{-1}$ (2.34% saturation) in the rainy season to 7.96 $ml.L^{-1}$ (160.37% saturation), fig. 2, with averages values of 2.66±1.61 $ml.L^{-1}$ (51.92±34.73%) in the rainy season and 4.02±1.08 $ml.L^{-1}$ (82.81±24.88%) in the dry season, table 1. The occurrence of very low dissolved oxygen, even with anoxic periods is explained by the increased production of organic matter within the ecosystem.

Nutrients (ammonium, nitrite, nitrate, phosphate and silicate) data can be seen in table 1. They were variable, but in general were higher in the rainy season and low tides. Nutrients levels generally were indicative of eutrophication. Nitrate the most variable can be seen in figure 2. It was also observed a trend to increase from spring to neap tide, due higher residence time of the organic pollution.

Table 1: Abiotic parameters at Barra das Jangadas estuary.

ENVIRONMENTAL PARAMETERS	DRY SEASON				RAINY SEASON			
	MINI-MUM	MAXI-MUM	MEAN	SD*	MINI-MUM	MAXI-MUM	MEAN	SD
Temperature (°C)	26.40	29.70	28.11	0.77	25.20	28.00	26.61	0.75
Salinity (PSU)	1.72	34.76	19.16	11.91	0.27	33.73	9.43	11.61
Dissolved Oxygen ($ml.L^{-1}$)	1.81	7.96	4.02	1.08	0.13	6.79	2.66	1.61
DO%	40.04	160.37	82.81	24.88	2.34	144.49	51.92	34.73
pH	6.75	8.30	7.61	0.57	6.12	8.76	7.32	0.66
Amonium-N ($\mu mol.L^{-1}$)	<0.02	3.02	0.68	0.96	0.30	8.75	3.60	2.96
Nitrite-N ($\mu mol.L^{-1}$)	0.05	0.99	0.40	0.27	0.13	1.41	0.75	0.36
Nitrate-N ($\mu mol.L^{-1}$)	0.76	9.10	3.63	2.69	0.33	12.55	5.07	3.05
Phosphate-P ($mmol.L^{-1}$)	<0.02	0.69	0.25	0.15	0.35	2.94	1.38	0.86
Silicate-Si ($\mu mol.L^{-1}$)	12.15	245.24	75.63	65.87	20.78	476.04	155.88	148.30

*SD= Standard Deviation

3.2 Chlorophyll-a

During this study, chlorophyll-a concentrations ranged from 5.91 $mg.m^{-3}$ (rainy season) to 158.60 $mg.m^{-3}$ (dry season), averaging 33.07+32.53 $mg.m^{-3}$ (dry season) and 20.32+13.2 $mg.m^{-3}$ (rainy season), fig. 3. Peak concentrations occurred during the dry season, mainly at spring tide.

3.3 Phytoplankton

A total of 125 phytoplankton infrageneric taxa were identified to the Barra das Jangadas estuary. Bacillariophyta was the most abundant taxa (44.0%) followed by Chlorophyta (33.6%), Cyanophyta (13.6%), Euglenophyta (4.8%), Dinophyta (3.2%) and Chromophyta (0.8%).

Few species dominated in the estuary outranking *Cyclotella meneghiniana*, *Microcystis flos-aquae, Oscillatoria* sp. and Sphaerocystis sp. The blue-green *Microcystis flos-aquae* is potentially toxic and decreases the water quality when occurring in dense blooms as it was observed in the present study.

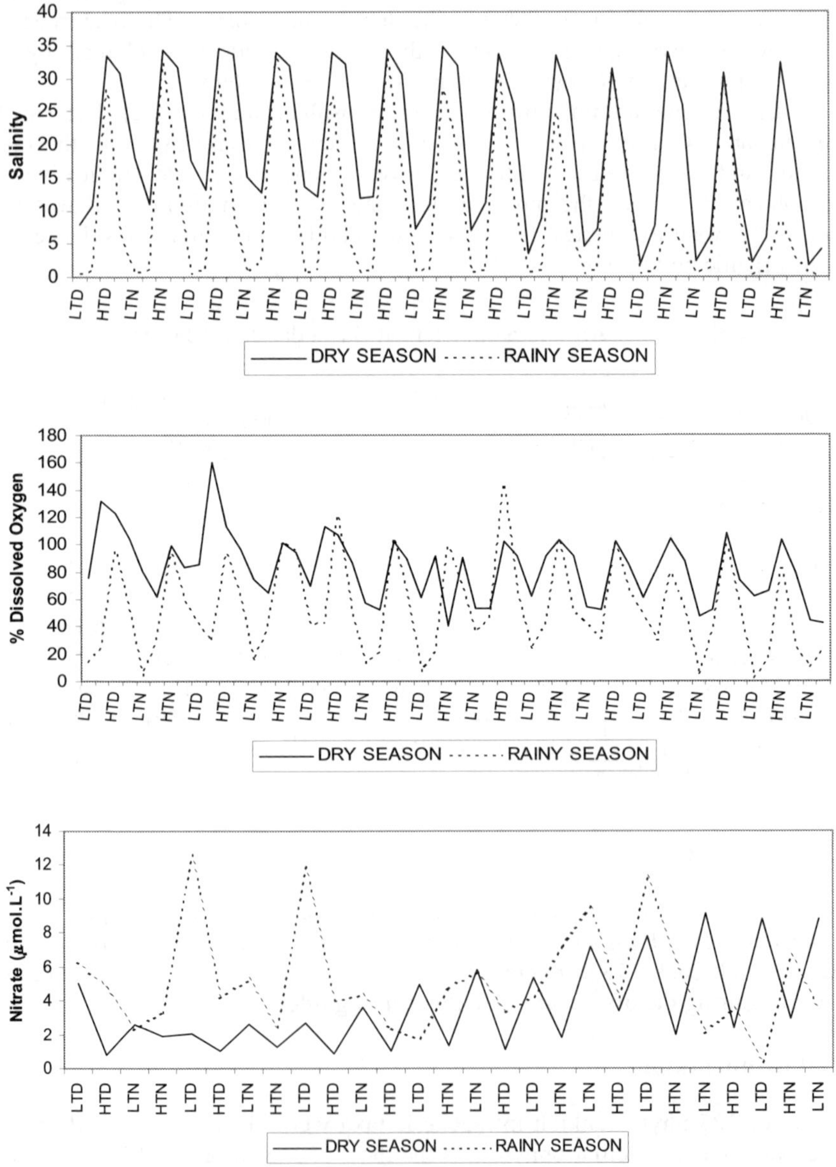

Figure 2: Main abiotic parameters in the Barra das Jangadas estuary. LT=low tide, HT=high tide, D=day, N=night.

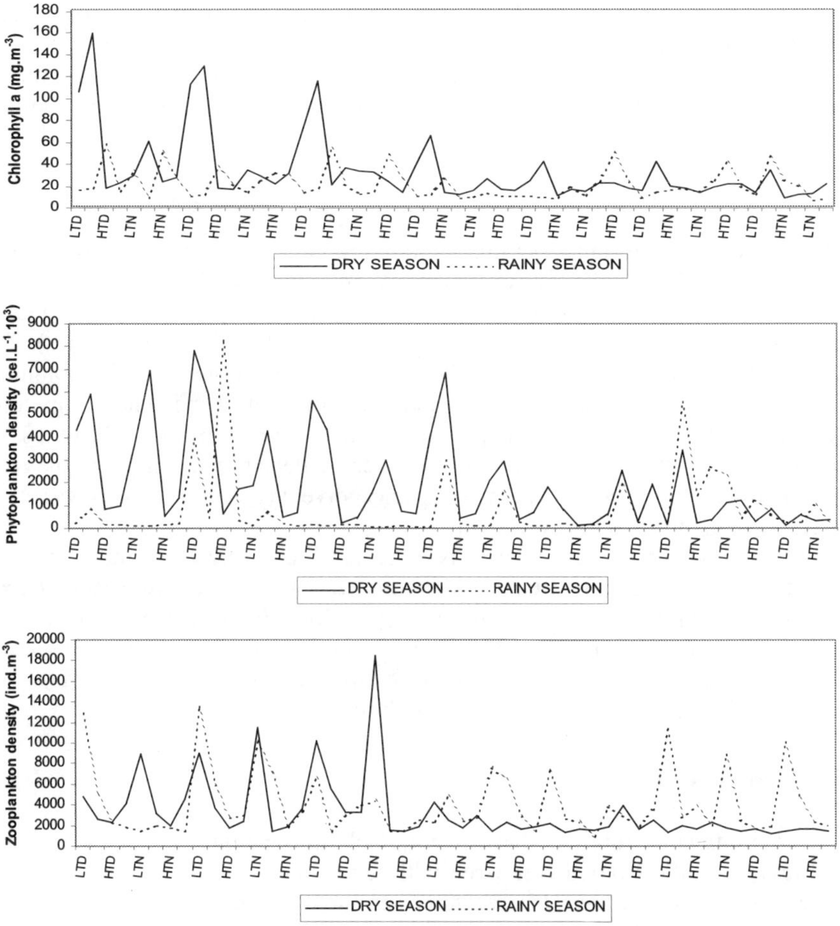

Figure 3: Chlorophyll-a, phytoplankton and zooplankton from the Barra das Jangadas estuary. LT=low tide, HT=high tide, D=day, N=night.

Species diversity index were under 2 bits.ind^{-1} and the evenness under 0.5 indicating an unbalanced system. This very low index is due the dominance of Cyclotella *meneghiniana* in the dry season and *Cyclotella meneghiniana, Microcystis flos-aquae,* and *Oscillatoria* in the rainy season.

During the dry season, the total abundance varied from 95.10^3 Cel.L^{-1} (high tide) to 7,830.10^3 Cel.L^{-1} (low tide), fig. 3, and this high density was due a bloom of *Cyclotellla maneghiniana*. Higher abundances occurred during flood and low tide. No pattern was observed in the temporal series, with irregular blooms of diatoms and phytoflagellates. During the rainy season, the abundance varied from 35.10^3 Cel.L^{-1} (low-tide) to 8,200.10^3 Cel.L^{-1} (high tide), fig. 3. During this season a pattern was observed with blooms of the diatom *Cyclotellla maneghiniana* from the first to the third day, followed by a *Sphaerocystis* sp.

(Chlorophycea) bloom (third to fifth day) and *Microcystis flos-aque* and *Oscillatoria* sp. (blue-greens) blooms from the fourth to the seventh day.

In general phytoplankton followed a pattern of decreases in biomass coupled with increases in diversity from low salinity waters (low tide) to high salinity (high tide).

3.4 Zooplankton

The zooplankton presented 87 taxa outranking Copepoda during the dry season and Rotifera during the rainy season. A common trend was the Copepoda dominance during high tide and rotifers at low tide. Copepoda outranked with 21 species, followed by Rotatoria (18 species) and Protozoa (10 species). The meroplankton was represented by Polychaeta larvae (dominated by spionids), Gastropoda and Bivalvia larvae and nauplius of Cirripedia, sometimes dominating the community. Zooplankton density varied from 1,300 to 18,500 ind.m^{-3}, both in the dry season, however average density was higher in the rainy season (4014.15$\pm$3104.74 ind.m^{-3}). Species diversity and evenness were low (<2.3 bits.ind^{-1}and < 0.5, respectively).

The zooplankton was essentially composed of typical marine euryhaline species. The most common Copepoda were *Parvocalanus crassirostris, Acartia lilljeborgi, Oithona hebes* and *Euterpina acutifrons*, in all life cycle stages. The rotifers were mainly represented by *Brachionus plicatilis, Brachionus angularis, Rotaria* spp., *Filinia longiseta, Lecane bulla*, among others. Many taxa were marine and occurred only once during high tide.

4 Discussion

The environmental forcings that control plankton dynamics in tropical estuaries in Brazil are little studied compared with temperate Atlantic estuaries. Tropical waters have a warmer temperature regime, including periods of warm temperature (>28°C), and are more frequently impacted by large rainfall events.

Besides the rain, the open marine area imposes large physical and chemical forcing on the estuarine ecosystem, due to tide and wind generated water exchange. This pulse created by the boundary also insures a large transport of organic material and nutrients subsidizing primary and secondary production in the estuarine area.

In the last decades, many coastal areas in Brazil have undergone increased eutrophication, mainly due to nitrate runoff from agriculture and sewage. The insidious nature of the eutrophication process means that in its early stages, the ecological effects are often difficult to distinguish against the normally high variation and dynamic nature of most estuaries. As a consequence, eutrophication is usually clearly recognized only towards the end-point of the process when ecological effects become obvious and dramatic.

The high amount of nutrients, mainly nitrate in the Barra das Jangadas estuary has stimulated phytoplankton growth and increased light attenuation. This eventually result in a decrease in oxygen concentration, and has a trend of anoxic system collapse, with the development of hydrogen-sulphide conditions, lethal to the benthic community. The Barra das Jangadas ecosystem showed low oxygen concentrations being the area classified as semi-polluted to polluted zone according to the classification of Macedo and Costa [17], only during high tide is the oxygen supersaturated.

Studies carried out by Souza and Tundisi [18] along the Jaboatão watershed showed a condition of environmental degradation, and in the urbanized areas worst water quality conditions were found, especially in the summer period, resulting from industrial and domestic effluents. The critical variables in their study were dissolved oxygen, fecal coliformes, and total phosphorus.

The changes in nutrients and dissolved oxygen concentrations caused an increase in numerical abundance of some phytoplankton species altering the ecosystem structure contributing to a decrease in the biodiversity of the area. The low estuarine diversity of phytoplankton, compared with that of coastal marine or oceanic waters, has been attributed to extreme dominance by a few forms able to prosper in an osmotically adverse environment with otherwise favorable growth conditions [20]. However, the frequent phytoplankton blooms and concomitant decrease in oxygen indicate that the Barra das Jangadas brackish water system has been considerably eutrophicated. Like phytoplankton, estuarine zooplankton communities have long been described as very abundant, but composed of few species [1, 20]. The large salinity variations within the estuary imply that most of the species occurring should be euryhaline. These species may be endemic to the estuary or may be carried out from the outside by tides, thus occurring only temporarily [21]. Copepod assemblages then typically decrease in biomass and increase in diversity with salinity [22]. When the salinity decreases Rotifera dominate the zooplankton community, many of which are organic pollution indicators. In general, zooplankton was dominated by Copepoda, which made up nearly 30% of the total number of taxa registered and 62% of total abundance. The dominance of Copepoda in Brazilian tropical estuaries has already been described by Tundisi [23]. The most abundant species found in the present research are typical of estuarine waters [24]. It must be observed in the Barra das Jangadas estuary that the enhanced productivity caused by wastewater input is not passed on to higher trophic levels as was demonstrated by Schwamborn et al. [25] to Guanabara Bay, where extreme eutrophication reduced the zooplankton productivity by causing recurring breakdowns of phyto- and zooplankton communities, probably related to occasional anoxia and peak ammonium concentrations.

References

[1] Day Jr, J. W., Hall, C. A. J., Kemp, W. M. & Yánñez-Arancibia, A. Zooplankton, the Drifting Consumers (Chapter 8). Estuarine Ecology. Willey-Interscience Publication: New York, pp.311-337, 1989.

[2] Flindt, M. R., Pardal, M. A., Lillebo, A. I., Martins, I., & Marques, J. C. Nutrient cycling and plant dynamics in estuaries: A brief review. Acta Oecologica, 20, pp. 237-248, 1999.

[3] Nixon, S. W. Coastal marine eutrophication: a definition, social causes, and future concerns. Ophelia, 41, pp. 199-219, 1995.

[4] Smith, V. H., Tilman, G. D. & Nekola, J. C. Eutrophication: impacts of excess nutrient inputs on freshwater, marine, and terrestrial ecosystems. Environmental Pollution, 100, pp. 179-196, 1999.

[5] Stolte, W., McCollin, T., Noordeloos, A. A. M. & Riegman, R. Effect of nitrogen source on the size distribution within marine phytoplankton populations. Journal of Experimental Marine Biology and Ecology, 184, pp. 83-97, 1994.

[6] Ottmann, F., Okuda, T., Silva, O. C., Araújo, J. V. A., Coelho, P. A., Paranaguá, M. N. & Eskinazi, E. Estudo da Barra das Jangadas – Parte V – Efeito da poluição sobre a ecologia do estuário. Trabalhos do Instituto Oceanográfico da UFPE, 7/8, pp. 7-16, 1966.

[7] Eskinazi, E. Estudo da Barra das Jangadas – Parte VI – Distribuição das diatomáceas. Trabalhos do Instituto Oceanográfico da UFPE, 7/8, pp. 17-32, 1966.

[8] Branco, E. S. Aspectos Ecológicos da Comunidade Fitoplanctônica no Sistema Estuarino de Barra das Jangadas. Dissertation (Master in Oceanography), Universidade Federal de Pernambuco, Recife, 2001.

[9] Lacerda, S. R. Série temporal do fitoplâncton no estuário de Barra das Jangadas (Jaboatão dos Guararapes – Pernambuco – Brasil). Thesis (PhD in Oceanography), Universidade Federal de Pernambuco, Recife. 2004.

[10] CPRH, Companhia Pernambucana de Controle da Poluição e Recursos Hídricos. Relatório Anual de Atividades. Recife, CPRH. 1995.

[11] Strickland, J. D. H. & Parsons, T. R. A manual of seawater analysis. Bulletin Fisheries Research Board of Canada, 125, pp.1-205, 1965.

[12] Strickland, J. D. H. & Parsons, T.R. A practical handbook of seawater analysis. Bulletin Fisheries Research Board of Canada, 167, pp. 207-211, 1972.

[13] Grasshoff, K., Ehrhardt, M. & Kremling, K. Methods of seawater analysis. Verlag Chemie, New York, 1983. 419p.

[14] Strickland, J. D. H. & Parsons, T. R. A. Production of organic matter in the primary stages of marine food chain. Chemical oceanography. ed. J. P. Riley & B. Kirrow, Academic Press: London, pp. 477-610, 1963.

[15] Shannon, C. E. A mathematical theory of communication. Bolletin Systematic Technology Journal., 27, pp. 379-423, 1948.

[16] Pielou, E. C. An introduction to Mathematical Ecology. Wiley-Intercience: New York, 1969. 286p.

[17] Macêdo, S. J. & Costa, K. M. P. Estudo ecológico da região de Itamaracá - Pernambuco - Brasil. Condições hidrológicas do estuário do Rio Botafogo. Ciêcia e. Cultura, 30 (7), pp. 346-368. 1978.

[18] Souza, A. D. G & Tundisi, J. G. Water quality in watershed of the Jaboatão river (Pernambuco, Brazil): a case study. Brazilian Archives of Biology and Technology, 46(4), pp. 711-721, 2003.

[19] Dolan, J. R. & Gallegos, C. L. Estuarine diversity of Tintinnids (planktonic ciliates). Journal of Plankton Research, 23 (9), p. 1009-1021, 2001.

[20] Riley, G. A. The plankton of estuaries. Estuaries. G. H. Lauff, American Association for the Advancement of Science: Washington, DC, pp. 316-326, 1967.

[21] Tundisi, T. M. Aspectos ecológicos do zooplâncton da região lagunar de Cananéia com especial referência aos copepodas (Crustácea). Tese de Doutorado, Departamento de Zoologia, Instituto de Biociências, Universidade de São Paulo, 1972. 191p.

[22] Mouny, P., Dauvin, J. C., Bessineton, C. & Elkaim, B. Biological components from the Seine estuary: first results. Hydrobiologia, 373/374, pp. 333-347, 1998.

[23] Tundisi, J. G. O plâncton estuarino. Contribuições avulsasdo Instituto. Oceanogáfico da Universidade de. São Paulo, série Oceanografia Biológica., 19, pp. 1-22. 1970.

[24] Björnberg, T. S. Copepoda. Atlas del zooplancton del Atlántico sudoccidental y métodos de trabajo con el zooplancton marino. D. Boltovskoy , INIDEP: Mar del Plata, pp.587-679, 1981.

[25] Schwamborn, R., Bonecker, S. L. C., Galvão, I. B., Silva, T. A. & Neumann-Leitão, S. Mesozooplankton grazing under conditions of extreme eutrophication in Guanabara Bay, brazil. Journal of Plankton Research, 26(9), pp. 983-992, 2004.

Section 19
Sustainable waste management

Use of material flow analysis for assessing solid waste management in Germany regarding sustainable solutions

N. Hartlieb, K.-R. Bräutigam, M. Achternbosch, C. Kupsch & G. Sardemann
Institute for Technology Assessment and Systems Analysis, Research Centre Karlsruhe, Germany

Abstract

Production and consumption activities lead to the depletion of limited resources and to the pressure on environmental sinks. Despite their adverse effects on the environment heavy metals like cadmium are still used in industry and consumer products. As a consequence a special treatment of the resulting wastes is necessary in many cases. Material flow analysis was used to assess waste management practices in Germany regarding sustainability with a focus on ecological aspects. As an example cadmium was traced from its production, through its various applications to the recycling and disposal of the used products. Balances were performed for the years 1995 until 2000. Cadmium is generated as a by-product of zinc production. In the observed timeframe zinc production in Germany did not change significantly leading to constant cadmium amounts. However, due to recent regulations and voluntary agreements of the industry cadmium containing products like pigments and stabilisers have been banned increasingly from the German market. The consumption of Ni/Cd cells has stayed constant. To reduce the environmental releases of cadmium different measures have been taken: Maximising zinc recycling and cutting back on the use of primary zinc; Substitution of cadmium in products where it is possible e.g. in pigments and stabilisers and by replacing Ni/Cd cells by lithium- or NiMH-batteries; Collection and recycling of products in order to reduce the amount of cadmium in domestic wastes. Emissions of cadmium into air and water bodies are declining. However, concentrations in soils and sediments show no reduction. Input of cadmium in agricultural soils occurs mainly via two pathways: atmospheric deposition and application of mineral fertilizers. According to various sources in the literature, both input pathways lie in the same order of magnitude.
Keywords: material flow analysis, cadmium, sustainable waste management.

1 Background

Production and consumption activities for the supply of presently about 6 billion people lead to the consumption of limited resources, the generation of material flows and to the pressure on environmental sinks. According to the recent knowledge the presently performed way of keeping house and way of living is not sustainable regarding ecological carrying capacities or resources inventories.

Despite their adverse effects on the environment heavy metals like cadmium, mercury and lead are still used in industry and consumer products. As a consequence a special treatment of the resulting wastes is necessary in many cases. Up to now the knowledge about the material household and the material flows of mercury, lead and cadmium associated with waste management measures is neither sufficient to assess the waste industry with respect to sustainability nor to work out recommendations for a material flow oriented waste management.

Material flow analysis (MFA) is an instrument capable of contributing to a sustainable waste management by delivering the required information.

2 Aim of project and approach

The project aims to assess waste management practices regarding ecological criteria for a sustainable development in Germany. This was done by identifying the main applications and related material flows of one indicator-substance (cadmium) starting from extraction and production and culminating in waste recovery or disposal. Cadmium balances were performed for the years 1995 until 2000.

The focus was set on input-pathways of cadmium in the environment by various applications and their most important waste flows. Regarding sustainable development, limitations of sources and sinks and their sustainable use are important indicators.

For compiling data, apart from an internet search, numerous technical journals and statistics were evaluated. In addition, data was collected by questionnaires sent to representatives from the industry and personal contacts to the industry.

3 Results

A summary of the results regarding cadmium balances for consumption, import and export in the years 1995 until 2000 are given in tables 1, 2 and 3.

3.1 Extraction of cadmium

Before using cadmium in various products, it has to be extracted and produced. Primary cadmium is mainly generated as by-product of the primary zinc production. Zinc concentrates/ores are mainly imported and contain on the average 0.2 % cadmium. In each of the years from 1995 to 2000 zinc ores and concentrates containing about 1100 to 1300 t of cadmium were imported. In addition a small share of cadmium was brought in via secondary materials like EAF-dust of the steel industry.

Since cadmium is toxic, recent regulations in the EU aspire to reduce or restrict the cadmium input in many applications. Therefore, with the exception of Ni/Cd batteries as an application, cadmium containing products are banned more and more from the German market due to recent legal regulations and voluntary agreements of the involved industry. Still, more than 1000 t of cadmium were annually separated and transformed to cadmium metal and alloys. The produced cadmium metal and alloys were kept in stock, exported, or brought to the domestic market.

3.2 Main applications of cadmium

3.2.1 Ni/Cd batteries

On a quantitative basis the most important flow of cadmium results from the use of cadmium for Ni/Cd batteries (NiCads). NiCads can be roughly divided in two categories portable, sealed cells and open, vented cells for industrial use.

More than 90 % of portable cells come on the market incorporated in electrical or electronic equipment (EEEq). The main applications by battery weight are cordless power tools and emergency lighting, but also cordless phones, remote control toys, and household appliances as dustbusters, shavers or tooth brushes. While there seems to be no real alternative for the use of Ni/Cd battery systems in power tools today, the share of NiCads used in other applications is ceasing. But even though the share of battery systems as NiMH and lithium is growing fast, the number of Ni/Cd cells sold in Germany remained approximately constant over the last 10 years because of the rapidly growing market of battery powered appliances.

Table 1: Cadmium consumption in Germany between 1995 and 2000. Range of share of cadmium in various applications and cadmium deposit in the total consumption of cadmium.

	Range in %
Ni/Cd batteries	**60-80**
Pigments	**4-15**
Stabilisers in PVC window profiles	**1-5**
Mineral fertilizers	**2-4**
Cadmium deposit	**15-20**

NiCads have the highest share in cadmium consumption (table 1), and regarding import and export (table 2 and 3). Since the production of portable Ni/Cd cells in Germany has stopped in 1999, increasing amounts have to be imported.

The European Union is discussing regulations, which will permit the use of cadmium in batteries in special applications only. However, even if batteries containing cadmium are no longer produced, the occurrence of cadmium in domestic wastes will continue for a long time due to the large stock of batteries which is still increasing.

Table 2: Cadmium import into Germany between 1995 and 2000. Range of share of cadmium extraction/production and cadmium in various applications in the total import of cadmium.

	Range in %
Cadmium contained in zinc ore and concentrates	**45-55**
Cadmium metal, raw cadmium and powder	**<1-10**
Cadmium oxide	**2-6**
Ni/Cd batteries	**32-42**
Pigments	**<1-2**
Stabilisers	**4-6**
PVC window profiles	**<1-2**
Mineral fertilizers	**<1-2**

3.2.2 Pigments, stabilisers and PVC window profiles

Until the year 2001, PVC stabiliser systems containing cadmium were used for the fabrication of window profiles. In 1980, the amount used for the production of these stabilisers was about 500 t, in 1995 less than 50 t and in 2000 less than 20 t. Import and export of stabilisers declined as well, having a small share concerning the total import and export (table 2 and 3). Meanwhile, due to voluntary agreements of the involved industry, stabilisers containing cadmium are no longer used in the European Union. However, the recycling of old windows leads to PVC-pellets, which still contain cadmium. These pellets have to be used for the production of new window profiles. The windows, which are not recycled, are exported, used as old windows in different application fields, disposed of or incinerated.

At the same time the production and consumption of pigments containing cadmium, their import and export has declined as well. Until 1980 the pigment production was one of the main applications fields for cadmium. While 1985 about 280 t of cadmium were used for pigment production, this value declined to 100 t in 1994 and further to 50 t in 2001.

3.2.3 Mineral fertilizers used in agriculture

Cadmium flows by mineral fertilizers regarding production, consumption, import and export have stayed constant from 1995 until 2000. The share of mineral fertilizers in cadmium import and export is negligible; nevertheless the share of fertilizer in cadmium consumption amounts to 2-4 % and exceeds the share of stabilisers in PVC window profiles (table 1, 2 and 3). This is due to the fact that the use of stabilisers has been cut down, while mineral fertilizer application needed to be retained constant.

Table 3: Cadmium export out of Germany between 1995 and 2000. Range of share of cadmium extraction/production and cadmium in various applications in the total export of cadmium.

	Range in %
Cadmium contained in zinc ore and concentrates	**5-15**
Cadmium metal, raw cadmium and powder	**25-50**
Ni/Cd batteries	**30-45**
Ni/Cd battery waste	**5-15**
Pigments	**<1-5**
Stabilisers	**2-8**
PVC window profiles	**<1-2**
Mineral fertilizers	**<1**

4 Discussion

4.1 Cadmium: steps on its way from the cradle to the grave

Cadmium can reach the environment through various phases of production, processing, usage and disposal processes. Possible sources for an environmental input are:

4.1.1 Production of zinc

The production of zinc is connected with emissions into air and water. A decrease of zinc consumption cannot be anticipated. In order to lower the cadmium emissions connected with zinc production, it should be aimed to maximize the share of secondary zinc related to the total production. However, according to information of the "WV-Metalle" [1] already today about 80 – 90 % of the zinc products are recycled at their end of life in Germany. Cadmium is a by-product resulting from the zinc production from ore. Since the demand for cadmium decreased clearly towards the end of the investigated period, a part of the cadmium has to be deposited. While from 1995 to 2000 about 15-20 % of the cadmium amount consumed in Germany was deposed (table 1), in the year 2001 this amount increased to about 50 %.

4.1.2 Production of products containing cadmium

With the use of cadmium for the fabrication of certain products cadmium emissions are connected, however, they are small compared to those of other cadmium emitters. Thus, within the European Union the emissions connected with the production of cadmium-containing products contribute with scarcely 4 % to the total cadmium emissions. Therefore, further restrictions of the production of cadmium-containing products will lead only to a small reduction of the emissions into the air. On the other hand a larger amount of cadmium would have to be deposited because of its reduced demand.

4.1.3 Recycling and disposal of products

In order to reduce the amount of NiCads found in domestic wastes an obligation to take back, recycle or properly dispose these batteries after use was set into force. Almost 90 % of the industrial Ni/Cd batteries put in circulation are collected, the cadmium is recovered domestically and used again for the production of new industrial batteries. Portable Ni/Cd cells which are seized over collecting systems like the German "GRS Batterien" are also recycled, however abroad. The export of NiCad waste to France for recycling lies steady within a range of 5-15 % of the total cadmium exported (table 3). Of this cadmium the largest share is recovered. This reduces the quantity of primary cadmium needed for production.

Nevertheless, despite considerable logistic efforts it is impossible to prevent the occurrence of NiCads in domestic wastes. According to a rough estimation the publicly collected household wastes and household type industrial wastes in Germany contain 100-150 t cadmium in the year 2001. For additionally resulting quantities of waste types similar to domestic wastes, which are not publicly collected for disposal, no representative analyses concerning their cadmium content are available. On the assumption that the cadmium concentration in this fraction corresponds to that of the household waste or the household type industrial waste, the total amount of cadmium within the waste to be disposed of can be estimated with 150-230 t. After a rough estimation of Recharge [2] approx. 80 t of cadmium within this waste are due to not properly disposed NiCads. Of the 150-230 t cadmium a share of approx. 46 % reaches the municipal solid waste incinerators (MSWI), the other approx. 54 % are deposed directly. Of the fractions treated within the MSWI, approximately 25 % of cadmium is contained in slags, the other 75 % can be found in the ashes, which are deposed and/or stored for further use in salt deposits.

Depending on their quality, slags from MSWI are used for road construction or for base sealings of landfill sites. It has to be mentioned that this type of use is potentially associated with a wide distribution of heavy metals. Thus, due to the leaching of heavy metals an environmental hazard can not be excluded on a long-term time scale.

4.2 Cadmium input into the environment

In order to reduce cadmium emissions and therewith the cadmium input into the environment, various measures have been taken since the Council resolution in 1988 [3]. To which extent the cadmium exposition of humans has been reduced hereby is unclear.

Due to measures taken, emissions of cadmium into air and water bodies are declining and as a result reduced cadmium concentrations in air and precipitation arise. However, cadmium is a stable environmental contaminant; it tends to accumulate in the biosphere, being preferentially stored in soils and sediments [4]. It has to be assumed that due to atmospheric deposition and the use of fertilizers a constant increase of heavy metal concentrations in soils is occurring to a small extent [5]. Therefore, although emissions are declining, recent measurements of soils, river- and ocean-sediments show problematic cadmium levels.

The main uptake of cadmium by humans occurs by food. The provisional tolerable weekly intake (PTWI) of cadmium was set at 7 μg kg^{-1} of body weight [6]. Due to results of the Belgian study CADMIBEL [7] it is recently discussed that this value is too high and it is recommended to reduce the value by half, therefore to a value of 3.5 μg kg^{-1} body weight (PWTI). According to the Enquete-Kommission [8] the weekly cadmium intake of an average adult ranges between 1 and 4 μg kg^{-1} body weight already.

In order to prevent any further increase of cadmium in agricultural soils which are likely to increase the dietary intake of future generations, the WHO recommended that airborne levels of cadmium should be as low as possible and not exceed 5 ng m^{-3} in rural areas and 10 ng m^{-3} in urban or industrial areas [9]. Air measurements in Germany in the years 1995 until 2000 show a reduction from 1.7 to 0.9 ng m^{-3} in industrial locations and from 1.1 to 0.7 ng m^{-3} in urban and rural regions [10]. The values are well below the proposed limits.

However, although emissions and cadmium concentrations in air and precipitation are declining, cadmium concentrations in foodstuff still sometimes exceed guideline levels [11]. On the other hand, cadmium levels in molluscs fall well below guideline levels, but show no clear reduction from 1996 to 2001 [12]. However, consumers of oil seeds, kidneys, molluscs and chocolate are warned to achieve high cadmium intakes [11].

Table 4: Cadmium flows into agricultural soils by the two input pathways atmospheric deposition and mineral fertilizer application according to data cited in literature. Values given in g ha^{-1} a^{-1}.

Atmospheric deposition		Mineral fertilizer	
1.5	[13]	1.2	[18]
1.7 - 5	[14]	1.5	[19]
2.1	[15]	1.7	[13]
2.3	[5]	1.7	[20]
3.9	[16]	5.6 - 18.1	[21]
4	[17]		

There is no doubt that the accumulation of heavy metals in soils is caused by anthropogenic inputs [5]. Input of cadmium in agricultural soils occurs mainly by two pathways: atmospheric deposition and application of mineral fertilizers. According to various sources in the literature, both input pathways lie in the same order of magnitude (table 4) although airborne levels of cadmium have already been declining.

However, from a food chain perspective, perhaps most important inputs of cadmium in soil are those that occur as a result of fertilization with fertilizers, which contain cadmium as an impurity [22]. Under these circumstances the cadmium is located in the immediate rooting zone and is also incorporated with plant nutrients, which stimulate proliferation of plant roots, thus enhancing crop access to the cadmium input.

The mass balance of cadmium in many fertilized agricultural soils is positive i.e. more cadmium is added in fertilizer and other sources than leaves the soil in food products, percolating waters or as soil particles through erosion [22]. If we wish to achieve a zero net cadmium addition to soils, it is debatable whether leaching or plant uptake is an environmentally acceptable way to minimise soil cadmium accumulation. The long-term goal needs to be minimisation of cadmium inputs to soil.

For reducing the environmental releases of cadmium various strategies are being suggested [3, 23], some of them already being implemented:

- Cut back on producing and consuming zinc
- Limitation of the uses of cadmium in cases where suitable alternatives do not exist
- Collection and recycling of products containing cadmium
- Prevent the flow of cadmium in the environment by using cadmium in a safe way.

Regarding regulations concerning the industrial use of cadmium leading to emissions from point sources, many measures have been already taken as has been mentioned in section 4.1. However, the diffuse distribution of cadmium and emissions of cadmium as a minor constituent is gaining of importance. For fertilizer application the next step is made: a proposal on an EU wide regulation on cadmium in fertilizers, reducing maximum cadmium concentrations in mineral fertilizers in three stages.

Table 5: Fields of human activity, some typical wastes and important waste flows related to cadmium. Selected activity fields taken from [24].

Activity field		Typical wastes	Wastes related to cadmium
AF1:	**Mobility and transportation**	Scrapped cars, wastes from transportation techniques	Ni/Cd batteries
AF2:	**Housing and construction**	Construction waste	PVC (windows), stabilisers, pigments
AF3:	**Nutrition and agriculture**	Organic wastes from households and agriculture, fertilizer	Mineral and organic fertilizers
AF4:	**Information and communication**	Electronic scrap, batteries	Ni/Cd batteries, solar cells

5 Outlook

In the preceding sections it is pointed out which cadmium flows arise in Germany with a special focus on cadmium containing products. For sustainability reasons it is inevitable to reduce the use of cadmium or other heavy metals such as lead or mercury to a minimum. These heavy metals can appear as by-products with the production of goods or they can be added intentionally as components of certain goods (e.g. cadmium in NiCads). In either case they emerge to the waste stream after the use of these products.

In order to assign such risky material flows to certain human activities (consumption patterns) and to derive measures to reduce or avoid them, waste flows are to be allocated to different activity fields according to the integrative sustainability concept of the HGF (Hermann von Helmholtz Association of National Research Centers) [24]. These activity fields are e.g. mobility /transportation, housing/construction, nutrition/agriculture. Waste management itself is no activity field on its own, but can be classified as a cross-section activity. A first attempt to assign waste flows to activity fields is shown in table 5.

References

[1] Zink – metallisches Multitalent. Recycling. Wirtschaftsvereinigung Metalle. www.wvmetalle.de/welcome.asp?page_id=185&sessionid=

[2] RECHARGE, *The flow of rechargeable batteries in the economy. The case study of portable nickel-cadmium batteries in Germany*, Final Draft, Brussels, November, 2004.

[3] Council Resolution of 25 January 1988 on a Community action programme to combat environmental pollution by cadmium Official Journal C 030, 04/02/1988.

[4] Anon., Task Force on Heavy metals emissions. Economic commission for Europe, Prague 1994. Cited in *Trace elements – their distribution and effects in the environment* eds. Markert & Friese, Elsevier, pp. 87-108, 2000.

[5] FAL: Eidgenössische Forschungsanstalt für Agrarökologie und Landbau, Zürich (eds) *Risikoanalyse zur Abfalldüngerverwertung in der Landwirtschaft. Teil 1: Grobbeurteilung*, Bericht, Juli 2001 im Auftrag des Bundesamtes für Landwirtschaft.

[6] FAO/WHO Food and Agriculture Organization of the United Nations/ World Health Organisation Cadmium. Geneva: WHO, *Environ Health Criteria* 134, 1992.

[7] Lauwerys R, Amery A, Bernard A, Bruaux P, Buchet JE, Claeys F, Plaen P de, Ducoffre G, Fagard R, Lijnen P, Nick L, Roels H, Rondia D, Saint-Remy A, Sartor F, Staessen J, Thijs L, Does environmental exposure to cadmium represent a health risk? CADMIBEL study. *Acta Clin Belg*, **46**, pp. 219-225, 1991.

[8] Enquete-Kommission „Schutz des Menschen und der Umwelt“ des Deutschen Bundestages, *Verantwortung für die Zukunft : Wege zum nachhaltigen Umgang mit Stoff- und Materialströmen*, Band 5, Economica Verlag, Bonn, 1994

[9] WHO, *Updating and Revision of the air quality guidelines for Europe*, Report on the WHO working group on inorganic air pollutants, EUR/ICP/EHAZ 94 05/MT04, 24-27 October 1994, Düsseldorf – Germany.

[10] Jahresmittelwerte für Blei und Cadmium im Schwebstaub Landesumweltamt Nordrhein-Westfalen, LUA-NRW. www.lua.nrw.de /luft/immissionen/ber_trend/disko2000.pdf

[11] Lebensmittelmonitoringbericht 1995 – 2002 und 2002, Bundesamt für Verbraucherschutz und Lebensmittelsicherheit (BVL), www.bvl.bund.de

[12] Meere – Schadstoffkonzentrationen in Organismen, Umweltdaten Deutschland online (UBA), www.env-it.de/umweltdaten/jsp/index.jsp

[13] European Commission, Directorate General Industry, A Study to Establish a Programme of Detailed Procedures for the Assessment of Risks to Health and the Environment from Cadmium in Fertilisers (ETD/99/502247), 2000.

[14] UMK-AMK-LABO-AG, Umweltministerkonferenz-Agrarministerkonferenz-Länderarbeitsgemeinschaft Bodenschutz-Arbeitsgruppe, *Cadmiumanreicherung in Böden/Einheitliche Bewertung von Düngemitteln,* Berichtsentwurf (Stand März 2000) zur Vorlage für die 26. ACK der UMK am 11./12.10.2000, Hannover.

[15] Zethner, G.; Goodchild R., *A Risk Assessment for Cadmium in Austria based on the Recommendations of ERM.* Final Report. Umweltbundesamt Österreich, 2000.

[16] LABO, Bund -/Länderarbeitsgemeinschaft Bodenschutz, Arbeitsgruppe „Schwermetalltransfer Boden/Pflanze“, *Eckpunkte zur Gefahrenbeurteilung des Wirkungspfades Bodenverunreinigungen /Altlasten – Pflanze*, Düsseldorf, Berlin, LABO Bodenschutz, p. 67, 1997.

[17] Grenzüberschreitender Transport und Deposition von Luftschadstoffen, EMEP Report 2000, „Umweltdaten Deutschland online“ des Umweltbundesamtes, www.env-it.de/umweltdaten/jsp/index.

[18] IVA Position Paper of Industrieverband Agrar (IVA) on the Draft Proposal relating to cadmium in fertilizers o the European Parliament and Council of 1. August 2003.

[19] Wilcke, W.; Döhler, H., *Schwermetalle in der Landwirtschaft. Quellen, Flüsse, Verbleib.* KTBL-Arbeitspapier 217, 1995.

[20] Smolders, E.; Schoeters, I. Merckx, R., *Risk Assessment, Cadmium Oxide.* CAS No. 1306-19-0, EINECS No. 215-146-2. Laboratory of Soil Fertility and Soil Biology, K.U. Leuven, Belgium, 1999.

[21] BMVEL Schütze, G.; Becker, R.; Dämmgen, U.; Nagel, H-D.; Schlutow, A.; Weigel, H-J., Risikoabschätzung der Cadmium-Belastung für Mensch und Umwelt infolge der Anwendung von cadmiumhaltigen Düngemitteln. *Landbauforschung Völkenrode* 2/3 (53), 64-170, 2003.

[22] McLaughlin, M.; & Hamon, R., Perspectives on inputs of cadmium to the food chain. In: *Environmental cadmium in the food chain: sources, pathways, and risk* (SCOPE) 60-65, 2001.

[23] Fthenakis V. M., Life cycle impact analysis of cadmium in CdTe PV production. *Renewable and Sustainable Energy Reviews* **8**, pp.303–334, 2004.

[24] Kopfmüller, J.; Brandl, V.; Jörissen, J.; Paetau, M.; Banse, G.; Coenen, R.; Grunwald, A., *Nachhaltige Entwicklung integrativ betrachtet. Konstitutive Elemente, Regeln, Indikatoren*, Edition sigma: Berlin, 2001.

Cement based floors with rubber addition

N. Quaranta, M. Caligaris, H. López & M. Regondi
Universidad Tecnológica Nacional,
Facultad Regional San Nicolás, Argentina

Abstract

In the present work, the characteristics of different cement based floors with the addition of a great amount of granular rubber, 16% in volume approximately, are studied.

During the three years that the experience went on, the samples were subjected to temperatures conditions varying between 43 °C and -2°C, to several episodes of strong wind and intense rain and to continuous crossing.

The samples were characterized by optical microscopy, scanning electron microscopy (SEM), electron diffraction analysis X-ray (EDAX), porosity and Vickers microhardness measurements.

The obtained results set up this application as an important tool for using this waste material which is nowadays disposed in landfills in Argentina.
Keywords: cement floor, rubber, scrap tires.

1 Introduction

The objective of reusing the rubber from scrap tires is to avoid the serious problem that its accumulation produces. These wastes occupy much space in the landfill in which they are disposed.

The rubber dust is used in several applications such as sports field drainage, race courses, road pavement improvement, among others. There exists a great advance in using rubber for plastic material products such as shoe soles, coating plates, and accessories for the automobile industry, but it is usually needed a grinding process and the removal of components as cloth or metal that comes from tire talons, increasing the costs of final products.

Mixing rubber with bitumen and asphalt filling is other important application [1, 2]. In this way, it can be used as binding material or as sealer layer in which case it is called asphalt rubber, or simply as a filling material, without interacting with other mixture components in which case it is called concrete or cement containing rubber.

Rubber addition to high-strength concrete was studied by F. Hernández and Barluenga [3], in order to reduce the risk of explosive spalling at high temperatures. Their results show that the temperatures reached of fire-tested specimens were reduced as the percentage of rubber was increased.

Siddique and Naik [4] present an overview of some of the research published regarding the use of scrap-tires in portland cement concrete. Disposal of tires has become one of the serious environmental problems and in the last years land filling is becoming unacceptable because of the rapid depletion of available sites for waste disposal, and for other potential problems like toxic emissions in the case of fire hazards, and vermin, rats and mosquitoes presence that find in used tires their breeding grounds. As reported by the authors the promising options are: i) use of tire rubber in asphalt concrete mixtures, ii) incineration of tires for production of steam, iii) reuse of ground tire rubber in a number of plastic and rubber products, and iv) use tires as a fuel for cement kiln and as feedstock for making carbon black.

The objective of the present work is to study the characteristics of different cement based floors with the addition of a great amount of granular rubber, 16% in volume approximately. The behavior of these materials after three years subject to inclemency and regular use is analyzed.

2 Experimental

2.1 Samples preparation

The scrap tires were treated with a reduction process in order to obtain small size particles with adequate characteristics to be incorporated to cement based floors. The tires were cut into pieces of 6 by 10 cm, approximately, from the tread zone, discarding those parts corresponding to the steel belts. These pieces were put into a kiln at 280 °C during 2 hours, to weaken them for making easier their subsequent grinding. The powders obtained after grinding had particle sizes smaller than 0.85 mm. They are composed by granular rubber and textile fiber particles coming from the reinforcement, as can be seen in Figure 1.

Four different mixtures were prepared. From now onwards they are identified as: Ce2, Ce2Ru, Ce1, and Ce1Ru. All of them contain six parts of sand. The mixtures identified with Ce2 have two parts of cement, and those with Ce1 have one part of cement and one of lime. Ru in the names indicates one and a half part of rubber in the mixture. Samples without rubber were prepared using the powders with the addition of 20% H_2O and the ones containing rubber with the addition of 25% H_2O.

Probes to be used as a reference of these materials were prepared in molds of 15cm x 10cm x 4cm, keeping the denomination of the mixtures. In order to observe the resistance of the floor to regular use, that is continuous walker crossing, and real meteorological conditions, other probes were also made. With this aim sectors of 50cm x 50cm of the different mixtures were incorporated during the construction of the doorway of the San Nicolás Regional Faculty, which constitutes the way in of the students. These sectors remained in use during three years. Figure 2 shows the location of the mentioned sectors in a frontal view of the building, and pieces of them after their removal.

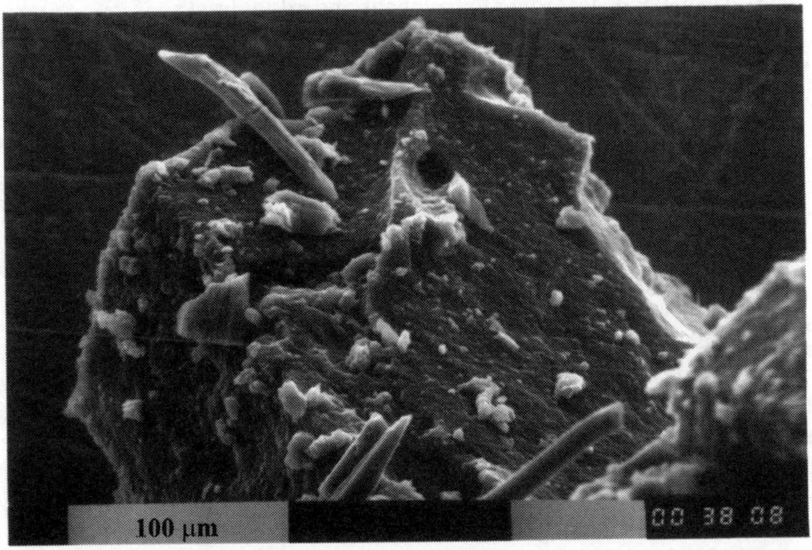

Figure 1: Rubber and textile fiber particles obtained after grinding.

Figure 2: (a) Frontal view of faculty building. (b) Pieces of removed sectors.

Once the floor probes were removed they were analyzed, together with reference samples without use, with traditional techniques. The used samples are identified as the corresponding mixture, with a preceding U.

2.2 Samples characterization

The samples were characterized by optical microscopy, scanning electron microscopy (SEM), electron diffraction analysis X-ray (EDAX), porosity, and Vickers microhardness measurements.

Porosity measurements: These determinations were carried out by Archimedes method, according to national standard for bricks.

Microhardness measurements: The hardness analyses were made with a Vickers indenter in an HMV-2000 Shimatzu equipment using loads of 300 g during 10 sec.

Microscopic analysis: The samples were observed by optical and scanning electron microscopies. The optical observations were made with a Metalloplan Leitz microscope. The SEM analysis was carried out through a Phillips 515 scanning electronic microscope with an X-ray detector.

3 Results and discussion

3.1 Surface characteristics

During the three years that the experience went on, the samples were subjected to temperatures conditions varying between 43°C and –2°C, to several episodes of strong wind and intense rain and to the continuous crossing, because during the analyzed period they were put in the only entrance for students. Surfaces without fissures or material shelling, with rubber particles still held in the structure were observed. Higher surface roughness in samples with rubber addition was determined. The rubber particles have a tendency to accumulate at the surface areas making the samples look dark.

Though structural differences characteristic of the different mixtures composition were found, similar behavior in materials with and without rubber were observed.

3.2 Workability and shrinkage

At mortar production moment the mixtures incorporating rubber particles achieved workabilities comparable to the others used as a comparative materials without rubber shreds. Some authors [5] mentioned that at rubber contents of 40% the concrete resulted not workable manually. This percentage is very high in relation to the used in this work, approximately 16%.

The observations of the reference samples suggest that the incorporation of rubber particles help in reducing shrinkage and the production of cracks. The probes without rubber, Ce2 and Ce1, presented volume shrinkages of about 6% and 5% respectively, while the specimens containing rubber particles, Ce2Ru and Ce1Ru, both showed volume shrinkages of about 3%.

The samples without rubber developed cracks having an average width of about 0.5 mm, while the rubber-probes have average crack widths of about 0.2-0.3 mm. In all cases the cracks density was smaller for rubbered samples.

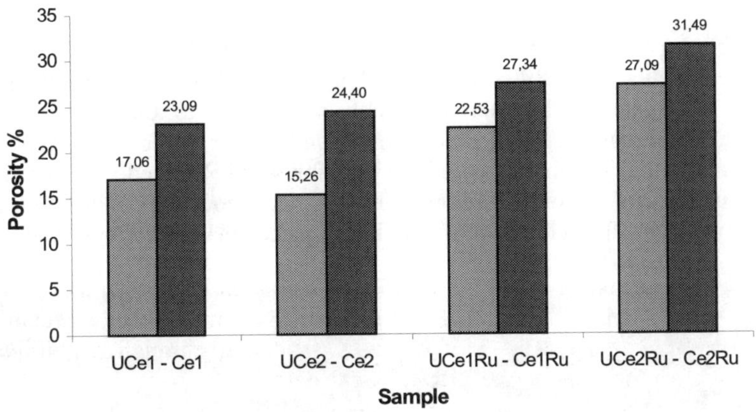

Figure 3: Samples porosity.

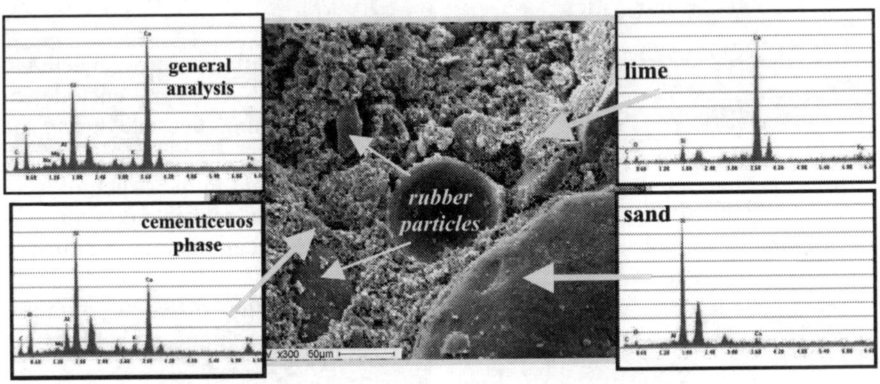

Figure 4: SEM and EDAX analysis of Ce1Ru sample.

3.3 Porosity

Figure 3 shows the results of the open porosity essays for samples with and without rubber addition, in reference and used samples.

As can be seen the open porosities of the reference samples result higher than the used ones in all cases. Taking into account the same samples with and without addition of rubber, it is possible to note that the presence of rubber particles conduces to more porous materials. Samples porosity increases about 4%-8% owing to the rubber incorporation. This may be due to the higher air content in the rubber-concrete mixtures. The non-polar nature of rubber particles and their tendency to entrap air in their surfaces, added to the fact that these particles repel water [5, 6], increase the air contents in rubber-concrete mixtures, producing materials with higher porosity.

3.4 Optical and scanning electron microscopies

The different phases present in the samples are clearly identified by SEM and EDAX techniques. Figure 4 shows a SEM photograph and the chemical analysis of each aggregate of the mixture which correspond to the more complex specimen which contain sand, lime, cement and rubber particles. Ca rich areas around sand grains in samples with lime addition were observed. It is possible to see the rubber shreds well incorporated into cementiceous matrix in all samples, the ones with lime as well as without, but with some areas containing pores.

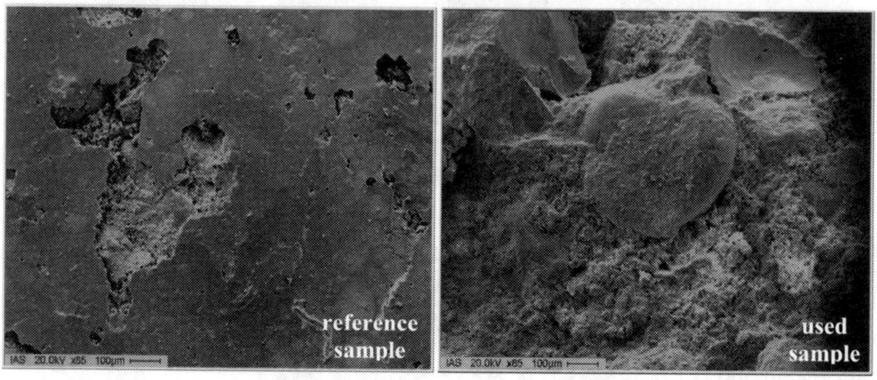

Figure 5: SEM photograph of Ce2 and UCe2 specimens.

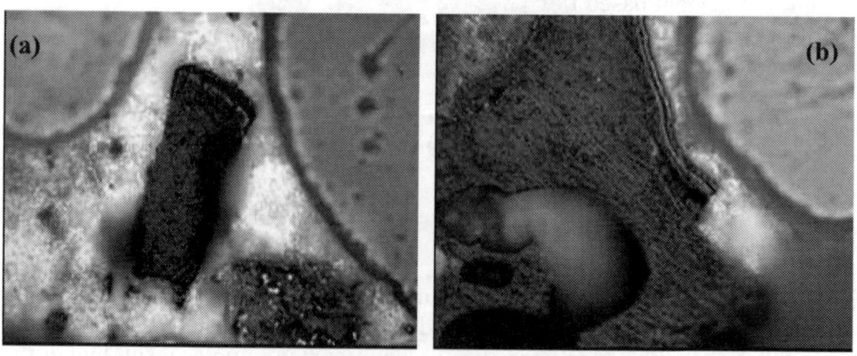

Figure 6: Optical microphotographs of rubbered samples.

At the superficial level of used samples some rubber particles loosening were observed, while the internal structure of the specimen keeps intact. The lime added samples showed higher wear levels after the three years of use. The general superficial aspect of the used samples is similar. Loss of part of the cement and/or lime phases what allows sand grains become the resistant area of the samples, was seen. This superficial change was noted in all samples. Figure 5 shows SEM analysis made on samples Ce2 and UCe2 where this fact can be clearly observed.

By optical microscopy technique it was seen the internal structure of the samples with more details due to the different colors of the present phases, which allows confirming the kind of contact existing between them. Furthermore, it is possible to observe the mentioned fact in relation to the higher porosities of the samples which contain rubber addition. Figure 6 (a) shows rubber particles separated from the cement matrix by pores, and in the case of the bigger added shreds (about 0.85 mm) it is possible to observe pores into them, Figure 6 (b).

3.5 Vickers microhardness

Materials microhardness was measured in different areas of the samples because these are specimens which have heterogeneous zones due to their composition.

The microhardness values obtained on the different homogeneous areas, for example sand grains, cement, lime, etc., are slightly lower than the corresponding ones to the pure phases. Values about 570 kg/mm^2 for sand were measured. In this case, no cracks formation around the indent was observed. In cement and cement-lime matrix the determined average values were 240 kg/mm^2 and 350 kg/mm^2 respectively. It can be observed the trend of these phases to form cracks around the indents, but this tendency diminishes toward the areas around rubber particles, suggesting the rubber presence gives more toughness to the specimens.

4 Conclusions

Samples of cement based floors with the addition of rubber from scrap tires were studied obtaining very good results in real meteorological conditions resistance just as continuous walker crossing resistance during three years.

It is possible to incorporate an important percentage of rubber wastes coming from used tires, in the production process of the construction industry. Into the structural material the rubber particles were distributed in a homogeneous way and immersed into the cementiceous matrix. Though the rubber addition increases the samples porosities, their behaviour during use was not altered.

Tire rubber could be used in applications that demand concrete properties which could reduce the disposal of used tires to a large extent.

The obtained results set up this application as an important tool for using this waste material which is nowadays disposed in landfills in Argentina.

Researches about process variables are required to optimize the characteristics of these rubbered materials, such as rubber particle size, percentage of rubber, type of cement, use of chemical and mineral additives, pretreatment of rubber shreds, etc.

Acknowledgements

The authors wish to thank the "Comisión de Investigaciones Científicas de la Provincia de Buenos Aires" for the financial support.

References

[1] R. Bortolotto Salini and A. F. Marcon, Utilizaçao de borracha reciclada de pneus em misturas asfálticas. *III Encontro Ibero-Americano de Unidades Ambientais do Setor Transportes*. Florianópolis, Brasil. 1998.

[2] S. Oda and J. Fernandes Junior, Evaluación de las Propiedades del Asfalto-Caucho para Utilización en Pavimentación Asfáltica. *Anales del IV Congreso de Ingeniería del Transporte. CIT 2000.* Eds. J. Colomer and A. García. Valencia. España. 2000.

[3] F. Hernández Olivares and G. Barluenga. Fire performance of recycled rubber-filled high-strength concrete. *Cement and Concrete Research* **34**, pp. 109-117, 2004.

[4] R. Siddique and T.R. Naik. Properties of concrete containing scrap-tire rubber – an overview. *Waste Management* **24(6),** pp. 563-569, 2004.

[5] Z. K. Khatib and F. M. Bayomy. Rubberized portland cement concrete. *ASCE Journal of Materials in Civil Engineering* **11(3)**, pp. 206-213, 1999. From reference [4].

[6] D. Fedroff, S. Ahmad and B. Z. Savas. Mechanical properties of concrete with ground waste tire rubber. *Transportation Research Board, Report No.1532*, Transportation Research Board, Washington DC, pp. 66-72, 1996. From reference [4].

Complex systems and slaughterhouse waste management

J.-H. Abraham
Universidad Popular Autonoma del Estado de Puebla, Mexico

Abstract

Environmental problems, such as pollution provoked by slaughterhouse wastes, can be examined with an integral, multidimensional and systemic approach. The objective was to design a strategy to use such wastes as organic fertilizers; this as a solution to the pollution and social problems they provoke. The methodology applied was the one proposed by García (1986, 1994) for the study of complex systems. The starting point was the conceptual shift of pollutant materials from "waste" to "byproducts". The research started with the construction of the system subject of study -the Slaughterhouse-Complex- considering certain key elements and the interactions between them; once the system was constructed, a diagnostic survey was conducted focusing on the identification of processes and mechanisms corresponding to the dynamics of the problem under study. Afterwards, an analysis of the dynamics of the system itself was performed, as well as of the changes that resulted from the processes of destructuration-restructuration arisen with the new stationary state reached by the system. Finally, it is suggested that with the proposed conceptual and structural changes, the new stationary state of the Slaughterhouse-Complex system will contribute to solve the environmental problems and to achieve a sustainable agricultural development
Keywords: complex systems, system dynamics, slaughterhouse waste products.

1 Introduction

The environmental problems in which humanity currently lives are extremely complex. This complexity is derived from the fact that there are really certain ecological, economic, political and social phenomena which are linked among themselves in a network of multiple interactions.

World scale environmental problems, such as desertification, greenhouse effect, poverty and hungry, ozone layer depletion and the loss of biodiversity, among others, can no longer be seen as isolated problems but as the result of interdependent processes derived from a conception of the world centered on economicist discernments and short-term benefit.

On local and regional scale, these problems can be manifested as water contamination, the loss of fertility of farmland and soil, excess energy consumption and pollution from urban wastes, among others.

As an example of the last problem indicated previously, we have the case of the slaughterhouses. Municipal slaughterhouse wastes are an important source of public health problems. In general, liquid wastes are unloaded in rivers or ravines and solid wastes are sent to landfill or exposed outdoors. However, collection and utilization of these materials provide wide benefits as economical as sanitary.

Complex problematic such as this, in which the physic-biological environment, manufacturing, technology, social organization, economy and culture are involved, is characterized by the confluence of multiple processes which interrelations constitute the structure of a working system as an organized whole, which, Apostel [1] and other researchers have called "complex system"

Faced with these situations of this multidimensional reality, new methodological approaches are necessary. New methodological approaches which are based on an integral, multidimensional and systemic vision of the problem as well as from its historical analysis so as to be able to understand its origins, are required.

On considering reality as a complex system, several authors, such as Garcia [2]; [3] and Novo [4] point out that a key task with which to adequately interpret the problem is fundamental in order to identify the system which is the object of the study; as well as the connecting elements, the flows and the guidelines which connect the systems behaviors.

The methodology has two objectives: first, to obtain a diagnosis of the functioning of the system; second, to be able to act on the system. To achieve the first objective, it is necessary to construct the system which is the object of the study. In order to do this, it is necessary to take from reality the elements which have an impact on the environmental problems which are being interpreted, to discover the interactions which occur amongst them and to identify the processes which take place. In order to achieve the second objective, there is a tendency to formulate policies aimed at stopping or reverting the deteriorating processes within the system studied.

The elements or components of the system are not independent in the measure in which they mutually determine each other. The elements in question must be those in which the relationships are more significant. This selection of the elements is determined by the questions which orient the research. The election of the limits must be carried out in such a way that the problem to be studied has a certain organization or structure. The structure is determined by the group of elements which come about among the elements. The study of the structure of the systems explains their historicity. The study of the structures of the systems has the study of the mechanisms for structuring and de-structuring as a central topic, which allows for the analysis of when and how a structure is transformed. The central study of the dynamics of the systems is the study of processes. The processes describe the changes which take place in the system. Once the system is constructed, the interactions between what remains within the system and what remains outside is taken into account through the conditions of the periphery or conditions of the limits. These conditions are specified in the form of flows. In the study of the flows, it is necessary to consider the speed of change. The speed of change is closely related with the temporal scale of the phenomena which are to be studied (Figure 1).

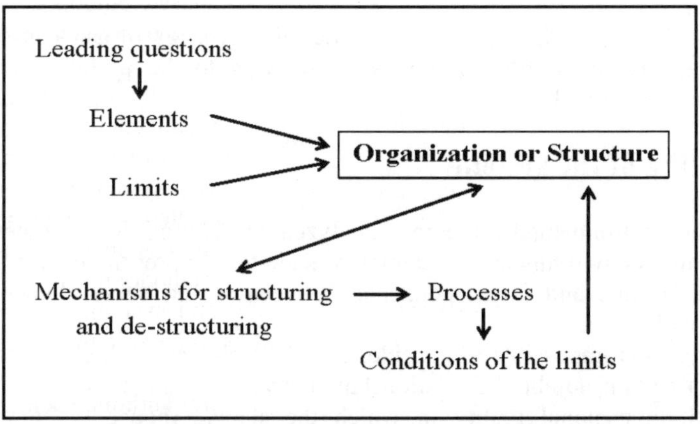

Figure 1: Components of the complex system.

The epistemic framework is the set of theories or theorizations which make up the "corpus" of knowledge based on which the study of a specific problem is approached. Thus the identification and selection of the data which is taken from the empirical reality is defined by it. In this way, the epistemic framework represents a certain conception of the world and on many occasions implicitly expresses the researcher's evaluating body. The observable factors are data from experience which have been interpreted under a specific epistemic framework.

2 Description of the problem

The city of Puebla, Mexico, is located in the central western part of the Mexican Republic.

On average, the Puebla's Municipal Slaughterhouse sacrifice 400 pigs, 175 head of cattle and 35 sheep and goats per day.

From this sacrifice, approximately 5,000 liters of blood, 3.3 m^3 of ruminal contents, 17,000 liters of effluents generated by the washing of the entrails, and 100 cm^3 of hoofs and bristles are produced.

Blood and effluents produced by the washing of the entrails are unloaded, without any treatment, at El Conde ravine.

Ruminal contents, hoofs and bristles are thrown at posterior zone of the slaughterhouse. Here, these wastes are exposed outdoors and human settlements are nearness.

In this way, the Municipal Slaughterhouse in Puebla, and its surrounding area may be considered a spatial expression of a reality which is intermeshed with social, political, economic, cultural and ecological situations. These situations are characterized by the convergence of processes which are not interdependent among themselves but which are interrelated and constitute a complex system which functions as an organized totality which is not static but is instead dynamic.

The objective of this approach is to design a strategy to use slaughterhouse wastes as organic fertilizers; this as a solution to the pollution and social problems they provoke.

3 Posing of the system

When the environmental problem is analyzed considering the slaughterhouse in relation to its environment, an attempt is made to interpret the manner in which the relationships and interdependence between it and some elements which interact with it come about.

Owing to is impossible to consider all of the elements which are part of the reality, a certain number of relationships between certain elements of concrete and multidimensional reality in which the slaughterhouse is immersed are established.

The conducting thread with which to define the relationships and the elements which come about in the environmental problems is established by the "leading questions". Waste products, such as blood, ruminal content, hoofs, bristles, which cause environmental contamination problems, once processed, could these be considered useful byproducts for agriculture in the production process of meat? And, what implications would this conceptual change have on the functional and structural relationships between the slaughterhouse and its environment?

Now, in order to refer to the Municipal slaughterhouse and the elements of the empirical reality which impact the environmental problems in question, the expression <u>Slaughterhouse-Complex</u> will be used. Both the limits and the elements or components of the <u>Slaughterhouse-Complex</u> were not well defined at the beginning of the research. Their characterization is elaborated based on leading questions and of a certain behavior in a specific number of social, ecological and/or productive activities which interact and are interdependent.

The selection of the elements for analysis is made on the basis of an interpretation of the function which they have within the organized totality which is strategic for the proposed analysis.

When the analysis of the <u>Slaughterhouse-Complex</u> is undertaken, blood, hoofs or ruminal content are not observed in an isolated manner but as "organic waste" or "organic fertilizer"; categories which are the result of a conceptual elaboration related to the productive, economic, social and ecological activities. The blood, hoofs and ruminal content are fact which are part of the empirical experience, while as the organic waste and organic fertilizers are observable and are interpreted in the context of a specific epistemic framework.

The challenge then, consists of going beyond the identification of the elements selected (description of the system) to the understanding of the process or processes which take place in the Slaughterhouse-Complex (interpretation of the system).

4 Construction of the Slaughterhouse-Complex system

The Slaughterhouse-Complex system is constructed based on the relationships which come about between the slaughterhouse and some elements or components in their environment: the operational systems related both to the process of slaughtering cattle, pigs, sheep and goats as well as the process of waste generation which occurs within the slaughterhouse, as well as the impact on the environment and society (environmental problems).

The environmental problem is not only the ecological damage or the contamination of water and soil, but also, it is related with social, political and economical processes such as the awareness of one's neighbors, and political and economic processes, such as urban development and municipal management, among others (Figure 2).

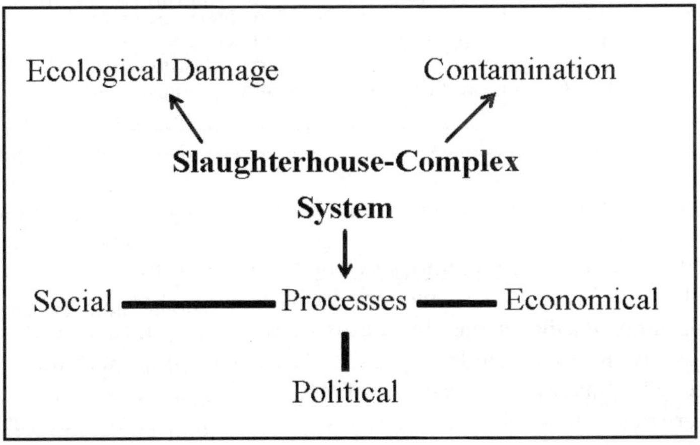

Figure 2: Construction of the Slaughterhouse-Complex system.

The Slaughterhouse is the connection between the physical environment and livestock production with society, which at the same time provides the means of appropriation, transformation, circulation and consumption of production. In these articulations, two general types of interactions come about. The ecological type interactions and the social-economic type interactions, in which the processes by which the animals are slaughtered play a determinate role generating processes of environmental and social deterioration (for instance. contamination and detrimental effects on the neighbors′ quality of life).

For methodological effects, a starting point may be a diagram with which to indicate the location of the Slaughterhouse-Complex within the empirical reality. Thus, some levels of *macro*, *meso* and *micro* organization can be established. The *macro* level is the totality of the empirical reality, in this case, the municipality of Puebla. Pue., at the *micro* level the slaughterhouse is defined by its "inside" elements. At the "*meso*" level the "portion" of empirical reality which includes elements from "outside" which interact with the slaughterhouse through the periphery conditions by means of the flow of matter, energy and information (Figure 3). In other words, the *meso* and *micro* levels correspond to the system which in the previous paragraph was denominated the Slaughterhouse-Complex.

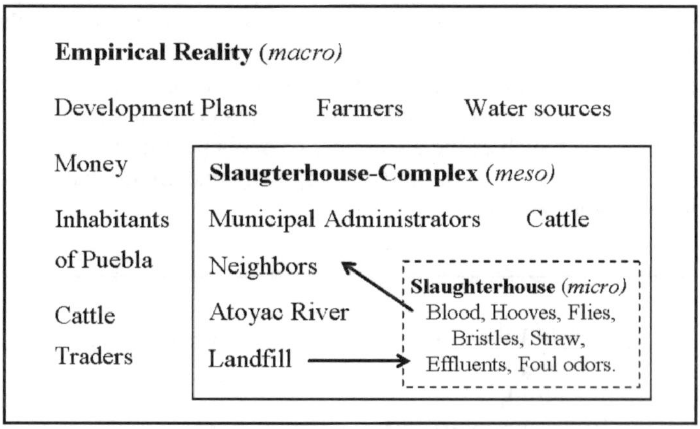

Figure 3: The Slaughterhouse-Complex system and its surrounding area.

The limits of the Slaughterhouse-Complex system are represented by the *meso* and *micro* levels. These two levels, as was previously pointed out, are interacting amongst themselves by means of flows. The flows which enter are represented by: livestock cattle, pigs, sheep and goats, drinkable water, the exit flows are effluents of the washing of cattle entrails, blood, hoofs, ruminal content, bristles, foul smells, noise and flies. This is the initial stationary state of the system.

Nevertheless, the conceptual shift of pollutant materials from wastes to byproducts carry on changing the conception of the slaughterhouse and considering it a center for the integral production of meat as well as of useable byproducts for agricultural reinvestment, then the flows change, new elements are incorporated and a new structure with new properties and relationships among its components is reached.

5 Dynamics of the Slaughterhouse-Complex system

The changes in the time in which the Slaughterhouse-Complex system arises are reflected as a consequence of the processes of structuring and de-structuring . In these processes, elements or components of the empirical reality which were not initially part of the Slaughterhouse-Complex may come to be important elements of the system once a new stationary state is reached (Figure 4).

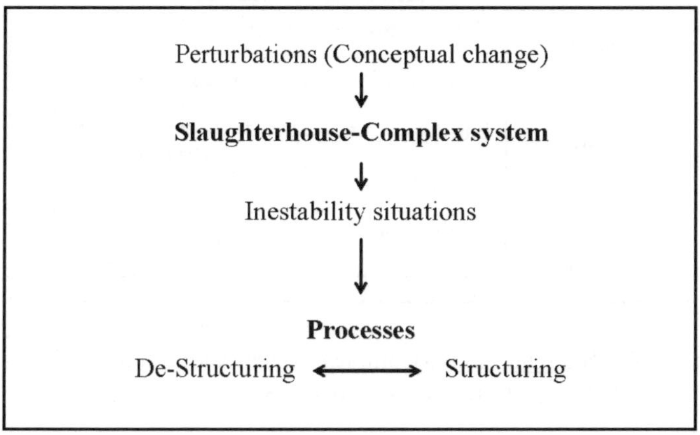

Figure 4: Dynamics of the Slaughterhouse-Complex system.

However, the posing derived from changes on conceptual level –wastes to byproducts- may lead the Slaughterhouse-Complex system to a situation of instability ("de-structuring") which may eventually lead to the making of a new stationary state. In the new stationary state, the structure and functioning of the Slaughterhouse-Complex system is different. Some of the elements which make up the system are new, while others disappear; additionally the conditions of the periphery, the limits and the relationship among them are different.

In this way, the set of internal relationships of the Slaughterhouse-Complex become disorganized. This is to say, on one hand some mechanisms come about which allow the slaughterhouse to become internally reorganized so that the waste products may be collected and now be considered byproducts in order that they may be processed and transformed into organic fertilizer. Additionally, the neighbors affected by the contaminated river begin to "disappear" from the Slaughterhouse-Complex system and turn into elements of the empirical reality which no longer fit into the new stationary state which the Slaughterhouse-Complex system would reach ("re-structuring").

On the other hand, the incorporation of new elements which exist in the empirical reality, as is the case of some farmers or nursery workers from the region who are interested in the purchase of these products, The Department of Parks and Gardens for self-consumption on the part of the Municipality; as well as the flow of money which occurs in the system due to the purchase/sale of the fertilizers leads to new types of relationships which will remain changeable for some time (figure 5).

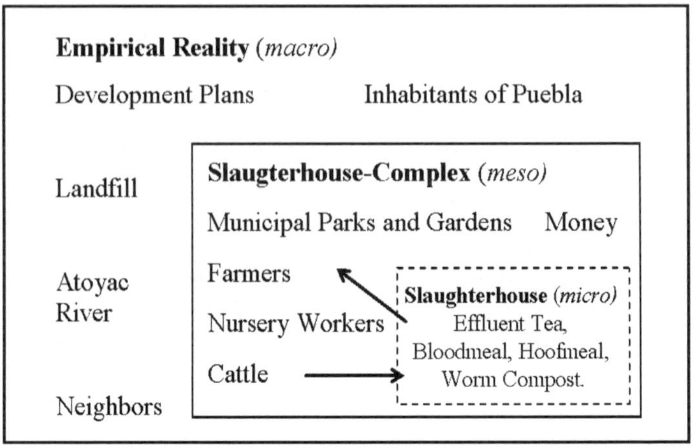

Figure 5: The Slaughterhouse-Complex system and its surrounding area after structuring-destructuring processes.

Now, in an as yet undetermined period of time, the Slaughterhouse-Complex will stabilize under a different structure.

Finally, this new state might contribute to the solution of environmental problems caused by waste generated by the slaughterhouse. The idea that this waste be considered a useful byproduct for agriculture (change in the conditions of the periphery) would be a factor which would fuel processes which would finally lead the Slaughterhouse-Complex to this new stationary state.

6 Conclusions

It is suggested that with the proposed conceptual and structural changes, the new stationary state of the Slaughterhouse-Complex system will contribute to solve the environmental problems and to achieve a sustainable agricultural development.

The theory of complex systems points out that the modification of a sector in a system introduces changes –to a lesser or greater extent, with different temporal scales- in the entire structure of the system (Garcia *et al*, [5]). In this way, when changing the function of the contaminant materials –from waste to subproducts- the relations between the members carried the system to the conformation of a new structure, with new properties and emergencies.

The conceptual change from “waste” to “subproducts” was the determining factor that led to the stating of an alternative handling model of the contaminant materials. This model corresponds to the proposal stated in this work of research.

The solution proposed in this work is to evoke, starting from a conceptual change, a change of organizational structure, in this way, the relations of the slaughterhouse with its surrounding changes. Also, the participation of other sectors of society is required, as well as the development of technological processes to make the most of the contaminant materials.

References

[1] Apostel, L., Comp., *Interdisciplinariedad. Problemas de la Enseñanza y de la Investigacion en las Universidades* [Interdisciplinary, Teaching and Research Problems in the Universities]. ANUIES: Mexico City, 1975.

[2] García, R. Conceptos básicos para el estudio de sistemas complejos (Basic concepts for the study of complex systems). (Chapter 11). *Los problemas del conocimiento y la perspectiva ambiental del desarrollo.* Coord. E. Leff [The problems of knowledge and the environmental perspective of development]. Coord. E. Leff, Siglo XXI: Mexico City, pp 381-409, 1986.

[3] García, R., Interdisciplinariedad y sistemas complejos (Interdisciplinarity and complex systems). (Chapter 2). *Ciencias Sociales y Formacion Ambiental.* Coord. E. Leff [Social Sciences and Environmental Formation]. Coord. E. Leff, Gedisa: Barcelona, pp 85-124, 1994.

[4] Novo, M. (Comp.). *El Análisis Interdisciplinar de la Problemática Ambiental.* Volume 1. [Interdisciplinary Analysis of Environmental Problems], Fundación Universidad-Empresa: Madrid, pp 21-58, 1997.

[5] García, R., Baraona, M., Sanz, C., Flores, A., Duval, G., Fernández, L. & M. Tarrio. *Modernización en el agro: ¿ventajas comparativas para quién? El caso de los cultivos comerciales en el Bajío* [Modernization in agriculture: comparative advantages for whom? The case of commercial crops in the Bajio], IFIAS, UNRISD, CINVESTAV/IPN: México City, 1988.

Author Index